International Rare
Book Prices

VOYAGES, TRAVEL
& EXPLORATION

1990

International Rare Book Prices

VOYAGES, TRAVEL & EXPLORATION

Series Editor: Michael Cole

1990

The Clique

© **The Clique Limited 1990**

7 Pulleyn Drive, York YO2 2DY, England

International Rare Book Prices — Voyages, Travel & Exploration

ISBN 1 870773 18 7

North America

Spoon River Press, P.O. Box 3676
Peoria, Illinois 61614, U.S.A.

Typesetting by Maxiprint, York, England
Printed and bound by Unwin Brothers Ltd., Woking, England

Contents

Introduction and Notes

Voyages, Travel & Exploration is the fifth title in the annual series *International Rare Book Prices*. The other titles in the series are *The Arts & Architecture, Early Printed Books, Modern First Editions, Science & Medicine, 19th Century Literature*.

The series, generally referred to as *IRBP*, provides annual records of the pricing levels of out-of-print, rare or antiquarian books within a number of specialty subject areas and gives likely sources and suppliers for such books in Britain and the United States of America. It is intended to be used by both the experienced bookman and the newcomer to book-collecting.

Sources of information:

The books recorded each year in the various subject volumes of *IRBP* have been selected from catalogues of books for sale issued during the previous year by numerous bookselling firms in Britain and the United States. These firms, listed at the end of this volume, range in nature from the highly specialized, handling books solely with closely defined subject areas, through to large concerns with expertise across a broad spectrum of interests.

Extent of coverage:

IRBP concentrates exclusively on books published in the English language and, throughout the series as a whole, encompasses books published between the 16th century and the 1970s.

The 30,000 or so separate titles recorded in the annual volumes of *IRBP* vary greatly from year to year although naturally there is a degree of overlap, particularly of the more frequently found titles. Consecutive annual volumes do not, therefore, merely update pricings from earlier years; they give substantially different listings of books on each occasion. The value of the *IRBP* volumes lies in providing records of an ever-increasing range of individual titles which have appeared for sale on the antiquarian or rare book market.

Emphasis is placed throughout on books falling within the lower to middle range of the pricing scale (£10 - £250; $20 - $500) rather than restricting selection to the unusually fine or expensive. In so doing, *IRBP* provides a realistic overview of the norm, rather than the exception, within the booktrade.

Authorship and cross-references:

Authors are listed alphabetically by surname.

Whenever possible, the works of each author are grouped together under a single form of name irrespective of the various combinations of initials, forenames and surnames by which the author is known.

Works published anonymously, or where the name of the author is not recorded on the title-page, are suitably cross-referenced by providing the main entry under the name of the author (when mentioned by the bookseller) with a corresponding entry under the first appropriate word of the title. In cases of unknown, or unmentioned, authorship, entry is made solely under the title.

Full-titles:

Editorial policy is to eschew, whenever possible, short-title records in favour of full-, or at least more complete and explanatory, titles. Short-title listings do little to convey the flavour, or even the content, of many books - particularly those published prior to the nineteenth century.

Descriptions:

Books are listed alphabetically, using the first word of the title ignoring, for alphabetical purposes, the definite and indefinite articles *the*, *a* and *an*. Within this alphabetical grouping of titles, variant editions are not necessarily arranged in chronological order, i.e., a 2nd, 3rd or 4th edition might well be listed prior to an earlier edition.

Subject to restrictions of space and to the provisos set out below, the substance of each catalogue entry giving details of the particular copy offered for sale has been recorded in full.

The listings have been made so as to conform to a uniform order of presentation, viz: Title; place of publication; publisher or printer; date; edition; size; collation; elements of content worthy of note; description of contents including faults, if any; description and condition of binding; bookseller; price; approximate price conversion from dollars to sterling or vice versa.

Abbreviations of description customary within the booktrade have generally been used. A list of these abbreviations will be found on page *x*.

Collations:

Collations, when provided by the bookseller, are repeated in toto although it should be borne in mind that booksellers employ differing practices in this respect; some by providing complete collations and others by indicating merely the number of pages in the main body of the work concerned. The same edition of the same title catalogued by two booksellers could therefore have two apparently different collations and care should be taken not to regard any collation recorded in *IRBP* as being a definitive or absolute record of total content.

Currency conversion:

IRBP lists books offered for sale priced in either pounds sterling (£) or United States dollars ($). For the benefit of readers unaccustomed to one or other of these currencies, an approximate conversion figure in the alternative currency has been provided in parentheses after each entry, as, for example, "**£100 [**≃ **$160]**", or, "**$60 [**≃ **£37]**". The conversion is based upon an exchange rate of £1 sterling ≃ US $1.60 (US $1 ≃ £0.625 sterling), the approximate rate applicable at the date of going to press.

It must be stressed that the conversion figures in parentheses are provided merely as an indication of the approximate pricing level in the currency with which the reader may be most familiar and that fluctuations in exchange rates will make these approximations inaccurate to a greater or lesser degree.

Acknowledgements:
We are indebted to those booksellers who have provided their catalogues during 1989 for the purposes of *IRBP*. A list of the contributing booksellers forms an appendix at the rear of this volume.

This appendix forms a handy reference of contacts in Britain and the United States with proven experience of handling books within the individual specialist fields encompassed by the series. The booksellers listed therein are able, between them, to offer advice on any aspect of the rare and antiquarian booktrade.

Many of the listed books will still, at the time of publication, be available for purchase. Readers with a possible interest in acquiring any of the items may well find it worth their while communicating with the booksellers concerned to obtain further and complete details.

Caveat:
Whilst the greatest care has been taken in transcribing entries from catalogues, it should be understood that it is inevitable that an occasional error will have passed unnoticed. Obvious mistakes, usually typographical in nature, observed in catalogues have been corrected. We have not questioned the accuracy in bibliographical matters of the cataloguers concerned.

The Clique

Abbreviations

advt(s)	advertisement(s)	iss	issue
addtn(s)	addition(s)	jnt(s)	joint(s)
a.e.g.	all edges gilt	lge	large
ALS	autograph letter signed	lea	leather
altrtns	alterations	lib	library
Amer	American	ltd	limited
bibliog(s)	bibliography(ies)	litho(s)	lithograph(s)
b/w	black & white	marg(s)	margin(s)
bndg	binding	ms(s)	manuscript(s)
bd(s)	board(s)	mrbld	marbled
b'plate	bookplate	mod	modern
ctlg(s)	catalogue(s)	mor	morocco
chromolitho(s)	chromo-lithograph(s)	mtd	mounted
ca	circa	n.d.	no date
cold	coloured	n.p.	no place
coll	collected	num	numerous
contemp	contemporary	obl	oblong
crnr(s)	corner(s)	occas	occasional(ly)
crrctd	corrected	orig	original
cvr(s)	cover(s)	p (pp)	page(s)
dec	decorated	perf	perforated
detchd	detached	pict	pictorial
diag(s)	diagram(s)	port(s)	portrait(s)
dw(s)	dust wrapper(s)	pres	presentation
edn(s)	edition(s)	ptd	printed
elab	elaborate	qtr	quarter
engv(s)	engraving(s)	rebnd	rebind/rebound
engvd	engraved	rec	recent
enlgd	enlarged	repr(d)	repair(ed)
esp	especially	rvsd	revised
ex lib	ex library	roy	royal
f (ff)	leaf(ves)	sep	separate
facs	facsimile	sev	several
fig(s)	figure(s)	sgnd	signed
fldg	folding	sgntr	signature
ft	foot	sl	slight/slightly
frontis	frontispiece	sm	small
hand-cold	hand-coloured	t.e.g.	top edge gilt
hd	head	TLS	typed letter signed
ill(s)	illustration(s)	unif	uniform
illust	illustrated	v	very
imp	impression	vell	vellum
imprvd	improved	vol(s)	volume(s)
inc	including	w'engvd	wood-engraved
inscrbd	inscribed	w'cut(s)	woodcut(s)
inscrptn	inscription	wrap(s)	wrapper(s)
intl	initial		

Voyages, Travel & Exploration 1989 Catalogue Prices

Abbey, J.R.

- Travel in Aquatint and Lithography 1770-1860 from the Library of J.R. Abbey. London: Dawsons, 1972. 2 vols. 4to. xiii,299; xiv,301-675 pp. Orig cloth. Dws.
(Frew Mackenzie) **£625 [≈ $1,000]**

Abbot, Abiel

- Letters Written in the Interior of Cuba, between the Mountains of Arcana, to the East, and of Cusco, to the West, in the Months of February, March, April, and May, 1828. Boston: 1829. xv,256 pp. Orig calf, somewhat rubbed, b'plate removed.
(Reese) **$250 [≈ £156]**
- Letters Written in the Interior of Cuba, between the Mountains of Arcana, to the East, and of Cusco, to the West, in ... 1828. Boston: Bowles & Dearborn, 1829. 1st edn. xvi,256 pp. Minor foxing at ends. Contemp cloth & mrbld bds, new label.
(Jenkins) **$225 [≈ £140]**

Abbot, George

- Sketches about Kurrah, Mannickpore. London: ptd by Engelmann, Graf & Coindet, 1831. Oblong folio. 2 ff, inc subscribers. 9 lithos, ptd on india paper & mtd. Some light marg stains. Old wrappers, some wear. Fldg case.
(Ximenes) **$2,000 [≈ £1,250]**

Abbot, Gorham D.

- Mexico, and the United States; Their Mutual Relations and Common Interests ... New York: Putnam, 1869. 8vo. xvi,392 pp. 2 steel engvd plates, 2 cold maps. Sm lib blind stamp on title. Orig green cloth gilt.
(Karmiole) **$125 [≈ £78]**

Abbott, Carlisle S.

- Recollections of a California Pioneer. New York: 1917. 235 pp. Frontis. Some spotting & foxing. Cloth.
(Reese) **$75 [≈ £46]**

Abbott, G.F.

- The Tale of a Tour in Macedonia. London: Edward Arnold, 1903. 8vo. xii,343 pp. Lge fldg map, num photo ills. Mod cloth.
(Piccadilly) **£24 [≈ $38]**

Abbott, S.

- Ardenmohr Among the Hills. Scenery and Sports in the Highlands. London: 1876. 8vo. Tinted plates. Orig bndg, sl rubbed, inner hinge sprung.
(Grayling) **£25 [≈ $40]**

Abel, Charles W.

- Savage Life in New Guinea. The Papuans in Many Moods. London: London Missionary Society, [1902]. 8vo. 221,2 advt pp. Photo frontis, 69 ills. Orig pict cloth.
(Bates & Hindmarch) **£18 [≈ $28]**

Abercrombie, W.R.

- Alaska, 1899: Copper River Exploring Expedition. Washington: GPO, 1900. 1st edn. 8vo. 169 pp. Lge fldg map, 168 photo views. Maroon cloth, orig spine relaid, spine lettering dulled. *(Terramedia)* **$75 [≈ £46]**
- Copper River Exploring Expedition. Washington: GPO, 1900. 1st edn. 8vo. Fldg map, 127 plates. Orig black cloth, spotted, spine tender. *(Parmer)* **$175 [≈ £109]**
- Copper River Exploring Expedition. Washington: GPO, 1900. 1st edn. 8vo. Fldg map, 168 photo. Half leather, mrbld bds.
(Parmer) **$200 [≈ £125]**

Aberigh-Mackay, George

- Twenty-One Days in India, being the Tour of Sir Ali Baba, K.C.B. London: 1880. 2nd edn. 8vo. Half calf. *(Farahar)* **£50 [≈ $80]**

Abert, James W.

- Through the Country of the Comanche Indians in ... 1845 ... Edited by John Galvin. San Francisco: 1970. Folio. [18],77 pp. 3 maps, 22 cold plates, other ills. Orig cloth

gilt. Inscrbd by the editor.
(Fenning) **£65 [≈ $104]**

About, Edmond
- Greece and the Greeks of the Present Day. New York: Dix, Edwards, 1857. Sm 8vo. xvi,360 pp. Cloth.   *(Zeno)* **£49.50 [≈ $80]**

Account ...
- Account of Denmark ... see Molesworth, Robert, Viscount.
- An Account of Switzerland ... see Stanyan, Abraham.
- An Account of the Province of Carolina ... see Wilson, Samuel.

Accum, Friedrich Christian (Frederick)
- Guide to the Chalybeate Spring of Thetford, exhibiting the General and Primary Effects of the Thetford Spa ... [London]: sold by T. Boys; at the Spa ..., 1819. 1st edn. 12mo. xiv,159,[i] pp. Fldg hand cold frontis, fldg plate. Orig bds, uncut, jnts rubbed.
(Finch) **£275 [≈ $440]**

An Accurate Description ...
- An Accurate Description of the United Netherlands ... see Carr, William.

Acerbi, Joseph
- Travels through Sweden ... London: for Joseph Mawman ..., 1802. 2 vols. 4to. Port, fldg map, 10 plain plates, 5 cold natural history plates, 6 dble plates of music. Lacks a sub-title in vol 2. Edges of some plates sl foxed. Mod qtr crushed mor.
(Hannas) **£550 [≈ $880]**
- Travels through Sweden ... London: for Joseph Mawman ..., 1802. The pirated edn on laid paper, without printer's imprint, & no cold plates. 2 vols. 4to. Port, fldg map, 16 plates, 6 dble plates of music. Lib stamps on plates, perf stamps on titles. Old style half calf.   *(Hannas)* **£750 [≈ $1,200]**

Ackerley, J.R.
- Hindoo Holiday. An Indian Journal. New York: Viking Press, 1932. 8vo. Text ills. Orig cloth, faded. Dw defective.
(Berkelouw) **$75 [≈ £46]**

Ackermann, Rudolph
- A History of the University of Oxford ... London: Ackermann, 1814. 2 vols. 4to. xiv,[ii],xxv, 275,[6]; 262,[6] pp. Half- titles. Port of Lord Grenville, 81 aquatint plates. Without the founders' plates. Occas sl offsetting. Later gilt dec mor, a.e.g.
(Frew Mackenzie) **£2,600 [≈ $4,160]**

Acts of Parliament
- An Act for Restraining and Preventing several Unwarrantable Schemes and Undertakings in His Majesty's Colonies and Plantations in America. London: John Baskett, 1741. Folio. 14 Geo. II, pp 681-688. Marks at hd. Disbound.
(Jarndyce) **£50 [≈ $80]**
- An Act for the Encouragement of the Whale Fishery in the Gulph and River of Saint Lawrence, and on the Coasts of His Majesty's Colonies in America. London: Mark Baskett, & assigns of Robert Baskett, 1764. Folio. 4 Geo III, pp 429-432 pp. Disbound.
(Jarndyce) **£50 [≈ $80]**
- An Act to Prevent Paper Bills of Credit, hereafter to be issued in any of His Majesty's Colonies or Plantations in America, from being declared to be a Legal Tender ... London: Baskett, 1764. Folio. 4 Geo III, pp 469-474. Disbound.   *(Jarndyce)* **£50 [≈ $80]**
- An Act to continue the Laws now in force for Regulating the Trade between the Subjects of His Majesty's Dominions and the Inhabitants of the Territories belonging to the United States of America ... London: 1788. Folio. 28 Geo II, pp 201-206. Disbound.
(Jarndyce) **£60 [≈ $96]**

Adam, W.
- The Gem of the Peak; or Matlock Bath and its Vicinity ... London: John & Charles Mozley, 1851. 5th edn. Sm 8vo. x,401,4 pp, advt leaf. Fldg map frontis, 7 tinted plates, text ills. Orig cloth gilt, spine sl darkened.
(Hollett) **£40 [≈ $64]**

Adams, A.L.
- Field and Forest Rambles with Notes and Observations on the Natural History of Eastern Canada. London: 1873. 8vo. xvi,333 pp. 3 maps, plates & text figs. Calf, lacks label.   *(Wheldon & Wesley)* **£75 [≈ $120]**

Adams, Ansel
- Yosemite and the Sierra Nevada. Photographs by Ansel Adams. Selections from the Works of John Muir. Edited by Charlotte E. Mauk. Boston: Houghton Mifflin, 1948. 1st edn. 4to. [xxii],132 pp. 64 ff of plates. Orig bndg. Dw sl chipped.
(Karmiole) **$125 [≈ £78]**

Adams, Henry Gardiner
- David Livingstone. London: 1881. 8vo. 306,4 pp. 21 plates, text figs. Orig pict cloth.
(Henly) **£18 [≈ $28]**

Adams, John
- Index Villaris: or, an Alphabetical Table of all the Cities, Market-Towns, Parishes, Villages, and Private Seats, in England and Wales ... London: A. Godbid & J. Playford, for the author, 1680. 1st edn. Folio. [xii], 412 pp. Contemp mor gilt, sl worn. Wing A.479.
(Pickering) **$1,200 [≈£750]**

Adams, Joseph
- Ten Thousand Miles through Canada. New York: [1912]. 310 pp. Fldg map, plates. Sl foxing. Orig gilt pict cloth.
(Reese) **$50 [≈£31]**

Adams, W.H. Davenport
- Egypt Past and Present, Described and Illustrated. With a Narrative of its Occupation by the British, and of Recent Events in the Soudan. London: T. Nelson & Sons, 1894. 12mo. [x],384 pp. Num plates & ills. Orig pict blue & maroon cloth gilt, sl worn.
(Terramedia) **$45 [≈£28]**
- Nelsons' Hand-Book to the Isle of Wight. London: T. Nelson & Sons, 1864. 8vo. Frontis, fldg cold map, 11 plates. Orig green cloth gilt.
(Sanders) **£25 [≈$40]**

Addison, G.A.
- Indian Reminiscences or the Bengal Moofussul Miscellany ... London: Bull, 1837. 1st edn. 8vo. xvi,339 pp. Orig cloth, unopened, edges rubbed, front cvr soiled, spine tears & chips.
(Worldwide Antiqu'n) **$65 [≈£40]**

Addison, Joseph
- Remarks on Several Parts of Italy, &c. In the Years 1701, 1702, 1703. The Second Edition. London: for J. Tonson, 1718. 8vo. [xii],x,410,[x] pp. Period panelled calf, rear free endpaper removed.
(Rankin) **£65 [≈$104]**
- Remarks on Several Parts of Italy &c. In the Years 1701, 1702, 1703 ... Third Edition. London: Tonson, 1726. 12mo. Contemp calf, rubbed.
(Falkner) **£25 [≈$40]**
- Remarks on Several Parts of Italy, &c. In the Years 1701 ... 1703. The Fifth Edition. London: Tonson, 1736. Lge 12mo. 304,[8] pp. Contemp calf gilt, a little worn but sound, lettered '4' on spine. *(Fenning)* **£24.50 [≈$40]**

Aflalo, F.G.
- The Sportsman's Book for India. London: Marshall, 1904. 8vo. xvi,567 pp. Fldg map frontis, 4 other maps, 41 photo ills. Orig red cloth gilt, t.e.g., spine sl sunned.
(Bates & Hindmarch) **£90 [≈$144]**

- Sunset Playgrounds. Fishing Days and Others in California and Canada. London: 1909. 251 pp. Ills. Cloth. *(Reese)* **$50 [≈£31]**

Agassiz, Louis
- A Journey in Brazil. Boston: 1868. xix,540 pp. Frontis, plates. Orig cloth, front hinge starting, sl rubbed. *(Reese)* **$150 [≈£93]**
- Lake Superior: its Physical Character, Vegetation, and Animals, compared with those of other and similar regions. With a Narrative of the Tour by J. Elliot Cabot. Boston: 1850. Roy 8vo. x,[ii],9-428 pp. Frontis, map, 15 plates. Title sl damaged. Orig cloth.
(Wheldon & Wesley) **£139 [≈$208]**

Aikin, John
- England Described: being a Delineation of Every County in England and Wales ... London: 1818. 8vo. vi,[i],499,[vii] pp. Fldg cold map. Orig half calf, rubbed, spine faded, label chipped. *(Bickersteth)* **£35 [≈$56]**

Ainsworth, William Francis
- Travels and Researches in Asia Minor, Mesopotamia, Chaldea, and Armenia. London: 1842. 2 vols in one. xi,[1],364, xi,[1],399 pp. Frontises, fldg maps, text ills. Tissue guards. Some foxing. Contemp polished calf, spine gilt extra, hinges sl worn.
(Reese) **$200 [≈£125]**
- Travels in the Track of the Ten Thousand Greeks ... London: Parker, 1844. 1st edn. 12mo. xv,248 pp. Fldg map. Perf lib stamp on title. Contemp qtr mor, rubbed at edges, hd of spine frayed.
(Terramedia) **$150 [≈£93]**

Ainsworth, William Francis (ed.)
- The Earth Delineated with Pen and Pencil; or, Voyages, Travels, and Adventures all Round the World ... London: Griffin, [ca 1875]. 4to. 820 pp. 200 ills by Dore & others. Contemp dark green calf by Bickers, elab gilt spine. *(Spelman)* **£45 [≈$72]**

Akeley, Carl E.
- In Brightest Africa. London: Heinemann, 1924. 1st UK edn. 8vo. xviii,[2],267 pp. Orig cloth, inside jnts weak.
(Fenning) **£28.50 [≈$46]**

Albert Victor, Prince & George, Prince of Wales
- The Cruise of Her Majesty's Ship 'Bacchante', 1879-1882. London: Macmillan, 1886. 1st edn. 2 vols. 8vo. xxvii,675; xii, 803 pp. Num plates, charts & maps (inc cold

frontis map). Orig pict blue cloth gilt, sm tear at hd of 1 spine.
(Terramedia) **$150 [≃ £93]**

Alcock, A.
- Naturalist in Indian Seas. London: Murray, 1902. 1st edn. 8vo. xxiv,328 pp. Fldg map, frontis, 98 plates & ills. Sl spotting at ends. Orig green cloth, spine sl rubbed & cockled.
(Gough) **£35 [≃ $56]**

Alderson, A.H.
- With the Mounted Infantry and the Mashonaland Field Force 1896. London: Methuen, 1898. xv,[1],308,48 advt pp. Fldg map, frontis, 9 plates, text diags. Front free endpaper excised. Orig cloth, sl worn, hinges weak. *(Parmer)* **$180 [≃ £112]**

Aldrich, Lorenzo D.
- A Journal of the Overland Route to California & The Gold Mines. Los Angeles: 1950. 93 pp. Cloth & bds, sl rubbed.
(Reese) **$85 [≃ £53]**

Aldridge, Olive M.
- The Retreat from Serbia through Montenegro and Albania. London: Minerva Publishing, 1916. 8vo. 113 pp. Fldg map. Orig ptd yellow cloth.
(Piccadilly) **£30 [≃ $48]**

Alexander, Boyd
- From the Niger to the Nile. London: 1907. 2 vols. Roy 8vo. Maps, ills. Orig cloth, used.
(Wheldon & Wesley) **£60 [≃ $96]**
- From the Niger to the Nile. London: Edward Arnold, 1907. 2 vols. Lge 8vo. xv, 358; xi, 395, 16 pp. Num ills & maps. Orig red cloth gilt, endpapers & edges foxed.
(Frew Mackenzie) **£165 [≃ $264]**
- From the Niger to the Nile. London: Edward Arnold, 1907. 1st edn. 2 vols. Lge 8vo. xv, 358; xi, 420, 16 advt pp. 2 fldg maps, num ills. Orig cloth gilt, spines v sl sunned.
(Hollett) **£150 [≃ $240]**

Alexander, Herbert
- Boyd Alexander's Last Journey. New York & London: Longmans, Green, 1912. 8vo. 296 pp. Fldg cold map, ills. Orig gilt dec blue cloth, partly unopened. *(Parmer)* **$60 [≃ £37]**

Alexander, William
- Picturesque Representations of the Dress and Manners of the Austrians. London: Murray, 1814. 1st edn. Trimmed 8vo. xv,3 pp. 50 cold plates, each with a leaf of text. Later red half mor, gilt dec spine, t.e.g., rubbed at edges &

extremities. *(Terramedia)* **$600 [≃ £375]**
- Picturesque Representations of the Dress and Manners of the Russians. London: for James Goodwin by W. Lewis, [ca 1820]. Roy 8vo. 64 hand cold plates. Contemp half calf, uncut, worn. *(Stewart)* **£475 [≃ $760]**

Allan, Robert
- The Sportsman in Ireland. London: Arnold, 1897. Sm 4to. Cold ills. Red half mor.
(Emerald Isle) **£75 [≃ $120]**

Allen, James & Schoolcraft, Henry
- Expedition to the Northwest Indians ... Washington: House Document 323, 1834. 68 pp. Fldg map. Half mor.
(Jenkins) **$450 [≃ £281]**

Allen, W.W. & Avery, R.B.
- California Gold Book. First Nugget. Its Discovery and Discoveries Discoverers and Some of the Results Proceeding Therefrom. San Francisco & Chicago: 1893. 439 pp. Ills. Orig cloth gilt. *(Reese)* **$150 [≃ £93]**

Allen, Zachariah
- The Practical Tourist, or Sketches of the State of the Useful Arts, and of Society, Scenery, &c. &c. in Great-Britain, France and Holland ... Boston: 1832. 2 vols. 363; 428 pp. Scattered foxing. Half mor, sl rubbed.
(Reese) **$225 [≃ £140]**

Allgood, Henry G.C.
- Stray Leaves from the Past of our Village: a History of Bethnal Green, from the Earliest Times to 1680 ... London: 1894. 8vo. vii,347, ix pp. Fldg genealogy. Advts. Orig cloth, faded & chafed. *(Coombes)* **£30 [≃ $48]**

Alli, Darogha Ubbas
- The Lucknow Album, containing a Series of Fifty Photographic Views ... Calcutta: G.H. Rouse, Baptist Mission Press, 1874. Lge 8vo. [vi],58 pp. Lge fldg map in pocket, 50 mtd albumen photos, each with mtd ptd caption. Orig gilt-titled cloth.
(Charles B. Wood) **$750 [≃ £468]**

Allom, Thomas
- Views on the Tyrol, from Drawings by T. Allom ... With Letterpress Descriptions, by a Companion of Hofer. London: Black & Armstrong, [ca 1830]. 4to. Engvd title, fldg map, 45 engvd plates. Dec blue cloth, sl rubbed, lacks front fly, contents loose in case.
(Moon) **£350 [≃ $560]**
- Views on the Tyrol, from Drawings by T.

Allom ... With Letterpress Descriptions, by a Companion of Hofer. London: Tilt, [ca 1830]. 8vo. 128 pp. Engvd title, fldg map (old repr without loss of ptd surface), 46 plates. Half calf, rubbed. *(Moon)* **£300 [≈ $480]**
- See also under Wright, Revd G.N.

Allom, Thomas & Rose, T.
- Westmorland, Cumberland, Durham and Northumberland Illustrated. London: F. Fisher ..., n.d. 4to. 22 pp. Title vignette, 215 steel engvd plates. Half mor gilt extra, sl rubbed. *(Hollett)* **£300 [≈ $480]**

Allport, Douglas
- Collections, Illustrative of the Geology, History, Antiquities and Associations, of Camberwell and the Neighbourhood. Camberwell: for the author, 1841. xvi,255,[4 subscribers] pp. 1 gathering loose. Frontis, 10 plates (5 hand cold). Orig green cloth. *(Box of Delights)* **£95 [≈ $152]**

Alsop, Richard (ed.)
- A Narrative of the Adventures and Sufferings of John R. Jewitt ... During a Captivity of Nearly Three Years Among the Savages of Nootka Sound ... Middletown [Ct.]: Seth Richards, 1815. 1st edn. 2nd (?) iss. 12mo. 204 pp. Frontis. Contemp calf, extremities rubbed. *(M & S Rare Books)* **$750 [≈ £468]**

Amedeo, Luigi, Duke of the Abruzzi
- On the "Polar Star" in the Arctic Sea. London: 1903. 1st English edn. 2 vols. 5 maps (2 fldg) in pocket, diags (part cold). Orig cloth, 1 rear cvr sl spotted. *(Parmer)* **$325 [≈ £203]**
- On the Polar Star in the Arctic Sea ... London: Hutchinson, 1903. 2 vols. Lge 8vo. 2 maps in pocket, 2 fldg panoramas, 16 plates, text ills. Orig dec cloth. *(High Latitude)* **$160 [≈ £100]**

The American Traveller ...
- See Cluny, Alexander.

Amundsen, Roald
- 'The North West Passage" being the Record of a Voyage of the Ship "Gjoa" 1903-1907 ... London: Constable, 1908. 1st edn in English. 2 vols. 8vo. xiii,335; ix,397 pp. 2 fldg maps, num plates. Orig dec cloth, t.e.g., trifling snag at hd of vol 1 spine. *(High Latitude)* **$395 [≈ £246]**
- The South Pole. An Account of the Norwegian Antarctic Expedition in the

'Fram', 1910-12. New York: Keedick; London: Murray, 1913. 1st Amer edn. 2 vols. 8vo. xxxv,392; x, 449 pp. Maps, num ills. Orig blue cloth gilt, sl wear to extremities. *(Parmer)* **$450 [≈ £281]**

Anburey, Thomas
- Travels through the Interior Parts of America. In a Series of Letters, by an Officer. London: 1789. 1st edn. 2 vols. Fldg plates & maps. Contemp calf, sl worn. *(Jenkins)* **$1,000 [≈ £625]**

Ancell, Samuel
- A Journal of the Blockade and Siege of Gibraltar ... 1779 to ... 1783 ... Cork: for the author by A. Edwards ..., 1793. 4th edn. 8vo. vi,[6],256 pp. Subscribers' list. New mor backed mrbld bds, uncut. *(Young's)* **£220 [≈ $352]**

Ancient Reliques ...
- See Storer, James Sargant & Greig, John.

The Andalusian Annual ...
- The Andalusian Annual for MDCCCXXXVII. Edited by Michael Burke Honan ... London: John Macrone, 1836. 1st edn. 4to. viii,162 pp. 12 hand cold plates. Occas sl foxing to text. Orig gilt dec brown cloth, a.e.g, spine relaid, new endpapers. *(Heritage)* **$1,000 [≈ £625]**

Anderson, Robert
- Deeside. Painted by William Smith. London: A. & C. Black Colour Book, 1911. 1st edn. Map, 20 cold plates. Orig dec cloth. *(Old Cathay)* **£33 [≈ $52]**

Anderson, Rufus
- The Hawaiian Islands: Their Progress and Condition under Missionary Labors. Boston: 1864. xxii,450,advt pp. 2 maps (1 fldg). Orig cloth, spine relaid, spine sunned. *(Reese)* **$175 [≈ £109]**

Anderson, William J.
- Architectural Sketches in Italy. Glasgow: for the author, [1890]. One of 150. Folio. Frontis & 41 plates, each with leaf of text. Orig cloth. *(Fenning)* **£45 [≈ $72]**

Andersson, Charles John
- Lake Ngami; or, Explorations and Discoveries during Four Years' Wanderings in the Wilds of Southwestern Africa. New York: Dix, Edwards, 1857. 1st Amer edn. 433,advt pp. Num ills. Orig embossed cloth, faded & rubbed. *(Parmer)* **$125 [≈ £78]**

- Lake Ngami: Four Years' Wanderings in the Wilds of Southwestern Africa. New York: 1857. 2nd edn. 433 pp. Fldg map, ills. Orig cloth. *(Trophy Room Books)* **$250 [≈£156]**
- Lake Ngami or Explorations and Discoveries during Four Years' Wanderings in the Wilds of South Western Africa. New York: 1857. 433, advt pp. 55 ills. Orig cloth, sl worn. *(Trophy Room Books)* **$225 [≈£140]**
- Notes of Travel in South-Western Africa. New York: 1875. 1st Amer edn. xi,318,advt pp. Text sl tanned. Orig gilt pict cloth, edge wear. *(Reese)* **$175 [≈£109]**
- Notes of Travel in South-Western Africa. New York: Putnam's, 1882. 2nd edn. 8vo. xi, 318 pp. Three qtr leather, sm spot on upper bd. *(Parmer)* **$100 [≈£62]**

Andree, S.A.
- Andree's Story. The Complete Record of his Polar Flight, 1897. From the Diaries and Journals ... found on White Island in the Summer of 1930 ... New York: 1930. 1st edn. Roy 8vo. xvi,390 pp. Frontis, 5 maps, 42 plates, 4 diags. Orig illust cloth, spine faded. *(Berkelouw)* **$75 [≈£46]**
- The Andree Diaries ... written during their Balloon Expedition to the North Pole in 1897 ... London: John Lane, [1931]. 1st London edn. 8vo. xx,[2],471 pp. 3 fldg maps, photo plates. Orig cloth, spine a bit faded. *(High Latitude)* **$50 [≈£31]**

Andrews, Clarence L.
- The Eskimo and his Reindeer in Alaska. Caldwell: Caxton, 1939. 1st edn. 8vo. 253 pp. Frontis map, photo plates. Orig dec cloth. Dw. Signed by the author. *(High Latitude)* **$60 [≈£37]**

Andrews, John
- Letters to a Young Gentleman, On his setting out for France: containing a Survey of Paris, and a Review of French Literature; with Rules and Directions for Travellers ... London: 1784. 1st edn. 8vo. [xiv],576 pp. Browned. Contemp half sheep, v sl worn. *(Finch)* **£75 [≈$120]**
- Letters to a Young Gentleman, on his setting out for France: containing a Survey of Paris, and a Review of French Literature; with Rules and Directions for Travellers ... London: J. Walter, 1784. 576 pp. Half-title. Contemp qtr calf, hinges cracking. *(C.R. Johnson)* **£120 [≈$192]**

Andrews, Roy Chapman
- Across Mongolian Plains ... New York: Appleton, 1921. 8vo. xxiv,276 pp. 40 ills inc

frontis. Title a bit foxed. Orig blue cloth gilt. *(Karmiole)* **$75 [≈£46]**
- Across Mongolian Plains. New York: 1921. 1st edn. 276 pp. Ills. Orig bndg. Dw. *(Trophy Room Books)* **$175 [≈£109]**
- Camps and Trails in China. New York: 1919. 334 pp. Ills. Orig cloth gilt. *(Trophy Room Books)* **$100 [≈£62]**
- Ends of the Earth. London: 1929. 1st edn. 8vo. Ills. Orig bndg. *(Grayling)* **£50 [≈$80]**
- Ends of the Earth. New York & London: Putnam's, 1929. 8vo. x,355 pp. Num plates. Orig black cloth. *(Terramedia)* **$75 [≈£46]**
- Ends of the Earth. London: 1929. 3rd imp. 8vo. Ills. Title foxed. Orig bndg, sl marked. *(Grayling)* **£40 [≈$64]**
- Ends of the Earth. New York: 1929. 3rd imp. 8vo. Ills. Orig cloth, sl marked. *(Grayling)* **£47 [≈$75]**
- On the Trail of Ancient Man. A Narrative of the Field Work of the Central Asiatic Expeditions. New York & London: Putnam's, 1926. 1st edn. 2nd printing. 8vo. xxiv,375 pp. Port, 58 photos. Orig green cloth. *(Parmer)* **$65 [≈£40]**
- Quest of the Snow Leopard. London: 1957. 155 pp. Ills. Orig bndg. Dw. *(Trophy Room Books)* **$40 [≈£25]**
- This Business of Exploring. London: 1935. 1st edn. 8vo. Ills. Sl foxing. Orig bndg, v sl rubbed. *(Grayling)* **£37 [≈$59]**
- Under a Lucky Star. A Lifetime of Adventure. London: 1945. 8vo. Orig bndg, sl rubbed. *(Grayling)* **£12 [≈$19]**

Anet, Claude
- Through Persia in a Motor-Car. By Russia and the Caucasus. Translated by M. Beresford Ryley. New York: Appleton, 1908. 1st edn. Lge 8vo. xvi,281 pp. Frontis, 35 plates. Sl foxed. Orig cloth, edges sl rubbed, spine ends frayed, lib number on spine. *(Worldwide Antiqu'n)* **$65 [≈£40]**

Angas, George French
- Polynesia; a Popular Description ... London: SPCK, 1866. 12mo. xii,436,4 advt pp. Fldg map, 6 plates, text engvs. Orig blue pict cloth, rubbed. *(Adelson)* **$175 [≈£109]**

Angeloni, Batista (pseud.)
- See Shebbeare, John.

Annabel, R.
- Hunting and Fishing in Alaska. New York: 1948. Ills. Orig bndg. *(Trophy Room Books)* **$200 [≈£125]**

Annandale, Nelson
- The Faroes and Iceland: Studies in Island Life. Oxford: Clarendon Press, 1905. 1st edn. 8vo. 24 plates. Orig cloth.
(Hannas) **£45 [≈ $72]**

Anson, George
- A Voyage round the World, in the Years MDCCXL, I, II, III, IV. By George Anson ... Compiled ... by Richard Walter. London: 1748. Large Paper. Lge thick 4to. 34,417 pp. 42 fldg plates (inc 3 fldg maps, 10 fldg plans). Contemp calf, gilt spine, untrimmed.
(Reese) **$1,500 [≈ £937]**
- A Voyage round the World, in the Years MDCCXL, I, II, III, IV. By George Anson ... London: 1776. 4to. xx,417,2 pp. 42 maps & plates. Mod qtr calf. *(Adelson)* **$400 [≈ £250]**

Ansted, David Thomas
- The Ionian Islands in the Year 1863. London: W.H. Allen, 1863. 8vo. xii,480 pp. Frontis, 3 maps, ills. Orig cloth, rebacked.
(Zeno) **£195 [≈ $312]**
- The Ionian Islands in the Year 1863. London: W.H. Allen, 1863. 8vo. xii,480 pp. Tinted frontis, 4 maps, ills in text. Sm lib stamp. Black cloth. *(Piccadilly)* **£125 [≈ $200]**

Antes, John
- Observations on the Manners and Customs of the Egyptians, the Overflowing of the Nile; with Remarks on the Plague ... London: Stockdale, 1800. 4to. 139,5 pp. Fldg map. Sl foxing. Orig bds, rubbed & soiled, lacks backstrip, untrimmed.
(Worldwide Antiqu'n) **$175 [≈ £109]**

Antiquarian ...
- The Antiquarian and Topographical Cabinet: containing a Series of Elegant Views of the Most Interesting Objects of Curiosity in Great britain. London: Murray ..., 1817-19. 6 vols. 8vo. 600 steel engvd half-page plates, with text beneath. Sl spotting. Lib cloth.
(Hollett) **£120 [≈ $192]**
- The Antiquarian and Topographical Cabinet ... see also Storer, James S. & Greig, John.
- Antiquarian Notices of Lupset ... see Hunter, Joseph.

Appleton, D., publisher
- Appleton's Hand-Book of American Travel. Western Tour. Embracing Eighteen Through Routes to the West .... Revised for the Autumn of 1873. New York: D. Appleton & Co, 1873. Sm 8vo. x,322,[2],21 advt pp. 9 maps. Orig red linen gilt, soiled, spine ends sl rubbed. *(Karmiole)* **$75 [≈ £46]**

Apponyi, Count H.
- My Big-Game Diary from India and the Himalayas. London: 1937. Ills. Orig cloth, rather rubbed. *(Grayling)* **£60 [≈ $96]**

Aramilev, I.
- Beyond the Ural Mountains. Adventures of a Siberian Hunter. London: 1961. 8vo. Ills. Orig bndg. Dw. *(Grayling)* **£30 [≈ $48]**

Arctic Miscellanies ...
- Arctic Miscellanies. A Souvenir of the late Polar Search by the Officers and Seamen of the Expedition. London: Colburn, 1852. 1st edn. xviii, 347 pp. Cold litho frontis. Contemp half calf, gilt spine, extremities rubbed. *(High Latitude)* **$325 [≈ £203]**

Arctic Pilot ...
- Arctic Pilot. Vol II. Iceland, Greenland Sea, Spitsbergen, and the East Coast of Greenland. Third Edition. London: HMSO, 1921. 8vo. Fldg map, plates, coast outlines in text. Orig ptd canvas. *(Hannas)* **£45 [≈ $72]**

The Arctic World ...
- The Arctic World: its Plants, Animals, and Natural Phenomena. With a Historical Sketch of Arctic Discovery. London: 1876. Folio. viii, [9]-276 pp. Orig gilt pict cloth, a few scrapes, 1 sm tear to cloth of front cvr, crnrs frayed.
(Reese) **$125 [≈ £78]**

Ari Thorgilsson Frodi
- The Book of the Settlement of Iceland. Second Edition. Translated from the Original Icelandic by Rev. T. Ellwood. Kendal: T. Wilson, 1908. 8vo. Frontis. No map in this edn. Orig blue cloth. *(Hannas)* **£30 [≈ $48]**

Arlington, L.C. & Lewisohn, William
- In Search of Old Peking. Peking: Henri Veitch, 1935. vi,382 pp. Cold map in pocket, port frontis, num plates & plans (some fldg). Orig maroon cloth. Pres inscrptn by Arlington. *(Lyon)* **£145 [≈ $232]**

Armitage, John
- The History of Brazil ... London: Smith, Elder, 1836. 1st edn. 2 vols in one. 8vo. xvi, 371; viii,297, 2 advt pp. 2 ports. New cloth, leather label. *(Adelson)* **$285 [≈ £178]**

Armstrong, A.N.
- Oregon: comprising a Brief History and Full Description of the Territories of Oregon and Washington ... Interspersed with Incidents of

Travel and Adventure. Chicago: 1857. 147 pp. Occas sl marg staining or smudging. Later three qtr mor.   *(Reese)* **$750 [≃ £468]**

Armstrong, Alexander
- A Personal Narrative of the Discovery of the North-West Passage ... while in Search of the Expedition under Sir John Franklin. London: Hurst & Blackett, 1857. xxii,[2],616 pp. Fldg map, tinted litho frontis. Rec half calf.
(High Latitude) **$495 [≃ £309]**

Armstrong, John
- The History of the Island of Minorca. London: for C. Davies, 1752. 1st edn. 8vo. xxviii, 260 pp. Fldg map, 2 fldg plates. Contemp gilt panelled calf, rebacked, label relaid.   *(Gough)* **£195 [≃ $312]**

Armstrong, M.J.
- An Actual Survey of the Great Post Roads between London and Edinburgh ... London: 1783. 2nd edn. Engvd general map, engvd title, 44 engvd strip maps. Mod half calf, new endpapers.   *(Henly)* **£240 [≃ $384]**

Armstrong, N.
- After Big Game in the Upper Yukon. London: 1937. 8vo. Ills. Orig cloth, badly faded, sl rubbed.   *(Grayling)* **£60 [≃ $96]**
- After Big Game in the Upper Yukon. London: 1937. 287 pp. 3 maps, ills. Orig bndg.   *(Trophy Room Books)* **$200 [≃ £125]**
- After Big Game in the Upper Yukon. London: 1937. 287 pp. 3 maps, ills. Orig bndg, cvrs v faded.
(Trophy Room Books) **$125 [≃ £78]**

Arrowsmith, A.
- A Comparative Atlas of Ancient and Modern Geography ... for the Use of Eton School. Eton: E.P. Williams, 1828. 4to. 53 maps, hand cold in outline. Orig calf backed bds, spine v worn, crnrs worn.
(Hollett) **£120 [≃ $192]**

Art and Nature under an Italian Sky ...
- See Dunbar, Margaret Juliana Maria.

Arundell, V.J.
- A Visit to the Seven Churches of Asia; with an Excursion into Pisidia; containing Remarks of the Geography and Antiquities of those Countries ... London: John Rodwell, 1828. 1st edn. 8vo. iv,340 pp. Fldg map, 13 fldg charts of inscrptns. Orig bds.
(Young's) **£70 [≃ $112]**

Ashbee, C.R.
- A Palestine Notebook. 1918-1923. London: Heinemann, 1923. 1st edn. 8vo. 278 pp. Frontis. Orig cloth, sl rubbed ex-lib, lib number on spine.
(Worldwide Antiqu'n) **$45 [≃ £28]**

Ashdown, Charles H.
- British Castles. London: A. & C. Black Colour Book, 1911. 1st edn. 32 cold plates. Orig cloth, t.e.g., v sl wear to extremities.
(Old Cathay) **£35 [≃ $56]**
- British Castles. London: Black, 1911. 4to. 208 pp. 32 cold plates. Inscrptn. Occas foxing. Orig dec cloth, t.e.g., some wear, front hinge tender. *(Monmouth)* **£15 [≃ $24]**

Ashe, Revd R.P.
- Chronicles of Uganda. London: Hodder & Stoughton, 1894. 1st edn. 8vo. xiv,477 pp. Frontis, num plates. Orig blue gilt pict cloth, sl soiled.   *(Terramedia)* **$150 [≃ £93]**

Asher & Adams
- New Topographical Atlas and Gazetteer of New York. New York: Asher & Adams, 1870. Elephant folio. 80,15 pp. Cold maps. Orig cloth, rebacked.   *(Jenkins)* **$300 [≃ £187]**

Asher, G.M.
- Henry Hudson the Navigator. The Original Documents in which his Career is Recorded ... London: Hakluyt Society, 1860. 8vo. [12], ccxviii, 292 pp. 2 fldg maps. Contemp calf, rebacked.   *(High Latitude)* **$90 [≃ £56]**

Ashley-Brown, W.
- On the Bombay Coast and Deccan, the Origin and History of the Bombay Diocese, a Record of 300 Years' Work for Christ in Western India. London: 1937. 8vo. Num plates, map endpapers. Orig cloth. *(Farahar)* **£15 [≃ $24]**

Ashmole, Elias
- The Antiquities of Berkshire ... London: E. Curll, 1719. 3 vols. Sm 4to. cxxviii, 580, 428 pp. 1 engvd plate, 1 engvd ill, sev fldg tables. Lacks port & plan. Contemp calf, rubbed.
(Ars Libri) **$275 [≃ £171]**

Askew, Alice & Claude
- The Stricken Land. Serbia as we saw it. London: Eveleigh Nash, 1916. 8vo. xvi,263 pp. Photos. Mod cloth.
(Piccadilly) **£18 [≃ $28]**

Atcherly, Roland
- A Trip to Boerland, or A Year's Travel, Sport and Gold-Digging in Transvaal. London:

Bentley, 1879. 1st edn. 8vo. x,267 pp. Ills. Orig pict mustard cloth, v rubbed & frayed.
(Terramedia) **$150 [≈£93]**

Atkinson, A.

- Ireland Exhibited to England in a Political and Moral Survey of her Population, and in a Statistical and Scenographic Tour of Certain Districts ... London: Baldwin, 1823. 2 vols. 8vo. Sl browning. Half calf.
(Emerald Isle) **£165 [≈$264]**

Atkinson, G.F.

- Curry and Rice ... The Ingredients of Social Life at 'our' Station in India. London: W. Thacker & Co, 1911. 4to. 40 cold plates. Orig dec cloth gilt, a.e.g., recased, new endpapers.
(Hollett) **£60 [≈$96]**

Atkinson, Thomas Witlam

- Oriental and Western Siberia ... London: Hurst & Blackett, 1858. 8vo. xi,611,2 advt pp. Fldg map (torn without loss), 20 litho & 32 w'engvd ills. Sl foxing. Ex-lib. Rec dark blue half leather.
(Bates & Hindmarch) **£150 [≈$240]**

- Travels in the Regions of the Upper and Lower Amoor and the Russian Acquisitions on the Confines of India and China. New York: Harper, 1860. 1st Amer edn. Tall 8vo. xii, 448, 4 advt pp. Fldg map, 83 ills. Orig cloth. *(Schoyer)* **$70 [≈£43]**

- Travels in the Regions of the Upper and Lower Amoor and the Russian Acquisitions on the Confines of India and China ... London: 1861. 2nd edn. xii,570,advt pp. Fldg map, tinted litho frontis (foxed), text ills. Three qtr calf, gilt spine.
(Reese) **$150 [≈£93]**

Atwater, Caleb

- Remarks Made on a Tour to Prairie du Chien; Thence to Washington City, in 1829. Columbus: 1831. 1st edn. 12mo. 296 pp. Contemp calf backed bds, front inner hinge weak, endpaper loose.
(M & S Rare Books) **$425 [≈£265]**

Audas, J.W.

- The Australian Bushland. Melbourne: 1950. 8vo. 711 pp. 8 cold & num other ills. Orig cloth, trifle used, endpapers tape-marked.
(Wheldon & Wesley) **£40 [≈$64]**

Auer, Harry A.

- Camp Fires in the Yukon. Cincinnati: 1916. 8vo. Ills. Orig bndg, v sl rubbed.
(Grayling) **£75 [≈$120]**

Austin, Alfred

- Haunts of Ancient Peace. Painted by Agnes Locke. London: A. & C. Black Colour Book, 1908. 1st edn thus. 20 cold plates. Orig dec blue cloth, t.e.g., spine ends v sl worn.
(Old Cathay) **£35 [≈$56]**

An Authentic Narrative ...

- An Authentic Narrative of Four Years' Residence at Tongataboo ... see Vason, George.

Ayrton, Edward & Loat, W.L.S.

- Pre-Dynastic Cemetery at El Mahasna. London: 31st Memoir of the Egypt Exploration Fund, 1911. Folio. viii,39 pp. 38 plates. Orig qtr cloth & bds, rubbed.
(Terramedia) **$75 [≈£46]**

B., R.

- The English Empire in America ... by R.B. (i.e. Richard Burton) ... see Crouch, Nathaniel.

Bache, Richard

- Notes on Colombia, taken in the years 1822-3. With an Itinerary of the Route from Caracas to Bogota; and an Appendix. Philadelphia: Carey & Lea, 1827. 8vo. 2 advt, viii, 9-303 pp. Fldg map, fldg plan. Orig calf, rebacked. *(Adelson)* **$450 [≈£281]**

Back, Sir George

- Narrative of the Arctic Land Expedition to the Mouth of the Great Fish River, and Along the Shores of the Arctic Ocean, in the Years 1833, 1834 and 1835. London: Murray, 1836. 1st edn. 8vo. Fldg map, 14 plates. Later cloth, v light wear to extremities.
(Parmer) **$495 [≈£309]**

- Narrative of the Arctic Land Expedition to the Mouth of the Great River, and Along the Shores of the Arctic Ocean in the Years 1833, '34, and '35. Philadelphia: 1836. 1st Amer edn. Lge 8vo. 456 pp. Fldg map. Cloth & bds, spine relaid. *(Reese)* **$300 [≈£187]**

Bacon, Sir Francis

- A Declaration of the Demeanor and Carriage of Sir Walter Raleigh ... see under Declaration.

Baden-Powell, B.H.

- The Indian Village Community, Examined with reference to the Physical, Ethnographic, and Historic Conditions of the Provinces ... London: 1896. 8vo. Fldg map. Orig cloth, sl worn. *(Farahar)* **£55 [≈$88]**

Baedeker, Karl

- Belgium and Holland. Leipzig: 1905. 14th edn. Orig cloth.
(Bates & Hindmarch) **£32 [≈ $51]**
- Belgium and Holland. Leipzig: 1910. 15th edn. Orig cloth, sm hole to front cvr, spine holed. *(Bates & Hindmarch)* **£18 [≈ $28]**
- Lower Egypt with the Fayum and the Peninsula of Sinai. Leipzig: 1878. 1st edn. Orig cloth.
(Bates & Hindmarch) **£130 [≈ $208]**
- Egypt. Part First. Leipsic: 1885. Sm 8vo. xiv, 538 pp. 16 maps, 30 plans, 7 views, num ills. Orig cloth, hinges starting, crnrs bumped.
(Berkelouw) **$150 [≈ £93]**
- Egypt. Leipzig: 1898. 4th remodelled edn. 12mo. 22 maps, 55 plans, 66 views & vignettes. A few fldg maps frayed. Orig cloth, worn. *(Worldwide Antiqu'n)* **$45 [≈ £28]**
- Egypt. Leipzig: 1902. 5th remodelled edn. 12mo. 23 maps, 66 plans, 59 vignettes. A few pencil underscorings. Orig cloth, sl rubbed, ex-lib externally unmarked.
(Worldwide Antiqu'n) **$75 [≈ £46]**
- Egypt and the Sudan. Leipzig: 1908. 6th edn. Orig cloth.
(Bates & Hindmarch) **£80 [≈ $128]**
- Egypt and the Sudan. Leipzig: 1914. 7th edn. cxc,458 pp. 22 maps, 85 plans, 55 vignettes. Orig cloth, lib number on spine.
(Worldwide Antiqu'n) **$65 [≈ £40]**
- Northern France ... Second Edition. Leipsic: Baedeker ..., 1894. 9 maps, 27 plans. Orig red cloth, front jnt v sl cracked.
(Piccadilly) **£18.50 [≈ $30]**
- Northern France. Leipzig: 1899. 3rd edn. Tear to 1st map without loss. Orig cloth.
(Bates & Hindmarch) **£28 [≈ $44]**
- Northern France. Leipzig: 1905. 4th edn. 1 fldg map torn without loss. Orig cloth.
(Bates & Hindmarch) **£25 [≈ $40]**
- Northern France. Leipzig: 1909. 5th edn. Some tears to map without loss. Orig cloth.
(Bates & Hindmarch) **£20 [≈ $32]**
- Paris and Environs. Leipzig: 1881. 7th edn. Orig cloth. *(Bates & Hindmarch)* **£40 [≈ $64]**
- Paris and Environs. Leipzig: 1888. 9th edn. Orig cloth. *(Bates & Hindmarch)* **£28 [≈ $44]**
- Paris and Environs. Leipzig: 1891. 10th edn. Orig cloth, hinges weak, virtually disbound.
(Bates & Hindmarch) **£24 [≈ $38]**
- Paris and Its Environs. Leipzig: 1907. 16th edn. Sm 8vo. Orig cloth gilt.
(Fenning) **£16.50 [≈ $27]**
- Paris and Environs ... Seventeenth revised English Edition. Leipzig: 1910. 14 maps, 41 plans, bound-in folder of street maps. Orig red cloth, spine sl marked, rear cvr sl marked.

(Piccadilly) **£12.50 [≈ $20]**
- Southern France. Leipzig: 1902. 4th edn. Orig cloth. *(Bates & Hindmarch)* **£25 [≈ $40]**
- Southern France. Leipzig: 1907. 5th edn. Orig cloth. *(Bates & Hindmarch)* **£25 [≈ $40]**
- Southern France. Leipzig: 1907. 5th edn. Sm 8vo. Orig cloth gilt. *(Fenning)* **£16.50 [≈ $27]**
- Southern France including Corsica. Fifth Edition. Leipsic & London: 1907. 33 maps, 49 plans. Orig red cloth, v sl rubbed.
(Piccadilly) **£16.50 [≈ $27]**
- Southern France. Leipzig: 1914. 6th edn. Orig cloth. *(Bates & Hindmarch)* **£25 [≈ $40]**
- Berlin and Its Environs. Leipzig: 1912. 5th edn. Sm 8vo. Orig cloth gilt. Dw.
(Fenning) **£16.50 [≈ $27]**
- Eastern Alps including the Bavarian Highlands ... Leipzig: 1895. 8th edn. Orig cloth, hinges splitting, spine frayed.
(Bates & Hindmarch) **£30 [≈ $48]**
- Munich and its Environs. Leipzig: 1950. Orig cloth. *(Bates & Hindmarch)* **£15 [≈ $24]**
- Northern Bavaria. Leipzig: 1951. Orig cloth, front cvr creased.
(Bates & Hindmarch) **£12 [≈ $19]**
- Northern Germany. Leipzig: 1925. 17th edn. 1 map torn without loss. Orig cloth, signs of wear. *(Bates & Hindmarch)* **£27 [≈ $43]**
- The Rhine from Rotterdam to Constance. Leipzig: 1892. 12th edn. Orig cloth, front hinge tender, cvrs & spine faded & stained.
(Bates & Hindmarch) **£23 [≈ $36]**
- The Rhine from Rotterdam to Constance. Leipzig: 1900. 14th edn. Orig cloth.
(Bates & Hindmarch) **£25 [≈ $40]**
- The Rhine including the Black Forest and the Vosges. Leipzig: 1911. 17th edn. Orig cloth. Front cvr creased.
(Bates & Hindmarch) **£17 [≈ $27]**
- The Rhine from the Dutch to the Alsatian Frontier. Leipzig: 1926. 18th edn. Orig cloth.
(Bates & Hindmarch) **£25 [≈ $40]**
- Southern Germany. Leipzig: 1910. 11h edn. Sm 8vo. Orig cloth gilt. Dw.
(Fenning) **£18.50 [≈ $30]**
- Southern Germany. Leipzig: 1910. xxx,364 pp. 36 maps, 45 plans. Frontis fldg map detached & reprd. Orig cloth gilt.
(Berkelouw) **$35 [≈ £21]**
- Southern Germany. Leipzig: 1914. 12th edn. Sm 8vo. Orig cloth gilt. Dw.
(Fenning) **£18.50 [≈ $30]**
- Southern Germany. Leipzig: 1929. 13th edn. Orig cloth. *(Bates & Hindmarch)* **£35 [≈ $56]**
- Greece: Handbook for Travellers. Leipzig, London & New York: 1905. 3rd rvsd edn. 12mo. 11 maps, 25 plans, panorama of

Athens. Orig red cloth, sl worn.
(Terramedia) **$75 [≈ £46]**
- Greece. Handbook for Travellers. Leipzig, 1909. 4th rvsd edn. cxxvi,447 pp. 16 maps, 30 plans, panorama of Athens. Orig red cloth. Dw sl soiled & torn without loss.
(Frew Mackenzie) **£90 [≈ $144]**
- Italy from the Alps to Naples. Leipzig: 1909. 2nd edn. Orig cloth.
(Bates & Hindmarch) **£22 [≈ $35]**
- Italy. Handbook for Travellers. Second Part: Central Italy and Rome. Thirteenth Revised Edition. Leipzig: 1900. Sm 8vo. lxxvi, 454, Rome Guide pp. Num fldg maps & plans. Orig red cloth, a little worn.
(Piccadilly) **£12.50 [≈ $20]**
- Northern Italy. Leipsic: 1895. 10th edn. Orig red cloth, minor stains on back cvr.
(Schoyer) **$25 [≈ £15]**
- Northern Italy. Leipzig: 1899. 11th edn. Orig cloth. *(Bates & Hindmarch)* **£23 [≈ $36]**
- Northern Italy. Leipzig: 1906. 13th edn. Orig cloth. *(Bates & Hindmarch)* **£20 [≈ $32]**
- Southern Italy, Sicily, and Excursions to the Lipari Islands ... Leipzig: 1875. 5th edn. 3 maps carelessly folded. Orig cloth, sm chip to spine. *(Bates & Hindmarch)* **£90 [≈ $144]**
- Southern Italy. Leipzig: 1903. 14th edn. Orig cloth. *(Bates & Hindmarch)* **£22 [≈ $35]**
- Southern Italy and Sicily ... Handbook for Travellers. Leipzig: Baedeker ..., 1912. 16th rvsd edn. 12mo. 30 maps & 34 plans. Orig cloth, sl rubbed, cvrs bent, hd of spine worn.
(Worldwide Antiqu'n) **$25 [≈ £15]**
- Norway, Sweden, and Denmark. Leipzig: 1895. 6th edn. 1 fldg map torn without loss. Front endpaper & rear endpaper (with half of index map) removed. Orig cloth.
(Bates & Hindmarch) **£30 [≈ $48]**
- Norway, Sweden, and Denmark. Leipzig: 1912. 10th edn. Orig cloth, spine faded.
(Bates & Hindmarch) **£24 [≈ $38]**
- La Russie. Manuel du Voyageur. Leipzig: Baedeker, 1897. 2nd edn. xlviii,447 pp. 14 maps, 22 plans. Orig red cloth.
(Frew Mackenzie) **£225 [≈ $360]**
- Spain and Portugal. Handbook for Travellers. Leipsic: Baedeker, 1898. 1st edn. 12mo. 6 maps & 46 plans. Orig cloth, a little rubbed & soiled, effects of silver-fish.
(Worldwide Antiqu'n) **$35 [≈ £21]**
- Spain and Portugal. Leipzig: Baedeker, 1913. 4th edn. Orig red cloth, hinges cracked.
(Schoyer) **$20 [≈ £12]**
- Switzerland and the adjacent portions of Italy, Savoy, and Tyrol. Leipzig: 1883. 10th edn. General map mtd on linen. Orig cloth, hinges v weak.

(Bates & Hindmarch) **£25 [≈ $40]**
- Switzerland and the adjacent portions of Italy, Savoy, and Tyrol. Leipzig: 1897. 17th edn. Orig cloth.
(Bates & Hindmarch) **£20 [≈ $32]**
- Switzerland and the adjacent portions of Italy, Savoy, and Tyrol. Leipzig: 1911. 24th edn. Orig cloth.
(Bates & Hindmarch) **£25 [≈ $40]**
- Switzerland and the adjacent portions of Italy, Savoy, and Tyrol. Leipzig: 1913. 25th edn. Orig cloth. *(Schoyer)* **£25 [≈ £15]**
- Switzerland together with Chamonix and the Italian Lakes. Leipzig: 1928. 27th edn. Orig cloth. *(Bates & Hindmarch)* **£25 [≈ $40]**
- The Traveller's Manual of Conversation. In Four Languages, English, French, German, Italian. Leipzig: 1878. Sm 8vo. x,332 pp. Orig cloth gilt, mrbld edges, exchange tables on endpapers. *(Berkelouw)* **$75 [≈ £46]**
- Traveller's Manual of Conversation. In Four Languages, English, French, German, Italian. Leipzig: [ca 1891]. Stereotype Edition. 331 pp. Orig cloth.
(Bates & Hindmarch) **£25 [≈ $40]**
- The United States with an Excursion into Mexico. Handbook for Travellers. Leipzig: 1899. 2nd rvsd edn. c,579 pp. 19 maps, 24 plans. Orig cloth, cvrs faded.
(Frew Mackenzie) **£125 [≈ $200]**

Baerlein, Henry
- The Birth of Yugoslavia. London: Leonard Parsons, 1922. 2 vols. 8vo. 308; 418 pp. Fldg map. Orig purple cloth, sl faded.
(Piccadilly) **£35 [≈ $56]**

Bagot, A.G.
- Sport and Travel in India and Central America. London: Chapman & Hall, 1897. 8vo. viii, 371 pp. Frontis (sl marked). Orig green cloth, t.e.g.
(Bates & Hindmarch) **£30 [≈ $48]**

Bagot, Richard
- The Italian Lakes. Painted by Ella Du Cane. London: A. & C. Black Colour Books, Twenty Shilling Series, 1905. Reprint. 68 cold plates. Orig dec blue cloth, t.e.g.
(Old Cathay) **£30 [≈ $48]**

Baikie, James
- Egyptian Papyri and Papyrus Hunting. New York & Chicago: Revell, [ca 1925]. 1st edn. Lge 8vo. 324 pp. 32 plates (4 cold). Orig cloth. Dw. *(Worldwide Antiqu'n)* **$90 [≈ £56]**

Baikie, William Balfour
- Narrative of an Exploring Voyage up the

Rivers Kwo'ra and Bi'nue (commonly known as the Niger and Tsadda) in 1854. London: Murray, 1856. 8vo. xvi,456 pp. Frontis, illust title, fldg map. Lacks plan of ship. Lacks half-title. Contemp cloth. *(Schoyer)* **$100 [≈ £62]**

Bailey, Henry, writing as Bula N'Zau
- Travel and Adventure in the Congo Free State and Its Big Game Shooting. London: 1894. 335 pp. Fldg map, ills. Orig green cloth.   *(Trophy Room Books)* **$500 [≈ £312]**

Bailey, Thomas
- Annals of Nottinghamshire and History of the County of Nottingham including the Borough. London: Simpkin, Marshall, [1852 - 55]. 4 vols in 2. 8vo. Fldg map, 16 steel engvs. Contemp half mor.
    (Waterfield's) **£85 [≈ $136]**

Baillie-Grohman, W.A.
- Camps in the Rockies. New York: 1882. 438 pp. Fldg map, ills. Orig bndg. Archibald Rogers's b'plate.
    (Trophy Room Books) **$225 [≈ £140]**
- Fifteen Years Sport and Life in the Hunting Grounds of Western America and British Columbia. London: 1900. 403 pp. 3 maps, 77 ills. Orig bndg.
    (Trophy Room Books) **$350 [≈ £218]**
- Sport in the Alps, Past and Present. The Chase of the Chamois, Red Deer, Bouquetin, Rose Deer, Capercalzie, &c. London: 1896. 8vo. ills. Sl foxing. Orig cloth, spine faded & frayed at ends.   *(Grayling)* **£50 [≈ $80]**
- Tyrol. Painted by E. Harrison Compton. London: A. & C. Black Colour Books, Six Shilling Series, 1908. 1st edn. 24 cold plates. Occas foxing, sometimes heavy. Orig dec grey-mauve cloth, t.e.g.
    (Old Cathay) **£36 [≈ $57]**
- Tyrol. Painted by E. Harrison Compton. London: A. & C. Black Colour Books, Six Shilling Series, 1908. 1st edn. 24 cold plates. Orig dec deep blue cloth, spine sl faded & worn at ends.   *(Old Cathay)* **£29 [≈ $46]**

Bain, J. Arthur
- Life and Explorations of Fridtjof Nansen. New Edition ... enlarged. London: Walter Scott, [ca 1897]. 8vo. xix,449,2 advt pp. 15 plates, text ills. Orig blue cloth gilt, sl wear to extremities.   *(Parmer)* **$75 [≈ £46]**

Baines, Thomas
- Explorations in South-West Africa. Being an Account of a Journey in the Years 1861 and 1862 from Walvisch Bay on the Western Coast to Lake Ngami and the Victoria Falls.

London: 1864. 1st edn. 535 pp. Fldg map, cold frontis, ills. Orig cloth.
    (Trophy Room Books) **$750 [≈ £468]**
- The Gold Regions of South Eastern Africa ... Accompanied by Biographical Sketch of the Author. LOndon & Cape Colony: 1877. 1st edn. 8vo. xxiv,240 pp. Fldg map in pocket, orig photo frontis port & 3 others, fldg facs letter. Orig cloth gilt, sl rubbed.
    (Frew Mackenzie) **£150 [≈ $240]**
- The Gold Regions of South Eastern Africa ... London: 1877. 240 pp. Fldg map in pocket, ills. Orig cloth gilt.
    (Trophy Room Books) **$650 [≈ £406]**
- The Gold Regions of South Eastern Africa. London: 1877. 240 pp. Fldg map in pocket, ills inc some mtd. Faint blindstamp on title. Orig cloth, partly unopened.
    (Trophy Room Books) **$650 [≈ £406]**
- History of the Commerce and Town of Liverpool ... London: 1852. Thick 8vo. xvi, 844, 12 subscribers, 13 pp. 2 fldg plans, 1 plate. Mor gilt, a.e.g., jnts cracking, spine ends sl defective.   *(Hollett)* **£75 [≈ $120]**
- Lancashire and Cheshire Past and Present ... London: William Mackenzie, [1868-69]. 4 vols. 4to. Engvd titles, 25 steel engvd plates. A little offsetting of plates. Mor gilt extra, heavy bevelled bds, a.e.g, rather rubbed & darkened.   *(Hollett)* **£225 [≈ $360]**
- Yorkshire. Past and Present ... London: [1871-77]. 2 vols in 4. 4to. Fldg cold map, 27 plates. Ends of vols foxed. Calf, vol 2 part 2 sl rubbed.   *(Henly)* **£120 [≈ $192]**

Baker, B. Granville
- The Walls of Constantinople. London: John Milne, 1910. 1st edn. Lge thick 8vo. [xi], 261, 1 pp. Num tissued plates. Orig maroon cloth.
    (Terramedia) **$75 [≈ £46]**

Baker, Ernest A. & Balch, Herbert E.
- The Netherworld of Mendip Explorations in the Great Caverns of Somerset, Yorkshire, Derbyshire & elsewhere. Clifton & London: 1907. 1st edn. 8vo. xii,172 pp. 56 plates. Trace of foxing on title & half-title, ink note on final endpaper. Orig cloth, uncut.
    (Claude Cox) **£65 [≈ $104]**
- The Netherworld of Mendip. Explorations in the Great Caverns of Somerset, Yorkshire, Derbyshire & elsewhere. Clifton: 1907. 1st edn. 8vo. Maps, plans & plates. Orig bndg.
    (Ambra) **£45 [≈ $72]**

Baker, James
- Turkey in Europe. London: Cassell, 1877. 8vo. xv,560 pp. 2 fldg maps. Cloth.

(Zeno) **£69.50 [≈ $112]**

Baker, Marcus
- Geographic Dictionary of Alaska. Second Edition. Washington: GPO, 1906. 8vo. 690,[2] pp. Rec cloth.
  (High Latitude) **$65 [≈ £40]**

Baker, Sir Samuel White
- The Albert N'Yanza Great Basin of the Nile, and Explorations of the Nile Sources. London: Macmillan, 1866. 1st edn. 2 vols. 8vo. xxx,395; ix,384 pp. 2 maps, port, 13 plates, ills. Brown half leather.
  (Bates & Hindmarch) **£115 [≈ $184]**
- The Albert Nyanza, Great Basin of the Nile. And Explorations of the Nile Sources. Philadelphia: Lippincott, 1870. New edn. 12mo. xxvii,499 pp. 2 fldg cold maps, num plates & ills (inc 1 tinted plate). Orig maroon cloth, sl worn.
  (Terramedia) **$75 [≈ £46]**
- The Albert N'Yanza Great Basin of the Nile Explorations of the Nile Sources. London: Macmillan, 1885. Sm 8vo. xxvi,499 pp. Cold map, 33 ills. Sl marg dampstaining. Orig cloth, edges rubbed, spine ends frayed.
  (Worldwide Antiqu'n) **$45 [≈ £28]**
- Eight Years Wanderings in Ceylon. New York: J.W. Lovell, 1881. 12mo. 323 pp. Frontis, plates. A few pp sl spotted. Orig dec brown cloth, top edge of spine sl frayed.
  (Terramedia) **$30 [≈ £18]**
- Eight Years in Ceylon. London: 1884. 8vo. Engvd plates. Orig elab gilt pict cloth, a.e.g., v sl rubbed.
  (Grayling) **£45 [≈ $72]**
- Exploration of the Nile Tributaries of Abyssinia. London: 1867. 1st edn. 596 pp. Ills. Half leather, spine gilt with 5 raised bands. *(Trophy Room Books)* **$450 [≈ £281]**
- Exploration of the Nile Tributaries of Abyssinia ... Connecticut: O.D. Case, 1868. 1st Amer edn. 8vo. 608 pp. Frontis, map, 15 plates. Rebound in cloth.
  (Berkelouw) **$150 [≈ £93]**
- Exploration of the Nile Tributaries of Abyssinia ... Hartford: Case, 1868. 8vo. 624 pp. 2 cold maps, 16 plates. Sl foxing. Orig cloth, sl rubbed.
  (Worldwide Antiqu'n) **$125 [≈ £78]**
- Ismailia; A Narrative of the Expedition to Central Africa for the Suppression of the Slave Trade ... London: Macmillan, 1874. 1st edn. 2 vols. 8vo. 448,55 advt; 588 pp. 2 maps, num plates. Orig pict green cloth.
  (Terramedia) **$450 [≈ £281]**
- Ismailia: A Narrative of the Expedition to Central Africa for the Suppression of the Slave-Trade ... New York: Harper, 1875. 1st Amer edn. 8vo. 542 pp. 2 maps, frontis port,

2 other frontis plates, num other tissued plates. Orig pict gilt brown cloth.
  (Terramedia) **$150 [≈ £93]**
- Ismailia. New York: 1875. 1st Amer edn. 542 pp. Ills. Orig green cloth gilt.
  (Trophy Room Books) **$200 [≈ £125]**
- Ismailia. A Narrative of the Expedition to Central Africa for the Suppression of the Slave Trade. London: 1879. 2nd edn. 8vo. Engvd plates. Some foxing. Orig bndg, a bit rubbed. *(Grayling)* **£25 [≈ $40]**
- The Rifle and Hound in Ceylon. Philadelphia: Lippincott, 1871. 12mo. 305, advt pp. Frontis, ills. Orig dec orange-brown cloth. *(Terramedia)* **$40 [≈ £25]**

Bakewell, R.
- Travels, comprising Observations made during a Residence in the Tarentaise, and various parts of the Grecian & Pennine Alps, & in Switzerland & Auvergne ... London: 1823. 1st edn. 2 vols. 8vo. 4 cold engvs, num text w'cuts. Three qtr calf.
  (Argosy) **$450 [≈ £281]**

Balch, H.E.
- Wookey Hole, its Caves and Cave Dwellers. OUP: 1914. Lge 4to. xiv,268 pp. 36 plates & num drawings by John Hassall. Orig cloth backed bds. Dw reprd.
  (Hollett) **£120 [≈ $192]**

Balch, Thomas Willing
- The Alaska Frontier. Philadelphia: Allen, Lane & Scott, 1903. 4to. xv,198 pp. Maps. Orig binder's cloth, t.e.g., few minor marks.
  (High Latitude) **$50 [≈ £31]**

Baldwin, C.E.
- The History and Development of the Port of Blyth. Newcastle: Reid, 1929. 4to. 141 pp. 9 fldg plans & charts, facs, ills. Orig bndg.
  (Book House) **£25 [≈ $40]**

Baldwin, Herbert
- A War Photographer in Thrace. An Account of Personal Experiences during the Turco-Balkan War 1912. London: Fisher Unwin, 1913. 8vo. 312 pp. 8vo. 36 photos. Orig cloth.
  (Zeno) **£39.50 [≈ $64]**

Baldwin, Thomas & Thomas, J.
- A New and Complete Gazeteer of the United States. Philadelphia: Lippincott, 1854. 1364 pp. Fldg map. Orig calf, later mor label.
  (Jenkins) **$450 [≈ £281]**

Baldwin, William Charles
- African Hunting and Adventure from Natal

to the Zambesi ... London: Bentley, 1894. 3rd edn. 8vo. x,428 pp. Fldg map, 17 plates. Orig brown cloth, sl rubbed.
(Adelson) **$160 [≈ £100]**

- African Hunting from Natal to the Zambezi ... London: Bentley, 1894. 3rd edn. 8vo. 428 pp. Fldg map, 6 tissued tinted plates, other ills. Crnr of 1 plate damp stained. Orig brown pict cloth, sl worn.
(Terramedia) **$180 [≈ £112]**

Balfour, Alice Blanch
- Twelve Hundred Miles in a Wagon [in South Africa]. With Illustrations by the Author. London: Edward Arnold, 1895. 1st edn. 8vo. Frontis, fldg map, 13 plates, text ills. 32 pp inserted ctlg. Orig cloth gilt, recased, spine sl faded.
(Sanders) **£28 [≈ $44]**

Bancroft, Edward
- An Essay on the Natural History of Guiana, in South America ... Together with an Account of ... Several Tribes of its Indian Inhabitants. London: Becket & De Hondt, 1769. [4],iv,402 pp. Frontis. Some wear at edges, occas foxing. Old calf, 19th c reback.
(Reese) **$800 [≈ £500]**

Bancroft, Hubert Howe
- History of Alaska 1730-1885. San Francisco: 1886. 1st edn. 8vo. 775 pp. Fldg map. Sheep, some spotting & scuffing.
(Parmer) **$125 [≈ £78]**
- Works. San Francisco, 1882-91. 39 vols. Maps & plates. Sheep, worn & soiled, 1 vol rebacked in cloth, sev cvrs detached.
(Parmer) **$950 [≈ £593]**

Banister, T. Roger
- The Coastwise Lights of China. An Illustrated Account of the Chinese Maritime Customs Lights Service. Shanghai: (1932). xviii, 243 pp. 2 maps, frontis, num ills. Orig leather backed green cloth gilt.
(Lyon) **£75 [≈ $120]**

Banks, Joseph
- Joseph Banks in Newfoundland and Labrador, 1766. His Diary, Manuscripts and Collections. Edited by A.M. Lysaght. London: 1971. 4to. xxviii, 458 pp. Frontis, 8 cold maps, 12 cold plates, 96 pp of half-tone ills, 6 line drawings, 6 text figs. Orig cloth. Dw.
(Wheldon & Wesley) **£50 [≈ $80]**

Bannerman, David A.
- The Canary Islands: Their History, Natural History and Scenery. London: Gurney & Jackson, 1922. 1st edn. 8vo. xv,365 pp. 4 maps, cold frontis by Roland Green, 2 cold

plates by Gronvold, 81 b/w ills. Orig cloth, faded, sm 'splash' on spine. His 1st book.
(Gough) **£95 [≈ $152]**

Barbe-Marbois, M.
- The History of Louisiana ... Philadelphia: Carey & Lea, 1830. 1st edn in English. [8 advt], xviii,[2], 17-455, [1 errata] pp. Some foxing. Orig drab bds, rebacked.
(Jenkins) **$350 [≈ £218]**

Barber, Samuel
- Beneath Helvellyn's Shade. Notes and Sketches in the Valley of Wythburn. London: Elliot Stock, 1892. 8vo. 166 pp. Orig pict green cloth, sl rubbed. *(Moon)* **£35 [≈ $56]**

Barclay, Revd James
- Barclay's Complete and Universal English Dictionary ... Liverpool: Nuttall, Fisher & Dixon, 1810. Thick 4to. 24 fldg maps. Contemp scribbling on endpapers. Contemp calf gilt, rubbed & bumped.
(Hollett) **£50 [≈ $80]**
- The Universal English Dictionary ... Pronouncing Dictionary ... Epitome of the History of England ... London: J. & F. Tallis, [ca 1845]. Thick 4to. 51 county maps by J. Archer, num steel engvd plates. Some spotting. Reversed calf, rather worn.
(Hollett) **£120 [≈ $192]**

Bard, Samuel A. (pseud.)
- See Squire, Ephrain George.

Baretti, Joseph
- A Journey from London to Genoa ... Third Edition. London: for T. Davies; & L. Davis, 1770. 4 vols. 8vo. Contemp mottled calf, gilt spines (sl bruised). John Cator's b'plates.
(Hannas) **£420 [≈ $672]**

Baring-Gould, Sabine
- A Book of the Rhine. New York: Macmillan, 1906. 12mo. xii,345 pp. Cold frontis, other cold plates by Trevor Hadden, num photo plates. Orig green cloth gilt, elab dec spine.
(Terramedia) **$25 [≈ £15]**
- The Deserts of Southern France. New York: Dodd Mead, 1894. 1st Amer edn. 2 vols. 8vo. xxii, 296; xii, 303 pp. Frontis, num plates. Orig pict cloth gilt, spine edges sl rubbed.
(Terramedia) **$75 [≈ £46]**
- Iceland: Its Scenes and Sagas. London: Smith, Elder, 1863. 1st edn. Lge 8vo. Fldg map, 4 cold & 12 plain plates, text ills. Rec half calf. *(Hannas)* **£190 [≈ $304]**

Barker, James P.
- The Log of the Limejuicer. The Experiences Under Sail of J.P. Barker, Master Mariner, as Told to Roland Barker. New York: Macmillan, 1936. 8vo. xiv,251 pp. Ills. Orig cloth. Dw sl torn. Author's pres copy.
(Terramedia) **$35 [≈£21]**

Barnes, George
- A Statistical Account of Ireland, founded on Historical Fact. Chronologically arranged ... Dublin: Hibernia-Press Office ..., 1811. 1st edn. 8vo. [6],[3]-77 pp, apparently complete thus. Rec wraps. *(Fenning)* **£85 [≈$136]**

Barnes, Hon. R. Gorell
- Babes in the African Forest. London: Longmans, Green, 1911. 1st edn. 12mo. xv,247 pp. Fldg map, frontis, num plates. Orig green cloth, photo inset on front cvr, sl dulled. *(Terramedia)* **$75 [≈£46]**
- Babes in the African Wood. London: Longmans, Green, 1911. 1st edn. 8vo. 247 pp. Fldg map, 69 photo ills. Orig green cloth, photo onlay on front cvr.
(Parmer) **$65 [≈£40]**

Barns, T. Alexander
- An African Eldorado [the Congo]. London: 1926. 229 pp. Map, 32 ills. Orig bndg.
(Trophy Room Books) **$65 [≈£40]**
- Angolan Sketches. London: Methuen, (1928). 1st edn. 8vo. xii,206 pp. 3 maps, 20 photo plates. Orig light blue cloth gilt, minor gouge on front cvr. *(Karmiole)* **$45 [≈£28]**
- The Wonderland of the Eastern Congo. The Region of the Snow-Crowned Volcanoes, the Pigmies, the Giant Gorilla, & the Okapi ... London & New York: Putnam's, [1922]. 1st edn. Lge thick 8vo. xxxv,288 pp. Fldg map, frontis, plates. Orig gilt pict light brown cloth. *(Terramedia)* **$200 [≈£125]**

Barratt, J., publisher
- A Description of the House and Gardens at Stourhead. Bath: ptd for & published by J. Barratt, 1822. 8vo. 32,2 advt pp. Frontis. Rec paper bds. *(Ambra)* **£47 [≈$75]**

Barrington, Daines
- The Possibility of Approaching the North Pole Asserted. A New Edition. With an Appendix ... on the North West Passage by Colonel Beaufoy ... Second Edition. London: 1818. 8vo. Half-title, 2 advt ff at end. Fldg map. Orig paper bds, label & spine sl defective. *(Hannas)* **£220 [≈$352]**
- The Possibility of Approaching the North Pole Asserted. A New Edition. With an Appendix ... on a North West Passage by Colonel Beaufoy ... Second Edition. London: 1818. 8vo. xxiv,258,4 advt pp. Fldg map. Old calf backed mrbld bds, outer hinges partly cracked. *(Karmiole)* **$250 [≈£156]**

Barrow, John
- Navigatio Britannica: Or a Complete System of Navigation ... London: for W. & J. Mount & T. Page, 1750. 1st (apparently only) edn. 4to. xv, [1], 296, 127,[1] pp. Fldg table, 12 fldg plates. Sm piece cut from title marg. Contemp calf, worn, spine ends sl defective. *(Ramer)* **$450 [≈£281]**

Barrow, Sir John
- A Chronological History of the Voyages into the Arctic Regions; undertaken ... for discovering ... Passage between the Atlantic and the Pacific. London: Murray, 1818. 1st edn. 8vo. Lge fldg map, 3 w'cut maps in text. Contemp calf gilt, spine sl worn.
(Hannas) **£180 [≈$288]**
- A Chronological History of Voyages into the Arctic Regions, undertaken for discovering ... a Passage from Atlantic to Pacific. London: 1818. 1st edn. [4],379,48 pp. Lge fldg map, plates. Half calf. *(Jenkins)* **$325 [≈£203]**
- A Tour Round Ireland Through the Sea Coast Counties in the Autumn of 1835. London: Murray, 1836. 1st edn. 8vo. 379,38 appendix pp. Antique style half calf.
(Emerald Isle) **£125 [≈$200]**

Barth, Henry
- Travels and Discoveries in North and Central Africa ... in the Years 1849-1855. London: Longman, Brown ..., 1857-58. 1st English edn. 5 vols. 8vo. 15 fldg maps, fldg w'cut plate, 58 (of 60) tinted litho plates, 117 other ills. Orig cloth, a little shaken.
(Fenning) **£450 [≈$720]**
- Travels and Discoveries in North and Central Africa ... New York: Harper, 1857. 3 vols. 8vo. 657; 709,2 advt; 800 pp. Fldg map, 62 plates. Orig blue cloth, sl rubbed.
(Adelson) **$485 [≈£303]**
- Travels and Discoveries in North and Central Africa ... With Notes ... by the American Editor. Philadelphia: Bradley, 1859. Sm 8vo. 538,6 advt pp. Fldg map, frontis, 15 ills. Orig cloth. *(Schoyer)* **$25 [≈£15]**

Barthelemy, D. & Milik, J.
- Discoveries in the Judaean Desert. I; Qumran Cave I. Oxford: Clarendon Press, [1956]. Reprint. Lge 4to. 160 pp. 37 plates. Orig cloth. *(Terramedia)* **$100 [≈£62]**

Bartholomew, J.G. (ed.)
- The Royal Atlas of England and Wales. Reduced from the Ordnance Survey ... London: George Newnes, [ca 1900]. Folio. xii,72 pp. 70 cold maps. Three qtr leather & cloth, crnrs scuffed. *(Schoyer)* **$150 [≈ £93]**

Bartlett, John R.
- Personal Narrative of Explorations and Incidents in Texas, New Mexico, California, Sonora and Chihuahua with the U.S. Boundary Commission. New York & London: 1856. 2 vols in one. Maps, lithos, ills. Orig elab gilt half mor.
  (Jenkins) **$485 [≈ £303]**

Bartlett, R.A. & Hale, R.T.
- The Last Voyage of the Karluk. The Flagship of Vilhjalmar Stefansson's Canadian Arctic Expedition of 1913-16. Boston: Small, Maynard, [1916]. 1st edn. 8vo. xii,329 pp. Map, photo frontis, num other photo plates. Orig blue cloth. *(Terramedia)* **$75 [≈ £46]**

Bartlett, W.H.
- Bible Scenes of Interest and Beauty: A Series of Ten Views in Palestine, with Descriptive Letterpress. London: Blackwood, [ca 1850]. 1st edn. Sm 4to. 24 pp. 10 plates by Bartlett. Sl foxing. Orig cloth, a.e.g., edges sl rubbed.
  (Worldwide Antiqu'n) **$70 [≈ £43]**
- Footsteps of Our Lord and His Apostles in Syria, Greece, and Italy ... London: Hall, Virtue, 1852. 2nd edn. Tall 8vo. vi,237,[16 advt] pp. 23 steel-engvd plates inc title & map, 24 text w'cuts. Orig cloth, a.e.g., ex lib, v rubbed, tear in spine.
  (Worldwide Antiqu'n) **$60 [≈ £37]**
- Footsteps of Our Lord and His Apostles in Syria, Greece, and Italy ... London: A. Hall, Virtue, 1851. 1st edn. Roy 8vo. iv,[2],237,16 advt pp. Addtnl engvd title, map, 21 engvd plates, 24 other ills. Orig cloth gilt, a.e.g., faded, spine reprd. *(Fenning)* **£45 [≈ $72]**
- Forty Days in the Desert, on the Track of the Israelites; or, A Journey from Cairo, by Wady Feiran, to Mount Sinai and Petra. London: Arthur Hall, [ca 1850]. Lge 8vo. [6], iv, 206, [6 advt] pp. 45 steel engvs inc fldg map & addtnl engvd title. Occas sl foxing. Orig cloth gilt. *(Karmiole)* **$175 [≈ £109]**
- Gleanings, Pictorial and Antiquarian, on the Overland Route. London: Hall, Virtue, 1851. 2nd edn. 8vo. vi,2 advt,256,[24 advt] pp. 28 steel engvd plates (1 fldg), 23 w'engvs. Sl foxed. Marg dampstain on a few plates. Orig cloth, lacks backstrip.
  (Worldwide Antiqu'n) **$115 [≈ £71]**

- The Nile Boat; or, Glimpses of the Land of Egypt. London: Hall, Virtue, 1849. Map, steel-engvd plates after Bartlett. Occas sl foxing. Three qtr leather, scuffed.
  (Parmer) **$250 [≈ £156]**
- The Nile Boat; or, Glimpses of the Land of Egypt. London: Hall, Virtue, 1849. 1st edn. Tall 8vo. viii,218,[4 advt] pp. 35 steel- engvd plates inc title, 17 w'cuts in text. Orig cloth, v rubbed, hd of spine missing.
  (Worldwide Antiqu'n) **$95 [≈ £59]**
- The Scenery and Antiquities of Ireland, Illustrated from Drawings by W.H. Bartlett ... (text by J. Stirling Coyne). London: [ca 1850]. 2 vols. 4to. Engvd titles, map, plates. Scattered foxing. Orig three qtr mor, rather worn. *(Reese)* **$500 [≈ £312]**
- The Scenery and Antiquities of Ireland ... Illustrated in One Hundred and Twenty Engravings, with Historical and Descriptive Text by J.S. Coyne and N.P. Willis. London: Virtue, [ca 1850]. 2 vols in one. Green half mor. *(Emerald Isle)* **£200 [≈ $320]**

Barton, George A.
- Archaeology and the Bible. Part I. Explorations. Part II. Translations ... Philadelphia: American Sunday-School Union, [1917]. 2nd edn. 8vo. 469 pp. 114 plates. Orig blue cloth with mtd photo view.
  (Terramedia) **$50 [≈ £31]**

Bartram, John & Kalm, Peter
- Observations ... made by Mr. John Bartram, in his Travels from Pensilvania to Onodago ... Annexed, a Curious Account of the Cataracts at Niagara by Mr. Peter Kalm ... London: 1751. title-leaf, [viii], [9]-94 pp. Fldg plan. Traces of foxing. Later three qtr calf.
  (Reese) **$4,000 [≈ £2,500]**

Bartram, William
- Travels through North and South Carolina, Georgia, East and West Florida ... Philadelphia: James & Johnson, 1791. 1st edn. 34,521 pp. Plates. Half of map in facs, facs restoration to 1 leaf, some marg reprs. Contemp calf, rebacked.
  (Jenkins) **$2,850 [≈ £1,781]**

Barttelot, W.G.
- The Life of Edmund Musgrave Barttelot, Captain and Brevet-Major Royal Fusiliers Commander of the Rear Column of the Emin Pasha Relief Expedition ... London: Bentley, 1890. 3rd edn. xi,413 pp. 6 ills inc 2 fldg maps. Orig cloth gilt, spine darkened, sl soiled. *(Hollett)* **£65 [≈ $104]**

Barzini, Luigi
- Pekin to Paris. An Account of Prince Borghese's Journey across Two Continents in a Motor-Car ... London: Grant Richards, 1907. 1st English edn. 645 pp. Port frontis, fldg map, photo ills. Orig pict dec blue cloth gilt, t.e.g., sl soiled & rubbed.
(Duck) £185 [≈ $296]

Bassompierre, Marshal de
- Memoirs of the Embassy of the Marshall de Bassompierre to the Court of England in 1626. Translated with Notes. London: Murray, 1819. 1st edn in English. 8vo. xx,154 pp. Perf lib stamp on title. Contemp calf, disbound.   *(Terramedia)* $40 [≈ £25]

Bates, Emily Catherine
- A Year in the Great Republic [North America]. London: Ward & Downey, 1887. 1st edn. 2 vols. 8vo. Orig sky-blue cloth dec in red on upper cvrs, 1 spine v sl marked.
(Burmester) £120 [≈ $192]

Bates, H.W.
- The Naturalist on the River Amazon. London: 1863. 1st edn. 2 vols. 8vo. Map, ills. Orig cloth.
(Wheldon & Wesley) £220 [≈ $352]

Batty, Robert
- French Scenery from Drawings made in 1819 by Captain Batty of the Grenadier Guards. London: Rodwell & Martin, 1822. Sm 4to. Engvd title, 64 engvd plates. Sl foxing. Three qtr mor.   *(Bernett)* $325 [≈ £203]
- French Scenery from Drawings made in 1819 ... London: 1822. Half-title. Engvd title, 64 engvd plates, engvd vignette. Tissue guards. Some foxing. Contemp three qtr polished calf, wear to extremities.
(Reese) $500 [≈ £312]

Baudier, Michel
- The History of the Court of the King of China. Out of French. London: H.B. for Christopher Hussey ..., 1682. 1st edn in English. 12mo. [x],102,[3 advt] pp. C2 with paper fault affecting 2 words. Some catchwords shaved. Disbound. Wing B.1165.
(Pickering) $250 [≈ £156]

Bauer, Paul
- Himalayan Quest. The German Expeditions to Siniolchum and Nanga Parbat. London: Nicholson & Watson, 1938. 1st edn. Sm 4to. 4 maps, 96 plates. Orig cloth. Price-clipped dw.   *(Hollett)* £35 [≈ $56]

Baum, James E.
- Savage Abyssinia. New York: 1927. 336 pp. Ills. Orig bndg.
(Trophy Room Books) $90 [≈ £56]
- Savage Abyssinia. New York: J.H. Sears, 1928. 8vo. xix,272 pp. Ca 30 photo plates. B'plate removed. Orig red cloth, moderate soiling, crnrs bumped. *(Parmer)* $30 [≈ £18]
- Unknown Ethiopia. New York: 1935. 2nd edn of 'Savage Abyssinia', retitled. 354 pp. Ills. Orig bndg.
(Trophy Room Books) $75 [≈ £46]

Baxter, Dow V., et al.
- On and Off Alaskan Trails. N.p.: privately ptd, 1937. 8vo. [vi],184,[1] pp. Photo plates, text ills, endpaper maps. Orig cloth.
(High Latitude) $60 [≈ £37]

Beadle, J.H.
- Life in Utah; or the Mysteries and Crimes of Mormonism ... Philadelphia: Natl Publ Co, 1870. Subscription Edition. 8vo. 540,advt pp. Fldg map. Sl foxing. Sm dampstain edge of 1st 30 pp. Orig green cloth gilt, sl rubbed.
(Parmer) $85 [≈ £53]

Beale, Edward F.
- Wagon Road from Fort Defiance to the Colorado River. Letter from the Secretary of War ... [Washington]: 1858. 87 pp. Lge fldg map. Disbound. *(Reese)* $325 [≈ £203]

Beattie, William
- The Castles and Abbeys of England ... London: Tilt & Bogue, 1842. 4to. xvi,352 pp. 9 engvd plates, num text w'cuts. Sl spotting. Orig cloth gilt, t.e.g., crnrs & spine ends sl worn, sl shaken.   *(Hollett)* £35 [≈ $56]
- The Castles and Abbeys of England ... Illustrated with upwards of Two Hundred and Fifty Engravings. London: Virtue, 1854. 8vo. 10 engvd plates. Some spotting. Brown cloth, shaken & worn.
(Waterfield's) £60 [≈ $96]
- The Danube: Its History, Scenery, and Topography ... Illustrated from Sketches ... Drawn by W.H. Bartlett. London: [1844]. Thick 4to. 236 pp. Port, map, 78 plates. Occas sl foxing. Contemp elab gilt mor, a.e.g., sl rubbed. *(Reese)* $750 [≈ £468]
- The Waldenses or Protestant Valleys of Piedmont, Dauphiny, and the Ban De La Roche ... Illustrated by W.H. Bartlett ... and W. Brockedon ... London: 1838. 4to. [6],216 pp. Port, fldg map, engvd title, 70 plates. Some heavy foxing. Contemp calf, a.e.g., sl worn.   *(Reese)* $400 [≈ £250]

Beatty, Charles
- The Journal of a Two Months Tour: with a View of Promoting Religion among the Frontier Inhabitants of Pensylvania ... London: 1768. 1st edn. viii,[9]-110 pp, advt leaf. A bit soiled, marg waterstain to a few ff. Three qtr crushed mor, spine gilt extra, sl rubbing.   *(Reese)* **$1,250 [≈ £781]**

Beaufort, Emily, Lady Strangford
- The Eastern Shores of the Adriatic in 1863. With a Visit to Montenegro. London: Bentley, 1864. Only edn. 8vo. 4 cold & engvd plates, photo of the chieftain Mirko. Occas sl foxing. Contemp calf, gilt spine, prize b'plate.
            (Trebizond) **$225 [≈ £140]**
- Egyptian Sepulchres and Syrian Shrines including some Stay in the Lebanon, at Palmyra and in Western Turkey. London: Longman ..., 1862. 2nd edn. 2 vols. 8vo. Fldg map, 6 chromolitho plates. Half mor, ex-lib, sl worn, v rubbed.
            (Worldwide Antiqu'n) **$75 [≈ £46]**

Beazley, C. Raymond
- A History of Exploration and Geographical Science from the Middle Years of the Fifteenth Century. Oxford: Univ Press, 1906. Thick 8vo. 12 maps. Orig cloth.
            (Stewart) **£20 [≈ $32]**

Beckett, John Angus
- Iceland Adventure. The Double Traverse of Vatnajokull by the Cambridge Expedition. London: Witherby, [1934]. 1st edn. 8vo. Map, 8 plates. Orig cloth.
            (Hannas) **£30 [≈ $48]**

Beckford, Peter
- Familiar Letters from Italy, to a Friend in England. Salisbury: 1805. 2 vols. xii,450; viii,454 pp, errata leaf. Occas sl foxing. Contemp calf gilt, minor shelf wear.
            (Reese) **$250 [≈ £156]**

Beckford, William
- Italy: with Sketches of Spain and Portugal. By the Author of "Vathek". London: Bentley, 1834. 1st edn. 2 vols. Lge 8vo. Half-titles. Orig paper bds, uncut, new spines, orig ptd labels remtd. Cloth box. Roger Senhouse's b'plate.   *(Hannas)* **£180 [≈ $288]**
- Italy; with Sketches of Spain and Portugal. London: Bentley, 1834. 2nd edn. 2 vols. 8vo. xvi,371; xv,381 pp. Orig cloth, rebacked.
            (Gough) **£45 [≈ $72]**
- Italy; with Sketches of Spain and Portugal. By the Author of "Vathek". Third Edition.

London: Bentley, 1835. 2 vols. 8vo. [2], xvi,371; xv,381 pp. Lacks half-titles. Contemp half calf, gilt spines.
            (Fenning) **£55 [≈ $88]**
- Italy, Spain, and Portugal. With an Excursion to the Monasteries of Alcobaca and Batalha. New York: Wiley & Putnam, 1845. 2 vols in one. Sm 8vo. xii,174; xii,256 pp. Contemp three qtr mor, jnts rubbed.
            (Schoyer) **$45 [≈ £28]**
- Recollections of an Excursion to the Monasteries of Alcobaca and Batalha. By the Author of "Vathek". London: Bentley, 1835. 1st edn. Tall 8vo. Half-title. Port. Orig bds, uncut, spine renewed.
            (Hartfield) **$425 [≈ £265]**
- The Travel-Diaries ... Edited with a Memoir and Notes by Guy Chapman ... Cambridge: 1928. 2 vols. Errata slip. 2 frontis, plates. Orig half cloth & paper bds, ptd paper labels, partly unopened, v sl edge wear.
            (Reese) **$75 [≈ £46]**

Beebe, William
- The Arcturus Adventure. An Account of the New York Zoological Society's First Oceanographic Expedition. Putnam, 1926. 8vo. xix,439 pp. 7 cold plates. Orig cloth gilt.
            (Hollett) **£75 [≈ $120]**
- Pheasant Jungles. New York: 1927. 8vo. xiii, 248 pp. 58 ills. Orig cloth.
            (Wheldon & Wesley) **£25 [≈ $40]**

Beechey, Frederick William
- Narrative of a Voyage to the Pacific and Beering's Strait, to co-operate with the Polar Expeditions ... London: Colburn & Bentley, 1831. 'Admiralty Edition'. 1st 8vo edn. 2 vols. 8vo. xxvii,472; iv,452 pp. 3 maps, 23 plates. Contemp gilt panelled calf.
            (Gough) **£475 [≈ $760]**
- Narrative of a Voyage to the Pacific and Beering's Strait, to co-operate with the Polar Expedition ... Philadelphia: Carey & Lea, 1832. 1st US edn. vi,[2],xi,493 pp. Moderately foxed. New paper bds, leather label.   *(High Latitude)* **$95 [≈ £59]**
- A Voyage of Discovery Towards the North Pole ... London: Bentley, 1843. 1st edn. 8vo. 351 pp. Fldg map (reprd), 5 plates (only, of 6, 1 being defective). Some foxing. Orig cloth, recased, new endpapers, waterstain on front cvr, wear on back.   *(Schoyer)* **$150 [≈ £93]**

Beechey, Frederick William & H.W.
- Proceedings of the Expedition to Explore the Northern Coast of Africa, from Tripoli Eastward, in 1821 and 1822. London: 1828. 1st edn. 4to. xxiv,572,xliii,5 pp. Lge fldg

map, 8 others, lge fldg plate, 12 others (water stained). Contemp half calf, rubbed.
(Claude Cox) **£190 [≈ $304]**

Beehler, W.H.
- The Cruise of the Brooklyn. A Journal of the Principal Events of a Three Years' Cruise in the U.S. Flagship Brooklyn, in the South Atlantic Station ... Philadelphia: Lippincott, 1885. 1st edn. 8vo. 341 pp. Num plates. Orig pict blue cloth gilt, t.e.g.
(Terramedia) **$125 [≈ £78]**

Beet, G.
- The Grand Old Days of the Diamond Fields. Cape Town: Maskew Miller, 1888. 8vo. xix,192 pp. Photo ills. Orig cloth.
(Gemmary) **$75 [≈ £46]**

Beeton, S.O. (ed.)
- Beeton's Dictionary of Geography. A Universal Gazetteer ... London: Ward Lock & Tyler, 1868. 15th thousand. Fat 8vo. 893,8 advt pp. Num fldg maps, plans, &c. 8vo. Orig cloth gilt, trifle rubbed. *(Hollett)* **£50 [≈ $80]**

Belcher, Sir Edward
- The Last of the Arctic Voyages; being a Narrative of the Expedition in H.M.S. Assistance ... in Search of Sir John Franklin ... London: Lovell Reeve, 1855. 1st edn. 2 vols. Lge 8vo. 4 fldg maps (1 with sl repr), 2 frontis, 34 plates. Later three qtr calf.
(Reese) **$1,350 [≈ £843]**
- The Last of the Arctic Voyages ... H.M.S. Assistance ... in Search of Sir John Franklin ... London: Lovell Reeve, 1855. 2 vols. 8vo. xx,383; viii,419 pp. 3 fldg maps, 36 plates, many cold. Full wine mor, gilt dentelles, t.e.g. *(High Latitude)* **$950 [≈ £593]**
- The Last of the Arctic Voyages ... H.M.S. Assistance ... in Search of Sir John Franklin ... London: Lovell Reeve, 1855. 2 vols. 4to. xx, 383, advt, 24; 419 pp. 4 maps (3 fldg, 2 in pocket), 36 plates (11 cold), 25 w'engvs. Orig blue cloth gilt, spines relaid.
(Parmer) **$1,250 [≈ £781]**
- Narrative of a Voyage Round the World ... during the Years 1836 - 1842 ... London: 1843. 2 vols. [xxiv],387,advt; [viii],474 pp. 3 fldg maps in front pocket. Plates (some v foxed). Orig cloth, 1 spine relaid, some wear to extremities, vol 2 spine ends chipped.
(Reese) **$750 [≈ £468]**
- Narrative of a Voyage round the World, performed in Her Majesty's Ship Sulphur ... London: 1843. 2 vols. [xxiv], 387, advt; [viii], 474 pp. 3 fldg maps in front pocket, plates (some v foxed). Orig cloth, vol 1 spine relaid, some wear to extremities.

(Reese) **$750 [≈ £468]**

Belcher, Henry
- Illustrations of the Scenery on the Line of the Whitby and Pickering Railway ... London: Longman ..., 1836. Sole edn. 8vo. viii, 115 pp. Errata slip. Addtnl engvd title, 12 engvd plates (occas sl spotting). Orig watered cloth, sm split in jnt. *(Bickersteth)* **£110 [≈ $176]**

Belhaven, Lord
- The Uneven Road [autobiography: childhood in India, career in Arabia]. London: 1955. 2 vols. 8vo. Plates. Orig cloth.
(Farahar) **£25 [≈ $40]**

Bell, Mrs Arthur G.
- Nuremberg. Painted by Arthur G. Bell. London: A. & C. Black Colour Book, 1905. 1st edn. 20 cold plates. Orig blue cloth dec in black & gilt, t.e.g., spine v sl discold.
(Old Cathay) **£33 [≈ $52]**

Bell, C.F. Moberly
- From Pharaoh to Fellah. Illustrated by Georges Montbard. London: Wells Gardner, Dalton, [1888]. 4to. frontis, num plates & ills. Orig dec red cloth gilt.
(Terramedia) **$50 [≈ £31]**

Bell, Gertrude
- Amurath to Amurath. London: Macmillan, 1924. 2nd edn. 8vo. xvii,370 pp. Lge fldg map, frontis. Orig blue cloth.
(Terramedia) **$50 [≈ £31]**
- Syria, the Desert and the Sown. New York: Dutton, 1907. 8vo. xvi,347 pp. Cold frontis, fldg map, ills. Sl foxed. Orig cloth, rubbed & soiled, spine ends frayed.
(Worldwide Antiqu'n) **$65 [≈ £40]**

Bell, Major Horace
- Reminiscences of a Ranger, or, Early Times in Southern California. Los Angeles: 1881. 1st edn. 8vo. 457 pp. Orig pict cloth, rubbed, a trifle loose.
(M & S Rare Books) **$250 [≈ £156]**

Bell, James Mackintosh
- The Wilds of Maoriland. London: Macmillan, 1914. 1st edn. 2 fldg maps, cold frontis, num plates. Orig pict blue cloth gilt.
(Terramedia) **$75 [≈ £46]**
- The Wilds of Maoriland. London: Macmillan, 1914. 8vo. xii,257 pp. 2 fldg maps, cold & b/w ills, 6 maps in text. Orig pict cloth, crnrs & ft of spine rubbed.
(Schoyer) **$60 [≈ £37]**

Bell, W.D.M.
- Bell of Africa. Autobiography, compiled by Col. Whelen. London: 1960. 1st edn. 236 pp. Ills. Orig bndg. Dw.
(Trophy Room Books) **$150 [≈ £93]**
- Wanderings of an Elephant Hunter. London: 1958. 2nd edn. 8vo. Orig bndg. Dw.
(Grayling) **£35 [≈ $56]**

Belloc, Hilaire
- The Historic Thames. Illustrated by A.R. Quinton. London: Dent, 1907. 1st edn. 59 cold plates. Orig dec cloth gilt, spine ends sl worn.   *(Old Cathay)* **£145 [≈ £232]**
- Sussex. Painted by Wilfrid Ball. London: A. & C. Black Colour Books, Twenty Shilling Series, 1906. 1st edn. Map, 75 cold plates. List of corrigenda opposite title. Orig dec cloth.   *(Old Cathay)* **£58 [≈ $92]**

Belo, Jane
- Trance in Bali. New York: 1960. xiii,284 pp. 108 ills. Orig silver dec red cloth. Dw.
(Lyon) **£65 [≈ $104]**

Belt, Thomas
- The Naturalist in Nicaragua: A Narrative ... London: Murray, 1874. Sm 8vo. 403,32 ctlg pp. Fldg map, 26 ills. Orig dec cloth, spine ends sl worn, ex-lib, new endpapers.
(Schoyer) **$65 [≈ £40]**

Beltrami, Giacomo Battista
- A Pilgrimage in Europe and America leading to the Discovery of the Sources of the Mississippi and Bloody River ... London: 1828. 1st edn in English. 2 vols. 8vo. Port, 1 map, 2 plans, 3 plates. Contemp half calf, rubbed, labels defective.
(Waterfield's) **£250 [≈ $400]**
- A Pilgrimage in Europe and America, leading to the Discovery of the Sources of the Mississippi ... London: 1828. 2 vols. lxxvi, 472; [545] pp. P 545 misnumbered 54. Fldg map, plans, port, plates. Lib blind stamp on titles. Some foxing to map & plates. Later half mor.   *(Reese)* **$500 [≈ £312]**

Belzoni, G.
- Narrative of the Operations and Recent Discoveries ... in Egypt and Nubia ... London: Murray, 1821-22. 2nd edn. 2 vols. Elephant folio & 4to text vol. Port, lge fldg map, 1 line engv; 44 lithos & engvs on 34 sheets. The folio vol sl dampstained. Rec mor.   *(Frew Mackenzie)* **£2,100 [≈ $3,360]**
- Narrative of the Operations and Recent Discoveries ... in Egypt and Nubia ...

London: Murray, 1821. 2nd edn. 4to. xix,533 pp. Port, lge fldg map, 1 line engv. Some underscoring in black & red pencil. Sl foxing. Contemp mor, jnts cracking, ex-lib.
(Worldwide Antiqu'n) **$250 [≈ £156]**

Benezet, Anthony
- A Short Account of the People called Quakers; Their Rise, Religious Principles and Settlement in America ... Philadelphia: Joseph Crukshank, 1780. 1st edn. 8vo. 27 pp. Sl foxing. Trimmed. Half mor gilt.
(Parmer) **$150 [≈ £93]**
- Some Historical Account of Guinea, Its Situation, Produce, and the General Disposition of its Inhabitants. With an Inquiry into ... the Slave Trade ... New Edition. London: 1788. xv, 131 [sic],1 advt pp. Title vignette. Some soiling to title. Later half mor.   *(Reese)* **$100 [≈ £62]**
- Some Historical Account of Guinea ... With an Inquiry into ... the Slave Trade ... London: Phillips, 1788. 8vo. xv,151 [sic],[1] pp. Sm title w'cut by Bewick ('Am I not a Man and a Brother'). Contemp pencil marginalia. Orig paper backed bds, paper spine split.
(Frew Mackenzie) **£125 [≈ $200]**

Benjamin, S.G.W.
- The Atlantic Islands as Resorts of Health and Pleasure. New York: 1878. 4to. 274,advt pp. Frontis, text ills. Orig pict cloth, ex lib with shelf number & b'plate, cloth soiled.
(Reese) **$100 [≈ £62]**
- Persia and the Persians. Boston & New York: Houghton Mifflin, Riverside Press, 1886. 1st edn. Sm 4to. xx,507 pp. Frontis, 56 ills. Orig cloth, sl rubbed, lib number on spine.
(Worldwide Antiqu'n) **$65 [≈ £40]**
- Persia and the Persians. Boston: Ticknor, 1887. Sm 4to. xx,507 pp. Num plates & text ills. Lib stamps on reverse of some plates. Lib buckram.   *(Worldwide Antiqu'n)* **$65 [≈ £40]**

Bennet, Ernest
- The Downfall of the Dervishes or the Avenging of Gordon. Being a Personal Narrative of the Final Soudan Campaign. London: 1899. 1st edn. Sm 8vo. xii,255 pp. 3 maps (2 fldg), port frontis. Orig red cloth gilt, sl worn.   *(Terramedia)* **$100 [≈ £62]**

Bennett, E.
- Shots and Snapshots in British East Africa. London: 1914. 312 pp. Fldg map, 51 ills. Orig bndg.
(Trophy Room Books) **$140 [≈ £87]**
- Shots and Snapshots in British East Africa. London: 1914. 8vo. Fldg map in pocket, num

ills. Sl foxing. Orig bndg, lower spine v sl marked.   *(Grayling)* **£105 [≈ $168]**

Bennett, George
- The History of Bandon and the Principal Towns in the West Riding of Cork. Enlarged Edition. Cork: Francis Guy, 1869. 8vo. viii, 572 pp. Erratum slip. 2 ports, tinted litho plate. Orig cloth gilt, sl worn, sl discold.
          (Fenning) **£135 [≈ $216]**

Bennett, James
- A Tewkesbury Guide. Containing a Sketch of the History of the Borough ... Description of the Abbey Church ... Tewkesbury: James Bennett, [1835]. Sm 8vo. Orig ptd bds, worn. crude repr to spine.   *(Ambra)* **£38 [≈ $60]**

Bensusan, S.L.
- Morocco. Painted by A.S. Forrest. London: A. & C. Black Colour Books, Twenty Shilling Series, 1904. 1st edn. 74 cold plates. Orig dec cloth, t.e.g.   *(Old Cathay)* **£55 [≈ $88]**
- Morocco. Painted by A.S. Forrest. London: A. & C. Black Colour Books, Twenty Shilling Series, 1904. 1st edn. 74 cold plates. Orig dec cloth, t.e.g., some rubbing to bds, browning to endpapers.   *(Old Cathay)* **£39 [≈ $62]**

Bent, James Theodore
- The Cyclades or Life among the Insular Greeks. London: Longmans, Green, 1885. 8vo. xx, 501 pp. Fldg map frontis. Orig blue cloth, edges rather rubbed, foredge foxed.
          (Piccadilly) **£32 [≈ $51]**
- The Ruined Cities of Mashonaland. Being a Record of Excavation & Exploration in 1891 ... London: 1893. New edn, with new preface. 8vo. xvii,427,advt pp. Fldg map, frontis, num plates & ills. Orig pict cloth, clean ex-lib.
          (Terramedia) **£150 [≈ $93]**
- The Ruined Cities of Mashonaland. Being a Record of Excavation and Exploration in 1891. London: Longmans, 1893. New edn. 8vo. xvi,427 pp. Fldg map, ills. Ex-lib. Rec red qtr leather.
     (Bates & Hindmarch) **£50 [≈ $80]**

Bent, N.
- Jungle Giants. MA: 1936. 253 pp. Ills. Orig red cloth.
          (Trophy Room Books) **$200 [≈ £125]**

Bentley, John
- Halifax, and its Gibbet-Law Placed in a True Light. Together with a Description of the Town ... Halifax: P. Darby, for John Bentley ..., [1761]. 1st edn. [ii],95 pp. Frontis. Mod half calf.   *(Hollett)* **£120 [≈ $192]**

- Halifax, and its Gibbet-Law ... see also Midgley, Samuel.

Bentley, Revd William Holman
- Dictionary and Grammar of the Kongo Language, as spoken at San Salvador ... Compiled and Prepared for the Baptist Mission on the Kongo River ... London: 1887. Thick 8vo. Orig bright blue cloth, some sl wear.   *(Farahar)* **£500 [≈ $800]**
- Pioneering on the Congo. New York: Revell, 1900. 2 vols. 8vo. 478; 448 pp. Fldg map, 206 ills. Orig pict cloth, sl soiled.
          (Schoyer) **$130 [≈ £81]**

Beresford, Lord Charles
- The Break-up of China, with an Account of its Present Commerce, Currency, Waterways, Armies, Railways, Politics and Future Prospects. London: 1899. Thick 8vo. 2 fldg maps, fldg table. Orig blue cloth.
          (Farahar) **£55 [≈ $88]**
- The Break-Up of China. London & New York: Harper, 1899. 1st edn. xviii,509,advt pp. 2 lge fldg maps. Orig blue cloth gilt.
          (Terramedia) **$80 [≈ £50]**

Bernacchi, Louis C.
- Saga of the 'Discovery'. London & Glasgow: Blackie, 1938. 1st cdn. 8vo. 240 pp. 3 maps, num photo plates. Orig blue cloth, somewhat tired, cvrs worn.   *(Parmer)* **$65 [≈ £40]**

Bernal, Ignacio
- The Olmec World. Translated from the Spanish by D. Hayden & Fernando Horcasitas. Berkeley & Los Angeles: Univ of Calif Press, 1969. 1st edn. Lge 4to. xiv,273 pp. Num plates. Cloth. Dw.
          (Terramedia) **$65 [≈ £40]**

Bernier, F.
- The History of the Late Revolution of the Empire of the Great Mogul ... London: 1676. 2nd edn. 2 vols in one. Fldg map. Faint marg stains at end of vol 2. Half calf, sl worn.
          (Farahar) **£225 [≈ $360]**

Bernier, J.E.
- Report on the Dominion of Canada Government Expedition to the Arctic Islands and Hudson Strait on board the D.G.S. 'Arctic'. Ottawa: Govt Printing Bureau, 1910. xxix, 529 pp. 4 fldg maps, num photo ills. Orig cloth, slight wear.
          (High Latitude) **$85 [≈ £53]**

Bertuchi, A.J.
- The Island of Rodriguez, A British Colony in

the Mascarenhas Group. London: 1923. 8vo.
Fldg map, plates. Orig cloth.
(Farahar) £55 [≈ $88]

Besley, H., printer
- The Handbook of Western Cornwall,
Penzance, Falmouth, and Neighbourhoods.
St. Michael's Mount, the Land's End, The
Logan Stone ... [Ca 1870]. 12mo. 24 pp advts.
Fldg map, 9 tinted lithos. Orig cloth, inner
hinges weak.   *(Ambra)* £35 [≈ $56]

Best, Elsdon
- Tuhoe The Children of the Mist. A Sketch of
... the Tuhoe Tribe of the Maori of New
Zealand ... New Plymouth, NZ: Avery, 1925.
1st edn. 2 vols. 8vo & oblong folio. Lge fldg
map in pocket. Genealogical tables. Orig
cloth.   *(Worldwide Antiqu'n)* $75 [≈ £46]

Bevan, Samuel
- Sand and Canvas: A Narrative of Adventures
in Egypt. With a Sojourn among the Artists in
Rome. London: Gilpin, 1884. 8vo. xii,370,2
advt pp. Num ills. Orig cloth, v rubbed, tears
& chips in spine, v soiled.
(Worldwide Antiqu'n) $55 [≈ £34]

Bey, F.
- The Story of Fergie Bey. London: 1930. 356
pp. Fldg map, ills. Orig bndg.
(Trophy Room Books) $225 [≈ £140]

Beynon, W.G.L.
- With Kelly to Chitral. London: Arnold,
1896. 1st edn. 160 pp. Fldg map, 8 plates.
Orig red cloth, sl marked & dulled.
(Box of Delights) £30 [≈ $48]

Bickmore, Albert S.
- Travels in the East Indian Archipelago. New
York: Appleton, 1869. 1st edn. 8vo. Fldg
map, 32 plates. Orig pict cloth gilt, gilt spine,
minor wear to spine extremities.
(Trebizond) $125 [≈ £78]

Bicknell, Arthur C.
- Travel and Adventure in Northern
Queensland. London: Longmans, Green,
1895. 1st edn. 8vo. xvi,219,24 advt pp. Num
plates, text ills. Orig pict green cloth gilt.
(Terramedia) $250 [≈ £156]
- Travel and Adventure in Northern
Queensland. London: Longmans, Green,
1895. 8vo. xiii,219,24 advt pp. Frontis, 24
plates. Orig pict green cloth gilt, rubbed.
(Adelson) $160 [≈ £100]

Bicknell, W.I.
- The Public Buildings of Paris and its
Environs, in the Middle of the Nineteenth
Century, Illustrated ... London: E.T. Brain &
Co, [ca 1849]. 1st edn. 8vo. vi,xxxii,235,[8]
pp. Addtnl engvd title, 150 plates. Sl
browned. Contemp cloth, spine relaid.
(Claude Cox) £75 [≈ $120]

Bigelow, Andrew
- Leaves from a Journal, or Sketches of a
Rambler in North Britain and Ireland.
Edinburgh: Oliver & Boyd, 1824. 1st edn in
book form. 16mo. 308 pp. Perf lib stamp on
title. Contemp calf, rebacked in brown
vellum.   *(Terramedia)* $25 [≈ £15]
- Travels in Malta and Sicily, with Sketches of
Gibraltar in 1827. Boston: Carter, Hendee &
Babcock, 1831. 1st edn. Oblong 4to. xxii, 528
pp. Hand cold chart frontis, 4 plates. Sl foxed
& spotted. Orig bds, v rubbed, lib cloth
reback.   *(Worldwide Antiqu'n)* $125 [≈ £78]

Bigham, Clive
- A Ride through Western Asia. London:
Macmillan, 1897. 1st edn. 8vo. xli,275 pp. 4
fldg cold maps, 34 plates. Orig cloth, edges
rubbed, spine ends frayed, ex-lib.
(Worldwide Antiqu'n) $45 [≈ £28]

Bingham, Hiram
- Inca Land: Explorations in the Highlands of
Peru. Boston & New York: Houghton
Mifflin, [1923]. 3rd imp. 8vo. xvi,365 pp.
Num maps & photo plates. Orig blue cloth.
(Terramedia) $100 [≈ £62]
- Machu Picchu. A Citadel of the Incas. Report
of the Explorations and Excavations ... New
Haven: Yale Univ Press for the Nat Geog
Soc, 1930. One of 500. 4to. xiv,244 pp. Lge
fldg map at end, 218 plates & text photos.
Orig red cloth over bds. Slip case rubbed.
(Karmiole) $750 [≈ £468]

Bingham, J. Elliott
- Narrative of the Expedition to China from the
Commencement of the War to the Present
Period ... London: Colburn, 1842. 1st edn. 2
vols. Lge 12mo. xvi,395; viii,424,[8 ctlg] pp.
3 plates (sl marg browning). Orig cloth,
uncut, sl soiled, spines darkened.
(Claude Cox) £120 [≈ $192]

Bingley, William
- Biographical Conversations on the most
Eminent Voyagers, of Different Nations,
from Columbus to Cook ... Designed for the
Use of Young Persons. London: 1856. 12mo.
xiii,[3], 360 pp. Text ills. Contemp calf gilt,
a.e.g., extremities worn. *(Reese)* $45 [≈ £28]

- A Tour round North Wales performed during the Summer of 1798. Sold by E. Williams & J. Deighton, Cambridge, 1800. 2 vols. 8vo. 2 frontis, 2 plates, 8 ff of music. Mod half calf.
  (Waterfield's) £155 [≈ $248]

Binion, Samuel Augustus
- Ancient Egypt or Mizraim. New York: Allen, 1887. One of 800 deluxe. 2 vols. Dble elephant folio. iv,72; iv,72 pp. 2 engvd titles, 72 plates (37 cold, 11 tinted). 1 plate with minor tear, 1 f minor fraying. Ex-lib. Orig qtr mor, cvrs detached.
  (Worldwide Antiqu'n) $1,950 [≈ £1,218]

Binney, Sir George
- With Seaplane and Sledge in the Arctic ... London: Hutchinson, [ca 1925]. 288 pp. Lge fldg map, 51 photo ills. Orig blue cloth. Sl chipped dw.
  (Karmiole) $85 [≈ £53]

Bird, Isabella Lucy
- The Golden Chersonese and the Way Thither. London: Murray, 1883. 1st edn. xvi, 384, [32 advt] pp. Frontis, fldg map, 10 plates. Mod half mor gilt.
  (Hollett) £95 [≈ $152]
- The Hawaiian Archipelago: Six Months among the Palm Groves, Coral Reefs and Volcanoes of the Sandwich Islands ... Third Edition. London: Murray, 1880. 32 pp ctlg. Num w'engvs. Orig gilt dec cloth.
  (Waterfield's) £80 [≈ $128]
- Journeys in Persia and Kurdistan. New York & London: Putnam's & John Murray, 1891. 1st edn. 2 vols. Sm 8vo. xiv,381; 409 pp. 2 fldg maps, 2 frontis, num plates. Clean ex-lib. Orig dec light blue cloth gilt, vol 1 sl shaken internally.
  (Terramedia) $300 [≈ £187]

Birge, John Kingsley
- The Bektashi Order of Dervishes. London: Luzac, 1937. 1st edn. Tall 8vo. 291 pp, errata slip. 32 photo plates. Endpapers sl foxed. Orig green cloth. Dw sl worn.
  (Frew Mackenzie) £90 [≈ $144]

Birkbeck, Morris
- Notes on a Journey through France. London: Phillips, 1815. 8vo. Bds.
  (Rostenberg & Stern) $160 [≈ £100]

Birkeland, Knud B.
- The Whalers of Akutan. An Account of Modern Whaling in the Aleutian Islands. New Haven: Yale Univ Press, 1926. [viii],171 pp. Plates. Orig cloth. Dw.
  (High Latitude) $85 [≈ £53]

Birket-Smith, Kaj & Laguna, Frederica de
- The Eyak Indians of the Copper River Delta, Alaska. Copenhagen: Levin & Munksgaard, 1938. 8vo. 591 pp. 18 plates, fldg graph. Ptd wraps.
  (High Latitude) $100 [≈ £62]

Bishop, Mrs J.F.
- Formerly Bird, Isabella Lucy, q.v.

Bisiker, Arthur
- Across Iceland. London: Edward Arnold, 1902. 1st edn. 8vo. xi,231,32 advt pp. 2 fldg maps, num ills. Advts spotted. Orig pict cloth gilt, spine faded.
  (Hollett) £75 [≈ $120]

Blachford, Robert
- The New West-India Pilot: containing Sailing Directions for the Gulfs of Florida and Mexico, Bay of Honduras, New Providence and Windward Passages ... London: [1818]. 2 ff, 55 pp. Later wraps.
  (Reese) $325 [≈ £203]

Black, A. & C.
- Black's Picturesque Guide to North Wales. Edinburgh: 1863. 8vo. iv,239,advt pp. Vignette title, 27 ills inc fldg railway map. Sl browning, endpapers sl soiled. Orig limp bds, worn, a touch loose.
  (Dillons) £15 [≈ $24]
- Blacks Guide to Scotland. London: 1892. 29th edn. 563,128 advt pp. Fldg map in pocket, maps, plans, w'engvs in text. Orig dec black cloth gilt, rear cvr sl damp stained.
  (Old Cathay) £29 [≈ $46]

Blackburn, Henry
- Artists and Arabs; or, Sketching in Sunshine. Boston: 1874. 12mo. 215,advt,errata pp. Ills. Occas foxing. Orig pict gilt cloth, some edge wear.
  (Reese) $75 [≈ £46]
- The Pyrenees: A Description of Summer Life at French Watering Places. London: Sampson Low ..., 1867. 1st edn. Lge 8vo. xvi,327,[4 advt] pp. Frontis, map, 111 ills by Gustave Dore. Occas sl spotting. Orig cloth gilt, bevelled bds, spine sl faded.
  (Hollett) £75 [≈ $120]

Blacker, L.V.S.
- On Secret Patrol in High Asia. Introduction by Major General Younghusband. London: 1922. 302 pp. Lge cold fldg map, ills. Orig bndg, moderate wear, almost no fading of spine.
  (Trophy Room Books) $200 [≈ £125]

Blackman, A.M.
- Luxor and its Temples. London: A. & C. Black, 1923. 1st edn. 8vo. Plates & text ills by Major Benton Fletcher. Orig cloth, rebacked,

sl soiled.   *(Worldwide Antiqu'n)* **$45 [≈£28]**

Blackmore, William
- Colorado: Its Resources, Parks and Prospects as a New Field for Emigration. London: Sampson Low, 1869. Folio. 217 pp. Map. 1 mtd photo (of William Gilpin). Orig cloth, rebacked. A few known copies have 2 maps & 4 photos.   *(Jenkins)* **$275 [≈£171]**

Blagdon, Francis William
- Paris As It Was and As It Is; or a Sketch of the French Capital ... By an English Traveller ... London: Baldwin, 1803. 1st edn. 2 vols. 8vo. [32],xxiv,460; [4],583,[1] pp. Contemp half roan, spines defective but bndgs strong.   *(Fenning)* **£55 [≈$88]**

Blaikie, John
- Among the Goths and the Vandals. London: Tinsley Bros, 1870. 1st edn. 8vo. [viii],270 pp. Orig bright green cloth.
        (Burmester) **£32 [≈$51]**
- Among the Goths and Vandals. London: Tinsley Bros, 1870. 1st edn. 8vo. Orig cloth.
        (Hannas) **£35 [≈$56]**

Blaikie, William G.
- The Personal Life of David Livingstone ... Chiefly from his Unpublished Journals and Correspondence ... Second Edition. London: Murray, 1881. 8vo. xix,526,24 advt pp. Fldg map, port. Rec calf backed mrbld bds.
        (Fenning) **£32.50 [≈$52]**

Blake, E. Vale (ed.)
- See Tyson, George E.

Blake, Euphemia
- Arctic Experiences: Containing Capt. George E. Tyson's Wonderful Drift on the Ice-Floe, a History of the Polaris Expedition ... New York: 1874. 1st edn. 8vo. 486,6 advt pp. Map, plates, ills. Three qtr calf, spine ends sl worn.   *(Parmer)* **$135 [≈£84]**

Bland-Sutton, J.
- Man and Beast in Eastern Ethiopia. London: 1911. 418 pp. 204 ills. Orig pict gilt bndg.
        (Trophy Room Books) **$275 [≈£171]**

Blashfield, Edwin H. & Evangeline
- Italian Cities. New York: Scribner's, 1900. 1st edn. 2 vols. 12mo. vi,296; vi,310, advt pp. Tipped-in photo views. Orig dec green cloth gilt, t.e.g.   *(Terramedia)* **$30 [≈£18]**

Blayney, Andrew
- Narrative of a Forced Journey through Spain and France, as a Prisoner of War, in the Years 1810 to 1814. London: E. Kerby, 1814. 1st edn. 2 vols. 8vo. xvi,495; viii,504 pp. 2 frontis. Sl spotting. Contemp half russia, gilt spines, jnts sl cracked.
        (Spelman) **£120 [≈$192]**

Blew, William C.A.
- Brighton and Its Coaches. A History of the London and Brighton Road. With Some Account of the Provincial Coaches ... London: Nimmo, 1894. Imperial 8vo. xxii,354 pp. 20 hand cold plates. Orig pict dec blue cloth gilt, t.e.g., spine sl marked.
        (Duck) **£195 [≈$312]**

Bligh, William
- A Voyage to the South Sea ... for the Purpose of Conveying the Bread-Fruit Tree to the West Indies ... Mutiny ... London: George Nicol, 1792. 1st edn. [viii],264 pp. Port frontis, 7 plates (plans, charts etc.). 2 sm reprs. Contemp calf gilt, sometime rebacked.   *(Frew Mackenzie)* **£3,250 [≈$5,200]**

Blomfield, Ezekiel
- A General View of the World, Geographical, Historical, and Philosophical ... Bungay: C. Brightly & T. Kinnersley, 1807. Sole edn. 2 vols. 4to. Frontis in vol 1, 21 maps, 36 engvd plates. 1 plate foxed. Orig diced calf, gilt spines, a little rubbed.
        (Bickersteth) **£40 [≈$64]**

Blunt, Lady Anne
- The Bedouin Tribes of the Euphrates. Edited with a Preface and Some Account of the Arabs and their Horses by W.S.B. New York: Harper, 1879. 8vo. 445 pp. Fldg map, frontis, num plates, fldg chart. Orig pict blue cloth gilt, poor ex-lib copy.
        (Terramedia) **$50 [≈£31]**

Blunt, John James
- Vestiges of Ancient Manners and Customs, Discoverable in Modern Italy and Sicily. London: Murray ..., 1823. only edn. 8vo. xvi, 293 pp. Half-title. 19th c half calf.
        (Young's) **£65 [≈$104]**

Blunt, Wilfred Scawen
- Ideas About India. London: Kegan Paul, 1885. 1st edn. 8vo. xxiii,202,44 advt pp. Frontis. Orig brown cloth gilt.
        (Gough) **£30 [≈$48]**
- My Diaries. Being a Personal Narrative of Events, 1888-1914. London: Martin Secker, 1919-20. 2 vols. 8vo. Orig blue cloth, spines faded, some shelfwear.
        (Parmer) **$125 [≈£78]**

- Secret History of the English Occupation of Egypt ... London: Fisher Unwin, 1907. 2nd edn, rvsd. 8vo. xii,606 pp. Orig blue cloth, unopened, some shelfwear, crnrs bumped. *(Parmer)* **$100 [≈ £62]**
- Secret History of the English Occupation of Egypt ... New York: Knopf, 1922. 1st Amer edn. 8vo. 416 pp. Frontis. Foredge sl stained. Orig bndg, paper label, cloth spine sl worn, bds sl stained. *(Parmer)* **$60 [≈ £37]**

Boas, Franz (ed.)
- Handbook of American Indian Languages. Washington: GPO, 1911-22. 1st edn. 2 vols. 8vo. 1069; 903 pp. Orig cloth, remains of b'plate on vol 1 pastedown. *(Schoyer)* **$100 [≈ £62]**

Bodie, William F.
- The Cruise of the Corwin ... see Muir, John.

Boemus, Joannes
- The Manners, Lawes and Customs of All Nations ... Written in Latin, and now newly translated into English, by Ed. Aston. London: 1611. 1st edn of this translation. 4to. Title soiled, lib stamp on verso. Minor stains elsewhere. Early calf, rebacked. STC 3198. *(Hannas)* **£750 [≈ $1,200]**

Boetticher, J.G.
- A Geographical, Historical, and Political Description of the Empire of Germany ... London: for John Stockdale, 1800. 1st edn. 4to. 390,viii,87 pp. Map frontis, 3 lge fldg maps, 23 plans. Contemp half calf, worn but sound, ft of spine chipped. *(Sotheran)* **£300 [≈ $480]**

Bogg, Edmund & Daykin, W.H.
- Nidderdale and the Vale of the Nidd from Nun Monkton to Great Whernside ... Leeds: E. Bogg, n.d. 4to. 56,advt pp. 32 full-page & over 20 other ills. Orig cloth backed ptd bds, sl soiled. *(Hollett)* **£75 [≈ $120]**

Boisgelin, Louis de
- Travels through Denmark and Sweden ... London: for Wilkie & Robinson ..., 1810. 1st edn. 2 vols. 4to. Half-titles, final errata leaf. 13 hand cold aquatint plates. A few ff foxed, as always. Later paper bds, cloth spines, uncut. *(Hannas)* **£650 [≈ $1,040]**

Bollaert, William
- Antiquarian, Ethnological and other Researches in New Granada, Ecuador, Peru and Chile ... London: Trubner, 1860. 8vo. 4,3-279 pp. Map, 17 plates. Brown mor bds,

rebacked. *(Adelson)* **$285 [≈ £178]**

Boller, Henry A.
- Among the Indians. Eight Years in the Far West: 1858-1866. Embracing Sketches of Montana and Salt Lake. Philadelphia: 1868. xvi, 17-428 pp. Lacks the map (not issued in all copies). Stamp on half-title, marg stain on title, spotting. Mod calf, gilt spine. *(Reese)* **$500 [≈ £312]**

Boner, Charles
- Chamois Hunting in the Mountains of Bavaria. London: 1853. viii,410 pp. Frontis, litho plates. Occas sl foxing, starting slightly between sgntrs. Contemp three qtr polished calf, some wear to extremities. *(Reese)* **$300 [≈ £187]**
- Chamois Hunting in the Mountains of Bavaria. London: 1853. 8vo. Tinted engvd plates, vignettes. Occas foxing. Orig cloth, spine strengthened. *(Grayling)* **£150 [≈ $240]**
- Transylvania; its Products and its People. London: 1865. 1st edn. 8vo. xiv,642 pp. Cold frontis, 5 fldg maps, 10 plates, num text ills. Sm stamp on title. Orig cloth. *(Fenning)* **£75 [≈ $120]**

Bonomi, Joseph
- Nineveh and Its Palaces. The Discoveries of Botta and Layard, applied to the Elucidation of Holy Writ. London: Ingram, Cooke, 1853. 2nd edn, rvsd. 8vo. xx,429 pp. 6 plates, 273 ills. Sl foxing. Endpapers sl water marked. Mor, a.e.g., edges rubbed. *(Thornton's)* **£28 [≈ $44]**
- Nineveh and Its Palaces. The Discoveries of Botta and Layard, applied to the Elucidation of Holy Writ. London: Ingram, Cooke, 1853. 2nd edn, rvsd. 8vo. xx,429 pp. 7 plates, 273 ills. Foxed. Rec paper bds. *(Fenning)* **£24.50 [≈ $40]**
- Nineveh and Its Palaces. The Discoveries of Botta and Layard, applied to the Elucidation of Holy Writ. London: Ingram, Cooke, 1853. 2nd edn, rvsd. 8vo. xx,429 pp. 8 plates, 273 ills. Half mor, elab gilt spine, sl rubbed. *(Worldwide Antiqu'n)* **$75 [≈ £46]**

Bonvalot, Gabriel
- Across Thibet ... New York: Cassell, 1892. 8vo. xiii,417 pp. Fldg map, 24 plates, num text ills. Orig pict cloth, rubbed. *(Adelson)* **$275 [≈ £171]**

Bonwick, James
- The Wild White Man and the Blacks of Victoria. Melbourne: Fergusson & Moore, 1863. 2nd edn. Sm 8vo. iv,90 pp. 2 plates.

Qtr cloth, slightly rubbed & spotted, ex-lib.
(Worldwide Antiqu'n) **$165 [≈ £103]**

Boon, Edward P.
- Catalogue of Books and Pamphlets principally relating to America. New York: 1870. 8vo. Contemp half mor, spine relaid. MS prices added. *(Waterfield's)* **£85 [≈ $136]**

Boothroyd, Benjamin
- The History of the Ancient Borough of Pontefract ... Pontefract: ptd by and for the author ..., 1807. Sole edn. 8vo. xvi,496,xxiv pp. Fldg town plan, 5 plates. Contemp tree calf. *(Young's)* **£78 [≈ $124]**

Borden, Mrs John
- The Cruise of the Northern Light. Explorations and Hunting in the Alaskan and Siberian Arctic. New York: Macmillan, 1928. Roy 8vo. xvi,318 pp. Port, over 80 photos, endpaper maps. Orig cloth gilt. Signed by the author. *(Berkelouw)* **$55 [≈ £34]**

Borden, W.W.
- Borden's Leadville. A Treatise on Leadville, Colorado. Reliable Information ... Containing the Different Routes ... New Albany: 1879. 39,10 advt pp. Wraps. *(Reese)* **$1,100 [≈ £687]**

Borlase, William
- Antiquities Historical and Monumental of the County of Cornwall. With a New Introduction by P. Pool and C. Thomas. London: 1769, facs reprint 1973. Folio. xxii, xvi, 464 pp. Ills. Orig cloth. *(Wheldon & Wesley)* **£50 [≈ $80]**

Borrow, George
- The Bible in Spain ... London: Murray, 1843. 1st edn. 3 vols. 8vo. xxiv, 370, [2 advt]; viii,398,[2 advt]; viii,391,[1 advt] pp. Half-titles. Inserted advt leaf on pale purple paper at end of vol 3. Contemp dark blue cloth, uncut, paper labels (sl rubbed). *(Gough)* **£225 [≈ $360]**
- The Romany Rye ... Second Edition. London: Murray, 1858. 2 vols. 8vo. xii,372; vii,375,[8 advt] pp. Contemp dark blue cloth, orig paper labels (a little chipped). *(Gough)* **£75 [≈ $120]**
- Wild Wales. London: Murray, 1862. 1st edn. 3 vols. Lge 12mo. xi,410, [2 blank], [32 advt dated Dec 1861, but lacking pp 19-20]; vii, 413, [2 blank]; viii, 474, [2 blank] pp. Half-title correctly in vol 1 only. Sl signs of use. Rec paper bds. *(Fenning)* **£115 [≈ $184]**

Boruwlaski, Joseph
- Memoirs of Count Boruwlaski: Containing a Sketch of his Travels ... Written by Himself. Durham: Francis Humble, 1820. Tall 8vo. xi, 391, [1 errata slip] pp. Subscribers' list at end. Frontis. Early three qtr calf, spine sometime relaid. *(Hartfield)* **$185 [≈ £115]**

Bosman, William
- A New and Accurate Description of the Coast of Guinea. London: 1721. 2nd English edn. [8],472 pp. Fldg map by Moll, 7 plates. Occas sl browning. Contemp calf, rebacked. *(Parmer)* **$850 [≈ £531]**

Bosset, C.P. de
- Parga, and the Ionian Islands; comprehending a Refutation of the Mis-statements ... on the Subject ... London: John Warren, 1821. xxii, [ii], '530' [≈ 534, inc pp 130A-130D]. 8vo. Half-title. 2 maps (some offsetting). Occas spotting. Mod half calf. *(Frew Mackenzie)* **£300 [≈ $480]**

Bossu, Jean Bernard
- Travels through that Part of North America formerly called Louisiana ... Added by the Translator a Systematic Account of all the Known Plants of English North America ... London: 1771. 2 vols. [8],407; [4],432 pp. Old marks removed. Later half calf, mrbld bds. *(Reese)* **$1,500 [≈ £937]**

Boswell, James
- An Account of Corsica ... Glasgow: 1768. 1st edn. Early copy, with D2r uncrrctd, E2 & Z3 cancels (other points). xxi,[3],382 pp. Fldg map. Lacks half-title. Occas v sl foxing or offsetting. Contemp calf, rebacked in contemp style, sm repr to hd of spine. *(Reese)* **$350 [≈ £218]**
- An Account of Corsica, the Journal of a Tour to that Island, and Memoirs of Pascal Paoli. Dublin: J. Exshaw, H. Saunders ..., 1768. 3rd edn. xii,282 pp. Contemp calf, raised bands, gilt label. *(Hartfield)* **$295 [≈ £184]**
- An Account of Corsica ... Third Edition. Dublin: J. Exshaw ..., 1768. 12mo. xii,282 pp. Contemp calf, raised bands, gilt label. *(Hartfield)* **$295 [≈ £184]**
- The Journal of a Tour to the Hebrides, with Samuel Johnson ... Second Edition, revised and corrected. London: Chas. Dilly, 1785. Tall 8vo. xxii,534,1 advt pp. Rebound in polished mor gilt, mrbld bds, orig label laid down. *(Hartfield)* **$395 [≈ £246]**
- The Journal of a Tour to the Hebrides, with Samuel Johnson ... Third Edition, revised

and corrected. London: Henry Baldwin for Charles Dilly, 1786. 8vo. xviii, 442, [1 advt] pp. Fldg map. Mod half calf gilt.
(Hollett) **£120 [≈ $192]**
- The Journal of a Tour to the Hebrides, with Samuel Johnson ... Fourth Edition, revised and corrected. London: Cadell & Davies, 1807. 8vo. [4],460 pp. Port. Contemp calf, little wear to ft of spine.
(Fenning) **£45 [≈ $72]**
- The Journal of the Tour to the Hebrides, with Samuel Johnson, LL.D. The Fourth Edition, Revised and Corrected. London: Cadell & Davies, 1807. 8vo. Port frontis (sl spotted). No half-title. Rec half calf.
(Clark) **£48 [≈ $76]**

Botero, Giovanni
- Relations of the most Famovs Kingdoms and Common-Weales thorovgh the World ... London: John Haviland, 1689. 3rd edn. 644,[2] pp. Prelim ff browned & stained. Lacks world map. Contemp calf, worn, rebacked. *(Jenkins)* **$250 [≈ £156]**

Boucard, A.
- Travels of a Naturalist. London: 1894. 204 pp. Cloth. *(Reese)* **$125 [≈ £78]**

Bouchette, Joseph
- A Topographical Dictionary of the Province of Lower Canada. London: 1832. 1st edn. Lge 4to. [12],384 pp. 6 fldg maps of Canada added at end. Contemp half calf.
(Jenkins) **$350 [≈ £218]**

Boulger, Demetrius C.
- The History of China. London: 1898. New & rvsd edn. 2 vols. 8vo. viii,734; 627 pp. Port ills. Orig maroon cloth, ex-lib.
(Terramedia) **$50 [≈ £31]**
- The History of China. London: Thacker, 1898. New & rvsd edn. 2 vols. 8vo. viii,[1], 734; [8], 627, 32 advt pp. Fldg map, 6 ports. Rec paper bds. *(Fenning)* **£65 [≈ $104]**

Bourgeois, C.
- Views in Switzerland Drawn from Nature by C. Bourgeois, and on Stone by A. Aglio. London: 1822. Folio. Litho title, 40 litho plates. Occas sl foxing, some minor marg damp staining. Orig bds, ptd paper label, bds worn & stained, front nearly detached, spine worn. *(Reese)* **$4,000 [≈ £2,500]**

Bourne, Benjamin Franklin
- The Captive in Patagonia: or, Life Among the Giants. A Personal Narrative ... Boston: 1853. 233 pp. Frontis, ills. Sl foxing, 1 sgntr

starting. Orig cloth. *(Reese)* **$125 [≈ £78]**

Bourne, H.R. Fox
- Civilization in Congoland: A Story of International Wrong-Doing. London: P.S. King & Son, 1903. 1st edn. 8vo. 311 pp. Lge fldg cold map. Orig green cloth, sl worn.
(Terramedia) **$50 [≈ £31]**

Bowdich, Thomas Edward
- Excursions in Madeira and Porto Santo, during the Autumn of 1823, while on his Third Voyage to Africa ... London: Whittaker, 1825. 4to. xii,278 pp. 23 plates (4 hand cold). Contemp gilt dec dark blue calf, rebacked, rubbed. *(Adelson)* **$575 [≈ £359]**

Bowditch, Nathaniel
- The New American Practical Navigator ... Newburyport: Edmund Blunt, 1807. 2nd edn. Thick 8vo. 679 pp. Fldg map, 10 plates. Occas foxing. Orig calf, hinge & ft of spine sl worn. *(Reese)* **$950 [≈ £593]**
- The New American Practical Navigator ... New York: E.M. Blunt, 1817. 4th edn. 8vo. xvi,597,13 advt pp. Fldg map, 11 plates. Orig calf, rebacked. *(Adelson)* **$285 [≈ £178]**

Bowen, F.C.
- The Golden Age of Sail: Indiamen, Packets and Clipper Ships ... With Illustrations from ... the Macpherson Collection. London: Halton & Truscott Smith, 1925. 1st edn. One of 1500. xv,86 pp. 92 plates (12 mtd cold). 1 p sl damaged. Orig cloth, v sl rubbed.
(Thornton's) **£75 [≈ $120]**

Bowring, Sir John
- The Kingdom and People of Siam; With a Narrative of the Mission to that Country in 1855. London: John W. Parker, 1857. 1st edn. 2 vols. Fldg map, 8 chromolitho & 6 engvd plates, 1 litho port, 3 fldg plates. Half leather, t.e.g., crnrs sl scuffed. Discreet ex-lib. *(Schoyer)* **$285 [≈ £178]**
- The Kingdom and People of Siam; With a Narrative of the Mission to that Country in 1855. London: John W. Parker, 1857. 2 vols. 8vo. xi,482,2 advt; vii,446,8 advt pp. Fldg map, 18 plates. Orig green cloth, spines faded. *(Adelson)* **$585 [≈ £365]**

Boyd, Louise A., et al.
- The Fiord Region of East Greenland. New York: Amer Geog Soc, 1935. 1st edn. 8vo. x, [2],369 pp. Frontis, maps, ills, tables. With sep slipcase containing 14 fldg maps.
(Parmer) **$85 [≈ £53]**

Boyde, Henry
- Several Voyages to Barbary ... see Morgan, John.

Boyes, J.
- The Company of Adventurers. East Africa: 1938. 318 pp. Ills. Orig bndg.
  (Trophy Room Books) **$300 [≈ £187]**

Boyle, Frederick
- The Savage Life. A Second Series of Camp Notes. London: Chapman & Hall, 1876. 1st edn. 8vo. viii,332 pp. Orig orange brown cloth.   *(Terramedia)* **$100 [≈ £62]**

Boyle, John, Earl of Orrery
- Letters from Italy, in the Years 1754 and 1755 ... Published from the Originals, with Explanatory Notes, by John Duncombe. London: for B. White, 1773. 1st edn. 8vo. Contemp half calf, gilt spine.
  (Ximenes) **$275 [≈ £171]**

Boyle, P.
- Boyle's Court and Country Guide, and Town Visiting Directory, corrected up to January 16, 1804 ... London: P. Boyle, [1804]. 12mo. 127, [v], 316 pp. Orig sheep, sl rubbed.
  (Bickersteth) **£35 [≈ $56]**

Boynton, Charles B. & Mason, T.B.
- A Journey through Kansas; with Sketches of Nebraska ... Cincinnati: 1855. 216 pp. Lacks map. Lib stamp, stained. Mod cloth, orig front wrap bound in.   *(Reese)* **$100 [≈ £62]**

Brackenridge, Henry Marie
- Recollections of Persons and Places in the West. Philadelphia: James Kay ... Pittsburgh: John L. Kay, [1834]. 1st edn. 12mo. 244 pp. Minor foxing & stains. Contemp cloth, later label, sl rubbed, unevenly faded, front inner hinge loosened.
  (M & S Rare Books) **$200 [≈ £125]**
- Views of Louisiana, together with a Journal of a Voyage up the Missouri in 1811. Pittsburgh: Cramer, Spear, Eichbaum, 1811. 1st edn. 304 pp. Later cloth over the orig bds, leather label.   *(Jenkins)* **$850 [≈ £531]**
- Views of Louisiana; together with a Journal of a Voyage up the Missouri River, in 1811. Pittsburgh: 1811. 304 pp. Inner marg of title reprd. Frequent underscorings in latter part of text. Antique half calf, mrbld bds.
  (Reese) **$850 [≈ £531]**
- Voyage to South America, performed by Order of the American Government, in the Years 1817 and 1818 in the Frigate Congress. Baltimore: for the author, 1819. 1st edn. 8vo.

351 pp, errata leaf. Fldg map (repr on verso). Contemp calf, sl worn. Cloth case.
  (Schoyer) **$250 [≈ £156]**
- Voyage to South America, performed by Order of the American Government in the Years 1817 and 1818, in the Frigate Congress. Baltimore: by the author, 1819. 2 vols. 8vo. xv, 17-351 pp, errata leaf; iv,5-381 pp. Fldg map (reprd). Orig calf, rebacked, ex-lib.   *(Adelson)* **$475 [≈ £296]**
- Voyage to South America, performed by Order of the Government in the Years 1817 & 1818 in the Frigate Congress. London: for John Miller ..., 1820. 1st English edn. 2 vols. 8vo. xviii,[2],331,40; [iv],317,2 advt pp. Rebound in half calf. *(Young's)* **£185 [≈ $296]**
- Voyage to South America, performed by order of the American Government, in the Years 1817 and 1818 ... Baltimore: the author, 1819. 2 vols. 352,errata leaf; 381 pp. Fldg hand cold map. Light foxing. Contemp mottled calf, sl wear to jnts.
  (Reese) **$500 [≈ £312]**

Bradbury, John
- Travels in the Interior of North America, in the Years 1809, 1810 ... Liverpool: 1817. 1st edn. 364 pp. Mor.
  (Jenkins) **$1,750 [≈ £1,093]**

Bradford, William J.A.
- Notes on the Northwest, or Valley of the Upper Missisippi [sic] ... New York: 1846. vi, 302 pp. Repr to title. Ex-lib. Over-size blindstamped cloth, leather label, spine chipped.   *(Reese)* **$125 [≈ £78]**

Bradley, A.G.
- Rivers and Streams of England. Painted by Sutton Palmer. London: A. & C. Black Colour Books, Twenty Shilling Series, 1909. 1st edn. Map, 75 cold plates. Some foxing to foredges. Orig dec cloth, t.e.g., v fine.
  (Old Cathay) **£75 [≈ $120]**

Bradley, Mary H.
- Caravans & Cannibals [Kenya & Uganda]. New York & London: Appleton, 1926. 1st edn. 8vo. 317 pp. Ills. Orig green cloth.
  (Terramedia) **$40 [≈ £25]**

Bradley-Birt, F.B.
- Chota Nagpore ... London: Smith, Elder, 1910. 2nd edn, enlgd. 8vo. xviii,327 pp. 120 b/w plates, 8 text figs. Orig cloth.
  (Gough) **£25 [≈ $40]**
- Chota Nagpore, A Little-Known Province of the Empire. Second Edition, revised and enlarged. London: 1910. 8vo. Fldg map,

plates. Orig cloth, spine sl sunned.
(Farahar) **£35 [≈ $56]**
- The Story of an Indian Upland. London: 1905. 8vo. Map, 20 plates. Orig dec cloth.
(Farahar) **£45 [≈ $72]**

Bradshaw's Handbook
- Bradshaw's Illustrated Handbook to Switzerland and the Tyrol; with Maps and Engravings. New Edition. London: 1897. Sq 12mo. xx,179,[32 advt] pp. 2 fldg maps, 4 plates. Orig red cloth gilt.
(Fenning) **£24.50 [≈ $40]**

Braine, A.
- A History of Kingswood Forest including all the Ancient Manors and Villages in the Neighbourhood. London: 1891. 1st edn. 8vo. Lge fldg map (folds sellotaped). Orig cloth, edges rubbed, inner hinges broken.
(Ambra) **£18 [≈ $28]**

Braithwaite, Captain John
- The History of the Revolutions in the Empire of Morocco, upon the Death of the late Emperor Muley Ishmael ... London: Darby & Browne, 1729. 1st edn. Lge 8vo. [xxiv],381 pp. Fldg map. Text possibly washed. Contemp speckled calf, later rebind.
(Schoyer) **$250 [≈ £156]**

Braithwaite, Richard
- See Brathwaite, Richard.

Brannon, George
- Vectis Scenery: being a Series of Original and Select Views ... of ... the Isle of Wight. Isle of Wight: 1829. 1st & 2nd series. Oblong 4to. Hand cold map, 49 engvd plates. Contemp half mor, gilt label, spine ends reprd, crnrs bumped. *(Spelman)* **£225 [≈ $360]**
- Vectis Scenery: being a Series of Original and Select Views ... of ... the Isle of Wight. Wooton Common, Isle of Wight: 1830. Oblong 4to. Hand cold map, 30 plates. Rebacked qtr leather. *(Henly)* **£200 [≈ $320]**

Bransby, James Hews
- A Descriptive and Historical Sketch of Beddgelert and Its Neighbourhood. London: T.M. Cradock, 1840. 12mo. 127,[i] pp. Orig cloth. *(Lamb)* **£18 [≈ $28]**

Brassey, Annie, Baroness
- Across the World in the Yacht 'Sunbeam'. Our Home on the Ocean for Eleven Months. New York: Henry Holt, 1889. 8vo. x,479 pp. Fldg map, frontis, num plates. Orig green cloth. *(Terramedia)* **$50 [≈ £31]**

- In the Trades, the Tropics, & the Roaring Forties. With Illustrations Engraved on Wood ... New York: Henry Holt, 1887. "Author's Edition". 8vo. xiv,532 pp. 292 w'engvs, inc 9 cold maps (2 fldg). Red & black title. Orig grey cloth gilt.
(Karmiole) **$65 [≈ £40]**
- Sunshine and Storm in the East, or Cruises to Cyprus and Constantinople ... London: Longmans, Green, 1880. 1st edn. xx,448 pp. Frontis, plates, ills. Lacks front free endpaper. Orig pict cloth in red & gilt.
(Wreden) **$95 [≈ £59]**
- A Voyage in the 'Sunbeam'. Our Home on the Ocean for Eleven Months ... London: Longmans, Green, 1879. xviii,492 pp. Frontis, plates. Orig gilt pict cloth, a.e.g., front jnt cracking, front cvr stained, pictures pasted to endpapers. *(Wreden)* **$85 [≈ £53]**

Brathwaite, Richard
- Drunken Barnaby's Four Journeys to the North of England. In Latin and English Meter. Together with Bessy Bell. London: S. Illidge, 1723. 3rd edn. 12mo. 175,index pp. Frontis, 5 engvs. Calf gilt, red label, considerable wear. *(Hartfield)* **$225 [≈ £140]**

Braun & Hogenberg
- Civitates Orbis Terrarum. The Towns of the World 1572-1618. With an Introduction by R.A. Skelton. New York & Cleveland: World Publ Co, 1966. 3 vols. Lge thick folio. Maps. Orig cloth. Dws. *(Moon)* **£350 [≈ $560]**

Breasted, James H.
- A History of Egypt. From the Earliest Times to the Persian Conquest. New York: Scribner's, 1928. Reprint of the 2nd rvsd edn of 1912. 2 vols. xxix,[314]; 634 pp. Lge fldg map at end, cold frontis, plates & maps. Later buckram, sl worn. *(Terramedia)* **$30 [≈ £18]**

Brebner, John Bartlet
- The Explorers of North America, 1492-1806. New York: Macmillan, 1933. 8vo. xv,502 pp. 4 fldg maps. Orig blue cloth.
(Terramedia) **$75 [≈ £46]**

Breckinridge, Robert J.
- Memoranda of Foreign Travel. Containing Notices of France, Germany, Switzerland, and Italy. Philadelphia: 1839. xii,342 pp. Light foxing with some soiling. Orig dec cloth gilt, faded, extremities worn, lacks front endsheet. *(Reese)* **$100 [≈ £62]**

Bredon, Juliet
- Peking: A Historical and Intimate

Description of its Chief Places of Interest.
Shanghai: Kelly & Walsh, 1922. 2nd edn,
rvsd & enlgd. 523 pp. Frontis, fldg maps &
plans, plates, ills. Orig ochre cloth gilt.
(*Lyon*) **£65 [≃ $104]**

Breen, Patrick
- The Diary of Patrick Breen. Recounting the
Ordeal of the Donner Party Snowbound in
the Sierra, 1846-47 ... [edited by] George R.
Stewart. San Francisco: Book Club of Calif
(Allen Press), 1946. One of300. Sm 8vo. 38,
(30) pp. Decs. Sl dusty. Orig cloth & bds.
(*Karmiole*) **$275 [≃ £171]**

Bremer, Fredrika
- Two Years in Switzerland and Italy.
Translated by Mary Howitt. London: Hurst
& Blackett, 1861. 1st edn. 2 vols. 8vo. [i], xii,
411; [ii],viii,412 pp. Orig orange cloth,
recased.   (*Piccadilly*) **£35 [≃ $56]**

Brett, Revd W.H.
- The Indian Tribes of Guiana; Their
Condition and Habits ... London: 1868. xiii,
500 pp. Fldg map (lib stamp on verso), plates
(some cold). Three qtr calf, mrbld bds,
extremities rubbed.   (*Reese*) **$250 [≃ £156]**

Brewer, J.N.
- The Beauties of Ireland ... Illustrated with
Engravings by J. & H.S. Storer, after ...
Drawings chiefly by Mr. Petrie ... London:
Sherwood, Jones & Co, 1825. 2 vols. 8vo. 24
plates. Orig cloth backed bds, uncut & largely
unopened, hd of vol 1 sl damaged.
(*Waterfield's*) **£185 [≃ $296]**
- The Picture of England; or, Historical and
Descriptive Delineations of the Most Curious
Works of Nature and Art in each County ...
London: 1820. Only edn. 2 vols. 8vo. 252
views on 84 plates (correct, ptd labels
incorrectly call for 272). Orig bds, sl worn.
(*Young's*) **£97 [≃ $155]**
- The Picture of England; or, Historical and
Descriptive Delineations of the Most Curious
Works of Nature and Art ... London: Harris
& Son, 1820. 2 vols. 12mo. xii, 384, [12]; [2],
416, [12] pp. 249 engvs on 83 pp. Half calf (ca
1900), gilt spine. (*Karmiole*) **$200 [≃ £125]**

Brewer, Josiah
- A Residence at Constantinople, in the Year
1827. With Notes to the Present Time. New
Haven: Durrie & Peck, 1830. 2nd edn. Sm
8vo. 384 pp. Fldg frontis, fldg cold map (both
torn without loss). Foxed & spotted. Contemp
mor, edges sl rubbed.
(*Worldwide Antiqu'n*) **$75 [≃ £46]**
- A Residence at Constantinople in the Years

1827. With Notes to the Present Time. New
Haven: 1830. 2nd edn. xii, 372 pp. Fldg
frontis, fldg map. Dampstain affecting plate &
about 60 pp. Occas sl foxing. Contemp
mottled calf, somewhat scuffed.
(*Reese*) **$100 [≃ £62]**

Brewster, John
- The Parochial History and Antiquities of
Stockton upon Tees ... Stockton:
Christopher, 1796. 1st subscribers edn. 4to.
x,178 pp. 7 plates & plans (1 fldg). Old half
calf gilt, edges rubbed.
(*Hollett*) **£165 [≃ $264]**

Brickell, John
- The Natural History of North Carolina. With
an Account of the Trade, Manners, and
Customs of the Christian and Indian
Inhabitants ... Dublin: 1737. xv,[1],408 pp.
Fldg map, 4 plates. Rebound in antique calf
& mrbld bds.   (*Reese*) **$3,000 [≃ £1,875]**

Bridgman, Frederick Arthur
- Winters in Algeria. New York: Harper, 1890.
1st edn. Wide 8vo. viii,262,advt pp. Frontis,
num plates & ills. Ex-lib. Orig pict green
cloth gilt, hd of spine frayed.
(*Terramedia*) **$25 [≃ £15]**

Brief ...
- A Brief State of the Province of Pennsylvania
... see Smith, William.

Bright, Richard
- Travels from Vienna through Lower
Hungary; with some Remarks on the state of
Vienna during the Congress in the year 1814.
Edinburgh: Constable ..., 1818. 1st edn. 4to.
xviii, 642, cii pp. 2 fldg maps, 10 plates.
Occas sl marks. Contemp calf, spine sl worn.
(*Frew Mackenzie*) **£350 [≃ $560]**

Brine, Lindesay
- Travels amongst American Indians. Their
Ancient Earthworks & Temples. Including a
Journey in Guatemala, Mexico & Yucatan ...
London: Sampson Low, 1894. 1st edn. 8vo.
xvi, 429 pp. Fldg map, num photo plates &
ills. Orig pict blue cloth gilt, spine edges worn
& frayed.   (*Terramedia*) **$100 [≃ £62]**

Brinkley, Capt. Frank
- Japan Described & Illustrated by the
Japanese. Boston: J.B. Millet, [1897-98]. 15
parts. Folio. 382 pp. 15 hand cold photos, 30
hand cold albumen prints, 15 full-page
chromolithos, over 200 halftones. Orig wraps
(sev chipped, 2 loose), cloth spines.
(*M & S Rare Books*) **$275 [≃ £171]**
- Japan Its History Arts and Literature. Boston

& Tokyo: (1901-02). Library Edition. One of 1000. 12 vols. 8vo. Lge fldg & other maps, 226 plates (many cold). Orig green cloth, t.e.g.   *(Bow Windows)* **£335 [≈ $536]**

Brinton, Daniel G.
- Notes on the Floridan Peninsula ... Philadelphia: Joseph Sabin, 1859. 1st edn. One of 100. 12mo. 202 pp. Orig cloth, ex-lib. Author's pres inscrptn.
          (M & S Rare Books) **$300 [≈ £187]**

Brissot de Warville, Jacques Pierre
- New Travels in the United States of America: including the Commerce of America with Europe. London: Jordan, 1794. 2 vols. 8vo. Port, fldg table. Qtr calf.
          (Rostenberg & Stern) **$425 [≈ £265]**

Britain Triumphant ...
- Britain Triumphant on the Plains of Waterloo. Being a Correct and Circumstantial Narrative of the Memorable Battle ... Burslem: John Tregortha, 1817. 8vo. iv,708 pp. Fldg hand cold sketch, fldg map (torn at fold), 6 ports. Leather & bds, new cloth spine.
          (Schoyer) **$200 [≈ £125]**

Britton, John
- The History and Antiquities of the Cathedral Church in Worcester illustrated by a Series of Engravings of Views, Elevations, Plans and Details ... London: Longman, 1835. 4to. 16 plates. Contemp half mor, a.e.g., a little scuffed.   *(Waterfield's)* **£50 [≈ $80]**

Britton, John & Brayley, E.W.
- The Beauties of England and Wales ... London: 1801-18. 19 vols bound in 26. Engvd titles, fldg maps, engvd plates. Occas foxing. 2 sgntrs starting. Three qtr calf, mrbld bds, some rubbing & wear to extremities.
          (Reese) **$2,000 [≈ £1,250]**
- Devonshire and Cornwall Illustrated. From Original Drawings by Thomas Allom, W.H. Bartlett ... London: 1832. 2 vols in one. 4to. 106; 48 pp. 2 maps, 2 engvd titles, 69 plates (each with 2 views). Dampstain on edge of plates. Orig three qtr leather, jnts & crnrs rubbed.   *(Schoyer)* **$400 [≈ £250]**

Brockett, L.P.
- Our Western Empire: or the New West beyond the Mississippi: the Latest and Most Comprehensive Work on the States and Territories West of the Mississippi ... Philadelphia: 1881. 1312 pp. Frontis, ills. Three qtr calf (worn) & cloth.
          (Reese) **$65 [≈ £40]**

Bromley, George Tisdale
- The Long Ago and the Later On. San Francisco: 1904. One of 150, sgnd. 289 pp. Cloth & bds.   *(Reese)* **$150 [≈ £93]**

Broodbank, Sir Joseph G.
- History of the Port of London. London: 1921. Large Paper. 2 vols. 8vo. xi,270; viii, 273-532 pp. 72 plates. Pict endpapers. Orig cloth, t.e.g. Typescript & cuttings inserted.
          (Coombes) **£46 [≈ $73]**

Brookes, Richard, M.D.
- Brookes' General Gazetteer Improved ... Philadelphia & Richmond: 1812. [Ca 800] pp. 8 fldg maps (1 sheet with a map on each side, making 9 maps). Orig calf, sl reprs.
          (Reese) **$500 [≈ £312]**
- A General Gazetteer; or, Compendious Geographical Dictionary ... revised ... by A.G. Findlay. London: Tegg, 1844. 2nd edn. Lge thick 8vo. xxiii,768 pp. Num fldg maps. Contemp calf gilt.   *(Hollett)* **£50 [≈ $80]**

Brookes, Richard, M.D. & Marshall, John
- The London General Gazetteer; or, Compendious Geographical Dictionary. London: Tegg, 1837. Thick 8vo. xiv,800 pp. 6 fldg maps. Half calf gilt, sl rubbed, jnts cracked.   *(Hollett)* **£50 [≈ $80]**

Brooks, Alfred H., et al.
- Reconnaissances in the Cape Nome and Norton Bay Regions, Alaska, in 1900. Washington: GPO, 1901. 4to. 222 pp. Maps (1 fldg), num photo ills. Orig ptd wraps.
          (High Latitude) **$50 [≈ £31]**

Brooks, V.
- Screed of a Safari Scribe. TN: privately ptd, 1947. 84 pp. Ills. Soft cvrs.
          (Trophy Room Books) **$200 [≈ £125]**

Brown, A. Samler
- Brown's Madeira, Canary Islands and Azores. A Practical and Complete Guide ... London: Sampson Low ..., 1903. 7th edn. 12mo. 16 individually paginated sections, 68 advt pp. 11 fldg maps, 6 fldg diags. Orig pict cloth, rubbed.   *(Schoyer)* **$40 [≈ £25]**

Brown, John
- The North-West Passage and the Plans for the Search for Sir John Franklin ... Second Edition, with a Sequel, including the Voyage of the "Fox". London: Stanford, 1860. xiii, 463, [ii],64,4 advt pp. 2 maps, frontis, fldg facs. Orig cloth.
          (High Latitude) **$425 [≈ £265]**

Brown, John Ross
- An American Family in Germany. Illustrated by the Author. New York: Harper, [1866]. xiv, 381, 2 advt pp. Ills. Orig cloth.
(Wreden) **$35 [≃ £21]**

Brown, L.
- Ethiopian Episode. London: 1965. 160 pp. Ills. Endpaper maps. Orig bndg. Dw.
(Trophy Room Books) **$90 [≃ £56]**

Brown, William Wells
- The American Fugitive in Europe ... With a Memoir of the Author. Boston: 1855. 1st edn. 12mo. 320 pp. Frontis. Orig cloth, v good ex-lib. Pres inscrptn by the author's daughter.
(M & S Rare Books) **$200 [≃ £12]**
- Three Years in Europe; or, Places I have seen and People I have met. With a Memoir of the Author by William Farmer. London: Charles Gilpin, 1852. 8vo. xxxii, 312 pp. Port. Occas sl spotting. Orig pict gilt cloth, sl marked & faded.   *(Gough)* **£80 [≃ $128]**

Browne, G.
- The Vanishing Tribes of Kenya ... Philadelphia: 1925. 8vo. 284 pp. 2 maps (1 fldg), frontis, num plates. Orig orange gilt pict cloth.   *(Terramedia)* **$150 [≃ £93]**

Browne, G. Waldo
- The New America and the Far East. Boston: Marshal Jones, [ca 1912]. 10 vols. Sm 4to. 1863 pp. 7 fldg maps, 250 plates (37 cold), 1122 text ills. Orig cloth, t.e.g., sl rubbed.
(Worldwide Antiqu'n) **$95 [≃ £59]**

Browne, James
- A History of the Highlands and of the Highland Clans. Glasgow: 1837-38. 1st edn. 4 vols. 8vo. 9 armorial plates, 1 other plate. Sm lib stamps on plates & some pp. Contents list & addtnl titles dated 1838 at end of vol 4. Orig cloth, ink nos. on spines.
(Bickersteth) **£48 [≃ $76]**

Browne, John Ross
- Adventures in Apache Country: A Tour through Arizona and Sonora. New York: Harper, 1869. 535 pp. Ills. Later mor, a.e.g.
(Jenkins) **$225 [≃ £140]**
- Crusoe's Island: A Ramble in the Footsteps of Alexander Selkirk. With Sketches of Adventure in California and Washoe. New York: Harper, 1867. 8vo. vii,9-436 pp. Num engvs. Orig brown cloth. Author's pres inscrptn.   *(Adelson)* **$250 [≃ £156]**
- Etchings of a Whaling Cruise, with Notes of a Sojourn on the Island of Zanzibar; and a

Brief History of the Whale Fishery ... London: 1846. 1st English edn. [xvi],580 pp. 8 plates, text ills. Lib stamp. Occas marg staining. Orig cloth, spine relaid.
(Reese) **$375 [≃ £234]**
- Etchings of a Whaling Cruise, with Notes of a Sojourn on the Island of Zanzibar and a Brief History of the Whale Fishery ... London: Murray, 1846. 1st English edn. 8vo. xiii,[1],580 pp. 8 plates, text ills. Washed. Later cloth & mrbld bds. Slipcase.
(Parmer) **$800 [≃ £500]**

Browne, Patrick
- The Civil and Natural History of Jamaica ... Illustrated with Forty-Nine Copper Plates ... By George Dionysius Ehret. London: 1789. 2nd edn. Lge thick folio. viii, 503, index pp. Fldg map, plates. Polished calf, raised bands, hinges reprd, extremities worn.
(Reese) **$1,500 [≃ £937]**

Brownlow, William G.
- Helps to the Study of Presbyterianism ... to which is added a Brief Account of the Life and Travels of the Author. Knoxville, Tenn.: F.S. Heiskell, 1834. 1st edn. 299 pp. Orig half calf, paper bds, lacks free endpapers.
(Jenkins) **$450 [≃ £281]**

Bruce, C.G.
- Himalayan Wanderer. London: 1934. 309 pp. 25 ills. Orig bndg.
(Trophy Room Books) **$200 [≃ £125]**
- Twenty Years in the Himalaya. London: 1910. 335 pp. Lge cold fldg map, 60 ills. Orig cloth.   *(Trophy Room Books)* **$375 [≃ £234]**

Bruce, James
- An Interesting Narrative of the Travels of James Bruce, Esq. into Abyssinia, to discover the Source of the Nile. Abridged from the Original Work by Samuel Shaw. Fourth Edition. London: H.D. Symonds, 1800. 12mo. 372 pp. Port (detached), 5 plates. Contemp calf.   *(Argosy)* **$150 [≃ £93]**
- An Interesting Narrative of the Travels of James Bruce, Esq. into Abyssinia, to discover the Source of the Nile. Abridged from the Original Work by Samuel Shaw. Fourth Edition. London: for H.P. Symonds, 1800. 12mo. Contemp half mor.
(Falkner) **£30 [≃ $48]**
- Travels to Discover the Source of the Nile, in the Years 1768-73. London: 1790. 1st edn. 5 vols. 4to. 3 maps, 58 plates. Contemp half calf, rebacked.
(Wheldon & Wesley) **£900 [≃ $1,440]**
- Travels to Discover the Source of the Nile, in

the Years 1768 ... 1773. Edinburgh: 1790. 1st edn. 5 vols. 4to. 10, lxxxiii, 535; viii,718; viii,759; viii,695; xiv,230,12 pp. 3 maps, 59 plates. Orig half calf gilt, rubbed, vol 1 rebacked.   *(Adelson)* **$1,575 [≈ £984]**

Bruce, John
- Historical View of Plans, for the Government of British India, and Regulation of Trade to the East Indies ... London: 1793. 1st edn. 4to. xiv,632 pp. Sev inscrptns. Contemp calf, rubbed & scuffed, jnts sl cracked, ft of spine worn. Also attributed to Lord Melville.
        (Pickering) **$400 [≈ £250]**

Brunton, Paul
- A Search in Ancient Egypt. London: Rider, [1936]. 1st edn. 8vo. Num photo plates. Orig maroon cloth, spine v sl sunned.
        (Terramedia) **$60 [≈ £37]**

Bryant, Edwin
- What I Saw in California: being the Journal of a Tour, by the Emigrant Route and South Pass of the Rocky Mountains ... in the Years 1846, 1847. New York: 1848. 455 pp. Some foxing. Orig cloth, spine worn.
        (Jenkins) **$225 [≈ £140]**

Bryant, William Cullen (ed.)
- Picturesque America: or The Land We Live In ... New York: Appleton, [1872]. 2 vols. Folio. viii,568; vi,576 pp. 49 tissued steel engvd plates, num w'engvd plates. Orig gilt dec mor, a.e.g.   *(Terramedia)* **$300 [≈ £187]**

Bryce, James
- Impressions of South Africa. New York: Century, 1897. 495,index pp. 3 fldg maps. Few lib stamps, lib pocket. Qtr leather.
        (Parmer) **$45 [≈ £28]**
- Transcaucasia and Ararat. Being Notes of a Vacation Tour in the Autumn of 1876. London: Macmillan, 1877. 1st edn. 12mo. x,420,36 advt pp. Map, frontis. Orig pict green cloth, clean ex-lib, hinges sl cracked internally.   *(Terramedia)* **$50 [≈ £31]**

Bryden, H. Anderson
- Gun and Camera in Southern Africa. A Year of Wandering in Bechuanaland, the Kalahari Desert and the Lake River Country. London: 1893. 544 pp. Fldg map, ills. Half red leather.
        (Trophy Room Books) **$250 [≈ £156]**
- Gun and Camera in Southern Africa. A Year of Wanderings in Bechuanaland, the Kalahari Desert, and the Lake River Country, Ngamiland ... London: Stanford, 1893. 8vo. xiv,544 pp. Fldg map, 35 plates. Orig pict cloth, sl rubbed.   *(Adelson)* **$225 [≈ £140]**

- Kloof and Karroo in the Cape Colony. Sport, Legend, Natural History. London: 1889. 434 pp. Ills. Orig pict gilt green cloth.
        (Trophy Room Books) **$450 [≈ £281]**

Brydone, Patrick
- A Tour through Sicily and Malta. In a Series of Letters to William beckford. A New Edition ... London: Cadell & Davis, 1806. 8vo. xii,387 pp. Fldg map (a few old reprs). Panelled calf gilt, by Sotheran, hd of spine chipped, jnts rubbed, label worn.
        (Schoyer) **$75 [≈ £46]**

Buch, Leopold von
- Travels through Norway and Lapland ... Translated from the Original German by John Black. With Notes ... London: Colburn, 1813. 1st English edn. 4to. 2 fldg maps (foxed). Lacks half-title & advt leaf. Early half mor.   *(Hannas)* **£200 [≈ $320]**
- Travels through Norway and Lapland ... Translated by J. Black, with Notes and Illustrations chiefly Mineralogical and Some Account of the Author by R. Jameson. London: 1813. 4to. xviii,460,[6] pp. 2 maps. New bds, uncut.
        (Wheldon & Wesley) **£200 [≈ $320]**

Buchanan, Revd Robert
- Jerusalem in 1860 ... see Cramb, John.

Buck, Edward J.
- Simla Past and Present. Bombay: 1925. 8vo. viii,342 pp. Port frontis, fldg map, num ills. Orig dec cloth, sl worn. Author's inscrptn.
        (Dillons) **£40 [≈ $64]**

Buckley, J.M.
- Travels in Three Continents, Europe, Africa, Asia. New York & Cincinnati: Eaton & Mains, [1894]. Lge 8vo. 614 pp. Num plates. Orig pict grey cloth, sl soiled. Author's pres copy.   *(Terramedia)* **$60 [≈ £37]**

Buckley, W.
- Big Game Hunting in Central Africa. London: 1930. 268 pp. Ills. Orig bndg.
        (Trophy Room Books) **$250 [≈ £156]**

Budge, E.A. Wallis
- Cook's Handbook for Egypt and the Egyptian Sudan. With Chapters on Egyptian Archaeology. Fourth Edition. London: Thomas Cook, 1921. 956 pp. 9 fldg maps, 182 plans & ills. Sm repr to title. Orig limp cloth gilt, hinges rubbed, new free endpapers.
        (Hollett) **£75 [≈ $120]**
- Cook's Handbook for Egypt and the Egyptian

Sudan. With Chapters on Egyptian Archaeology. Fourth Edition. London: Thomas Cook, 1921. 956 pp. 9 maps, 182 plans & text ills. Orig bndg.
(Thornton's) **£40 [≈ $64]**
- The Dwellers on the Nile. Or, Chapters on the Life, Literature, History and Customs of the Ancient Egyptians. London: RTS, By-Paths of Bible Knowledge Series, 1885. 1st edn. 12mo. 204 pp. Fldg frontis, ills. Three qtr leather, jnts v tender.
(Schoyer) **$45 [≈ £28]**
- The Dwellers on the Nile. Chapters on the Life, History, Religion and Literature of the Ancient Egyptians. London: RTS, 1926. 8vo. 326 pp. 11 plates, 38 ills. Orig blue cloth, tiny tear hd of spine. *(Terramedia)* **$60 [≈ £37]**
- The Life of Takla Haymanot in the Version of Dabra Libanos ... London: privately ptd for Lady Meux, 1906. One of 250. 2 vols. V lge 4to. 165 chromolitho plates. Orig maroon cloth. *(Frew Mackenzie)* **£425 [≈ $680]**
- Osiris and the Egyptian Resurrection. London & New York: Warner & Putnam's, 1911. 1st edn. Tall 8vo. xxix,404; viii,440 pp. 2 cold fldg frontis, num plates. Orig pict red cloth gilt, ex-lib with minor wear.
(Terramedia) **$200 [≈ £125]**

Bula N'Zau
- Pseudonym used by Henry Bailey, q.v.

Bullett, Gerald
- Germany. With a Chapter on German Tourism and Mountaineering by Anthony Bertram. Painted by E.T. and E. Harrison Compton. London: A. & C. Black, 1930. 1st edn thus. Map, 32 cold plates. Orig cloth.
(Old Cathay) **£23 [≈ $36]**

Bullock, W.H.
- Across Mexico in 1865 ... London & Cambridge: Macmillan, 1866. 1st edn. [8],396, [4 advt] pp. Cold frontis map, 8 sepia lithos. Stamp erased from title. Orig green cloth. *(Jenkins)* **$400 [≈ £250]**

Bullock, William
- Sketch of a Journey through the Western States of North America ... in 1827. With a Description of ... Cincinnati ... London: 1827. 1st edn. 12mo. Half-title,31,8,135 pp. Fldg map (a few reprs to verso). Lacks the US map. Orig bds, untrimmed, disbound.
(M & S Rare Books) **$375 [≈ £234]**
- Sketch of a Journey through the Western States of North America ... in 1827 ... London: 1827. xxxi,viii,135 pp. Fldg linen backed plan, fldg map. Lib blindstamps. Orig

bds, rebacked in cloth. Half mor box. Author's pres copy. *(Reese)* **$1,250 [≈ £781]**

Bulpett, C.
- A Winter Picnic Party in Wildest Africa. Being a Sketch of a Winter's Trip to Some of the Unknown Waters of the Upper Nile. London: Edward Arnold, 1907. 1st edn. 8vo. 246 pp. Fldg map, num plates. Orig maroon cloth, sl worn. *(Terramedia)* **$100 [≈ £62]**

Bulwer, Sir Henry Lytton
- France, Social, Literary, Political ... [with the sequel] The Monarchy and the Middle Classes. Paris: Galignani, 1834-36. 2 vols. 8vo. xx,375; xx,350 pp. 3 maps, 6 tables. Old half leather, rubbed, newly rebacked.
(Piccadilly) **£55 [≈ $88]**

Bulwer-Lytton, Edward George Earle, 1st Baron Lytton
- England and the English. New York: Harper, 1833. 1st Amer edn. 2 vols. 12mo. 243,8 advt; 220,8 advt pp. Later cloth.
(Schoyer) **$25 [≈ £15]**

Bunbury, Charles J.F.
- Journal of a Residence at the Cape of Good Hope with Excursions into the Interior, and Notes on the Natural History and Native Tribes. London: Murray, 1848. 8vo. xii,297, [i] pp. Occas foxing of plates. Contemp half calf. *(Lamb)* **£80 [≈ $128]**

Burchell, William J.
- The South African Drawings. Johannesburg: Witwatersrand Univ Press, 1938-52. One of 300. 2 vols. Sm folio. 43 plates. Half leather. Dws. *(Thornton's)* **£450 [≈ $720]**
- Travels in the Interior of Southern Africa. London: 1822-24. 2 vols. 4to. Lge fldg map, 20 hand cold aquatint plates, num other ills. Sl offsetting onto some plates. Contemp calf gilt, jnts cracked. Marquis of Stafford's arms on cvrs.
(Wheldon & Wesley) **£2,000 [≈ $3,200]**

Burckhardt, John Lewis
- Travels in Arabia ... London: Colburn ..., 1829. 1st edn. 2 vols. 8vo. xxi,452; ii,431 pp. 5 fldg maps. Some foxing & spotting, esp plates. Lib stamps on reverse of plates. Lib buckram, rebacked in cloth, sl tears in spines, lib number on spine.
(Worldwide Antiqu'n) **$325 [≈ £203]**
- Travels in Nubia. London: Society for Promoting Discovery in the Interior Parts of Africa, 1819. 1st edn. 4to. 543,2 advt pp. Half-title. Port frontis, 3 maps (2 fldg). Minimal marg spotting. Half leather, mrbld

bds. *(Trophy Room Books)* **$1,250** [≈ £781]

Burges, Barthalomew
- A Series of Indostan Letters by a Traveller, containing a Striking Account of the Manners and Customs of the Gentoo Nations ... New York: 1817. xxi,147 pp. Calf & bds.
(Reese) **$250** [≈ £156]

Burgoyne, John
- A State of the Expedition from Canada ... London: 1780. 2nd edn. ix,[1],191,[1],civ pp. 6 fldg maps (with orig colouring of troop movements). Contemp calf, outer hinges cracked, front bd loose.
(Reese) **$1,500** [≈ £937]

Burke, W.S.
- The Indian Field Shikar Book. Calcutta & Simla: Thacker & Spink, 1920. 5th edn. 585, advt pp. A few underlinings. Orig (leather backed) green cloth gilt. *(Lyon)* **£55** [≈ $88]

Burnaby, Andrew
- Travels through the Middle Settlements in North-America, in the Years 1759 and 1760, with Observations upon the State of the Colonies. London: 1775. 4to. viii,106 pp, errata leaf. Sm hole in title not affecting text. Later half calf & cloth. *(Reese)* **$600** [≈ £375]

Burnaby, Captain Fred (Frederick Gustavus)
- On Horseback Through Asia Minor. London: 1877. 1st edn. 2 vols. 352; 399 pp. Maps. Elab gilt leather.
(Trophy Room Books) **$425** [≈ £265]
- On Horseback Through Asia Minor. London: 1877. 1st edn. 2 vols. 352; 399 pp. Maps (1 with sm tear). Orig green cloth, vol 1 recased.
(Trophy Room Books) **$350** [≈ £218]
- On Horseback through Asia Minor. London: Sampson Low, 1877. 2nd edn. 2 vols. 8vo. 3 fldg map, frontis photo in vol 1. Orig pict cloth gilt, gilt lettering added to spines by previous owner. *(Trebizond)* **$225** [≈ £140]

Burnby, John
- An Historical Description of the Cathedral and Metropolitical Church of Christ, Canterbury ... Canterbury: T. Smith & Son ..., 1772. 1st edn. 8vo. vi,3-105,[1] pp. Half-title. Frontis. 19th c red half roan, trifle rubbed. *(Burmester)* **£60** [≈ $96]

Burnes, Sir Alexander
- Cabool. Being a Personal Narrative of a Journey to an Residence in that City, in the Years 1836, 7 and 8. London: 1842. 398 pp.

Frontis, 10 plates, 1 fldg plate. Orig cloth.
(Trophy Room Books) **$500** [≈ £312]
- Travels into Bokhara being the Account of a Journey from India to Cabool, Tartary and Persia ... London: 1834. 2 vols. Frontis, ills. Some foxing in vol 3. Half leather gilt, sl wear, hd of vol 3 spine chipped.
(Trophy Room Books) **$800** [≈ £500]

Burnet, David G.
- To Messrs. Anthony Dey, Wm. H. Sumner and George Curtis, Esquires. In Compliance with Your Request to Furnish a Brief Account of Texas ... [New York: 1830?]. Fldg folio. 4 pp. Old fold marks. Cloth case.
(Reese) **$5,000** [≈ £3,125]

Burnet, Gilbert
- Some Letters. Containing, an Account of what seemed most Remarkable in Switzerland, Italy, &c ... Rotterdam: Abraham Acher, 1686. 1st edn. 8vo. 307,[i] pp. Errata leaf. Title a little dusty. Contemp calf, lightly rubbed, 2 sm holes in backstrip. Wing B.5915. *(Clark)* **£120** [≈ $192]
- Some Letters Containing an Account of what seemed most Remarkable in Travelling through Switzerland, Italy, Some Parts of Germany ... This Edition was Corrected ... by the Author. London: 1689. 1st English ptd edn. 12mo. Title dust soiled. Mod calf. Wing B.5921. *(Hannas)* **£65** [≈ $104]
- Some Letters, Containing an Account of what seem'd most remarkable in travelling thro' Switzerland, Italy, Some Parts of Germany ... London: for J. Lacy, 1729. 8vo. [ii],xxvi, 355,[xv advt] pp. Contemp calf, red mor label, extremities rubbed, jnt ends just cracking. *(Finch)* **£90** [≈ $144]
- Three Letters Concerning the Present State of Italy, written in the Year 1687 ... Being a Supplement to Dr. Burnets Letters. [London]: ptd in the year, 1688. 1st edn (?). Sm 8vo. [16],191,[1] pp. Contemp calf, rebacked. Wing B.5931.
(Hannas) **£45** [≈ $72]

Burnett, Frank
- Through Polynesia and Papua. Wanderings with a Camera in Southern Seas. London: Francis Griffiths, 1911. 8vo. xv,197 pp. 148 photo ills. Orig red cloth.
(Schoyer) **$45** [≈ £28]

Burney, James
- A Chronological History of the Discoveries in the South Sea or Pacific Ocean ... London: 1803-17. 5 vols. Lge 4to. xii,[viii],392; vi, [x],482; [viii],438; xviii,580; viii,338 pp. 41 maps & plates. Blindstamp on text ff only.

Mod mor gilt. *(Sotheran)* **£7,500 [≈ $12,000]**

Burnham, J.
- The Rim of Mystery. New York: 1929. 281 pp. Fldg map, 60 ills. Orig bndg.
(Trophy Room Books) **$175 [≈ £109]**

Burr, Agnes Rush
- Alaska: Our Beautiful Northland of Opportunity. Boston: Page Co, 1920. 2nd imp. Map, 54 plates (6 cold). Orig pict green cloth gilt.   *(Terramedia)* **$35 [≈ £21]**

Burrard, Major G.
- Big Game Hunting in the Himalayas and Tibet. London: 1925. 8vo. Ills. Orig bndg, sl worn & marked.   *(Grayling)* **£100 [≈ $160]**
- Big Game Hunting in the Himalayas and Tibet. London: Herbert Jenkins, 1925. 8vo. 320 pp. Frontis, 8 maps & charts, 23 photo ills. Edge tears to frontis without loss. Occas sl foxing. Orig blue cloth gilt.
(Bates & Hindmarch) **£175 [≈ $280]**
- Big Game Hunting in the Himalayas and Tibet. London: [ca 1925]. 320 pp. 8 maps, num ills. Orig bndg.
(Trophy Room Books) **$250 [≈ £156]**

Burrows, Ronald M.
- The Discoveries in Crete. And their bearing on the History of Ancient Civilization. New York: Dutton, 1907. 8vo. 244 pp. Fldg chart, other ills. Orig bndg, sl worn.
(Terramedia) **$30 [≈ £18]**

Burton, Isabel
- A.E.I. - Arabia, Egypt, India. A Narrative of Travel. London & Belfast, 1879. 1st edn. 8vo. viii,488 pp. 2 cold maps, 15 plates. Orig cloth, edges rubbed, spine ends chipped, tears in spine, lib number on spine.
(Worldwide Antiqu'n) **$95 [≈ £59]**
- The Inner Life of Syria, Palestine, and the Holy Land, from my private Journal ... London: 1875. 2 vols. x,376; 340 pp. Ports, fldg map, 2 chromolitho plates. Lib marks. Contemp three qtr calf, extremities worn, 1 bd nearly detached.   *(Reese)* **$300 [≈ £187]**
- The Life of Captain Sir Richard F. Burton ... By His Wife ... London: Chapman & Hall, 1893. 2 vols. 8vo. Frontis ports, 5 maps, 2 cold & 16 b/w plates, 11 text ills. Orig dec cloth, crnrs bumped, spine starting.
(Berkelouw) **$200 [≈ £125]**

Burton, John
- Monasticon   Eboracense: and   the Ecclesiastical   History   of   Yorkshire   ... London: for the author by N. Nickson ...,

1758. 1st edn. Folio. xii,448,[35] pp. Fldg map, 2 fldg plans, correct. Contemp calf gilt, gilt spine, upper hinge tender. Trench Chiswell's b'plate.   *(Hollett)* **£250 [≈ $400]**

Burton, Sir Richard Francis
- A Plain and Literal Translation of the Arabian Nights Entertainments ... London: Burton Club, [1903]. One of 1000. 17 vols. 8vo. Num plates. Orig gold & silver dec cloth, sl worn, the gilt tarnished.
(Farahar) **£250 [≈ $400]**
- Camoens: His Life and his Lusiads. London: Quaritch, 1881. 1st edn, 1st iss. 2 vols. 12mo. viii,366; (367)-738 pp. Orig gilt dec green cloth, rubbed.   *(Adelson)* **$200 [≈ £125]**
- The Captivity of Hans Stade of Hesse, in A.D. 1547-1555, among the Wild Tribes of Eastern Brazil. Translated by Albert Tootal ... and annotated by Richard F. Burton. London: Hakluyt Society, 1874. 8vo. 4,xcvi, 169 pp. Lib stamp on half-title verso. Orig blue cloth.   *(Adelson)* **$175 [≈ £109]**
- The City of the Saints and across the Rocky Mountains to California. London: Longman, Green ..., 1861. 1st edn. 8vo. xii, 707 pp. Fldg map, fldg plan, 8 plates. New qtr mor.   *(Adelson)* **$425 [≈ £265]**
- First Footsteps in East Africa. London: 1856. 1st edn, 1st iss. 648 pp. 2 maps, 4 cold plates., 7 text ills. Polished calf, 'Townsend House' in gilt on cvrs, minor wear to spine.
(Trophy Room Books) **$850 [≈ £531]**
- First Footsteps in East Africa ... London: Longman ..., 1856. 1st edn, 2nd iss. 8vo. xli, 648 pp. 2 maps, 4 cold plates. Orig red cloth, front cvr rubbed.   *(Adelson)* **$925 [≈ £578]**
- First Footsteps in East Africa or an Exploration of Harrar. London: 1856. 1st edn. 648 pp. Ills, some cold. Half leather, raised bands, gilt dec spine.
(Trophy Room Books) **$1,250 [≈ £781]**
- First Footsteps in East Africa ... London: Longman, Brown ..., 1856. 1st edn. xl,648,24 advt pp. 2 maps, 4 cold plates. A little fingering & spotting. Mod half levant mor gilt.   *(Hollett)* **£350 [≈ $560]**
- First Footsteps in East Africa. London: 1894. Memorial Edition. 2 vols. 209; 276 pp. Orig pict gilt black cloth.
(Trophy Room Books) **$250 [≈ £156]**
- First Footsteps in East Africa. Time Life: 1982. 2 vols. 209; 276 pp. Orig imitation leather.   *(Trophy Room Books)* **$150 [≈ £93]**
- Goa, and the Blue Mountains: or Six Months of Sick Leave. London: Bentley, 1851. 1st edn. 8vo. Fldg map, 4 tinted litho plates. A few pencil notes. Orig buff cloth, recased, crnrs a little worn, some wear to jnts & spine

ends. *(Clark)* £270 [≃ $432]
- The Gold Mines of Midian and the Ruined Midianite Cities. A Fortnight's Tour in Northwestern Arabia. London: 1878. 1st edn. 398 pp. Fldg map, ills. Orig red cloth.
(Trophy Room Books) $800 [≃ £500]
- The Gold-Mines of Midian and the Ruined Midianite Cities ... London: Kegan Paul, 1878. 1st edn. 8vo. xvi,398,32 advt pp. Fldg map. Some ff carelessly opened. Orig red cloth. *(Adelson)* £625 [≃ £390]
- The Highlands of Brazil ... London: Tinsley Bros, 1869. 1st edn. 2 vols. xii,443; viii,478 pp. Half-titles. 2 frontis, fldg map, title vignettes. Three qtr levant mor gilt by Bayntun, orig cloth from upper bd & spine at end of vol 1. *(Hollett)* £375 [≃ $600]
- Lacerda's Journey to Cazembe in 1798 ... London: John Murray, for the Royal Geog Society, 1873. 1st edn. [viii],271 pp. Lge fldg map. Orig blue cloth gilt, hinges & spine ends worn, jnts tender. *(Hollett)* £120 [≃ $192]
- The Lake Regions of Central Africa. London: 1860. 1st edn. 2 vols. 412; 468 pp. Advts at rear. Fldg map, ills. Orig cloth, recased, new endpapers.
(Trophy Room Books) $1,250 [≃ £781]
- The Lake Regions of Central Africa. New York: Harper, 1860. 1st Amer edn. 8vo. 572,4 advt pp. Fldg map, 12 plates. Orig cloth, rubbed, spine ends starting.
(Adelson) $160 [≃ £100]
- The Lake Regions of Central Africa, a Picture of Exploration. New York: Harper & Bros, 1860. 1st Amer edn. 8vo. Fldg map, 35 w'cut ills. Orig maroon cloth, gilt lettering, crnrs a little worn, spine ends frayed, gilt faded.
(Clark) £130 [≃ $208]
- The Lands of Cazembe. Lacerda's Journey to Cazembe in 1798. Translated and Annotated by Burton. London: Royal Geographical Society, 1873. 1st edn. Orig bndg.
(Trophy Room Books) $350 [≃ £218]
- The Lands of Cazembe. Lacerda's Journey to Cazembe in 1798. Translated and annotated by Capt. R.F. Burton ... London: RGS, 1873. 8vo. vii, 272 pp. Fldg map. Orig blue cloth, sl rubbed. *(Adelson)* $285 [≃ £178]
- A Mission to Gelele, King of Dahome ... London: 1864. 1st edn. Orig bndg.
(Trophy Room Books) $1,000 [≃ £625]
- A Mission to Gelele, King of Dahomey. London: 1893. Memorial Edition. 2 vols. 8vo. 256; 305 pp. 2 frontis. Orig black gilt pict cloth, 1/2 inch tears at top right crnr of both spines. *(Terramedia)* $100 [≃ £62]
- Personal Narrative of a Mission to El-Medinah and Meccah. New York: Putnam, 1856. 1st Amer edn. xvi,492 pp. Tinted litho

frontis & title, fldg map. Orig cloth gilt, a few unobtrusive ex-lib marks.
(Reese) $275 [≃ £171]
- Personal Narrative of a Pilgrimage to El-Medinah and Meccah ... New York: Putnam, 1856. 1st Amer edn. Sm 8vo. 492 pp. Fldg map (sl defective), 2 tinted plates. Sl foxed & spotted. Orig cloth, edges sl rubbed, spine ends sl frayed.
(Worldwide Antiqu'n) $125 [≃ £78]
- Personal Narrative of a Pilgrimage to Mecca and Medina. Leipzig: Bernhard Tauchnitz, 1874. 3 vols. 8vo. Three qtr calf, sm stain on 1 cvr. *(Book Block)* $375 [≃ £234]
- Personal Narrative of a Mission to Al-Madinah and Meccah. London: 1893. Memorial Edition. 2 vols. 8vo. 436; 479 pp. Fldg map, 2 frontis, 15 other plates, text ills. Orig pict gilt black cloth, hinges cracked internally, 1 flyleaf loose.
(Terramedia) $150 [≃ £93]
- Selected Papers on Anthropology Travel and Exploration. Edited by N.M. Penzer. London: 1924. 240 pp. Orig cloth.
(Trophy Room Books) $150 [≃ £93]
- Selected Papers on Anthropology Travel and Exploration. Edited by N.M. Penzer. London: 1924. One of 100. 240 pp. Orig cloth. *(Trophy Room Books)* $450 [≃ £281]
- Sind Revisited ... London: 1871. 1st edn. 2 vols. Sm hole in front free endpaper vol 2. Lib bndg. *(Trophy Room Books)* $200 [≃ £125]
- Two Trips to Gorilla Land and the Cataracts of the Congo. London: 1876. 1st edn. 2 vols. 261; 255 pp. Fldg map, ills. Almost imperceptible blindstamp on titles. Orig cloth, minimal wear.
(Trophy Room Books) $1,250 [≃ £781]
- Ultima Thule; or, a Summer in Iceland. London: Nimmo, 1875. 1st edn. 2 vols. 8vo. xx,380,16 advt; vi,[11],408 pp. 2 fldg maps, 11 plates, text ills. Three qtr leather gilt, by Macdonald, sl worn. *(Parmer)* $500 [≃ £312]
- Unexplored Syria ... London: Tinsley, 1872. 1st edn. 2 vols. 8vo. xx,360; viii,400 pp. Fldg map, 25 plates. Half yellow calf by Sangorski, rubbed, hinges worn but intact.
(Adelson) $525 [≃ £328]
- Wanderings in Three Continents. Edited, with a Preface, by W.H. Wilkins ... London: Hutchinson, 1901. 1st edn. xiii,313 pp. Port, 4 plates. Orig red buckram, rubbed, spine faded. *(Adelson)* $155 [≃ £96]
- Wanderings in West Africa From Liverpool to Fernando Po. London: 1863. 1st edn. 2 vols. 295; 303 pp. Orig cloth.
(Trophy Room Books) $1,150 [≃ £718]
- The Works. London: Tylston & Edwards, 1894-94. Memorial Edition. 7 vols. Num

maps, plates, text ills. Some pencil marks. Half mor, sl rubbed & scuffed.

(Worldwide Antiqu'n) **$750 [≈ £468]**

Busbecq, Ogier Ghiselin de
- The Four Epistles of Busbequius concerning his Embassy into Turkey. Being Remarks upon the Religion, Customs, Riches, Strength and Government of that People ... London: 1694. 1st edn in English. 16mo. [viii],420,advt pp. Few ff sl browned. Contemp calf, rebacked.

(Terramedia) **$300 [≈ £187]**
- Travels into Turkey. Translated from the original Latin of the learned A.G. Busbequius. Third Edition. Glasgow: Robert Urie, 1761. 12mo. 283,4 advt pp. Old name on title. Calf, worn, cvrs detached. Boxed.

(Schoyer) **$60 [≈ £37]**

Butler, Alban
- Travels through France & Italy, and Part of Austrian, French & Dutch Netherlands, during the Years 1745 and 1746 ... Edinburgh: John Moir ..., 1803. 1st edn. 8vo. 472 pp. Rec cloth.   *(Young's)* **£45 [≈ $72]**

Butler, Elizabeth
- Letters from the Holy Land. London: Black, 1903. 1st edn. One of 200, sgnd. 4to. x,84 pp. 16 cold plates. Sl foxed. Orig cloth, sl rubbed & soiled.   *(Worldwide Antiqu'n)* **$75 [≈ £46]**

Butler, H.
- South African Sketches. Illustrative of the Wild Life of a Hunter on the Frontier of the Cape Colony. London: 1841. 15 pp. 15 full-page plates showing 31 cold scenes. Tissues. Half leather, fine.

(Trophy Room Books) **$1,500 [≈ £937]**

Butler, S.
- An Atlas of Ancient Geography. London: [1848]. 8vo. Engvd title, 22 dble page maps, hand cold in outline. Sm hole in plate 8. New half calf.   *(Henly)* **£45 [≈ $72]**

Butler, Samuel, 1835-1902
- Alps and Sanctuaries of Piedmont and the Canton Ticino. London: David Bogue, 1882 [1881]. 1st edn, 1st iss. 4to. Final advt leaf. Frontis on india paper, num ills. Orig brown cloth, blocked in black & gilt, t.e.g., soiled, extremities sl worn, new endpapers.

(Sanders) **£65 [≈ $104]**

Butler, Col. Sir W.F.
- The Campaign of the Cataracts. Being a Personal Narrative of the Great Nile Expedition of 1884-5. London: Sampson,

Low, Marston, 1887. 1st edn. 8vo. vii,389 pp. Lge fldg map, frontis, num plates & ills. Orig light blue gilt pict cloth.

(Terramedia) **$350 [≈ £218]**
- The Great Lone Land: A Narrative of Travel and Adventure in the Northwest of America. London: Sampson Low, Marston, 1873. 4th edn. 386 pp. Fldg map, ills. Minimal foxing. Three qtr leather.   *(Parmer)* **$125 [≈ £78]**
- The Wild North Land: being the Story of a Winter Journey, with Dogs, across Northern North America. London: Sampson Low, 1874. 2nd edn. 8vo. xii,358,48 advt pp. Frontis, fldg map, 15 ills. Mod half calf gilt.   *(Hollett)* **£55 [≈ $88]**
- The Wild North Land ... Philadelphia: Porter & Coates, 1874. 4th edn. 358 pp. Frontis, fldg map (tears reprd), 15 ills. Orig pict gilt green cloth, moderate wear to all edges.   *(Parmer)* **$80 [≈ £50]**

Buttrick, Tilly, Jr.
- Voyages, Travels and Discoveries of ... Boston: 1831. 12mo. 58 pp. Some foxing. Self-wraps, stitched. Clamshell case.

(Reese) **$2,750 [≈ £1,718]**
- Voyages, Travels and Discoveries of ... Boston: 1831. 1st edn. 58 pp. Sl foxing. Self-wraps, stitched as issued. Clamshell case.

(Jenkins) **$2,750 [≈ £1,718]**

Buxton, E.N.
- Short Stalks or Hunting Camps North South East and West. London: 1892. 399 pp. 70 ills. Orig bndg.

(Trophy Room Books) **$250 [≈ £156]**
- Short Stalks. Hunting Camps, North, South, East and West. London: 1893. 8vo. ills. Half mor.   *(Grayling)* **£45 [≈ $72]**
- Short Stalks: or Hunting Camps, North, South, East, and West. Second Edition. London: 1893. 8vo. [xiv],405 pp. 25 full-page & 43 other text ills. Orig illust buckram, spine (as usual) browned.

(Bow Windows) **£40 [≈ $64]**
- Short Stalks Second Series. London: 1898. 226 pp. 2 fldg pocket maps (front & rear). Num ills. Orig bndg.

(Trophy Room Books) **$250 [≈ £156]**

Buxton, Thomas Fowell
- The African Slave Trade. London: Murray, 1839. 1st edn. 8vo. xv,240,8 advt pp. Fldg map, cold in outline. Orig green cloth, "With a Map" embossed at ft of spine, sm repr at edge of spine.   *(Gough)* **£250 [≈ $400]**

Byrd, Richard Evelyn
- Discovery. The Story of the Second Byrd

Antarctic Expedition ... New York: 1935. 1st edn. 8vo. xxiv,406 pp. Frontis, map, plates, endpaper maps. Orig cloth, spine faded, sm stain on lower spine. dw. Sgnd by the author.
(Berkelouw) **$100 [≈ £62]**

- Little America. Aerial Exploration in the Antarctic. The Flight to the South Pole. New York: 1930. 1st edn. 8vo. xvi,422 pp. Port, 4 maps, 55 plates, illust endpapers. Orig cloth gilt. Dw partly missing. Sgnd by the author.
(Berkelouw) **$100 [≈ £62]**

- Skyward. New York: Putnam's, 1928. One of 500, sgnd. Lge 8vo. xv,348 pp. Fldg map, plates. 2 pieces of cloth from the plane Josephine Ford fixed to pastedown. Orig blue cloth over paper bds, gilt spine. Orig box.
(Heritage) **$300 [≈ £187]**

- Skyward. New York: 1928. 1st edn. 1st iss, with gravure port. Thick 8vo. xvi,348 pp. Port frontis, plates, endpaper maps. Orig cloth gilt. Dw. Author's sgnd pres copy.
(Berkelouw) **$175 [≈ £109]**

- Skyward. New York: 1928. 1st edn. 1st iss, with gravure port. Thick 8vo. xvi,348 pp. Port frontis, plates, endpaper maps. Orig cloth gilt. *(Berkelouw)* **$75 [≈ £46]**

Byrne, P.

- A Picturesque Handbook to Carlingford Bay and Vicinity ... Newry & Dublin: 1846. Map, ills. Orig cloth, rebacked.
(Emerald Isle) **£45 [≈ $72]**

Byron, George Gordon, Lord

- Narrative of Lord Byron's Voyage to Corsica and Sardinia during the Summer and Autumn of of the Year 1821. Paris: Galignani, 1825. 8vo. Contemp half roan, rather rubbed. A fabrication. *(Waterfield's)* **£30 [≈ $48]**

Byron, John

- The Narrative of the Honourable John Byron (Commodore of a Late Expedition round the World) ... Second Edition. London: S. Baker & G. Leigh, 1768. 8vo. [2],viii,257 pp. Frontis (foxed & with stamp on verso). Lib b'plate. 19th c half mor, spine rubbed & reprd. *(Spelman)* **£50 [≈ $80]**

- The Narrative of the Honourable John Byron (Commodore in a Late Expedition round the World) ... London: 1768. 2nd edn. viii,257 pp. Frontis. Front free endsheet nearly detached. Contemp calf, raised bands, jnts worn, spine ends chipped.
(Reese) **$300 [≈ £180]**

- The Narrative of the Honourable John Byron (Commodore of a Late Expedition Round the World) ... Coast of Patagonia ... Description of St. Jago de Chili ... London: 1768. [i]-vii,

257 pp. Frontis. Orig calf gilt, spine reprd.
(Reese) **$500 [≈ £312]**

Cable, Mildred & French, Francesca

- The Gobi Desert. London: 1942. 8vo. Fldg map, 3 cold & num other plates. Orig cloth.
(Farahar) **£25 [≈ $40]**

- The Making of a Pioneer, Percy Mather of Central Asia. London: 1935. 8vo. Fldg map, plates. Orig cloth. *(Farahar)* **£20 [≈ $32]**

- Something Happened. London: 1933. 8vo. Fldg map, frontis. Orig cloth, spine sl worn.
(Farahar) **£18 [≈ $28]**

- Through Jade Gate and Central Asia. An Account of Journeys in Kansu, Turkestan and the Gobi Desert. London: 1927. 1st edn. 8vo. Fldg map, plates. Orig cloth, sl worn.
(Farahar) **£25 [≈ $40]**

Cadell, W.A.

- A Journey in Carniola, Italy, and France, in the Years 1817, 1818 ... Edinburgh: Constable, 1820. 1st edn. 2 vols. 8vo. viii, 554; 424 pp. Lge fldg map, 32 plates (some fldg). Occas sl soiling. Contemp calf gilt, rebacked. *(Frew Mackenzie)* **£180 [≈ $288]**

Caine, W.S.

- A Trip Round the World in 1887-8. London: 1892. 398 pp. Frontis, ills. Some foxing. Orig cloth gilt, soiled & loose. *(Reese)* **$85 [≈ £53]**

Calderwood, W.L.

- The Salmon Rivers and Lochs of Scotland. London: Edward Arnold, 1909. One of 250 Large Paper. 4to. x,442 pp. 4 cold & 34 other plates. Orig 2-tone cloth, t.e.g.
(Egglishaw) **£150 [≈ $240]**

Callcott, Lady

- See Graham, Maria.

Calvert, Albert F.

- Spain. An Historical and Descriptive Account of its Architecture, Landscape, and Arts. London: Batsford, 1924. 2 vols. Lge 4to. 46 cold plates, over 1700 ills. Orig cloth gilt. Dws. *(Hollett)* **£75 [≈ $120]**

Calvert, Frederick, 6th Baron Baltimore

- A Tour to the East, in the Years 1763 and 1764. With Remarks on the City of Constantinople and the Turks ... London: Richardson & Clark, 1767. 1st edn. 8vo. Engvd title, lge fldg plan (torn without loss in inner marg), 4 plates. Mod mor, gilt spine.
(Trebizond) **$525 [≈ £328]**

Cambridge, Ada
- Thirty Years in Australia. London: Methuen, 1903. 8vo. vii,304 pp. Orig bndg.
(Schoyer) **$50 [≃ £31]**

Camden, William
- Britannia. Translated into English by Edmund Gibson. London: 1695. 1st edn. Folio. Engvd port & title, 50 maps by Robert Morden, plates, 65 w'cut text ills. Some offsetting. Short tear in crnr of 1 map just affecting engvd surface. Contemp calf, rebacked. *(Henly)* **£1,600 [≃ $2,560]**
- Britannia ... Enlarged by the Latest Discoveries by Richard Gough. The Second Edition ... London: 1806. 4 vols. Folio. Port, fldg pedigree, 52 fldg maps by Cary & 5 others, 103 plates, others in text. Sl signs of use. Old calf, rebacked, a little rubbed.
(Bow Windows) **£1,350 [≃ $2,160]**
- Remaines, concerning Britaine ... Reviewed, corrected, and encreased. London: Iohn Legatt for Simon Waterson, 1614. 4to. Sm hole through lower portion of 1st 3rd of text. Later sheep, sl rubbed. STC 4522. Early MS notes. *(Sanders)* **£175 [≃ $280]**
- Remains Concerning Britaine ... The Fifth Impression, with many Rare Antiquities Never Before Imprinted ... London: Thomas Harper for John Waterson, 1636. Sm 4to. [6],420,[2] pp. Num w'cut coats-of-arms. Some old marg stains. Old calf, rebacked. STC 4525. *(Karmiole)* **$250 [≃ £156]**
- Remaines Concerning Britaine ... The Fifth Impression, with many Rare Antiquities never Before Imprinted. By the Industry and Care of John Philpot. London: 1636. Sm 4to. [6],420, [2] pp. Num w'cut arms. Some old marg stains. Old calf, rebacked. STC 4525.
(Karmiole) **$250 [≃ £156]**
- Remaines Concerning Britain ... The sixth Impression, with many rare Antiquities never before imprinted ... London: 1657. Sm 4to. [iv], 334 [=410], [2] pp. Port frontis. 19th c polished speckled calf, gilt spine, a.e.g., by Bedford. Sm reprs. Wing C.374A.
(Clark) **£185 [≃ $296]**
- Remains Concerning Britain. London: John Russell Smith, Library of Old Authors, 1870. 8vo. Port. A bit browned. Orig red cloth, gilt spine, sl rubbed. *(Clark)* **£18 [≃ $28]**

Cameron, Verney Lovett
- Across Africa. London: Daldy, Isbister, 1877. 2 vols. 8vo. xvi,389,4 advt; xii,366,8 advt pp. Fldg map, 33 plates. Orig blue pict cloth, sl rubbed. *(Adelson)* **$300 [≃ £187]**
- Across Africa. New York: Harper, 1877. 1st Amer edn. 8vo. xvi,508,8 advt pp. Fldg map

in pocket, frontis, num tissued plates & other ills. Orig orange brown gilt pict cloth.
(Terramedia) **$150 [≃ £93]**

Camm, Bede
- Forgotten Shrines. An Account of some old Catholic Halls and Families in England ... London: 1910. 1st edn. 4to. xvi,411,[2] pp. Ca 150 ills & plates. Orig cloth gilt, t.e.g., silk marker. *(Fenning)* **£45 [≃ $72]**

Campbell, Archibald
- A Voyage around the World, from 1806 to 1812; in which Japan, Kamschatka, the Aleutian Islands, and the Sandwich Islands were visited ... Edinburgh: 1816. 288 pp. Fldg map. 1st few pp loose. Sl browning. Three qtr calf & bds. *(Reese)* **$1,350 [≃ £843]**
- A Voyage around the World, from 1806 to 1812. New York: 1817. 204 pp. Lacks map. Old calf, hinges broken but cords sound.
(Reese) **$400 [≃ £250]**

Campbell, Donald
- A Narrative of the Extraordinary Adventures, and Sufferings by Shipwreck & Imprisonment ... Overland Journey to India ... London: Strahan ..., 1801. 4th edn. 8vo. xi, 259 pp. Frontis. Orig bds, rebacked.
(Young's) **£58 [≃ $92]**

Campbell, Dugald
- Wanderings in Central Africa. London: 1929. 8vo. 284 pp. Frontis, num plates. Orig orange gilt pict cloth. *(Terramedia)* **$50 [≃ £31]**
- Wanderings in Widest Africa. London: RTS, [1931]. Reprint of the 1st edn of 1930. 8vo. [xi], 223 pp. Fldg map, frontis, num plates. Orig blue gilt cloth.
(Terramedia) **$50 [≃ £31]**

Campbell, John
- Lives of the Admirals, and Other Eminent British Seamen. Containing their Personal Histories; and a Detail of all their Public Services ... London: 1742-44. 4 vols. Lib stamps. Orig calf, gilt spines.
(Reese) **$850 [≃ £531]**
- Lives of the Admirals and other Eminent British Seamen ... Second Edition ... London: 1750. 4 vols. [With] A Continuation ... New Edition. London: 1781. Together 5 vols. 8vo. 4 frontis, 6 fldg maps. Contemp calf, sl rubbed, spine ends sl worn, some jnts cracked but firm. *(Bickersteth)* **£120 [≃ $192]**

Campbell, Revd John
- Travels in South Africa [1st Journey] ... London: for Black, Parry & Co, 1815. 3rd

edn, crrctd. 8vo. 400 pp. Fldg map, 8 plates (1 fldg). Sl browning. Contemp qtr mor, disbound.   *(Terramedia)* **$70 [≈ £43]**

- Travels in South Africa ... Narrative of a Second Journey in the Interior of that Country. London: Francis Westley, 1822. 1st edn. 2 vols. 8vo. 322; 384 pp. Fldg cold map, 12 hand cold plates. Contemp half mor, sl rubbed & frayed. *(Terramedia)* **$750 [≈ £468]**

- Travels in South Africa ... Narrative of a Second Journey in the Interior of that Country. London: 1822. 2 vols in one. xii, 322; 384 pp. Fldg cold map, 12 cold aquatint plates. Lacks half-title & dedic leaf. Contemp calf gilt, some wear to extremities.
                        (Reese) **$800 [≈ £500]**

Campbell, Marius R., et al.

- Guidebook of the Western United States ... Washington: 1915. 4 vols. Num maps, ills. Orig limp pebbled mor gilt, extremities a bit dry.   *(Reese)* **$200 [≈ £125]**

- Guidebook of the Western United States. Washington: 1916. 1st edn. 3 vols. Almost 80 fldg maps, ills. Cloth.
                        (Jenkins) **$200 [≈ £125]**

Campbell, Dr. Thomas

- A Philosophical Survey of the South of Ireland, in a Series of Letters to John Watkinson, M.D. London: Strahan, 1777. Plate at end. Diced calf, rebacked.
                (Emerald Isle) **£150 [≈ $240]**

- A Philosophical Survey of the South of Ireland, in a Series of Letters to John Watkinson, M.D. Dublin: for W. Whitestone ..., 1778. 1st Irish edn. 8vo. xvi, 478, [2 blank] pp. 6 plates (2 fldg). Rec calf backed mrbld bds.   *(Fenning)* **£125 [≈ $200]**

Campbell, Col. Walter

- My Indian Journal. London: 1864. 8vo. Cold map on title, engvd plates (sl foxed). Mod half mor.   *(Grayling)* **£85 [≈ $136]**

Campbell, Captain Walter, of Skipness

- The Old Forest Ranger: or, Wild Sports of India on the Neilgherry Hills, in the Jungles and on the Plains. Second Edition. London: Jeremiah How, 1845. 8vo. 8 plates, ills on addtnl engvd title, all mtd on canvas. Rather finger marked. Red half mor. *(Hannas)* **£45 [≈ $72]**

Campbell, Wilfred

- Canada. Painted by T. Mower Martin. London: A. & C. Black Colour Books, Twenty Shilling Series, 1907. 1st edn. 77 cold plates. Orig dec cloth, v fine.
                (Old Cathay) **£95 [≈ $152]**

- Canada. Painted by T. Mower Martin. London: A. & C. Black Colour Books, Twenty Shilling Series, 1907. 1st edn. 77 cold plates. Orig dec cloth, browning to endpapers, v.g.   *(Old Cathay)* **£45 [≈ $72]**

- Canada. Painted by T. Mower Martin. London: A. & C. Black Colour Books, Twenty Shilling Series, 1907. 1st edn. 77 cold plates. Orig dec cloth, spine sl faded, upper bd somewhat bowed.
                (Old Cathay) **£40 [≈ $64]**

Campenhausen, Baron

- Travels through Several Provinces of the Russian Empire ... London: Richard Phillips, 1808. 128 pp. Occas foxing. Mod half cloth, t.e.g.   *(Reese)* **$150 [≈ £93]**

Campion, J.S.

- On the Frontier. Reminiscences of Wild Sports, Personal Adventures, and Strange Scenes ... London: 1878. xvi, 372, 32 advt pp. Port, plates (2 reprd in tape). Cloth, minor chipping. Plain dw.   *(Reese)* **$150 [≈ £93]**

Candler, Edmund

- The Long Road to Baghdad. London: Cassell, 1919. 1st edn. 2 vols. 8vo. 19 maps & plans, 16 plates. Orig cloth gilt.
                        (Hollett) **£45 [≈ $72]**

Cane, Claude

- Summer and Fall in Western Alaska: The Record of a trip to Cook's Inlet after Big Game. London: Horace Cox, 1903. 1st edn. viii, 191 pp. 26 ills. Orig dec cloth gilt.
                (Hollett) **£180 [≈ $288]**

Cantwell, John C.

- Report of the Operations of the U.S. Revenue Steamer Nunivak on the Yukon River Station, Alaska 1899-1901. Washington: GPO, 1904. 8vo. 325 pp. Num photo plates. Half mor.   *(Parmer)* **$175 [≈ £109]**

Capper, B.P.

- A Compendious Geographical Dictionary ... Fourth Edition. Corrected and Enlarged. London: 1813. Sm 8vo. Fldg world map, 7 other fldg maps, all hand cold in outline, fldg plan of the solar system. Contemp dark green straight grained mor gilt, a.e.g., spine sl rubbed.   *(Sanders)* **£125 [≈ $200]**

Capper, John

- The Three Presidencies of India: A History of the Rise and Progress of the British Indian Possession ... London: Ingram, Cooke, 1853. 1st edn. 8vo. xii, 492, 4 advt pp. Fldg map (torn without loss), num engvs. Sl foxed. Orig

cloth, crnrs rubbed.
(Worldwide Antiqu'n) **$35 [≈ £21]**

Cardinell, Charles
- Adventures on the Plains. San Francisco: 1922. 1st sep iss (one of 150). 15 pp. Ptd wraps.   *(Reese)* **$75 [≈ £46]**

Cardonnel, Adam de
- Picturesque Antiquities of Scotland. London: for the author, 1788-93. 2 parts in 1 vol. 4to. 50 pp text. 100 etchings. With the introduction to parts 3 & 4 (which were never published). Lacks title to 2nd part. Contemp calf, worn, spine damaged.
(Stewart) **£185 [≈ $296]**

Carew, Richard
- The Survey of Cornwall. London: S.S. for John Jaggard, 1602. 1st edn. 4to. Intl blank leaf, errata leaf. Table at end misbound. Tear in title reprd, single worm hole through last qtr of the book. Minor stains. Contemp limp vellum. STC 4615. *(Hannas)* **£500 [≈ $800]**

Carey, Edith F.
- The Channel Islands. Painted by Henry B. Wimbush. London: A. & C. Black, 1924. 2nd edn, rvsd. Map, 32 cold plates. Foxing throughout. Orig cloth.
(Old Cathay) **£13 [≈ $20]**

Carleton, George W.
- Our Artist in Cuba. Fifty Drawings on Wood. Leaves from the Sketch-Book of a Traveler, during the Winter of 1864-5. New York: 1865. viii pp, 50 ff. Orig cloth gilt, sl sunned, sl edge wear. Author's pres copy.
(Reese) **$250 [≈ £156]**
- Our Artist in Peru. [Fifty Drawings on Wood.] Leaves from the Sketch-Book of a Traveller, during the Winter of 1865-6. New York: 1866. viii pp, 50 ff. Orig cloth gilt, some wear to extremities.
(Reese) **$175 [≈ £109]**

Carlisle, The Earl of
- Diary in Turkish and Greek Waters. Edited by C.C. Felton. Boston: Hickling, Swan & Brown, 1855. 1st edn. 8vo. xviii,299 pp. Frontis, plates & ills. Orig cloth.
(Worldwide Antiqu'n) **$75 [≈ £46]**

Carne, John
- Syria, the Holy Land, Asia Minor &c. Illustrated ... London: [1836-38]. 3 vols in two. 80; 76; 100 pp. Engvd titles, 117 engvd plates after Bartlett et al. Occas sl foxing. Contemp three qtr calf, extremities worn.
(Reese) **$750 [≈ £468]**

- Syria, the Holy Land & Asia Minor Illustrated ... London: [1842]. 3 vols in one. 4to. 2 maps, 2 (of 3) engvd titles, port, 113 (of 117) plates. Lacks 6 ff of text. Occas marg foxing. Contemp half calf, spine worn, bds just holding.   *(Fenning)* **£185 [≈ $296]**
- Syria, the Holy Land & Asia Minor illustrated ... London: Peter Jackson, late Fisher, Son, & Co ... [ca 1842]. 3 vols in one. 4to. 3 vignette titles, 2 maps, 118 plates. 1st & last few ff foxed, some offsetting. Purple half calf, gilt spine, minor rubbing.
(Heritage) **$600 [≈ £375]**

Carne, Louis de
- Travels in Indo-China and the Chinese Empire with a Notice of the Author by Count de Carne. Translated from the French. London: Chapman & Hall, 1872. 1st edn in English. xxi, [1], 365 pp. Fldg map, 6 plates. Orig cloth, lower crnr of upper cvr waterstained.   *(Claude Cox)* **£55 [≈ $88]**

Carpenter, G.D.H.
- A Naturalist on Lake Victoria with an Account of Sleeping Sickness and the Tse-Tse Fly. London: 1920. 8vo. Map, 2 cold plates, 7 charts, 87 ills. Orig cloth, trifle used, front cvr string-marked.
(Wheldon & Wesley) **£58 [≈ $92]**

Carpenter, R.
- Game Trails from Alaska to Africa. Privately ptd: 1938. One of 850. Orig bndg. Sgnd by the author.
(Trophy Room Books) **$150 [≈ £93]**
- Game Trails from Alaska to Africa. Privately ptd: 1938. One of 850. Orig bndg.
(Trophy Room Books) **$100 [≈ £62]**

Carr, Mrs Comyns
- North Italian Folk. Sketches of Town and Country Life. London: 1878. 1st edn. 8vo. Illust by Randolph Caldecott. Orig dec cloth, cvrs sl marked. *(Robertshaw)* **£12.50 [≈ $20]**

Carr, H.R.C. & Lister, G.A. (eds.)
- The Mountains of Snowdonia in History, the Sciences, Literature and Sport. London: 1948. 2nd edn. 8vo. xiii,312 pp. 50 ills & diags. Orig cloth, faded.
(Wheldon & Wesley) **£18 [≈ $28]**

Carr, Sir John
- A Northern Summer; or Travels round the Baltic, through Denmark, Sweden, Russia, Prussia, and Part of Germany, in the Year 1804. London: 1805. 1st edn. Half-title. 11 sepia aquatint plates (1 fldg with sm tear), plus 1 inserted plate. Contemp calf, sl

rubbed. *(Hannas)* **£380 [≈ $608]**

- A Northern Summer; or Travels round the Baltic, through Denmark, Sweden, Russia, Prussia, and Part of Germany, in the Year 1804. London: 1805. 1st edn. 4to. xii,480 pp. 11 tinted plates. Marking & wear. Old calf, worn, rough hinge repr.
(Hollett) **£150 [≈ $240]**

- A Northern Summer: or Travels round the Baltick, through Denmark, Sweden, Russia, prussia, and Part of Germany, in the Year 1804. Second Connecticut Edition. New London: 1806. 330,advt pp. Occas foxing, pp darkened. Contemp calf, worn.
(Reese) **$85 [≈ £53]**

- The Stranger in France: or, a Tour from Devonshire to Paris ... London: J. Johnson, 1803. 4to. 12 aquatint plates, tinted by hand with a sepia wash. Contemp calf, dble labels (1 defective), front jnt cracked. From the Earl of Durham's library.
(Waterfield's) **£150 [≈ $240]**

- The Stranger in Ireland, or A Tour in the Southern and Western Parts of the Country in 1805. London: Phillips, 1806. 4to. Sepia aquatints. Contemp diced calf gilt, rebacked.
(Emerald Isle) **£350 [≈ $560]**

Carr, William
- An Accurate Description of the United Netherlands ... Written by an English Gentleman. London: for Timothy Childe, 1691. 1st edn. 2 parts in one vol. Sm 8vo. 5 fldg plates. Half calf, crnrs worn, rebacked. Wing C.632. *(Hannas)* **£160 [≈ $256]**

Carranza, Domingo Gonzales
- A Geographical Description of the Coasts, Harbours, and Sea Ports of the Spanish West-Indies ... Translated from a Curious and Authentic Manuscript ... London: 1740. [xii], 124, [8] pp. 5 fldg maps & plans. Title soiled. Antique half calf. *(Reese)* **$1,850 [≈ £1,156]**

Carruthers, D.
- Beyond the Caspian. London: 1949. 290 pp. Fldg map, 6 cold plates, ills. Orig bndg.
(Trophy Room Books) **$175 [≈ £109]**

Carson, Blanche M.
- From Cairo to the Cataract. Boston: L.C. Page, 1909. 1st edn. 12mo. 330 pp. Num photo plates. Orig pict green cloth.
(Terramedia) **$35 [≈ £21]**

Carstensen, A. Riis
- Two Summers in Greenland ... London: 1890. xxxi, 185 pp. Frontis, fldg map, title vignette, ills. Orig pict gilt cloth, extremities

bumped. *(Reese)* **$200 [≈ £125]**

Carter, Nathaniel H.
- Letters from Europe, comprising the Journal of a Tour ... New York: 1827. 528 pp. Occas foxing, sgntr starting. Orig sheep, scuffed & worn, ex-lib with b'plate. *(Reese)* **$75 [≈ £46]**

Carus, C.G.
- The King of Saxony's Journey through England and Scotland in the Year 1844 ... Translated by S.C. Davison. London: Chapman & Hall, 1846. 8vo, Orig cloth.
(Waterfield's) **£50 [≈ $80]**

Carvalho, S.N.
- Incidents of Travel and Adventure in the Far West; with Col. Fremont's Last Expedition across the Rocky Mountains ... New York: 1857. 2nd edn. [xvi],[17]-380,advt pp. Dedic leaf (pp v-vi) excised as usual. Frontis. Occas foxing. Orig cloth, sl worn.
(Reese) **$250 [≈ £156]**

Carver, Jonathan
- The New Universal Traveller. Containing a Full and Distinct Account of all the Empires, Kingdoms, and States, in the Known World ... London: G. Robinson, 1779. Folio. iv, 668, 6 pp. Frontis, 18 maps, 37 plates. Orig calf, rebacked, gilt spine, orig label.
(Adelson) **$750 [≈ £468]**

Cary, John
- Cary's British Traveller; or, an abridged Edition of his New Itinerary ... London: for J. Cary, 1803. 470 pp. Fldg map frontis. New cloth backed mrbld bds, leather label.
(Box of Delights) **£40 [≈ $64]**

- New and Correct English Atlas; being a New Set of County Maps from Actual Surveys. London: 1787. 4to. Engvd title, dedic, subscribers list, general map & 45 county maps, all hand cold. Contemp calf, spine relaid, lower hinge starting to crack.
(Henly) **£475 [≈ $760]**

- Cary's New Itinerary: or, an Accurate Delineation of the Great Roads, both Direct and Cross, throughout England and Wales ... London: for John Cary, 1798. 1st edn. 2nd iss, with 48 pp index. 8vo. Engvd title & dedic leaf. Part only of the map. Contemp qtr calf. *(Young's)* **£40 [≈ $64]**

- Cary's New Itinerary: or, an Accurate Delineation of the Great Roads ... Third Edition with Improvements. London: for J. Cary, 1806. Fldg map torn without loss. Orig bds, worn, jnts breaking.
(Waterfield's) **£50 [≈ $80]**

- New Pocket Plan of London, Westminster and Southwark ... London: 1830. Cold map, dissected on canvas, fldg into orig mrbld slipcase with orig paper label. Some wear on slipcase.   *(Coombes)* £45 [≈ $72]
- A Survey of the High Roads from London. London: 1799. Sm 4to. Engvd title, general map, general plan, 80 strip maps, all hand cold. Sheep, a little rubbed.
          (Henly) £350 [≈ $560]

Casati, Gaetano
- Ten Years in Equatoria and the Return with Emin Pasha. London: Warne, 1891. 2 vols. 8vo. xxi,376; xvi,347 pp. 4 maps, 60 plates. Orig pict cloth, 1 spine starting.
          (Adelson) $285 [≈ £178]

Casey, Charles
- Two Years on the Farm of Uncle Sam. London: Bentley, 1852. 1st edn. 8vo. x,311 pp. Orig claret cloth, gilt spine, faded, spine sl dull.   *(Burmester)* £55 [≈ $88]

Caspipina's Letters ...
- See Duche, Jacob.

Cassas, L.F.
- Travels in Istria and Dalmatia, Drawn up from the Itinerary of L.F. Cassas ... London: Richard Phillips, 1805. iv,124 pp. 6 plates, fldg frontis map. Occas foxing & offsetting from plates. Mod half cloth, t.e.g.
          (Reese) $125 [≈ £78]

Castellan, Antoine L.
- Turkey, being a Description of the Manners, Customs, Dresses and Other Peculiarities Characteristic of the Inhabitants of the Turkish Empire ... Philadelphia: 1829. 3 vols. 12mo. 24 cold plates by Shoberl. Foxing. Contemp three qtr calf, scuffed.
          (Reese) $450 [≈ £281]

Castletown, Lord
- "Ego". Random Records of Sport Service and Travel in Many Lands ... London: 1923. 8vo. Orig cloth.   *(Grayling)* £50 [≈ $80]

Cater, Revd J.
- Bisley Bits; or, Records of a Surrey Corner. London: 1892. 8vo. 127 pp. 14 ills inc fldg map & fldg picture. Orig cloth.
          (Coombes) £21 [≈ $33]

Catlin, George
- Catlin's Notes of Eight Years' Travels and Residence in Europe with his North American Indian Collection. London: the author, 1848. 2nd edn. 2 vols. Ills. Orig pict cloth gilt.   *(Jenkins)* $525 [≈ £328]
- O-kee-pa: A Religious Ceremony; and Other Customs of the Mandans. London: Trubner, 1867. 1st edn. Lge 8vo. 52 pp. Folium Reservatum sheet laid in. 13 cold plates. Orig dec red cloth.
          (W. Thomas Taylor) $5,500 [≈ £3,437]

Catlow, Agnes & Maria E.
- Sketching Rambles; or, Nature in the Alps and Appenines. Illustrated ... by the Authors. London: James Hogg, [1831]. Only edn. 2 vols. 8vo. xii,[ii], 374,[ii]; viii, [ii], 368 pp. 2 cold litho frontis, 18 tinted lithos. Orig cloth gilt, sl dulled.   *(Blackwell's)* £250 [≈ $400]

Cave, Henry W.
- The Ruined Cities of Ceylon. A New Edition. London: 1900. 8vo. 165,6 pp. 65 photo ills on 64 plates. Orig gilt illust cloth, t.e.g., rebacked.   *(Bow Windows)* £52 [≈ $83]

Cayley, Cornelius, Junior
- A Tour through Holland, Flanders, and Part of France ... New Edition. Leeds: James Nichols, 1815. vi,97 pp. Sl dog-eared. Plain paper wraps, grubby & worn.
          (Box of Delights) £20 [≈ $32]

Cella, Paolo Della
- Narrative of an Expedition from Tripoli in Barbary, to the Western Frontier of Egypt, in 1817, by the Bey of Tripoli ... London: 1822. 8vo. Fldg map (foxed), text ills. Sl browning. Half calf, worming affecting bds.
          (Farahar) £36 [≈ $57]

Cesnola, Louis Palma Di
- Cyprus: Its Ancient Cities, Tombs and Temples. A Narrative of Researches and Excavations ... New York: Harper, 1878. 2nd edn. 8vo. xix,456,[3 advt] pp. 59 plates & num ills & maps. V sl foxing. Orig cloth, t.e.g., sl rubbed.
          (Worldwide Antiqu'n) $65 [≈ £40]
- Cyprus: Its Ancient Cities, Tombs, and Temples. A Narrative of Researches and Excavations ... New York: Harper, 1878. 3rd edn. 8vo. xix,456,[3 advt] pp. 59 plates & num ills & maps. Orig cloth, t.e.g., sl rubbed.
          (Worldwide Antiqu'n) $120 [≈ £75]

Chalmers, P.
- Sport and Travels in East Africa. Two Visits by HRH The Prince of Wales in 1928 and 1930. New York: 1934. 273 pp. Fldg map, ills. Orig bndg.
          (Trophy Room Books) $80 [≈ £50]

Chalmers, P.R.
- Mine Eyes to the Hills. An Anthology of the Highland Forest. London: A. & C. Black, 1931. 1st edn. Roy 8vo. xv,368 pp. 8 cold plates, text ills. Orig cloth.
(Egglishaw) £36 [≈ $57]

Chamberlain, G.
- African Hunting among the Thongas. New York: 1923. 286 pp. Ills. Orig bndg.
(Trophy Room Books) $85 [≈ £53]

Chamberlayne, Edward
- Angliae Notitia or the Present State of England ... London: 1700. 3 parts in one vol. 8vo. 600 pp. Port frontis (sl cropped at hd). Some browning & foxing. Later calf gilt, spine relaid, lacks 1 crnr.
(Dillons) £95 [≈ $152]

Chamberlayne, Edward & John
- Angliae Notitia: or the Present State of England ... London: T.H. for S. Smith & B. Walford ..., 1704. 3 parts in one vol. 8vo. [xx], 647, [9] pp. Front endpaper rather stained & sl torn. Old calf, a little worn, ft of spine defective, sl shaken. *(Hollett)* £65 [≈ $104]

Chambers, Robert
- Tracings of Iceland & The Faroe Islands. London: Chambers, 1856. 1st edn. Sm 8vo. [4], 85 pp. Frontis, 2 maps, i vignette in text. Orig ptd wraps, rubbed.
(Hannas) £55 [≈ $88]

Champion, F.W.
- With a Camera in Tiger-Land. Garden City: Doubleday, 1928. 1st edn. 4to. xviii,226 pp. Orig cloth, front hinge cracked internally and shaken. *(Terramedia)* $40 [≈ £25]
- With a Camera in Tiger-Land. London: Chatto & Windus, 1928. 1st edn. Sm 4to. xviii, 228 pp. 74 plates. Orig cloth, sl rubbed.
(Worldwide Antiqu'n) $45 [≈ £28]

Chancellor, E. Beresford
- Lost London. Illustrated by J. Crowther. London: Constable & Houghton Mifflin, 1926. One of 1025. Cold & b/w plates. Orig bndg. *(Old Cathay)* £39 [≈ $62]

Chandler, John, of Orford
- Coasting Directions for the North and South Channels of the River Thames: also Directions from Lowestoff-Roads to the Downs ... British Channel ... London: 1778. Only edn. 4to. [ii],28,[i advt] pp. Fldg chart. Orig wraps, sl worn & fragile. Mor backed case. *(Finch)* £250 [≈ $400]

Chandless, William
- A Visit to Salt Lake, being a Journey across the Plains and a residence in the Mormon Settlements at Utah. London: 1857. 1st edn. 346 pp. Fldg map. Orig cloth, reprd.
(Jenkins) $285 [≈ £178]

Chanler, William Astor
- Through Jungle and Desert. London: 1896. 535 pp. Num maps & ills. Orig pict gilt cloth.
(Trophy Room Books) $850 [≈ £531]

Chanter, C.
- Ferny Combes. A Ramble after Ferns in the Glens and Valleys of Devonshire. London: 1856. 2nd edn. Sm 8vo. viii,118 pp. Map, 8 hand cold plates. Orig cloth, fine.
(Wheldon & Wesley) £30 [≈ $48]

Chapin, Frederick
- Mountaineering in Colorado. Boston: 1889. 1st edn. 168 pp. Ills. Contemp pres mor gilt, a.e.g. Author's sgnd inscrptn.
(Jenkins) $350 [≈ £218]

Chapman, Abel
- The Borders and Beyond. Arctic ... Cheviot ... Tropic. London: Gurney & Jackson, 1924. 1st edn. 19 cold plates by Ridell, 170 sketches by Chapman. Mod half levant mor gilt.
(Hollett) £85 [≈ $136]
- The Borders and Beyond. Arctic Cheviot Tropic. London: 1924. 489 pp. 17 cold plates by Riddell, 170 sketches by Chapman. Orig bndg. *(Trophy Room Books)* $200 [≈ £125]
- Memories of Four Score Years less Two. 1851 to 1929. London: 1930. 8vo. Cold & other plates, text ills. Orig bndg.
(Grayling) £30 [≈ $48]
- Memories of Fourscore Years less Two, 1851-1929. With a Memoir by G. Bolam. London: 1930. xxviii,257 pp. 8vo. Port, 24 cold & 3 plain plates, 81 figs. Orig cloth.
(Wheldon & Wesley) £40 [≈ $64]
- Memories of Fourscore Years less Two, 1851-1929. London: Gurney & Jackson, 1930. 8vo. xxviii,257 pp. 24 cold & 4 plain plates, 81 text ills. Orig cloth, t.e.g.
(Egglishaw) £35 [≈ $56]
- On Safari. Big-Game Hunting in British East Africa. London: Edward Arnold, 1908. 8vo. xvi,340,4 advt pp. Over 170 ills. Orig pict gilt grey cloth, *(Parmer)* $120 [≈ £75]
- Retrospect. Reminiscences and Impressions of a Hunter-Naturalist in Three Continents, 1851-1928. London: Gurney & Jackson, 1928. xx, 353 pp. 20 cold & 34 plain plates, text ills. Orig cloth, t.e.g.
(Egglishaw) £40 [≈ $64]

- Retrospect: Reminiscences and Impressions of a Hunter-Naturalist in Three Continents, 1851-1928. London: Gurney & Jackson, 1928. 1st edn. 8vo. 353 pp. Cold frontis, plates & ills. Orig green cloth gilt.
  (Terramedia) **$100 [≈ £62]**
- Savage Sudan. Its Wild Tribes, Big Game and Bird Life. London: 1921. 452 pp. 248 ills. Orig cloth, virtually mint.
  (Trophy Room Books) **$350 [≈ £218]**
- Savage Sudan. Its Wild tribes, Big Game and Bird Life. London: 1921. 452 pp. 248 ills. Orig cloth, front upper crnr dented, crnrs worn. *(Trophy Room Books)* **$75 [≈ £46]**
- Savage Sudan. Its Wild Tribes, Big Game and Bird-Life. London: 1921. 8vo. Ills. Orig cloth. *(Grayling)* **£130 [≈ $208]**
- Wild Norway. With Chapters on Spitzbergen, Denmark &c. London: 1897. 8vo. Ills. Orig bndg, sl rubbed & bumped.
  (Grayling) **£120 [≈ $192]**

Chapman, F. Spencer
- Northern Lights - The Official Account of the British Arctic Air-Route. London: Chatto & Windus, 1933. Later printing. xv,[1],304 pp. Frontis, fldg map, 63 plates, ills. Orig cloth, edges foxed, spine faded.
  (Parmer) **$65 [≈ £40]**

Chapman, George T.
- Chapman's Centenary Memorial of Captain Cook's Description of New Zealand. Auckland: Geo. T. Chapman, 1870. 4to. xx,21-160,4 pp. 5 fldg maps, facs, 16 plates. Orig red cloth, rubbed & faded.
  (Adelson) **$85 [≈ £53]**

Chapman, W. & L.
- Wilderness Wanderers. Adventures among Wild Animals in Rocky Mountain Solitudes. London: 1937. Roy 8vo. Ills. Orig cloth, spine ends rubbed. *(Grayling)* **£40 [≈ $64]**

Charcot, Jean
- The Voyage of the 'Why Not?' in the Antarctic ... Toronto: Musson Book Co, [1911]. 1st Canadian edn. viii,315 pp. Map, fldg frontis, photo plates. Orig gilt dec cloth, white penguin on spine. Dw reprd & intact.
  (High Latitude) **$425 [≈ £265]**

Chardin, Sir John
- The Travels of Sir John Chardin into Persia and the East Indies ... London: Christopher Bateman, 1691. Folio. 13, 417, 8, 154, 5 pp. Fldg map, 18 plates. Orig panelled calf.
  (Adelson) **$1,400 [≈ £875]**
- Travels in Persia. London: Argonaut Press,

1927. 3rd edn. One of 975. 4to. xxx,290 pp. 7 plates, 2 text ills. Orig vellum backed cloth.
  (Worldwide Antiqu'n) **$225 [≈ £140]**

Charters ...
- Charters and General Laws of the Colony and Province of Massachusetts Bay. Boston: T.B. Wait, 1814. 1st edn. 8vo. vii,868 pp. Occas browning. Contemp calf, rebacked.
  (Gough) **£100 [≈ $160]**

Chase, C. Thurston
- A Manual of School-Houses and Cottages for the People of the South. Washington: 1868. 83 pp. Plans, ills. Some browning. Orig cloth gilt, hd of spine chipped, extremities worn.
  (Reese) **$275 [≈ £171]**

Chastellux, Francois J.
- Travels in North America, in the Years 1780, 1781, and 1782. London: 1787. 1st English edn. 2 vols. 462; 432 pp. 2 fldg maps, 3 plates. Contemp calf, rebacked, 1 hinge tender. *(Reese)* **$1,000 [≈ £625]**

Chateaubriand, Francois A. de
- Travels in America and Italy ... London: 1826. 1st English edn. 2 vols. Occas foxing. Half cloth & paper bds, paper labels, new endpapers, crnrs bumped.
  (Reese) **$175 [≈ £109]**
- Travels in Greece, Palestine, Egypt, and Barbary, during the years 1806 and 1807 ... Translated from the French by Frederick Shoberl. London: 1812. 2nd edn. 2 vols. 2 maps (1 fldg). Orig bds, uncut, spines repapered. *(Farahar)* **£145 [≈ $232]**

Chateauvieux, Mons.
- Italy, Its Agriculture &c. Being Letters written ... in Italy in the Years 1812 & 1813. Translated by Edward Rigby. Norwich: Burks & Kinnerbrook, 1819. 8vo. xiv, [ii], 358, i pp. Contemp calf gilt, spine trifle faded. *(Hollett)* **£40 [≈ $64]**

Cheadle, W.B.
- Cheadle's Journal of a Trip across Canada 1862 - 1863. Ottawa: 1931. 311 pp. Fldg map. Ills. Limp cloth. *(Reese)* **$100 [≈ £62]**

Cheesman, R.E.
- In Unknown Arabia. London: Macmillan, 1926. 1st edn. Lge 8vo. xx,447 pp. 3 maps, frontis, num photo plates. Orig pict green cloth gilt, bevelled edges, t.e.g., sl spotted.
  (Terramedia) **$400 [≈ £250]**

Cheever, George B.
- Wanderings of a Pilgrim in the Shadow of Mont Blanc. London: Wiley & Putnam, 1845. 1st English edn (Amer sheets with a new title- page). Sq 8vo. x,166,[14 advt] pp. Sl foxing. Orig green cloth.
(Burmester) **£60 [≃ $96]**

Cheever, Henry T.
- Life in the Sandwich Islands: or, the Heart of the Pacific, as it was and is. New York: A.S. Barnes, 1851. 1st edn. 12mo. 355 pp. Engvd title, map, 5 plates. Sl foxing. Orig pict cloth, rubbed.
(Adelson) **$185 [≃£115]**

Cheltenham and its Vicinity ...
- Cheltenham and its Vicinity. Described in a Series of Letters Written during a Prolonged Visit ... By a Convalescent. Cheltenham: M.Q. Henriques, [1850]. Sm 8vo. Vignette title, fldg plan, 1 other plate. Orig cloth.
(Ambra) **£20 [≃ $32]**

Cherry-Garrard, Apsley
- The Worst Journey in the World. New York: Doran, [ca 1923]. 1st Amer edn. 2 vols. lxiv, 300, [4]; vii, 301-585 pp. 5 maps (2 fldg), num ills (some cold). Orig cloth spines & paper cvrd bds, minor chipping to spine labels.
(Parmer) **$350 [≃£218]**
- The Worst Journey in the World. New York: Doran, [ca 1923]. 1st Amer edn. 2 vols. lxiv, 300,[4]; vii,301-585 pp. 5 maps (2 fldg), num ills (some cold). Orig cloth spines & paper cvrd bds, soiled, bumped, showing wear.
(Parmer) **$295 [≃£184]**

Chesney, Francis Rawdon
- The Russo-Turkish Campaigns of 1828 and 1829. With a View of the Present State of Affairs in the East. With an Appendix ... New York: Redfield, 1854. 1st Amer edn. 12mo. xxiv, 360,advt pp. 2 fldg maps. Perf lib stamp on title. Orig green cloth, sl worn.
(Terramedia) **$50 [≃£31]**

Chilcott, John
- Chilcott's New Guide to Bristol, Clifton and the Hotwells. Bristol: J. Chilcott, 1826. 12mo. 2 fldg maps, w'engvd frontis. Contemp calf. Pres inscrptn. *(Waterfield's)* **£50 [≃ $80]**

Child, Mrs Lydia
- An Appeal in Favor of that Class of Americans called Africans. New York: John S. Taylor, 1836. 12mo. 216 pp. Occas foxing. Orig brown cloth, somewhat worn.
(Terramedia) **$60 [≃£37]**

Childers, Erskine
- In the Ranks of the C.I.V. A Narrative and Diary of Personal Experiences ... in South Africa. London: Smith, 1901. 3rd imp. Ills. Orig cloth.
(Emerald Isle) **£25 [≃ $40]**

Chilvers, Hedley A.
- The Seven Wonders of Southern Africa. Johannesburg: Administration of the South African Railways and Harbours, 1929. 386, index pp. Maps, 18 cold plates, photo ills. Orig red cloth, hinges started, ripple in cloth of spine.
(Parmer) **$45 [≃£28]**

The Chinese Traveller ...
- The Chinese Traveller. Containing a Geographical, Commercial, and Political History of China ... London: for E. & C. Dilly, 1772. 1st edn. 2 vols. 12mo. Port of Confucius, fldg map, 1 plate, fldg ptd table. Marg wormhole 1st sgntr vol 1. Orig sheep, mor labels.
(Bickersteth) **£190 [≃ $304]**
- The Chinese Traveller. Containing a Geographical, Commercial, and Political History of China ... Second Edition ... London: for E. & C. Dilly, 1775. 2 vols. 12mo. Fldg map (sl chipped), fldg chart, 4 plates. Contemp calf, gilt dec spines, sl worn. Slipcase.
(Heritage) **$450 [≃£281]**

Christaller, Revd J.G.
- A Dictionary of the Asante and Fante Language called Tshi (Chwee, Twi), with a Grammatical Introduction and Appendices of the Geography of the Gold Coast ... Basel: 1881. 8vo. Lacks f.e.p. Orig publisher's bds & cloth spine.
(Farahar) **£200 [≃ $320]**

The Christian Keepsake ...
- See Ellis, William (ed.).

Christian, F.W.
- The Caroline Islands. Travel in the Sea of the Little Lands ... London: Methuen, 1899. xiv, 412 pp. Lge folding map, num ills. Moderately foxed. Orig dec green cloth.
(Karmiole) **$65 [≃£40]**

Christianographie ...
- See Pagitt, Ephraim.

Christie, Dugald
- Thirty Years in Moukden, 1883-1913, being the Experiences and Recollections of Dugald Christie, C.M.G. edited by his Wife. London: 1914. 8vo. 2 fldg maps, plates. Orig cloth.
(Farahar) **£25 [≃ $40]**

Christmas, H.
- Shores and Islands of the Mediterranean ... London: Bentley, 1851. 1st edn. 3 vols. 8vo. xx,324; vii,326; viii,324 pp. 3 frontis. Occas foxing. Contemp prize calf gilt.
(Gough) **£295 [≈ $472]**
- The Shores and the Islands of the Mediterranean; Including a Visit to the Seven Churches of Asia. London: 1851. 1st edn. 3 vols. 8vo. 3 frontis. Contemp prize calf gilt.
(Gough) **£195 [≈ $312]**

Christy, C.
- Big Game and Pygmies. London: 1924. 8vo. Ills. Orig cloth. *(Grayling)* **£70 [≈ $112]**
- Big Game and Pygmies. London: 1924. 8vo. Ills. Orig cloth, restored, new endpapers.
(Grayling) **£60 [≈ $96]**

Chubb, T.A.
- A Descriptive Catalogue of the Printed Maps of Gloucestershire 1577-1911. London: 1912. 8vo. Ills. Rec cloth. *(Ambra)* **£64 [≈ $102]**
- A Descriptive List of the Printed Maps of Norfolk 1574-1916 ... Norwich: Jarrold, 1928. 8vo. xvi, 289 pp. Orig cloth, spine faded. *(Lamb)* **£85 [≈ $136]**
- The Printed Maps in the Atlases of Great Britain and Ireland: A Bibliography, 1579-1870 ... London: 1927, reprinted 1977. 4to. xvii,479 pp. Frontis. Orig cloth.
(Bow Windows) **£60 [≈ $96]**

The Church Rambler ...
- See Lewis, Harold.

Churchill, Lord Randolph
- Men, Mines & Animals in South Africa. London: 1892. 1st edn. 8vo. xv,337 pp. Fldg map, frontis, num plates & ills. Orig pict maroon cloth, lge chip from hd of spine.
(Terramedia) **$150 [≈ £93]**

Churchill, Winston Spencer
- My African Journey. London: Hodder & Stoughton, 1908. 1st edn. 8vo. xiii,226,[18 advt] pp. 3 maps, 47 plates. Orig pict red cloth, spine faded, a few sl spots to cvrs, flyleaves browned, edges sl foxed.
(Heritage) **$600 [≈ £375]**
- The River War. An Historical Account of the Reconquest of the Soudan. London: Longmans, 1899. 1st edn. 2 vols. 8vo. xxiii, 462; xiv,499 pp. 7 ports, 20 fldg maps, text ills. A few ff sl foxed. New crushed levant gilt.
(Adelson) **$1,200 [≈ £750]**
- The River War. An Historical Account of the Reconquest of the Soudan. London: Longmans, 1899. 2 vols. 8vo. xxiii,462; xiii,

499 pp. 2 frontis, 34 maps & plans, 56 ills. Ex-lib. Some dampstaining vol 1. Rec red half mor. *(Bates & Hindmarch)* **£450 [≈ $720]**
- The Story of the Malakand Field Force. London: Longmans, 1899. Silver Library edn. 8vo. xvi,337 pp. Frontis, 2 fldg & 4 other maps. Orig bndg.
(Bates & Hindmarch) **£60 [≈ $96]**

Churchward, William B.
- My Consulate in Samoa. A Record of Four Years' Sojourn in the Navigators Islands ... London: Bentley, 1887. 1st edn. 8vo. xii,403 pp. Lib stamp on title. Orig pict mustard cloth, spine sl soiled & frayed at edges.
(Terramedia) **$75 [≈ £46]**

Churchyard, Thomas
- The Worthines of Wales, a Poem ... London: reptd from the edn of 1567, for Thomas Evans, 1776. 2nd edn. 8vo. xv,[i],128 pp. Half- title. Title dusty. Old cloth, gilt label, worn. *(Burmester)* **£45 [≈ $72]**

Churton, E.
- The Railroad Book of England: Historical, Topographical, and Picturesque ... London: Churton, 1851. 1st edn. 4to. 590 pp. Vignette ills. Lacks map. Orig cloth, rebacked.
(Book House) **£45 [≈ $72]**

Chute, Chaloner W.
- A History of the Vyne in Hampshire, being a Short Account of the Building and Antiquities of that House ... Winchester: 1888. 1st edn. 4to. Frontis, 13 plates, text ills. Orig half vellum, t.e.g., hd of spine torn.
(Robertshaw) **£20 [≈ $32]**

Claridge, W. Walton
- A History of the Gold Coast & Ashanti. From the Earliest Times ... London: Murray, 1915. 1st edn. 2 vols. 8vo. xx,649; xv,638 pp. 2 fldg frontis maps, 1 other map. Orig pict green cloth, spines sl faded.
(Terramedia) **$275 [≈ £171]**

Clark, A.H.
- The Invasion of New Zealand by People, Plants and Animals: the South Island. New Brunswick: 1949. 8vo. xiv,465 pp. 82 ills. Orig cloth. *(Wheldon & Wesley)* **£25 [≈ $40]**

Clark, Edward L.
- Daleth or the Homestead of the Nations. Egypt Illustrated. Boston: Ticknor & Fields, 1864. 1st edn. 8vo. x,289 pp. 15 plates (12 cold), num text ills. Orig cloth, t.e.g., edges sl rubbed, spine ends frayed, sl tear in spine.
(Worldwide Antiqu'n) **$95 [≈ £59]**

- Daleth, or Homestead of the Nations: Egypt Illustrated. Boston: Ticknor, 1864. 8vo. x, 289 pp. 14 litho plates (mostly cold or tinted). Ex-lib with minimal markings. Orig pict green cloth gilt, front hinge sl shaken.
(Terramedia) $100 [≈£62]

- Daleth, or the Homestead of the Nations. Egypt Illustrated. Boston: Ticknor & Fields, 1864. Lge 8vo. xii,290 pp. 82 ills inc 12 cold lithos.Orig green cloth gilt, t.e.g.
(Karmiole) $150 [≈£93]

Clark, Francis E.
- Our Journey Around the World An Illustrated Record of a Year's Travel ... Hartford: 1895. 641,advt pp. Fldg map, port, ills. Orig gilt pict cloth, some edge wear.
(Reese) $60 [≈£37]

Clark, J.D.
- Kalambo Falls, Prehistoric Site. Cambridge: Univ Press, 1969-74. 2 vols. Lge 8vo & 4to. xvi,253; xiii.420 pp. Num plates & charts, some fldg. Orig cloth. Dws.
(Terramedia) $200 [≈£125]

Clark, James L.
- Trails of the Hunted. Boston: Little, Brown, 1928. 1st edn. 8vo. xiii,309,1 pp. Frontis, num plates. Orig brown cloth.
(Terramedia) $75 [≈£46]

Clark, Joseph G.
- Lights and Shadows of Sailor Life ... Boston: Benj. B. Mussey & Co, 1848. 2nd edn. 12mo. xii,13-324 pp. 6 plates. Orig gilt dec red cloth. *(Adelson)* $175 [≈£109]

Clark, Robert Sterling & Sowerby, A. de C.
- Through Shen-Kan: The Account of the Clark Expedition in North China, 1908-9. Edited by Major C.H. Chepmell. London: Fisher Unwin, 1912. iii,247 pp. Map frontis, plates (some cold), maps (1 fldg in pocket). Orig cloth, cvrs sl stained, hd of spine worn.
(Lyon) £245 [≈$392]

Clarke, Asa B.
- Travels in Mexico and California: comprising a Journal of a Tour from Brazos Santiago, through Central Mexico ... the Country of the Apaches. Boston: Wright & Hasty, 1852. 1st edn. 138 pp. Orig ptd wraps, fine. Half mor slipcase. *(Jenkins)* $1,500 [≈£937]

Clarke, Charles
- Architectura Ecclesiastica Londini; or Graphical Survey of the Cathedral, Collegiate and Parochial Churches in London ...

London: John Booth, 1820. 1st edn. Large Paper. Folio. 123 plates on india paper. Occas marg foxing. Contemp elab gilt mor by Mackenzie. *(Spelman)* £350 [≈$560]

Clarke, Edward Daniel
- The Life and Remains ... see Otter, W.
- Scandinavia. London: for T. Cadell, Travels in Various Countries of Europe, Asia and Africa Series, Vols 11 & 12, 1824. 2 vols. 8vo. 580; 492 pp. 4 fldg maps, num vignettes. Mod cloth, leather labels.
(Piccadilly) £55 [≈$88]
- Travels in Various Countries of Europe Asia and Africa ... Part the First Russia, Tartary and Turkey. London: 1810. Thick 4to. xxviii,759 pp. Fldg maps, port, plates. Some foxing, 2 captions shaved. Contemp three qtr calf, gilt spine, extremities worn, jnts tender.
(Reese) $150 [≈£93]
- Travels in Russia, Tartary, and Turkey. New Edition. Aberdeen: Clark; Ipswich: Burton, 1848. Sm 8vo. 383 pp. Frontis. Sl foxing. Orig cloth, a little rubbed.
(Worldwide Antiqu'n) $65 [≈£40]

Clarke, George
- Pompeii. London: Charles Knight, 1831-32. 1st edn. 2 vols. 12mo. x,323; xii,324 pp. 8 steel engvs, 293 w'engvs in text. Contemp polished calf, mor labels, by Hering, extremities sl rubbed.
(Claude Cox) £25 [≈$40]

Clarke, Joseph
- Japan at First Hand. New York: 1918. 8vo. 482 pp. Frontis, plates. Orig brown cloth.
(Terramedia) $25 [≈£15]

Clarke, Samuel, 1599-1683
- A Mirrour or Looking-Glasse both for Saints, and Sinners. London: 1657. 4to. [16], 702,[10], [2nd part] A Geographical Description of ... the Known World 218,[8] pp. 2 engvd titles (the 1st stained & reprd). Sl marg reprs. Antique half calf. Wing C.4551.
(Reese) $750 [≈£468]

Clarke, Susie C.
- The Round Trip from the Hub to the Golden Gate. Boston: [1890]. 193 pp. Gilt cloth.
(Reese) $55 [≈£34]

Clarke, W.T.
- Norfolk & Suffolk. Painted by A. Heaton Cooper. London: A. & C. Black Colour Books, Twenty Shilling Series, 1921. 1st edn. 40 cold plates. Orig blind dec plain blue cloth, minor wear to ft of spine.
(Old Cathay) £33 [≈$52]

Clarkson, Thomas
- Memoirs of the Private and Public Life of William Penn. London: 1813. 1st edn. 2 vols. 8vo. Occas spotting. Binder's cloth.
(Farahar) £85 [≈ $136]

Clay, John
- My Life on the Range. Chicago: privately printed, [1924]. 1st edn. 8vo. 366 pp. Ills. Orig cloth, t.e.g., untrimmed & mostly unopened. Sgnd pres inscrptn by the author.
(Schoyer) $300 [≈ £187]

Clayton, Captain J.W.
- Il Pellegrino; or, "Wanderings and Wonderings." London: T. Cautley Newby ..., 1863. 1st edn. 2 vols. 8vo. viii,323; 319 pp. Contemp red half calf, raised bands, elab gilt spines, dble labels. *(Young's)* £64 [≈ $102]

Cleveland, Richard J.
- Voyages and Commercial Enterprises of the Sons of New England. New York: Leavitt & Allen, 1855. 8vo. 407 pp. Frontis. Sl foxing. Orig pict cloth, faded. *(Adelson)* $70 [≈ £43]

Clifford, Charles Cavendish
- A Tour [to Iceland] Twenty Years Ago, by Umbra. London: F. Shoberl, 1863. Privately ptd. 8vo. 108 pp. Fldg frontis. Orig ptd wraps. Sgntr of Arthur Russel, a member of the expedition. *(Hannas)* £250 [≈ $400]

Clifton, Violet
- The Book of Talbot. London: Faber, 1933. 1st British edn. 8vo. xi,1,3-439 pp. Frontis port, maps. Orig purple cloth gilt, t.e.g.
(Parmer) $45 [≈ £28]

Clinton-Baddeley, V.C.
- Devon. Painted by Sutton Palmer. London: A. & C. Black, 1928. 2nd edn. Map, 32 cold plates. Orig cloth. Dw.
(Old Cathay) £18 [≈ $28]

Cluny, Alexander
- The American Traveller ... By an Old and Experienced Trader. London: for E. & C. Dilly; & J. Almon, 1769. 1st edn. State with dedic sgnd in type. 4to. Frontis, lge fldg map. Some foxing. 19th c cloth, backstrip defective. *(Ximenes)* $3,000 [≈ £1,875]

Coan, Frederick G.
- Yesterdays in Persia and Kurdistan. Claremont, CA: Saunders Studio Press, 1939. 1st edn. 8vo. xvi,284 pp. Frontis, 28 plates, endpaper maps. Orig cloth, spine ends sl rubbed. *(Worldwide Antiqu'n)* $55 [≈ £34]

Coates, Charles
- The History and Antiquities of Reading. London: for the author, by J. Nichols & Son, 1802. 1st edn. 4to. [xiv], 464, [supplement xciv] pp, inc subscribers. Fldg plan, 8 aquatint plates. Lacks supplement title-leaf. Orig mottled calf, rebacked, spine relaid.
(Bickersteth) £120 [≈ $192]

Coates, Dandeson
- The New Zealanders and their Lands. The Report of the Select Committee of the House of Commons on New Zealand, considered in a Letter to Lord Stanley. Second Edition, with Additions ... London: Hatchard, 1844. 8vo. 72 pp. Wrappers.
(Fenning) £125 [≈ $200]

Cobbett, James P.
- Journal of a Tour in Italy, and also in part of France and Switzerland ... London: 11 Bolt Court, Fleet-Street, 1830. 1st edn. 8vo. 12 advt pp at end. Lib stamp on title. Orig cloth backed bds, paper label, uncut, label chipped, endpapers renewed. *(Clark)* £70 [≈ $112]

Cobbett, William
- Rural Rides ... New Edition. With Notes by Pitt Cobbett. London: 1893. 2 vols. xlviii, 406; 407 pp. Half-titles. Later three qtr crushed levant & linen, partly unopened.
(Reese) $150 [≈ £93]
- Rural Rides ... Tours in Scotland ... Letters from Ireland ... Edited ... by G.D.H. and Margaret Cole. London: 1930. 1st edn thus. One of 1000. 3 vols. Lge 8vo. Map, num vignettes by John Nash. 1 or 2 marks, name erased from blank in each vol. Orig bndg.
(Bow Windows) £225 [≈ $360]
- Cobbett's Tour In Scotland, and the Four Northern Counties of England: in the Autumn of the Year 1832. London: 11 Bolt Court, 1833. 1st edn. 12mo. Contemp half calf, headband worn. *(Hannas)* £140 [≈ $224]

Cobbold, R.
- Innermost Asia: A Record of Sport in the Pamirs. London: 1900. 354 pp. Lge cold fldg map. Num ills. Orig bndg.
(Trophy Room Books) $500 [≈ £312]

Cobham, Sir Alan
- Twenty Thousand Miles in a Flying-Boat. My Flight round Africa. London: Harrap, 1930. 1st edn. 8vo. 250 pp. Fldg map, 46 ills. Orig cloth, sl marked.
(Claude Cox) £18 [≈ $28]

Cochrane, John Dundas
- Narrative of a Pedestrian Journey through Russia and Siberian Tartary, from the Frontiers of China to the Frozen Sea and Kamtchatka ... London: 1824. xvi,[2],564 pp. Half-title. 2 fldg maps. Sl used. Contemp three qtr calf, a bit worn & rubbed, jnts reprd.
(Reese) **$500** [≈ £312]

Cockburn, John
- A Journey Over Land, from the Gulf of Honduras to the Great South-Sea ... London: for C. Rivington, 1735. 1st edn. viii,349,[3] pp. Some soiling & spotting. Three qtr green mor gilt extra, t.e.g., edges rubbed.
(Reese) **$950** [≈ £593]

Codman, John
- Ten Months in Brazil: with Notes on the Paraguayan War. New York: 1872. 218 pp. Frontis, plates. Orig cloth gilt. Author's inscrptn. *(Reese)* **$150** [≈ £93]

Coffin, Charles Carleton
- Our New Way Round the World. Boston: Estes & Lauriat, 1880. 1st edn. Lge 8vo. xix, 508 pp. Num ills. Orig cloth, hd of spine sl torn. *(Worldwide Antiqu'n)* **$45** [≈ £28]

Coghlan, Francis
- The Iron Road Book and Railway Companion from London to Birmingham, Manchester, and Liverpool ... Second Edition, Corrected. London: A.H. Baily, [1838?]. 12mo. i-iv, [ii], 3-64, 55-180 pp, advt leaf. Fldg plate, 12 maps. A bit used. Orig pict gilt cloth, sl worn.
(Duck) **£110** [≈ $176]

Coke, Henry J.
- A Ride over the Rocky Mountains to Oregon and California, with a Glance at Some of the Tropical Islands including the West Indies and the Sandwich Isles. London: Bentley, 1852. 388 pp. Frontis port. Orig polished calf, mrbld bds, spine reprd.
(Jenkins) **$225** [≈ £140]

Colange, Leo De
- Voyages and Travels, or Scenes in Many Lands. Boston: Walker & Co, [1887]. 2 vols. Lge 4to. 576; 576 pp. 23 steel engvs & photogravures, num other plates & ills. Contemp half mor, a.e.g., rubbed, crnrs sl worn. *(Terramedia)* **$100** [≈ £62]

Colbert, Elias & Chamberlin, Everett
- Chicago and the Great Conflagration. With Numerous Illustrations by Chapin & Gulick, from Photographic Views Taken on the Spot. Cincinnati: C.F. Vent, 1872. 8vo. 528 pp. 36

w'cut ills, inc fldg map. Some text foxing. Orig green cloth gilt. *(Karmiole)* **$45** [≈ £28]

Colby, Col.
- Ordnance Survey of the County of Londonderry. Volume I [all published]. Dublin: Hodges, 1837. 4to. Cold & other plates. Half leather.
(Emerald Isle) **£150** [≈ $240]

Cole, Mrs Henry Warwick
- A Lady's Tour round Monte Rosa; with Visits to the Italian Valleys of Anzasca, Mastalone ... London: 1859. x,402 pp. Cold title vignette, 4 chromolitho plates (inc frontis), fldg map, text ills. Ink notes. Three qtr polished calf, rubbed, spine sunned.
(Reese) **$125** [≈ £78]

Colenso, John W.
- Ten Weeks in Natal. A Journal of a First Tour of Visitation among the Colonists & Zulu Kafirs of Natal. Cambridge: Macmillan, 1855. 12mo. xxxii, 271, 16, 16 advt pp. Fldg map, 4 plates. Orig cloth, backed in calf.
(Adelson) **$260** [≈ £162]

Coles, John
- Summer Travelling in Iceland ... London: Murray, 1882. 1st edn. Tall 8vo. x,269 pp. Fldg map, 19 plates. Orig cloth gilt, sl worn, front jnt just cracking. *(Hollett)* **£75** [≈ $120]

Collenette, C.L.
- A History of Richmond Park: with an Account of its Birds and Animals. London: 1937. One of 600. 4to. xii,164 pp. Fldg map, 5 plates. Sl foxing. Orig cloth. *(Coombes)* **£18** [≈ $28]

Collins, Francis
- Voyages to Portugal, Spain, Sicily, Malta, Asia-Minor, Egypt, &c. &c. from 1796 to 1801 ... Philadelphia: 1809. 1st Amer edn. xi, [13]-335 pp. Some soiling, dampstaining, occas foxing. Later cloth.
(Reese) **$150** [≈ £93]

Collins, Gilbert
- Far Eastern Jaunts. London: Methuen, [1924]. 1st edn. 8vo. 282 pp. Num photo plates. Orig green cloth.
(Terramedia) **$50** [≈ £31]

Collins, John
- The City and Scenery of Newport, Rhode Island. Burlington, N.J.: 1857. Oblong folio. 8 pp. Map, 13 tinted litho plates. Some plates with minor foxing. Wraps, front wrap soiled & reprd, rear wrap supplied. Cloth box.
(Reese) **$2,500** [≈ £1,562]

Collins, Percy McDonough
- A Voyage Down the Amoor. With a Land Journey through Siberia and Incidental Notices of Manchooria, Kamschatka, and Japan. New York: 1860. 1st edn. 8vo. 390 pp. 4 litho plates. Foxing on plates & tissue guards. Orig cloth. *(Schoyer)* **$125 [≈ £78]**
- A Voyage down the Amoor: With a Land Journey through Siberia, and incidental Notices of Manchooria, Kamschatka, & Japan. New York: Appleton, 1860. 1st edn. 8vo. 4, 390, 2 advt pp. 4 plates. Orig brown cloth. *(Adelson)* **$100 [≈ £62]**

Collins, W.W.
- Cathedral Cities of Italy. New York: Dodd Mead, 1913. 8vo. viii,4,395 pp. Cold frontis, num cold plates. Orig dec pict red cloth gilt. *(Terramedia)* **$35 [≈ £21]**
- Cathedral Cities of Spain. London: Heinemann, 1909. Sm 4to. xii,255 pp. 60 cold plates, with guards. Orig yellow cloth, sl discold. *(Piccadilly)* **£25 [≈ $40]**

Collis, Septima M.
- A Woman's Trip to Alaska, being an Account of a Voyage through the Inland Seas of the Sitkan Archipelago in 1890. New York: Cassell, 1890. 1st edn. 8vo. xiv,194 pp. Fldg cold frontis, ills. Orig cloth, some shelf wear. *(Parmer)* **$95 [≈ £59]**

Colquhoun, Archibald R.
- China in Transformation. Second Edition. London: 1898. 8vo. 4 fldg maps, text maps & diags. Orig blue cloth gilt. *(Farahar)* **£55 [≈ $88]**
- The 'Overland' to China. London: Harper & Bros, 1900. 2nd edn. Thick 8vo. xii,465 pp. 4 maps, 36 ills. Orig cloth gilt, extremities sl worn. *(Hollett)* **£120 [≈ $192]**

Colquhoun, J.
- The Moor and the Loch. Instructions in all Highland Sports ... London: 1851. 8vo. Engvd plates. Orig cloth, spine ends chipped & torn. *(Grayling)* **£25 [≈ $40]**

Colson, Nathaniel
- The Mariners New Kalendar. Containing the Principles of Arithmetick and Geometry ... Directions for Sailing into Some Principal Harbours. London: Thomas Page, William & Fisher Mount, 1724. 132 pp. W'cuts, tables. Some stains. Contemp calf. *(Karmiole)* **$300 [≈ £187]**

Colt, Mrs Miriam Davis
- Went to Kansas: being a Thrilling Account of an Ill-Fated Expedition to that Fairy Land, and its Sad Results ... Watertown: 1862. 1st edn. 294 pp. Orig cloth. *(Jenkins)* **$285 [≈ £178]**

Colton, J.H.
- The State of Indiana Delineated: Geographical, Historical, Statistical & Commercial, with a Brief View of Internal Improvements. New York: 1838. 93 pp. Fldg map. Orig bds, ptd label. *(Jenkins)* **$950 [≈ £593]**

Colton, Walter
- Deck and Port; or, Incidents of a Cruise in the United States Frigate Congress to California ... New York: 1850. 1st edn. 408 pp. Map, 4 cold plates, port. Ptd endpapers as noted by Howes. Occas foxing & spots. Orig cloth gilt, worn at extremities, hinge cracked. *(Reese)* **$125 [≈ £78]**
- Deck and Port ... New York: A.S. Barnes & Co, 1850. 1st edn. Sm 8vo. 408,advt pp. Map, 5 plates (4 cold), text ills. Orig dark brown cloth gilt, rebacked, gilt titling relaid, lower edge of front cvr waterstained. *(Karmiole)* **$150 [≈ £93]**
- Land and Lee in the Bosphorus and Aegean; or, Views of Constantinople and Athens, edited by Henry T. Cheever. New York: Barnes ..., 1851. 1st edn. Sm 8vo. 366,11 advt pp. 2 plates. Sl foxed. Orig cloth, sl rubbed. *(Worldwide Antiqu'n)* **$65 [≈ £40]**

Columbus, Christopher
- The Columbus Letter of 1493. A Facsimile of the Copy in the William L. Clements Library with a New Translation into English by Frank E. Robbins ... Ann Arbor: 1952. One of 1000. 17, [8] pp. Facsimiles. Orig cloth backed pict bds. *(Reese)* **$45 [≈ £28]**
- Fac-Simile of the Spanish Quarto Letter of Columbus giving an Account of the First Voyage ... [New York: 1903]. 4to. [8] pp. Facsimiles. Orig ptd wraps, string-tied. Intended to accompany vol 7 of Thacher's work on Columbus, New York: 1903, ltd to 100 sets. *(Reese)* **$75 [≈ £46]**
- The Latin Letter of Columbus Printed in 1493 and Announcing the Discovery of America Reproduced in Facsimile, with a Preface. London: Quaritch, 1893. Sm 4to. vi, [10] pp. Orig ptd wraps, stained, worn at spine. *(Reese)* **$75 [≈ £46]**
- Letter of Christopher Columbus, The Great Benefactor of the Present Age, concerning the Newly Discovered Islands of India upon the Ganges ... Facsimile Reprint of the Original Edition ... Albany: 1900. [19],translation 14 pp. Ills. Orig wraps, unopened. *(Reese)* **$75 [≈ £46]**

Colvin, Ian D.
- The Cape of Adventure. London: Jack, 1912. 459,index pp. Ills. Orig blue cloth, spine faded, some wear. *(Parmer)* **$50 [≈ £31]**

Comeau, N.A.
- Life and Sport on the Lower St. Lawrence. Quebec: 1909. 1st edn. 8vo. Orig ptd wraps, spine reprd, new label.
(Grayling) **£50 [≈ $80]**

A Companion of Hofer (pseud.)
- Views on the Tyrol ... see Allom, Thomas.

Compilation ...
- Compilation of Narratives of Exploration in Alaska. Washington: GPO, 1900. Thick 4to. [2], vii, 3-856 pp. 27 fldg maps, 33 plates. Old (orig?) half mor, a bit rubbed.
(High Latitude) **$on395 [≈ £246] aw**

The Compleat Histdnory ...
- The Compleat History of Thamas Kouli Khan, (at present called Schah Nadir) Sovereign of Persia. London: for J. Brindley, S. Birt ..., 1742. 1st edn in English. 12mo. Frontis port, fldg map. Contemp calf gilt, gilt spine. *(Ximenes)* **$375 [≈ £234]**

Conder, Claude Regnier
- The Latin Kingdom of Jerusalem. 1099 to 1291 A.D. London: Palestine Exploration Fund, 1897. 8vo. 442 pp. 2 maps in pocket. Sl yellowing of endpapers. Orig blue cloth gilt. *(Terramedia)* **$100 [≈ £62]**
- Tent Work in Palestine. A Record of Discovery and Adventure ... New York: Appleton, 1878. 2 vols. xxvi,382; viii,352 pp. 32 engvd ills, inc 2 frontis & 1 map. Orig olive cloth stamped in gold & black, extremities sl rubbed, inner hinges partly cracked.
(Karmiole) **$100 [≈ £62]**

Conder, Josiah
- Greece. London: James Duncan, Modern Traveller Series, 1826. 2 vols. 12mo. 275; 336 pp. Fldg map, 7 engvs. Old calf, rebacked.
(Piccadilly) **£45 [≈ $72]**
- Palestine; or, the Holy Land. London: for James Duncan, Modern Traveller Series Vol 1, 1824. 1st edn. 16mo. iv,356 pp. Fldg map, 3 plates. Last 20 ff with front edge browned & brittle, sm hole in last leaf. Blue mor, elab gilt spine, edges sl rubbed.
(Worldwide Antiqu'n) **$45 [≈ £28]**
- Russia. London: for James Duncan, Modern Traveller Series Vol 17, 1825. 1st edn. 16mo. iv, 338 pp. 2 fldg maps, 2 plates. Sl foxing. Half mor, edges sl rubbed.
(Worldwide Antiqu'n) **$75 [≈ £46]**

- Syria and Asia Minor. London: for James Duncan, Modern Traveller Series Vol 2, 1824. 1st edn. 16mo. iv,356 pp. Fldg map, 5 plates. Blue mor, elab gilt spine, edges rubbed, front hinges starting.
(Worldwide Antiqu'n) **$65 [≈ £40]**

The Conquest of Canada ...
- See Warburton, G.D.

Consett, Matthew
- A Tour through Sweden ... London: for J. Johnson ...& R. Christopher at Stockton, 1789. 1st edn. 4to. [xvi], '157' [= 158, pp 143-158 misnumbered 142-157] pp. 8 full page plates (7 on copper) by Thomas Bewick. Some foxing. Orig bds, spotted, spine defective. *(Frew Mackenzie)* **£420 [≈ $672]**
- A Tour through Sweden ... London: for J. Johnson ..., 1789. 1st edn. 2nd iss, with London imprint on cancel title. 4to. Half-title. Subscribers' list. 7 engvd plates on 6 sheets by Thomas Bewick & Ralph Beilby. Orig bds, uncut, ptd spine label.
(Hannas) **£650 [≈ $1,040]**

Conway, Derwent (pseud. of Henry David Inglis)
- Switzerland, the South of France, and the Pyrenees in 1830. London: Constable's Miscellany, 1831. 1st edn. 2 vols. 12mo. Fldg map, addtnl engvd title. Orig green linen bds, paper label. *(Claude Cox)* **£20 [≈ $32]**

Conway, J.
- Forays Among Salmon and Deer. London: 1861. 1st edn. 8vo. Orig cloth, spine just sl snagged. *(Grayling)* **£45 [≈ $72]**

Conway, Sir William Martin
- The Alps. Painted by A.D. McCormick. London: A. & C. Black, 1904. 8vo. 294 pp. Num tissued cold plates. Orig pict green cloth, sl worn. *(Terramedia)* **$50 [≈ £31]**
- The Alps. Painted by A.D. McCormick. London: A. & C. Black Colour Books, Twenty Shilling Series, 1904. 1st edn. 70 cold plates. Orig dec cloth, t.e.g., shows some signs of age. *(Old Cathay)* **£33 [≈ $52]**
- The Alps from End to End. Westminster: 1895. 8vo. 403 pp. Frontis & 99 other plates by A.D. M'Cormick. Contemp half calf, front jnt cracked. *(Argosy)* **$125 [≈ £78]**
- Climbing & Exploration in the Bolivian Andes. A Record of Climbing & Exploration in the Cordillera Real in the Years 1898 & 1900. New York & London: Harpers, 1901. 8vo. 405 pp. Num plates. Orig pict grey cloth, sl soiled, sl frayed at hd.

(Terramedia) **$150 [≃ £93]**
- Early Dutch and English Voyages to Spitsbergen in the Seventeenth Century ... London: Hakluyt Society, 1904. xvi,191 pp. 2 fldg maps, 4 plates. Orig cloth.
(High Latitude) **$80 [≃ £50]**

Conwell, Eugene A.
- A Ramble Round Trim, amongst its Ruins and Antiquities, with Short Notices of its Celebrated Characters. Dublin: Gill, 1878. Ills. Mod cloth backed bds, orig front wrapper bound in.
(Emerald Isle) **£75 [≃ $120]**

Conybeare, W.J. & Howson, J.S.
- The Life and Epistles of St. Paul. London: Longman ..., 1864. 2 vols. 4to. Engvd titles with vignette views, maps, 32 steel engvd views of Greece, Rome and the Middle East by Bartlett & others. Period polished calf gilt, elab gilt spines.   *(Rankin)* **£100 [≃ $160]**

Cook, Frederick A.
- My Attainment of the Pole. New York: Polar Publ Co, 1911. 1st edn. xx, 1, [1], 604 pp. Frontis, 49 ills. Orig illust brown cloth over bds,   *(Parmer)* **$145 [≃ £90]**
- My Attainment of the Pole. New York & London: Mitchell Kennerley, 1913. "Press" Edition. 3rd printing. 610 pp. Ills. Orig dec blue cloth, sl worn. Author's sgnd pres inscrptn.   *(Parmer)* **$125 [≃ £78]**
- To the Top of the Continent. Discovery, Exploration and Adventure in Subarctic Alaska. The First Ascent of Mt. McKinley, 1903-1906. New York: Doubleday, Page, 1908. 1st edn. 8vo. xxi,[3],321 pp. Photo plates. Orig cloth, t.e.g., spine spotted.
(High Latitude) **$150 [≃ £93]**

Cook, Captain James
- Atlas to the Second Voyage towards the South Pole and round the World. London: Strahan & Cadell, 1777. Folio. 63 plates. Sl dampstain to crnr of last few plates. Orig bds, rebacked in calf, worm holes in the bds (only).
(Frew Mackenzie) **£1,800 [≃ $2,880]**
- The Journals of Captain James Cook on his Voyages of Discovery. Edited by J.C. Beaglehole. Cambridge: Univ Press for the Hakluyt Society, 1967-74. 4 vols in 5. Lge 8vo, plus a portfolio of 58 maps, & addendum leaflets. Orig cloth. Dws.
(Frew Mackenzie) **£375 [≃ $600]**
- The Three Voyages of Captain James Cook Round the World ... London: for Longman ..., 1821. 1st edn thus. 7 vols. 8vo. Frontis port, fldg map, 2 fldg ff of tables, 24 aquatint

plates. Occas sl foxing. Contemp half calf, gilt spines, extremities sl rubbed. Slipcase.
(Heritage) **$900 [≃ £562]**
- A Voyage to the Pacific Ocean ... under the direction of Capt. Cook, Clerke, & Gore, in the years 1776,7,8,9, & 80 ... Leigh: Wm. Reid, for Constable, 1813. 3 vols. Sm 8vo. 28 plates inc fldg map. Some browning. 1 sm marg wormhole. Contemp half calf, gilt spine
(Frew Mackenzie) **£175 [≃ $280]**
- The Voyages of Captain James Cook Round the World. Comprehending a History of the South Sea Islands. London: Jaques & Wright, 1825. 2 vols. 8vo. 488; 457 pp. 11 (only, of 13) plates. Contemp half mor gilt, v rubbed.
(Terramedia) **$150 [≃ £93]**
- The Voyages of Captain James Cook Round the World; Comprehending a History of the South Sea Islands. London: Jaques & Wright, 1825. 2 vols in one. ii,488; ii,458 pp. 13 plates. Sl foxed. Contemp mor, gilt spine, edges rubbed, cvrs detached.
(Worldwide Antiqu'n) **$195 [≃ £121]**
- The Voyages of Captain James Cook Round the World; Comprehending a History of the South Sea Islands. London: Jaques & Wright, 1825. 2 vols in one. 8vo. ii,498; ii,458 pp. 13 plates. Sl foxing. Contemp mor, elab gilt spine, cvrs detached, edges rubbed.
(Worldwide Antiqu'n) **$195 [≃ £121]**
- The Three Voyages of Captain James Cook. London: 1842. 2 vols. 4to. Addtnl engvd title page & vignette, 2 frontis, 3 maps, num text w'cuts. Contemp calf, spines relaid, new labels, a.e.g.   *(Henly)* **£220 [≃ $352]**

Cook, Captain James & King, Captain James
- A Voyage to the Pacific Ocean ... for making Discoveries in the Northern Hemisphere ... London: Nicol & Cadell, 1784. 1st edn. 3 vols 4to & atlas lge folio. 24 maps & plates, + atlas 63 maps & plates. Text new half calf. Atlas half calf, rubbed, spine ends chipped.
(Adelson) **$5,500 [≃ £3,437]**

Cook, Joel
- The Mediterranean and Borderlands. Philadelphia: Winston, 1910. 1st edn. 2 vols. 8vo. vii,609; v,648 pp. 50 plates. Orig elab gilt cloth, sl rubbed.
(Worldwide Antiqu'n) **$45 [≃ £28]**

Cook, John A.
- Pursuing the Whale. A Quarter-Century of Whaling in the Arctic. Boston: Houghton Mifflin, 1926. 1st edn. 8vo. x, 344 pp. Frontis, 15 plates, ports. Orig dec grey cloth.
(Parmer) **$60 [≃ £37]**

Cook, Sir Theodore Andrea
- Old Touraine. The Life and History of the Chateaux of the Loire. London: 1928. 8th edn. 2 vols. Sm 8vo. xxiv, 287; xv, 279 pp. Fldg map, fldg charts, num photo plates. Orig gilt dec blue cloth. *(Terramedia)* **$25 [≈ £15]**

Cooke, Alan & Holland, Clive
- The Exploration of Northern Canada 500 to 1920. A Chronology. Toronto: Arctic History Press, [ca 1978]. One of 1100. 8vo. 349 pp. Lge fldg map in pocket, 25 pp of maps. Padded leatherette.
(High Latitude) **$150 [≈ £93]**

Cooke, George Alexander
- Topographical and Statistical Description of the County of Somerset. London: for Sherwood, Neely & Jones, 1820. 1st edn (?). 12mo. Fldg map, 2 plates (foxed) with 4 views. Stamp on title. Contemp qtr roan.
(Hannas) **£25 [≈ $40]**

Cooke, Thomas L.
- The Picture of Parsontown [Birr] in the King's County [Co. Offaly], containing the History ... With its Description at the Present Day. Dublin: W. De Veaux, 1826. 1st edn. 8vo. 259 pp, errata leaf. 9 plates. Orig (?) cloth backed bds, uncut, spine sl worn.
(Fenning) **£285 [≈ $456]**

Cooley, William D.
- The History of Maritime and Inland Discovery. London: Lardner's Cabinet Cyclopaedia, 1830-30-34. 1st edn vols 1 & 2, new (2nd) edn vol 3. 3 vols. Sm 8vo. Orig cloth, ptd paper labels. *(Fenning)* **£45 [≈ $72]**

Coolidge, W.A.B.
- Blacks Guide to Switzerland. With Cycling Supplement by Charles L. Freeston. London: (1901). 8 cold maps, 4 b/w photos. Orig green cloth, spine discold.
(Old Cathay) **£33 [≈ $52]**

Cooper, A. Heaton
- The Norwegian Fjords. London: A. & C. Black Colour Books, Six Shilling Series, 1907. 1st edn. 24 cold plates. Orig cloth, t.e.g. *(Old Cathay)* **£33 [≈ $52]**
- The Norwegian Fjords. London: A. & C. Black Colour Books, Six Shilling Series, 1907. 1st edn. 24 cold plates. Orig cloth, t.e.g., spine sl discold with sm tear at hd.
(Old Cathay) **£29 [≈ $46]**

Cooper, Elizabeth
- The Harim and the Purdah. Studies of

Oriental Women. New York: Century, [ca 1915]. 8vo. 309 pp. Frontis, num photo plates. Orig pict blue cloth gilt, t.e.g., spine a bit dulled. *(Terramedia)* **$50 [≈ £31]**

Cooper, Frederick H.
- The Handbook for Delhi with Index and Two Maps ... Lahore: T.C. McCarthy, at the Lahore Chronicle Press, 1865. Roy 8vo. [9],v,168 pp. 3 [sic] fldg maps. A few sm reprs. Orig green cloth gilt, sl stained, recased & reprd. *(Fenning)* **£85 [≈ $136]**

Cooper, Reginald Davis
- Hunting & Hunted in the Belgian Congo. Edited by Keith Johnston. London: Smith, Elder, 1914. 1st edn. Lge 8vo. 263 pp. Fldg map, plates. Orig pict cloth, spine sl sunned & lettering sl faded.
(Terramedia) **$150 [≈ £93]**
- Hunting and Hunted in the Belgian Congo. London: 1914. 8vo. Ills. Some foxing. Orig cloth, restored. *(Grayling)* **£40 [≈ $64]**

Copway, George
- Running Sketches of Men and Places, in England, France, Germany, Belgium, and Scotland. New York: 1851. 346 pp. Port, ills. Orig cloth gilt, some wear to jnts.
(Reese) **$125 [≈ £78]**

Corbett, Jim
- Maneaters of Kumaon. New York: OUP, 1946. 1st American edn. Orig cloth. Dw.
(Terramedia) **$35 [≈ £21]**

Cordier, H.
- Ser Marco Polo. Notes and Addenda to Sir Henry Yule's Edition containing the Results of Recent Research and Discovery. London: 1920. 161 pp. Frontis. Orig bndg, v fine.
(Trophy Room Books) **$150 [≈ £93]**

Corner, Miss
- The History of China and India Pictorial and Descriptive. London: Washbourne, 1847. 3rd edn. xxii,402 pp. 2 fldg maps, 31 lithos, num w'cuts. 1 plate frayed and marked. Orig green cloth gilt, a.e.g., rebacked.
(Bates & Hindmarch) **£70 [≈ $112]**
- The History of China & India: Pictorial & Descriptive. London: Dean & Co, n.d. iii,iii, 393 pp. Fldg maps, cold frontis, cold plates, w'engvs, text ills. Orig indigo calf gilt, rebacked. *(Lyon)* **£125 [≈ $200]**

'Cosmopolite'
- The Sportsman in Ireland. London: 1897. 8vo. Cold & other plates. Half vellum, rather

grubby. *(Grayling)* £25 [≈ $40]

Cotman, John Sell
- Architectural Antiquities of Normandy ... see Turner, Dawson.

Cotton, W. & Dallas, J.
- Notes and Gleanings: A Monthly Magazine devoted chiefly to subjects connected with the Counties of Devon & Cornwall. London: 1888-92. 5 vols in 2 (all publ). 8vo. 2 vols bound without titles, as usual. Binder's cloth. *(Ambra)* £60 [≈ $96]

Cottrell, Charles Herbert
- Recollections of Siberia in the Years 1840 and 1841. London: John Parker, 1842. 1st edn. Tall 8vo. xii,410,[16 ctlg dated Jan 1843] pp. Fldg map. 1 sgntr pulling slightly. Orig bndg, crnrs sl bumped. *(Schoyer)* $125 [≈ £78]

Coudenhove, Hans
- My African Neighbours. Man, Bird & Beast in Nyasaland. Boston: Little, Brown, 1925. 8vo. xiv, 245 pp. Frontis & other photo plates. Orig maroon cloth. *(Terramedia)* $50 [≈ £31]

Coulter, John
- Adventures on the Western Coast of South America and the Interior of california ... London: Longman ..., 1847. 2 vols. 8vo. xxiv, 288; xii, 278 pp. Perf stamps on titles. Orig cloth, rebacked, leather labels. *(Adelson)* $475 [≈ £296]

Coustos, John
- The Sufferings of John Coustos for Free-Masonry, and for his Refusing to turn Roman Catholic, in the Inquisition at Lisbon ... London: W. Strahan for the author, 1746. 1st edn. 8vo. 50,400 pp. Port frontis, 3 fldg plates. Few sl stains, minor foxing. Contemp calf, jnts cracking. *(Ramer)* $650 [≈ £406]

Coutant, Charles G.
- The History of Wyoming. From the Earliest Known Discoveries. In Three Volumes. Vol.I [all published]. Laramie: 1899. 1st edn. xxiv, 712 pp. Frontis, plates. Orig three qtr mor gilt. *(Wreden)* $250 [≈ £156]

Covarrubias, Miguel
- Island of Bali. New York: Knopf, 1937. 3rd edn. 8vo. xxv, 417, x pp. Fldg map, 4 cold plates, 82 plates, num text ills. Orig cloth, sl rubbed & soiled.
(Worldwide Antiqu'n) $45 [≈ £28]
- Island of Bali. New York: 1938. 3rd printing.

xxv, 417, x pp. Fldg map, cold frontis, plates, ills. With an album of photos by Rose Covarrubias. Orig black & yellow dec cloth gilt. *(Lyon)* £45 [≈ $72]

Cowles, Raymond
- Zulu Journal: Field Notes of a Naturalist in South Africa. Berkeley: Univ of Calif Press, 1959. 1st edn. xxi,267 pp. Maps, photo plates. Orig cloth. Dw.
(Terramedia) $25 [≈ £15]

Cox, E.H.M.
- Farrer's Last Journey: Upper Burma, 1919-20. Together with a Complete List of all the Rhododendrons Collected ... London: Dulau, 1926. 1st edn. 8vo. xix, 244 pp. Num photo plates. Orig maroon cloth.
(Terramedia) $125 [≈ £78]
- Plant-Hunting in China. London: 1945. 8vo. 230 pp. Cold frontis, 24 plain plates. Orig cloth. *(Terramedia)* £18 [≈ $28]

Cox, James
- Historical and Biographical Record of the Cattle Industry and the Cattlemen of Texas and Adjacent Territory. St Louis: Woodward & Tiernan, 1895. Lge thick folio. 743 pp. 272 ills. Index ff worn & reprd. Lacks the cold plate as usual. Later calf.
(Jenkins) $4,500 [≈ £2,812]

Cox, R.H.
- The Green Roads of England. London: (1934). 4th edn. 8vo. xii,196 pp. 9 cold maps, 24 other ills. Sl foxing. Orig cloth.
(Bow Windows) £20 [≈ $32]

Cox, Ross
- Adventures on the Columbia River, including Six Years on the Western Side of the Rocky Mountains, among the Various Tribes of Indians hitherto unknown ... New York: Harper, 1832. 1st edn. 335 pp. Sm tear in crnr of title. Contemp calf, wear to spine. *(Jenkins)* $300 [≈ £187]
- Adventures on the Columbia River, including ... Six Years on the Western Side of the Rocky Mountains, among Various Tribes of Indians hitherto unknown ... London: Colburn & Bentley, 1832. 2 vols. xx,333; 350 pp. Vol 2 title in facs. Orig cloth, leather labels.
(Jenkins) $300 [≈ £187]

Cox, Samuel S.
- Diversions of a Diplomat in Turkey. New York: 1887. 8vo. xix,685 pp. Frontis, num plates (2 cold), ills. Orig pict red cloth gilt, spine v sunned. *(Terramedia)* $75 [≈ £46]

- Diversions of a Diplomat in Turkey. New York: Webster, 1887. 1st edn. 8vo. xix,685 pp. Num plates (2 chromolitho), ills. Orig cloth, sl rubbed.
(Worldwide Antiqu'n) **$65 [≈ £40]**

Coxe, William

- Account of the Russian Discoveries between Asia and America. To which are added, the Conquest of Siberia ... London: 1780. 1st edn. 4to. xxii,344,[14],[2] pp. 4 fldg maps. Fldg view. Occas browning. Contemp calf, early reback, jnts sl rubbed. Half mor slipcase.
(Reese) **$1,800 [≈ £1,125]**
- Travels into Poland, Russia, Sweden, and Denmark ... In Two [three] Volumes. London: 1784-90. 1st edn. 3 vols. 4to. Subscribers' list. Final advt leaf. Genealogical table on C5. 26 maps & plates. Contemp blind-tooled calf, gilt spines. The Boulton copy.
(Hannas) **£850 [≈ $1,360]**
- Travels in Switzerland, and in the Country of the Grisons: in a Series of Letters to William Melmoth, Esq. ... London: Cadell, 1791. 2nd edn. 3 vols. 8vo. 2 fldg maps, 5 plates. Half calf gilt, bds a little rubbed & scraped.
(Hollett) **£130 [≈ $208]**

Coyne, J.S. & Willis, N.P.

- The Scenery and Antiquities of Ireland ... see Bartlett, W.H.

Coyner, David H.

- The Lost Trappers; A Collection of Interesting Scenes and Events in the Rocky Mountains; together with a Short Description of California: also, Some Account of the Fur Trade ... Cincinnati & Philadelphia: 1856. [16], [17]-255 pp. Sl used. Later cloth.
(Reese) **$150 [≈ £93]**

Crabb, George

- Universal Historical Dictionary, or Explanation of the Names of Persons and Places ... Enlarged Edition ... London: Baldwin & Cradock, 1833. 2 vols. 4to. 40 plates at end of vol 1. Rec cloth.
(Schoyer) **$100 [≈ £62]**

Crabb, James

- The Gipsies' Advocate; or Observations on the Origin, Character, Manners, and Habits of the English Gipsies. Third Edition, with Additions. London: Nisbet, 1832. 8vo. xii, 199, [1] pp. Half-title. Orig cloth, spine reprd.
(Spelman) **£45 [≈ $72]**

Craig, Lulu Alice

- Glimpses of Sunshine and Shade in the Far North or my Travels in the Land of the Midnight Sun. Cincinnati: Editor Pub. Co., 1900. 8vo. ix, 123 pp. Photo plates, 3 other cold plates. Orig white cloth, minor soil. Author's pres inscrptn.
(High Latitude) **$65 [≈ £40]**

Crakes, Sylvester, Jr.

- Five Years a Captive among the Blackfeet Indians ... Columbus: 1858. 244 pp. Plates. Frontis. Light scattered foxing. Mottled calf, rebacked, front hinge a bit worn.
(Reese) **$850 [≈ £531]**

Cramb, John

- Jerusalem in 1860: a Series of Photographic Views ... With Descriptive Letterpress by the Rev. Robert Buchanan. Glasgow: William Collins, 1860. Folio. [6] pp. 12 mtd albumen prints. Orig gilt dec cloth, hinges cracked, disbound due to gutta-percha bndg.
(Charles B. Wood) **$1,000 [≈ £625]**

Cramer, Zadok

- The Navigator, Containing Directions for Navigating the Monongahela, Allegheny, Ohio and Mississippi Rivers ... Pittsburgh: published by Cramer, Spears & Eichbaum, 1817. 9th edn. 12mo. 307 pp. V sm hole in 1 plate. Orig half calf. Cloth traycase.
(Schoyer) **$700 [≈ £437]**

Crane, Leo

- Desert Drums: The Pueblo Indians of New Mexico, 1540-1928. Boston: Little, Brown, 1928. 1st edn. 8vo. x,393 pp. Fldg map, frontis, num plates. Orig blue cloth with cold pict onlays.
(Terramedia) **$65 [≈ £40]**

Crane, Louise

- China in Sign and Symbol. A Panorama of Chinese Life, Past and Present. Shanghai: 1926. xx, 227 pp. Num plates (mostly cold, 1 fldg). Orig dec cream cloth gilt.
(Lyon) **£250 [≈ $400]**

Cranworth, Lord

- Kenya Chronicles. London: 1939. 368 pp. Ills. Orig bndg.
(Trophy Room Books) **$175 [≈ £109]**
- Profit and Sport in British East Africa. London: 1901. 502 pp. Maps, cold frontis by Millais, ills. Rebound in cloth, leather label.
(Trophy Room Books) **$150 [≈ £93]**
- Profit & Sport in British East Africa. A Second Edition, Revised & Enlarged, of "A Colony in the Making". London: 1919. 8vo. Cold frontis, ills. Stamp on title. Orig bndg, sl rubbed & marked. *(Grayling)* **£38 [≈ $60]**

Craven, Lady Elizabeth
- A Journey through the Crimea to Constantinople. London: Robinson, 1789. 4to. 327 pp. Directions to binder. Fldg frontis map (sl foxed), 6 plates (1 fldg). Orig calf, rebacked, orig label.
(Terramedia) **$600 [≈ £375]**
- A Journey through the Crimea to Constantinople .. Dublin: for H. Chamberlaine ..., 1789. 8vo. 8,415 pp. 2 fldg plates. Sl foxing. Contemp calf, edges v rubbed, lacks front endpaper.
(Worldwide Antiqu'n) **$75 [≈ £46]**

Craven, Richard Keppel
- A Tour through the Southern Provinces of the Kingdom of Naples ... London: Rodwell & Martin, 1821. 1st edn. 4to. [xii],449 pp. 14 engvd plates. Occas spotting & browning. Half calf, mrbld bds, spine sl rubbed, upper jnt a bit weak.
(Frew Mackenzie) **£150 [≈ $240]**

Crawford, Charles H.
- Scenes of Earlier Days in Crossing the Plains to Oregon and Experiences of Western Life. Petaluma: 1898. 186 pp. Port, ills. Black cloth. Lightly stained, as are most copies. Cloth case.   *(Reese)* **$350 [≈ £218]**
- Scenes of Earlier Days in Crossing the Plains to Oregon, and Experiences of Western Life. Petaluma: J.T. Studdert, 1898. 186 pp. Port, ills. Orig cloth.   *(Jenkins)* **$200 [≈ £125]**

Crawford, Dan
- Back to the Long Grass. My Link with Livingstone. New York: Doran, [ca 1920]. 8vo. 373 pp. 3 maps, 34 ills. Orig bndg.
(Schoyer) **$25 [≈ £15]**

Crawford, Reginald
- Windabyne ... see Ranken, George (ed.).

Crawfurd, Oswald
- Portugal Old and New. London: Kegan Paul, 1880. 8vo. xii,386 pp. 2 maps (1 fldg, sl torn without loss), 8 w'engvs. Orig dec red cloth, spine sl marked & sl rubbed, endpapers cracked.   *(Piccadilly)* **£25 [≈ $40]**
- Round the Calendar in Portugal. London: Chapman & Hall, 1890. Sm 4to. x,316 pp. Ills. Sl foxing. Orig green cloth gilt, v sl splashed.   *(Piccadilly)* **£30 [≈ $48]**

Creswicke, L.
- South Africa and the Transvaal War ... London: 1900-02. 1st edn. 8 vols. 8vo. 64 cold plates, 137 other plates, 63 ports, fldg maps, other ills. Foredge of a few ff sl bent.

Orig pict cloth, some cvrs dustmarked or sl stained, 2 sm pinholes in 1 cvr.
(Bow Windows) **£95 [≈ $152]**

Crichton, Andrew
- History of Arabia, Ancient and Modern ... Edinburgh: Oliver & Boyd; London: Simpkin & Marshall, 1833. 1st edn. 2 vols. 12mo. 464; 464 pp. Engvd titles, fldg map (sl torn), 8 engvs. 1st & last few ff foxed. Cloth, sl rubbed & soiled.   *(Worldwide Antiqu'n)* **$85 [≈ £53]**

Crichton, Andrew & Wheaton, Henry
- Scandinavia, Ancient and Modern ... London: Oliver & Boyd, 1838. 2 vols. Sm 8vo. 400; 432 pp. Fldg map, 12 engvs. Orig brown cloth, recased. *(Piccadilly)* **£28 [≈ $44]**

Croasdaile, Henry E.
- Scenes on Pacific Shores; with a Trip across South America. London: 1873. 173 pp. Frontis. Orig cloth. Family assoc copy.
(Reese) **$225 [≈ £140]**

Crofutt, George
- Crofutt's New Overland Tourist and Pacific Coast Guide ... over the Union, Central, and Southern Pacific Railroads ... Chicago: 1879. 321, advt pp. Maps, fldg plates. Limp cloth, some wear.   *(Reese)* **$150 [≈ £93]**

Croly, George
- The Holy Land ... see Roberts, David.

Cromer, Earl of
- Modern Egypt. New York: 1908. 2 vols. 8vo. 594; 600. Fldg map, port frontis. Orig green cloth.   *(Terramedia)* **$50 [≈ £31]**
- Modern Egypt. New York: Macmillan, 1909. 2 vols. 8vo. xviii,594; xiv,600. Fldg map, port frontis. Orig green cloth, t.e.g., sm stain vol 1 spine.   *(Schoyer)* **$30 [≈ £18]**

Cromwell, Thomas Kitson
- Excursions in the County of Kent. London: Longmans ..., 1822. Vol I [all published]. Frontis, addtnl engvd title, fldg map, fldg plan, 45 plates. Contemp calf, rebacked, crnrs reprd.   *(Waterfield's)* **£85 [≈ $136]**
- Excursions through Suffolk, illustrated with Engravings. London: Longman, 1819. 2 vols in one. Sm 8vo in 6s. v,224; 198 pp. Fldg map, 2 engvd titles, 16 engvd plates. Occas sl browning. Mod half levant mor gilt.
(Hollett) **£95 [≈ $152]**
- Excursions in the County of Surrey. London: Longmans ..., 1821. Frontis, addtnl engvd title, 2 plans, 42 plates. Contemp calf, rebacked.   *(Waterfield's)* **£85 [≈ $136]**

- Excursions in the County of Sussex. London: Longmans ..., 1822. Frontis, addtnl engvd title, 2 maps, 44 plates. Contemp calf, rebacked.   *(Waterfield's)* **£85 [≈ $136]**

Crossing, William
- Gems in a Granite Setting: Beauties of the Lone Land of Dartmoor. Plymouth: 1905. 2nd edn. Roy 8vo. Num ills. New cloth.
        (Ambra) **£40 [≈ $64]**
- A Hundred Years on Dartmoor. Plymouth: 1901. 4th edn. Roy 8vo. Title & last leaf sl spotty. Orig bndg.   *(Ambra)* **£17 [≈ $27]**
- The Old Stone Crosses of the Dartmoor Borders. With Notices of the Scenery and Traditions of the District. Exeter: 1892. 1st edn. 8vo. Map, frontis, 14 plates. Orig cloth.
        (Ambra) **£60 [≈ $96]**

Crouch, Nathaniel
- The English Empire in America: or A Prospect of His Majesties Dominions ... By R.B. [i.e. Richard Burton, pseud.]. London: 1685. [4],209,[1] pp. Map, 2 plates. Text trimmed close, occas marg tears, not affecting text. title mtd. Calf, rebacked. Wing C.7319.
        (Reese) **$1,500 [≈ £937]**

Crow, Carl
- The Travellers' Handbook for China (including Hong Kong). Shanghai: 1921. 3rd edn, rvsd. vi,314,x pp. 9 fldg maps & plans, num ills. Orig cloth.   *(Lyon)* **£45 [≈ $72]**

Cudahy, J.
- Mananaland. Adventuring with Rifle and Camera through California and Mexico. New York: 1928. 250 pp. 30 ills. Orig bndg.
        (Trophy Room Books) **$350 [≈ £218]**

Cumberland, S.
- Sport on the Pamirs and Turkestan Steppes. London: 1895. 278 pp. Fldg map, ills. Orig pict gilt cloth.
        (Trophy Room Books) **$350 [≈ £218]**

Cumming, Fortescue
- Sketches of a Tour to the Western Country ... A Voyage down the Ohio and Mississippi Rivers ... Pittsburgh: Cramer, Spear, & Eichbaum, 1810. 1st edn. 504 pp. Sl foxing. Calf, usual wear.   *(Jenkins)* **$850 [≈ £531]**

Cumming, Roualeyn Gordon
- Five Years of a Hunter's Life in the Far Interior of South Africa ... London: Murray, 1850. 1st edn. 2 vols. 8vo. xvi,386; x,370 pp. Map, 14 plates, 2 vignettes. Half mor, rubbed.   *(Adelson)* **£425 [≈ £265]**

- Five Years of a Hunter's Life in the Far Interior of South Africa. New York: Harper & Bros, 1852. 2 vols. foxed. Free endpapers of vol 1 excised. Orig cloth, soiled, spine ends worn.   *(Parmer)* **$125 [≈ £78]**
- Five Years of a Hunter's Life in the Far Interior of South Africa ... New York: Harper & Bros, 1874. 2 vols. 12mo. xiv,526; viii, 303, 4 advt pp. Orig maroon cloth.
        (Terramedia) **$100 [≈ £62]**
- A Hunter's Life in South Africa ... London: 1850. 2nd edn. 2 vols. Engvd plates. Sl foxing. Mod qtr mor, orig gilt designs preserved on upper cvrs.
        (Grayling) **£40 [≈ $64]**

Cummings, Alfred Hayman
- Churches and Antiquities of Cury and Gunwalloe, in the Lizard District, including Local Traditions. London: 1875. 1st edn. 8vo. Ills. Portion cut from endpaper. Orig cloth, spine sl rubbed. *(Ambra)* **£34 [≈ $54]**

Cunynghame, Sir Arthur Thurlow
- Travels in the Eastern Caucasus, on the Caspian and Black Seas, especially in Daghestan, and on the Frontiers of Persia and Turkey ... London: Murray, 1872. 1st edn. 8vo. 2 fldg maps, 6 (of 7) plates, 19 text ills. Sl offsetting. Ex-lib. Orig cloth, sl worn.
        (Worldwide Antiqu'n) **£135 [≈ £84]**

Currie, Donald
- Thoughts upon the Present and Future of South Africa, and Central and Eastern Africa. A Paper. London: 1877. 54 pp. Disbound.
        (Jarndyce) **£35 [≈ $56]**

Curtin, Walter R.
- Yukon Voyage. Unofficial Log of the Steamer Yukoner. Caldwell: Caxton, 1938. 8vo. 299 pp. Photo ills. Orig cloth, extremities worn.
        (High Latitude) **$40 [≈ £25]**

Curtis, Charles & Richard
- Hunting in Africa East & West. Boston: Houghton Mifflin, 1925. 1st edn. Frontis, num plates. Orig orange cloth, sl worn.
        (Terramedia) **$80 [≈ £50]**

Curtis, George William
- Howadji in Syria. New York: Harper & Bros, 1852. 12mo. 304 pp. Sl foxed. Orig leather, a.e.g., sl edgeworn.   *(Parmer)* **$65 [≈ £40]**
- Nile Notes of a Howadji. New York: Harper, 1851. 1st edn. Sm 8vo. 320 pp. Engvd title. Sl foxing. Orig cloth, edges sl rubbed.
        (Worldwide Antiqu'n) **$35 [≈ £21]**
- Nile Notes of a Howadji. New York: Harper

& Bros, 1854. 12mo. 320 pp. Sl foxed. Leather, a.e.g., some wear to extremities & hinge.   *(Parmer)* **$65 [≈ £40]**

Curtis, William Elroy
- Around the Black Sea: Asia Minor, Armenia, Caucasus, Circassia, Daghestan, the Crimea, Roumania. New York: Hodder & Stoughton, [1911]. Sm 8vo. 456 pp. Lge fldg map, num plates. Orig pict light brown cloth, front hinge cracked internally, spine sl stained.
          (Terramedia) **$60 [≈ £37]**
- The Capitals of Spanish America. New York: 1888. 715 pp. Mtd photo frontis, ills. Three qtr mor, spine gilt extra, t.e.g., rear bd detached, front hinge weak. Pres copy.
          (Reese) **$100 [≈ £62]**

Curtiss, Daniel S.
- Western Portraiture, and Emigrant's Guide: A Description of Wisconsin, Illinois, and Iowa; with Remarks on Minnesota, and Other Territories. New York: 1852. 351,18 advt pp. Lge fldg map. Cloth, sl stained.
          (Reese) **$225 [≈ £140]**

Curwen, J.C.
- Observations on the State of Ireland. Principally Directed to Agriculture and Rural Population; in a Series of Letters written on a Tour ... London: 1818. 1st edn. 2 vols. xix, 435; xii, 366 pp. Occas browning & spotting. Contemp calf gilt, sl worn & scratched.
          (Dillons) **£125 [≈ $200]**

Curzon of Kedlestone, Marquis
- British Government in India. The Story of the Viceroys and Government Houses. London: Cassell, 1925. 2nd imp. 2 vols. 4to. xix,259; x,268 pp. Num ills. Orig blue cloth gilt, spine ends sl frayed.
          (Bates & Hindmarch) **£40 [≈ $64]**
- Leaves from a Viceroy's Note-Book and Other papers. London: Macmillan, 1926. 8vo. x,414, 2 advt pp. Frontis, photo ills. Orig blue cloth gilt.
          (Bates & Hindmarch) **£18 [≈ $28]**

Curzon, G.N.
- Tales of Travel. London: 1923. 8vo. Plates. Faint spotting at beginning & end. Orig cloth.
          (Farahar) **£30 [≈ $48]**

Curzon, Robert
- Armenia: a Year at Erzeroom, and on the Frontiers of Russia, Turkey, and Persia. London: Murray, 1854. 3rd edn. 12mo. Map, title vignette, 5 full-page & 2 text ills. Orig cloth gilt, gilt spine, sm nick on front cvr.
          (Trebizond) **£120 [≈ £75]**

- Visits to Monasteries in the Levant. London: Murray, 1849. 1st edn. 8vo. xxx,449 pp. Frontis, 15 plates, title vignette. Orig black cloth gilt, spine ends sl worn, tear in lower jnt reprd.   *(Burmester)* **£120 [≈ $192]**

Cutler, Carl C.
- The Story of the American Clipper Ship Greyhounds of the Sea ... New York: 1930. Thick 4to. xxvii,592 pp. Maps, plates (some cold). Scattered fox marks. Orig cloth gilt, sl edge wear.   *(Reese)* **$150 [≈ £93]**

Cutler, Jervis
- A Topographical Description of the State of Ohio, Indiana Territory, and Louisiana, comprehending the Ohio and Mississippi Rivers ... Boston: 1812. 1st edn. 219,errata pp. 5 w'cut plates. Half calf.
          (Jenkins) **$2,000 [≈ £1,250]**

Cutler, Manasseh
- An Explanation of the Map which delineates that Part of the Federal Lands, comprehended between Pennsylvania West Line, the Rivers Ohio and Sioto; and Lake Erie ... Newport: for Peter Edes, [1788]. 24 pp. Light lib blind stamp. Later half calf.
          (Reese) **$3,000 [≈ £1,875]**

Cutting, Suydam
- The Fire Ox and Other Years. London: 1947. Roy 8vo. xviii,393 pp. 3 maps, 3 cold plates, 128 pp of photos.Orig cloth.
          (Wheldon & Wesley) **£30 [≈ $48]**

Dahl, K.
- In Savage Australia. A Hunting and Collecting Expedition to Arnhem Land and Dampier Land. London: 1927. 8vo. Ills. Orig bndg.   *(Grayling)* **£40 [≈ $64]**

Dale, Harrison
- Ireland. Painted by A. Heaton Cooper. London: A. & C. Black, 1927. 1st edn thus. Map, 32 cold plates. Orig cloth.
          (Old Cathay) **£20 [≈ $32]**

Dall, William H.
- Pacific Coast Pilot Alaska Part I. Washington: GPO, US Coast & Geodetic Survey, 1883. 4to. [2],viii,[2],333 pp. 29 charts & views, many fldg. Old (orig?) half calf, well rubbed.
          (High Latitude) **$95 [≈ £59]**
- Tribes of the Extreme Northwest. Part I [all published]. Washington: 1876. 106 pp. Lge fldg map (minor splitting). Ills. Orig ptd wraps, minor chipping.
          (Jenkins) **$275 [≈ £171]**

Dallas, George Mifflin
- A Series of Letters from London, Written During the Years 1856,'57,'58,'59, and '60. Edited by his Daughter Julia. Philadelphia: Lippincott, 1869. 2 vols in one. 264; 226,6 advt pp. Orig cloth, spine extremities sl frayed. *(Karmiole)* **$35** [≈ £21]

Dallaway, James
- Constantinople Ancient and Modern, with Excursions to the Shores and Islands of the Archipelago and to the Troad. London: Bensley for Cadell & Davies, 1797. 1st edn. Engvd title with vignette, 10 aquatint plates inc map. Minor offsetting. Contemp russia, rebacked. *(Frew Mackenzie)* **£395** [≈ $632]

Dally, Frank Fether
- The Channel Islands. A Guide ... Second Edition. London: Stanford, 1860. 16mo. viii, 263, 4 advt pp. Fldg map. Orig blue cloth, spine sl cocked with sl stain.
(Schoyer) **$50** [≈ £31]

Dalzel, Archibald
- The History of Dahomy, an Inland Kingdom of Africa. Compiled from Authentic Memoirs; with an Introduction and Notes. London: for the author, 1793. 1st edn. 4to. xxxvi, xxvi, 230 pp. Lge fldg map, 6 plates. Sm marg water stain, few sl marks. Rebound in calf, uncut.
(Frew Mackenzie) **£495** [≈ $792]

Damberger, Christian Frederick (pseud.)
- Travels through the Interior of Africa ... Charlestown: 1801. xxiv,523 pp. Fldg map. Occas foxing. Orig mottled calf, rear cvr defective, jnts worn but cords sound. Pseudonym of Zacharias Taurinius. An imaginary voyage. *(Reese)* **$275** [≈ £171]

Dana, Edmund
- Geographical Sketches on the Western Country: Designed for Emigrants and Settlers: Being the Result of Extensive Researches and Remarks. Cincinnati: Looker, Reynolds, 1819. 1st edn. 12mo. 312 pp. Few crnrs v sl stained. Orig calf, sl rubbed, lacks f.e.p. *(Schoyer)* **$850** [≈ £531]
- Geographical Sketches on the Western Country, Designed for Emigrants and Settlers. Cincinnati: Looker, Reynolds, 1819. 1st edn. 312 pp. Orig calf, mor label. Slipcase. *(Jenkins)* **$1,000** [≈ £625]

Dana, Richard Henry
- To Cuba and Back. A Vacation Voyage. Boston: 1859. 288,advt pp. Orig cloth, rubbed. *(Reese)* **$125** [≈ £78]

- To Cuba and Back. A Vacation Voyage. London: Smith, Elder, 1859. 1st British edn. 24 advt pp bound in at end. Orig blue cloth, sl worn, lower jnt splitting, contents shaken. *(Sanders)* **£22** [≈ $35]
- Two Years Before the Mast. Los Angeles: Ward Ritchie, 1964. 2 vols. 8vo. 552 pp. 8 cold plates, charts, text ills, map endpapers. Slipcase. *(Parmer)* **$95** [≈ £59]

The Dangers of Europe ...
- The Dangers of Europe, from the Growing Power of France, with some Free Thoughts on Remedies ... Third Edition. London: 1702. Sm 4to. 36 pp. Later wraps. *(Reese)* **$225** [≈ £140]

The Danish Laws ...
- The Danish Laws: or, the Code of Christian the Fifth. Faithfully translated for the Use of the English Inhabitants of the Danish Settlements in America. London: for N. Gibson, 1756. 1st edn in English. 8vo. viii, 476, [4] pp. Contemp calf, upper jnt sl tender. *(Burmester)* **£500** [≈ $800]

Darby, William
- A Tour from the City of New York, to Detroit, in the Michigan Territory. New York: Kirk & Marcein, 1819. 8vo. viii,errata,9-228, lxiii,7 pp. 3 fldg maps. Some waterstaining & foxing. Half mor. *(Adelson)* **$160** [≈ £100]

Darley, Felix O.C.
- Sketches Abroad with Pen and Pencil. New York: 1868. Sm 4to. vii,191 pp. Frontis, plates, text ills. A couple of sgntrs starting or loose. Orig pict gilt cloth, a bit soiled, wear to extremities. *(Reese)* **$125** [≈ £78]

Darley, Henry
- Slaves and Ivory. A Record of Adventure and Exploration in the Unknown Sudan, and Among the Abyssinian Slave-Raiders ... London: Witherby, 1926. Thick 8vo. xvii,219, advt pp. 2 maps, 7 photo plates. Orig green cloth, gilt spine. *(Karmiole)* **$60** [≈ £37]

Darling, F.F.
- A Naturalist on Rona. Oxford: (1939). 8vo. x,137 pp. Map, 28 plates. Orig cloth. *(Wheldon & Wesley)* **£20** [≈ $32]

Darrah, H.
- Sport in the Highlands of Kashmir. An Eight Month's Trip in Baltistan and Ladakh. Together with Hints to Guidance of Sportsmen. London: Rowland Ward, 1908.

506 pp. Fldg pocket map. Orig bndg.
(Trophy Room Books) **$550 [≈ £343]**

Darwin, Charles

- Charles Darwin and the Voyage of the "Beagle". Edited by N. Barlow. London: 1945. 8vo. 279 pp. Map, 15 plates. Orig cloth.   *(Wheldon & Wesley)* **£28 [≈ $44]**

- Journal of Researches into the Geology and Natural History of the Various Countries visited by H.M.S. Beagle ... London: 1840. 1st edn, 3rd iss. 8vo. [iv],[vii],xiv,629,[16 advt dated Aug 1839] pp. 2 fldg maps. Orig cloth, spine reprd. Freeman 12, bndg variant a.
(Rootenberg) **$1,500 [≈ £937]**

- Journal of Researches ... London: 1845. 2nd edn, crrctd with addtns. Cr 8vo. viii,519 pp. Orig red cloth, trifle used, inner jnt cracked. Freeman 14c.
(Wheldon & Wesley) **£100 [≈ $160]**

- Journal of Researches into the Natural History and Geology of the Countries Visited during the Voyage of the H.M.S. Beagle ... New York: Harper, 1846. 1st Amer edn. 2 vols. Scattered foxing. Ugly later cloth. Freeman 16.   *(Reese)* **$150 [≈ £93]**

- Journal of Researches ... London: 1860. 10th thousand. 8vo. xv,519 pp. Orig green cloth, spine reprd, inner jnts taped. Freeman 20.
(Wheldon & Wesley) **£85 [≈ $136]**

- A Naturalist's Voyage. Journal of Researches into the Natural History and Geology of the Countries visited during the Voyage of H.M.S. "Beagle" ... London: Murray, 1889. 8vo. x,519,[4 advt] pp. Port. Orig cloth gilt, rhea hunt on cvr, 3/6 on spine. Freeman 49.
(Blackwell's) **£45 [≈ $72]**

- A Naturalist's Voyage. Journal of Researches into the Natural History and Geology of the Countries visited during the Voyage of H.M.S. Beagle. New Edition. London: 1890. Cr 8vo. xi,500 pp. Port & title sl foxed. Orig cloth, sl worn. Freeman 58.
(Wheldon & Wesley) **£20 [≈ $32]**

- Journal of Researches ... during the Voyage of H.M.S. "Beagle". London: Minerva Library, 1894. 12th edn. 8vo. 492 pp. 16 plates & text figs. Orig cloth. Freeman 77.
(Wheldon & Wesley) **£25 [≈ $40]**

- Journal of Researches into the Natural History and Geology of the Countries visited during the Voyage of H.M.S. "Beagle" ... New Edition. London: Murray, 1901. 8vo. xvi, 521, [7 advt] pp. 26 ills. Orig cloth. Freeman 97.   *(Blackwell's)* **£25 [≈ $40]**

- Journal of Researches ... London: 1913. New edn. 8vo. 2 maps, 105 ills. Orig cloth. Freeman 125.
(Wheldon & Wesley) **£35 [≈ $56]**

Darwin, Charles, Fitzroy, R. & King, P.P.

- Narrative of the Surveying Voyage of H.M. Ships Adventure and Beagle between the Years 1826 and 1836. London: 1839-40. 4 vols (inc vol 2 Appendix). 8vo. 12 maps, 44 plates. Vol 1 plates water stained, vol 2 trifle foxed. Mod half mor. Freeman 10.
(Wheldon & Wesley) **£1,800 [≈ $2,880]**

Dauncey, John

- A Compendious Chronicle of the Kingdom of Portugal ... Together with a Cosmographical Description of the Dominions of Portugal. London: 1661. 1st edn. 12mo. [xvi], 216, [4 advt] pp. Frontis. Rather cropped, worn & browned. 18th c calf, spine relaid. Wing D.289.   *(Burmester)* **£80 [≈ $128]**

Daunt, A.

- With Pack & Rifle in the Far South West. Adventures in New Mexico, Arizona and Central America. London: 1886. 8vo. Engvd plates. Orig pict gilt cloth, a.e.g., v sl rubbed.
(Grayling) **£35 [≈ $56]**

Dautremer, Joseph

- Burma Under British Rule. New York & London: Scribner's & Unwin, [1913]. 1st edn. 8vo. 391 pp. Num plates. Occas foxing. Orig blue cloth.   *(Terramedia)* **$40 [≈ £25]**

Davenport, A.H. & Greig, E.H., supposed authors.

- A Narrative of the Cruise of the Yacht Maria among the Feroe Islands in the Summer of 1854. London: Longman, Brown ..., 1855. 1st edn. Lge 8vo. Map, 10 tinted plates. Orig dec blue cloth. Pres copy inscrbd 'from the authors'.   *(Hannas)* **£320 [≈ $512]**

Davenport, Henry E.

- Rovings on Land and Sea. Boston: 1860. 316 pp. Frontis, text ills. Stamp on title. Orig cloth, spotted, spine worn & sunned.
(Reese) **$75 [≈ £46]**

David-Neel, Alexandra

- My Journey to Lhasa. The Personal Story of the only White Woman Who Succeeded in Entering the Forbidden City. New York & London: Harper, 1927. 1st edn. 8vo. xviii, 310, advt pp. Num photo ills, map endpaper. Orig maroon cloth.   *(Parmer)* **$65 [≈ £40]**

Davidson, George

- The Alaska Boundary. San Francisco: Alaska Packers Association, 1903. Lge 8vo. 235 pp. 2 lge fldg maps, frontis port. Orig cloth.
(High Latitude) **$100 [≈ £62]**

Davidson, Norman J.
- Modern Exploration Sport & Travel ... London: Seeley Service, 1932. 8vo. 318,10 advt pp. Frontis, 36 ills. Orig bndg. Dw.
(Bates & Hindmarch) **£35 [≈ $56]**

Davie, John C.
- Letters from Paraguay: Describing the Settlements of Monte Video and Buenos Ayres ... London: Robinson, 1805. 8vo. viii,293,2 advt pp. Orig bds, rebacked in calf.
(Adelson) **$225 [≈ £140]**

Davies, E.W.L.
- Algiers in 1857. Its Accessibility, Climate and Resources described with especial reference to English Invalids. London: 1858. 1st edn. 8vo. 4 litho plates. Orig orange cloth.
(Robertshaw) **£60 [≈ $96]**

Davies, G. Christopher
- Norfolk Broads and Rivers, or the Water-Ways, Lagoons and Decoys of East Anglia. London: 1884. 8vo. Ills. Orig bndg, sl rubbed. *(Grayling)* **£35 [≈ $56]**
- On Dutch Waterways. The Cruise of the S.S. Atalanta on the Rivers and Canals of Holland & the North of Belgium. London: Jarrold, (1886). Deluxe iss with 12 photogravures. 4to. 379, 1 pp. 12 photogravures, 38 text ills. Orig dec cloth gilt, t.e.g., hinges weak.
(Charles B. Wood) **$300 [≈ £187]**

Davies, General Henry
- Ten Days on the Plains. New York: Crocker & Co, n.d. [187-?]. 1st edn. 88 pp. Fldg map. Lacks the photos issued in some copies. Half cloth & bds, scuffed & worn, cvrs nearly detached. *(Reese)* **$1,750 [≈ £1,093]**

Davis, F.H.
- Myths and Legends of Japan. London: 1913. 1st edn. 8vo. 432 pp. 32 cold ills by Evelyn Paul. Sl spotting, a few tears. Orig elab dec cloth, t.e.g. *(Bow Windows)* **£80 [≈ $128]**

Davis, John Francis
- The Chinese: A General Description of the Empire of China and its Inhabitants. New York: Harper, Harper's Family Library, 1836. 2 vols. 12mo. 384; 440,4 advt pp. Fldg map, 25 w'cut ills. Orig light brown ptd cloth, sl soiled. *(Karmiole)* **$60 [≈ £37]**
- The Chinese: A General Description of the Empire of China and its Inhabitants. London: Knight, 1836. 1st edn. 2 vols. 8vo. iv, 420; iv, 480 pp. 54 ills. Sl offsetting. Ex-lib. Orig cloth, worn, spine chips.
(Worldwide Antiqu'n) **$110 [≈ £68]**

- The Chinese: A General Description of China and its Inhabitants. London: 1844. New edn. 3 vols. 16mo. Ills. Sl trace of foxing. Three qtr calf, a bit scuffed, some edge wear. *(Reese)* **$75 [≈ £46]**
- The Chinese: A General Description of China and its Inhabitants. London: Charles Knight, 1844-45. New edn. 4 vols in 2 (inc the supplementary vol Sketches in China, 1845). 8vo. 58 ills. Contemp half calf, sl rubbed, hd of 1 spine worn.
(Young's) **£95 [≈ $152]**
- Han Koong Tsew, or the Sorrows of Han: a Chinese Tragedy. Translated from the Original with Notes. London: Oriental Translation Fund, 1829. 4to. viii,18 pp. 4 pp of Chinese text inc engvd pres leaf. Binder's cloth. *(Farahar)* **£50 [≈ $80]**

Davis, Nathan
- Carthage and her Remains: Being an Account of the Excavations and Researches on the Site of the Phoenician Metropolis in Africa ... London: Bentley, 1861. 1st edn. 8vo. xvi,632 pp. 32 plates (inc 2 fldg maps & 1 hand cold plate). Contemp calf gilt. Slipcase.
(Karmiole) **$175 [≈ £109]**
- Ruined Cities within Numidian and Carthaginian Territories. London: Murray, 1862. 1st edn. 8vo. 391 pp. Fldg map, frontis, title vignette, 10 plates. Orig orange brown cloth, minor tear at top crnr of spine.
(Terramedia) **$125 [≈ £78]**

Davis, R.C.
- Reminiscences of a Voyage Round the World. Ann Arbor: Chase's Steam printing House, 1869. 331,[5] pp. Orig cloth gilt, extremities sl chipped & frayed. *(Reese)* **$450 [≈ £281]**

Davis, Richard Harding
- Three Gringos in Venezuela and Central America. New York: Harper, 1896. 1st edn. 8vo. 2 maps, 42 full-page ills, over 60 text ills. Orig dec cloth gilt, spine foxed.
(Trebizond) **$95 [≈ £59]**

Davis, Theodore M.
- Excavations Biban El Moluk: The Tomb of Hatshopsitu ... London: Constable, 1906. 1st edn. Folio. xv,112 pp. 15 plates (7 cold). Occas foxing. Orig green cloth gilt, bevelled edges, tear at hd of spine.
(Terramedia) **$400 [≈ £250]**
- Excavations Biban El Moluk: The Tomb of Queen Tiyi ... London: Constable, 1910. 1st edn. Folio. xxiv,45 pp. 35 plates (3 tinted, 1 cold). Appreciable foxing. Orig green cloth gilt, bevelled edges.
(Terramedia) **$500 [≈ £312]**

- Excavations Biban El Moluk: The Tomb of Spitah: The Monkey Tomb and the Gold Tomb ... London: Constable, 1908. 1st edn. Folio. 28 plates (12 cold), 46 text ills. 1st few ff sl foxed. Orig green cloth gilt, bevelled edges, spine ends sl frayed.
(*Terramedia*) **$400 [≈ £250]**

Davis, W.W.H.
- El Gringo: or, New Mexico and her People. New York: 1857. 432 pp. Cloth, extremities sl worn. (*Reese*) **$275 [≈ £171]**

Deakin, Ralph
- A Tour of the Prince of Wales to Africa and South America. Philadelphia: [1926]. Lge 8vo. 302 pp. Frontis, 46 other photo plates. Orig blue cloth gilt. (*Terramedia*) **$40 [≈ £25]**

De Amicis, Edmondo
- Constantinople. Translated from the Fifteenth Italian Edition by Maria H. Lansdale. Philadelphia: 1896. 1st edn thus. 2 vols. 8vo. 303; 307 pp. Orig elab gilt dec red cloth, t.e.g.
(*Terramedia*) **$75 [≈ £46]**
- Holland. Translated from the Thirteenth Edition of the Italian by Helen Zimmern. Philadelphia: Winston Co, [1894]. 2 vols. 8vo. 273; 275 pp. Fldg map, num tissued photo plates. Orig elab gilt dec red cloth, spine sl rubbed. (*Terramedia*) **$30 [≈ £18]**
- Morocco, Its People and Places. Philadelphia: Henry Coates, 1897. 2 vols. 8vo. viii,253; viii,225 pp. Orig elab gilt dec green cloth. (*Terramedia*) **$60 [≈ £37]**

De Beerski, P. Jeannerat
- Angkor, Ruins in Cambodia. London: Grant Richards, 1923. 1st edn. 8vo. 304 pp. Frontis, plates. Orig maroon cloth.
(*Terramedia*) **$50 [≈ £31]**

De Berneaud, Arsienne Thiebaut
- A Voyage to the Isle of Elba: with Notices of the Other Islands in the Tyrrhenian Sea. Translated from the French ... by William Jerdan. London: Longman ..., 1814. 1st edn in English. 8vo. Fldg map. Occas spotting. Contemp calf, rebacked, crnrs worn.
(*Clark*) **£85 [≈ $136]**

Declaration ...
- A Declaration of the Demeanor and Carriage of Sir Walter Raleigh, Knight, as well in his Voyage, as in, and since, his return ... London: 1618. 63 pp. With blank A1. Crushed green mor gilt. STC 20652.5. Said to have been written by Francis Bacon.
(*Reese*) **$1,250 [≈ £781]**

Decle, Lionel
- Three Years in Savage Africa. London: 1898. 594 pp. Cold fldg map, 100 ills. Orig bndg.
(*Trophy Room Books*) **$275 [≈ £171]**
- Three Years in Savage Africa. Introduction by Henry M. Stanley. London: 1900. New edn. 8vo. 593 pp. 3 fldg maps, frontis, num photo plates & ills. Orig dec orange brown cloth gilt, ex-lib with sm tear at hd of spine.
(*Terramedia*) **$100 [≈ £62]**

De Cort, Henry
- Six Views in Chudleigh, Devonshire. London: 1817. All published. 4to. 6 loose etched plates engvd by G. Hollis after De Court. Some spotting.
(*Ambra*) **£110 [≈ $176]**

de Filippi, F.
- Ruwenzori. An Account of the Expedition. London: 1908. 408 pp. Lge fldg panorama, gravures with tissue guards, num ills. Orig cloth, hinges weak.
(*Trophy Room Books*) **$750 [≈ £468]**

Defoe, Daniel
- A New Voyage round the World, by a Course never sailed before. being a Voyage undertaken by some Merchants, who afterwards proposed the Setting up an East-India Company in Flanders. London: 1725. 1st edn. 8vo. Frontis, 3 plates. Old calf, a.e.g., rebacked. (*Clark*) **£420 [≈ $672]**
- A Tour through the Whole Island of Great Britain ... Continued ... Brought Down to the Present Time ... Seventh Edition, with very great Additions . . London: Rivington ..., 1769. 4 vols. Tall 12mo. Contemp polished calf, rebacked. (*Hartfield*) **£425 [≈ £265]**

Delany, M.C.
- The Historical Geography of the Wealden Iron Industry. London: Benn, 1921. 62 pp. Maps. Orig wraps, cvrs rather grubby.
(*Book House*) **£25 [≈ $40]**

Les Delices de Windsor ...
- See Pote, Joseph.

Dellenbaugh, Frederick
- The Romance of the Colorado River ... New York: Putnam, 1902. 1st edn. 8vo. xxxv, 399, [4 advt] pp. Num ills. Orig pict cloth, new endpapers. (*Hollett*) **£85 [≈ $136]**

Dellon, Gabriel
- The History of the Inquisition, as it is Exercised at Goa ... With an Account of His Deliverance. London: 1688. 1st English edn.

2nd iss, with bookseller's name on title. Sm 4to. [6],70 pp. Margs shaved, pages darkened. Antique half calf. Wing D.942.
(Reese) **$450 [≈ £281]**

Denham, Dixon & Clapperton, Hugh
- Narrative of Travels & Discoveries in Northern & Central Africa, in the Years 1822, 1823 & 1824 ... London: Murray, 1826. 1st edn. 2 parts in one vol. 4to. xlviii, 333; [iv], 269 pp. Fldg map, 37 plates (1 hand cold), 6 vignettes. Contemp mor gilt, hinges reprd.
(Terramedia) **$1,000 [≈ £625]**
- Narrative of Travels and Discoveries in Northern and Central Africa, in the Years 1822, 1823 and 1824 ... London: 1826. Thick 4to. xlviii,335; [2],269,[3] pp. 44 plates (1 cold), maps (1 fldg), vignettes. Occas foxing. Three qtr cloth & paper bds, soiled, edgeworn.
(Reese) **$850 [≈ £531]**
- Narrative of Travels & Discoveries in Northern and Central Africa. Boston: Cummings, Hilliard & Co, 1826. 1st Amer edn (?). lxiv,255, iv,104,112 pp. 2 fldg maps. Sl foxing. Half cloth & bds, paper label, hd of spine chipped, ft torn, hinge weak.
(Parmer) **$300 [≈ £187]**
- Narrative of Travels and Discoveries in Northern and Central Africa in the Years 1822, 1823 and 1824 ... London: Murray, 1828. 3rd edn. 2 vols. 8vo. xii,[2],471; iv,467 pp. 15 plates & maps (1 cold, 3 fldg). Mod calf gilt, lacks labels.
(Parmer) **$300 [≈ £187]**

Dennis, George
- The Cities and Cemeteries of Etruria. London: Murray, 1848. 2 vols. 8vo. 2 maps (1 fldg), 3 tinted plates. Orig dark green cloth.
(Waterfield's) **£90 [≈ $144]**
- The Cities and Cemeteries of Etruria. Revised Edition, Recording the Most Recent Discoveries ...L: Murray, 1878. 2 vols. Lge 8vo. Cold frontis, 2 fldg maps, num ills. Orig cloth gilt, spines sl faded, extremities rubbed.
(Karmiole) **$175 [≈ £109]**

Denny, Arthur A.
- Pioneer Days of the Puget Sound. Seattle: 1888. 83 pp. Sticker & ills pasted on title, sm piece missing from marg of 1st page, some pencil underscoring. Lacks errata called for by Howes. Orig cloth. Inscrbd pres copy from the author.
(Reese) **$200 [≈ £125]**

Dent, Emma
- Annals of Winchcombe and Sudeley. London: 1877. 4to. Num ills, some cold. Orig cloth gilt, hinges & edges sl rubbed.
(Ambra) **£52 [≈ $83]**

D'Orleans, Prince Henri
- From Tonkin to India By the Sources of the Irawadi January '95 - January '96. New York: Dodd, Mead, 1898. 1st Amer edn. Tall 8vo. xii, 467 pp. Fldg map, etchings. Light soil, endpapers renewed. *(Parmer)* **$250 [≈ £156]**

Depons, F
- Travels in Part of South America, during the Years 1801, 1802, 1803, & 1804 ... London: Richard Phillips, 1806. 157,[1],index pp. Fldg frontis map, fldg plan. Scattered foxing & tanning. Mod half cloth, t.e.g.
(Reese) **$150 [≈ £93]**

De Prorok, Byron Khun
- Digging for Lost African Gods. The Record of Five Years Archaeological Excavation in North Africa. With Notes and Translations by E.F. Allen. New York & London: Putnam's, 1926. 1st edn. 8vo. xv,369 pp. Num photo plates. Orig bndg.
(Terramedia) **$45 [≈ £28]**

De Selincourt, Beryl & Henderson, May Sturge
- Venice. Illustrated by Reginald Barratt. London: Chatto & Windus, 1907. One of 310 Large Paper, this copy unnumbered. 30 cold plates. Title browned, occas sl foxing. Orig parchment cvrd bds gilt, t.e.g., parchment somewhat soiled. *(Clark)* **£24 [≈ $38]**

De Smet, Pierre Jean
- Letters and Sketches: with a Narrative of a Year's Residence among the Indian Tribes of the Rocky Mountains. Philadelphia: 1843. ix, 244, 12 pp. 13 plates (inc the fldg allegorical plate, often lacking). Faint damp stain. Orig pict cloth, spine relaid, some edgewear.
(Reese) **$1,750 [≈ £1,093]**
- Letters and Sketches with a Narrative of a Year's Residence among the Indian Tribes of the Rocky Mountains. Philadelphia: Fithian, 1843. 8vo. Frontis & 11 litho plates, & the fldg allegorical plate. Occas light foxing & staining. Orig black pict cloth.
(W. Thomas Taylor) **$1,500 [≈ £937]**

Dewar, G.A.B.
- Life and Sport in Hampshire. London: 1908. 8vo. xii, 274 pp. 14 plates (inc 2 cold, by Thorburn). Blank upper qtr of half-title cut away. Orig cloth.
(Wheldon & Wesley) **£30 [≈ $48]**

Dewar, T.R.
- A Ramble Round the Globe ... London: Chatto & Windus, 1894. Sm 8vo. xvi,316,36 pp. Frontis, over 200 ills. Orig dec cloth.

(Berkelouw) **$75 [≈ £46]**

De Wet, Christian R.
- Three Years' War (October 1899 - June 1902). Westminster: Constable, 1902. 520,advt pp. Frontis, fldg map. Partly unopened.   *(Parmer)* **$100 [≈ £62]**
- Three Years' War [Boer War]. New York: Scribner's, 1902. 8vo. x, 448 pp. Fldg map, frontis port. Orig brown cloth gilt.
(Terramedia) **$30 [≈ £18]**

Dewey, Orville
- The Old World and the New; or, a Journal of Reflections and Observations made on a Tour in Europe. New York: 1836. 1st edn. 2 vols. 12mo. Foxed. Orig cloth, paper labels.
(Argosy) **$60 [≈ £37]**

De Windt, Harry
- From Paris to New York by Land. London: 1904. 311 pp. Fldg maps, frontis. Occas trace of foxing. Orig pict gilt cloth, rubbed.
(Reese) **$100 [≈ £62]**
- From Paris to New York by Land. New York: 1904. 8vo. 2 fldg maps, 84 photo ills. Orig pict cloth gilt.   *(Henly)* **£28 [≈ $44]**
- Through the Gold-Fields of Alaska to Bering Straits. London: Chatto & Windus, 1898. 1st edn. 8vo. viii, 312, [32 advt dated Jan 1898] pp. Lge fldg map, 32 plates. Orig cloth, rather marked & bumped.   *(Hollett)* **£120 [≈ $192]**
- Through the Gold-Fields of Alaska to Bering Straits. London: Chatto & Windus, 1898. 8vo. viii, 312 pp. Lge fldg map, num photo plates. Orig dec cloth, t.e.g.
(High Latitude) **$70 [≈ £43]**

Dexter, T.F.G. & Henry
- Cornish Crosses Christian & Pagan. With Some Observations on the Tau Cross, Thor's Hammer, and the Cult of the Axe. London: 1938. 1st edn. 4to. Ills. Orig bndg. Dw sl worn.   *(Ambra)* **£69 [≈ $110]**

Dibdin, Thomas Frognall
- A Bibliographical Antiquarian and Picturesque Tour in France and Germany. London: for the author ..., 1821. 1st edn. 3 vols. Lge 8vo. Addtnl title dated 1823, num plates. Perf & rubber stamps on titles. Some plates offset. Lib half mor, extremities rubbed.   *(Hannas)* **£380 [≈ $608]**
- A Bibliographical, Antiquarian and Picturesque Tour in France and Germany. London: Jennings & Major, 1829. 2nd edn. 3 vols. 421; 428; 481 pp. Frontis ports, 33 autographs. Occas sl foxing. Red cloth, grey cloth spines replaced, facs paper labels.

(Hartfield) **$265 [≈ £165]**
- A Bibliographical Antiquarian and Picturesque Tour in France and Germany. London: Robert Jennings ..., 1829. 2nd edn. 3 vols. 8vo. Plates, text ills. Rec cloth.
(Young's) **£70 [≈ $112]**
- A Bibliographical, Antiquarian and Picturesque Tour in France and Germany. London: 1829. 2nd edn. 3 vols. 8vo. 11 plates. Minor spotting. Contemp pink half calf, mor labels, rather rubbed.
(Waterfield's) **£200 [≈ $320]**

Dicey, Thomas
- An Historical Account of Guernsey ... London: for the author, & sold by J. Newbery, 1751. 1st edn, 1st iss. 12mo. List of subscribers, with leaf of addtnl subscribers. A few ink spots on title. Later mrbld bds, rebacked.   *(Trebizond)* **$475 [≈ £296]**
- An Historical Account of Guernsey. London: 1751. 1st edn. 12mo. Contemp sheep, upper cover detached, spine defective.
(Robertshaw) **£115 [≈ $184]**
- An Historical Account of Guernsey. New Edition. London: 1797. 4to. Map, 5 plates (foxed). Contemp calf, rebacked. Duke of York's copy, sold May 1827.
(Robertshaw) **£80 [≈ $128]**

Dickens, Charles
- Pictures from Italy. London: Bradbury & Evans, 1846. 1st edn. [270],[2] pp. Orig blue cloth gilt.   *(Jenkins)* **$225 [≈ £140]**

Dickey, Herbert Spencer
- My Jungle Book [expedition on the Amazon and Orinoco]. Boston: Little, Brown, 1932. 8vo. xii, 298 pp. 19 ills. Orig green cloth, spine faded. Dw sl chipped.
(Karmiole) **$45 [≈ £28]**

Dickinson, F.
- Lake Victoria to Khartoum with Rifle and Camera. London: 1910. 334 pp. Ills. Orig bndg.   *(Trophy Room Books)* **$260 [≈ £162]**

Dickinson, T.
- Narrative of the Operations for the Recovery of the Public Stores and Treasures sunk in H.M.S. Thetis ... London: Longman ..., 1836. 1st edn. 8vo. xvi,91 pp. 2 charts (1 fldg), frontis, 2 plates. Contemp cloth, uncut.
(Gough) **£135 [≈ $216]**

Dickson, H.R.P.
- Arab of the Desert. London: Allen & Unwin, 1949. 1st edn. 8vo. 648,index pp. Errata slip. Fldg maps (9 on 7 sheets), 6 genealogical

trees, num ills. Sm piece missing from 1 map
marg. Unpleasant stain on front bd.
(Parmer) **$75 [≈£46]**
- The Arab of the Desert: A Glimpse into
Badawin Life in Kuwait and Saudi Arabia.
London: Allen & Unwin, [1951]. 2nd edn.
8vo. 664 pp. 11 fldg maps & charts in pocket,
frontis, other photo plates (inc 8 cold plates).
Orig orange cloth, red label.
(Terramedia) **$300 [≈£187]**
- Kuwait and her Neighbours. London: Allen
& Unwin, 1956. 1st edn. 8vo. 627 pp. 8 maps
& charts in rear pocket, cold frontis, num
plates, some cold. Orig orange cloth, green
spine label.   *(Terramedia)* **$300 [≈£187]**

Dietz, Arthur Arnold
- Mad Rush for Gold in Frozen North. Los
Angeles: Times-Mirror, 1914. 8vo. 281 pp.
Frontis, ills. Orig dec cloth.
(High Latitude) **$55 [≈£34]**

Dieulafoy, Jane
- At Susa. The Ancient Capital of the King of
Persia. Narrative of Travel through Western
Persia ... Translated ... by Frank Listow
White. Philadelphia: Gebbie, 1890. 1st US
edn. Folio. vi,266 pp. Num ills. Qtr mor,
worn, lacks backstrip, internally good ex-lib.
(Worldwide Antiqu'n) **$95 [≈£59]**

Digges, Sir Dudley, 1583-1639
- A Discourse of Sea-Ports; principally of the
Port and Haven of Dover: Written by Sir
Walter Raleigh and Address'd to Queen
Elizabeth ... London: John Nutt, 1700. 1st
edn. Sm 4to. [iv], 16 pp. Sewed as issued,
uncut, crnrs sl creased, sl chipped & dusty.
Wing D.1458.   *(Bickersteth)* **£300 [≈$480]**

Directories
- Bennett's Business Directory of
Gloucestershire. 1909. 8vo. 80 pp. Rec cloth.
(Ambra) **£28 [≈$44]**
- Kelly's Directory of Bristol. 1938. Lacks
map. Orig cloth, faded, inner hinges weak.
(Ambra) **£18 [≈$28]**
- Kelly's Directory of Devonshire & Cornwall.
London: 1923. 8vo. 1 fldg map (only, of 2,
lacks map of Devonshire). Orig cloth, inner
hinges weak.   *(Ambra)* **£60 [≈$96]**
- Kelly's Directory of Devonshire. 1910. Fldg
map. Orig cloth, partly faded, top outer hinge
split.   *(Ambra)* **£42 [≈$67]**
- Kelly's Directory of Dorsetshire. 1927. 8vo.
Fldg map. Orig cloth, top bd sl spotted.
(Ambra) **£32 [≈$51]**
- Kelly's Directory of Dorsetshire. 1907. 8vo.
Fldg map. 1 page torn & lacking lower qtr.

Orig cloth, rubbed at edges, inner hinges
split.   *(Ambra)* **£24 [≈$38]**
- Kelly's Directory of Gloucestershire. 1902.
8vo. Fldg map. 2 tears to 1st leaf without loss.
Orig cloth, damped.   *(Ambra)* **£38 [≈$60]**
- Kelly's Directory of Hampshire, Wiltshire,
Dorsetshire and the Isle of Wight. London:
1907. 8vo. 3 fldg maps. Orig cloth, partly
faded, inner hinges split, amateur repr to
spine.   *(Ambra)* **£60 [≈$96]**
- Kelly's Directory of Somersetshire and the
City of Bristol. London: 1914. 8vo. 2 fldg
maps (1 partly torn). Orig cloth, spine relaid.
(Ambra) **£58 [≈$92]**
- Kelly's Directory of Somersetshire. 1939.
8vo. Cold fldg map. New cloth. Extracted
from a larger work.   *(Ambra)* **£27 [≈$43]**
- Kelly's Directory of Somersetshire. 1889.
8vo. Fldg map. Orig cloth, sl spotted, edges
rubbed.   *(Ambra)* **£72 [≈$115]**
- Kelly's Directory of Wiltshire. 1927. 8vo.
Lacks map. Orig cloth. *(Ambra)* **£30 [≈$48]**
- Kelly's Directory of Wiltshire. 1923. 8vo.
Fldg map. Orig cloth. *(Ambra)* **£28 [≈$44]**
- Mathew's Annual Bristol Directory, for the
Year 1814 ... 12mo. New cloth.
(Ambra) **£45 [≈$72]**
- Mathew's Annual Directory for the City &
County of Bristol, including Clifton,
Bedminster, and Surrounding Villages. 1862.
12mo. Advts. Orig embossed cloth, inner
hinges split.   *(Ambra)* **£42 [≈$67]**
- New Directory of Stroud and District, 1908.
Stroud: Harry Harmer, 1908. 8vo. Fldg map,
street plan, num ills & advts. Orig cloth
backed paper bds.   *(Ambra)* **£35 [≈$56]**
- Pigot's Directory of Monmouthshire. 1844.
Lacks map. New cloth. *(Ambra)* **£46 [≈$73]**
- Sheffield Directory and Guide ... John
Blackwell, 1828. 8vo. lxxxii, 18, 4 advt,
19-202, [ii] pp, plus advt ff, many with engvd
trade cards etc. Old calf rubbed & worn, v
shaken, some sections loose.
(Hollett) **£130 [≈$208]**
- See also White, William.

Distant, W.L.
- A Naturalist in the Transvaal. London: R.H.
Porter, 1892. 1st edn. xvi,277 pp. 4
chromolithos, 1 litho, 30 plates. Orig pict
cloth gilt.   *(Hollett)* **£120 [≈$192]**

Disturnell, John
- The Northern Traveller; Containing the
Hudson River Guide, and Tour to the
Springs, Lake George and Canada, Passing
through Lake Champlain ... New York: J.
Disturnell, 1844. 16mo. 84 pp. Frontis, 2

maps. Text a bit foxed. Orig blue cloth gilt, soiled. *(Karmiole)* **$65 [≈ £40]**

Ditchfield, P.H.
- The Cottages & Village Life of Rural England. Illustrated by A.R. Quinton. London: Dent, 1912. 1st edn. 52 cold plates, 19 line ills. Orig dec cloth, sometime partly rebound. *(Old Cathay)* **£75 [≈ $120]**

Ditson, George Leighton
- Circassia; or, A Tour to the Caucasus. New York & London: Stringer & Townsend, Newby, 1850. 1st edn. 8vo. 453, appendix pp. Frontis. Some yellowing. Orig brown cloth, spine ends sl worn.
(Terramedia) **$60 [≈ £37]**

Diver, Maud
- The Hero of Herat, A Frontier Biography [of Major Eldred Pottinger] in Romantic Form. London: 1912. 8vo. Fldg map, port frontis. Orig cloth, upper jnt worn.
(Farahar) **£20 [≈ $32]**
- The Judgment of the Sword, The Tale of the Kabul Tragedy, and of the part played therein by Major Eldred Pottinger, the Hero of Herat. London: 1913. 8vo. 2 fldg maps, plates. Orig cloth. *(Farahar)* **£25 [≈ $40]**

Dixon, Winifred H.
- Westward Hoboes. Ups and Downs of Frontier Motoring. New York: 1921. 377 pp. Frontis, ills. Gilt pict cloth, hinges weak.
(Reese) **$50 [≈ £31]**

Dobson, G.
- St. Petersburg. Painted by F. De Haenen. London: A. & C. Black Colour Book, 1910. 1st edn. Map, 16 cold & 16 b/w plates. yellow & black dec cloth, 1 or 2 sl stains.
(Old Cathay) **£49 [≈ $78]**

Doddridge, Sir John
- The History of the Ancient and Modern State of the Principality of Wales, Dutchy of Cornwall, and Earldome of Chester. London: Tho. Harper ..., 1630. 1st edn. 4to. Lacks final blank leaf. Title browned, a few headlines just shaved. Mod scarlet half mor. STC 6982. *(Hannas)* **£150 [≈ $240]**

Doddridge, Joseph
- Notes on the Settlement and Indian Wars of Virginia and Pennsylvania, 1763-1783, with a View of the First Settlers of the Western Country. Wellsburgh, Va.: Gazette Office, 1824. 1st edn. 316 pp. Mod half mor gilt.
(Jenkins) **$375 [≈ £234]**

Dodge, Bayard
- The Fihrist of Al-Nadim. New York & London: 1970. 2 vols. 8vo. 570; 1149 pp. Orig purple cloth. *(Terramedia)* **$50 [≈ £31]**

Dodwell, Edward
- A Classical and Topographical Tour through Greece, during the Years 1801, 1805, and 1806. London: Rodwell & Martin, 1819. 2 vols. 4to. xii,587,errata; vii,537,errata pp. Fldg map, 66 plates (2 cold), text w'cuts. Contemp diced russia, reprd, crnrs rubbed.
(Frew Mackenzie) **£950 [≈ $1,520]**

Doe, Brian
- Southern Arabia. New York: 1971. 4to. 287 pp. Num photo ills & drawings. Orig bndg. Dw. *(Terramedia)* **$40 [≈ £25]**

Doke, Clement M.
- The Lanbas of Northern Rhodesia: a Study of their Customs and Beliefs. London: Harrap, 1931. 1st edn. 8vo. 408 pp. Map, 110 ills. Orig cloth. *(Fenning)* **£35 [≈ $56]**
- The Lanbas of Northern Rhodesia. A Study of their Customs and Beliefs. London: Harrap, 1931. 1st edn. 8vo. Map, 110 ills. Orig cloth gilt, sl marked.
(Hollett) **£60 [≈ $96]**

Domenech, E.
- Missionary Adventures in Texas and Mexico, a Personal Narrative of Six Years' Sojourn ... London: Longmans ..., 1858. 1st English edn. 8vo. xvi,366,[24] pp. Lge fldg map of Texas. Contemp diced calf, sl shelfwear.
(W. Thomas Taylor) **$600 [≈ £375]**
- Missionary Adventures in Texas and Mexico. A Personal Narrative of Six Years Sojourn in those Regions. Translated from the French ... London: Longman ..., 1858. 1st English edn. 8vo. xv, 366 pp. Lacks map(?). Half calf, rehinged. *(Young's)* **£55 [≈ $88]**

Domville-Fife, Charles W.
- Among Wild Tribes of the Amazons. An Account of Exploration & Adventure on the Mighty Amazon & Its Confluents ... Philadelphia: Lippincott, 1925. 1st Amer edn. 8vo. 6 maps, 27 ills. Orig red cloth gilt.
(Karmiole) **$75 [≈ £46]**

Doughty, Charles Montague
- Travels in Arabia Deserta. Cambridge: Univ Press, 1888. 1st edn. 2 vols. Maps (fldg map in vol 1 pocket), ills. Minor scattered foxing. Orig gilt dec cloth, sl rubbed, inner hinges cracked but sound. Cloth case (defective).
(Reese) **$2,000 [≈ £1,250]**

- Travels in Arabia Deserta ... London: Cape, 1923. 2 vols. 623; 690 pp. Fldg linen backed map in pocket. Gilt faded, some tenderness to hinges. *(Parmer)* **$75 [≈ £46]**
- Travels in Arabia Deserta ... Introduction by T.E. Lawrence ... London: Cape & Medici Society, 1926. 2 vols in one. 8vo. Fldg map, port, num plates, text ills. Orig cloth, spine sl dull & minimally nicked.
  (Sanders) **£28 [≈ $44]**
- Travels in Arabia Deserta ... Introduction by T.E. Lawrence ... Thin-Paper Edition in One Volume, Complete & Unabridged. London: Cape & Medici Society, 1926. 1,[iii], 623, [ii], 690 pp. Fldg map. Orig cloth, new endpapers. *(Lamb)* **£20 [≈ $32]**
- Travels in Arabia Deserta ... Introduction by T.E. Lawrence ... Thin-Paper Edition in One Volume, Complete & Unabridged. London: Cape, 1926. 8vo. xliv,690 pp. Maps, ills. Sl scuff to bottom edge. *(Parmer)* **$65 [≈ £40]**
- Travels in Arabia Deserta ... London: Cape, 1949. 3rd printing of 1936 "New and Definitive" edn. 2 vols. Lge 8vo. 2 fldg maps, 9 plates. Orig cloth. Dws.
  (Parmer) **$195 [≈ £121]**
- Travels in Arabia Deserta. With Illustrations made on the spot by Edy Legrand. New York: Heritage, [1953]. Abridged edn. Lge 8vo. xxi,453 pp. Num plates. Orig white cloth. Slipcase. *(Terramedia)* **$50 [≈ £31]**

Doughty, Marion
- Afoot through the Kashmir Valleys. London: Sands & Co, 1902. 1st edn. 8vo. xxxii,276 pp. 40 ills. Orig cloth gilt. *(Hollett)* **£65 [≈ $104]**

Douglas, Francis
- A General Description of the East Coast of Scotland, from Edinburgh to Cullen ... Universities ... Trade and Manufactures ... Paisley: for the author ..., 1782. 1st edn. 12mo. [viii], 310, xiv pp. Contemp sheep, rebacked. *(Burmester)* **£175 [≈ $280]**

Douglass, William
- A Summary, Historical and Political, of the First Planting, Progressive Improvements, and Present State of the British Settlements in North-America ... Boston: 1749-51 [i.e. 1752]. 2 vols. [vi], 568; [ii], 416 pp. Top marg shaved sl close in sev ff. Half calf.
  (Reese) **$2,750 [≈ £1,718]**

Down, E.J.
- The Bushman. London: Charles Griffin, 1931. 1st edn. 4to. xii,130 pp. Frontis, 33 plates. Lib stamp on title. Orig maroon cloth.
  (Terramedia) **$75 [≈ £46]**

Downing, Clement
- A Compendious History of the Indian Wars; with An Account of ... Angria the Pyrate ... London: for T. Cooper, 1737. 1st edn. 12mo. iv, 238 pp. Title trimmed sl short not affecting text. Contemp sprinkled calf gilt, mor label, jnts just cracked.
  (Finch) **£275 [≈ $440]**

Downing, George
- A Discourse written by ... the King of Great Britain's Envoy Extraordinary to the States of the United Provinces ... added a Relation ... by a Meaner Hand. London: for John Luttome, 1672. 2nd edn, JCB iss 'A'. 12mo. 31,139,[4] pp. Rec calf by Middleton.
  (Reese) **$650 [≈ £406]**

Dracopoli, I.N.
- Through Jubaland to the Lorian Swamp. An Adventurous Journey of Exploration and Sport. Philadelphia: Lippincott, 1914. 1st edn. 8vo. 317 pp. Fldg cold map, frontis, num other photo plates. Orig orange pict cloth, lower half of spine v stained & bumped.
  (Terramedia) **$100 [≈ £62]**

Drake, Daniel
- Natural and Statistical View, or Picture of Cincinnati in the Miami Country ... Cincinnati: 1815. 251,[4] pp. 2 fldg maps. Scattered foxing. Orig ptd bds, stained, spine chipped. Cloth box. *(Reese)* **$1,000 [≈ £625]**
- Natural and Statistical View, or Picture of Cincinnati and the Miami Country ... With an Appendix ... Cincinnati: 1815. 12mo. 251, [5] pp. Lacks plan & map. Scattered foxing, minor stains. Contemp tree calf, some wear.
  (Hemlock) **$225 [≈ £140]**
- A Practical Treatise on the History, Prevention, and Treatment of Epidemic Cholera. Designed both for the Profession and the People. Cincinnati: Corey & Fairbank, 1832. 1st edn. 12mo. 180 pp. Orig cloth, paper label. Author's pres inscrptn.
  (Hemlock) **$900 [≈ £562]**

Drayson, A.W.
- Sporting Scenes amongst the Kaffirs of South Africa. London: 1860. 2nd edn. Engvd plates by Joseph Wolf. Mod half mor, edges trimmed sl unevenly. *(Grayling)* **£50 [≈ $80]**

Drummond, Alexander
- Travels through Different Cities of Germany, Italy, Greece and Several Parts of Asia ... London: for the author, 1754. Folio. 311 pp. Fldg frontis, 18 maps & plans, 16 plates, sev fldg. Sl stain, marg foxing. Contemp calf, sl worn & rubbed, hinges cracked.

(Sotheran) **£850 [≈ $1,360]**

Drunken Barnaby's Four Journeys ...
- See Brathwaite, Richard.

Dubois, Felix
- Timbuctoo the Mysterious. Translated by D. White. London: Heinemann, 1897. 8vo. xi,377 pp. 11 maps & plans, title vignette, num plates & ills. Orig pict green cloth gilt, rubbed, hd of spine sl chipped.
(Terramedia) **£150 [≈ £93]**
- Timbuctoo the Mysterious. Translated from the French by Diana White. London: Heinemann, 1897. 1st edn. Lge 8vo. xii,377 pp. 11 maps & plans, 153 ills. A little fingering, 1 sm lib stamp. Mod half mor gilt.
(Hollett) **£75 [≈ $120]**

Dubourdieu, John
- Statistical Survey of the County of Antrim, with Observations on the Means of Improvement ... for the consideration of the Dublin Society. Dublin: Graisberry, 1812. Plates. Contemp half calf.
(Emerald Isle) **£200 [≈ $320]**
- Statistical Survey of the County of Down. Dublin: Graisberry, 1802. Map, frontis. Half calf.   *(Emerald Isle)* **£200 [≈ $320]**

Du Cane, Florence
- The Canary Islands. Painted by Ella Du Cane. London: A. & C. Black Colour Book, 1911. 1st edn. Cold plates. Orig white cloth, endpapers browned, v fine.
(Old Cathay) **£45 [≈ $72]**
- The Canary Islands. Painted by Ella Du Cane. London: A. & C. Black Colour Book, 1911. 1st edn. Cold plates. Orig red cloth, spine faded.   *(Old Cathay)* **£20 [≈ $32]**

Ducarel, A.C.
- Some Account of the Town, Church, and Archiepiscopal Palace of Croydon, in the County of Surrey, from its Foundation to the Year 1783. London: Bibliotheca Topographica Britannica No. XII, 1783. 4to. viii,80,158 pp. 10 plates. Lib marks. 3 reprs. Qtr mor.   *(Coombes)* **£45 [≈ $72]**

Du Chaillu, Paul B.
- Explorations & Adventures in Equatorial Africa. London: Murray, 1861. 2nd edn. 8vo. xviii, 489 pp. 74 w'engvd plates. Fldg map supplied in facs. Orig pict black cloth gilt. Ex libris the Marquis of Londonderry.
(Gough) **£48 [≈ $76]**
- Explorations and Adventures in Equatorial Africa ... London: 1861. 2nd edn. 8vo. xviii,

479 pp. Fldg map (reprd), frontis, 72 ills. New cloth. *(Wheldon & Wesley)* **£85 [≈ $136]**
- A Journey to Ashango-Land. And Further Penetration into Equatorial Africa. New York: Appleton, 1867. 1st Amer edn. Tall 8vo. xxiv, 501, advt pp. Fldg map, frontis, plates. Orig pict blue cloth, hd of spine sl frayed, front cvr & endpapers sl stained, sl shaken.   *(Terramedia)* **$125 [≈ £78]**
- The Land of the Midnight Sun. New York: 1881-82. Vol 1 1st edn. 2 vols. 8vo. Frontis & 234 ills, map. Orig gilt pict cloth.
(Argosy) **$100 [≈ £62]**
- The Land of the Midnight Sun. Summer and Winter Journeys ... New York: 1882. 2 vols. Fldg map in pocket of vol 1, 2 frontis, plates, text ills. Orig pict gilt cloth, sl edge wear.
(Reese) **$125 [≈ £78]**
- The Land of the Midnight Sun. New York: Harper, 1882. 2 vols. Fldg map in pocket, 235 ills. Orig gilt pict blue cloth.
(Parmer) **$150 [≈ £93]**
- The Land of the Midnight Sun. Summer and Winter Journeys ... New York & London: Harper, 1899. 2 vols. 8vo. xvi,441; xi,ii,474 pp. Fldg map in pocket, 2 frontis, num plates. Orig pict gilt grey cloth, back cvr of vol 1 & maps stained.   *(Terramedia)* **$40 [≈ £25]**
- The Viking Age ... New York: Scribner's, 1889. 1st edn. 2 vols. 8vo. Frontises, maps, num text ills. Contemp red half mor, uncut, crnrs & jnts rubbed. *(Hannas)* **£75 [≈ $120]**
- The Viking Age ... New York: Scribner, 1890. 2 vols. 8vo. Over 1300 text ills. Orig cloth.   *(Berkelouw)* **$125 [≈ £78]**

Duchaussois, P.
- The Grey Nuns in the Far North (1867 - 1917). Toronto: McClelland & Stewart, 1919. 1st edn. 8vo. 287 pp. 46 photo ills. Orig cloth, spine ends sl worn.   *(Parmer)* **$75 [≈ £46]**
- Mid Snow & Ice: The Apostles of the Northwest. London: Burns, Oates & Washbourne, 1923. 1st edn. 8vo. xiii,328 pp. Lge fldg map, num plates. Orig pict blue cloth.   *(Terramedia)* **$75 [≈ £46]**

Duche, Jacob
- Caspipina's Letters; containing Observations upon a Variety of Subjects ... added, the Life and Character of Wm. Penn, Esq. Bath: 1777. 1st English edn. 2 vols in one. 8vo. [xii],188; 236 pp. No half-title. Minor stains. Contemp calf, rebacked, crnrs sl worn.
(Clark) **£85 [≈ $136]**

Duck, John N.
- The Natural History of Portishead: Comprising a Guide to the Locality, with an

Appendix ... Ornithological, Entomological and Botanical ... Bristol: 1852. 12mo. 3 engvd views. Lacks map (never bound in). Orig cloth, sl loose.   *(Ambra)* £60 [≈ $96]

Duckworth, Francis
- Chester. Painted by E. Harrison Compton. London: A. & C. Black Colour Book, 1910. 1st edn. Map, 20 cold plates. Orig dec cloth, fine.   *(Old Cathay)* £39 [≈ $62]
- The Cotswolds. Painted by G.F. Nicholls. London: A. & C. Black Colour Books, Six Shillings Series, 1908. 1st edn. Map, 24 cold plates. Orig dec cloth, t.e.g., some rubbing to front bd, some browning to endpapers.   *(Old Cathay)* £25 [≈ $40]

Duff, H.L.
- Nyasaland under the Foreign Office. London: 1903. 1st edn. 8vo. 422 pp. Frontis, num plates & maps. Orig pict green cloth gilt, sl soiled.   *(Terramedia)* $100 [≈ £62]

Dufferin, Lord
- Letters from High Latitudes. Being Some Account of a Voyage ... to Iceland, Jan Mayen, & Spitzbergen in 1856. London: Murray, 1856. 1st edn. 8vo. xx,424 pp. Fldg chart (torn without loss), 3 maps, 11 w'engvs. Orig cloth gilt, uncut, rubbed, extremities sl worn.   *(Claude Cox)* £65 [≈ $104]
- Letters from High Latitudes. Being Some Account of a Voyage in the Schooner Yacht "Foam", 85 O.M. to Iceland, Jan Mayen & Spitzbergen in 1856. London: Murray, 1857. 2nd edn. 8vo. xvii,2,425 pp. 3 maps, plates, ills. Contemp half mor, spine sl rubbed & darkened.   *(Terramedia)* $100 [≈ £62]
- Letters from High Latitudes ... to Iceland, Jan Meyen and Spitzbergen. London: Murray, 1895. 10th edn. Ills. Blue cloth gilt.   *(Emerald Isle)* £15 [≈ $24]
- A Yacht Voyage (Letters from High Latitudes). Boston: Ticknor & Fields, 1859. 8vo. x,ll,406,16 advt pp. Orig cloth, spine ends & crnrs worn.   *(Parmer)* $60 [≈ £37]

Duffield, A.J.
- Recollections of Travel Abroad. London: 1889. 1st edn. 8vo. xiv,327 pp. Cold fldg map. Some spotting of foredge & endpapers. Cutting on pastedown. Orig illust cloth gilt.   *(Bow Windows)* £70 [≈ $112]

Dufton, Henry
- Narrative of a Journey through Abyssinia in 1862-3. With an Appendix ... Second Edition. London: Chapman & Hall, 1867. 8vo. xiv, 337 pp. 3 fldg cold maps. Later cloth, orig

backstrip laid down.   *(Schoyer)* $80 [≈ £50]

Dugdale, William
- Monasticon Anglicanum: or, the History of the Ancient Abbies, Monasteries ... Corrected ... by an Eminent Hand. London: 1718. 3 parts in one vol. Folio. xvi,375,[9] pp. Addtnl engvd title, 103 plates (1 tear reprd). Contemp calf, rebacked, crnrs rubbed.   *(Karmiole)* $500 [≈ £312]

Dugmore, A. Radclyffe
- Camera Adventures in the African Wilds ... New York: Doubleday, 1910. 1st edn. Frontis, num photo plates. Orig pict green cloth gilt.   *(Terramedia)* $100 [≈ £62]
- Camera Adventures in the African Wilds. London: 1910. 4to. xviii, 231 pp. Map, num photo ills. Orig cloth.   *(Wheldon & Wesley)* £30 [≈ $48]
- Wild Life and the Camera. London: 1912. 332 pp. Ills. Cloth.   *(Reese)* $40 [≈ £25]
- The Wonderland of Big Game being an Account of Two Trips through Tanganyika and Kenya. London: 1925. Roy 8vo. Map, num plates. Orig cloth, sl worn.   *(Farahar)* £40 [≈ $64]
- The Wonderland of Big Game: Two Trips through Tanganyika and Kenya. London: 1925. 288 pp. 2 maps, 60 ills. Orig bndg.   *(Trophy Room Books)* $80 [≈ £500]

Du Mont, Sieur
- A New Voyage to the Levant ... London: for T. Goodman, 1702. 3rd edn. Sm 8vo. [xxii],416 pp. 8 fldg plates. Sl foxing. Half mor.   *(Worldwide Antiqu'n)* $375 [≈ £234]

Dunbar, Margaret Juliana Maria
- Art and Nature under an Italian Sky. Second Edition. Edinburgh: 1853. 8vo. Engvd frontis. Orig green cloth, spine darkened.   *(Robertshaw)* £18 [≈ $28]

Dunbar, Seymour
- A History of Travel in America ... Indianopolis: Bobbs-Merril, [1915]. 4 vols. 8vo. 1531 pp. 4 cold frontis, num plates & ills, some cold. Orig blue cloth gilt, spines sl spotted.   *(Terramedia)* $100 [≈ £62]

Duncan, James
- The Scotch Itinerary, containing the Roads through Scotland, on a New Plan ... Glasgow: for James & Andrew Duncan, 1808. 2nd edn, enlgd. Tall thin 12mo. [xiv],74,74,28 pp. 2 fldg maps (each with sm tear, no loss). Orig pink bds, ptd label. *(Burmester)* £75 [≈ $120]

Duncumb, John
- Collections towards the History and Antiquities of the County of Hereford. Hereford: E.G. Wright, 1804. 2 vols. 4to. 17 plates & maps (inc an addtnl plate, not called for). Contemp calf, rebacked. Vol 2 part 2 was never published. *(Waterfield's)* **£400 [≈ $640]**

Dunham, Jacob
- Journal of Voyages ... Twice Captured by the English ... Cast Away and Residing with Indians ... New York: 1850. 243 pp. Port, plates. Foxed. Limp cloth gilt, t.e.g., a bit spotted & worn at spine.
(Reese) **$450 [≈ £281]**

Dunham, Samuel A.
- The History of Poland. London: Lardner's Cabinet Cyclopaedia, 1831. 1st edn. Sm 8vo. Orig cloth, ptd paper label.
(Fenning) **£18.50 [≈ $30]**
- The History of Spain and Portugal. London: Lardner's Cabinet Cyclopaedia, 1832-33. 1st edn. 5 vols. Sm 8vo. Orig cloth, ptd paper labels. *(Fenning)* **£32.50 [≈ $52]**
- History of the Germanic Empire. London: Lardner's Cabinet Cyclopaedia, 1834-35. 1st edn. 3 vols. Sm 8vo. Orig cloth, ptd paper labels. *(Fenning)* **£24.50 [≈ $40]**

Dunkin, Robert
- See "Snaffle".

Dunmore, The Earl of
- The Pamirs. London: 1893. 2nd edn. 2 vols. 360; 352 pp. Lge cold fldg map. Orig blue silk cloth, silver pict dec front cvrs.
(Trophy Room Books) **$750 [≈ £468]**

Dunn, Robert
- The Shameless Diary of an Explorer. New York: Outing Pub. Co., 1907. 12mo. viii,297 pp. 2 fldg maps, photo plates. Orig cloth, front endpaper removed.
(High Latitude) **$100 [≈ £62]**

Dunton, John, London mariner
- A true journall of the Sally Fleet, with the Proceedings of the Voyage ... London: John Dawson for Thomas Nicholes, 1637. 1st & only sep edn. 4to. [2 ff],25,[1] pp,[9 ff]. Lge fldg plan. Sm repr to title. Later calf, inner dentelles gilt, edges sl worn. STC 7357.
(Ramer) **$1,250 [≈ £781]**

Dupin, Charles
- A Tour through the Naval and Military Establishments of Great Britain, in the years 1816-17-18-19 and 1820 ... London: for Sir

Richard Phillips, 1822. 1st English edn. 8vo. iv, 116 pp. 2 plates (1 browned around 1 fold & reprd). Rec paper cvrd bds.
(Young's) **£35 [≈ $56]**
- Two Excursions to the Ports of England, Scotland, and Ireland, in 1816, 1817, and 1818; with a Description of the Breakwater at Plymouth, and of the Caledonian Canal ... London: Sir Richard Phillips, 1819. 1st English edn. 108 pp. 2 plates (1 cold). Rec half calf. *(Young's)* **£48 [≈ $76]**

Durand, A.
- The Making of a Frontier. Five Year's Experiences and Adventures in Gilgit, Hunza, Nagar, Chitral and the Eastern Hindu Kush. London: 1900. 298 pp. Map, port, ills. Orig cloth, recased, new endpapers.
(Trophy Room Books) **$275 [≈ £171]**

Durand, J.P.L.
- A Voyage to Senegal ... London: Richard Phillips, 1806. 181,index pp. Fldg frontis map, 6 plates. Scattered foxing, some offsetting from plates. Mod half cloth, t.e.g.
(Reese) **$200 [≈ £125]**

Durbin, John P.
- Observations in the East. Chiefly in Egypt, Palestine, Syria, and Asia Minor. New York: Harper, 1847. 2 vols. 12mo. xi,347; x, 299 pp. Num tissued engvs & maps. Sl damp stain at crnr. Contemp calf.
(Terramedia) **$80 [≈ £50]**

Dutt, William
- The Norfolk Broads. London: 1903. 1st edn. 8vo. viii,379 pp. 48 cold & 29 b/w ills by Frank Southgate. Foredge spotted. Orig blue cloth gilt. *(Gough)* **£45 [≈ $72]**

Dwight, Nathaniel
- A Short but Comprehensive System of the Geography of the World: by Way of Question and Answer ... Seventh Connecticut Edition ... Hartford: 1807. 216 pp. 12mo. Half calf & paper over bds, rubbed. *(Reese)* **$40 [≈ £25]**

Eachard, Laurence
- See Echard, Laurence.

Eardley-Wilmot, Sainthill
- Forest Life and Sport in India. New York & London: Longmans & Edward Arnold, [1910]. 1st edn. 8vo. vii,324 pp. Frontis, plates. Orig pict red cloth gilt, covers spotted & discold. *(Terramedia)* **$75 [≈ £46]**

Earhart, Amelia
- The Fun of It. Random Records of my own Flying and of Women in Aviation. New York: Harcourt, Brace, (1932). 6th printing. x,220 pp. Frontis, 30 plates. Orig cloth. Dw. Sgnd by the author on front endpaper.
(Berkelouw) **$300 [≈£187]**

Earl, George Windsor
- The Eastern Seas, or Voyages and Adventures in the Indian Archipelago, in 1832-33-34 ... London: Wm. A. Allen, 1837. 1st edn. 8vo. xii,461 pp. 4 fldg maps. Later cloth & bds, orig spine title laid down.
(Schoyer) **$200 [≈£125]**

Earle, Augustus
- A Narrative of Nine Month's Residence in New Zealand, in 1827; together with a Journal of a Residence in Tristan D'Acunha ... London: Longman ..., 1832. 1st edn. 8vo. xi, 371, 16 advt pp. 7 aquatint plates (sl foxing). Half mor gilt.
(Adelson) **$550 [≈£343]**

The Earthquake of Juan Fernandez ...
- See Sutcliffe, Thomas.

Earwaker, J.P.
- East Cheshire Past and Present ... London: for the author, 1877. 1st edn. 2 vols. Lge thick 4to. 253 plates & ills. Orig cloth gilt, crnrs bumped. *(Hollett)* **£120 [≈$192]**

Eastern Hospitals and English Nurses ...
- See Taylor, Fanny M.

Eastman, George
- Chronicles of an African Trip. Privately ptd: 1927. 1st edn. Tall 8vo. 87 pp. 26 photo plates. Minor general wear. Author's inscrptn. *(Terramedia)* **$60 [≈£37]**
- Chronicles of an African Trip. Privately printed: 1927. 8vo. Ills. Orig cloth backed bds. Pres letter from the chairman of Kodak inserted. *(Grayling)* **£65 [≈$104]**

Easton, John
- An Unfrequented Highway, Through Sikkim and Tibet to Chumolaori. London: Scholartis Press, 1928. One of 960. 4to. xii,134 pp. 16 plates. Orig red cloth, spine sl faded.
(Karmiole) **$150 [≈£93]**

Ebers, G.
- Egypt: Descriptive, Historical and Picturesque. Translated from the Original German by Clara Bell. London & New York: Cassell, Petter, Galpin, [ca 1878]. 2 vols.

Folio. xxiv,314; xxii,388 pp. Num plates & ills. Orig cloth gilt, a.e.g., spine ends frayed, edges rubbed.
(Worldwide Antiqu'n) **$125 [≈£78]**
- Egypt: Descriptive, Historical and Picturesque. Translated from the Original German by Clara Bell. London, Paris, Melbourne: Cassell, [ca 1878]. 1st edn. 2 vols. Folio. Num engvs. Orig cloth gilt, a.e.g., edges sl rubbed & soiled, externally unmarked ex-lib *(Worldwide Antiqu'n)* **$125 [≈£78]**
- Egypt. Descriptive, Historical and Picturesque. Translated from the Original German by Clara Bell ... London & New York: Cassell, [1880-83]. 1st edn. 2 vols. Folio. 314; 388 pp. Num plates & ills. Contemp half mor, gilt dec spine, a.e.g., sl rubbed. *(Terramedia)* **$300 [≈£187]**

Echard, Laurence
- The Classical Geographical Dictionary ... London: for J. Tonson ..., 1715. 1st edn. 12mo. Unpaginated. Rec half calf.
(Young's) **£48 [≈$76]**
- The Gazetteer's: or Newsman's Interpreter. Being a Geographical Index ... London: for Tho. Salusbury, 1693. 2nd edn. 12mo. Contemp calf, gilt spine, short crack in 1 jnt, sl rubbed. Wing E.145.
(Young's) **£120 [≈$192]**
- The Gazetteer's: or Newsman's Interpreter. Being a Geographical Index ... Seventh Edition ... London: for John Nicholson & Samuel Ballard, 1704. 12mo. [376] pp. Orig sheep, rebacked. *(Bickersteth)* **£55 [≈$88]**
- The Gazetteer's, or Newsman's Interpreter. Being a Geographical Index of all the Considerable Provinces, Cities ... in Europe ... Asia, Africa and America ... London: for S. Ballard ..., 1741. 15th & 8th edns. 2 parts in one vol. 8vo. Old calf, raised bands.
(Young's) **£46 [≈$73]**
- The Gazetteer's: or Newsman's Interpreter. Being a Geographical Index ... Sixteenth Edition. 1744. [With the] ... Second Part ... Ninth Edition. 1744. 2 parts in one vol. 12mo. [276]; [228] pp. Orig sheep, rebacked. *(Bickersteth)* **£38 [≈$60]**

Eddis, William
- Letters from America, Historical and Descriptive; comprising Occurrences from 1769, to 1777, inclusive. London: for the author ..., 1792. Title,xii,455 pp, errata & subscribers list, addendum. Occas hint of foxing. Later 3 qtr calf, spine relaid. H.C. Lodge b'plate. *(Reese)* **$675 [≈£421]**

Eddy, John W.
- Hunting the Alaska Brown Bear. The Story of a Sportsman's Adventures in an Unknown Valley after the Largest Carnivorous Animal in the World. New York & London: Putnam's, 1930. 1st edn. 8vo. xv,253 pp. Maps, ills. Orig cloth, spine sl faded. Author's pres copy.
                    (Terramedia) **$150 [≈ £93]**

Edrehi, Moses
- An Historical Account of the Ten Tribes. Settled Beyond the River Sambatyon, in the East ... Philadelphia: Isaac Edrehi, 5613 [1853]. 8vo. 290,[40] pp. Frontis. Orig purple cloth, crnrs sl rubbed.
                    (Karmiole) **$125 [≈ £78]**

Edwardes, Charles
- Letters from Crete. Letters Written during the Spring of 1886. London: Bentley, 1887. 8vo. xiv,394 pp. Cloth.
                    (Zeno) **£67.50 [≈ $108]**

Edwardes, Herbert B.
- A Year on the Punjab Frontier in 1848-9. London: 1851. 1st edn. 2 vols. 607; 734 pp. 2 frontis (cold in vol 2), 6 other plates inc 2 fldg & 2 cold, 3 fldg plans & facs, fldg litho map. Half leather.
                    (Trophy Room Books) **$700 [≈ £437]**
- A Year on the Punjab Frontier, in 1848-9. London: Bentley, 1851. 1st edn. 2 vols. 8vo. 2 maps, 7 plates (4 cold). Half mor gilt.
                    (Hollett) **£140 [≈ $224]**

Edwards, Amelia B.
- A Midsummer Ramble in the Dolomites. London: Routledge, 1889. 2nd edn. xxiv, 389 pp. Cold fldg map, 9 plates, 18 text ills. Prize label on pastedown. Orig pict blue cloth gilt & silvered.   *(Hollett)* **£75 [≈ $120]**
- Pharaohs, Fellahs and Explorers. New York: Harper, 1891. 1st edn. 8vo. xviii,325 pp. Num plates & text ills. Orig cloth, edges a little rubbed, back cvr sl soiled.
                    (Worldwide Antiqu'n) **$28 [≈ £17]**
- Pharaohs, Fellahs and Explorers. New York: Harper, 1892. xix,[1],325,advt pp. Num plates & text ills. Orig dec cloth gilt, minor shelf wear & soiling. *(Parmer)* **$110 [≈ £68]**
- A Thousand Miles up the Nile. London: Longmans, Green, 1877. 1st edn. xxv,732 pp. 2 fldg maps, frontis, 70 plates, num text figs. Some re-tipped pp sl skewed. Three qtr leather & cloth, orig gilt dec spine laid in, crnrs worn.   *(Parmer)* **$250 [≈ £156]**
- A Thousand Miles Up the Nile. London: Routledge, 1889. 2nd edn. 8vo. xxviii,499 pp.

Num ills. V sl foxing. Orig pict dec cloth, sl rubbed.   *(Worldwide Antiqu'n)* **$28 [≈ £17]**
- A Thousand Miles Up the Nile. London & Glasgow: Routledge, 1890. Sm 4to. xxvii,499 pp. Num ills. Orig pict dec cloth, sl rubbed.
                    (Worldwide Antiqu'n) **$32 [≈ £20]**
- A Thousand Miles up the Nile. London: Routledge, 1899. Lge 8vo. 499 pp. Num plates & ills. Orig pict tan cloth.
                    (Terramedia) **$50 [≈ £31]**
- Untrodden Peaks and Unfrequented Valleys: a Midsummer Ramble in the Dolomites. London: 1873. 1st edn. 8vo. xxvi, 385, [1 blank] pp. Fldg map, 9 full-page & 18 other ills. Sl marking. Orig green cloth, worn, spine ends & jnts a little torn.
                    (Bow Windows) **£150 [≈ $240]**

Edwards, Bryan
- A Historical Survey of the French Colony in the Island of St. Domingo ... and ... Transactions of the British Army in that Island to the end of 1794. London: 1797. 1st edn. 4to. xxiii,247 pp. Fldg map. Few sm marg reprs, perf lib stamp. New period style calf, uncut.   *(Young's)* **£150 [≈ $240]**
- The History Civil and Commercial, of the British Colonies in the West Indies ... London: 1798. Sm 4to. [v]-xvi, 373, [7] pp. Half-title. Fldg map, frontis. Sl soiling, v good ex-lib. Mottled calf, hinges sl worn, hd of spine chipped.   *(Reese)* **$350 [≈ £218]**
- The History, Civil and Commercial, of the British Colonies in the West Indies. London: 1801. 3rd edn. 3 vols. 8vo. xxiv,xxiii, 576; viii, 617; xxxii, 477 pp. 22 maps & plates. Some inner marg stains to plates vol 1. Marg perf lib stamps. New period style calf.
                    (Young's) **£400 [≈ $640]**
- The Proceedings of the Governor and Assembly of Jamaica, in regard to the Maroon Negroes ... prefixed, an Introductory Account ... of the Maroons ... London: Stockdale, 1796. 1st edn. 8vo. lxxxix,[i], 109,[1 advt] pp. Frontis. Contemp calf, rubbed, spine worn.
                    (Frew Mackenzie) **£220 [≈ $352]**

Edwards, Deltus M.
- The Toll of the Arctic Seas. New York & London: Henry Holt, 1910. 1st edn. 8vo. x,449 pp. 4 maps, 24 plates. Orig red cloth.
                    (Parmer) **$95 [≈ £59]**

Edwards, George Wharton
- Alsace-Lorraine. Philadelphia: Penn, [1918]. 4to. 344 pp. Cold frontis, num tissued plates, many cold. Occas sl foxing. Orig dec blue cloth, sl dulled. *(Terramedia)* **$25 [≈ £15]**
- Holland of Today. New York: Moffat, 1909.

2nd printing. 4to. xi,217 pp. Cold frontis, 55 plates, many tissued & cold. Orig dark green cloth with heavily embossed pict on front cvr & spine. *(Terramedia)* **$50 [≈ £31]**
- Vanished Halls and Cathedrals of France. London: Skeffington, 1917. 4to. 324 pp. 32 cold & b/w plates, tissues. Orig elab gilt blue cloth, t.e.g. *(Piccadilly)* **£35 [≈ $56]**
- Vanished Towers and Chimes of Flanders. Philadelphia: Penn, 1916. 1st edn. Tall 4to. 211,1 pp. Cold frontis, engvd cold title, 29 other tissued plates, mostly cold, some tinted. Orig gilt dec pict green cloth.
(Terramedia) **$40 [≈ £25]**

Edwards, John
- The Tour of the Dove; or a Visit to Dovedale, &c. A Poem ... Second Edition. London: Longman ..., [1825?]. Orig ptd bds, backstrip v worn. *(Waterfield's)* **£20 [≈ $32]**

Edwards, Tudor
- British Cities - Bristol. London: Batsford, 1951. 1st edn. Num photo ills. Orig bndg. Dw by Brian Cook. *(Old Cathay)* **£17 [≈ $27]**

Egan, Howard
- Pioneering the West, 1846 to 1878. Richmond, Ut.: 1917. 302 pp. Cloth.
(Reese) **$125 [≈ £78]**

Egan, P.M.
- History, Guide and Directory of the County and City of Waterford. Kilkenny: Egan, 1893. Ca 800 pp. Orig bndg.
(Emerald Isle) **£75 [≈ $120]**

Elder, William
- Biography of Elisha Kent Kane. Philadelphia: Childs & Peterson, 1858. 416, subscribers pp. Orig gilt titled brown cloth, wear & chipping to spine ends, sl rubbed.
(Parmer) **$40 [≈ £25]**

Elizabeth [Tonna, later Phelan], Charlotte
- Letters from Ireland. MDCCCXXXVII. By Charlotte Elizabeth. London: Seeley ..., 1838. Only edn. 8vo. [vi],436 pp. Contemp half mor, a little rubbed. *(Young's)* **£42 [≈ $67]**
- Letters from Ireland MDCCCXXXVII. London: Seeley & Burnside, 1838. 1st edn. 8vo. 4 advt pp at end. Orig brown cloth, backstrip laid down, cloth marked.
(Clark) **£36 [≈ $57]**

Elkington, E. Way
- The Savage South Seas. Painted by Norman H. Hardie. London: A. & C. Black Colour Books, Twenty Shilling Series, 1907. 1st edn.

68 cold plates. Orig dec green cloth, t.e.g., v fine. *(Old Cathay)* **£85 [≈ $136]**
- The Savage South Seas. Painted by Norman H. Hardie. London: A. & C. Black Colour Books, Twenty Shilling Series, 1907. 1st edn. 68 cold plates. Orig dec cerulean blue cloth, v minor chipping to front bd & spine.
(Old Cathay) **£75 [≈ $120]**
- The Savage South Seas. Painted by Norman H. Hardie. London: A. & C. Black Colour Books, Twenty Shilling Series, 1907. 1st edn. 68 cold plates. Orig dec cloth, shaken.
(Old Cathay) **£39 [≈ $62]**

Elliadi, M.N.
- Crete, Past and Present. With Additional Chapters by Sir Arthur Evans ... London: Heath Cranton, 1933. 8vo. 224 pp. Lge fldg map, num photos. Orig blue cloth. Dw reprd.
(Piccadilly) **£25 [≈ $40]**

Ellicott, Andrew
- The Journal ... for Determining the Boundary between the United States and the Possessions of His Catholic Majesty in America ... Philadelphia: 1803 [sic]. 1st edn. 4to. 299,151,[1] pp. Errata leaf. 14 maps (some reprs). Browning of text. Contemp bds, rebacked with leather.
(M & S Rare Books) **$2,200 [≈ £1,375]**
- The Journal ... for Determining the Boundary between the U.S. and the Possessions of His Catholic Majesty. Philadelphia: William Fry, 1814 [sic]. 1st edn. 4to. 299, 151,errata pp. 14 fldg maps & charts. Contemp calf, rebacked.
(Jenkins) **$2,750 [≈ £1,718]**

Elliot, Charles W.
- Remarkable Characters and Places of the Holy Land ... Hartford: Burr ..., 1867. 1st edn. 8vo. 640 pp. Cold map, 12 steel engvd plates. Sl foxing. Half mor, sl rubbed, spine sl discold. *(Worldwide Antiqu'n)* **$95 [≈ £59]**

Elliot, G.F. Scott
- A Naturalist in Mid-Africa. Being an Account of a Journey to the Mountains of the Moon & Tanganyika. London: 1896. 1st edn. 8vo. xvi,413 pp. 3 lge cold fldg maps, frontis, num views. Orig pict brown cloth gilt, sl rubbed, front hinge cracked internally.
(Terramedia) **$650 [≈ £406]**

Elliott, Grace Dalrymple
- Journal of My Life during the French Revolution. London: Bentley, 1859. 1st edn. 8vo. 28 pp ctlg. Port frontis, 2 other port plates. Occas minor spotting. Orig pink blind stamped cloth, gilt spine, extremities sl worn.
(Clark) **£35 [≈ $56]**

Elliott, Henry
- Our Arctic Province. Alaska & the Seal Islands. New York: Scribner's, 1886. 8vo. 465 pp. Lge fldg map, num plates. Orig pict black cloth, hinges sl shaken, sl worn. Author's pres copy to John A. Ryder & orig port drawing of author by Ryder tipped-in.
(Terramedia) **$200 [≈ £125]**

Elliott, Robert
- Views of the East; comprising India, Canton, and the Shores of the Red Sea ... London: Fisher, 1833. 1st edn. 2 vols. Sm 4to. 240 pp. 59 (of 60) steel engvd views. Contemp green mor & mrbld bds.
(Worldwide Antiqu'n) **$225 [≈ £140]**

Ellis, Arthur Charles
- An Historical Survey of Torquay ... Torquay: [1930]. 2nd edn. 4to. Num ills. Orig cloth.
(Ambra) **£60 [≈ $96]**

Ellis, Henry
- Journal of the Proceedings of the Late Embassy to China ... London: Murray, 1817. 1st edn. 4to. 526 pp, errata leaf. 3 maps (1 with sm tear without loss), frontis port of Lord Amherst, 7 hand cold plates. Sl foxing to maps. Orig bds, rebacked in cloth.
(Heritage) **$750 [≈ £468]**
- Journal of the Proceedings of the Late Embassy to China ... London: Murray, 1817. 526 pp. Fldg map, port frontis, cold ills. Some page reprs & foxing. Half calf, rebacked.
(Lyon) **£425 [≈ $680]**

Ellis, Richard
- History of Thornbury Castle. London: 1839. 1st edn. 8vo. Addtnl litho title, 2 fldg litho plans, fldg view, 1 other plate. Contemp qtr cloth, paper bds, few marks to cvrs, sl shaken.
(Ambra) **£32 [≈ $51]**

Ellis, William
- Polynesian Researches, during a Residence of nearly Six Years in the South Sea Islands ... London: Fisher & Jackson, 1829. 1st edn. 2 vols. 8vo. xvi,536; viii,576 pp. 2 maps, 8 plates (sl foxed). Contemp half calf, green labels.
(Adelson) **$450 [≈ £281]**

Ellis, William (ed.)
- The Christian Keepsake, and Missionary Annual. 1837. London: Fisher, Son, & Co, [1837]. 1st edn. 8vo. 206,[6 advt] pp. 16 engvd plates, inc addtnl vignette title. Orig straight-grained pale brown mor, a.e.g.
(Fenning) **£45 [≈ $72]**

Ellsberg, Ed.
- Under the Red Sea Sun. New York: Dodd, Mead, 1946. 1st edn. 8vo. ix,500 pp. Orig bndg.
(Terramedia) **$60 [≈ £37]**

Elmes, James
- Metropolitan Improvements ... see Shepherd, Thomas H.

Elwin, Verrier
- The Baiga, with a Foreword by J.H. Hutton. London: 1939. 8vo. 3 maps, num plates. Orig cloth, spine sunned.   *(Farahar)* **£45 [≈ $72]**
- Bondo Highlander. Indian OUP: 1950. Roy 8vo. Cold plate, num other plates, endpaper maps. Orig cloth.   *(Farahar)* **£45 [≈ $72]**
- Maria Murder and Suicide. Second Edition. Bombay: OUP, 1950. 8vo. Num plates, endpaper maps. Orig cloth.
(Farahar) **£35 [≈ $56]**
- The Muria and their Ghotul. Bombay: OUP, 1947. Roy 8vo. Num plates, text maps. Orig cloth.   *(Farahar)* **£60 [≈ $96]**
- Myths of Middle India. Madras: OUP, 1949. 8vo. Orig cloth.   *(Farahar)* **£40 [≈ $64]**
- Phulmat of the Hills. A Tale of the Gonds. London: 1937. Cr 8vo. Orig cloth, spine sunned.   *(Farahar)* **£18 [≈ $28]**
- The Religion of an Indian Tribe. India: 1955. 1st edn. 8vo. 1 cold plate, num other plates, 2 text maps. Calico.   *(Farahar)* **£45 [≈ $72]**
- Tribal Myths of Orissa. Calcutta: OUP, 1954. 8vo. Orig cloth. *(Farahar)* **£40 [≈ $64]**

Emerson, James
- Letters from the Aegean. London: Colburn, 1829. Sole edn. 2 vols. 8vo. Fldg map (silked), aquatint frontis in vol 2. Early staining of some margs. Contemp mrbld bds, uncut, rebacked, early lib labels.
(Trebizond) **$325 [≈ £203]**

Emory, William H.
- Report on the United States & Mexican Boundary Survey. Volume 1 [only]. Washington: House of Representatives, 1857. 4to. 174 pp. 3 fldg charts, 76 plates (inc 12 cold plates & 10 steel engvs). 1 cold plate v foxed. Orig brown cloth, rebacked.
(Terramedia) **$300 [≈ £187]**

England and the English ...
- See Bulwer-Lytton, Edward George Earle, 1st Baron Lytton.

Englefield, Sir Henry C.
- A Description of the Principal Picturesque Beauties of the Antiquities and Geological

Phenomena of the Isle of Wight ... London:
1816. Large Paper. Folio. Port (spotted), 3
maps, 46 plates. Sl dampstain to 1 map. Half
calf. Baron Northwick's b'plate.
(Henly) **£450 [≈ $720]**
- A Walk through Southampton. Southampton:
T. Baker, 1801. 1st edn. 8vo. [xii],100 pp. 6
litho plates (3 tinted). Contemp half calf,
mrbld bds.   *(Gough)* **£90 [≈ $144]**

An Englishman in Paris ...
- An Englishman in Paris. Notes and
Recollections. New York: Appleton, 1892.
3rd edn. 2 vols. 8vo. xv,332; xv,352 pp. Orig
dec blue cloth gilt. *(Terramedia)* **$40 [≈ £25]**

The Englishwoman in Russia ...
- The Englishwoman in Russia ... London:
Murray, 1855. 5th thousand. 8vo. xv,350,32
advt pp. 6 plates. Orig cloth, sl 'pulled' at hd.
(Gough) **£25 [≈ $40]**

An Entire and Complete History ...
- An Entire and Complete History, Political
and Personal of the Boroughs of Great Britain
... see Oldfield, Thomas Hinton Burley.

Eothen ...
- See Kinglake, Alexander William.

Erman, Adolf
- Travels in Siberia ... Translated from the
German by W.D. Cooley. London: Longman,
Brown, 1848. 1st edn in English. 2 vols. 8vo.
xi, 495; ix, 536 pp. Fldg map. Orig brown
cloth, spine sunned & chipped at edges.
(Terramedia) **$250 [≈ £156]**

Erskine, John Elphinstone
- Journal of a Cruise among the Islands of the
Western Pacific ... London: 1853. 1st edn.
8vo. vi,[i],488,32 advt pp. Errata slip. Fldg
chart, 4 tinted lithos, 3 full page w'engvs, 11
text ills. Occas foxing. Lib blind stamp on
title. Orig cloth, spine relaid.
(Frew Mackenzie) **£300 [≈ $480]**

Erskine, Mrs Stuart
- Trans-Jordan. Some Impressions ... London:
1924. 8vo. 126,advt pp. Num ills. Some
foxing. Orig cloth.   *(Dillons)* **£18 [≈ $28]**

Essay ...
- An Essay on the Natural History of Guiana ...
see Bancroft, Edward.

Eustace, John Chetwode
- A Tour through Italy ... London: J.
Mawman, 1813. 1st edn. 2 vols. Final advt

leaf in vol 1. 8 plates in vol 1 (some foxing).
4to. Rec bds.   *(Clark)* **£90 [≈ $144]**

Evans, Estwick
- A Pedestrious Tour, of Four Thousand
Miles, through the Western States and
Territories, during the Winter and Spring of
1818 ... Concord, NH: Joseph C. Spear,
1819. 1st edn. 256 pp. W'cut frontis. Ptd bds,
backstrip worn.   *(Jenkins)* **$1,250 [≈ £781]**

Evans, G.P.
- Big-Game Shooting in Upper Burma.
London: Longmans, 1912. 8vo. ix,240 pp.
Frontis, fldg map, 10 fldg ills. Orig bndg, 2
ring marks on front cvr.
(Bates & Hindmarch) **£75 [≈ $120]**

Evans, John
- Letters written during a Tour through South
Wales in the year 1803 and at other Times ...
London: Baldwin, 1804. 8vo. Orig bds,
rebacked retaining orig ptd label.
(Waterfield's) **£90 [≈ $144]**

Evans-Pritchard,
- Witchcraft, Oracles and Magic among the
Azande. OUP: [1968]. 1st edn. 8vo. xxv,558 pp.
Ills. Orig bndg. Dw. *(Terramedia)* **$50 [≈ £31]**

Everest, Robert
- A Journey through Norway, Lapland, and
Part of Sweden ... London: Underwood,
1829. 1st edn. 8vo. Frontis, table, general
map (probably inserted), 6 cold geological
maps. Contemp calf gilt, rebacked.
(Hannas) **£190 [≈ $304]**

Everitt, E.B.
- Tour of the St. Elmo's. From the Nutmeg
State to the Golden Gate. N.p.: 1883. 227 pp.
Cloth gilt, a trifle soiled. *(Reese)* **$100 [≈ £62]**

Evermann, Barton Warren
- Investigations of the Aquatic Resources &
Fisheries of Porto Rico ... in 1889.
Washington: GPO, 1900. 1st edn. 4to. vi,350
pp. Fldg map, 49 cold plates (sev chipped at
1 crnr). Orig cloth, back hinge internally
cracked.   *(Terramedia)* **$150 [≈ £93]**

Excursions ...
- Excursions in the County of Kent / Surrey /
Sussex ... see Cromwell, T.K.

An Explanation of the Map ...
- An Explanation of the Map which delineates
that Part of the Federal Lands ... see Cutler,
Manasseh.

Faber, M.
- Sketches of the Internal State of France. Translated from the French. London: Murray ..., 1811. 8vo. xii,300 pp. Mod cloth. *(Piccadilly)* **£32 [≈ $51]**

Fabricius, Friedrich Ernst von
- The Genuine Letters of Baron Fabricius ... To Charles XII of Sweden ... Residence in Turkey. London: Becket & De Hondt, 1761. 1st English edn. 8vo. Contemp mottled calf. B'plate & sgntr of Sir James Colquhoun of Luss. *(Hannas)* **£130 [≈ $208]**

A Faggot of French Sticks ...
- See Head, Sir Francis Bond.

Fair France ...
- See Mulock, Dinah Maria.

Fairbanks, George R.
- The History and Antiquities of the City of St. Augustine, Florida ... New York: 1858. 200 pp. 7 plates. Orig cloth gilt, spine ends chipped. *(Reese)* **$125 [≈ £78]**

Fairchild, David
- Garden Islands of the Great East. Collecting Seeds from the Philippines and Netherlands India in the Junk "Cheng Ho". New York: Scribner's, 1943. 1st edn. 8vo. Frontis, plates. Some foxing on top edge. Orig cloth. Dw. *(Wreden)* **$35 [≈ £21]**

Falconer, John D.
- The Geology and Geography of Northern Nigeria. London: 1911. 1st edn. 8vo. xiv,[2], 295 pp. Lge fldg map in pocket, 4 maps, 24 plates. Orig cloth, t.e.g. *(Fenning)* **£45 [≈ $72]**

Falconer, Thomas
- Notes of a Journey through Texas and New Mexico in the Years 1841 and 1842. London: Journal of the Royal Geographic Society, 1843. [23] pp. *(Jenkins)* **$1,750 [≈ £1,093]**

Falkonberg, B.E. (B. Solymos)
- Desert Life. Recollections of an Expedition in the Soudan. London: W.H. Allen, 1880. 8vo. xi,[1],382 pp. Prize calf, edges worn, hd chipped. *(Parmer)* **$75 [≈ £46]**

Falle, Philip
- An Account of the Island of Jersey, with an Appendix of Records. To which are added Notes and Illustrations by the Rev. Edward Durell. Jersey: 1837. 1st edn. 8vo. Near contemp cloth. Sgntr on title of Sir James de Sausmarez. *(Robertshaw)* **£65 [≈ $104]**

Farini, G.
- Through the Kalahari Desert. A Journey to Lake Ngami and Back. London: 1886. 1st edn. 475 pp. Lge fldg map. Orig bndg. *(Trophy Room Books)* **$450 [≈ £281]**

Farman, Elbert E.
- Along the Nile. An Account of the Visit to Egypt of General Ulysses S. Grant and his Tour through that Country. New York: Grafton Press, 1908. Sm 8vo. xvii,339,corrigenda pp. Frontis, num photo plates. Orig green cloth gilt, sl worn. *(Terramedia)* **$40 [≈ £25]**
- Egypt and its Betrayal. New York: Grafton Press, [1908]. 1st edn. 8vo. xix,349 pp. Fldg map, frontis, num photo plates. Orig green cloth gilt. *(Terramedia)* **$75 [≈ £46]**

Farmer ...
- The Farmer's Tour ... see Young, Arthur.

Farrelly, M.J.
- The Settlement after the War in South Africa. New York: Macmillan, 1900. 8vo. xv, [1], 323 pp. Orig red cloth, some wear to spine ends & crnrs. *(Parmer)* **$60 [≈ £37]**

Farrer, Reginald
- On the Eaves of the World. London: Edwin Arnold, 1917. 1st edn. 2 vols. 8vo. xii,311; viii,328 pp. Fldg map, num photo plates. Orig blue cloth, rubbed & dulled. *(Terramedia)* **$200 [≈ £125]**
- On the Eaves of the World. London: 1917. 1st imp. 2 vols. 8vo. Map, 64 plates. Lower marg of 1 plain somewhat trimmed. Orig cloth, back cvr somewhat stained. *(Wheldon & Wesley)* **£75 [≈ $120]**
- On the Eaves of the World. London: 1926. 2nd imp. 2 vols. 8vo. Map, 64 plates. Sl foxing. Orig blue cloth, inner jnts vol 1 reprd. *(Wheldon & Wesley)* **£65 [≈ $104]**
- The Rainbow Bridge. London: Edwin Arnold, 1921. 1st edn. 8vo. xi,383 pp. Fldg map, num photo plates. Orig blue cloth, hd of spine sl chipped. *(Terramedia)* **$125 [≈ £78]**
- The Rainbow Bridge. London: 1922. 2nd imp. 8vo. xi,383 pp. Map, 16 ills. Sl foxing. Orig blue cloth. *(Wheldon & Wesley)* **£60 [≈ $96]**
- Vasanta the Beautiful, a Homily in Four Acts. Privately printed: 1913. 8vo. 84 pp. A little minor foxing. Orig wraps, cvrs trifle faded. *(Wheldon & Wesley)* **£35 [≈ $56]**

Farrer, Richard Ridley
- A Tour in Greece. 1880. Edinburgh & London: Blackwood, 1882. 1st edn. Sm 4to.

xi, 216 pp. Fldg map, 27 plates. Orig cloth, unopened, sl rubbed.
(Worldwide Antiqu'n) **$125 [≈ £78]**

Faulds, Henry
- Nine Years in Nipon Sketches of Japanese Life and Manners. London: 1887. 2nd edn. xii, [9]-304 pp. Frontis, text ills. Front free endsheet excised, a few fox marks. Contemp polished calf gilt, a.e.g. *(Reese)* **$100 [≈ £62]**

Fay, Theodore S.
- Views in New-York and its Environs ... with Historical, Topographical & Critical Illustrations ... New York: Peabody, 1831 [-34]. 1st edn. 6 parts (only, of 8). 4to. 50 pp. 12 plates (only, of 15) inc vignette title. Foxed. Contemp calf & mrbld bds.
(M & S Rare Books) **$950 [≈ £593]**

Fearnside, William Gray & Harrel, Thomas
- The Great Metropolis: or, Views and History of London in the Nineteenth Century ... Illustrated with Splendid Steel Engravings. London: D. Omer Smith, [ca 1860]. Roy 8vo. [4],219 pp. Addtnl engvd title, frontis, 33 plates (1 more than listed). Orig cloth gilt.
(Claude Cox) **£100 [≈ $160]**

Featherstonehaugh, G.W.
- A Canoe Voyage up the Minnay Sotor: With an Account of the Lead & Copper Deposits of Wisconsin ... London: Bentley, 1847. 2 vols. 8vo. xiv,416; 349 pp. 2 frontis, 2 fldg maps mtd on cloth. Late 19th c qtr mor, gilt spines, labels, by Morrel.
(Terramedia) **$900 [≈ £562]**
- Geological Report of an Examination made in 1834 of the Elevated Country between the Missouri and Red Rivers ... Washington: 1835. 8vo. 97 pp. Fldg cold section (nearly 10 feet long). Sm lib stamp in text & title verso. Rebound in qtr calf, new endpapers.
(Henly) **£120 [≈ $192]**

Fedden, Katharine & Romilly
- The Basque Country. London: A. & C. Black Colour Book, 1921. 1st edn. 24 cold ills, num text ills. Orig cloth, spine faded.
(Old Cathay) **£25 [≈ $40]**

Fell, R.
- A Tour through the Batavian Republic during the latter part of the Year 1800 ... London: for R. Phillips ..., 1801. 8vo. xii, 395, [i advt] pp. Contemp bds, uncut, crnrs worn, rebacked. *(Hollett)* **£60 [≈ $96]**

Fellowes, W.D.
- A Visit to the Monastery of La Trappe, in 1817 ...he Fourth Edition. London: Thomas M'Lean, 1823. Large Paper. Roy 8vo. xii,188 pp. 15 ills (inc 13 hand cold aquatint plates). Contemp purple mor elab gilt, a.e.g. Littlecote House copy.
(Spelman) **£400 [≈ $640]**

Fellows, Sir Charles
- A Journal written during an Excursion in Asia Minor. London: Murray, 1839. 1st edn. Roy 8vo. x,[1],347 pp. Dble-page map, 21 litho plates (sl foxed). Rec calf backed bds.
(Fenning) **£165 [≈ $264]**

Felton, Mrs
- American Life. A Narrative of Two Years' City and Country Residence in the United States. Bolton Percy: for the authoress, 1843. 3rd thousand, with an addtnl chapter. Sm 8vo. 136 pp. Fldg plan of Manhattan. Orig purple-brown cloth, a bit faded & rubbed.
(Burmester) **£65 [≈ $104]**

Felton, C.C.
- Greece, Ancient and Modern. Lectures Delivered before the Lowell Institute. Boston: Ticknor & Fields, 1867. 2 vols. Tall 8vo. vi,511; iv,549 pp. Frontis. Sl foxing. Orig cloth, sl worn.
(Worldwide Antiqu'n) **$95 [≈ £59]**

Female Life among the Mormons ...
- See Ward, M.N.

Fergusson, W.N.
- Adventure, Sport and Travel on the Tibetan Steppes. London: Constable, 1911. 1st edn. Lge 8vo. xvi,343 pp. Frontis port, 2 fldg maps, 75 ills. Mod half calf gilt.
(Hollett) **£155 [≈ $248]**
- Adventure, Sport and Travel on the Tibetan Steppes. London: 1911. 342 pp. Ills. Fine ex-lib. *(Trophy Room Books)* **$150 [≈ £93]**
- Adventure, Sport and Travel on the Tibetan Steppes. London: Constable, 1911. 8vo. xvi, 343 pp. Frontis, 2 fldg maps, num ills. Orig pict cloth.
(Bates & Hindmarch) **£175 [≈ $280]**

Fermor, Patrick Leigh
- The Traveller's Tree. A Journey through the Caribbean Islands. London: Murray, 1950. 8vo. xi,403 pp. 43 photo ills. Orig bndg.
(Bates & Hindmarch) **£24 [≈ $38]**

Ferrier, J.P.
- Caravan Journeys and Wanderings in Persia,

Afghanistan, Turkistan and Beloochistan with Historical Notices of the Countries lying between Russia and India. London: 1856. 534 pp. Lge fldg map, ills. Orig cloth.
(Trophy Room Books) **$650 [≈ £406]**
- History of the Afghans. London: 1858. 491 pp. Fldg map, map in text. Half leather.
(Trophy Room Books) **$600 [≈ £375]**

Ferriman, Z. Duckett
- Home Life in Hellas. Greece and the Greeks. London: MIlls & Boon, 1910. 8vo. [x], 338 pp. Photo ills. Orig blue cloth, dec spine faded.   *(Piccadilly)* **£25 [≈ $40]**

Ferris, Cornelia
- The Mormons at Home; with Some Incidents of Travel from Missouri to California, 1852 - 53. New York: 1856. 299 pp. Cloth, spine ends chipped, lacks front endpaper.
(Reese) **$125 [≈ £78]**

Ferris, Warren Angus
- Life in the Rocky Mountains 1830-1835. Salt Lake City: [ca 1940]. Rvsd edn. 4to. 284 pp. Frontis, fldg map, ills. Buckram gilt, a bit soiled.   *(Reese)* **$125 [≈ £78]**

Few ...
- A Few Days in Paris: Remarks Characteristic of Several Distinguished Personages. London: Wilson, 1802. 8vo. Title remargd. Wraps.   *(Rostenberg & Stern)* **$165 [≈ £103]**
- A Few Months in the East ... see Forsyth, Joseph Bell.

Field, Henry M.
- From Egypt to Japan. New York: 1877. 424 pp. Orig cloth, worn, spine ends chipped, some glue residue on rear cvr.
(Reese) **$45 [≈ £28]**
- Gibraltar. New York: Scribner's, 1888. 1st edn. 8vo. viii,139,advt pp. Frontis, plates, ills. Orig cloth, ex-lib with labels inside cvrs.
(Terramedia) **$30 [≈ £18]**
- Old Spain and New Spain. New York: 1888. 303 pp. Cold map. Orig cloth, t.e.g., spine ends sl chipped. Author's pres inscrptn.
(Reese) **$50 [≈ £31]**
- On the Desert: with a Brief Review of Recent Events in Egypt. New York: 1883. ii, 330, advt pp. Fldg cold map. Some pencil marginalia. Orig cloth, t.e.g., edgeworn, spine ends fraying, front hinge starting. Author's pres inscrptn.   *(Reese)* **$50 [≈ £31]**
- Summer Pictures: From Copenhagen to Venice. New York: 1859. 291,advt pp. Orig cloth, spotted, spine ends chipped. Author's pres copy to his sister.   *(Reese)* **$65 [≈ £40]**

Fielding, Henry
- The Journal of a Voyage to Lisbon. London: A. Millar, 1755. 1st published edn. 8vo. [ii], iv, 228 pp. Half-title removed or not bound in. Title sl wrinkled. Occas browning. Orig blue paper wraps, untrimmed, backstrip wraps largely deficient but stitching secure.
(Clark) **£250 [≈ $400]**
- The Journal of a Voyage to Lisbon. London: for A. Millar, 1755. 1st published edn. 12mo. xvii, [1],240, 193-228 pp. Some sl darkening. Contemp polished calf, spine gilt extra, spine extremities quite chipped.
(Reese) **$350 [≈ £218]**
- The Journal of a Voyage to Lisbon. Cambridge: at the Riverside Press, 1902. One of 300, this copy unnumbered. Tall 8vo. 215 pp. Port frontis, Orig cloth & bds, paper label, unopened.   *(Schoyer)* **$100 [≈ £62]**

Fielding, T.H.
- British Castles ... London: Howlett & Brimmer, 1825. 1st edn. Oblong 4to. 73 pp. 25 cold aquatint views. Contemp red half roan, rebacked.   *(Gough)* **£495 [≈ $792]**

Fife, C.W. Domville
- Savage Life in the Black Sudan. An Account of an Adventurous Journey of Exploration ... Philadelphia: 1927. 8vo. 284 pp. 2 fldg maps, frontis, num photo plates. Orig pict black cloth gilt.   *(Terramedia)* **$120 [≈ £75]**

Filson, John
- The Discovery, Settlement, and Present State of Kentucky ... London: Stockdale, 1793. 1st sep English edn. 8vo. 68 pp. Lacks the map, half-title, & advt ff. Disbound.
(Bickersteth) **£120 [≈ $192]**

Finden, W. & E.
- Landscape Illustrations of the Bible, consisting of Views of the Most Remarkable Places mentioned in the Old and New Testaments ... With Descriptions by Revd. T.H. Horne. London: Murray, 1836. 2 vols. Lge 4to. 2 engvd titles, 97 plates. Contemp half mor gilt, a.e.g.   *(Hollett)* **£260 [≈ $416]**
- The Ports Harbours and Watering Places and The Coast Scenery of Great Britain. London: 1844. 2 vols in one. 4to. Port, 2 addtnl titles, 123 plates. Contemp calf, spine relaid.
(Henly) **£450 [≈ $720]**

Findlay, F.R.N.
- Big Game Shooting and Travel in South-East Africa. London: 1903. 8vo. Fldg map, ills. Orig buckram, spine ends rubbed.
(Grayling) **£200 [≈ $320]**

- Big Game Shooting and Travel in South-East Africa. London: 1903. 313 pp. 86 ills. Orig bndg. *(Trophy Room Books)* **$500 [≈£312]**

Finlayson, Duncan
- Traits of American-Indian Life and Characters. By a Fur Trader. London: 1853. 218 pp. Three qtr leather & bds. At one time attributed to Duncan Finlayson, but now generally agreed to be by Peter Skene Ogden. *(Reese)* **$1,750 [≈£1,093]**

First Russian Railroad ...
- First Russian Railroad from St. Petersburg to Zarscoe-Selo and Pawlowsk, Established by Imperial Decree of 21st March, 1836 ... Translated from the Russian. St. Petersburg, 1837. London: Skipper & East, [March 1837]. 44 pp. Dampstain. Orig wraps, worn. *(Duck)* **£350 [≈$560]**

Fischer, Christian August
- Letters Written during a Journey to Montpelier. Performed in the Autumn of 1804. London: Richard Phillips, 1806. 87,index pp. Mod half cloth, t.e.g. *(Reese)* **$85 [≈£53]**
- Travels to Hyeres, in the South of France, performed in the Spring of 1806. London: Richard Phillips, 1806. 76 pp. Mod half cloth, t.e.g. *(Reese)* **$85 [≈£53]**

Fischer, Christian Augustus
- A Picture of Madrid: taken on the Spot. London: for J. Mawman; J.G. Bernard, printer, 1808. 1st edn in English. 8vo. Sl foxing. Orig light blue bds, drab paper backstrip, ptd paper label, unopened. *(Ximenes)* **$350 [≈£218]**

Fisher, Alexander
- A Journal of a Voyage of Discovery to the Arctic Regions, in His Majesty's Ships Hecla and Gripper, in the Years 1819 & 1820. London: Longman ..., 1821. 3rd edn. 8vo. xi, 320 pp. Fldg chart (torn in marg), map, 5 w'cut ills. Orig bds, uncut. *(Young's)* **£150 [≈$240]**

Fisher, Ruth B.
- On the Borders of Pigmy Land. London: Marshall Bros, [ca 1905]. 3rd edn. 8vo. ix, [1],215 pp. 32 photo plates. Occas sl foxing. Orig green cloth, crnrs bumped, rubbed. *(Parmer)* **$35 [≈£21]**

Fisk, James Liberty
- Expedition of Captain Fisk to the Rocky Mountains. Letter from the Secretary of War ... Washington: 38th Cong. 1st Sess., 1864.

38 pp. Disbound. *(Reese)* **$125 [≈£78]**

Fisk, Wilbur
- Travels on the Continent of Europe ... Third Edition. New York: 1838. Thick 8vo. xv, [9]-688 pp. Plates. Light to heavy foxing, marg dampstain. Orig calf, scuffed, 1 crnr gnawed. *(Reese)* **$85 [≈£53]**

Fittler, James & Nattes, John Claude
- Scotia Depicta; or, the Antiquities, Castles, Public Buildings ... of Scotland ... London: Bensley, 1804. Oblong folio. 6 pp prelim text, subscribers' leaf. Frontis, 48 engvd plates, each with ptd text, engvd tailpiece. Contemp green mor, ft of spine reprd. *(Spelman)* **£450 [≈$720]**

Fitz-Stephen, William
- Fitz-Stephen's Description of the City of London, Newly translated out of the Latin original ... By an Antiquary [Samuel Pegge, the elder]. London: for B. White, 1772. 4to. ix, 81 pp. Disbound. *(Bickersteth)* **£50 [≈$80]**

Fitzgerald, E.A.
- The Highest Andes. A Record of the First Ascent of Aconcagua & Tupungato in Argentina and the Exploration of the Surrounding Valleys ... New York: Scribner's, 1899. 1st edn. Lge 8vo. xvi,390 pp. 2 fldg cold maps, frontis, num other plates. Orig pict cloth gilt. *(Terramedia)* **$200 [≈£125]**

Fitzgerald, Sybil
- In the Track of the Moors. Sketches in Spain and Northern Africa. London: Dent, 1905. 1st edn. 4to. x,204 pp. 63 cold plates & 42 text ills by August Fitzgerald. Orig pict cloth, t.e.g., sl rubbed. *(Worldwide Antiqu'n)* **$60 [≈£37]**
- In the Track of the Moors. Sketches in Spain and Northern Africa. London: Dent, 1905. Cold frontis, 62 cold plates. Orig dec cloth, backstrip sunned, bds sl stained. *(John Smith)* **£40 [≈$64]**

Fitzgerald, Sybil & Augustine
- Naples. London: A. & C. Black Colour Books, Twenty Shilling Series, 1904. 1st edn. 80 cold plates. Orig dec cloth, t.e.g., spine v sl faded as usual. *(Old Cathay)* **£50 [≈$80]**
- Naples. London: A. & C. Black Colour Books, Twenty Shilling Series, 1904. 1st edn. 80 cold plates. Orig dec cloth, t.e.g., lower half of spine worn. *(Old Cathay)* **£23 [≈$36]**

Fitzpatrick, J.P.
- The Transvaal from Within. A Private Record of Public Affairs. New York: Stokes, 1899. 1st edn. 8vo. xiv,452 pp. Orig blue cloth, some wear & spotting.
(Parmer) **$50 [≃ £31]**

Flack, A.
- A Hunter's Experiences in the Southern States of America ... London: 1866. 8vo. Crnr torn from endpaper. Orig cloth, spine relaid. Sgnd by author on title.
(Grayling) **£85 [≃ $136]**

Fletcher, F.W.F.
- Sport on the Nilgiris and in Wynaad. London: 1911. 1st edn. 8vo. Map, 18 plates. Orig cloth. *(Robertshaw)* **£40 [≃ $64]**
- Sport on the Nilgiris and Wynaad. London: 1911. 8vo. Fldg map, photo plates. Orig cloth, sl marked & rubbed.
(Grayling) **£25 [≃ $40]**

Fletcher, James
- The History of Poland ... With a Narrative of the Recent Events ... London: Cochrane & Pickersgill, 1831. 1st edn. 8vo. 428,16 ctlg pp. Fldg map (with one inch tear), 2 ports (foxed). Silk over bds, spine relaid, crnrs bumped. *(Schoyer)* **$110 [≃ £68]**

Flinders, Matthew
- Narrative of His Voyage in the Schooner Francis ... Golden Cockerel Press: 1946. One of 750. Folio. 102 pp. Engvs by John Buckland Wright. Orig green buckram, t.e.g.
(Bow Windows) **£205 [≃ $328]**

Floyer, E.
- Unexplored Baluchistan. London: 1882. 507 pp. Fldg map, mtd photo frontis, ills. Orig cloth, nice ex-lib, recased, new endpapers.
(Trophy Room Books) **$750 [≃ £468]**

Foa, E.
- After Big Game in Central Africa. London: 1899. 278 pp. Map, ills. Orig bndg.
(Trophy Room Books) **$750 [≃ £468]**

Fogg, William Perry
- Arabistan: or the Land of "The Arabian Nights." Being Travels through Egypt, Arabia, and Persia, to Bagdad. Hartford &c.: by subscription only, 1875. 1st edn. Sm 8vo. 350 pp. 88 ills. Orig cloth, sl rubbed, spine ends sl frayed.
(Worldwide Antiqu'n) **$125 [≃ £78]**
- The Land of 'The Arabian Nights'. Being Travels through Egypt, Arabia and Persia to

Baghdad. New York: Scribner's, 1882. 1st Amer edn. Sm 8vo. [xxii],350,advt pp. Frontis, num plates & ills. Lib stamp on title. Orig pict red cloth gilt, sl shaken.
(Terramedia) **$20 [≃ £12]**

Folsom, George F.
- Mexico in 1842 ... To which is added an Account of Texas and Yucatan, and of the Santa Fe Expedition. New York: 1842. 1st edn. 256 pp. Lacks map. Orig cloth, gilt spine, extremities sl chipped.
(Jenkins) **$750 [≃ £468]**

Foran, W.
- African Odyssey. The Life of Verney Lovett Cameron. London: 1937. 389 pp. Ills. Orig bndg. *(Trophy Room Books)* **$250 [≃ £156]**

Forbes, Alexander
- Northernmost Labrador Mapped From the Air. New York: Amer Geog Soc, 1938. 1st edn. xix, [1], 255 pp. Frontis, ills. Orig grey cloth, some age-darkening to spine & map case. *(Parmer)* **$65 [≃ £40]**

Forbes, Allan
- Towns of New England and Old England, Ireland and Scotland. Connecting Links between Cities and Towns of New England and Those of the Same Name in England ... New York: 1921. 1st book edn. 4to. 225, 225 pp. Three qtr crushed levant, t.e.g., light line across cvr. *(Schoyer)* **$85 [≃ £53]**

Forbes, Sir Charles Stewart
- Iceland; its Volcanoes, Geysers, and Glaciers. London: Murray, 1860. 1st edn. 8vo. Fldg map, title vignette, 8 plates inc frontis, text ills. Contemp half calf, upper jnt weak.
(Hannas) **£120 [≃ $192]**

Forbes, E.F.
- Five Years in China. From 1842 to 1847. With an Account of the Occupation of the Islands of Lubuan and Borneo ... London: Bentley, 1848. 1st edn. 8vo. x,405 pp. Hand cold frontis, 21 other ills. Qtr mor, rebacked.
(Terramedia) **$400 [≃ £250]**

Forbes, Henry O.
- A Naturalist's Wanderings in the Eastern Archipelago. A Narrative of Travel and Exploration from 1878 to 1883. New York: 1885. 8vo. 6 maps (3 fldg), 2 maps in text, cold frontis, plates. Orig pict cloth gilt, sm tear at hd of spine. *(Farahar)* **£175 [≃ $280]**

Forbes, James David
- Norway and Its Glaciers, visited in 1851.

Edinburgh: Adam & Charles Black, 1853. 1st edn. Lge 8vo. Fldg cold map, 11 chromolitho plates, 1 plain plate, text ills. Half-title, errata leaf. Orig cloth, uncut, sl snags at spine ends. Labels removed from endpapers.
(Hannas) **£180 [≈ $288]**

Forbes, Rosita
- Conflict Angora to Afghanistan. London: Cassell, 1931. 8vo. xxvi,302 pp. 48 photo ills. Orig bndg. *(Bates & Hindmarch)* **£40 [≈ $64]**
- From Red Sea to Blue Nile: Abyssinian Adventure. New York: McCauley Co, [1925]. 1st edn. 8vo. 386 pp. Frontis, num photo plates. Orig pict blue cloth gilt. Author's inscrptn & photo. *(Terramedia)* **$50 [≈ £31]**
- Secret of the Sahara: Kufara. New York: Doran, 1921. fldg map, 54 photo ills. Orig dec green cloth over bds, bds sl worn at crnrs. Dw sl chipped & torn. *(Parmer)* **$46 [≈ £28]**

Forbes, W. Cameron
- The Philippine Islands. Boston & New York: Houghton, Mifflin, 1928. 1st edn. 2 vols. 8vo. xiv,620; vii,638 pp. Fldg map in pocket. Num plates. Contemp buckram, a bit rubbed. Lib bookplate. *(Terramedia)* **$100 [≈ £62]**

Ford, Eric H.
- Shepton Mallet Somerset. An Historical and Postal Survey. Bournemouth: bound & published by the author, 1958. One of 200. 8vo. Orig bndg. *(Ambra)* **£28 [≈ $44]**

Ford, Ford Madox
- Great Trade Route. New York: OUP, 1937. 1st iss. 408 pp. Cold frontis, b/w ills. Orig cloth, sl shelfwear. *(Parmer)* **$95 [≈ £59]**

Ford, Richard
- Gatherings from Spain. By the Author of the Handbook of Spain ... New Edition. London: Murray, 1851. Sm 8vo. x,342,32 advt pp. Occas marks. Sev crnr tips folded. Orig red embossed cloth, dull & marked, crnr tips & spine ends sl rubbed.
(Bow Windows) **£65 [≈ $104]**

Forester, Thomas
- Norway and Its Scenery, comprising the Journal of a Tour by Edward Price ... and a Road-Book for Tourists. London: 1853. 1st edn. 8vo. 21 mezzotint plates engvd by David Lucas. Early prize calf gilt.
(Robertshaw) **£50 [≈ $80]**
- Norway and Its Scenery ... Journal of a Tour by Edward Price. London: Bohn, 1853. 1st edn. 8vo. 21 plates. Contemp half calf.
(Gough) **£50 [≈ $80]**

Formilli, C.T.G.
- The Stones of Italy. London: A. & C. Black, 1927. 8vo. xvi,247 pp. Map, 32 cold ills. Edges sl foxed. Orig dec grey cloth.
(Piccadilly) **£25 [≈ $40]**

Forster, Charles
- Sinai Photographed, or Contemporary Records of Israel in the Wilderness, with an Appendix. London: Bentley, 1862. 1st edn. Folio. xx, 348 pp. Map, 19 mtd photos, 5 plates (4 tinted), 1 glyphograph plate. Minor lib marks. Orig cloth, moderate wear.
(Worldwide Antiqu'n) **$650 [≈ £406]**

Forster, John Reinold
- Observations made during a Voyage Round the World ... London: G. Robinson, 1778. 1st edn. 4to. Title,dedic, [i]-iii,[i]-iv, [9]-649, errata, subscribers pp. Fldg map, fldg chart. New cloth backed bds, uncut.
(Frew Mackenzie) **£1,500 [≈ $2,400]**

Forsyth, J.
- The Highlands of Central India. Notes on their Forests and Wild Tribes, Natural History and Sports. New York: Dutton, 1920. New edn. 8vo. xi,387 pp. Fldg map, frontis, plates. Orig red cloth.
(Terramedia) **$100 [≈ £62]**

Forsyth, Joseph
- Remarks on Antiquities, Arts, and Letters during an Excursion in Italy in the Years 1802 and 1803. London: for T. Cadell, 1813. 1st edn. 8vo. [vii],387 pp. Contemp half calf.
(Young's) **£70 [≈ $112]**
- Remarks on Antiquities, Arts, and Letters during an Excursion in Italy, in the Years 1802 and 1803. Second Edition. London: Murray, 1816. 2nd edn, with a biographical notice. 8vo. Contemp vellum, gilt spine, mor label, bds sl bowed, jnt ends split, label chipped. *(Clark)* **£45 [≈ $72]**

Forsyth, Joseph Bell
- A Few Months in the East; or, a Glimpse of the Red, the Dead, and the Black Seas. By a Canadian. Quebec & London: 1861. [14],181 pp. 4 cold litho plates. Orig cloth gilt, spine ends chipped, sm crack in 1 jnt. Author's pres inscrptn. *(Reese)* **$200 [≈ £125]**

Fortune, Robert
- A Residence among the Chinese: Inland, on the Coast, and at Sea ... A Third Visit to China from 1853 to 1856 ... London: Murray, 1857. 1st edn. 8vo. [xvi],440 pp. Frontis, 5 plates, 17 text ills. Contemp half calf, rebacked. *(Bickersteth)* **£145 [≈ $232]**

- A Residence among the Chinese: Inland, on the Coast, and at Sea ... A Third Visit to China from 1853 to 1856 ... London: Murray, 1857. 1st edn. xvi,440 pp. 5 w'engvd plates, 18 vignettes. Occas sl marg soiling. Orig cloth, rubbed & faded, recased.
  (Claude Cox) **£75 [≈ $120]**
- Three Years' Wanderings in the Northern Provinces of China ... Second Edition. London: Murray, 1847. xxiv,[2],420,[16 ctlg dated June 1847] pp. Map, addtnl pict title, 3 litho plates (spotted), ills. Orig cloth, uncut, rebacked, most of orig backstrip preserved.
  (Claude Cox) **£75 [≈ $120]**
- Yedo and Peking. A Narrative of a Journey to the Capitals of Japan and China. London: 1863. 8vo. xvi,395 pp. Map, 9 plates. Mod half calf. *(Wheldon & Wesley)* **£150 [≈ $240]**

Forty Days in the Desert ...
- See Bartlett, W.H.

Foster, Birket
- In Rustic England. Painted by Birket Foster. With Critical Notes by A.B. Daryll, edited by W. Shaw Sparrow. London: Hodder & Stoughton, 1906. 25 cold plates. Orig bndg.
  (Old Cathay) **£55 [≈ $88]**

Fothergill, Edward
- Five Years in the Sudan. London: 1911. 323 pp. Ills. Orig bndg.
  (Trophy Room Books) **$250 [≈ £156]**
- Five Years in the Sudan. New York: Appleton, 1911. 1st Amer edn. 8vo. xvi,327 pp. Tissued frontis, num photo plates. Orig orange maroon cloth.
  (Terramedia) **$200 [≈ £125]**

Fox, Sir Frank
- Australia. Painted by Percy F.S. Spence. London: A. & C. Black Colour Books, Twenty Shilling Series, 1910. 1st edn. Cold plates. Orig dec cloth, v fine.
  (Old Cathay) **£100 [≈ $160]**
- Australia. Painted by Percy F.S. Spence. London: A. & C. Black Colour Books, Twenty Shilling Series, 1910. 1st edn. Cold plates. Orig dec cloth, fine.
  (Old Cathay) **£90 [≈ $144]**
- Australia. Painted by Percy F.S. Spence. London: A. & C. Black Colour Books, Twenty Shilling Series, 1910. 1st edn. Cold plates. Orig dec cloth, crnrs bruised.
  (Old Cathay) **£85 [≈ $136]**
- Australia. Illustrated by Percy F.S. Spence and F.K. Giles. London: A. & C. Black, 1927. 2nd edn. 32 cold plates. Orig cloth.
  (Old Cathay) **£25 [≈ $40]**

- England. London: A. & C. Black Colour Books, Twenty Shilling Series, 1918. 1st edn thus. 64 cold plates. Orig dec cloth, inscrptn on f.e.p.
  (Old Cathay) **£45 [≈ $72]**
- Italy. London: A. & C. Black Colour Book, 1915. 1st edn. 32 cold plates. Orig plain red gilt dec cloth, spine faded, occas spotting to bds.
  (Old Cathay) **£23 [≈ $36]**
- Switzerland. London: A. & C. Black Colour Book, 1915. 1st edn. 32 cold plates. Orig red cloth gilt, minor fading to spine & rear bd.
  (Old Cathay) **£23 [≈ $36]**
- Switzerland. Painted by J. & M. Hardwicke Lewis, A. D. McCormick ... London: A. & C. Black Colour Books, Twenty Shilling Series, 1917. 2nd edn. 64 cold plates. Orig cloth dec with alpine landscape.
  (Old Cathay) **£45 [≈ $72]**
- Switzerland. With 32 Illustrations in Colour by J. & M. Hardwicke Lewis, A. D. McCormick ... London: A. & C. Black, 1930. Orig red cloth gilt, spine sl faded.
  (Sanders) **£18 [≈ $28]**

Fox, Robert
- The History of Godmanchester, in the County of Huntingdon ... London: Baldwin & Cradock, 1831. Sole edn. 8vo. [xvi],391,xxxvi pp. Frontis. Orig cloth, rebacked. *(Bickersteth)* **£40 [≈ $64]**

Fox, William
- A Brief Description of the Wesleyan Missions on the Western Coast of Africa. London: Aylott & Jones, 1851. xx,624,[1] pp. Fldg map, 6 cold plates. Some text missing in a few spots. Contemp half leather, gilt title, raised bands. *(Parmer)* **$250 [≈ £156]**

Framjee, Dosabhoy
- The Parsees: their History, Manners, Customs, and Religion. London: Smith, Elder, 1858. 1st edn. xv,286,16 ctlg pp. Orig cloth. *(Wreden)* **$75 [≈ £46]**

Franck, Harry
- Wandering in Northern China. New York & London: Century Co, [1923]. 8vo. 502 pp. Num photo plates. Orig green cloth, a bit soiled. *(Terramedia)* **$35 [≈ £21]**

Francklin, William
- Military Memoirs of Mr. George Thomas ... North-West of India ... interspersed, Geographical and Statistical Accounts of several of the States composing the Interior of the Peninsula ... London: 1805. 8vo. Fldg map, port, 1 plate. Sl spotted. Orig paper bds.
  (Farahar) **£225 [≈ $360]**

- Observations made on a Tour from Bengal to Persia in the Years 1786-7 ... London: Cadell, 1790. 2nd edn. 8vo. viii,351 pp. Sl foxed & spotted. Contemp calf, v worn.
(Worldwide Antiqu'n) **$145 [≈ £90]**

Franklin, G.E.
- Palestine. Depicted and Described. London: Dent; New York: Dutton, 1911. 1st edn. 8vo. xx, 218 pp. 95 plates. Sl foxing. Orig cloth, t.e.g., sl rubbed.
(Worldwide Antiqu'n) **$65 [≈ £40]**

Franklin, Lady Jane
- A Letter to Viscount Palmerston ... With an Appendix. London: 1857. 1st edn. 8vo. 36 pp. Mod wraps. Lady Franklin's sgntr loosely inserted.
(Robertshaw) **£15 [≈ $24]**

Franklin, Sir John
- Narrative of a Journey to the Shores of the Polar Sea ... London: Murray, 1823. 1st edn. 4to. xvi,768 pp. 4 fldg maps, 30 plates (11 cold). Leather, orig spine relaid, some scuffing & bumping especially to crnrs.
(Parmer) **$650 [≈ £406]**
- Narrative of a Journey ... Polar Sea ... Third Edition. London: 1824. 2 vols. 8vo. 3 (of 4, lacks map III) fldg maps. Contemp mor gilt, a.e.g.
(Fenning) **£32.50 [≈ $52]**
- Narrative of a Journey to the Shores of the Polar Sea ... in 1819-20-21-22. Third Edition. London: Murray, 1824. 2 vols. 8vo. xix,370; iv,[1],399 pp. Half-titles. 4 lge fldg maps (1 cold in outline). Contemp mor gilt, gilt spines, a.e.g.
(Fenning) **£135 [≈ $216]**
- Narrative of a Journey to the Shores of the Polar Sea ... London: Murray, 1824. 3rd edn. 2 vols. xix,370; iv,1,399 pp. 3 fldg maps. Leather gilt, raised bands, mrbld endpapers, v sl wear.
(Parmer) **$500 [≈ £312]**
- Narrative of a Second Expedition to the Shores of the Polar Sea, 1825-1827. London: 1828. 1st edn. [24],320,[157] pp. 6 maps, 31 plates. Contemp half mor.
(Jenkins) **$850 [≈ £531]**
- Narrative of a Second Expedition to the Shores of the Polar Sea, in the Years 1825 ... 1827. Philadelphia: Lea & Carey, 1828. 1st US edn. xxi,23-318 pp. Fldg map frontis. Occas sl foxing, minor tear in map without loss. Orig cloth backed paper bds, uncut.
(High Latitude) **$150 [≈ £93]**
- Narrative of a Second Expedition to the Shores of the Polar Sea, in the Years 1825, 1826, and 1827 ... London: Murray, 1828. Thick 4to. xxiv,320,clvii pp. 6 fldg maps (few sl reprs), 31 plates. Occas foxing. Orig cloth, chipped spine relaid, new endpapers.

(Reese) **$1,000 [≈ £625]**
- Thirty Years in the Arctic Regions: A Narrative of the Explorations ... Philadelphia: Potter, [ca 1859]. 480 pp. Orig brown cloth, some wear to extremities.
(Parmer) **$125 [≈ £78]**

Fransham, John
- The Entertaining Traveller; or, the Whole World in Miniature ... New Edition ... London: for Henry Holmes, 1767. 1st edn under this title. 2 vols. 12mo. Leaf of directions in vol 2. 2 frontis, 4 plates. Contemp calf, rebacked, a bit worn.
(Ximenes) **$400 [≈ £250]**

Fraser, Mrs Hugh
- A Diplomatist's Wife in Japan. London: 1899. 1st edn. 2 vols. 8vo. 250 ills. Some finger & other marks, a few crnrs creased, tiny pin & rust holes in title & frontis vol 1. Orig gilt dec cloth, t.e.g., recased, new endpapers, cvrs partly sunned & marked.
(Bow Windows) **£135 [≈ $216]**
- Letters from Japan. A Record of Modern Life in the Island Empire. New York: 1904. 2 vols in one. Thick 8vo. Frontis, num ills. Ex lib. Orig pict blue cloth.
(Terramedia) **$30 [≈ £18]**

Fraser, Sir Hugh
- Amid the High Hills. London: 1923. 1st edn. 8vo. Cold & other plates, text ills. Orig bndg.
(Grayling) **£40 [≈ $64]**

Fraser, J.D.
- The Gold Fever or Two Years in Alaska. A True Narrative of Actual Events as Experienced by the Author. N.p.: the author, [ca 1923]. 8vo. 100 pp. Orig ptd wraps.
(High Latitude) **$100 [≈ £62]**

Fraser, James B.
- Persia. Historical and Descriptive Account of Persia ... New York: Harper, 1860. 12mo. 346 pp. Engvd title, fldg map, 6 plates, 1 text ill. Ex-lib. Orig cloth, edges rubbed, spine ends chipped.
(Worldwide Antiqu'n) **$55 [≈ £34]**

Fraser, R.W.
- Turkey. Ancient and Modern ... Edinburgh: Black, 1854. 1st edn. Sm 8vo. xv,540 pp. 2 fldg maps, frontis. Orig cloth, edges rubbed, tears in spine.
(Worldwide Antiqu'n) **$65 [≈ £40]**

Frederickson, A.D.
- Ad Orientem. London: W.H. Allen, 1889. 1st

edn. xii,388 pp. Fldg cold map (edge sl soiled), 26 litho plates (many tinted or cold). Half-title sl soiled. Mod half levant mor gilt.
                                    (Hollett) **£175 [≈ $280]**

Freeling, Arthur
- Freeling's Grand Junction Railway Companion to Liverpool, Manchester, and Birmingham ... London & Liverpool: 1838. 2nd edn, 2nd or subsequent iss. 12mo. 192,[32,4,8 advt] pp. 2 fldg maps, gradient profiles, fldg timetable. Some marks. Orig cloth, sl worn.   *(Duck)* **£120 [≈ $192]**

Freeman, Edward A.
- The History of Sicily from the Earliest Times. Oxford: 1891. 1st edn. 4 vols. 8vo. Maps. Orig cloth.   *(Robertshaw)* **£55 [≈ $88]**

Freeman, Richard A.
- Travels & Life in Ashanti & Jaman. New York: Stokes, 1898. 1st Amer edn. Lge 8vo. xx, 559 pp. Cold fldg map, frontis, other photo plates & ills. Orig pict orange cloth, ex-lib, sl soiled, labels removed.
                                    (Terramedia) **$150 [≈ £93]**

Fremont, John C.
- Narrative of the Exploring Expedition to the Rocky Mountains, in 1842, and to Oregon and North Carolina, in 1843-44. London: Wiley & Putnam, 1846. 1st English edn. 8vo. 324 pp. Lge fldg linen backed map, 4 litho views. Orig blue cloth.
                                    (Jenkins) **$450 [≈ £281]**
- Narrative of the Exploring Expedition to the Rocky Mountains, in the Year1842, and to Oregon and North California, in the Years 1843-44. London: Wiley & Putnam, 1846. 1st English edn. 8vo. 324 pp. Fldg linen backed map, 4 litho plates. Calf gilt, sl rubbed.
                                    (Heritage) **$500 [≈ £312]**
- Oregon and California. The Exploring Expedition to the Rocky Mountains, Oregon and California ... Buffalo: 1851. 456 pp. Cloth, worn at headbands.
                                    (Reese) **$75 [≈ £46]**
- Report of the Exploring Expedition to the Rocky Mountains in the Year 1842, and to Oregon and North California in the Years 1843 - 44. Washington: 1845. The House iss. 583 pp. 5 maps, 22 plates. Lib stamps. Minor but persistent dampstain. Later half mor.
                                    (Reese) **$550 [≈ £343]**
- Report of the Exploring Expedition to the Rocky Mountains in the Year 1842, and to Oregon and North California in the Years 1843-'44. Washington: Gales & Seaton, 1845. Senate edn. 8vo. 693 pp. 2 maps (1 reprd), 23 plates. Occas damp stains. Linen.

                                    (Parmer) **$650 [≈ £406]**

French, B.F. (compiler)
- Historical Collections of Louisiana ... Compiled with Historical and Biographical Notes ... by B.F. French. New York: Wiley & Putnam, 1846-53. 5 vols. Port vol 5, fldg map vol 4. Occas foxing. Unobtrusive lib stamps. Lacks map in vol 2. Three qtr mor.
                                    (Reese) **$1,250 [≈ £781]**

French, George
- The History of Col. Parke's Administration whilst he was Captain-General and Chief Governor of the Leeward Islands ... London: 1717. x,427 pp. Port. Antique calf.
                                    (Reese) **$900 [≈ £562]**

French, L.H.
- Nome Nuggets. Some of the Experiences of a Party of Gold Seekers in North-Western Alaska in 1900. New York: Mantross, Clark & Emmons, 1901. Thin 8vo. xxi,[3],25-102 pp. Photo ills. Orig cloth.
                                    (High Latitude) **$65 [≈ £40]**

French-Sheldon, Mrs M. (Bebe Bwana)
- Sultan to Sultan: Adventures among the Masai. Boston: 1892. 1st edn. Numbered & inscrbd by author & publisher. Lge 8vo. 435 pp. Frontis port, num plates & ills. Orig dec red cloth gilt, bevelled edges, sl worn.
                                    (Terramedia) **$150 [≈ £93]**
- Sultan to Sultan. Adventures among the Masai and Other tribes of East Africa. Boston: Arena, 1892. Roy 8vo. x,434 pp. Port, 27 plates, num text ills. Orig cloth, faded.   *(Berkelouw)* **$125 [≈ £78]**

Frere, George
- A Short History of Barbados, from its First Discovery and Settlement, to the End of the Year 1767. London: for J. Dodsley ..., 1768. 1st edn. 8vo. viii,121,[2] pp. Lib stamp on title marg. New period style calf.
                                    (Young's) **£190 [≈ $304]**

Freshfield, Mrs Henry
- A Summer Tour in the Grisons and the Italian Valleys of the Bernina. London: 1862. 1st edn. 8vo. [x],292 pp. 2 fldg maps, 4 tinted litho plates. Orig cloth gilt, uncut, short tear in cloth at edge of upper cvr.
                                    (Bickersteth) **£110 [≈ $176]**

Freyberg, H.
- Out of Africa. London: 1935. 8vo. Ills. Light foxing. Orig bndg, cvrs a bit grubby.
                                    (Grayling) **£20 [≈ $32]**

Freygang, Madame de

- Letters from the Caucasus and Georgia; to which are added, the Account of a Journey into Persia ... From the French. London: 1823. 1st edn in English. xiv, 414 pp. Errata. 2 maps, plates. Lacks half-title. Foxing & offsetting of plates. Contemp three qtr calf, rubbed. *(Reese)* **$275 [≈£171]**

Frobenius, Leo

- The Childhood of Man. A Popular Account of the Lives, Customs & Thoughts of the Primitive Races. London: Staley & Co, 1909. 8vo. [xviii],504 pp. Frontis, ills. Orig pict blue cloth gilt, sl worn.
 (Terramedia) **$50 [≈£31]**
- The Voice of Africa. Being an Account of the Travels of the German Inner African Exploration Expedition in the years 1910 - 1912. Translated by Rudolf Blind. London: 1913. 1st edn. 2 vols. Sm 4to. 4 maps & tables, 70 plates, 200 text ills. Orig cloth, v sl worn. *(Hollett)* **£120 [≈$192]**

Fuentes, Manual A.

- Lima or Sketches of the Capital of Peru, Historical, Stetestical [sic], Administrative, Commercial and Moral. Paris: 1866. 4to. ix,224 pp. 44 tinted litho plates, num text ills. Orig cloth backed pict paper bds, some wear, bds soiled, inner hinges broken.
 (Reese) **$300 [≈£187]**

A Full Account ...

- A Full Account of the late Dreadful Earthquake at Port Royal in Jamaica, written in Two Letters from the Minister at that Place ... London: for Tonson, & Baldwyn, 1692. 4to. 2 pp broadsheet. Sl trimmed, not affecting text. Cloth case. Wing F.2267.
 (Reese) **$1,350 [≈£843]**

Fullarton, William

- A View of the English Interests in India, and an Account of the Military Operations in the Southern Parts of the Peninsula ... London: 1787. 1st edn. 8vo. Fldg plan. Contemp tree calf, gilt spine, jnts reprd.
 (Farahar) **£180 [≈$288]**

Fuller, George N.

- Historic Michigan: Land of the Great Lakes ... (Dayton, Ohio): Nat Hist Assoc, [ca 1924]. 3 vols. 4to. 540, xxvi; x, 541-1064,x; 664 pp. Photos & ports. Orig blue cloth gilt, inner hinge vol 2 cracked. *(Karmiole)* **$85 [≈£53]**

Fullerton, Alice

- To Persia for Flowers. London: OUP, 1938. 1st edn. 8vo. xvi,195 pp. 12 plates. Orig

cloth. Dw torn.
 (Worldwide Antiqu'n) **$35 [≈£21]**

Fulleylove, John

- Oxford. With Notes by T. Humphrey Ward. London: Fine Art Society, 1889. 1st edn. Lge 4to. 30 mtd plates, 10 text ills. Damp mark in left hand crnr of all mounts, not affecting plates. Orig brown bevelled buckram.,
 (Gough) **£65 [≈$104]**

Funston, Frederick

- Memories of Two Wars: Cuban and Philippine Experiences. London: Constable, 1912. xv,451 pp. Port frontis, 33 plates. Orig cloth. *(Box of Delights)* **£25 [≈$40]**

Furlong, Charles Wellington

- The Gateway to the Sahara. New York: Scribner's, 1909. 306 pp. Ills. Date on title. Orig blue cloth over bds, some wear to spine ends. *(Parmer)* **$40 [≈£25]**

Fytche, Albert

- Burma Past and Present with Personal reminiscences of the Country. London: Kegan Paul, 1878. 1st edn. 2 vols in one. 8vo. xiv, 355; viii, 348 pp. Fldg cold map (short tear, no loss), 20 ills inc 10 chromolitho. Orig blue cloth stamped in black & gilt, sl stain. *(Frew Mackenzie)* **£185 [≈$296]**

G., S.T.

- The Australian Sketchbook ... see Gill, Samuel Thomas.

Gadow, Hans

- Through Southern Mexico, being an Account of the Travels of a Naturalist. London: Witherby, 1908. 8vo. xvi,527 pp. 4 maps, 170 ills. Orig red buckram gilt, backstrip sl faded. *(Blackwell's)* **£80 [≈$128]**

Gage, J.

- The History and Antiquities of Hengrave in Suffolk. London: 1822. 4to. Frontis, 29 plates (4 cold). Contemp vellum, spine reprd.
 (Stewart) **£175 [≈$280]**

Gage, W.L.

- Palestine, Historical and Descriptive. Or, the Home of God's People. Boston: 1883. Wide 8vo. 557 pp. Num plates. Orig dec brown cloth. *(Terramedia)* **$50 [≈£31]**

Gallatin, Albert

- A Memoir of the North-Eastern Boundary (of the United States), in Connexion with Mr. Jay's Map. New York: for the New York Hist

Soc, 1843. 1st edn. 8vo. iii,74 pp. With Jay's hand cold fldg map. Orig orange ptd wraps, fine.   *(Gough)* **£195 [≈ $312]**

Galloway, Joseph
- Letters to a Nobleman, on the Conduct of the War in the Middle Colonies. The Second Edition. London: J. Wilkie, 1779. 101 pp. Fldg map. Disbound.
                  (Jarndyce) **£260 [≈ $416]**

Galton, Sir Francis
- The Art of Travel; or Shifts and Contrivances available in Wild Countries. London: Murray, 1860. 3rd edn, rvsd & enlgd. 8vo. xviii,298 pp. Num text w'cuts. Orig cloth, rubbed, spine ends chipped.
                  (Adelson) **$200 [≈ £125]**
- Narrative of an Explorer in Tropical South Africa being an Account of a Visit to Damaraland in 1851 ... London: Ward Lock, Minerva Lib, 1889. 8vo. xviii, [2], 320 pp. Map, text ills. Polished blue prize calf, sl rubbed, hd of spine sl worn.
                  (Claude Cox) **£25 [≈ $40]**

Galton, Sir Francis (ed.)
- Vacation Tourists and Notes of Travel in 1862-63. London: Macmillan, 1864. Sole edn. 8vo. viii,418 pp. Contemp half calf.
                  (Bickersteth) **£85 [≈ $136]**

Gardiner, Allen F.
- Narrative of a Journey to the Zoolu Country, in South Africa ... London: 1836. iv, 412 pp. 2 fldg maps, plates (some cold, inc frontis). Occas trace of foxing. Contemp polished calf, spine relaid, some edge wear.
                  (Reese) **$450 [≈ £281]**

Gardner, Alexander
- Memoirs of Alexander Gardner, Soldier and Traveller. Edited by H. Pearse. Introduction by R. Temple. London: 1898. 359 pp. Frontis, text maps. Orig cloth.
                  (Trophy Room Books) **$600 [≈ £375]**

Gardner, George Peabody, Jr.
- Chiefly the Orient. An Undigested Journal ... 27 July 1910 - 10 June 1911. [Norwood, Ma.]: 1912. x,378 pp. Frontis, photo ills. Orig cloth gilt with pict onlay, some edge wear. Author's inscrptn.   *(Reese)* **$125 [≈ £78]**

Garlake, Peter S.
- Great Zimbabwe. Introduction by Mortimer Wheeler. New York: Stein & Day, 1973. 1st edn. 4to. 224 pp. Num plates & ills, many cold. Orig cloth. Dw.
                  (Terramedia) **$85 [≈ £53]**

Garner, R.
- The Natural History of the County of Stafford ... London: 1844. 8vo. xii,551 pp. Fldg geological map, frontis, 8 plates, 19 ills. Orig cloth., rather worn. Pres copy. Without the 61-page Supplement publ in 1860.
                  (Wheldon & Wesley) **£60 [≈ $96]**
- The Natural History of the County of Stafford ... London: 1844-60. 1st edn. 8vo. vii, 551, 61 pp. Hand cold geological map, 9 plates, 19 text engvs. Orig cloth, spine faded.
                  (Henly) **£95 [≈ $152]**

Garrard, Lewis H.
- Wah-To-Yah and the Taos Trail. Glendale: 1938. 377 pp. Fldg map. Cloth.
                  (Reese) **$100 [≈ £62]**

Garstin, Crosbie
- Samuel Kelly - An Eighteenth Century Seaman. New York: Stokes, 1925. 1st edn. Large Paper. 8vo. 320 pp. 24 plates. Orig cloth gilt, t.e.g.   *(Parmer)* **$60 [≈ £37]**

Garstin, Sir William
- Report upon the Basin of the Upper Nile with Proposals for the Improvement of that River ... Cairo: National Printing Dept, 1904. Sm folio. vi,[i],196, 55,42 pp. 4 plans in pocket, 37 plans, 46 pp of photo plates. Orig qtr cloth, sl soiled.
                  (Frew Mackenzie) **£140 [≈ $224]**

Gaspey, William
- Tallis's Illustrated London; in Commemoration of the Great Exhibition of all Nations in 1851 ... With Historical and Descriptive Letter-press. London & New York: John Tallis, [1851-52]. 12mo. vii,320 pp. 75 plates, 2 addtnl engvd titles. Orig leather gilt, sl worn. *(Schoyer)* **$165 [≈ £103]**

Gates, R.R.
- A Botanist in the Amazon Valley; an Account of the Flora and Fauna in the Land of Floods. London: 1927. Cr 8vo. 203 pp. Map, 10 plates. Orig cloth, trifle used.
                  (Wheldon & Wesley) **£45 [≈ $72]**

Gatherings from Spain ...
- See Ford, Richard.

Gatke, Heinrich
- Heligoland as an Ornithological Observatory. Edinburgh: David Douglas, 1895. 1st edn. Imperial 8vo. xii,599,20 illust ctlg pp. Port, num ills. Orig pict green cloth gilt, sl bumped.   *(Gough)* **£48 [≈ $76]**

Gay, Susan E.
- Old Falmouth. The Story of the Town from the Killigrews to the Earliest Part of the 19th Century. London: 1903. 1st edn. 8vo. Orig cloth, inner hinges weak.
(Ambra) **£42 [≈ $67]**

Geddie, Revd John
- Missionary Life Among the Cannibals: being the Life of the Rev. John Geddie, D.D., First Missionary to the New Hebrides ... Toronto: 1882. 512 pp. Map, port, ills. Sgntr starting. Orig cloth gilt, rubbed. *(Reese)* **$125 [≈ £78]**

Gehrts, Miss A.
- A Camera Actress in the Wilds of Togoland ... Philadelphia: Lippincott, 1915. 1st edn. 8vo. 314 pp. Fldg map, num plates. Orig pict light blue cloth. *(Terramedia)* **$75 [≈ £46]**

Geikie, Cunningham
- The Holy Land and the Bible. A Book of Scripture Illustrations Gathered in Palestine. London: James Pott, 1888. 2 vols. 8vo. viii,560; vii,544 pp. Orig blue cloth gilt.
(Terramedia) **$50 [≈ £31]**
- The Holy Land and the Bible. A Book of Scripture Illustrations Gathered in Palestine. New York: Alden, 1888. 2 vols in one. 8vo. 656,li pp. Fldg cold map, 84 plates. Orig cloth. *(Worldwide Antiqu'n)* **$65 [≈ £40]**

Geil, William Edgar
- The Great Wall of China. New York: Sturgis & Walton, 1909. 1st edn. 8vo. xvi,393 pp. Frontis, num photo views. Orig pict maroon cloth. *(Terramedia)* **$100 [≈ £62]**
- The Isle that is called Patmos. Phil: A.J. Rowland, 1897. 1st edn. 4to. xii,195 pp. Frontis port, num photo plates. Lib stamps on title & plate versos. Orig pict orange-brown cloth, spine worn.
(Terramedia) **$50 [≈ £31]**

Gell, Sir William
- Pompeiana: The Topography, Edifices and Ornaments of Pompeii. London: for Rodwell & Martin, 1817-19. 1st edn. Tall 8vo. xxxi, 273,[iii] pp. 80 plates. A few spots. Contemp green half calf gilt, rubbed, edges scraped.
(Hollett) **£140 [≈ $224]**
- Pompeiana: The Topography, Edifices, and Ornaments of Pompeii. London: 1817-19. xxviii, 273, [ii] pp. Maps, plans, plates. Tissue guards. Scattered foxing. Orig gilt dec calf, rebacked, a.e.g. *(Reese)* **$250 [≈ £156]**
- The Topography of Rome and its Vicinity. New Edition, revised and enlarged by Edward Bunbury. London: Bohn, 1846.

viii,499 pp. Fldg map frontis, 2 maps, 2 facs. Blue cloth, faded, recased.
(Piccadilly) **£18 [≈ $28]**

General ...
- A General Survey of that Part of the Island of St. Christophers, which formerly belonged to France; and was yielded up to Great britain for Ever, by the late Treaty of Utrecht ... London: 1722. 48 pp. Half calf & bds.
(Reese) **$750 [≈ £468]**
- General View of the Agriculture of the County of Norfolk ... see Young, Arthur.

Gent, Thomas
- The Antient and Modern History of the Famous City of York ... York: 1730. 1st edn. 1st imp, with crown w'cut on p 84. Fcap 8vo. viii,256, [8 addenda, subscribers, advt] pp. Fldg plan, fldg view, 6 ills. Lacks inserted w'cut at p 171 as usual. Rec leather.
(Spelman) **£90 [≈ $144]**

Gentleman ...
- A Gentleman's Tour through Monmouthshire ... see Wyndham, Henry Penryddocke.

A Geographical Description ...
- A Geographical Description of ... the Spanish West-Indies ... see Carranza, Domingo Gonzales.

Gerard, Francis
- Picturesque Dublin Old and New. London: Hutchinson, 1898. 429 pp. 91 ills by Rose Barton. Orig bndg.
(Emerald Isle) **£45 [≈ $72]**

Gerstaecker, Frederick
- Gerstaecker's Travels. Rio de Janeiro - Buenos Ayres - Ride through the Pampas - Winter Journey across the Cordilleras - Chili - Valparaiso - California and the Gold Fields. London: Nelson, 1854. 8vo. 9-290 pp. 2 plates. New cloth, ex-lib.
(Adelson) **$285 [≈ £178]**
- Wild Sports in the Far West. London: Routledge, 1859. New edn. 8vo. vi,314 pp. 8 plates by Harrison Weir. Orig red cloth, recased. *(Young's)* **£35 [≈ $56]**

Giaever, John
- The White Desert ... The Official Account of the Norwegian - British - Swedish Antarctic Expedition. London: Chatto & Windus, 1954. 1st English edn. 304 pp. Maps, ills. Orig cloth. Dw worn. *(Parmer)* **$40 [≈ £25]**

Gibbons, A. St.H.
- Africa from North to South through Marotseland. London: 1904. 2 vols. 276; 270 pp. Lge fldg maps in rear pockets of both vols. Ills. Orig cloth, sl worn.
(Trophy Room Books) **$750 [≈ £468]**

Gibbons, Phebe Earle
- French and Belgians. Philadelphia: Lippincott, 1879. 1st edn. 8vo. Orig cloth gilt, gilt spine, bright.
(Trebizond) **$65 [≈ £40]**

Gibson, John
- The History of Glasgow, from the Earliest Accounts to the Present Time ... Glasgow: for the author ..., 1777. 1st edn. 8vo. viii, [ii], 391 pp. Fldg plan. Old sheep, jnts cracked.
(Young's) **£88 [≈ $140]**

Gibson, T.A. & G.M.
- Etymological Geography ... Second Edition, Greatly Enlarged ... Edinburgh: 1840. 12mo. xii, 163, [1] pp, advt leaf. Tear in title reprd. Orig calf, rebacked. *(Bickersteth)* **£45 [≈ $72]**

Giffen, J. Kelly
- The Egyptian Sudan, Illustrated. Fleming H. Revell: 1905. 3rd edn. 8vo. 252 pp. Orig dec cloth, sl dull.   *(Moon)* **£25 [≈ $40]**

Gilbert, J. & Churchill, G.C.
- The Dolomite Mountains. Excursions through Tyrol, Carinthis, Carniola, & Friuli ... With a Geological Chapter ... London: 1864. 1st edn. 8vo. xx,576 pp. 2 cold fldg maps, 6 cold litho plates, 27 text ills. Some marks. Orig cloth, spine ends worn, little loose.   *(Bow Windows)* **£155 [≈ $248]**

Gilbert, Linney
- India Illustrated ... London: for the Proprietor, n.d. Tall 8vo. viii,232 pp. 22 steel engvd plates after William Daniell. Orig cloth gilt, recased, spine darkened & creased.
(Hollett) **£50 [≈ $80]**

Gilbert, Paul & Bryson, C.L.
- Chicago & Its Makers. A Narrative of Events from the Day of the First White Man to the Inception of the Second World's Fair. Chicago: 1929. One of 2000. Lge 4to. xvi,1085 pp. Frontis, num ills. Orig cloth gilt, raised bands.   *(Terramedia)* **$150 [≈ £93]**

Giles, Herbert Allen
- A Chinese Biographical Dictionary. London: Quaritch; Shanghai: Kelly & Walsh, 1897-98. 1st edn. 2 vols. 8vo. xvii,1022 pp.. Orig cloth,

both spines taped in cloth, ex-lib.
(Worldwide Antiqu'n) **$45 [≈ £28]**

Gill, Isobel Sarah
- Six Months in Ascension. An Unscientific Account of a Scientific Expedition. Second Edition. London: Murray, 1880. Sm 8vo. liv, 285, [32 ctlg dated Sept 1888] pp. Map. Orig dec cloth, rubbed, sl shaken, rear hinge reprd.
(Schoyer) **$45 [≈ £28]**

Gill, Samuel Thomas
- The Australian Sketchbook by S.T.G. [Melbourne]: Hamel & Ferguson, [1865]. Oblong folio. Cold litho title, 24 cold litho plates. V sl crnr wear to a few plates. Loose sheets laid in a fldg cloth box.
(Reese) **$6,000 [≈ £3,750]**

Gill, Revd William
- Gems from the Coral Islands ... Philadelphia: Presbyterian Board of Publication, [1855]. 12mo. 285 pp. 13 w'cut plates. Orig pict gilt cloth.   *(Schoyer)* **$60 [≈ £37]**
- Gems from the Coral Islands ... Philadelphia: [1855]. 285 pp. Frontis, plates. Orig pict gilt cloth, dull.   *(Reese)* **$175 [≈ £109]**
- Gems from the Coral Islands ... London: Ward & Co ..., 1856. 1st edn. 2 vols. 8vo. xvi,ii,243; xvii,320 pp. 31 maps & ills. Orig cloth gilt, 2 inner jnts strengthened, spine ends chipped.   *(Young's)* **£60 [≈ $96]**
- Gems from the Coral Islands ... London: [ca 1860?]. New & cheap edn. Sm 8vo. viii,344 pp. Charts, ills. Orig green cloth.
(Bow Windows) **£40 [≈ $64]**

Gillingwater, Edmund
- An Historical Account of the Ancient Town of Lowestoft ... London: G.G.J. & J. Robinson ... sold by W. Stevenson, Norwich, [1790]. 4to. xv,485,[i errata],[4 index] pp. Half-title. Subscribers. Few sm reprs without loss. Mod mor gilt, uncut.
(Lamb) **£180 [≈ $288]**
- An Historical Account of the Ancient Town of Lowestoft ... London: G.G.J. & J. Robinson ... sold by W. Stevenson, Norwich, [1790]. 4to. xv,485,[i errata],[4 index] pp. Half-title (sl spotted). Subscribers. End of index sl spotted. Mod calf, mor label.
(Lamb) **£200 [≈ $320]**

Gilliss, J.M.
- The U.S. Naval Astronomical Expedition to the Southern hemisphere, during the Years 1849-'50-51-'52 ... Chile ... Philadelphia: 1856. 2 vols. Lge 4to. xiii,556; xi,300 pp. 53 maps & plates (inc 15 cold). Some foxing of

plates. Orig cloth, rebacked, some wear.
(Reese) **$650 [≈£406]**

Gillmor, Frances & Wetherill, Louisa Wade

- Traders to the Navajos. The Story of the Wetherills of Kayenta. Boston: Houghton Mifflin, 1934. 1st edn. 8vo. [6],266 pp. 8 plates. Endpapers & title sl foxed. Orig cloth. Chipped dw. *(Karmiole)* **$40 [≈£25]**

Gillmore, Parker

- The Great Thirst Land: A Ride through Natal, Orange Free State, Transvaal and Kalahari Desert. London, Paris & New York: [1876]. 1st edn. 8vo. 466 pp. Frontis. Orig dec brown cloth gilt, sl rubbed & soiled.
(Terramedia) **$100 [≈£62]**
- Gun, Rod, and Saddle. Personal Experiences. By Ubique. New York: 1871. 275,advt pp. Orig cloth gilt, trace of rubbing & edgewear. Lindley Eberstadt b'plate.
(Reese) **$85 [≈£53]**
- The Hunter's Arcadia [Bechuanaland]. London: 1886. 8vo. Ills. Orig cloth.
(Grayling) **£30 [≈$48]**
- Prairie and Forest: a Description of the Game of North America, with Personal Adventures in their Pursuit. London: Chapman & Hall, 1874. 8vo. x,383 pp. 13 plates, text ills. Orig green cloth, sl rubbed.
(Adelson) **$100 [≈£62]**
- Prairie Farms and Prairie Folk. London: Hurst & Blackett, 1872. 1st edn. 2 vols. 8vo. 2 frontis. Title vignettes. 16 pp ctlg vol 1. Occas sl foxing. Mod half calf.
(Bickersteth) **£165 [≈$264]**
- Through Gasa Land and the Land of the Portuguese Aggression: A Journey of a Hunter in Search of Gold & Ivory. London: [1890]. 1st edn. 8vo. 349 pp. Fldg cold map, frontis. Orig pict red cloth gilt, unopened, spine darkened & worn at edges.
(Terramedia) **$150 [≈£93]**

Gilly, William

- Narrative of an Excursion to the Mountains of Piemont, in the Year MDCCCXXIII. And Researches among the Vaudois, or Waldenses, Protestant Inhabitants of the Cottian Alps ... London: 1826. 3rd edn. 8vo. xxiii,295,86 pp. 2 maps, 2 facs. Rebacked mrbld bds, label *(Young's)* **£60 [≈$96]**
- Narrative of an Excursion to Mountains of Piemont, in the Year MDCCCXXIII. And Researches among the Vaudois, or Waldenses, Protestant Inhabitants of the Cottian Alps ... London: 1827. 4th edn. 8vo. xiv,2,307,88 pp. 10 plates, 2 maps, 2 facs.

Near contemp half calf.
(Young's) **£70 [≈$112]**

Gilpin, William

- Observations Relative Chiefly to Picturesque Beauty ... particularly the High-Lands of Scotland. London: Blamire, 1789. 1st edn. 2 vols. 8vo. xi,221; [2],196, xx,[i] pp. 40 plates. Contemp tree calf, gilt spines, sl chipping, upper hinges cracked but firm.
(Spelman) **£160 [≈$256]**
- Observations Relative Chiefly to Picturesque Beauty ... particularly the High-Lands of Scotland. London: Blamire, 1789. 1st edn. 2 vols. 8vo. xi,221; [2],196, xx,[i] pp. 40 plates. 19th c bds, linen spines, paper labels, linen sl creased, labels sl chipped.
(Spelman) **£120 [≈$192]**
- Observations on the Western Parts of England, relative Chiefly to Picturesque Beauty ... Beauties of the Isle of Wight. London: 1798. xvi, 359, advt pp. 18 plates. Occas trace of foxing. Contemp three qtr calf, rebacked.
(Reese) **$200 [≈£125]**

Gilpin, William, of Colorado

- The Central Gold Region. The Grain, Pastoral, and Gold Regions of North America ... Philadelphia: 1860. 194 pp. 6 maps. Cloth, backstrip relaid, worn at edges & backstrip.
(Reese) **$400 [≈£250]**

Glaisher, Ernest H.

- A Journey on the Berbice River and Wieroonie Creek. Georgetown: "Argosy" Press, 1885. 8vo in 4s. Orig ptd bds, sl soiled, rebacked in cloth. Author's pres inscrptn.
(Sanders) **£25 [≈$40]**

Glasgow and Its Environs ...

- Glasgow and Its Environs: Past and Present; with a Description of its Leading Mercantile Houses and Commercial Enterprises. Stratten: 1891. 4to. 365 pp. Engvs & w'cuts. Orig dec bndg, cvrs a little marked.
(Book House) **£35 [≈$56]**

Gleanings of a Wanderer ...

- Gleanings of a Wanderer, in Various Parts of England, Scotland, & North Wales made during an Excursion in the Year 1804 ... London: Richard Phillips, 1805. 182 pp. Plate. Occas trace of foxing. Mod half cloth, t.e.g. *(Reese)* **$85 [≈£53]**

Gleig, George R.

- The Life of Major-General Sir Thomas Munro, Bart. and K.C.B. late Governor of Madras ... New Edition. London: 1831. 2 vols. 8vo. Fldg hand cold map, port.

Contemp calf, gilt arms, sl worn.
(Farahar) **£75 [≈ $120]**

Glenister, A.G.
- The Birds of the Malay Peninsula, Singapore & Penang. London: OUP, [1959]. Reprint of 1951 edn. 8vo. 282 pp. Cold plates. Orig bndg. Dw.   *(Terramedia)* **$50 [≈ £31]**

Glover, Stephen
- The Peak Guide, containing the Topographical, Statistical, and General History of Buxton, Chatsworth, Edensor ... Edited by Thomas Noble ... Derby: Mozley, 1830. 8vo. Map, fldg plan, 2 fldg tables, 2 plates, num text vignettes. Publisher's (?) cloth.   *(Waterfield's)* **£65 [≈ $104]**

Gobat, Samuel
- Journal of Three Years' Residence in Abyssinia ... Accompanied with a Biographical Sketch of Bishop Gobat. New York: Dodd, 1850. 12mo. 480pp. Litho frontis, fldg map. Occas foxing. Orig bndg, hd of spine chipped, crnr sl bumped.
(Schoyer) **$50 [≈ £31]**

Goding, John
- Norman's History of Cheltenham. London: 1863. 8vo. Steel & w'engvs. Orig ptd paper bds, worn, top bd loose. *(Ambra)* **£40 [≈ $64]**

Godley, John Robert
- Letters from America. London: Murray, 1844. 1st edn. 2 vols. 8vo. xxiii,272; viii, 243,5 advt pp. Half-titles. Orig blue cloth, a little stained, labels chipped.
(Young's) **£115 [≈ $184]**

Godman, F. du Cane
- Natural History of the Azores, or Western Islands. London: 1870. 8vo. vii,358 pp. 2 maps. Cloth.
(Wheldon & Wesley) **£50 [≈ $80]**

Godsell, Philip H.
- Red Hunters of the Snows: An Account of Thirty Years' Experience with the Primitive Indian and Eskimo Tribes of the Canadian North-West ... Toronto: Ryerson Press, 1938. 8vo. 324 pp. Fldg map. Orig cloth, spine faded.   *(Parmer)* **$95 [≈ £59]**

Godwin, G. & Britton, J.
- The Churches of London ... London: Tilt, 1838. 1st edn. 2 vols. 58 plates. Orig cloth, gilt spines.   *(Gough)* **£195 [≈ $312]**

Goff, R.C. & Clarissa
- Florence and Some Tuscan Cities. London: A. & C. Black Colour Books, Twenty Shilling Series, 1905. 1st edn. Cold plates. V sl yellowing of text. Orig dec cloth, sl wear to spine ends.   *(Old Cathay)* **£40 [≈ $64]**

Goldring, Douglas
- The Loire. A Record of a Pilgrimage from Gerbier de Joncs to St. Nazaire. London: Constable, 1913. 8vo. xxii,332 pp. 8 cold plates, num text ills. Orig dec grey cloth.
(Piccadilly) **£24 [≈ $38]**

Goodisson, William
- A Historical and Topographical Essay upon the Islands of Corfu, Leucadia, Cephalonia, Ithaca, and Zante ... London: Underwood, 1822. 1st edn. 8vo. xxiv,267 pp, leaf of directions & errata. 4 pp subscribers. 4 maps, 8 litho plates. Rec paper bds, uncut.
(Fenning) **£135 [≈ $216]**

Goodman, E.J.
- New Ground in Norway: Ringerike, Telemarken, Saetersdalen. London: Newnes, 1896. 1st edn. xvi,224,24 advt pp. Fldg map, 56 ills from photos by Paul Lange. Orig pict gilt cloth.   *(Box of Delights)* **£25 [≈ $40]**

Goodrich-Freer, A.
- Inner Jerusalem. New York: Dutton, 1904. 8vo. 388 pp. Num photo plates. Orig cloth, sl rubbed.   *(Terramedia)* **$100 [≈ £62]**

Goodridge, Charles Medyett
- Narrative of a Voyage to the South Seas, and the Shipwreck of The Prince of Wales Cutter, with an Account of Two Years Residence on an Uninhabited Island ... Exeter: 1843. 5th edn. 8vo. 172 pp. Port. Errata slip. Subscribers. Orig cloth gilt, inner hinge reprd.   *(Moon)* **£48 [≈ $76]**

Goodspeed, Thomas Harper
- Plant Hunters in the Andes. New York: 1941. 1st edn. 8vo. xvi,429 pp. 75 plates. Orig cloth, spine faded.   *(Henly)* **£65 [≈ $104]**
- Plant Hunters in the Andes. London: 1961. 8vo. ix,378 pp. Num photos, endpaper maps. Orig cloth. Dw.
(Wheldon & Wesley) **£30 [≈ $48]**

Gordon, Lady Duff
- Letters from Egypt ... New York & London: 1903. Rvsd edn, with new intro by George Meredith. xvi,383,advt pp. Port, plates. Three qtr mor & silk bds by MacDonald, some sm tears at untrimmed foredge.

(Reese) $60 [≈ £37]

Gordon, Charles George
- The Journals of Major-General C.G. Gordon, C.B. at Khartoum. Printed from the Original MSS ... Boston: 1885. 1st Amer edn. Sm 8vo. lxiv, 79 pp. Frontis, fldg map, sev plans. Orig green cloth gilt, sl worn.
(Terramedia) $75 [≈ £46]

Gordon, George
- An Introduction to Geography, Astronomy, and Dialling ... London: J. Senex ..., 1726. 1st edn. 8vo. [xii],iv,[iv], 188,40 pp. 11 engvs on 10 fldg plates. 19th c half calf, rubbed, rebacked.
(Burmester) £175 [≈ $280]

Gordon, Henry William
- Events in the Life of Charles George Gordon. From Its Beginning to Its End. London: Kegan Paul, 1886. 1st edn. 8vo. 463 pp. Num plates, ills, & maps (inc 3 fldg). Contemp red mor gilt, sl rubbed.
(Terramedia) $125 [≈ £78]

Gordon, Jan & Cora
- Two Vagabonds in Albania. London: John Lane, [1927]. 1st edn. 8vo. xii,304 pp. Cold frontis, plates & ills. Orig pict gilt blue cloth.
(Terramedia) $50 [≈ £31]

Gordon, Revd M.L., M.D.
- American [medical] Missionary in Japan. Boston: Houghton Mifflin, 1892. 8vo. 276 pp. Orig bndg. (Xerxes) $65 [≈ £40]

Gordon, Patrick
- Geography Anatomiz'd: or, the Geographical Grammar ... London: John Nicholson ..., 1708. 5th edn. 8vo. [xxvi],428,[4] pp. Red & black title. 16 fldg maps by Robert Morden (inc America with California an island). Contemp panelled calf, jnts & hd of spine reprd. (Frew Mackenzie) £260 [≈ $416]

Gordon, Seton
- Amid Snowy Wastes. Wild Life on the Spitsbergen Archipelago. London: Cassell, 1922. xiv,206 pp. 2 maps, num photo plates. Orig dec cloth, spine faded.
(High Latitude) $50 [≈ £31]
- Amid Snowy Wastes. Wild Life on the Spitsbergen Archipelago. London: Cassell, 1922. 1st edn. 8vo. xiv,206 pp. 2 maps, num ills. Orig cloth gilt. (Hollett) £60 [≈ $96]
- Hebridean Memories. London: 1923. 8vo. xii, 179 pp. Frontis, 62 plates. A little foxing. Orig cloth, trifle used.
(Wheldon & Wesley) £25 [≈ $40]

Gorer, Geoffrey
- Himalayan Village. An Account of the Lepchas of Sikkim. London: Joseph, 1938. 8vo. 510 pp. Photo frontis, 31 photo ills. Orig bndg, a little bumped & worn.
(Bates & Hindmarch) £25 [≈ $40]
- Himalayan Village: An Account of the Lepchas of Sikkim. London: Michael Joseph, [1938]. 1st edn. 8vo. 510 pp. Plates. Orig green cloth, sl worn.
(Terramedia) $50 [≈ £31]

Gorges, Sir Ferdinando
- America Painted to the Life ... London: 1659. 1st edn. 4 parts in one. Sm 4to. [2], 51,[3],57, [5],236,[4], 52,[17],[3] pp. Fldg frontis, fldg map, plate preceding 4th part. Sev margs shaved, not affecting text. Foxing of pt 4. Calf by Middleton. Sion College copy.
(Reese) $12,500 [≈ £7,812]

The Gospel According to Luke ...
- The Gospel According to Luke, translated into the Cherokee Language. Park Hill [Indian Territory]: Mission Press, Edwin Archer printer, 1850. 16mo. 134 pp. Light brown cloth, spine label.
(Terramedia) $300 [≈ £187]

Goss, P.H.
- Letters from Alabama ... chiefly relating to Natural History. London: Richard Clay, 1855. 1st edn. 12,306 pp. Orig blue cloth.
(Jenkins) $950 [≈ £593]

Gosse, P.H.
- A Naturalist's Rambles on the Devonshire Coast. London: 1853. 1st edn. 8vo. xvi,451 pp. 28 plates (12 cold). Orig cloth, spine faded, 1 hinge worn. (Baldwin) £35 [≈ $56]
- A Naturalist's Ramblings on the Devonshire Coast. London: 1853. 8vo. xvi,451 pp. 28 plates (12 cold). Inserted advts dated Dec 1857. Cream endpapers. A little minor foxing. Orig blue cloth.
(Wheldon & Wesley) £50 [≈ $80]
- A Naturalist's Ramblings on the Devonshire Coast. London: 1853. 1st edn. 8vo. xvi,451 pp. 28 plates (12 cold). Inserted advts dated Dec 1860. Orig green cloth, spine evenly faded. Freeman & Wertheimer 58g.
(Fenning) £75 [≈ $120]
- Tenby: A Sea-Side Holiday. London: 1856. 12mo. 400 pp. 20 cold & 4 plain plates. Orig cloth. (Henly) £100 [≈ $160]

Gostling, William
- A Walk about the City of Canterbury ... Canterbury: ptd by Simmons & Kirkby,

1777. 2nd edn, enlgd & illust. 8vo. 402,[16] pp. Fldg map (reprd), 20 plates. Some offsetting. Contemp calf, rehinged.
(Young's) **£120 [≈ $192]**

Gough, Sir Charles & Innes, Arthur D.
- The Sikhs and the Sikh Wars. The Rise, Conquest, and Annexation of the Punjab State. London: Innes, 1897. 8vo. xiv,304 pp. Fldg map frontis, 12 maps & plans. Ex-lib. Maroon half leather.
(Bates & Hindmarch) **£90 [≈ $144]**

Gouldsbury, Charles Elphinstone
- Life in the Indian Police. London: 1912. 285 pp. Ills. Orig cloth.
(Trophy Room Books) **$150 [≈ £93]**
- Tigerland. Reminiscences of Forty Years' Sport and Adventures in Bengal. London: Chapman & Hall, 1913. 8vo. xvii,262,6 advt pp. Photo frontis, 23 photo ills. Orig green cloth gilt, front top crnr bumped & ragged.
(Bates & Hindmarch) **£45 [≈ $72]**

Gouldsbury, Cullen & Sheane, H.
- The Great Plateau of Northern Rhodesia Being Some Impression of the Tanganyika Plateau. London: 1911. 352 pp. Fldg map, ills. Rec half leather gilt, orig front cvr preserved inside.
(Trophy Room Books) **$500 [≈ £312]**

Graah, Wilhelm A.
- Narrative of an Expedition to the East Coast of Greenland ... In Search of the Lost Colonies ... Translated from the Danish ... London: John W. Parker, 1837. [16],199,[1], [16] pp. Lge fldg map (foxed). Orig cloth, largely unopened.   *(Reese)* **$350 [≈ £218]**

Graham, Maria [Lady Callcott]
- Journal of a Residence in Chile. During the Year 1822. And a Voyage from Chile to Brazil in 1823. London: Longman, Hurst ..., 1824. 1st edn. 4to. v,1,512 pp. Frontis, 13 plates & text ills. Perf lib stamp on title. Plates foxed. Rec mor.   *(Terramedia)* **$500 [≈ £312]**
- Letter on India. London: 1814. 8vo. 2 maps (1 fldg), 8 plates (spotted with some offsetting onto text). Contemp red straight grained calf, gilt spine, upper hinge worn at ft.
(Farahar) **£160 [≈ $256]**

Graham, Stephen
- Through Russian Central Asia. London: Cassell, 1916. 1st edn. 8vo. xii,279,1 pp. Fldg map, frontis, num photo plates. Orig blue cloth.   *(Terramedia)* **$50 [≈ £31]**

Grainge, William
- Nidderdale; or, an Historical, Topographical and Descriptive Sketch of the Valley of the Nidd ... Pateley Bridge: Thomas Thorpe, 1863. 1st edn, deluxe iss. xii,231, [5] pp. 4 tinted litho plates. Orig gilt dec navy cloth, faded, spine ends chipped.
(Box of Delights) **£60 [≈ $96]**

Grant, Christina P.
- The Syrian Desert. Caravans, Travel and Exploration. London: A. & C. Black, 1937. 1st edn. 8vo. xv,410 pp. 3 fldg maps, frontis, plates. Orig brown cloth.
(Terramedia) **$60 [≈ £37]**

Grant, John Cameron
- The Ethiopian - a Narrative of the Society of Human Leopards. New York: Black Hawk Press, 1935. xv,287 pp. Port frontis. Olive cloth, paper label.   *(Parmer)* **$50 [≈ £31]**

Grant, Robert
- The Expediency Maintained of continuing the System by which the Trade and Government of India are now regulated ... London: for Black, Parry ... & J. Hatchard, 1813. 1st edn. 8vo. [iv],xix,[i blank],404 pp, inc 2 fldg tables. Orig bds, sl worn.
(Pickering) **$850 [≈ £531]**

Grattan, Thomas Colley
- The History of the Netherlands. London: Lardner's Cabinet Cyclopaedia, 1830. 1st edn. Sm 8vo. Orig cloth, ptd paper label.
(Fenning) **£18.50 [≈ $30]**

Graves, Samuel Robert
- A Yachting Cruise in the Baltic. London: Longman, Green ..., 1863. 1st edn. 8vo. Half-title. Fldg tinted frontis, 10 plates (sl foxed), w'cuts in text. Orig dec cloth, rebacked in blue mor.   *(Hannas)* **£70 [≈ $112]**

Gray, A.B.
- Charter of the Texas Western Railroad Company ... Survey of Route from Eastern Borders of Texas to California. Cincinnati: Porter, Thrall, & Chapman, 1855. 40 pp. Fldg map. Half mor.
(Reese) **$1,750 [≈ £1,093]**

Gray, Mrs Hamilton
- Tour to the Sepulchres of Etruria, in 1839. London: 1843. 3rd edn. xi,541 pp. Maps (some cold, some fldg), cold frontis, plates. Contemp three qtr mor. *(Reese)* **$85 [≈ £53]**

Gray, Hugh
- Letters from Canada, written during a Residence there in the Years 1806, 1807, and 1808 ... London: Longman ..., 1809. 8vo. 16, 406 pp. Fldg map, 3 fldg tables. Contemp calf, rebacked.   *(Adelson)* **$375 [≈£234]**

Gray, John Alfred
- At the Court of the Amir. London: Bentley, 1895. 1st edn. 8vo. xvi,[2],523 pp. Gravure frontis, 3 plates. Ink splash across 1 opening. Orig cloth, rubbed, gilt faded, torn Mudie's label on upper cvr. *(Claude Cox)* **£18 [≈$28]**

Gray, William
- Travels in Western Africa, in the Years 1818, 19, 20, and 21, from the River Gambia ... London: Murray, 1825. 1st edn. 8vo. xvi, 413 pp. Fldg map, 14 plates. Sl foxing. Orig cloth backed bds, some chipping & cracking to spine.   *(Adelson)* **$425 [≈£265]**

Greece ...
- Greece. Modern Traveller Series ... see Conder, James.

Greely, Adolphus W.
- Report on the Proceedings of the United States Expedition to Lady Franklin Bay, Grinnell Land. Washington: GPO, 1888. 2 vols. 4to. viii,545; v,738 pp. Fldg maps, charts, plates. Orig brown cloth, all edges showing wear.   *(Parmer)* **$200 [≈£125]**
- Three Years of Arctic Service. An Account of the Lady Franklin Bay Expedition of 1881-1884. New York: Scribner's, 1886. 2 vols. 8vo. xxv,428; xii,[2],444 pp. Lge fldg map in pocket, num plates, maps, ills. Orig dec cloth.   *(High Latitude)* **$175 [≈£109]**
- Three Years of Arctic Service. An Account of the Lady Franklin Bay Expedition of 1881-84 ... New York: Scribner's, 1886. 1st edn. 2 vols. Lge 8vo. xv,428; xii,444 pp. 8 maps (only, of 9, lacks pocket map), num plates. Orig cloth, sl worn.
 (Terramedia) **$120 [≈£75]**
- Three Years of Arctic Service. An Account of the Lady Franklin Bay Expedition of 1881 - 1884 and the Attainment of the Farthest North. New York: 1886. 2 vols. 428; 444 pp. Fldg maps. Orig dec cloth.
 (Reese) **$275 [≈£171]**

Green, Samuel G.
- French Pictures Drawn with Pen and Pencil. London: RTS, [1878]. Imperial 8vo. xii,212,8 advt pp. Orig pict blue cloth, lacks front free endpaper.   *(Claude Cox)* **£20 [≈$32]**

Green, Valentine
- The History and Antiquities of the City and Suburbs of Worcester. London: for the author by W. Bulmer & Co ..., 1796. 1st edn. 2 vols. 4to. Port, fldg town plan (sl torn in fold), 24 plates (mostly rather browned or foxed). A few spots. Later buckram..
 (Hollett) **£110 [≈$176]**
- A Survey of the City of Worcester ... Worcester: J. Butler for S. Gamidge, 1764. 1st edn. 8vo. [iv],vii,[i],252 pp. 16 engvd plates, mostly fldg. Contemp half calf, bds, label, sl rubbed, spine chipped at hd.
 (Clark) **£110 [≈$176]**

Greenaway, T.
- Farming in India, considered as a Pursuit for European Settlers of a Superior Class, with Plans for the Construction of Dams, Tanks, Weirs and Sluices. London: Smith, Elder, 1864. xvi,132 pp. 7 text ills. Orig green cloth gilt, partly unopened.
 (Blackwell's) **£35 [≈$56]**

Greene, F.V.
- The Russian Army and Its Campaigns in Turkey in 1877-1878. New York: Appleton, 1879. 1st edn. 2 vols (text & atlas). Lge 8vo. Orig green cloth gilt, ex-lib.
 (Terramedia) **$125 [≈£78]**

Greene, Max
- The Kanzas Region ... Scenery, Climate, Wild Productions, and Commercial Resources, interspersed with Incidents of Travel. New York: 1856. 1st edn. 192,[12] pp. Map, ills. Orig cloth, extremities sl worn..
 (Jenkins) **$450 [≈£281]**

Greenhow, Robert
- The History of Oregon and California, and the Other Territories on the Northwest Coast of America. Boston: Little & Brown, 1845. 2nd edn, enlgd. [2],xviii,[2],492 pp. Lge fldg map. Later cloth.   *(Jenkins)* **$250 [≈£156]**

Greenwood, James
- Curiosities of Savage Life. London: S.O. Beeton, 1863. 8vo. xiv,418 pp. 9 cold plates, num text engvs. Mod qtr calf.
 (Adelson) **$225 [≈£140]**

Gregg, Josiah
- Commerce of the Prairies: or the Journal of a Santa Fe Trader during Eight Expeditions across the Great Western Prairies, and a Residence of nearly Nine Years in Northern Mexico. New York: 1844. 2 vols. 2 fldg maps, 6 plates. Orig pict gilt cloth, sl worn.
 (Reese) **$2,000 [≈£1,250]**

- Commerce of the Prairies: or the Journal of a Santa Fe Trader during Eight Expeditions across the Great Western Prairies. New York: 1844. 1st edn. 2 vols. 1 map (only, of 2), plates. Contemp half mor, extremities chipped.   *(Jenkins)* **$800 [≈ £500]**

Gregorovius, Ferdinand
- Corsica in its Picturesque, Social, and Historical Aspects: The Record of a Tour in the Summer of 1852. Translated by Russell Martineau. London: 1855. 1st English edn. 8vo. Orig cloth, spine faded, front inner hinge weak.   *(Robertshaw)* **£32 [≈ $51]**

Gregson, Matthew
- Portfolio ... of Fragments ... of the Duchy of Lancaster. Second Edition, with Additions. Liverpool: C.A. Worrall, 1824. 3 parts in 1 vol. Folio. x,302,cviii pp. Num engvd plates & ports, ca 1600 ills. Late 19th c blind-tooled "gothic" calf.   *(Gough)* **£235 [≈ $376]**

Greig, E.H.
- See Davenport, A.H. & Greig, E.H.

Grenfell, Francis W.
- Three Weeks in Moscow. London: privately ptd, 1896. Only edn. 8vo. [viii], 152 pp. Frontis, 10 ills. Foxed. Compliment slip inserted. Orig red ruled & titled parchment, t.e.g., upper cvr smeared.
                    (Bow Windows) **£48 [≈ $76]**

Grew, J.
- Sport and Travel in the Far East. New York: 1910. 253 pp. 80 ills. Orig bndg.
            (Trophy Room Books) **$100 [≈ £62]**

Gribble, Francis
- Montreux. Painted by J. Hardwicke Lewis and May Hardwicke Lewis. London: A. & C. Black Colour Book, 1908. 1st edn. 20 cold plates. Orig cloth, t.e.g. Fine.
                    (Old Cathay) **£39 [≈ $62]**
- Montreux. Painted by J. Hardwicke Lewis and May Hardwicke Lewis. London: A. & C. Black Colour Book, 1908. 1st edn. 20 cold plates. Orig cloth, t.e.g. Good.
                    (Old Cathay) **£19 [≈ $30]**

Griffis, William Elliot
- The Mikado's Empire. New York: 1890. 6th edn. 8vo. 661 pp. Num ills. Orig cloth, edges sl rubbed, spine ends frayed.
            (Worldwide Antiqu'n) **$65 [≈ £40]**
- The Mikado's Empire. New York: 1900. 9th edn. 8vo. 651 pp. Num ills. Lib label. Orig orange-brown cloth, front cover a bit stained.

                    (Terramedia) **$40 [≈ £25]**
- The Mikado's Empire. New York: 1903. 10th edn, with 6 supplementary chapters. 2 vols. 8vo. 695 pp. Frontis, plates. Sl foxing to prelims vol 1, & endpapers of both vols. Orig bndg, sl worn & soiled, hd of spine sl frayed.
                    (Dillons) **£45 [≈ $72]**
- Townsend Harris. First American Envoy in Japan. Boston: Houghton, Mifflin, 1895. 8vo. xii, 352 pp. Frontis port. Orig green cloth, spine a bit soiled.   *(Karmiole)* **$50 [≈ £31]**

Griffith, Charles
- The Present State and Prospects of the Port Phillip District of New South Wales. Dublin: Curry; London: Longman ...; Edinburgh: Fraser, 1845. 1st edn. 8vo. vi, 202, 2 advt pp. Frontis, text ills. A bit frayed & damped at edges. Orig cloth, v rubbed, rebacked.
            (Worldwide Antiqu'n) **$225 [≈ £140]**

Griggs, Robert F.
- The Valley of Ten Thousand Smokes. Washington: National Geographic Society, 1922. Lge 8vo. xiii,[3],340 pp. Fldg map, fldg frontis, num photo ills. Orig cloth, minor wear, upper crnr bruised.
                    (High Latitude) **$50 [≈ £31]**

Grimshaw, Beatrice
- Fiji and its Possibilities. New York: Doubleday, Page, 1907. 1st Amer edn. Tall 8vo. xiii,315 pp. Port, 83 photo ills. Orig bndg. Publ in England as 'From Fiji to the Cannibal Islands'.   *(Schoyer)* **$40 [≈ £25]**
- In the Strange South Seas. London: Hutchinson, 1908. 8vo. x,382 pp. 56 plates. Orig cloth gilt.   *(Karmiole)* **$65 [≈ £40]**
- In the Strange South Seas. Philadelphia: Lippincott; London: Hutchinson, 1908. 1st edn. 8vo. x,381 pp. Photo plates. Orig pict blue cloth gilt, front hinge cracked internally.
                    (Terramedia) **$60 [≈ £37]**

Grimwood, Ethel St. Claire
- My Three Years in Manipur, and Escape from the Recent Mutiny. London: Bentley, 1891. 2nd edn. 8vo. 321 pp. Port frontis, title vignette, ills. Orig cloth gilt, front hinge cracked internally. *(Terramedia)* **$80 [≈ £50]**

Grinnell, Joseph B.
- Sketches of the West, or the Home of the Badgers: comprising an early History of Wisconsin, with a Series of Familiar letters and remarks ... New York: 1847. 48 pp. Fldg map. Orig ptd wraps, bound into half mor. Lib b'plate.   *(Reese)* **$1,000 [≈ £625]**

Griswold, Mrs Stephen M.
- A Woman's Pilgrimage to the Holy Land ... Hartford: Burr & Hyde, 1871. 1st edn. 8vo. 423 pp. 40 ills. Some foxing & spotting. Orig cloth, a.e.g., sl rubbed & faded.
(Worldwide Antiqu'n) **$45** [≈ £28]

Grose, Francis
- The Antiquities of England & Wales. London: M. Cooper, 1773-87. 1st edn. Thick Paper edn. 4 vols. Folio. Engvd frontises, title-vignettes, num plates & plans. Contemp tree calf gilt, elab gilt spines, hinges of 2 vols reprd. *(Hartfield)* **£850** [≈ £531]
- The Antiquities of Ireland. London: Hooper, 1791. 2 vols. 4to. Plates. Diced russia, spine gilt extra, in the Zaehnsdorf style, spines relaid. *(Emerald Isle)* **£365** [≈ $584]

Grosvenor, Edwin A.
- Constantinople. With an Introduction by General Lew Wallace. Boston: Roberts bros, 1895. 2 vols. Lge 8vo. xxii,812 pp. Num ills, fldg map. Orig blue cloth gilt, extremities sl rubbed. *(Karmiole)* **$50** [≈ £31]

Gue, Benjamin F.
- History of Iowa. From the Earliest Times to the Beginning of the Twentieth Century. New York: Century History Co, [1903]. 4 vols. Orig light green cloth, spine lettering sl faded. *(Terramedia)* **$100** [≈ £62]

Guenther, K.
- A Naturalist in Brazil. The Fauna and Flora and the People of Brazil. Translated by B. Miall. London: 1931. Roy 8vo. 400 pp. 32 plates & text figs. Orig cloth.
(Wheldon & Wesley) **£35** [≈ $56]

Guillemard, F.H.H.
- The Cruise of the Marchesa to Kamschatka & New Guinea with Notices of Formosa, Liu-Kiu and Various Islands of the Malay Archipelago. London: Murray, 1889. 2nd edn. xx,455 pp. 14 maps, 139 w'engvd ills. Orig cloth gilt, uncut, rubbed at extremities.
(Claude Cox) **£55** [≈ $88]

Gully, John
- New Zealand Scenery Chromolithographed after Original Water-Colour Drawings ... With Descriptive Letterpress by Dr. Julius Von Haast. London: Marcus Ward, 1877. 1st edn. Elephant folio. Perf lib stamp on title. Sl wear. 15 chromo plates. Orig cloth, rebacked.
(M & S Rare Books) **$3,500** [≈ £2,187]

Gunnison, J.W.
- The Mormons, or, Latter-Day Saints, in the Valley of the Great Salt Lake ... a Residence among them. Philadelphia: 1856. ix, [i], 13-168, advt pp. Dampstain to advts. Orig cloth, sunned, spine ends worn.
(Reese) **$100** [≈ £62]

Gunther, R.T.
- Oxford Gardens based upon Daubeny's Popular Guide to the Physick Garden of Oxford ... Oxford: Parker, 1912. Cr 8vo. xv,288 pp. Planting charts, 33 ills. Orig gilt dec blue cloth. *(Blackwell's)* **£50** [≈ $80]

Guppy, H.B.
- Observations of a Naturalist in the Pacific between 1896 and 1899. London: 1903 - 06. 2 vols. 8vo. Maps, ills. Orig cloth. Sl worn & reprd dws.
(Wheldon & Wesley) **£100** [≈ $160]

Gurney, John Henry
- Rambles of a Naturalist in Egypt and other Countries ... with ... Ornithological Notes. London: Jarrold, [ca 1880]. 8vo. 307,advt pp. Orig pict gilt maroon cloth, spine sl sunned, edges frayed, sm tear at ft of spine.
(Terramedia) **$100** [≈ £62]

Guthrie, Maria
- A Tour, performed in the years 1795-6, through the Taurida, or Crimea, the Antient Kingdom of Bosphorus ... London: Nichols ..., 1802. Only edn. 4to. xxiv,446,[2] pp. Lge fldg map, plan, 3 engvd plates, 8 plates of medals, text ills. Orig bds, uncut, spine sl worn. *(Young's)* **£230** [≈ $368]
- A Tour performed in the Years 1795-6, through the Taurida, or Crimea, the Ancient Kingdom of Bosphorus ... London: Cadell & Davies, 1802. 4to. xxiv,446,[2] pp. 2 fldg maps, 11 plates. Occas foxing. Contemp half calf, rebacked, new endpapers.
(Frew Mackenzie) **£200** [≈ $320]

H., T.
- A Short Way to Know the World ... see Harris, T.

Habersham, A.W.
- The North Pacific Surveying and Exploring Expedition; or, My Last Cruise ... Philadelphia: 1857. 507,advt pp. Frontis, addtnl engvd title, plates, ills. Waterstains to about half the plates. Orig pict cloth, spine gilt extra, some wear to extremities.
(Reese) **$250** [≈ £156]

Hadfield, William
- Brazil and the River Plate in 1868: showing the Progress of those Countries since his former Visit in 1853. London: Bates, Hendy, 1869. 1st edn. [2],272,[11 advt] pp. 4 w'engvd plates. Orig cloth gilt, extremities sl rubbed.
(Karmiole) **$175 [≈£109]**
- Brazil and the River Plate in 1868. Showing the Progress of those Countries since his former visit in 1853. London: Bates, Hendy & Co, 1869. 8vo. 271, 11 advt pp. 4 plates. Orig pict blue cloth, spine ends chipped.
(Adelson) **$225 [≈£140]**
- Brazil, the River Plate, and the Falkland Islands; with the Cape Horn Route to Australia ... Illustrated ... from the Drawings of Sir Charles Hotham ... London: Longman ..., 1854. 8vo. vi,384 pp. 3 fldg maps, port, text ills. Half calf, rubbed.
(Adelson) **$375 [≈£234]**

Hafen, Le Roy R.
- Colorado. The Story of a Western Commonwealth. Denver: The Peerless Publishing Co, 1933. 8vo. 328 pp. Num ills. Orig green cloth gilt, spine extremities sl rubbed. Author's pres copy.
(Karmiole) **$75 [≈£46]**

Haig, M.R.
- The Indus Delta Country. A Memoir chiefly on its ancient Geography and History. London: 1894. 1st edn. 8vo. 148 pp. 3 maps. Orig cloth. *(Robertshaw)* **£20 [≈$32]**

Hailey, Lord
- An African Survey. Oxford: 1938. 8vo. xxviii, 1837 pp. 6 maps. Orig cloth, sl soiled & worn.
(Dillons) **£35 [≈$56]**

Hakluyt, Richard
- The Principal Navigations Voyages Traffiques & Discoveries of the English Nation ... Glasgow: James MacLehose, 1903. One of 1000. 12 vols. 8vo. Num maps & plates. Orig pict cloth, rubbed, spines faded, ex lib. *(Adelson)* **$275 [≈£171]**

Hales, A.G.
- Campaign Pictures of the War in South Africa (1899-1900). Letters from the Front. London: Cassell, 1900. 8vo. xi,303,20 advt pp. Frontis. Orig red cloth gilt.
(Bates & Hindmarch) **£20 [≈$32]**

Halifax, and its Gibbet-Law ...
- See Bentley, John.

Halkett, John
- Statement Respecting the Earl of Selkirk's Settlement upon the Red River, in North America ... London: Murray, 1817. The 'imprinted issue", after the unimprinted issue of the same year. 194,[ii],c pp. Fldg map. Contemp bds, rebacked.
(Reese) **$750 [≈£468]**

Hall, Captain Basil, R.N.
- Account of a Voyage of Discovery to the West Coast of Corea, and the Great Loo-Choo Island ... London: Murray, 1818. 1st edn. 4to. xv,1,222, cxxx,72 pp. 9 cold plates & 6 other plates & maps (2 fldg). Contemp calf, front hinge cracked.
(Terramedia) **$900 [≈£562]**
- Extracts from a Journal, written on the Coasts of Chili, Peru, and Mexico, in the Years 1820, 1821, 1822. Edinburgh: Constable, 1824. 1st edn. 2 vols. 12mo. xvi,335; xii,380 pp. Fldg map (torn). Contemp half calf, rubbed, vol 1 front cvr re-attached.
(Schoyer) **$125 [≈£78]**
- Extracts from a Journal written on the Coasts of Chili, Peru, and Mexico, in the Years 1820, 1821, 1822. Edinburgh: Constable, 1824. 2nd edn. 2 vols. xvii,372; xii,288,65 pp. Fldg map. Dec red mor.
(Parmer) **$200 [≈£125]**
- Extracts from a Journal, written on the Coasts of Chili, Peru, and Mexico ... Reprinted from the last [i.e. first] London Edition. Boston: Wells & Lilly, 1824. 2 vols in one. 12mo. xii,244; vii,230 pp. Dampstain on top crnr. Contemp three qtr calf, v rubbed.
(Schoyer) **$45 [≈£28]**
- Forty Etchings made from Sketches with the Camera Lucida, in North America, in 1827 and 1828. London: Simpkin & Marshall ..., 1829. 1st edn. Sm folio. [ii],iv pp. 40 etchings on 20 ff, each with a descriptive leaf of text. Orig ptd bds, old cloth reback.
(Charles B. Wood) **$350 [≈£218]**
- Patchwork. London: Moxon, 1841. 1st edn. 3 vols. Lacks half-titles in vol 2 & 3 (not called for in vol 1). Contemp half calf, spines sl darkened & lacking labels.
(Burmester) **£45 [≈$72]**
- Schloss Hainfeld; or, a Winter in Lower Styria. Edinburgh: Robert Cadell ..., 1836. 1st edn. Lge 12mo. Name on title. Contemp half calf, upper jnt sl damaged.
(Hannas) **£35 [≈$56]**

Hall, Charles Francis
- Arctic Researches and Life among the Esquimaux: being the Narrative of an Expedition in Search of Sir John Franklin in

the Years 1860, 1861 and 1862. New York: Harper, 1865. 1st US edn. xxviii, 595 pp. Addtnl engvd title, fldg map, ills. Orig cloth, minor wear. *(High Latitude)* **$110 [≈ £68]**

- Arctic Researches and Life among the Esquimaux: being the Narrative of an Expedition in Search of Sir John Franklin in the Years 1860, 1861 and 1862. New York: 1866. Thick 8vo. xvi, 595 pp. Engvd title, ills. Lacks map. Orig cloth, spine ends worn.
(Reese) **$125 [≈ £78]**

- Narrative of the North Polar Expedition U.S. Ship Polaris, Captain Charles Francis Hall Commanding. Edited by Rear Adm. C.H. Davis. Washington: GPO, 1876. 4to. 696 pp. Num plates & maps. Orig cloth, minor wear.
(High Latitude) **$100 [≈ £62]**

- Narrative of the Second Arctic Expedition made by Charles F. Hall ... during the Years 1864-69 ... Edited by J.E. Nourse. Washington: 1879. 1st edn. 4to. 644 pp. Fldg maps, lge fldg linen backed map in pocket, photo plates. Orig calf, spine chipped.
(Jenkins) **$225 [≈ £140]**

Hall, Francis
- Colombia: Its Present State ... and Inducements to Emigration. London: Baldwin, 1824. 1st edn. [4], 154 pp. Fldg map. Lib stamp on title. Half mor.
(Jenkins) **$200 [≈ £125]**

- Travels in Canada and the United States in 1816 and 1817. London: Longman ..., 1818. 1st edn. 8vo. Fldg map. Sl staining. half calf. *(Falkner)* **£85 [≈ $136]**

- Travels in Canada & the United States in 1816 & 1817. London: Longman, Hurst, 1818. 1st edn. 8vo. 534 pp. Fldg map (sl foxed). Contemp calf, rebacked, orig label, bumped. *(Terramedia)* **$300 [≈ £187]**

Hall, Revd George
- The History of Chesterfield, and its Charities ... Chesterfield: John Ford, 1823. 8vo. viii,132,[xii] pp. 4 plates. Some light soiling. 19th c half calf, gilt spine.
(Frew Mackenzie) **£75 [≈ $120]**

Hall, H.R.
- Aegean Archaeology: Introduction to the Archaeology of Prehistoric Greece. London: Philip Lee Warner; New York: Putnam's, 1915. 8vo. Fldg map, cold frontis, plates, ills. 1 leaf loose. Orig pict blue cloth.
(Terramedia) **$50 [≈ £31]**

Hall, Mary
- A Woman's Trek from the Cape to Cairo. London: Methuen, [1907]. 1st edn. 8vo.

424,40 advt pp. Fldg map, num plates. Orig blue cloth, sl rubbed. Author's pres copy.
(Terramedia) **$75 [≈ £46]**

Hall, Mrs Newman
- Through the Tyrol to Venice. London: James Nisbet, 1860. 8vo. 388 pp. Frontis. Orig brown cloth gilt, jnts sl loose.
(Piccadilly) **£20 [≈ $32]**

Hall, R.
- The Highland Sportsman. A Compendious Sporting Guide to the Highlands of Scotland. London: 1882. 8vo. Ills. Qtr mor.
(Grayling) **£50 [≈ $80]**

Hall, Richard Nicklin
- Great Zimbabwe, Mashonaland, Rhodesia ... London: Methuen, (1905). 1st edn. Tall 8vo. xliii, 459 pp. 200 ills, maps, plans, inc fldg cold map. Orig pict gilt cloth, spine sunned, lacks rear free endpaper, rear hinge reprd.
(Schoyer) **$75 [≈ £46]**

Hall, Richard Nicklin & Neal, W.G.
- The Ancient Ruins of Rhodesia (Monomotapae Imperium). London: Methuen, 1902. 1st edn. 8vo. 396, advt pp. Fldg map in pocket, frontis, num plates. Foxing. Marg pencil marks. Orig pict blue cloth gilt, spine edges sl worn, inner hinges cracked. *(Terramedia)* **$100 [≈ £62]**

- The Ancient Ruins of Rhodesia (Monomotapae Imperium). London: Methuen, 1902. 8vo. xxvii, 396 pp. 13 maps & plans (inc 1 lge fldg linen backed), 36 ills. Ex-lib. Rec red qtr leather.
(Bates & Hindmarch) **£85 [≈ $136]**

Hall, S.C.
- A Week at Killarney, with Descriptions of the Routes Thither from Dublin, Cork, etc. London: Virtue, 1865. Sm 4to. Ills. Orig green cloth, sl worn.
(Emerald Isle) **£25 [≈ $40]**

Hall, Mr. & Mrs. S.C.
- Ireland, its Scenery, Character, etc. London: How, 1841-43. 1st edn. 3 vols. Contemp half calf. *(Emerald Isle)* **£150 [≈ $240]**

- Ireland; Its Scenery, Character, etc. New Edition. Philadelphia: Gebbie & Barrie, [ca 1860]. 3 vols. 8vo. 13 chromolitho views, 18 cold maps, 609 plates & ills. Orig green cloth gilt. *(Gough)* **£175 [≈ $280]**

Hallifax, and its Gibbet-Law ...
- See Midgley, Samuel.

Hallock, Charles
- Our New Alaska: or, the Seward Purchase Vindicated. New York: Forest & Stream, 1886. 8vo. viii,[2],9-209 pp. Fldg map, ills. Orig cloth.   *(High Latitude)* **$35 [≈ £21]**

Hamilton, John P.
- Travels through the Interior Provinces of Columbia. London: Murray, 1827. 2 vols. 8vo. 4, 332; 4,256, errata pp. Fldg map, 7 plates. Mod buckram, ex-lib.
    (Adelson) **$375 [≈ £234]**

Hamilton, Thomas
- Men and Manners in America. By the Author of 'Cyril Thornton,' etc. Edinburgh: Blackwood; London: Cadell, 1833. 1st edn. 2 vols. 8vo. Contemp calf, gilt spines, mor labels (1 lacking), somewhat scuffed.
    (Trebizond) **$120 [≈ £75]**

Hamilton, Vereker M. & Fasson, Stewart M.
- Scenes in Ceylon. London: Chapman & Hall; Colombo: H.W. & A.W. Cave, [1881]. 1st edn. Oblong folio. 4 pp prelims, errata slip. 20 litho plates. Accompanying text. Crease in title. Orig morocco backed cloth, cold paper onlay, extremities rubbed, speckled fading.
    (Claude Cox) **£230 [≈ $368]**

Hamilton, William, 1755-1797
- Letters Concerning the Northern Coast of the County of Antrim ... Antiquities, Customs, Natural History, of the Basaltes. Dublin: Bonham, 1790. Map, plates. Diced calf, rebacked.   *(Emerald Isle)* **£150 [≈ $240]**
- Letters Concerning the Northern Coast of the County of Antrim ... Belfast: Simms & McIntyre, 1822. Map, plates. Half leather.
    (Emerald Isle) **£95 [≈ $152]**

Hamlin, Cyrus
- Among the Turks. New York: American Tract Society, 1877. Sm 8vo. 378,advt pp. Orig mustard cloth.
    (Terramedia) **$50 [≈ £31]**

Hammer, S.C.
- Norway. Painted by A. Heaton Cooper. London: A. & C. Black, 1928. 1st edn. Map, 32 cold plates. Orig cloth.
    (Old Cathay) **£16 [≈ $25]**

Hanbury, David T.
- Sport & Travel in the Northland of Canada. New York & London: Macmillan & Arnold, 1904. 1st edn. 8vo. 319 pp. 2 fldg maps, tissued cold & other plates. Orig maroon

cloth, t.e.g., bottom of front cvr sl spotted.
    (Terramedia) **$200 [≈ £125]**

Handcock, William D.
- The History and Antiquities of Tallaght, Co. Dublin. Dublin: Hodges, 1899. 2nd edn, rvsd. 160 pp. Orig cloth.
    (Emerald Isle) **£35 [≈ $56]**

Hanson, Charles Henry
- The Land of Greece described and illustrated. London: T. Nelson & Sons, 1886. 1st edn. Lge 8vo. 400 pp. Addtnl vignette title, 3 maps, 44 ills. Orig pict cloth, a.e.g.
    (Schoyer) **$45 [≈ £28]**

Harcourt, Edward Vernon
- A Sketch of Madeira; containing Information for the Traveller, or Invalid Visitor. London: Murray, 1851. 1st edn. 8vo. xvi,176, [4],32 advt pp. 2 fldg maps (1 sl creased), frontis, engvd title vignette, 4 engvs. Prelims sl spotted. Orig orange cloth.
    (Frew Mackenzie) **£98 [≈ $156]**

Harding, W.M.
- Trans-Atlantic Sketches, by "Porte Plume." New York: 1879. 87 pp. Title vignette. Limp cloth gilt, a bit sunned. *(Reese)* **$75 [≈ £46]**

Hardy, Philip Dixon
- The Northern Tourist, or Stranger's Guide to the North and West of Ireland. Dublin: Curry, 1830. 12mo. 394 pp. Map, plates. Green calf.   *(Emerald Isle)* **£75 [≈ $120]**

Hare, Augustus J.C.
- Walks in London. London: 1878. 1st edn. 2 vols. 8vo. Num w'engvd text ills. Orig cloth.
    (Robertshaw) **£15 [≈ $24]**

Hargrave, James
- The Hargrave Correspondence 1821-1843. Toronto: Champlain Society, 1938. One of 550. 8vo. xxvi,472,[xii] pp. Fldg map in pocket, 3 plates. Orig cloth, spine sl faded.
    (Parmer) **$175 [≈ £109]**

Hargraves, Edward Hammond
- Australia and Its Gold Fields ... London: H. Ingram & Co, 1855. 8vo. xvi,240 pp. Fldg map, port frontis. Sl smudge marks on fly leaf. Orig bead grain blue cloth, Australian arms in gilt on front cvr, v bright.
    (Moon) **£600 [≈ $960]**

Hargrove, Ely
- The Ancient Customs of the Forest of Knaresborough ... Knaresborough: ptd by

Hargrove & Sons, 1808. 1st edn. 12mo. 71,[1] pp. Frontis. Last few ff dog-eared, last leaf somewhat soiled. Stitched as issued, uncut.
(Burmester) **£38 [≈ $60]**
- The History of the Castle, Town and Forest of Knaresborough, with Harrogate, and its Medicinal Waters. York: W. Blanchard; & sold by E. Hargrove ..., 1789. 4th edn, enlgd. 12mo. 330 pp. Fldg hand cold map, 7 plates. Contemp calf, gilt spine. Colquhoun b'plate.
(Ximenes) **$325 [≈ £203]**

Harkin, William
- Scenery and Antiquities of North West Donegal. Londonderry: Irvine, 1893. 120 pp. Ills, advts. Orig cloth.
(Emerald Isle) **£50 [≈ $80]**

Harland, J. (ed.)
- Historical Account of the Cistercian Abbey of Salley in Craven, Yorkshire ... London: J. Russell Smith; Clitheroe: Wm. Whewell, 1853. 1st edn. [ii],107 pp. Litho title in red & black, frontis, fldg plan, 10 litho plates. Orig cloth gilt.
(Hollett) **£65 [≈ $104]**

Harm, Ray
- Ray Harm's African Sketchbook. Edited by Robert Emmett McDowell. Louisville, New York: Frame House Gallery, [1973]. 1st edn. Oblong folio. xxix pp. 80 plates, many cold. Orig cloth. Broken slipcase. Inscribed by the artist.
(Terramedia) **$100 [≈ £62]**

Harmon, Daniel W.
- A Journal of Voyages and Travels in the Interiour of North America ... from Montreal nearly to the Pacific Ocean ... Andover: 1820. 1st edn. 432 pp. Port, fldg map. Usual browning, some staining. Sl offsetting. No errata slip. Orig calf, front hinge cracking.
(Reese) **$850 [≈ £531]**
- A Journal of Voyages and Travels in the Interior of North America. Andover, Mass.: 1820. 1st edn. 432 pp. Port. Lacks map. Contemp calf.
(Jenkins) **$385 [≈ £240]**

Harnett, Legh
- Two Lectures on British Columbia. Victoria: 1868. 50 pp. 2 sm stains. Self-wraps, later tape spine.
(Reese) **$1,250 [≈ £781]**

Harris, Charles T.
- Memories of Manhattan in the Sixties & Seventies. New York: Derrydale Press, 1928. One of 1000. Orig cloth & bds, front hinge sl cracked internally. *(Terramedia)* **$50 [≈ £31]**

Harris, George Herbert
- The Faroe Islands. Birmingham: Cornish Bros, 1927. 1st edn. 8vo. Orig cloth backed paper.
(Hannas) **£45 [≈ $72]**

H[arris?], T.
- A Short Way to Know the World: or the Rudiments of Geography: being a New Familiar Method of teaching Youth the Knowledge of the Globe ... By T.H. The Second Edition, with Additions. London: 1712. 12mo. 2 plates. Contemp calf, gilt spine worn. Rolle b'plate. *(Hannas)* **£120 [≈ $192]**

Harris, William Cornwallis
- The Highlands of Ethiopia. London: Longman ..., 1844. 3 vols. 8vo. Fldg map, chromolitho dedic, 3 title vignettes, 3 litho frontis (1 cold). Occas light soiling. Orig plum cloth, spines & extremities darkened.
(Frew Mackenzie) **£450 [≈ $720]**
- The Highlands of Ethiopia. From the First London Edition. New York: J. Winchester, New World Press, [ca 1844]. 1st Amer edn. 8vo. xii, 392 pp. 6 lithos, inc hand cold frontis. Some text foxing. Orig brown gilt stamped cloth, extremities sl frayed.
(Karmiole) **$125 [≈ £78]**
- The Wild Sports of Southern Africa. London: Murray, 1839. xxiv,387 pp. Fldg map, 7 plates. Leather gilt, mrbld endpapers.
(Parmer) **$500 [≈ £312]**
- The Wild Sports of Southern Africa: being the Narrative of an Expedition from the Cape of Good Hope ... Third Edition. London: William Pickering, 1841. Roy 8vo. xvi,359,[i advt] pp. Map, 26 hand cold litho plates inc title. Orig cloth gilt, a.e.g., fine.
(Blackwell's) **£700 [≈ $1,120]**
- The Wild Sports of Southern Africa. London: 1852. 5th edn. 8vo. xvi,359 pp. Cold title vignette, cold frontis, 24 cold plates. 1 plate somewhat foxed. Mod qtr calf, qtr leather slipcase. *(Wheldon & Wesley)* **£480 [≈ $768]**

Harrison, E.S.
- Nome and the Seward Peninsula. A Book of Information about Northwestern Alaska. Seattle: Metropolitan Press, [ca 1905]. 8vo. [vi], 132, 12 advt pp. Fldg map, num photo ills. Orig stiff ptd wraps.
(High Latitude) **$75 [≈ £46]**

Harrison, Thomas Skelton
- The Homely Diary of a Diplomat in the East 1897-1899. Boston & New York: 1917. 1st edn. xxix, 364 pp. 41 plates, num text ills. Orig cloth, t.e.g., partly unopened, sl rubbed.
(Worldwide Antiqu'n) **£65 [≈ £40]**

Harrisse, Henry
- Bibliotheca Americana Vetustissima. A Description of Works relating to America published between the Years 1492 and 1551. New York: 1866. Thick 4to. 519 pp. Some staining, a few ff chipped & dogeared. Later cloth.   *(Reese)* **$300 [≈ £187]**

Harrod, W.
- The History of Mansfield and its Environs. Mansfield: the author, 1801. 1st edn. Sm 4to. iv,64,56 pp. 17 MS appendix pp. 17 plates (2 cold, most fldg). Contemp calf gilt, rebacked.   *(Gough)* **£275 [≈ $440]**

Hartlib, Samuel
- The Reformed Commonwealth of Bees ... with The Reformed Virginian Silk-Worm ... London: 1655.Sm 4to. iv, 62, [2], [iv],40 pp. W'cuts. Title soiled & mtd. Sl soiling & staining. Sm hole in last 2 ff, with sl loss of text. New calf, antique style.
        (Wheldon & Wesley) **£750 [≈ $1,200]**
- The Reformed Virginian Silk-Worm, Or, a Rare and New Discovery ... for the feeding of Silk-worms in the Woods, on the Mulberry-Tree leaves in Virginia ... London: 1655. [4], 40 pp. Calf.   *(Reese)* **$2,750 [≈ £1,718]**

Hartwig. G.
- The Polar World ... New York: Harper, 1869. 1st Amer edn. xvi,[17]-486,advt pp. 163 ills. Orig dec brown cloth gilt, some shelf wear.   *(Parmer)* **$100 [≈ £62]**
- The Polar World ... London: 1874. 2nd edn. xviii,548 pp. Fldg cold maps, frontis, plates (some tinted). Scattered foxing & darkening. Three qtr calf & cloth, scuffed, worn at extremities, cloth soiled, repairs to outer hinge, prize b'plate.   *(Reese)* **$50 [≈ £31]**

Harvey, E.G.
- Mullyon: its History, Scenery & Antiquities; Narratives of Shipwrecks & its Coast ... Truro & London: 1875. 8vo. Dble page map, frontis, 4 w'engvd plates. Orig cloth gilt, a.e.g.   *(Ambra)* **£46 [≈ $73]**

Harvey, M.
- Newfoundland As It Is in 1894 ... A Handbook and Tourists' Guide. London: Kegan, Paul ..., 1894. 8vo. [9 advt], 298, [22 advt] pp. Fldg cold map. Orig red cloth gilt, cvrs waterstained.   *(Moon)* **£100 [≈ $160]**
- Text-Book of Newfoundland History, for the Use of Schools and Academies. Boston: Doyle & Whittle, 1885. 8vo. 202 pp. Fldg map, ills. Orig dec ptd brown cloth, faint string mark to back cvr. Author's pres inscrptn to his

brother.   *(Moon)* **£100 [≈ $160]**

Haskell, William R.
- Two Years in the Klondike and Alaskan Gold-Fields. A Thrilling Narrative of Personal Experience and Adventure ... Hartford, CT: Hartford Pub Co, 1898. 8vo. xxxii, 33-558 pp. 24 photo plates. Lacks map. Orig cloth.   *(High Latitude)* **$65 [≈ £40]**

Haslund, Henning
- Tents in Mongolia (Yabonah). Adventures and Experiences among the Nomads of Central Asia. New York: Dutton, [1934]. 1st edn. Lge 8vo. 366 pp. Num photo plates. Orig cloth.   *(Terramedia)* **$35 [≈ £21]**

Hassaurek, Friedrich
- Four Years among Spanish Americans. New York: Hurd & Houghton, 1867. 1st edn. 8vo. Orig cloth, gilt spine, spine extremities worn.   *(Trebizond)* **$100 [≈ £62]**
- Four Years among Spanish-Americans. New York: 1868. 401 pp. Orig cloth.
        (Reese) **$125 [≈ £78]**

Hassell, John
- Tour of the Grand Junction ... London: for J. Hassell, 1819. 8vo. Hand cold aquatint frontis, 23 hand cold aquatint plates. Blank marg of 1 plate reprd. Contemp russia gilt, jnts reprd, sm repr to ft of spine. Duchess of St Albans's copy.   *(Spelman)* **£480 [≈ $768]**

Hasselquist, Frederick
- Voyages and Travels in the Levant; in the Years 1749, 50, 51, 52 ... Published ... by Charles Linnaeus ... London: Davis & Reymers, 1766. Sm 8vo. viii,456 pp. Fldg map frontis. Lower part of book affected by dampstaining. Rec half mor.
        (Worldwide Antiqu'n) **$225 [≈ £140]**

Hattersley, C.W.
- The Baganda at Home. With One Hundred Pictures of Life and Work in Uganda. London: RTS, 1908. 1st edn. 8vo. xvi,227,advt pp. Num photo plates. Orig pict cloth, rear hinge sl cracked.
        (Terramedia) **$100 [≈ £62]**

Hatton, Frank
- North Borneo. Explorations and Adventures on the Equator ... London: Sampson Low, 1885. 8vo. xiv, 342 pp. 18 plates, 26 text ills. Lacks frontis port. Contemp three qtr mor, v rubbed, edges worn, shaken.
        (Schoyer) **$40 [≈ £25]**

Haughton, H.L.
- Sport & Folklore in the Himalaya. London: 1913. 8vo. Ills. Endpapers sl scuffed & marked. Orig pict gilt cloth, sl rubbed.
(Grayling) £90 [≈ $144]

Hawes, Charles Boardman
- Whaling. New York: Doubleday, Page, 1924. 1st edn. 8vo. 358 pp. 8 cold plates. Orig blue cloth gilt, t.e.g.   *(Parmer)* $165 [≈ £103]

Hawes, J.
- The Religion of the East, with Impressions of Foreign Travel. Hartford: Belknap & Hammersley, 1845. 1st edn. 8vo. 215 pp. 2 tinted plates. Orig cloth, edges rubbed, spine ends chipped, tears in spine.
(Worldwide Antiqu'n) $75 [≈ £46]

Hawes, Robert & Loder, Robert
- The History of Framlingham in the County of Suffolk ... Woodbridge: R. Loder, 1798. [One of 250]. 4to. xii,453 pp. 2 pp subscribers. Port frontis, 10 plates. Contemp qtr calf, uncut, largely unopened, rebacked.
(Lamb) £180 [≈ $288]

Hawkesworth, John
- An Account of the Voyages undertaken by Order of his Present Majesty for Making Discoveries in the Southern Hemisphere ... Captain Cook ... Third Edition. London: Strahan & Cadell, 1785. 4 vols. 8vo. 2 fldg charts, 11 fldg plates. Orig sheep, vol 2 spine relaid.   *(Bickersteth)* £485 [≈ $776]

Hawks, Francis Lister
- Narrative of the Expeditions of an American Squadron ... see Perry, M.C.

Hay, A.
- The History of Chichester. Chichester: 1804. 8vo. xiv,605,16 pp. Calf, jnts becoming weak.
(Henly) £85 [≈ $136]

Hayes, Isaac I.
- An Arctic Boat Journey. Boston: Taggard & Chase, 1860. 1st edn. Sm 8vo. xvii,375 pp. Sm tear in 1 fldg map. Orig gilt dec brown cloth, spine ends chipped, spine leaning, edges worn.   *(Parmer)* $60 [≈ £37]

Haynes, Alfred E.
- Man-Hunting in the Desert, being a Narrative of the Palmer Search Expedition (1882, 1883). London: 1894. xxii,305 pp. Maps, port, plates. Occas trace of foxing. Contemp three qtr polished calf, some wear to extremities.   *(Reese)* $350 [≈ £218]

Haywood, A.H.W.
- Through Timbuctu & Across the Sahara. An Account of an Adventurous Journey of Exploration from Sierra Leone to the Source of the Niger ... London: 1912. 1st edn. 8vo. 349 pp. Fldg cold map, num plates. Orig pict red cloth gilt.   *(Terramedia)* $125 [≈ £78]

Hazard, Samuel
- Santo Domingo, Past and Present; with a Glance at Hayti. New York: Harper, 1873. 1st edn. 8vo. Advt leaf. Fldg map, frontis, 24 full-page & num text ills. Orig dec cloth gilt, gilt spine.   *(Trebizond)* $110 [≈ £68]

Head, Sir Francis Bond
- A Faggot of French Sticks. By the author of 'Bubbles from the Brunnen of Nassau'. London: Murray, 1852. 1st edn. 2 vols. 8vo. 463; 455, [32 ctlg dated Oct 1851] pp. Orig mrbld blue cloth blocked in gold, by Remnant & Edmonds, hinges & spine ends rubbed.
(Claude Cox) £30 [≈ $48]
- A Fortnight in Ireland. London: Murray, 1852. 8vo. [8], 400, 16 advt pp. Fldg map, text ills. Orig cloth gilt.
(Bickersteth) £58.50 [≈ $94]
- The Life of Bruce, the African Traveller. London: 1830. 16mo. vii,535 pp. Port, 2 fldg maps. Occas sl foxing. Contemp three qtr polished calf, lacks label, rubbed, extremities worn.   *(Reese)* $60 [≈ £37]
- The Life of Bruce, the African Traveller ... Third Edition. London: Murray, 1838. 8vo. Frontis (guard tissue intact), 2 maps (1 fldg). Contemp calf, a.e.g., spine relaid.
(Waterfield's) £45 [≈ $72]
- A Narrative [of his despatches from Upper Canada]. London: Murray, 1839. 1st edn. 8vo. viii, 488,38 appendix, [8 advt dated February 1839] pp. Errata slip. Sl foxed. Orig gilt dec green cloth, worn, bumped & soiled, spine faded, hinges well started.
(Parmer) $300 [≈ £187]
- A Narrative [of his administration of Upper Canada]. Second Edition. London: Murray, 1839. 8vo. viii,488 pp, advt leaf, 38 pp, 8 ctlg pp. Sewing of some sections loose, occas spotting. Orig cloth, faded.
(Bickersteth) £55 [≈ $88]
- Rough Notes Taken During Rapid Journeys Across the Pampas and among the Andes. London: Murray, 1826. 2nd edn. 8vo. 309 pp. Orig bds, label, spine ends chipped, new endpapers.   *(Schoyer)* $100 [≈ £62]

Head, Sir George
- Rome. A Tour of Many Days. London: Longmans ..., 1849. 1st edn. 3 vols. 8vo. Orig

maroon cloth, uncut, spines faded & frayed at ends with sl loss at hd. *(Clark)* **£40 [≃ $64]**

Healy, M.A.
- Report of the Cruise of the Revenue Marine Steamer Corwin in the Arctic Ocean. Washington: GPO, 1887. 1st edn (?). Lge 4to. 2 lge fldg maps, 43 plates (inc 4 cold). Orig black cloth, sl soiled & sl frayed at edges. *(Terramedia)* **$160 [≃ £100]**
- Report of the Cruise of the Revenue Steamer Corwin in the Arctic Ocean ... Washington: GPO, 1889. Some minor flaws. Later cloth. *(Parmer)* **$75 [≃ £46]**

Hearn, Lafcadio
- Exotics and Retrospectives. Boston: Little, Brown, 1898. 1st Waedn. 12mo. 299 pp. 4 plates, 13 text ills. Orig pict cloth, t.e.g., spine sunned. *(Schoyer)* **$50 [≃ £31]**
- Glimpses of Unfamiliar Japan. Boston & New York: Houghton, Mifflin, [1922]. 2 vols. Sm 8vo. x,[342]; 699 pp. Orig pict black cloth, sl worn. *(Terramedia)* **$50 [≃ £31]**
- Historical Sketch Book and Guide to New Orleans and Environs. With Map ... Edited and Compiled by Several Leading Writers of the New Orleans Press. New York: Will H. Coleman, 1885. Sm 8vo. [4],324 pp. Ills. Orig brown cloth, sl frayed. Without the map (often lacking). *(Karmiole)* **$250 [≃ £156]**
- A Japanese Miscellany. London: Sampson Low ..., 1901. 1st English edn. Sm 8vo. [x],305, [1 blank] pp. 8 plates, 5 text ills. Some marg browning. 2 blank crnr tips torn away. Old repr to flyleaf. Orig pict cloth, t.e.g. *(Bow Windows)* **£75 [≃ $120]**

Hearne, Samuel
- A Journey from Prince of Wales Fort in Hudson's Bay, to the Northern Ocean ... London: 1795. Folio. xliv,458 pp. Lge fldg map, 3 fldg charts, 2 plates (1 fldg). Faint lib stamps, marg dampstain to a few ff inc 1 fldg chart & fldg plate. Antique half calf. *(Reese)* **$2,750 [≃ £1,718]**
- A Journey from Prince of Wales's Fort in Hudson's Bay, to the Northern Ocean. Amsterdam & New York: 1968. Facs reprint of the 1795 edn. xliv,458 pp. 8 plates & maps. *(Parmer)* **$100 [≃ £62]**

Hearne, Thomas
- The History and Antiquities of Glastonbury ... Oxford: 1722. 1st edn. 8vo. 349 pp. Frontis & 4 plates (3 fldg). Half calf. One of 150. *(Argosy)* **$250 [≃ £15]**

Heath, Arthur H.
- Sketches of Vanishing China. London: 1927. 1st edn. Lge 4to. 184 pp. 24 cold mtd plates. Orig bndg, spine split. *(Moorhead)* **£20 [≃ $32]**

Heath, Charles
- Historical and Descriptive Accounts of the Ancient and Present State of Ragland Castle ... Monmouth: 1806. 8vo. 150 pp. Disbound. *(Ambra)* **£33 [≃ $52]**

Heath, F.G.
- Autumnal Leaves [New Forest]. London: 1885. 3rd edn. 8vo. 352 pp. 12 cold plates. Flyleaf defective. Orig cloth. *(Wheldon & Wesley)* **£18 [≃ $28]**
- Autumnal Leaves [New Forest]. London: 1899. 4th edn. 8vo. xvi,352 pp. 12 cold plates. Orig cloth, faded. *(Wheldon & Wesley)* **£18 [≃ $28]**

Heber, Reginald
- The Life of Reginald Heber, D.D. Lord Bishop of Calcutta. By his Widow [Amelia Heber] ... Poems ... Journal of his Tour in Norway ... London: 1830. Only edn. 2 vols. 4to. xv,684; viii,636 pp. Port, fldg map, 2 plates. 19th c half calf, gilt spines, mor labels. *(Young's)* **£95 [≃ $152]**
- Narrative of a Journey through the Upper Provinces of India from Calcutta to Bombay 1824-25. Philadelphia: 1829. 402; 522 pp. Orig bds. *(Trophy Room Books)* **$200 [≃ £125]**
- Narrative of a Journey through the Upper Provinces of India from Calcutta to Bombay, 1824-1825 ... London: Murray, 1844. 2 vols. Sm 8vo. viii,311,1 advt; iv,304 pp. Contemp half calf, a little worn. *(Bates & Hindmarch)* **£45 [≃ $72]**

Hector, James
- Handbook of New Zealand. Wellington: 1883. 3rd edn. 8vo. viii,147 pp. 2 fldg maps, 12 charts. Orig limp cloth cvrd bds, rehinged. *(Young's)* **£28 [≃ $44]**

Hedin, Sven
- Big Horse's Flight. The Trail of War in Central Asia. London: Macmillan, 1936. 1st English edn. xv,248 pp. Map, num ills. Foredge spotted. Orig cloth gilt. Dw. *(Hollett)* **£65 [≃ $104]**
- Central Asia and Tibet. Towards the Holy City of Lassa. London: Hurst & Blackett, 1903. 1st English edn. 2 vols. Thick 8vo. xvii, 608; xlv, 664 pp. 5 maps on 4 sheets, 8 cold plates, 420 ills. Some spotting. Orig cloth gilt,

rather worn.   *(Hollett)* £195 [≈ $312]
- Jehol City of Emperors. London: 1932. Roy
  8vo. Map, plates. Orig cloth.
          (Farahar) £35 [≈ $56]
- Jehol City of Emperors. Translated by E.G.
  Nash. London: 1932. 8vo. xiv,278 pp. 62
  plates, 4 line ills. Orig cloth, internally v sl
  weak. Dw soiled & faded on spine.
          (Dillons) £65 [≈ $104]
- My Life as an Explorer. New York: 1925. 1st
  Amer edn. Roy 8vo. Num text ills. Orig cloth.
          (Farahar) £50 [≈ $80]
- My Life as an Explorer. Translated from the
  Swedish by Alhild Huebsch. New York: Boni
  & Liveright, 1925. 1st edn. 8vo. 544 pp. Cold
  frontis, num ills. Orig cloth, sl rubbed,
  unevenly faded
          (Worldwide Antiqu'n) $22 [≈ £13]
- Overland to India. London: Macmillan,
  1910. 1st edn. 2 vols. Thick 8vo. 2 maps, 308
  ills. Orig cloth gilt, rather rubbed & worn, a
  trifle shaken.   *(Hollett)* £120 [≈ $192]
- The Silk Road. London: Routledge, 1938. 1st
  English edn. vii,322 pp. Map, 31 plates.
  Foredge spotted. Orig cloth. Dw rather
  chipped & torn at edges.
          (Hollett) £75 [≈ $120]
- The Silk Road. Translated from the Swedish
  by F.H. Lyon. New York: Dutton, 1938. 1st
  US edn. 8vo. viii,322 pp. Fldg map, 31
  plates, ills. Orig cloth.
          (Worldwide Antiqu'n) $65 [≈ £40]
- Trans-Himalaya. Discoveries and Adventures
  in Tibet. London: Macmillan, 1909-13. 1st
  edn. 3 vols. 8vo. xxiii,436; xvii, 441, advt;
  xxv, 426, advt pp. Num maps & plates. Orig
  gilt pict maroon cloth, t.e.g., spine of vol 1
  sunned & rubbed at one edge.
          (Terramedia) $350 [≈ £218]

Hedley, John
- Tramps in Mongolia. London: Fisher
  Unwin, 1910. Lge 8vo. xii, 371, [ctlg xv,87,2]
  pp. Fldg map, num photo ills. Orig pict gilt
  green cloth, t.e.g.
          (Frew Mackenzie) £80 [≈ $128]

Heim, Arnold & Gansser, August
- The Throne of the Gods. An Account of the
  First Swiss Expedition to the Himalayas.
  New York: Macmillan, 1939. 1st edn.
  xxvi,236 pp. 2 lge fldg plates, lge map in
  pocket, num ills. Orig green cloth, spine sl
  faded.   *(Karmiole)* $150 [≈ £93]

Heine, Heinrich
- A Trip to the Brocken. Translated by R.
  McLintock. London: Macmillan ..., 1881. 1st
  edn of this translation. 8vo. Orig cloth, uncut.

          (Hannas) £25 [≈ $40]

Helms, Anthony Zachariah
- Travels from Buenos Ayres, by Potosi, to
  Lima. With Notes by the Translator,
  containing Topographical Descriptions of the
  Spanish. London: Phillips, 1806. 1st English
  edn. 12mo. xii,287 pp. Fldg map. New three
  qtr calf.   *(Jenkins)* $225 [≈ £140]
- Travels from Buenos Ayres, by Potosi, to
  Lima ... London: Richard Phillips, 1807. 92
  pp. Scattered foxing. Mod half cloth, t.e.g.
          (Reese) $200 [≈ £125]

Hemans, H.N.
- The Log of a Native Commissioner. Work
  and Sport in Southern Rhodesia. London:
  1935. 8vo. Ills. Orig bndg, sl rubbed.
          (Grayling) £40 [≈ $64]

Hemingway, Joseph
- Panorama of the Beauties, Curiosities, &
  Antiquities of North Wales ... Second
  Edition. London: Groombridge, 1835. Lge
  12mo. viii, 314, vi pp. Fldg map, 4 plates.
  Orig roan, gilt spine.
          (Fenning) £38.50 [≈ $62]

Henderson, Alice Palmer
- The Rainbow's End: Alaska. New York:
  Stone, 1898. 296 pp. Frontis, plates. Orig gilt
  dec blue cloth.   *(Parmer)* $125 [≈ £78]

Henderson, Ebenezer
- Iceland; or the Journal of a Residence in that
  Island, during the Years 1814 and 1815 ...
  Edinburgh: 1818. 1st edn. 2 vols. 8vo. Half-
  titles. Fldg map, 16 plates. List of plates calls
  for 14 only. Many edges stained especially on
  plates. Orig bds, uncut.
          (Hannas) £140 [≈ $224]
- Iceland: or the Journal of a residence in that
  Island, during the Years 1814 and 1815 ...
  Abridged from the Second Edinburgh Edition
  ... Boston: 1831. xii,[9]-252 pp. Fldg frontis
  map, plates. Sl foxing. Orig cloth, paper label,
  sunned, a bit worn.   *(Reese)* $125 [≈ £78]

Henderson, John
- Jamaica. Painted by A.S. Forrest. London: A.
  & C. Black Colour Books, Six Shilling Series,
  1906. 1st edn. 24 cold plates. Orig cloth,
  t.e.g.; bndg poor, f.e.p. missing, ochre on
  spine faded.   *(Old Cathay)* £19 [≈ $30]
- The West Indies. Painted by A.S. Forrest.
  London: A. & C. Black Colour Books,
  Twenty Shilling Series, 1905. 1st edn. 74 cold
  plates. Orig dec cloth, spine unfaded.
          (Old Cathay) £75 [≈ $120]

- The West Indies. Painted by A.S. Forrest.
London: A. & C. Black Colour Books,
Twenty Shilling Series, 1905. 1st edn. 74 cold
plates. Orig dec cloth, spine browned, bds
faded, worn & discold.
(Old Cathay) **£50 [≈ $80]**

Hennepin, Louis
- A New Discovery of a Vast Country in
America ... between New France and New
Mexico. London: Bentley, 1698. 1st edn in
English. 2 vols in one. Lacks maps. Calf.
(Jenkins) **$750 [≈ £468]**

Henry, Alexander
- Travels and Adventures in Canada and the
Indian Territories, between the Years 1760
and 1776. In Two Parts. New York: 1809.
330 pp, errata leaf. Port. Moderate foxing.
Contemp calf, rebacked.
(Reese) **$1,250 [≈ £781]**

Henshall, Audrey Shore
- The Chambered Tombs of Scotland.
Edinburgh: UP, 1963-72. 1st edn. 2 vols. 4to.
[xvi],456; [xvi],656 pp. Num plates, photos &
plans. Orig green cloth. Dws.
(Terramedia) **$300 [≈ £187]**

Henson, Matthew A.
- A Negro Explorer at the North Pole. With a
Foreword by Robert E. Peary ... New York:
Stokes, (1912). 1st edn. xx,200 pp. 7 photo
ills. Minor repr to 1 plate marg, minor foxing
in frontis margs. Orig cloth, photo onlay.
(High Latitude) **$250 [≈ £156]**

Herbert, Agnes
- Two Dianas in Somaliland. Record of a
Shooting Trip. London: 1908. 1st edn. 8vo.
306, advt pp. Frontis, num plates. Orig red
cloth.   *(Terramedia)* **$125 [≈ £78]**

Herbert, George & Kingsley, George Henry
- South Sea Bubbles. By the Earl [of Pembroke]
and the Doctor. London: 1872. 312, advt pp.
Orig cloth gilt, soiled. *(Reese)* **$275 [≈ £171]**

Herdman, W.G.
- Pictorial Relics of Ancient Liverpool.
Liverpool: 1878. 2 vols. Folio. xix,60,68,xvi
pp. 109 views on 70 autotype plates. Text
rather spotted in places. Half red mor gilt,
rather marked, spines worn.
(Hollett) **£175 [≈ $280]**

Heriot, George
- Travels through the Canadas ... London: for
Richard Phillips, 1807. 1st edn. Lge 4to.

xii,602 pp. Fldg cold map, fldg frontis, 26
plates (5 fldg). Frontis & map rehinged, marg
dampstains, some foxing & offsetting, ex-lib.
Half calf & bds. *(Wreden)* **$1,800 [≈ £1,125]**
- Travels through the Canadas ... Philadelphia:
M. Carey, 1813. 1st Amer edn. 12mo. Lacks
flyleaves. Orig drab ptd bds, sl wear to upper
jnt.   *(Ximenes)* **$650 [≈ £406]**

Herndon, William Lewis & Gibbon, Lardner
- Exploration of the Valley of the Amazon.
Made Under Direction of the Navy
Department. Washington: A.O.P. Nicholson,
House of Representatives, 1854. 2 vols. 8vo.
339; 417 pp. 52 plates. Occas foxing. Maroon
cloth, 1 bd sunned & yellowed.
(Terramedia) **$100 [≈ £62]**

Hervey, Harry
- Travels in French Indo-China. London:
1928. 1st edn. 8vo. 286 pp. Map, 12 plates.
Orig cloth.   *(Fenning)* **£14.50 [≈ $24]**

Hervey, Maurice H.
- Dark Days in Chile. An Account of the
Revolution of 1891. London: Edward Arnold,
1891-92. 1st edn. 8vo. x,336 (inc advts) pp.
Frontis port, 14 other plates. Orig blue cloth,
hd of spine sl chipped.
(Terramedia) **$100 [≈ £62]**

Hewett, Sir J.
- Jungle Trails in Northern India.
Reminiscences of Hunting in India. London:
Methuen, 1938. 8vo. 278 pp. Frontis, 41
photo ills, map endpapers. Orig bndg.
(Bates & Hindmarch) **£40 [≈ $64]**

Heyerdahl, Thor
- The American Indians in the Pacific. The
Theory behind the Kon-Tiki Expedition.
London: Allen & Unwin, 1952. 1st edn. Lge
8vo. xvi,821 pp. 11 maps, 91 plates. Light
waterstain across crnr of 1st 50 ff. Orig cloth,
new endpapers.   *(Claude Cox)* **£35 [≈ $56]**
- The Art of Easter Island. Garden City, New
York: Doubleday, 1975. 4to. 350 pp. 15 cold
& 320 b/w plates. Orig light green linen.
Chipped dw.   *(Karmiole)* **$65 [≈ £40]**

Heylyn, Peter
- Cosmographie in Foure Bookes ... London:
for Henry Sale, 1652. Folio. 324,274,257,197
pp. Engvd title. Lacks the maps. Rebound in
blue mor.   *(Terramedia)* **$400 [≈ £250]**
- Cosmography, in Four Books ... Revised,
Corrected, and Inlarged by the Author
himself immediately before his Death.

London: 1670. Folio. [xiv],1095,[xliii] pp. Addtnl engvd title (mtd), 4 maps (sl cropped). Occas marks. Rec half calf. Wing H.1693. *(Clark)* **£450 [≃ $720]**

- [Greek title: Microcosmos]. A Little Description of the Great World. The Fourth Edition, Revised. Oxford: 1629. Sm 4to. 10 ff, 807 pp, 3,[4] ff, the last blank. Contemp panelled calf, spine gilt in compartments, red label. STC 13279. *(Hemlock)* **$200 [≃ £125]**

Hichens, Robert
- The Near East. Dalmatia, Greece and Constantinople. Illustrated by Jules Guerin. New York: Century Co, 1913. Sm folio. x,268 pp. Cold & b/w plates & photos, all with tissues. Orig dec blue cloth, edges v sl rubbed. *(Piccadilly)* **£40 [≃ $64]**
- The Near East: Dalmatia, Greece and Constantinople. Illustrated by Jules Guerin. New York: Century Co, 1913. 1st edn. Tall 4to. x,268 pp. 50 tissued plates, many cold. Orig pict cloth. *(Terramedia)* **$50 [≃ £31]**

Hildreth, Richard
- Japan and the Japanese. Revised ... by the Author. Boston: Bradley, Dayton & Co, 1860. 586 pp. Foxed. Orig cloth. *(Wreden)* **$75 [≃ £46]**

Hill, Alex. Staveley
- From Home to Home: Autumn Wandering in the North-West, in the Years 1881, 1882, 1883, 1884. London: Sampson Low ..., 1885. 2nd edn. 8vo. [x], 432, 32 advt pp. 2 fldg maps, 34 ills. Orig gilt dec cloth. *(Young's)* **£48 [≃ $76]**

Hill, Joseph
- The History of Warner's Ranch & its Environs. Los Angeles: privately ptd, 1927. 1st edn. One of 1000. 4to. x,221 pp. Frontis, other ills. Orig maroon cloth, paper spine label, sl worn. *(Terramedia)* **$60 [≃ £37]**

Hillard, George Stillmann
- Six Months in Italy. Boston: Ticknor, 1854. 3rd edn. 2 vols. 12mo. xi,432; vi,455,8 advt pp. Orig brown cloth, hd of spine chipped, ex-lib. *(Terramedia)* **$40 [≃ £25]**

Hilprecht, H.V.
- The Excavations in Assyria and Babylonia. Philadelphia: A.J. Holman, 1904. 8vo. 2 fldg maps in pocket, num ills. Orig rec cloth gilt. *(Karmiole)* **$45 [≃ £28]**
- Explorations in Bible Lands during the 19th Century. Philadelphia: Holman, 1903. 1st edn. Sm 4to. xxiv,810 pp. 4 fldg maps in

pocket, num ills. Orig cloth, t.e.g., sl rubbed. *(Worldwide Antiqu'n)* **$65 [≃ £40]**

Hinchcliff, Thomas W.
- South American Sketches: or a Visit to Rio de Janeiro, the Organ Mountains, La Plata, and the Parma ... London: Longman, Green, 1863. 1st edn. xviii,[2],414 pp. Fldg cold map, frontis, 5 plates (4 cold). Half calf, spine worn. *(Jenkins)* **$200 [≃ £125]**
- South American Sketches; or a Visit to Rio Janeiro, the Organ Mountains, La Plata, and the Parana ... London: Longman, Green ..., 1863. 8vo. xix,414 pp. Fldg cold map, 5 plates (4 cold). New cloth, leather label. *(Adelson)* **$375 [≃ £234]**

Hind, Arthur M.
- Wenceslaus Hollar and his Views of London and Windsor in the Seventeenth Century. London: 1922. 4to. xiv,92 pp. Frontis, 96 ills. Orig cloth, uncut. *(Coombes)* **£110 [≃ $176]**
- Wenceslaus Hollar and his Views of London and Windsor in the Seventeenth Century. London: 1922. 1st edn. Cr 4to. [xvi],92 pp. Port, 96 ills on 65 plates. B'plate. Orig buckram, t.e.g.. *(Bow Windows)* **£115 [≃ $184]**

Hind, Henry Y.
- North-West Territory: Reports of Progress, together with a Preliminary Report on the Assiniboine and Saskatchewan Exploring Expedition. Toronto: John Lovell, 1859. 1st edn. Lge folio. 202 pp. Fldg cold maps, plates. Lacks 1 plate. *(Jenkins)* **$275 [≃ £171]**

Hinde, Sidney L.
- The Fall of the Congo Arabs. New York: Thomas Whittaker, 1897. 8vo. viii,308 pp. Lge fldg map, 2 other maps, 2 ports, some other ills. Orig cloth gilt, endpapers renewed. *(Fenning)* **£28.50 [≃ $46]**

Hine, Reginald L.
- The History of Hitchin. London: Allen & Unwin, 1927. 1st edn. One of 1107, signed. 2 vols. 8vo. 375; 536 pp. Cold plate, num ills. Orig cloth, t.e.g. *(Claude Cox)* **£55 [≃ $88]**
- Hitchin Worthies, Four Centuries of English Life. London: (1932). 1st edn. One of 1021, this copy unnumbered. 8vo. 399,[1] pp. 4 cold & 65 other plates, num text ills. Minor spots. Orig cloth. Dw. *(Bow Windows)* **£45 [≃ $72]**

Hines, Gustavus
- Life on the Plains of the Pacific. Oregon: Its History, Condition and Prospects ... Personal

Adventures ... Auburn: Derby & Miller, 1851. 1st printing under this title. 8vo. 437, [7 advt] pp. Frontis port. Orig cloth, gilt spine.   *(Karmiole)* **$50 [≈ £31]**
- Wild Life in Oregon ... New York: Hurst & Co, [1881]. Arlington Edition. 12mo. 437,advt pp. Frontis. Orig dec maroon cloth.
                         (Terramedia) **$25 [≈ £15]**

Historical ...
- A Historical Account of His Majesty's Visit to Scotland ... see Mudie, Robert.
- An Historical Account of the Discovery of the Island of Madeira, abridged from the Portugueze Original ... Present State ... London: for J. Payne ..., 1750. 1st edn. 8vo. [ii],x,88 pp. Old pencil marg notes. Contemp calf backed bds, sl worn. Imaginary voyage.
                         (Burmester) **£450 [≈ $720]**
- An Historical and Descriptive Account of Iceland ... see Nicoll, James.
- Historical Collections of Louisiana ... see French, B.F. (compiler).
- An Historical Description of St. Paul's Cathedral ... London: for J. Newbery ..., 1759. 5th (?) edn. 8vo. iv,56 pp. Inner marg defect just touching 1 letter. Disbound.
                         (Young's) **£58 [≈ $92]**
- An Historical Description of the Cathedral and Metropolitical Church of Christ, Canterbury ... see Burnby, John.
- An Historical Description of the Tower of London and its Curiosities. Giving an Account of its Foundation ... Government ... Spoils of the Spanish Armada ... Armory ... Jewel Office ... Mint ... London: for J. Newbery ..., 1759. 8vo. 71 pp. Unbound, uncut.   *(Young's)* **£95 [≈ $152]**
- Historical Sketch Book and Guide to New Orleans ... see Hearn, Lafcadio.
- Historical View of Plans, for the Government of British India ... see Bruce, John.

History ...
- The History and Description of Colchester ... see Strutt, Joseph or Benjamin.
- History of American Missions to the Heathen, From their Commencement to the Present Time. Worcester: Spooner & Howland, 1840. 1st edn. Tall 8vo. 726 pp. Frontis, num w'cut maps & text ills. Orig elab blind stamped black cloth, gilt spine.
                         (Karmiole) **£150 [≈ $93]**
- The History of Ayder Ali Khan ... see Maistre De La Tour, --.
- The History of Barbados ... see Rochefort, C. de.
- The History of Maritime and Inland

Discovery ... see Cooley, William D.
- The History of Poland ... see Dunham, Samuel A.
- The History of Spain and Portugal ... see Dunham, Samuel A.
- History of Switzerland. London: Lardner's Cabinet Cyclopaedia, 1832. 1st edn. Sm 8vo. Orig cloth, ptd paper label.
                         (Fenning) **£24.50 [≈ $40]**
- The History of the Court of the King of China ... see Baudier, Michel.

Hitchcock, Edward
- Sketch of the Scenery of Massachusetts. Northampton: 1842. 4to. 75 pp. 14 lithos (1 fldg), 45 text w'cuts. Scattered foxing, sometimes heavy on text pp but only sl affecting lithos. Orig cloth gilt, rebacked.
                         (Reese) **$850 [≈ £531]**

Hittel, John S.
- The Resources of California ... and the Past and Future Development of the State. San Francisco: A. Roman & Co, 1863. 1st edn. 8vo. xvi,464 pp. Orig purple cloth gilt, spine extremities sl rubbed. *(Karmiole)* **$85 [≈ £53]**

Hittell, John S.
- The Resources of California, comprising the Society, Climate, salubrity, Scenery, Commerce, and Industry of the State. San Francisco: 1874. 6th edn, with addtns. 443 pp. Cloth, extremities worn, backstrip reprd.
                         (Reese) **$100 [≈ £62]**

Hoare, Sir Richard Colt
- Recollections Abroad, during the Year 1790. Sicily and Malta. Bath: 1817. 4to. One of 50, numbered & sgnd. xxxii,247 pp. Map. A few sm marg reprs to 1 leaf, occas sl foxing or staining. Contemp mrbld bds, rebacked in mor.   *(Reese)* **$600 [≈ £375]**

Hobart Pasha, Augustus Charles
- Sketches from my Life. London: Longmans, Green, 1886. 12mo. viii,282 pp. Frontis. Orig dec brown cloth, hinges cracked but holding.
                         (Parmer) **$95 [≈ £59]**

Hobson, J.A.
- The War in South Africa: Its Causes and Effects. New York & London: Macmillan, 1900. 1st edn. 8vo. viii,324 pp. Orig maroon cloth.   *(Terramedia)* **$50 [≈ £31]**

Hodson, A.
- Trekking the Great Thirst: Sport and Travel in the Kalahari Desert. London: 1913. 3rd edn. 359 pp. Fldg map, ills. Orig bndg.

(Trophy Room Books) $150 [≈ £93]

Hoe, Robert
- Catalogue of the Library of Robert Hoe of New York ... to be sold at Auction ... by the Anderson Auction Company. New York: 1911-12. 4 parts in 8 vols. 8vo. Orig ptd wraps.   *(Waterfield's)* £125 [≈ $200]

Hoffmann, W.
- With Stanley in Africa. London: 1938. 284 pp. Ills, endpaper maps. Orig cloth. Dw.
    (Trophy Room Books) $95 [≈ £59]

Hofland, Barbara
- Africa Described, in its Ancient and Present State ... London: 1828. 12mo. viii, 291 pp. Fldg map. Preliminary sheet excised. Orig polished calf, elab gilt, a.e.g., gilt inner dentelles, extremities worn, sm tear at hd of spine, spotted.   *(Reese)* $85 [≈ £53]

Hogarth, D.G.
- The Life of Charles M. Doughty. Garden City: Doubleday, Doran, 1929. 216 pp. Fldg map, ills. Dw chipped & worn.
    (Parmer) $50 [≈ £31]

Holberg, Baron Ludvig
- An Introduction to Universal History. Translated from the Latin. With Notes ... By Gregory Sharpe. The Second Edition, Corrected and Enlarged ... London: Millar, Ward, & Linde, 1758. 8vo. xxxi,341 pp. 5 fldg maps, 1 plate. Orig calf, red mor label.
    (Bickersteth) £115 [≈ $184]

Holbrook, Silas P.
- Sketches, by a Traveller. Boston: Carter & Hendee, 1830. 1st edn. [4],315 pp. Orig cloth, paper label.   *(Jenkins)* $200 [≈ £125]

Holder, Charles F.
- Life in the Open. Sport with Rod, Gun, Horse & Hound in Southern California. New York: Putnam's, 1906. 1st edn. Lge 8vo. xv, 401, advt pp. Frontis, num photo plates & vignettes. Orig pict green cloth, t.e.g.
    (Terramedia) $40 [≈ £25]

Hole, S. Reynolds
- A Little Tour in Ireland. Being a Visit to Dublin, Galway, Connemara ... By an Oxonian. With Illustrations by John Leech. London: Bradbury & Evans, 1859. Hand cold frontis, w'cut text ills. Sl spotting, edges of 1 leaf reprd. Orig pict green cloth gilt, recased.
    (Hollett) £45 [≈ $72]

Holland, Clive
- Denmark. Painted by A. Heaton Cooper. London: A. & C. Black, 1928. 1st edn. Map, 32 cold plates. Orig cloth.
    (Old Cathay) £19 [≈ $30]
- Warwickshire. Painted by Frederick Whitehead. London: A. & C. Black Colour Books, Twenty Shilling Series, 1906. 1st edn. Map, 75 cold plates. Orig dec cloth.
    (Old Cathay) £75 [≈ $120]
- Warwickshire. Painted by Frederick Whitehead. London: A. & C. Black Colour Books, Twenty Shilling Series, 1906. 1st edn. Map, 75 cold plates. Orig dec cloth, significant wear to spine ends, some minor rubbing to front bd, rear bd somewhat battered.   *(Old Cathay)* £53 [≈ $84]
- Warwickshire - The Land of Shakespeare. Painted by Fred Whitehead. London: A. & C. Black, 1922. 2nd edn, rvsd. Map, 32 cold plates. Orig cloth. *(Old Cathay)* £17 [≈ $27]
- Wessex. Painted by Walter Tyndale. London: A. & C. Black Colour Books, Twenty Shilling Series, 1906. 1st edn. Map, 75 cold plates. Orig green, ochre & black dec cloth, v bright.
    (Old Cathay) £65 [≈ $104]

Holland, Henry Richard Fox, Baron
- Foreign Reminiscences, by Henry Richard Lord Holland; Edited by his son Henry Edward Lord Holland. Paris: Galignani, 1851. 78 pp. Disbound.
    (Jarndyce) £25 [≈ $40]

Holland, P.
- Select Views of the Lakes in Cumberland, Westmorland & Lancashire ... Engraved by C. Rosenberg. Liverpool, 1792. Only edn. Oblong sm 4to. Engvd title/dedic (v soiled), 20 aquatint plates each with text leaf. Last plate edges reprd, verso soiled. Later cloth.
    (Hollett) £380 [≈ $608]

Holley, Mary Austin
- Texas: Observations Historical, Geographical, and Descriptive, in a Series of Letters written during a Visit to Austin's County. Baltimore: 1833. 1st edn. 167 pp. Map in facs. Orig cloth, mild wear to cvrs. Half mor slipcase.
    (Jenkins) $2,850 [≈ £1,781]

Holm, Fritz
- My Nestorian Adventure in China. A Popular Account of the Holm-Nestorian Expedition in Sian-Fu and its Results ... New York: Fleming H. Revell, 1923. Lge 8vo. 336 pp. Ills. Orig cloth, sl soiled.
    (Karmiole) $50 [≈ £31]

Holmes, G.
- Sketches of Some of the Southern Counties of Ireland, collected during a Tour in the Autumn of 1797. London: 1801. vii, 210, 1 pp. 7 plates. 1 page remargd at hd. Orig mrbld bds, rebacked.
  (Emerald Isle) **£175 [≈ $280]**

Holmes, John
- Historical Sketches of the Missions of the United Brethren for propagating the Gospel among the Heathen ... Dublin: R. Napper, 1818. [8], 472 pp. Contemp diced calf, jnts worn, some rubbing.   *(Reese)* **$250 [≈ £156]**

Holton, Isaac
- New Granada: Twenty Months in the Andes. New York: Harper, 1857. 8vo. xiv,605 pp. Dble page cold frontis, maps, num plates & ills. Orig brown cloth, ex-lib, spine worn, fly leaves damp stained at ft.
  (Terramedia) **$40 [≈ £25]**

Holub, Emil
- Seven Years in South Africa: Travels, Researches, and Hunting Adventures, between the Diamond-Fields and the Zambesi (1872-79). Boston: 1881. 2 vols. 8vo. xi,426; xi,479 pp. Fldg map, num plates. Orig pict cloth, rubbed, back cvr vol 1 stained.
  (Adelson) **$325 [≈ £203]**

Holyoake, George Jacob
- Among the Americans and a Stranger in America. Chicago: 1881. 1st Amer edn. 246 pp. Orig cloth. Orig ptd dw, sunned on spine, rubbed, splitting on front edge. Half mor box.
  (Reese) **$500 [≈ £312]**

Home, Gordon
- Normandy. The Scenery and Romance of Its Ancient Towns. London: Dent, 1905. 8vo. xiv, 248 pp. 24 cold plates. Orig dec blue cloth, t.e.g.   *(Piccadilly)* **£21 [≈ $33]**
- Yorkshire. Coast and Moorland Scenes. London: A. & C. Black Colour Book, 1904. 1st edn. Map, 32 cold plates. Orig cloth, t.e.g., browning to endpapers.
  (Old Cathay) **£33 [≈ $52]**
- Yorkshire. London: A. & C. Black Colour Books, Twenty Shilling Series, 1908. 1st edn. Map, 71 cold plates. Orig dec cloth, minor rubbing & wear to bds.
  (Old Cathay) **£39 [≈ $62]**
- Yorkshire. Vales and Wolds. London: A. & C. Black Colour Book, 1908. 1st edn. Map, 20 cold plates. Orig gilt dec blue cloth, t.e.g.
  (Old Cathay) **£30 [≈ $48]**
- Yorkshire. London: A. & C. Black Colour

Books, Twenty Shilling Series, 1908. 1st edn. Map, 71 cold plates. Orig dec cloth, hinges tender, wear to extremities.
  (Old Cathay) **£33 [≈ $52]**
- Yorkshire. London: A. & C. Black, 1925. 2nd edn. Map, 32 cold plates. Orig cloth, some browning to endpapers.
  (Old Cathay) **£15 [≈ $24]**

Honan, Michael Burke (ed.)
- See under Andalusian Annual.

Hone, Percy
- Southern Rhodesia. London: George Bell, 1909. 1st edn. 8vo. xv,406 pp. Fldg map, frontis & other photo plates. Orig cloth, spine sunned.   *(Terramedia)* **$50 [≈ £31]**

Hoo Peih Seang
- The Ceremonial Usages of the Chinese, B.C. 1121 ... Being an Abridge of the Chow Le Classic ... Translated ... by William Raymond Gingell ... London: Smith, Elder, 1852. 1st edn. Slim 4to. Title, dedic, errata slip, [ii], ii, 107, [8]pp. Orig yellow cloth, sl soiled.
  (Frew Mackenzie) **£325 [≈ $520]**

Hood, Thomas
- Up the Rhine. Frankfort: 1840. 16mo. vi, 300 pp. Plates. 1 sgntr detached. Orig ptd bds, rubbed, crudely rebacked with tape. Slipcase.
  (Reese) **$50 [≈ £31]**

Hooker, Sir Joseph Dalton & Ball, John
- Journal of a Tour in Marocco and the Great Atlas. London: Macmillan, 1878. 1st edn. 8vo. xvi,489,[40 advt] pp. Fldg map, 9 plates, 13 text engvs. Sl foxing. Orig cloth, edges rubbed, spine ends frayed, lib number on spine, sl shaken.
  (Worldwide Antiqu'n) **$150 [≈ £93]**

Hooker, Le Roy
- The Africanders. A Century of Dutch-English Feud in South Africa. Chicago & New York: Rand McNally, 1900. 279,advt pp. 16 ills. Orig dec green cloth.
  (Parmer) **$65 [≈ £40]**

Hooker, Sir William Jackson
- Journal of a Tour in Iceland in the Summer of 1809. Yarmouth: ptd by J. Keymer. Not published, 1811. 1st edn, 1st iss (Yarmouth). 8vo. Errata leaf. Cold frontis & 3 plates (2 fldg). Lacks half-title. Mod crushed mor gilt.
  (Hannas) **£350 [≈ $560]**
- Journal of a Tour in Iceland, in the Summer of 1809. London: for Longman, Hurst ... by J. Keymer, Yarmouth, 1813. 2nd edn, with

addtns. 1st complete edn. 2 vols. 8vo. Half-titles. Cold frontis, 7 plates & maps (offset), 1 table. Contemp calf, rebacked. Pres copy.
(Hannas) **£280 [≈ $448]**

Hooper, W.H.
- Ten Months among the Tents of the Tuski ... London: Murray, 1853. xv,417 pp. Fldg map, 6 plates (inc 4 tinted lithos). Orig dec cloth, minor wear.   *(High Latitude)* **$425 [≈ £265]**

Hope Edwards, E.C.
- Eau-de-Nil; A Chronicle. London: Bentley, 1882. 1st edn. 8vo. viii,319 pp. Orig pict gilt blue cloth, inner hinges cracked.
(Terramedia) **$50 [≈ £31]**

Hope, Sir W.H. St. John
- Cowdray and Easebourne Priory in the County of Sussex. London: Country Life, 1919. One of 400. Folio. xiv, 144 pp. Mtd cold frontis, 53 plates. Orig half vellum, gilt spine, somewhat rubbed & marked.
(Gough) **£100 [≈ $160]**

Hore, Edward Coode
- Tanganyika: Eleven Years in Central Africa. London: Edward Stanford, 1892. 1st edn. 8vo. 306 pp. Lge fldg frontis, title vignette, plates. Orig pict blue cloth, front hinge internally cracked, spine edges sl rubbed.
(Terramedia) **$150 [≈ £93]**
- Tanganyika: Eleven Years in Central Africa. London: Edward Stanford, 1892. 2nd edn. 8vo. xv,306 pp. Fldg frontis, 3 maps, 9 plates. repr to frontis. Blindstamp on title. Orig pict cloth, rubbed.   *(Adelson)* **$150 [≈ £93]**
- Tanganyika: Eleven Years in Central Africa. London: 1892. 8vo. 2 maps, fldg panorama frontis, plates. Half calf.
(Farahar) **£125 [≈ $200]**

Hornaday, William T.
- Camp-Fires in the Canadian Rockies. New York: Scribner's, 1907. Lge 8vo. xvii, 353, advt pp. 2 maps, 70 photo ills. Orig gilt dec cloth, photo onlay.   *(Parmer)* **$125 [≈ £78]**
- Campfires in the Canadian Rockies. Illustrations by John M. Phillips. New York: Scribner's, 1916. 8vo. 353,advt pp. 2 maps, num plates. Orig blue cloth, photo onlay.
(Terramedia) **$75 [≈ £46]**
- Camp Fires on Desert and Lava. New York: 1908. 1st edn. 366 pp. Cold frontis, ills. Orig bndg.   *(Trophy Room Books)* **$150 [≈ £93]**
- Camp Fires on Desert and Lava. New York: 1908. 366 pp. Cold frontis by Rungius, ills. Orig bndg.
(Trophy Room Books) **$150 [≈ £93]**

Hornby, Lady
- Constantinople during the Crimean War. London: 1863. xvi, 500 pp. 4 chromolitho plates. Scattered foxing, marg inkstain. Contemp three qtr polished calf, bds edgeworn & rubbed, endsheets loosened.
(Reese) **$125 [≈ £78]**

Horne, Melville
- Letters on Missions. Andover: Flagg & Gould, 1815. 216 pp. Some offset. Leather.
(Parmer) **$65 [≈ £40]**

Horne, T.H.
- Landscape Illustrations of the Bible ... see Finden, W. & E.

Horsfield, T.W.
- The History, Antiquities and Topography of the County of Sussex. Lewes: Sussex Press, 1835. 1st edn. 2 vols. 4to. Subscribers' list. Indexes. Port frontises, 2 fldg maps (reprd), 54 plates, text ills. Some foxing, stains, tears. Contemp half roan, sl worn, rebacked.
(Bow Windows) **£275 [≈ $440]**

Horsford, Eben Norton
- The Defences of Norumbega. Boston & New York: Houghton, Mifflin ..., 1891. 1st edn. Lge 4to. Fine paper. 20 plates & maps. Orig cloth, t.e.g.   *(Hannas)* **£120 [≈ $192]**
- Discovery of America by Northmen. Boston & New York: Houghton Mifflin ..., 1888. 1st edn. Lge 4to. Fine paper. 15 maps, 2 plates. Orig dec cloth, t.e.g. *(Hannas)* **£150 [≈ $240]**
- The Discovery of the Ancient City of Norumbega. Cambridge [Mass.]: privately ptd, [1889?]. 1st edn. One of 250. Fine paper. Lge 4to. 20 plates & maps. Orig cloth, t.e.g.
(Hannas) **£140 [≈ $224]**
- The Problem of the Northmen ... Second Edition. Boston & New York: Houghton, Mifflin ..., 1890. Fine paper. Lge 4to. 8 plates & maps. Orig cloth, t.e.g.
(Hannas) **£75 [≈ $120]**

Horsford, Eben Norton & Cornelia
- Leif's House in Vinland [and] Graves of the Northmen. Boston: Damrell & Upham, 1893. 1st edn. Lge 4to. 4 plates & maps. Text ills. Orig cloth, t.e.g.   *(Hannas)* **£85 [≈ $136]**

Hosie, Sir Alexander
- On the Trail of the Opium Poppy. A Narrative of Travel in the Chief Opium-Producing Provinces of China. Boston: [ca 1915]. 2 vols. viii,300; 307 pp. 2 frontis, 2 fldg maps, plates. Orig green cloth gilt.
(Lyon) **£250 [≈ $400]**

Hosmer, James K.
- History of the Expedition of Captains Lewis and Clark 1804-5-6. Reprinted from the Edition of 1812. With Introduction and Index ... Chicago: 1904. One of 75 Large Paper. 2 vols. Lge 8vo. lviii,500; xiv,584 pp. 8 plates. Vellum-like spines sl soiled.
(Karmiole) $200 [≈ £125]

Hotchkiss, Charles F.
- On the Ebb: A Few Log-Lines from an Old Salt. New Haven: 1878. 127 pp. Cloth.
(Reese) $175 [≈ £109]

The Hotels of Europe ...
- The Hotels of Europe, 1876. With Maps and Railway and Steamship Routes. London: Henry Herbert, [1876]. Imperial 8vo. [lxviii],212 pp. 16 dble-page cold maps, num pict advts within dec chromolitho borders. Orig dec green cloth gilt.
(Gough) £100 [≈ $160]

Hotoman, Francois
- Franco-Gallia: or, An Account of the Ancient Free State of France, and Most other parts of Europe, before the Loss of their Liberties. London: 1738. 2nd English edn. 8vo. Sl staining & browning. Contemp calf, rubbed, jnts cracked but firm.
(Robertshaw) £30 [≈ $48]

Hotten, John Camden
- Abyssinia and its People: or Life in the Land of Prester John. London: 1868. Sm 8vo. 384,advt pp. Lge cold fldg map, cold frontis, 7 plates. Orig cloth gilt, spine ends worn.
(Terramedia) $75 [≈ £46]

Hourst, Lieutenant
- French Enterprise in Africa. The Personal Narrative of Lieut. Hourst of his Exploration of the Niger. Translated by Bell (D'Anvers). London: 1898. 1st edn. 8vo. xvi, 520 pp. Frontis, photo ills. Lacks map. Other minor defects.
(Terramedia) $150 [≈ £93]

Houstoun, Matilda
- Texas and the Gulf of Mexico; or, Yachting in the New World. Philadelphia: Zieber, 1845. 1st Amer edn. 288 pp. Orig cloth.
(Jenkins) $600 [≈ £375]

Howard, John
- An Account of the Principal Lazarettos in Europe ... Second Edition, with Additions. London: J. Johnson ..., 1791. 4to. 22 plates, 1 fldg table. Advt leaf misbound in Appendix. Minor marg tears & waterstains. Half-title browned. Sl offsetting. Rec qtr calf.

(Blackwell's) £200 [≈ $320]
- An Account of the Principal Lazarettos in Europe ... London: 1791. 2nd edn, with addtns. 4to. 259,[13],32 pp. 22 fldg plates, table. Contemp polished calf, rubbed, rebacked, new endpapers.
(Hollett) £295 [≈ $472]

Howay, Frederic W. (ed.)
- Voyages of the "Columbia" to the Northwest Coast 1787-1790 and 1790-1793. [Boston]: The Massachusetts Hist Soc, 1941. Lge 8vo. xxxiv, 518 pp. 14 plates. Orig black cloth over bds.
(Karmiole) $100 [≈ £62]

Howe, Octavius Thorndike
- Argonauts of '49. History and Adventures of the Emigrant Companies from Massachusetts 1849-1850. Cambridge: Harvard Univ Press, 1923. Lge 8vo. [6],222 pp. Ills. Orig blue cloth over bds, extremities sl rubbed.
(Karmiole) $45 [≈ £28]

Howell, Frederick W.W.
- Icelandic Pictures drawn with Pen and Pencil. London: RTS, 1893. 1st edn. Sm folio. 176,8 illust ctlg pp. Map, w'engvs. Some spotting of 1st & final ff. Orig pict cloth.
(Claude Cox) £25 [≈ $40]

Howells, William Dean
- Italian Journeys. London: Sampson, Low ..., 1868. 1st English edn. 8vo. 24 pp ctlg at end. Orig brown cloth, gilt spine, uncut & almost entirely unopened, extremities sl rubbed.
(Clark) £36 [≈ $57]

Howison, John
- Sketches of Upper Canada, Domestic, Local, and Characteristic ... added, Practical Details for the Information of Emigrants of Every Class ... Edinburgh: Oliver & Boyd ..., 1821. 1st edn. 8vo. xvi,339 pp. Half-title. Orig bds, jnts cracking.
(Young's) £200 [≈ $320]

Howitt, E.
- Selections from Letters written during a Tour through the United States, in the Summer and Autumn of 1819 ... Nottingham: J. Dunn, [1820]. [22], 230 pp. Sm stain on crnr of a few ff. Orig bds, backstrip defective, front bd nearly detached. Cloth slipcase.
(Reese) $500 [≈ £312]

Howitt, William
- Land, Labor and Gold; or, Two Years in Victoria: with Visits to Sydney and Van Dieman's Land. Boston: 1855. 1st Amer edn. 2 vols. 441; 426 pp. Occas foxing. Orig cloth.
(Reese) $300 [≈ £187]

- Visits to Remarkable Places: Old Halls, Battle Fields, and Scenes Illustrative of Striking Passages in English History and Poetry. London: 1840. vii,[1],528,advt pp. Title vignette, text ills. Orig cloth gilt, spine ends chipped, crnrs bumped. *(Reese)* **$60 [≈ £37]**

Hubback, T.
- Elephant and Seladang Hunting in the Federated Malay States. London: Rowland Ward, 1905. 289 pp. Num ills. Orig red cloth. *(Trophy Room Books)* **$750 [≈ £468]**

Hubback, T.R.
- To Far Western Alaska for Big Game. London: 1929. 8vo. Ills. Lib stamp on endpaper. Lacks map from pocket. Orig bndg, spine sl faded. *(Grayling)* **£60 [≈ $96]**

Hubbard, Arthur John & George
- Neolithic Dew-Ponds and Cattle-Ways. Second Edition. London: Longmans, Green, 1907. 8vo. xxiv,116 pp. 29 photo plates. Endpapers marked. Orig green cloth, sl rubbed & stained. *(Gough)* **£25 [≈ $40]**

Hubner, Le Baron de
- A Ramble round the World, 1871. Translated by Lady Herbert. London: Macmillan, 1874. 1st edn. 2 vols. Lge 8vo. Orig green cloth, spines relaid. *(Claude Cox)* **£28 [≈ $44]**

Huc, Evariste
- The Chinese Empire; forming a Sequel to the Work entitled " Recollections of a Journey through Tartary and Thibet". London: Longman ..., 1855. 2 vols. 8vo. xxxii,421; viii,440 pp. Fldg map. Contemp half mor, 1 cvr detached, lacks labels. *(Worldwide Antiqu'n)* **$145 [≈ £90]**
- The Chinese Empire: forming a Sequel to the Work entitled " Recollections of a Journey through Tartary and Thibet". Second Edition. London: Longman ..., 1855. 2 vols. 8vo. xxxii, 421, [2 advt]; viii,440 pp. Fldg map. Some foxing. Rec buckram bds. *(Fenning)* **£55 [≈ $88]**
- A Journey through the Chinese Empire. New York: Harper, 1855. 1st US edn. 2 vols. Sm 8vo. 421; 422 pp. Fldg map. Lower right hand crnr dampstained. Sl foxing. Lib buckram. *(Worldwide Antiqu'n)* **$95 [≈ £59]**
- A Journey through the Chinese Empire. New York: Harper, 1855. 2 vols. 12mo. 421; 422 pp. Fldg map. Orig bndg. *(Schoyer)* **$70 [≈ £43]**
- A Journey through the Chinese Empire. New York: Harper, 1878. 2 vols. 12mo. xxvi,421; vi,422,10 advt pp. Orig green cloth.

(Terramedia) **$100 [≈ £62]**
- Recollections of a Journey through Tartary, Thibet, and China during the Years 1844, 1845 and 1846, a Condensed Translation by Mrs. Percy Sinnett. London: Longman ..., 1852. Sm 8vo. viii,313 pp. Half mor, worn, cvrs loose. *(Worldwide Antiqu'n)* **$30 [≈ £18]**
- Travels in Tartary, Thibet, and China, during the Years 1844-5-6 ... London: National Illustrated Library, [1852]. Vol 1 3rd edn, vol 2 2nd edn. 2 vols. 8vo. 2 frontis, addtnl illust titles, fldg map (sm tear at fold). Orig orange cloth, sm nicks at spine ends *(Claude Cox)* **£60 [≈ $96]**
- Travels in Tartary, Thibet, and China, during the Years 1844-5-6 ... London: National Illustrated Library, [ca 1856]. 2nd edn. 2 vols in one. 12mo. 292; 304 pp. Fldg map, 100 w'engvs. Half leather by Sangorski & Sutcliffe. *(Parmer)* **$80 [≈ £50]**

Hudson, W.H.
- The Naturalist in La Plata. London: Chapman & Hall, 1892. 1st edn. 8vo. vii,1, 388, 40 advt pp. Frontis & other ills. Orig cloth gilt. *(Terramedia)* **$200 [≈ £125]**

Hughes, Griffith
- The Natural History of Barbadoes in Ten Books. London: for the author, 1750. Folio. Lge fldg map, 30 engvd plates, vignette views. Some minimal spotting. Contemp ink inscrptn on title. Contemp speckled calf, rebacked. *(Farahar)* **£1,150 [≈ $1,840]**

Hughes, John
- An Itinerary of Provence and the Rhone made during the Year 1819, with Etchings by the Author. London: Cawthorn, 1822. vi,293 pp. 13 plates. A little foxing. Half calf, mrbld bds, crnrs & edges rubbed. *(Box of Delights)* **£50 [≈ $80]**

Hughes, John T.
- Doniphan's Expedition: containing an Account of the Conquest of New Mexico ... Cincinnati: James, 1848. 1st book edn. 407 pp. Fldg map, plan, plates. Orig cloth, chipped. Association inscrptn. *(Jenkins)* **$375 [≈ £234]**

Hughes, Revd T.S.
- Travels in Greece and Albania. Second Edition with Considerable Additions. London: Colburn & Bentley, 1830. 2 vols. 8vo. [i], xvi,511; [ii],xii,512 pp. Cold frontis, 2 fldg maps, 6 fldg plates, other plates & vignettes. Half calf, mrbld sides, v sl rubbed. *(Piccadilly)* **£380 [≈ $608]**

Hughes, Thomas (ed.)
- G.T.T. Gone to Texas: Letters from Our Boys. London: Macmillan, 1884. 1st edn. 228 pp. Orig cloth.   *(Jenkins)* **$285 [≈ £178]**

Hugo, Victor
- Excursions along the Banks of the Rhine. London: Colburn, 1843. 1st English edn. 8vo. xiv,418 pp. Title marg reprd. Cloth, spine faded.   *(Young's)* **£33 [≈ $52]**

Huish, Marcus B.
- Happy England. Painted by Helen Allingham. London: A. & C. Black Colour Books, Twenty Shilling Series, 1903. 1st edn. 81 cold plates. Orig dec cloth, t.e.g.
        (Old Cathay) **£125 [≈ $200]**

Humbert, Aime
- Japan and the Japanese Illustrated ... London: Bentley, 1874. 1st edn in English. 4to. [xx],378,[2] pp. 200 ills. Some foxing & other marks. 1 gathering a little loose. Orig illust cloth, rather dull & marked, inner hinges torn.   *(Bow Windows)* **£295 [≈ $472]**
- Japan and the Japanese Illustrated ... New York: Appleton, 1874. 4to. xviii,378,[2 advt] pp. 207 ills. Orig elab dec pict cloth, spine relaid, crnrs worn.   *(Schoyer)* **$95 [≈ £59]**

Humboldt, Alexander von & Bonpland, Aime
- Personal Narrative of Travels to the Equinoctial Regions of the New Continent during the Years 1799-1804. Translated ... by Helen Maria Williams. London: 1814. 1st edn. 2 vols. xii,li,289; 299 pp. Frontis map, 2 tables. Mod qtr mor. The 1st 2 of 7 vols.
        (Terramedia) **$250 [≈ £156]**
- Personal Narrative of Travels to the Equinoctial Regions of the New Continent, during the Years 1799 - 1804 ... London: 1814-20. 1st English edn. 7 vols in 9. 8 fldg maps. Some minor foxing. Orig cloth & bds.
        (Reese) **$1,750 [≈ £1,093]**
- Personal Narrative of Travels to the Equinoctial Regions of America, during the Years 1799-1804. Translated ... by Thomasina Ross. London: Bell, 1889. 3 vols. 8vo. Green half calf, gilt spines sl faded.
        (Frew Mackenzie) **£135 [≈ $216]**

Hunt, John
- The Ascent of Everest. [London: 1953]. xx, [300] pp. Cold frontis, photo ills. Orig cloth.
        (Reese) **$30 [≈ £18]**
- The Conquest of Everest ... with a Chapter on the Final Assault by Sir Edmund Hillary ... New York: 1954. xx,300 pp. Cold frontis, text ills, maps. Orig pict cloth. Dw.
        (Reese) **$30 [≈ £18]**

Hunt, Rockwell D.
- California and Californians. Chicago: Lewis Publ Co, 1926. 1st edn. 5 vols. Lge 8vo. xlix,569; x,590; 493; 504; 536 pp. Num photo plates. Orig brown cloth.
        (Terramedia) **$150 [≈ £93]**

Hunt, S.L. & Kenny, A.S.
- Tropical Trials. A Hand-Book for Women in the Tropics. London: 1883. 1st edn. Sm 8vo. xii, 461,[1],[6 advt] pp. A few crnrs folded, a few dust marks. Orig illust cloth gilt, v sl marked.   *(Bow Windows)* **£36 [≈ $57]**

Hunter, John D.
- Manners and Customs of Several Indian Tribes Located West of the Mississippi ... Philadelphia: 1823. viii,[11]-402 pp. Occas foxing. Later cloth. Sgntr of David Gelston on title.   *(Reese)* **$450 [≈ £281]**
- Manners and Customs of Several Indian Tribes Located West of the Mississippi ... Philadelphia: for the author, 1823. 1st edn. 8vo. 402 pp. Contemp calf, front cvr nearly loose.   *(M & S Rare Books)* **$400 [≈ £250]**
- Memoirs of a Captivity Among the Indians of North America ... London: 1823. 1st English edn (of 'Manners and Customs', retitled). 8vo. 9,447 pp. Orig cloth backed bds, uncut, spine faded, minor wear.
        (M & S Rare Books) **$300 [≈ £187]**
- Memoirs of a Captivity Among the Indians of North America. London: Longman, 1823. 1st English edn. 447 pp. Three qtr calf, preserving orig mrbld bds & gilt dec spine.   *(Jenkins)* **$200 [≈ £125]**

Hunter, Joseph
- Antiquarian Notices of Lupset, the Heath, Sharlston, and Ackton, in the County of York. Privately ptd: 1851. Sm 4to. [vi],107 pp. Tinted litho frontis. Orig cloth gilt, a.e.g., extremities a trifle rubbed.
        (Hollett) **£87.50 [≈ $142]**
- Hallamshire. The History and Topography of Sheffield in the County of York ... New enlarged edition by Rev. A. Gatty. Sheffield: 1869. Folio. xv,[iii],508 pp. 26 plates (some rather spotted). Orig cloth gilt, a little spotted, jnts & crnrs worn.
        (Hollett) **£120 [≈ $192]**

Huntington, Archer M.
- A Notebook in Northern Spain. New York: Putnam's, 1898. 4to. xiv,264 pp. Num ills. Orig red linen gilt.   *(Karmiole)* **$65 [≈ £40]**

Huntly, Marquis of
- Travel, Sport and Politics in the East of Europe. London: 1887. 8vo. Ills. Orig bndg.
(Grayling) £35 [≈ $56]

Huntt, Henry
- A Visit to the Red Sulphur Spring of Virginia, during the Summer of 1837: with Observations on the Water. Boston: Dutton & Wentworth, 1839. Roy 8vo. 40 pp. Frontis. Some marg waterstains. Lacks wraps, folded lengthwise at some time.
(Xerxes) $125 [≈ £78]

Hurd, William
- A New Universal History of the Religious Rites, Ceremonies, and Customs of the Whole World ... London: Alexander Hogg, [1799?]. Folio. 704,xii,[4 subscribers] pp. 60 plates. Contemp tree calf, lightly scraped in places, front jnt split, cvr partly detached.
(Schoyer) $375 [≈ £234]

Huson, Gordon
- The Faroes in Pictures. London: Allen & Unwin, 1946. Photo ills. Oblong 4to.
(Hannas) £30 [≈ $48]

Hutchings, James Mason
- Scenes of Wonder and Curiosity in California. A Tourist's Guide to the Yosemite Valley ... New York & San Francisco: Roman, 1870. Rvsd edn, 1st printing. 8vo. 292 pp. Frontis, over 100 engvd text ills. 19th c gift mor gilt, a.e.g., sl rubbed
(Heritage) $250 [≈ £156]

Hutchinson, Alex H.
- Try Lapland. A Fresh Field for Summer Tourists. London: 1870. x,228 pp. Fldg map, ills. Orig dec pebbled cloth gilt, a bit soiled, crnrs bumped, partly unopened.
(Reese) $85 [≈ £53]

Hutchinson, J.
- A Botanist in Southern Africa. Foreword by Field Marshal Smuts. London: 1946. Roy 8vo. xii, 686 pp. Cold port, num ills. Orig cloth, trifle used.
(Wheldon & Wesley) £60 [≈ $96]

Hutchinson, Thomas J.
- Buenos Ayres and Argentine Gleanings: with Extracts for a Diary of Salado Exploration in 1862 and 1863. London: Stanford, 1865. xxiv, 322, [2] pp. 3 fldg maps, 8 w'engvd plates, 16 text ills. A few ff sl foxed. Orig cloth, minor shelfwear.
(Jenkins) $250 [≈ £156]

- Impressions of West Africa. With Remarks on the Diseases of the Climate ... London: Longman, Brown ..., 1858. 1st edn. 8vo. xvi, 313, [6 advt] pp. Frontis, engvd vignette title, 2 text diags. Sl browning. Rec calf backed mrbld bds.
(Fenning) £85 [≈ $136]

Hutchinson, Walter (ed.)
- Hutchinson's Beautiful Britain ... London: Hutchinson: [1920s]. 4 vols. Num cold plates, ca 2000 ills. Orig pict gilt dec green cloth.
(Old Cathay) £49 [≈ $78]

Hutchison, Isobel W.
- Stepping Stones from Alaska to Asia. London: Blackie, 1937. 8vo. x,246 pp. Fldg map, 4 cold & other plates. Orig cloth.
(High Latitude) $30 [≈ £18]

Hutchison, J.
- A Botanist in Southern Africa. London: Gawthorn, 1946. 1st edn. Imperial 8vo. xii, 686 pp. 2 fldg maps, fldg chart, 532 ills. Orig green cloth gilt.
(Gough) £50 [≈ $80]

Hutton, William
- A Journey from Birmingham to London. Birmingham: Pearson & Rollason; sold by Baldwin & Lowndes, London, 1785. 12mo. Frontis. Some spotting. Contemp calf gilt, Signet Library stamp, rebacked.
(Jarndyce) £110 [≈ $176]

Huxley, Elspeth
- White Man's Country: Lord Delamere and the making of Kenya. London: Macmillan, 1935. 1st edn. 2 vols. 8vo. xiii,315; vii,333 pp. 4 fldg maps, 24 plates. Orig cloth, spines faded, bds sl spotted.
(Fenning) £38.50 [≈ $62]

Huxley, Thomas Henry
- Diary of the Voyage of H.M.S. Rattlesnake. Edited from the Unpublished MS. by Julian Huxley. London: 1935. 1st edn. 8vo. [viii], 372 pp. Map, cold frontis, 12 plates. A few marks. Orig cloth. Prize label. Dw torn & partly frayed away.
(Bow Windows) £70 [≈ $112]
- Diary of the Voyage of H.M.S. Rattlesnake. Edited from the Unpublished MS. by Julian Huxley. London: 1935. Roy 8vo. 372 pp. Map, 13 plates. Cloth.
(Wheldon & Wesley) £45 [≈ $72]

Hylton, Lord
- Notes on the History of the Parish of Kilmersdon. In the County of Somerset. Taunton: 1910. 1st edn. 8vo. Ills, maps, pedigrees. Orig bndg.
(Ambra) £34 [≈ $54]

Ibn Battuta
- The Travels ... Translated ... with Notes ... by the Rev. Samuel Lee. London: Oriental Translation Fund, 1829. 4to. xix,243 pp, inc engvd pres leaf. Mod half calf.
(Farahar) **£160 [≈ $256]**
- Travels in Asia and Africa 1325-1354. Translated and selected by H.A.R. Gibb. London: Routledge, Broadway Traveller's Series, 1963. 5th imp. 8vo. vii,398 pp. 4 maps, 4 plates. Orig maroon cloth, gilt dec spine. *(Terramedia)* **$75 [≈ £46]**

Ides, E. Ysbrants
- Three Years Travels from Moscow over-land to China ... London: Freeman & Walthoe, 1706. 1st English edn. 4to. [12],210 pp. Addtnl engvd title, lge fldg map, 30 plates. Occas sl foxing. Contemp panelled calf, v sm repr to hd of spine. *(Spelman)* **£580 [≈ $928]**

Imlay, George
- A Topographical Description of the Western Territory of North America ... Discovery, Settlement and Present State of Kentucky ... London: 1793. 2nd edn, rvsd & enlgd. xvi,433, index pp. 3 fldg maps, fldg table. Antique half calf, mrbld bds.
(Reese) **$950 [≈ £593]**

In Perils of Mine Own Countrymen ...
- See McNamara, John J.

Inchbold, A.C.
- Under the Syrian Sun. London: 1902. 2 vols. Orig bndg, spines v sunned.
(Terramedia) **$50 [≈ £31]**

Incidents of Travel in Greece ...
- See Stephens, John L.

Ingham, G. Thomas
- Digging Gold among the Rockies, or, Exciting Adventures of Wild Life in Leadville, Black Hills and the Gunnison Country ... Philadelphia: Hubbard Brothers, [1880]. 1st edn. 12mo. 508 pp. Ills. 1 loose sgntr. Some fingerprints. Orig dec cloth, edges rubbed. *(Schoyer)* **$115 [≈ £71]**

Inglis, Henry David
- The Channel Islands of Jersey, Guernsey, Alderney, Sark, Herm and Jethou. London: 1844. 4th edn. Ptd title states 'Fifth edition, 1838'. 8vo. Engvd title, frontis, 2 maps. Orig cloth backed bds, paper spine label soiled.
(Robertshaw) **£58 [≈ $92]**
- See also under his pseudonym, Derwent Conway.

Inglis, The Hon. James
- Tent Life in Tigerland with which is incorporated Sport and Work on the Nepaul Frontier. London: Sampson Low, 1892. 8vo. xxiv,690 pp. 22 chromolithos. Orig cloth, recased. *(Bates & Hindmarch)* **£115 [≈ $184]**

Inglis, Lady Julia
- The Siege of Lucknow: a Diary. London: Osgood, 1892. 1st edn. viii, 240 pp. Orig black cloth, upper cvr sl bubbled.
(Box of Delights) **£30 [≈ $48]**

Ingram, James
- Memorials of Oxford. The Engravings by John Le Keux, from Drawings by F. Mackenzie. Oxford: 1837. 1st edn. Large Paper. 3 vols. 4to. 3 frontis, plan, 97 plates, vignette text ills. Occas sl foxing. Contemp mor, gilt spines, a.e.g., sl rubbed.
(Sanders) **£550 [≈ $880]**

Ingrams, Harold
- Arabia and the Isles. London: Murray, 1942. 1st edn. Roy 8vo. xvi,367 pp. 2 maps, num photo ills. Orig cloth.
(Bickersteth) **£25 [≈ $40]**

Inman, Henry
- The Old Santa Fe Trail. The Story of a Great Highway. New York & London: Macmillan, 1898. 3rd printing. 8vo. xvi,493,advt pp. Fldg map, sev plate ills by Frederick Remington. Orig pict brown cloth.
(Terramedia) **$100 [≈ £62]**

Inman, Henry & Cody, William
- The Great Salt Lake Trail. New York & London: Macmillan, 1898. 1st edn. 8vo. 529, advt pp. Fldg map, frontis, num plates & ills. Orig pict green cloth, t.e.g.
(Terramedia) **$200 [≈ £125]**

Inquiry ...
- An Inquiry into the Causes of the Insurrection of the Negroes in the Island of St. Domingo. To which are added, Observations of M. Garran-Coulon on the same Subject ... London: 1792. Sl foxing, a few ff detached. Wraps. *(Reese)* **$150 [≈ £93]**

Interesting Tracts ...
- Interesting Tracts, relating to the Island of Jamaica, consisting of Curious State- Papers, Councils of War, Letters, Petitions, Narratives ... St. Jago de la Vega: 1800. 4to. vi,300 pp. Contemp calf, rebacked.
(Reese) **$2,500 [≈ £1,562]**

Ireland, Alleyne
- The Far Eastern Tropics. Studies in the Administration of Tropical Dependencies ... Boston & New York: Houghton, Mifflin, 1905. 1st edn. Fldg map in pocket. Orig green cloth. *(Terramedia)* **$30 [≈£18]**

Ireland, John B.
- Wall-Street to Cashmere. A Journal of Five Years in Asia, Africa, and Europe ... New York: Rollo, 1859. 1st edn. 8vo. xviii,531 pp. Over 70 plates (1 hand cold). Sl foxed. Orig cloth, v rubbed, spine ends chipped, sl shaken. *(Worldwide Antiqu'n)* **$95 [≈£59]**

Ireland, Samuel
- A Picturesque Tour through Holland, Brabant, and Part of France; made in the Autumn of 1789 ... London: Egerton, 1790. 1st edn. 2 vols. Lge 8vo. xvi,210 pp; vi,210 pp. 2 engvd titles, 47 plates (3 more than called for in list of plates). Old mor, rebacked. *(Karmiole)* **$600 [≈£375]**

Ireland, William Henry
- France for the last Seven Years; or, the Bourbons. London: Whittaker, 1822. 1st edn. 8vo. xvi,439 pp. Sl foxing. Orig blue bds, drab spine, ptd label, spine ends sl worn, rubbed. *(Burmester)* **£60 [≈$96]**

Irving, Washington
- Astoria; or, Enterprise beyond the Rocky Mountains. Paris: Baudry's European Library, 1836. 1st continental edn. 336 pp. B'plate. Three qtr calf. *(Reese)* **$200 [≈£125]**
- Captain Bonneville, or Enterprises beyond the Rocky Mountains. A Sequel to "Astoria". London: 1837. 2nd London edn, with altered title. 3 vols. Occas v sl foxing. Later half vellum, paper labels. *(Reese)* **$150 [≈£93]**
- The Rocky Mountains: or, Scenes, Incidents and Adventures in the Far West ... Phila: 1837. 1st Amer edn. 2 vols. 2 maps (foxed, torn at folds). Title-page of vol 1 torn, removing the "The". Staining & foxing. Orig cloth. *(Reese)* **$200 [≈£125]**
- A Tour on the Prairies. Philadelphia: 1835. 1st edn, 1st iss. 274 pp. Orig cloth, paper label, a bit worn. BAL 10140. *(Jenkins)* **$250 [≈£156]**
- A Tour on the Prairies. Philadelphia: Carey, Lea, & Blanchard, 1835. 1st Amer edn, State A with 1st state of the paper spine label. 12mo. 274,24 ctlg pp. Normal expected foxing. Orig green cloth bds, sl rubbed, sgntr removed from pastedown. Cloth case. *(Schoyer)* **$165 [≈£103]**
- A Tour on the Prairies. London: Murray,

1835. 1st edn. 8vo. xiii,335 pp. 19th c half calf, sl rubbed. *(Young's)* **£70 [≈$112]**

Irwin, David
- Alone Across the Top of the World. The Authorized Story of the Arctic Journey. As Told to Jack O'Brien. Chicago: John Winston Co, [1935]. 1st edn. 8vo. x,254 pp. Frontis & other photo plates. Orig pict green cloth. Author's inscrptn. *(Terramedia)* **$35 [≈£21]**

Irwin, Eyles
- Occasional Epistles. Written during a Journey from London to Busrah, in the Gulf of Persia, in the years 1780 and 1781. To William Hayley. London: J. Dodsley, 1783. 4to. Half-title. Frontis. Disbound. *(Jarndyce)* **£250 [≈$400]**
- A Series of Adventures in the Course of a Voyage up the Red-Sea, on the Coasts of Arabia and Egypt ... London: Dodsley, 1780. 1st edn. 4to. xvi,400 pp. Half-title. 4 maps, 2 plates. Some waterstains. Three qtr leather. *(Schoyer)* **$325 [≈£203]**

Italy ...
- Italy from the Alps to Mount Etna. Its Arts: Its Cities: Its Lakes: Its Rivers. London: William Glaisher, 1903. Sm 4to. viii, 392 pp. Num w'cut ills. Orig dec blue cloth gilt, a.e.g. *(Piccadilly)* **£18 [≈$28]**
- Italy: with Sketches of Spain and Portugal ... see Beckford, William.

Izacke, Richard
- Remarkable Antiquities of the City of Exeter ... London: Rowland Reynolds, 1681. 2nd edn. 8vo. [vi],191,[lxiii] pp. Frontis (sm hole), fldg map (sm repr without loss), arms in margs of text. Old sheep, rebacked, crnrs sl worn. Wing I1111. *(Clark)* **£110 [≈$176]**

Jackson, A.V.W.
- From Constantinople to the Home of Omar Khayyam. Travels in Transcaucasia and Northern Persia for Historic and Literary Research. New York: Macmillan, 1911. 1st edn. 8vo. xxxii,317,advt pp. Lge fldg map, cold frontis, num plates. Orig cloth gilt, pict onlay. *(Terramedia)* **$125 [≈£78]**
- Persia Past and Present. A Book of Travel and Research. New York & London: Macmillan, 1906. 8vo. xxxi,471,advt pp. Fldg map, num photo plates. Orig blue cloth, ex-lib, hinges sl shaken. *(Terramedia)* **$75 [≈£46]**

Jackson, E.L.
- St. Helena: The Historic Island. London: Ward, Lock, [ca 1903?]. 343 pp. Erratum slip.

Photo plates. 1 plate rather wrinkled. Covers rough, somewhat worn & spotted.
(Parmer) **$65 [≈ £40]**

Jackson, Edith
- Annals of Ealing from the Twelfth Century to the Present Time. London: 1898. 4to. xvi, 348 pp. Sl foxing. Orig buckram, uncut, cvrs sl marked.   *(Coombes)* **£40 [≈ $64]**

Jackson, Frederick George
- The Great Frozen Land (Bolshaia Zemelskija Tundra). Narrative of a Winter Journey Across the Tundras & a Sojourn Among the Samoyads ... London: Macmillan, 1895. 1st edn. 8vo. xviii, 2, 297, advt pp. 3 fldg maps, frontis, other ills. Lib stamp on title. Orig pict cloth.   *(Terramedia)* **$100 [≈ £62]**
- A Thousand Days in the Arctic ... London: Harper, 1899. 2 vols. 8vo. xxi,551; xv,580 pp. Num fldg maps, ills. Orig cloth, recased, new endpapers, gilt lib stamp on vol 1 front cvr.
(High Latitude) **$150 [≈ £93]**
- A Thousand Days in the Arctic. New York & London: Harper, 1899. 1st edn. Thick 8vo. xxiii, 940 pp. Frontis, 5 fldg maps, 15 plates. Sm piece torn from title. Orig dec bndg, front hinge tender.   *(Parmer)* **$110 [≈ £68]**

Jackson, Hamilton
- The Shores of the Adriatic. New York: Dutton, 1906-08. 1st American edn. 2 vols. 8vo. xiv,358; xv,420 pp. Num plates. Orig dec red cloth gilt. Vol 1 The Italian Side; Vol 2 The Austrian Side.
(Terramedia) **$125 [≈ £78]**

Jackson, James Grey
- An Account of the Empire of Marocco, and the District of Suse ... added, an Account of Timbuctoo ... Philadelphia: Francis Nichols, 1810. 1st Amer edn. 12mo. xx,242 pp. 2 fldg maps (stain on crnr). New cloth.
(Schoyer) **$100 [≈ £62]**

Jackson, Rowland
- The History of the Town & Township of Barnsley in Yorkshire ... London: 1858. 8vo. 248 pp. 9 pedigrees, facs of charter, vignette title. Foxing to prelims. Half mor, t.e.g., gilt dec spine sl worn, bds v sl worn. William Boyne's b'plate.   *(Dillons)* **£95 [≈ $152]**

Jackson, Sheldon
- Alaska, and Missions on the North Pacific Coast. New York: Dodd, Mead, [ca 1880]. 12mo. 400 pp. Fldg map, plates, ills. Orig cloth, minor wear.
(High Latitude) **$45 [≈ £28]**

Jaekel, Blair
- The Land of the Tamed Turk or the Balkan States Today. A Narrative of Travel ... Boston: Page & Co, 1910. 12mo. xiv,295 pp. Fldg map, frontis, num plates. Orig gilt & cold dec cloth.   *(Terramedia)* **$30 [≈ £18]**

James, Edith A. Coulson
- Bologna. Its History, Antiquities and Art. London: Henry Frowde, 1909. Lge 8vo. xxviii, 410 pp. Fldg cold map, 116 ills. pict cloth.   *(Schoyer)* **$65 [≈ £40]**

James, Edwin
- Account of an Expedition from Pittsburgh to the Rocky Mountains, performed in the Years 1819, 1820 ... Under the Command of Major S.H. Long ... London: 1823. 1st English edn. 3 vols. 8vo. Fldg map, chart, 8 plates. Contemp three qtr leather, rebacked. Cloth case.   *(Schoyer)* **$1,900 [≈ £1,187]**

James, Frank L.
- The Wild Tribes of the Soudan. An Account of Travel and Sport chiefly in the Base Country ... New York: 1883. 280 pp. 2 lge cold fldg maps, ills. Orig elab gilt dec bndg.
(Trophy Room Books) **$350 [≈ £218]**
- The Wild Tribes of the Soudan. An Account of Personal Experiences and Adventures ... Second Edition. With ... a Chapter ... by Sir Samuel Baker. London: Murray, 1884. 8vo. xxxiv, 265, [2,32 advt] pp. Fldg map, 21 full page & other ills. Orig pict cloth.
(Fenning) **£45 [≈ $72]**
- The Wild Tribes of the Soudan. Personal Experiences and Adventures ... Second Edition. With ... a Chapter ... by Sir Samuel Baker. London: 1884. 8vo. Engvd plates & text ills. Orig cloth, sl rubbed & dulled.
(Grayling) **£70 [≈ $112]**

James, George W.
- The Wonders of the Colorado Desert (Southern California) ... including an Account of a Recent Journey made down the Overflow of the Colorado River to the Mysterious Salton Sea. Boston: 1906. 2 vols. 4 maps, 33 plates, 300 ills. Orig cloth gilt, t.e.g.   *(Reese)* **$150 [≈ £93]**

James, H.E.M.
- The Long White Mountain, or a Journey in Manchuria ... London: Longmans, 1888. 8vo. 502 pp. Fldg map, cold frontis, num plates. Appreciable foxing. Orig pict mustard cloth, hd of spine chipped.
(Terramedia) **$150 [≈ £93]**
- The Long White Mountain, or a Journey in

Manchuria ... London: 1888. 1st edn. 8vo. 502 pp. Fldg map, cold frontis, plates, ills. Occas sl foxing. Rebacked in qtr mor.
(Terramedia) **$220 [≈£137]**

James, John Thomas
- Journal of a Tour in Germany, Sweden, Russia, Poland, during the Years 1813 and 1814. London: Murray, 1816. 1st edn. 4to. viii, [4],527 pp. Vignette title, 18 aquatint plates. Rebound in dark blue calf, gilt spine, a.e.g. *(Spelman)* **£225 [≈$360]**
- Journal of a Tour in Germany, Sweden, Russia, Poland, in 1813-14. Third Edition. London: Murray, 1819. 2 vols. 8vo. Final colophon leaf in vol 1. 12 aquatint plates. Contemp maroon calf gilt, spines faded. *(Hannas)* **£130 [≈$208]**
- Journal of a Tour in Germany, Sweden, Russia, Poland, in 1813-14. London: 1819. 3rd edn. 2 vols. xvi,470; iv,447 pp. 2 frontis, plates. Occas sl foxing or soiling, offsetting from plates. Contemp polished calf gilt, lacks 1 label, wear to jnts & edges.
(Reese) **$150 [≈£93]**

Jameson, James
- The Story of the Rear Column of the Emin Pasha Relief Expedition. Edited by Mrs. J.S. Jameson. London: R.H. Porter, 1890. 1st edn. 8vo. xxxii, [3], 455 pp. Lge fldg map on 2 sheets, port, plates, ills. Orig cloth gilt. *(Fenning)* **£75 [≈$120]**
- The Story of the Rear Column of the Emin Pasha Relief Expedition. New York: Lovell Co, [1890?]. Thick 8vo. xxxii,455 pp. 2 fldg maps (1 torn, missing section), num ills. Orig pict green cloth, sl shaken.
(Terramedia) **$125 [≈£78]**

Janson, Charles W.
- The Stranger in America: containing Observations made during a long Residence in that Country. London: 1807. 1st edn. 22,500 pp. 9 tinted plates. Orig half calf, mrbld bds, sl outer wear, hinges strengthened. *(Jenkins)* **$850 [≈£531]**

Jaques, Mary J.
- Texan Ranch Life, with Three Months through Mexico in a Prairie Schooner. London: Cox, 1894. 1st edn. Sm folio. xii,363 pp. Ills. Orig pict cloth gilt.
(Jenkins) **$1,575 [≈£984]**

Jarves, James J.
- History of the Hawaiian Islands ... Third Edition. Honolulu: Charles Edwin Hitchcock, 1847. 8vo. 240 pp. Ills. New leather backed bds.

(M & S Rare Books) **$425 [≈£265]**

Jay, W.M.L.
- My Winter in Cuba. New York: 1871. [viii], [9]-296 pp. Orig dec cloth gilt, extremities a bit rubbed. *(Reese)* **$85 [≈£53]**

Jebb, Mrs
- A Strange Career. Life and Adventures of John Gladwyn Jebb. By His Widow. London: 1894. 335,[32] pp. Port. Orig gilt pict cloth, a bit soiled, some edge wear.
(Reese) **$100 [≈£62]**

Jefferson, Joseph
- The Autobiography of Joseph Jefferson. London: [1890]. 501 pp. Plates. Port laid in. Three qtr mor, spine gilt extra, sl rubbed.
(Reese) **$75 [≈£46]**

Jeffery, W., publisher
- London Parishes; containing the Situation, Antiquity, and Re-Building, of the Churches within the Bills of Mortality ... London: 1824. 12mo. [ii],156 pp. Some foxing. Sl loss to crnr of 1 leaf. Orig bds, paper label, later (?) cloth spine, edges worn.
(Coombes) **£40 [≈$64]**

Jefferys, Thomas
- The Natural and Civil History of the French Dominions in North America and South America. London: 1760. 2 vols in one. 18 fldg maps & plans (a few with minor reprs). Calf over orig bds. *(Jenkins)* **$7,500 [≈£4,687]**

Jekyll, Gertrude
- Old West Surrey. London: Longman, Green, 1904. 1st edn. 8vo. xx,320 pp. Num photo ills. Orig green buckram gilt.
(Gough) **£50 [≈$80]**

Jenkins, Lady
- Sport and Travel in Both Tibets. London: 1909. Imperial 8vo. 25 cold plates. Lib stamp on title verso & endpapers. Orig cloth, spotted & sl rubbed. *(Grayling)* **£80 [≈$128]**

Jephson, A.J. Mountenay
- Emin Pasha and the Rebellion at the Equator. New York: Scribner's, 1891. 8vo. xxi, 490 pp. Fldg map & fldg facs in pocket at end. Frontis port, num plates. Orig cloth, rear cvr stained.
(Terramedia) **$100 [≈£62]**

Jerrold, Alice (Mrs Adolphe Smith)
- A Cruise in the Acorn ... London: Marcus Ward, 1875. Sm 4to. 140,4 advt pp. 6 mtd chromolithos. Orig green cloth stamped in

gold & black, cold onlay, spine extremities a
bit rubbed.   *(Karmiole)* **$65 [≈ £40]**

Jessen, B.
- W.N. McMillin's Expeditions and Big Game
Hunting in Southern Sudan, Abyssinia and
East Africa. London: privately ptd, 1906. 415
pp. Fldg map in pocket, 112 ills. Orig bndg.
(Trophy Room Books) **$1,500 [≈ £937]**

Jewitt, John R.
- A Narrative of the Adventures and Sufferings
... see Alsop, Richard (ed.).

Jocelyn, Lord
- Six Months with the Chinese Expedition or,
Leaves from a Soldier's Note-Book. London:
Murray, 1841. 5th edn. 8vo. xv,155,4 advt
pp. 2 fldg plans. Orig cloth.
(Bates & Hindmarch) **£50 [≈ $80]**

Jochelson, Waldemar
- History, Ethnology and Anthropology of the
Aleut. Washington: Carnegie Inst, 1933. Lge
4to. v,[3],91 pp. Photo ills. Orig ptd wraps.
(High Latitude) **$85 [≈ £53]**

Johnshoy, J. Walter
- Apaurak in Alaska. Social Pioneering among
the Eskimos. Translated and Compiled from
the Records of the Reverend T.L. Brevig,
Pioneer Missionary to the Eskimos of Alaska
... Philadelphia: [ca 1944]. 8vo. xvii,19-325
pp. Photo ills. Orig cloth.
(High Latitude) **$50 [≈ £31]**

Johnson, B.
- Descriptive Particulars of the Ancient and
Present State of the Palace of the Savoy: now
the Site of the Bridge of Waterloo ... Third
Edition, improved and enlarged. London:
1817. 8vo. 19 pp. Orig wraps, uncut, some
wear on cvrs.   *(Coombes)* **£21 [≈ $33]**

Johnson, M.
- Camera Trails in Africa. New York: 1924.
8vo. 342 pp. 32 plates. Orig dec cloth.
(Wheldon & Wesley) **£20 [≈ $32]**

Johnson, Samuel
- A Journey to the Western Isles of Scotland.
London: Strahan & Cadell, 1775. 1st edn. 1st
iss. No half-title called for in 1st iss. 8vo.
Title, 384 pp, 12-line errata leaf. D8 & U4
cancels. Errata crrctd in ink in text. Orig
speckled calf, new label & endpapers.
(Bickersteth) **£275 [≈ $440]**
- A Journey to the Western Islands of Scotland.
London: for W. Strahan ..., 1775. 1st edn.

2nd iss, with 6-line errata. 8vo. [iv], 384 pp.
Last few ff sl stained. Calf, rebacked.
(Young's) **£148 [≈ $236]**
- A Journey to the Western Islands of Scotland.
London: 1775. The concealed 2nd edn
(sometimes called the 2nd iss of the 1st edn,
but most of the book was reset). 6-line errata.
8vo. Sm erasure hole in title. Occas browning.
Contemp calf, rebacked.
(Sanders) **£120 [≈ $192]**
- A Journey to the Western Islands of Scotland.
London: J. Pope, 1775. Pirated edn. 12mo.
268 pp. Contemp calf, rebacked.
(Hartfield) **$395 [≈ £246]**
- A Journey to the Western Islands of Scotland.
Baltimore: Philip H. Nicklin; Boston:
Farrand, Mallory; Albany: E. Earle;
Philadelphia: B.B. Hopkins, 1810. 1st Amer
edn. 12mo. Contemp calf, gilt spine, mor
label.   *(Trebizond)* **$350 [≈ £218]**
- A Journey to the Western Islands of Scotland.
First American Edition. Baltimore: 1810.
8vo. [4], 284 pp. Orig 2-toned bds (green &
orange), uncut, cvrs nearly loose.
(M & S Rare Books) **$200 [≈ £125]**
- A Journey to the Western Islands of Scotland.
Baltimore: Nicklin & Co. ..., 1810. 1st Amer
edn. Sm 12mo. [1],284 pp. Contemp calf,
worn but sound, new label.
(Hartfield) **$295 [≈ £184]**
- A Journey to the Western Islands of Scotland.
Baltimore: Philip H. Nicklin; Boston:
Farrand, Mallory; Albany: E. Earle;
Philadelphia: B.B. Hopkins, 1810. 1st Amer
edn. 12mo. Occas foxing. Contemp calf, gilt
spine, mor label, a bit worn.
(Trebizond) **$175 [≈ £109]**

Johnson, Thomas Broadwood
- Tramps around the Mountains of the Moon
and through the Back Gate of the Congo
State. Boston: Dana Estes, 1909. 8vo.
xxiii,316 pp. 2 maps, 48 plates. Orig pict
cloth.   *(Schoyer)* **$50 [≈ £31]**

Johnson, Virginia W.
- Genoa the Superb. The City of Columbus.
London: (1892). 1st edn. 8vo. xiv,298 pp. 20
photo plates. A few sl marks. Orig dec cream
cloth, dull.   *(Bow Windows)* **£55 [≈ $88]**

Johnston, Sir Harry H.
- British Central Africa. An Attempt to Give
Some Account of a Portion of the Territories
Under British Influence North of the
Zambezi. New York: Edward Arnold, 1897.
4to. xix,544 pp. 6 fldg maps, 220 ills. Orig
pict embossed cloth, rubbed, wear to spine.
(Adelson) **$285 [≈ £178]**

- British Central Africa: An Attempt to Give Some Account of a Portion of the Territories Under British Influence North of the Zambezi. London: [1906]. 3rd edn. 4to. 544 pp. Frontis & num plates (6 cold, 4 fldg). Orig red cloth gilt. *(Terramedia)* **$150 [≈ £93]**
- George Grenfell and the Congo ... London: Hutchinson, 1908. 2 vols. 8vo. xxiii,496; xx, 493 pp. 14 maps, 496 photo ills. Orig cloth, ex-lib, shaken, a little tatty. *(Bates & Hindmarch)* **£50 [≈ $80]**
- A History and Description of the British Empire in Africa. (Britain Across the Seas: Africa). London: [1910]. 1st edn. 8vo. 429 pp. Num cold maps & plates. Orig pict red cloth gilt. *(Terramedia)* **$150 [≈ £93]**
- A History and Description of the British Empire in Africa. London: National Society's Depository, Britain Across the Seas: Africa series, [1910]. 1st edn. 8vo. xix,429 pp. Erratum slip. 7 maps, ca 250 ills. Orig cloth gilt. *(Fenning)* **£45 [≈ $72]**
- Liberia. London: Hutchinson, 1906. 1st edn. 2 vols. 8vo. xxviii,[520]; xvi,-1183 pp. 22 maps (4 fldg), num plates (28 cold), ills. Orig pict maroon cloth, vol 1 front cvr sl warped. *(Terramedia)* **$300 [≈ £187]**
- Liberia. London: Hutchinson, 1906. 2 vols. Sm 4to. xxviii,xvi,1183 pp. 22 maps, 28 cold ills, 24 botanical drawings, 402 other ills. Orig cloth. *(Egglishaw)* **£120 [≈ $192]**
- Liberia. London: Hutchinson, 1906. 2 vols. 8vo. xxviii,520; xvi,662 pp. 22 maps, 28 cold ills, 24 botanical drawings, 402 other ills. Ex-lib. Rec blue half leather. *(Bates & Hindmarch)* **£90 [≈ $144]**
- The Nile Quest. A Record of the Exploration of the Nile and its Basin. London: Lawrence & Bullen, 1903. Thick 8vo. xv, 341 pp. Frontis port, 73 plates. Orig dec green cloth gilt, hinges sl rubbed. *(Hollett)* **£65 [≈ $104]**
- The River Congo from its Mouth to Bolobo. With a General Description of the Natural History and Anthropology of its Western Basin. London: Sampson, Low, 1895. 4th & cheaper edn, rvsd. 12mo. 300 pp. Over 70 ills. Orig maroon cloth, sl worn. *(Terramedia)* **$75 [≈ £46]**
- The Uganda Protectorate ... London: Hutchinson, 1902. 1st edn. 2 vols. Lge 8vo. xix,470; xiii,471-1018 pp. 9 maps, 48 cold plates, 506 ills, dec endpapers. Mod three qtr black levant mor gilt. *(Hollett)* **£295 [≈ $472]**
- The Uganda Protectorate. London: Hutchinson, 1902. 1st edn. 2 vols. Imperial 8vo. xx,470; xiv,471-1018 pp. 9 maps, 48 cold plates, 506 b/w ills. Occas marking at some lower margs. Orig black cloth gilt. *(Gough)* **£375 [≈ $600]**

- The Uganda Protectorate ... New York & London: Dodd, Mead, & Hutchinson, 1902. 1st edn. 2 vols. 4to. xix,[470]; [xiii],-1018 pp. 9 fldg maps, num plates (48 cold). Orig red cloth, spines sl dulled. *(Terramedia)* **$500 [≈ £312]**

Johnston, James
- Reality Versus Romance in South Central Africa. Being a Journey across the Continent from Benguella on the West ... to the Mouth of the Zambezi. New York & Chicago: [1893]. 1st edn. Lge 8vo. 353. Fldg map, frontis, 51 photogravures. Orig cloth, sl worn & soiled. *(Terramedia)* **$100 [≈ £62]**

Johnston, Joseph E.
- Reports of the Secretary of War with Reconnaissances of Routes from San Antonio to El Paso ... and from Fort Smith to Santa Fe ... Washington: SED 64, 1850. 1st edn. 250 pp. 2 fldg maps, 72 plates, some cold. Half calf. *(Jenkins)* **$775 [≈ £484]**

Johnston, Philip Mainwaring
- Old Camberwell: its History and Antiquities. Camberwell: for the author by J.R. Wigzell, [1919]. 139 pp. 16 plates. Orig bndg. *(Box of Delights)* **£20 [≈ $32]**

Johnston, Robert
- Travels through Part of the Russian Empire and Country of Poland ... London: Stockdale, 1815. 1st edn. 4to. [3]-7, [3], 460 pp, binder's leaf. 2 maps, 1 uncold & 20 cold plates. Lacks half-title. Contemp mrbld bds, rubbed, later calf spine & crnrs worn. *(M & S Rare Books)* **$600 [≈ £375]**

Johnston, William G.
- Experiences of a Forty-Niner. Pittsburgh: 1892. 1st edn. Lge 8vo. 390 pp. Frontis port, 13 plates. A few tissue guards loose. Orig gilt dec green cloth. With the extra blue-print map laid in, but not the extra port. Sgnd pres slip by Johnston laid in. *(Schoyer)* **$700 [≈ £437]**

Jones, Charles C., Jr.
- Antiquities of the Southern Indians, Particularly of the Georgia tribes. New York: Appleton, 1873. 1st edn. Lge 8vo. 532 pp. 30 full-page plates, 3 w'cuts. Orig green cloth, backstrip relaid. *(Schoyer)* **$200 [≈ £125]**

Jones, Fortier
- With Serbia into Exile. An American's Adventures in the Army that Cannot Die. New York: Century, 1916. 1st edn. Sm 8vo. 447 pp. Num photo plates. Orig pict grey

cloth, sl worn.   *(Terramedia)* **$30 [≈ £18]**

Jones, George Matthew
- Travels in Norway, Sweden, Finland, Russia, and Turkey ... London: Murray, 1827. 1st edn. 2 vols. 8vo. Fldg map. 2 tables. Lacks errata ff & half-title. Contemp half calf, rebacked. B'plate of Brisbane of Brisbane.
       (Hannas) **£140 [≈ $224]**

Jones, M.
- Dr. Kane - The Arctic Hero. London: Nelson, 1890. 16mo. 128 pp. Num ills. Orig dec red cloth, light wear, sl soiling.
       (Parmer) **$60 [≈ £37]**

Jones, Owen Glynne
- Rock-Climbing in the English Lake District. With a Memoir and Portrait of the Author ... Keswick: G.P. Abraham & Sons, 1900. 2nd edn. Lge 8vo. lxiv,322,[9 advt] pp. Port frontis, 31 plates, 9 diags. Orig cloth gilt, extremities sl rubbed. *(Hollett)* **£120 [≈ $192]**

Jones, William Carey
- Report of the Secretary of the Interior, communicating a Copy of the Report of ... Special Agent to Examine the Subject of Land Titles in California. Washington: 1851. 136 pp. Lge fldg map (the 1st ptd city map of San Francisco). Disbound. Cloth box.
       (Reese) **$900 [≈ £562]**

Josephus, Flavius
- The Works ... With great diligence Revised and Amended, according to the excellent French Translation of Monsieur Arnaud L'Andilly ... London: Herringman, 1683. 4to. Map. rebound in cloth, inner hinge cracked at title.   *(Thornton's)* **£125 [≈ $200]**
- The Whole Works ... Translated by Sir Roger L'Estrange ... Dundee: Henry Galbraith, 1766. Folio. 779 pp. Title backed. Some trimming. Lacks the map & plates. Rebound in cloth.   *(Thornton's)* **£160 [≈ $256]**

Josselyn, John
- An Account of Two Voyages to New-England ... London: for Giles Widdows, 1674. [4],279, [3] pp. Licence & errata ff, advts. V sl browning. 19th c polished calf gilt, sm repr to cvr. Half mor slipcase.
       (Reese) **$5,500 [≈ £3,437]**

Journal ...
- Journal of a Few Months' Residence in Portugal ... see Quillinan, Dorothy.
- A Journal of the late Expedition to Carthagena ... see Smollett, Tobias.

Journey ...
- A Journey through Scotland ... see Macky, John.
- A Journey to Mequinez ... see Windus, John.
- A Journey to the Western Isles of Scotland ... see Johnson, Samuel.

Joyce, Weston St.John
- The Neighbourhood of Dublin: its Topography, Antiquities and Historical Associations ... Dublin: Gill, 1939. 8vo. xx, 512 pp. Fldg maps, num ills. Orig cloth.
       (Fenning) **£38.50 [≈ $62]**

Judge, Charles J.
- An American Missionary. Baltimore & New York: John Murphy Co, 1904. 1st edn. xv,294 pp. Fldg map, photo plates. Orig gilt dec red cloth, light shelfwear & soiling.
       (Parmer) **$125 [≈ £78]**

Jungman, Beatrix
- Norway. Painted by Nico Jungman. London: A. & C. Black Colour Books, Twenty Shilling Series, 1905. 1st edn. Cold plates. Orig dec cloth, top qtr inch of spine v sl faded, else v fine.   *(Old Cathay)* **£85 [≈ $136]**
- Norway. Painted by Nico Jungman. London: A. & C. Black Colour Books, Twenty Shilling Series, 1905. 1st edn. Cold plates. Orig dec cloth, sunning & hence discoloration to spine.
       (Old Cathay) **£50 [≈ $80]**

Junker, Wilhelm
- Travels in Africa, 1879-1883. London: 1891. 8vo. viii,471,index pp. Map, num ills. Lib stamp on title. Lib marks on spine.
       (Rittenhouse) **$125 [≈ £78]**

Junod, H.A.
- The Life of a South African Tribe. New York: University Books, 1962. 2 vols. Roy 8vo. 14 plates, num text ills. Orig cloth, slipcase.   *(Berkelouw)* **$100 [≈ £62]**

Kalm, Peter
- Travels in North America. Edited by Adolph B. Benson. New York: 1937. 2 vols. Maps. Orig cloth.   *(Jenkins)* **$125 [≈ £78]**

Kane, Elisha Kent
- Arctic Explorations in the Years 1853, '54, '55. Philadelphia: Childs & Peterson, 1857. 2 vols. 8vo. 464; 467 pp. 2 engvd titles, 3 maps (2 fldg), 20 engvd plates. Calf, a little rubbed & scraped.   *(Hollett)* **£85 [≈ $136]**
- The U.S. Grinnell Expedition in Search of Sir John Franklin. A Personal Narrative. New York: Harper, 1854. xi,13-552 pp. 3 maps, 12

plates. Orig cloth, faded.
(High Latitude) **$85 [≈ £53]**

Kane, Paul
- Wanderings of an Artist among the Indians of North America. London: 1859. 1st edn. [18], 455, [8] pp. 3 cold plates (only, of 8). Lacks map. Foxed. Orig cloth, worn.
(Jenkins) **$285 [≈ £178]**

Kaye, John William
- History of the War in Afghanistan from Unpublished Letters and Journals ... London: Bentley, 1851. 1st edn. 2 vols. 8vo. Vol 1 title torn without loss. Sl foxing. Contemp half mor, edges v rubbed, a few nicks on vol 1 spine. *(Worldwide Antiqu'n)* **$145 [≈ £90]**

Kearsley's Guide ...
- Kearsley's Stranger's Guide, or a Companion through London and Westminster, and the Country Round. London: [1791]. 1st edn. 8vo. 2 fldg maps. Contemp half calf.
(Robertshaw) **£36 [≈ $57]**

Kearton, Cherry & Barnes, J.
- Through Central Africa from East to West. London: 1915. Roy 8vo. xviii,283 pp. Map, cold frontis, 8 photogravures, 160 photos by Kearton. Orig cloth.
(Wheldon & Wesley) **£35 [≈ $56]**

Keate, George
- An Account of the Pelew Islands ... Composed from the Journals ... of Captain Henry Wilson ... London: G. Nicol, 1788. 1st edn. Lge 4to. xxviii,378,[2] pp. Port frontis, fldg map, 15 plates. Contemp calf.
(Karmiole) **$500 [≈ £312]**
- An Account of the Pelew Islands ... Composed from the Journals ... of Captain Henry Wilson, and Some of his Officers ... London: for Captain Wilson, 1788. 2nd edn. 4to. xxvii,[1],378 pp. Port, fldg map, 15 plates. Contemp calf, rebacked, sl scorched.
(Reese) **$400 [≈ £250]**
- An Account of the Pelew Islands in the Western Pacific Ocean. Dublin: Luke White, 1788. Port, map. Contemp Irish calf.
(Emerald Isle) **£150 [≈ $240]**
- An Account of the Pelew Islands ... Composed from the Journals ... of Captain Henry Wilson, and Some of his Officers ... Philadelphia: 1789. 20,256 pp. Calf, sl wear to front hinge. *(Reese)* **$350 [≈ £218]**
- Sketches from Nature; taken, and coloured, in a Journey to Margate. Published from the Original Designs. London: Dodsley, 1779. 1st edn. 2 vols. 8vo. [vi],207,[i]; [ii],223,[i] pp.

Occas sl browning. Contemp half calf, minor wear to extremities, jnts cracked.
(Clark) **£95 [≈ $152]**
- Sketches from Nature, taken and coloured in a Journey to Margate. Published from the Original Designs. The Fifth Edition. London: T. Hurst, 1802. 8vo. viii,[6],261 pp. Frontis & engvd ills, sev by Bewick. Occas foxing. Later tree calf, gilt spine, lemon edges. *(Spelman)* **£65 [≈ $104]**

Keating, William H.
- Narrative of an Expedition to the Source of St. Peter's River, etc., in the Year 1823 under the Command of Stephen H. Long. Philadelphia: 1824. 1st edn. 2 vols. 15 litho plates. Lacks the map. Half calf, mrbld bds, mor labels. *(Jenkins)* **$225 [≈ £140]**

Keatinge, Maurice
- Travels in Europe and Africa ... London: Colburn, 1816. 1st edn. 4to. xvi,346; [ii], 274 pp. Frontis & 33 other sepia aquatint plates. Sl offsetting from plates. Contemp black mor, rebacked, gilt dec spine.
(Terramedia) **$800 [≈ £500]**

Keeler, N.E.
- A Trip to Alaska and the Klondike in the Summer of 1905. Cincinnati: Ebert & Richardson, 1906. 1st edn. 8vo. 115 pp. 10 plates. Marg dampstain on last 2 pp. Orig brown wraps, chipped.
(Parmer) **$125 [≈ £78]**

Keely, Robert N. & Davis, G.G.
- In Arctic Seas. The Voyage of 'Kite', with the Peary Expedition. Together with a Transcript of the Log of the Kite. Philadelphia: Hartranft, 1892. 1st edn. 8vo. vii, 542 pp. Fldg map, num photo plates & ills. Orig dec white cloth, sl soiled, front hinge cracked. *(Terramedia)* **$100 [≈ £62]**

Kelly, R. Talbot
- Burma. London: A. & C. Black Colour Books, Twenty Shilling Series, 1905. 1st edn. 75 cold plates. Endpapers sl foxed. Orig dec cloth, t.e.g., spine sl faded.
(Old Cathay) **£60 [≈ $96]**
- Burma. London: A. & C. Black, 1933. 2nd edn, rvsd. 32 cold plates. Inscrptn on f.e.p. Orig cloth. *(Old Cathay)* **£19 [≈ $30]**
- Egypt. London: A. & C. Black Colour Books, 1902. One of 500, sgnd by Kelly. 75 cold plates. Orig dec cloth, t.e.g., almost fine.
(Old Cathay) **£165 [≈ $264]**
- Egypt. London: A. & C. Black Colour Books, Twenty Shilling Series, 1902. 1st edn. Cold

plates. Orig dec cloth, t.e.g., sl shaken.
(Old Cathay) **£33 [≈ $52]**
- Egypt. London: A. & C. Black Colour Books,
Twenty Shilling Series, 1902. 1st edn. Cold
plates. Orig dec cloth, t.e.g., fine.
(Old Cathay) **£50 [≈ $80]**
- Egypt. London: A. & C. Black Colour Books,
Twenty Shilling Series, 1903. Cold plates.
Foxing, inscrptn on endpapers. Orig dec
cloth. *(Old Cathay)* **£45 [≈ $72]**
- Egypt. London: A. & C. Black Colour Books,
Twenty Shilling Series, 1906. Cold plates.
Orig dec cloth, front bd & spine worn badly
in places. *(Old Cathay)* **£15 [≈ $24]**
- Egypt. London: A. & C. Black Colour Books,
Twenty Shilling Series, 1912. Cold plates.
Orig dec cloth. *(Old Cathay)* **£28 [≈ $44]**

Kelman, John
- From Damascus to Palmyra. With Color
Plate Illustrations by Margaret Thomas.
London: A. & C. Black, 1908. 8vo. 367 pp.
Fldg map, num plates. Orig pict blue & white
cloth. *(Terramedia)* **$40 [≈ £25]**
- The Holy Land. Painted by John Fulleylove.
London: A. & C. Black Colour Books,
Twenty Shilling Series, 1902. 1st edn. 92
plates, mostly cold. Inkstaining to foredges.
Orig dec cloth, t.e.g. Dw with half inch loss
to hd of spine. *(Old Cathay)* **£29 [≈ $46]**
- The Holy Land. Painted by John Fulleylove.
London: A. & C. Black 1902. 8vo. 301 pp.
Cold frontis, num other cold plates. Contemp
half mor gilt. *(Terramedia)* **$60 [≈ £37]**
- The Holy Land. Painted by John Fulleylove.
London: A. & C. Black Colour Books,
Twenty Shilling Series, 1912. 92 plates,
mostly cold. Occas foxing, esp to endpapers.
Orig dec cloth. *(Old Cathay)* **£33 [≈ $52]**

Kemp, E.G.
- The Face of China. London: Chatto &
Windus, 1909. 48 cold plates, 16 sepia ills.
Orig bndg. *(Old Cathay)* **£36 [≈ $57]**
- The Face of Manchuria, Korea, and Russian
Turkistan. London: Chatto & Windus, 1910.
Tall 8vo. Fldg map, cold frontis & plates.
Orig green cloth gilt, front cover sl stained.
(Terramedia) **$70 [≈ £43]**
- The Face of Manchuria, Korea, and Russian
Turkestan. London: Chatto & Windus, 1910.
Cold frontis & 23 cold plates. Orig dec cloth
gilt, hd of spine bumped.
(John Smith) **£45 [≈ $72]**

Kendall, George W.
- Narrative of the Texan Santa Fe Expedition
... New York: Harper, 1844. 1st edn. 1st iss,
with 1844 at ft of spines. 2 vols. Fldg map, 5

plates. Orig cloth. *(Jenkins)* **$650 [≈ £406]**
- Narrative of the Texan Santa fe Expedition.
New York: Harper, 1856. 7th edn, with
addtns. 2 vols. 8vo. 452; 442 pp. Fldg map
(tear reprd), 5 plates. Occas sl foxing. Orig
black cloth.
(W. Thomas Taylor) **$2,500 [≈ £1,562]**
- Narrative of an Expedition across the Great
South-Western Prairies, from Texas to Santa
Fe. London: 1845. 1st English printing. 2
vols. Map, 2 plates. Orig cloth gilt.
(Jenkins) **$475 [≈ £296]**

Kennan, George
- Tent Life in Siberia ... New York: Putnam;
London: Low, Son, & Marston, 1871. 8vo.
x,425 pp. Fldg map. Orig cloth.
(Worldwide Antiqu'n) **$24 [≈ £15]**

Kennedy, Edward B.
- The Black Police of Queensland:
Reminiscences of Official Work and Personal
Adventures in the Early Days of the Colony.
London: Murray, 1902. 1st edn. xviii,280 pp.
Frontis, 19 plates. Orig dec brown cloth, sl
faded. *(Box of Delights)* **£30 [≈ $48]**

Kennedy, James
- A Description of the Antiquities and
Curiosities in Wilton House ... see Pembroke,
Thomas Herbert, 8th Earl of.

Kennedy, William
- Texas: Its Geography, Natural History, and
Topography. New York: 1844. 1st Amer edn.
118 pp. Half mor. *(Jenkins)* **$750 [≈ £468]**
- Texas: The Rise, Progress, and Prospects of
the Republic of Texas. London: Hastings,
1841. 1st edn. 2 vols. Maps supplied from a
later edn. Later half mor.
(Jenkins) **$1,250 [≈ £781]**

Kennett, Basil
- Romae Antiquae Notitia: or, the Antiquities
of Rome ... with Copper Cuts of the Principal
Buildings ... London: Swall & Child, 1696.
1st edn. 8vo. [xl],368,[24] pp. Final errata
leaf. 10 plates, some fldg. Contemp calf, spine
ends sl worn. Wing K.298.
(Clark) **£85 [≈ $136]**
- Romae Antiquae Notitia: or, The Antiquities
of Rome ... The Fourth Edition Revised and
Corrected. London: Child & Knaplock, 1708.
8vo. [xvi],375,[26] pp, advt leaf. Port, title
vignette, 14 plates, some fldg. Orig panelled
calf, rebacked. *(Bickersteth)* **£55 [≈ $88]**
- Romae Antiquae Notitia: or, the Antiquities
of Rome ... London: for T. Child ..., 1717.
6th edn. 8vo. xxx,375,26 advt pp. Port

frontis, 13 plates. Red & black title. Contemp panelled calf, rebacked.
(Young's) £46 [≈ $73]

Kennion, R.L.
- By Mountain, Lake and Plain. Sport in Eastern Persia. London: 1911. 8vo. Cold frontis, num plates. Sl foxing. Orig bndg, sl rubbed. *(Grayling)* £155 [≈ $248]
- By Mountain, Lake and Plain. Sketches of Sport in Eastern Persia. London: 1911. Ills. Orig bndg.
(Trophy Room Books) $300 [≈ £187]
- Sport and Life in the Further Himalaya. London: 1910. 330 pp. Ills. Orig pict gilt bndg. *(Trophy Room Books)* $350 [≈ £218]

Kenyon, Kathleen M.
- Excavations at Jericho: Volume I: The Tombs Excavated in 1952-4 ... London: for the School of British Archaeology in Jerusalem, 1960. 1st edn. 4to. xii,583 pp. 43 plates, num ills. Orig maroon cloth.
(Terramedia) $250 [≈ £156]

Keppel, George
- Personal Narrative of a Journey from India to England, by Bussorah, Bagdad, the Ruins of Babylon ... in the Year 1824. London: Colburn, 1827. 1st edn. 4to. xii,340 pp. Fldg map, 3 cold plates, 8 text engvs. 3 marg tears reprd. Orig bds, sometime rebacked in calf.
(Frew Mackenzie) £325 [≈ $520]

Keppel, Henry
- The Expedition to Borneo of 'H.M.S. Dido' for the Suppression of Piracy: with Extracts from the Journal of James Brooke ... London: Chapman & Hall, 1846. 2nd edn. 2 vols. 8vo. Half-titles. 6 maps & plans, table, 11 plates. Some soiling. Orig cloth, uncut.
(Trebizond) $375 [≈ £234]
- The Expedition to Borneo of H.M.S. Dido for the Suppression of Piracy. With Extracts from the Journal of James Brooke, Esq. of Sarawak. New York: Harper, 1846. 16mo. xii, 413 pp. Fldg map. Qtr mor, rebacked.
(Terramedia) $200 [≈ £125]

Ker, J.G.
- A Naturalist in the Gran Chaco (S. America). London: 1950. 8vo. 240 pp. Map, 24 plates. Orig cloth. *(Wheldon & Wesley)* £30 [≈ $48]

Kerner, Robert J.
- Northeastern Asia. A Selected Bibliography ... Berkeley: Univ of Calif Press; London: Cambridge UP, 1939. 1st edn. 2 vols. 8vo. Ex-lib. Orig cloth, edges sl rubbed.

(Worldwide Antiqu'n) $125 [≈ £78]

Kerr, M.
- The Far Interior. London: 1887. 2 vols. 318; 318 pp. Fldg map, num ills. Barely visible blindstamp on titles. Orig cloth.
(Trophy Room Books) $850 [≈ £531]
- The Far Interior. London: 1887. 2 vols. 318; 318 pp. Fldg map, num ills. Orig cloth, sl wear to spine ends.
(Trophy Room Books) $750 [≈ £468]

Keys, A.E.
- A History of Eastington, near Stonehouse in Gloucestershire. London: [1953]. One of 220. Orig bndg. Sgnd by the author & ALS inserted. *(Ambra)* £20 [≈ $32]

Kidder, Daniel P.
- Sketches of Residence and Travels in Brazil ... Philadelphia: 1845. 2 vols. 369; 404 pp. Maps, 2 frontis, plates (tanned as usual). Orig cloth gilt, Imperial arms on cvrs, faded, hd of spines chipped. *(Reese)* $325 [≈ £203]
- Sketches of Residence and Travels in Brazil ... Philadelphia: Sorin & Ball, 1845. 2 vols. 8vo. xvi,19-369; viii,9-404 pp. Map, 10 plates. Mod cloth, leather labels.
(Adelson) $375 [≈ £234]

Kilby, Henry
- Trips to Algeria, Holland, the North Cape, etc ... London: H.R. Allenson, 1895. 1st edn. 8vo. 132 pp. Num litho ills, many full page. Orig pict stiff wraps. *(Hannas)* £85 [≈ $136]

Kindersley, Jemima
- Letters from the Island of Teneriffe, Brazil, the Cape of Good Hope and the East Indies. London: J. Nourse, 1777. [4],302 pp. Frontis. Half-title. Contemp calf, red label.
(Karmiole) $350 [≈ £218]

King, Jessie M.
- The City of the West [: Edinburgh]. Edinburgh: Foulis, 1911. 1st edn. 8vo. 26 plates, mtd as drawings, all by King, with text on versos. Orig cold ptd wraps over plain stiff wraps. *(Fenning)* £24.50 [≈ $40]

King, Leonard W. & Hall, H.R.
- Egypt and Western Asia in the Light of Recent Discoveries. London: SPCK, 1907. 1st edn. 4to. 480 pp. Num plates. Orig red cloth gilt, bevelled edges.
(Terramedia) $125 [≈ £78]

King, Thomas Butler
- California: The Wonder of the Age ... New

York: 1850. Unauthorized edn. 34 pp. Orig
wraps, sl darkened, lib mark on front cvr.
(Reese) **$85 [≈ £53]**

Kingdon-Ward, F.
- Pilgrimage for Plants. London: 1960. 8vo. 21
plates. Lib stamps on title & verso. Orig
bndg. Dw.   *(Henly)* **£20 [≈ $32]**
- Plant Hunting in the Wilds. London: [1931].
8vo. 79 pp. 8 plates. Orig cloth. Dw.
(Henly) **£17 [≈ $27]**
- Plant Hunting on the Edge of the World.
London: 1930. 1st edn. 8vo. 383 pp. Orig
black cloth.   *(Henly)* **£68 [≈ $108]**
- The Romance of Plant Hunting. London:
1933. 2nd edn. Cr 8vo. x,227,4 advt pp. Map,
8 plates. Orig cloth.   *(Henly)* **£11 [≈ $17]**

Kinglake, Alexander William
- Eothen, or Traces of Travel brought Home
from the East. London: John Ollivier, 1845.
2nd edn. 8vo. xi,178 pp. 2 hand cold plates (1
fldg). Mod half mor. *(Hollett)* **£120 [≈ $192]**
- Eothen, or Traces of Travel brought Home
from the East. London: 1845. 2nd edn. xi,418
pp. Fldg chromolitho frontis (cold partly by
hand), chromolitho plate. Contemp three qtr
mor, mrbld bds, gilt spine.
(Reese) **$250 [≈ £156]**
- Eothen. London: John Ollivier ..., 1845. 3rd
edn. 8vo. xiii,424 pp. Cold fldg frontis. 1
gathering a little loose. Contemp red calf, gilt
dec spine.   *(Young's)* **£35 [≈ $56]**

Kingsley, Charles
- At Last: A Christmas in the West Indies. New
York: 1871. 1st Amer edn. xii, [13]-465, advt
pp. Frontis, plates, text ills. Occas sl foxing.
Orig cloth gilt, some wear to extremities, hd
of spine sl frayed.   *(Reese)* **$125 [≈ £78]**

Kingsley, Mary H.
- Travels in West Africa. London: Macmillan,
1897. 1st edn. Thick 8vo. xvi,743,8 advt pp.
2 litho plates, 45 full-page ills. Orig red cloth
gilt, rather used & faded, hinges badly
cracked.   *(Hollett)* **£65 [≈ $104]**
- Travels in West Africa: Congo Francais,
Corisco, and Cameroons. London:
Macmillan, 1897. 1st edn. 8vo. xvi,743,advt
pp. Num plates & ills. Last few ff foxed. Orig
maroon cloth gilt, top crnr of spine v rubbed
& sl discold, rear hinge shaken.
(Terramedia) **$200 [≈ £125]**
- Travels in West Africa, Congo Francais,
Corisco and Cameroons. London: 1897. 2nd
thousand. 8vo. xvi,743 pp. 18 plates, ills.
Some foxing, a few lib stamps. Buckram,
leather back.

(Wheldon & Wesley) **£50 [≈ $80]**
- Travels in West Africa. London: 1897. 2nd
edn. 8vo. Ills. Some foxing. Orig bndg.
(Grayling) **£20 [≈ $32]**
- West African Studies. London: 1899. 8vo.
xxiv,639 pp. Map (reprd), frontis, 23 plates.
Some sm lib stamps. Edges lightly trimmed.
Rebound in buckram, mor back.
(Wheldon & Wesley) **£40 [≈ $64]**

Kingston, W.H.G.
- Western Wanderings, or a Pleasure Tour in
the Canadas. London: 1856. 1st edn. 2 vols.
8vo. 2 frontis. Sl foxing. Sl dampstaining in
vol 1. Orig cloth, spines relaid.
(Henly) **£54 [≈ $86]**

Kinloch, A.A.
- Large Game Shooting in Thibet, the
Himalayas, Northern and Central India.
London: 1892. 3rd edn, rvsd & enlgd. Sm
folio. Ills. Orig bndg, v sl rubbed, 2 crnrs
bumped.   *(Grayling)* **£170 [≈ $272]**

Kinsey, William M.
- Portugal Illustrated. [London]: 1828. xvii,
500 pp. Fldg map, fldg frontis, plates (some
cold), tables. Scattered foxing, especially to
b/w plates (cold plates are clean). Contemp
polished calf gilt, gilt inner dentelles,
rebacked.   *(Reese)* **$650 [≈ £406]**

Kirby, John
- The Suffolk Traveller: or, A Journey through
Suffolk ... Ipswich: John Bagnall, 1735. 1st
edn. 8vo. [iv],206 pp,errata leaf. Orig mrbld
bds, new calf spine, untrimmed.
(Bickersteth) **£160 [≈ $256]**

Kirk, Robert C.
- Twelve Months in Klondike. London:
Heinemann, 1899. 1st edn. xii,273 pp. 24
plates inc map & port. Minimal foxing to
endpapers.   *(Parmer)* **$135 [≈ £84]**

Kirke, Henry
- Twenty-Five Years in British Guiana.
London: 1898. 1st edn. 8vo. xi,364 pp. Fldg
map (a little torn), 20 ills. Num pencil
marginalia. Orig cloth.
(Bow Windows) **£36 [≈ $57]**
- Twenty-Five Years in British Guiana.
London: Sampson Low, Marston, 1898. 1st
edn. 8vo. x,364 pp. Fldg map, 20 plates. Orig
bndg, partly unopened. *(Schoyer)* **$60 [≈ £37]**

Kitching, A.L.
- On the Backwaters of the Nile. Studies of
some Child Races of Central Africa. New

York & London: Scribners; Fisher, Unwin, 1912. 8vo. xxiv,295 pp. Fldg map, num plates. Orig pict black cloth gilt, ex-lib.
(Terramedia) **$75 [≈ £46]**

Kittenberger, K.
- Big Game Hunting and Collecting in East Africa 1760-1926. New York: 1929. 342 pp. Fldg map, 200 ills. Orig bndg.
(Trophy Room Books) **$160 [≈ £100]**

Kneeland, Samuel
- The Wonders of the Yosemite Valley, and of California. With Original Photographic Illustrations by John P. Soule. Third Edition, revised and enlarged. Boston, 1872. 4to. 98 pp. 2 maps, 10 mtd albumen prints. Orig gilt dec cloth, a.e.g.
(Charles B. Wood) **$400 [≈ £250]**

Knight, Charles (ed.)
- Old England: a Pictorial Museum of Regal, Ecclesiastical, Municipal, Baronial and Popular Antiquities. London: James Sangster, [1860?]. 2 vols. Folio. 24 cold plates. Contemp half calf, rubbed, rear cvrs marked.
(Waterfield's) **£60 [≈ $96]**

Knight, E.F.
- The Awakening of Turkey. A History of the Turkish Revolution. Philadelphia & London: Lippincott & Milne, 1909. 1st edn. 8vo. x,355 pp. Frontis port & other tissued plates. Orig dec cloth gilt. *(Terramedia)* **£60 [≈ £37]**
- Madagascar in War Time. The Times's Special Correspondent's Experiences among the Hovas during the French Invasion of 1895. London: 1896. 8vo. Fldg map, 4 plates, text ills. Orig cloth, sl worn.
(Farahar) **£80 [≈ $128]**

Knight, Francis A.
- The Heart of Mendip. London: 1915. 1st edn. 8vo. Num ills. Orig cloth.
(Ambra) **£24 [≈ $38]**

Knight, Henry G.
- Saracenic and Norman Remains: to illustrate the Normans in Sicily. London: Murray, [1840]. Elephant folio. ii,1,6 pp. Engvd title & 29 litho plates (3 cold, 1 tinted). Ex-lib with perf stamp on title, sm stamps on plates. Orig mor & cloth, spine ends worn.
(Terramedia) **$1,000 [≈ £625]**

Knox, Alexander
- The Ballynahinch Mineral Waters ... together with Notices of the Scenery, Antiquities and Natural History. Belfast: Lamont Bros, 1846. 47,[vi] pp. Orig yellow ptd wraps, tipped into

bds. *(Emerald Isle)* **£75 [≈ $120]**
- A History of County Down ... Geography, Topography, Antiquities and Natural History. Dublin: Hodges, 1875. 724 pp. Cold map. Orig bndg.
(Emerald Isle) **£110 [≈ $176]**
- The Irish Watering Places. Their Climate, Scenery and Accomodations ... Analyses of their Principal Springs ... and the Various Forms of Disease to which they are adapted ... Dublin: Curry, 1845. 336 pp. Contemp travelling bndg, with flap & tie.
(Emerald Isle) **£50 [≈ $80]**

Knox, Alexander A.
- The New Playground, or Wanderings in Algeria. London: Kegan Paul, 1883. Sm 8vo. 482 pp. Orig cloth. *(Terramedia)* **$50 [≈ £31]**

Knox, Arthur E.
- Ornithological Rambles in Sussex ... London: Van Voorst, 1849. 1st edn. Cr 8vo. vi,250,ctlg pp. 4 plates. Orig cloth gilt.
(Egglishaw) **£25 [≈ $40]**
- Ornithological Rambles in Sussex. London: 1850. 2nd edn. 8vo. x,254 pp. 4 plates. Occas sl foxing. Orig cloth, trifle used.
(Wheldon & Wesley) **£20 [≈ $32]**
- Ornithological Rambles in Sussex ... Third Edition. London: 1855. 8vo. xii,260 pp, advt leaf. 4 tinted litho plates. Orig gilt illust cloth.
(Bow Windows) **£40 [≈ $64]**

Knox, Charles
- Traditions of Western Germany. The Black Forest, the Neckar, the Odenwald, the Taunus, the Rhine, and the Moselle. London: Saunders & Otley, 1841. 3 vols. 8vo. viii,328; viii, 312; [6],308 pp. Orig dec green cloth, spine extremities sl chipped.
(Karmiole) **$75 [≈ £46]**

Knox, John P.
- A Historical Account of St. Thomas, W.I. ... St. Croix and St. Johns; Slave Insurrections ... Emancipation ... New York: 1852. xii, [13]-271 pp. Frontis, fldg map (torn, 1 panel lacking), charts, tables. Lib stamp & bookplate. Orig cloth. *(Reese)* **$275 [≈ £171]**

Knox, Robert
- An Historical Relation of the Island of Ceylon ... London: Richard Chiswell, 1681. 1st edn. Folio. Licence leaf, xxii,189 pp, advt leaf. Fldg map & 14 plates (only, of 15). Maps & some plates reprd at margs. Occas marg tears. Contemp calf, rebacked.
(Gough) **£375 [≈ $600]**
- An Historical Relation of the Island of Ceylon

... London: 1681. 1st edn. Lge 4to. [20],189,[3] pp. Fldg map & 15 plates. Occas foxing, few sm stains. Many plates tears mended on versos & sm pieces missing from margs. Lacks port. Contemp style three qtr calf gilt.   *(Reese)* **$650 [≈ £406]**

Knox, Thomas W.

- The Oriental World. A Record of Recent Travel, Adventure, and Exploration ... Hartford: 1877. 8vo. 694 pp. Num ills. Orig cloth, edges rubbed, spine ends frayed.
(Worldwide Antiqu'n) **$65 [≈ £40]**

- Overland through Asia. Pictures of Siberian, Chinese and Tartar Life. Travels and Adventures ... Hartford, CT: 1870. 1st edn. 8vo. 608 pp. Map, nearly 200 ills. Orig cloth, edges rubbed, spine ends frayed, some tears in spine.   *(Worldwide Antiqu'n)* **$125 [≈ £78]**

Koebel, W.H.

- Argentina, Past and Present. London: A. & C. Black Colour Books, Twenty Shilling Series, 1914. 2nd edn. Fldg map, 96 ills (64 from b/w photos, 32 cold by E.W. Christmas). Front free endpaper clipped at the top. Orig dec cloth, front cvr sl marked.
(Old Cathay) **£65 [≈ $104]**

- In the Maoriland Bush. London: Stanley Paul, [ca 1920]. 1st edn (?). 8vo. 316 pp. 32 b/w plates. Some foxing. Orig pict cloth gilt.
(Gough) **£18 [≈ $28]**

Koehl, H., Fitzmaurice, J.C. & Von Hunefeld, G.

- The Three Musketeers of the Air. Their Conquest of the Atlantic from East to West ... New York: Putnam's, 1928. Authors' Autograph Edition, one of 260, sgnd. Roy 8vo. 2,xii,330 pp. Frontis, 30 plates. Orig half cloth & bds, uncut, spotted, top spine worn.
(Berkelouw) **$250 [≈ £156]**

Kollmann, Paul

- The Victoria Nyanza. The Land, the Races and their Customs ... London: Swan Sonnenschein, 1899. 8vo. ix,254 pp. Fldg map, num text ills. Perf stamp on title. Orig red cloth.   *(Adelson)* **$175 [≈ £109]**

Kotzebue, August von

- Travels through Italy in the Years 1804 and 1805 ... London: for Richard Phillips, 1806. 1st English edn. 4 vols. Sm 8vo. xix, 279; xvi,302; xii,263; xvi,331 pp. Sl foxing. Pink half calf over mrbld bds, gilt dec spines, sl rubbed.   *(Heritage)* **$400 [≈ £250]**

Kotzebue, Otto Von

- A New Voyage Round the World, in the

Years 1823, 24, and 26. London: Colburn & Bentley, 1830. 1st edn in English. 2 vols. Upper marg of a few ff in vol 2 nibbled. Three qtr calf, worn & chipped.
(Jenkins) **$385 [≈ £240]**

Kouwenhoven, John A.

- The Columbia Historical Portrait of New York. An Essay in Graphic History in Honor of the Tricentennial of New York City ... New York: Doubleday, 1953. Sq 4to. 550 pp. Num ills. Orig bndg. *(Bernett)* **$200 [≈ £125]**

Krascheninnikov, Stephan Petrovich

- The History of Kamtschatka, and the Kurilski Islands ... Gloucester: R. Raikes for T. Jefferys, 1764. 1st English edn. 4to. vii,[1],280,index pp. 2 fldg maps, 5 plates (2 fldg). Some offset from plates. Light foxing to endpapers. Calf, rebacked.
(Parmer) **$2,000 [≈ £1,250]**

- The History of Kamtschatka, and the Kurilski Islands ... London: T. Jefferys, 1764. 1st English edn. 4to. vi,[errata leaf], 9-280,8 pp. 2 fldg maps, 5 plates. Orig calf, gilt spine, red label.
(Adelson) **$2,250 [≈ £1,406]**

Krist, Gustav

- Alone Through the Forbidden Land. Journey in Disguise through Soviet Central Asia. London: 1938. 8vo. Plates. Orig cloth.
(Farahar) **£20 [≈ $32]**

Krohn, William O.

- In Borneo Jungles. Among the Dyak Headhunters. Indianopolis: Bobbs-Merrill, [1927]. [12],328 pp. Num plates & maps. 1 leaf opened roughly. Orig blue cloth gilt. Dw sl chipped.   *(Karmiole)* **$45 [≈ £28]**

Kumm, H. Karl W.

- From Hausaland to Egypt through the Sudan. London: Constable, 1910. 1st edn. Tall 8vo. xi, 324 pp. Fldg map, frontis, num photo plates (inc 6 cold plates of butterflies). Orig pict orange brown cloth, sl soiled.
(Terramedia) **$100 [≈ £62]**

Kuttner, Charles Gottlob

- Travels through Denmark, Sweden, Austria, and Part of Italy, in 1798 & 1799. London: Richard Phillips, 1805. iv,200 pp. Fldg frontis map (somewhat foxed). Mod half cloth, t.e.g.   *(Reese)* **$100 [≈ £62]**

L., B.J.

- A Short Outline of the History of Russia. Edinburgh: privately ptd [T. & A. Constable], 1900. 2 vols. 4to. Orig plum cloth.

(Rankin) £65 [≈ $104]

L., H.A., 'The Old Shekarry'
- See Leveson, Henry Astbury.

Laborde, Leon de
- Journey through Arabia Petraea, to Mount Sinai, and the Excavated City of Petra, the Edom of the Prophecies. London: 1838. 2nd English edn. xxviii,340 pp. Maps (1 fldg), frontis, plates, title vignette. Orig three qtr calf, a bit worn at extremities.
(Reese) $225 [≈ £140]

Lacaille, A.D.
- The Stone Age in Scotland. OUP: 1954. Lge 8vo. 345 pp. Num plates. Orig blue cloth. Chipped dw. *(Terramedia)* $120 [≈ £75]

Lacombe, Jean de
- A Compendium of the East. Being an Account of Voyages to the Grand Indies ... London: Golden Cockerel Press, 1937. One of 300. Tall 4to. 210 pp. Num plates. Orig black cloth over dec cloth.
(Karmiole) $200 [≈ £125]

Ladue, Joseph
- Klondyke Facts being a Complete Guide Book to the Great Gold Regions of the Yukon and Klondyke and the Northwest Territories. Montreal: John Lovell, [1897]. 12mo. 205 pp. Maps (1 fldg), plates. Orig dec cloth, minor wear. *(High Latitude)* $175 [≈ £109]

A Lady's Tour round Monte Rosa ...
- See Cole, Mrs Henry Warwick.

La Farge, John
- Reminiscences of the South Seas. Garden City: Doubleday Page, 1912. Lge 8vo. 480 pp. 48 ills (32 cold). Orig green cloth gilt, pict onlay. *(Parmer)* $125 [≈ £78]

Laing, John
- A Voyage to Spitzbergen; containing an Account of that Country ... Second Edition, Corrected and Enlarged. Edinburgh: for Adam Black, 1818. 12mo. Orig bds, paper label, backstrip worn.
(Hannas) £180 [≈ $288]

Laing, Samuel
- Journal of a Residence in Norway during the Years 1834, 1835 & 1836. London: Longman ..., 1837. 2nd edn. 8vo. xii,482,32 advt pp. Orig cloth gilt, recased, new endpapers.
(Hollett) £35 [≈ $56]
- Journal of a Residence in Norway during the

Years 1834, 1835 and 1836 ... London: Longman ..., 1837. 2nd edn. 8vo. xii,482,advt pp. Mod half calf. *(Piccadilly)* £55 [≈ $88]
- Journal of a Residence in Norway during the Years 1834, 1835 and 1836 ... London: Longman ..., 1837. 2nd edn. 8vo. xii,482,14 advt pp. 1st gathering a little loose. Orig cloth, gilt spine. *(Young's)* £65 [≈ $104]
- Observations on the Social & Political State of Denmark, and the Duchies of Sleswick and Holstein, in 1851. London: Longman, Brown ..., 1852. 8vo. xvi,446 pp. Map. Mod cloth.
(Piccadilly) £35 [≈ $56]

Lally Tollendal, Thomas Arthur, Comte
- Memoirs of Count Lally, from his embarking for the East Indies ... to his being sent Prisoner of War to England ... London: Charles Kiernan, for F. Newbery, 1766. 1st edn. 8vo. Fldg map. Contemp calf, worn.
(Hannas) £150 [≈ $240]

Lamartine, Alphonse de
- De Lamartine's Visit to the Holy Land, or, Recollections of the East ... Translated by T. Phipson. London: [ca 1840]. 2 vols in one. 8vo. vii,470; 297,advt pp. 2 fldg maps, 2 frontis, num other tissued steel engvs, some by Bartlett. Orig cloth, uncut, v sl worn.
(Terramedia) $100 [≈ £62]
- The Life and Times of Christopher Columbus. Edinburgh: Bibliotheca Curiosa, 1887. One of 350. 2 vols. 12mo. 64; 78 pp. Orig ptd wraps, sl chipped.
(Reese) $100 [≈ £62]

Lambert, H.C.M.
- History of Banstead in Surrey. London: 1912-31. 2 vols. 8vo. 380; viii,128 pp. Lge fldg map. 18 ills. Orig cloth, faded.
(Coombes) £45 [≈ $72]

Lambert, John
- Travels through Canada, and the United States ... 1806, 1807, & 1808 ... Third Edition, Corrected and Improved. London: 1816. 2 vols. 8vo. Maps & plates (2 maps & 5 plates cold). Contemp calf, hinges cracked but firm. *(M & S Rare Books)* $725 [≈ £453]

Lamont, James
- Seasons with the Sea-Horses; or, Sporting Adventures in the Northern Seas. London: Hurst & Blackett, 1861. 1st edn. 8vo. Fldg map & 8 plates (inc title). 1 section sprung. Contemp half calf gilt.
(Hannas) £85 [≈ $136]

La Motraye, Aubry de
- Travels through Europe, Asia, and Part of Africa ... London: for the author & E. Symon ..., 1723-32. Only English edn. 3 vols. Folio. Privilege leaf. Subscribers. 57 engvd plates & maps (some by Hogarth). Occas marking. Contemp calf gilt, 2 vols rebacked, 1 rebound.
(Young's) **£825 [≈ $1,320]**

Lamplough, A.O. & Francis, R.
- Cairo and its Environs. London: Sir Joseph Causton, 1909. 1st edn. 8vo. xxi,191 pp. 51 cold plates. Orig cloth, t.e.g., sl rubbed.
(Worldwide Antiqu'n) **$45 [≈ £28]**

Lanciani, Rodolf
- Wanderings through Ancient Roman Churches. Boston & New York: Houghton Mifflin, 1924. 1st edn. Lge 8vo. xvi,325 pp. Num photo plates. Orig red cloth gilt, t.e.g., spine lettering sl dulled.
(Terramedia) **$50 [≈ £31]**

Lander, Richard
- Records of Captain Clapperton's Last Expedition to Africa ... with the Subsequent Adventures of the Author. London: Colburn & Bentley, 1830. 1st edn. 2 vols. 8vo. xxiii, 310, [2 advt]; vi,293,16 advt pp. Port, 6 ills. Orig bds, uncut, rebacked to style.
(Fenning) **£225 [≈ $360]**

Lander, Richard & John
- Journal of an Expedition to Explore the Course and Termination of the Niger ... London: 1832. 1st edn. 3 vols. 16mo. Fldg map, plates, text ills. Dampstain to frontis in vols 2 & 3, vol 1 port loose. Contemp three qtr polished calf gilt, rubbed, edgeworn.
(Reese) **$375 [≈ £234]**

Landon, Percival
- Lhasa: An Account of the Country and People of Central Tibet ... London: Hurst & Blackett, 1905. 2 vols. 8vo. 414; 426 pp. Fldg map, num plates. Orig maroon cloth, spines much sunned & sl soiled.
(Terramedia) **$175 [≈ £109]**
- The Opening of Tibet ... New York: Doubleday, 1905. 1st American edn. 4to. xv, 484 pp. Cold frontis, num plates. Orig green cloth, vg ex-lib.   *(Terramedia)* **$80 [≈ £50]**

Landor, A. Henry Savage
- See Savage-Landor, A. Henry.

Landscape Illustrations ...
- Landscape Illustrations of the Waverley Novels with Descriptions of the Views.

London: Charles Tilt, 1832. Large Paper. 2 vols. Folio. [4],80 ff. 80 steel engvd india proof plates (all clean). Contemp green mor gilt, a.e.g.   *(Karmiole)* **$300 [≈ £187]**

Landt, Jorgen
- A Description of the Faroe Islands ... London: for Longman, Hurst ..., 1810. 1st English edn. 8vo. Fldg map, 2 plates. Contemp calf, sl worn, rebacked.
(Hannas) **£350 [≈ $560]**

Lane, Edward William
- An Account of the Manners and Customs of the Modern Egyptians ... London: Charles Knight, 1837-36. 2 vols. 12mo. xx,418; viii, 429 pp. 107 ills. Orig purple cloth, spines sunned, remnants of lib spine labels.
(Schoyer) **$80 [≈ £50]**

Langdon, William B.
- A Descriptive Catalogue of the Chinese Collection, now exhibiting at St. George's Place, Hyde Park Corner, London ... London: for the proprietor ..., 1842. 1st English edn. 1st iss (?). i-x,11-150 pp. 4 w'engvd plates. Orig cloth.
(Duck) **£55 [≈ $88]**

Lange, Algot
- The Lower Amazon. A Narrative of Explorations in the Little Known Regions of the State of Pare' on the Lower Amazon ... New York & London: Putnams, 1914. 1st edn. Sm 8vo. xxv,468 pp. Frontis, num plates & maps (1 lge fldg). Orig green cloth.
(Terramedia) **$50 [≈ £31]**

Langford, J.A.
- Staffordshire and Warwickshire Past and Present. London: Wm. Mackenzie, n.d. 4 vols. 4to. 23 maps, 28 engvd plates & ports. Orig dec cloth gilt, faded, some wear, jnts cracking.   *(Hollett)* **£85 [≈ $136]**

Lansdell, Henry
- Russian Central Asia. Boston: Houghton, Mifflin, 1885. 1st edn. 2 vols. 8vo. xxix, iii,687; xv,i,732 pp. 2 fldg maps, mtd photo frontis, num plates. Vol 1 frontis loose & brittle at edges. Orig pict grey cloth gilt.
(Terramedia) **$250 [≈ £156]**
- Through Siberia. London: 1882. 1st edn. 2 vols. 8vo. Mtd frontis photo of the author, 2 fldg maps, 22 plates, 21 ills. Orig pict cloth. With addtnl copy of the frontis photo on a ptd mount.   *(Argosy)* **$175 [≈ £109]**
- Through Siberia. London: Sampson Low, 1882. 1st edn. 2 vols. 8vo. xvi,[ii],391; ix, [iii],404 pp. 2 fldg maps, 2 frontis (1 a photo),

21 plates, 21 text ills. Occas foxing. Orig pict cloth in black, silver & gold, sl rubbed, spine ends sl worn. *(Sotheran)* **£250 [≈ $400]**

- Through Siberia. London: Sampson Low, 1882. 1st edn. 2 vols. 8vo. xvi,2,391; ix,2, 404 pp. 2 fldg maps, frontis, num plates. Some sl dampstains in vol 1. Orig pict blue cloth gilt. *(Terramedia)* **$250 [≈ £156]**

Lardner, E.G. Dion
- Soldiering and Sport in Uganda 1909-1910. London: Walter Scott, 1912. 1st edn. 8vo. xxi, 289 pp. Fldg map, frontis, num photo plates. Orig pict blue cloth gilt. *(Terramedia)* **$150 [≈ £93]**

Larpenteur, Charles
- Forty Years a Fur Trader on the Upper Missouri: The Personal Narrative of ... 1833-1872. New York: Francis P. Harper, 1898. 1st edn. One of 950. 2 vols. Contemp three qtr scarlet mor, mrbld bds, t.e.g. Alfred Henry Lewis's b'plate. *(Jenkins)* **$400 [≈ £250]**

Larsen, Helge & Rainey, Froelich
- Ipiutak and the Arctic Whale Hunting Culture. New York: Amer Mus of Nat His Anthropological Papers Vol 42, 1948. 4to. 276 pp. Fldg map, 101 plates, text ills. Orig ptd wraps. *(High Latitude)* **$95 [≈ £59]**

Las Casas, The Count de
- Memorial de Sainte Helene. Journal of the Private Life and Conversations of the Emperor Napoleon at Saint Helena. London: 1823. 1st edn in English. 8 vols in 4. 8vo. Plate, 3 fldg plans & views. Sl marg dampstain vol 3. Orig diced calf, 1 spine relaid, sl rubbed. *(Bickersteth)* **£110 [≈ $176]**

Latham, Robert Gordon
- Norway and the Norwegians. London: Bentley, 1840. 1st edn. 2 vols. 12mo. Sl foxing at ends. Contemp half calf. *(Hannas)* **£75 [≈ $120]**

Latham, Wilfrid
- The States of the River Plate. London: Longmans, Green, 1868. 2nd edn. 8vo. x,381,2 advt pp. Fldg map. New cloth. *(Adelson)* **$275 [≈ £171]**

Latouche, John (i.e. Crawford, O., J. & F.)
- Travels in Portugal. By John Latouche [pseud.]. London: Ward, Lock & Tyler, [1875]. 1st edn. 8vo. viii,354 pp, advt leaf. 5 woodburytype ills. Lib stamp on title. Orig green cloth, a little rubbed. *(Frew Mackenzie)* **£48 [≈ $76]**

- Travels in Portugal. With Illustrations by the Right Hon. T. Sotheron Estcourt. Second Edition. London: Ward, Lock, & Tyler, [ca 1875]. 8vo. xvi,356 pp. 5 mtd photos of Estcourt's paintings. Orig dark green cloth gilt, extremities rubbed & sl frayed. *(Karmiole)* **$40 [≈ £25]**

Latrobe, C.I.
- Journal of a Visit to South Africa in 1815 and 1816 ... London: L.B. Seeley, 1818. 1st edn. 4to. vii,[1],406 pp. Lge fldg map, 4 charts, 12 cold plates. Sm stain on verso of map & verso of sketch plate at p 358. Qtr leather, mrbld bds. *(Parmer)* **$1,600 [≈ £1,000]**
- Journal of a Visit to South Africa in 1815 and 1816 ... New York: James Eastburn, 1818. 1st Amer edn. vii,395 pp. Usual foxing. Three qtr leather & mrbld paper, rubbed, spine label chipped. *(Parmer)* **$125 [≈ £78]**

Latrobe, J.A.
- Scripture Illustrations: being a Series of Engravings on Steel and Wood, illustrative of the Geography and Topography of the Bible. London: for L. & G. Seeley ..., 1838. 4to. v, 256 pp. 84 plates. A few spots. Old half mor gilt, cloth faded, jnts cracked. *(Hollett)* **£120 [≈ $192]**

Laurie, Robert & Whittle, James
- The London Directory, or a New and Improved Plan of London, Westminster & Southwark ... London: 1781. Cold dissected linen-backed map. Stain on 1 section of table. V worn slipcase. Unlisted variant of Howgego 166. *(Coombes)* **£50 [≈ $80]**
- New Travellers Companion. London: 1807. 2nd edn. Roy 8vo. Dble-page engvd title, map of England & Wales, 24 dble-page maps hand cold in outline. Limp mor, rebacked. *(Henly)* **£180 [≈ $288]**

Laurie, Thomas
- Dr. Grant and the Mountain Nestorians. Boston: Gould & Lincoln, 1853. 1st edn. Sm 8vo. xii,418,[6 advt] pp. Fldg map, 7 plates. Some foxing & spotting. Orig cloth, edges rubbed, sl soiled, spine ends frayed. *(Worldwide Antiqu'n)* **$75 [≈ £46]**

Laut, A.C.
- The Story of the Trapper. Toronto: 1902. 8vo. Ills. Orig bndg. *(Grayling)* **£35 [≈ $56]**

Lawrence, A.B.
- A History of Texas; or, the Emigrant's Guide to the New Republic. New York: William W. Allen, 1840. 1st edn, 1st iss. 275 pp. Frontis view of Austin. Some foxing. Orig cloth, sl

reprs to spine.   *(Jenkins)* **$475 [≈£296]**
- History of Texas, or the Emigrant's Guide to
the New Republic, By a Resident Emigrant ...
New York: 1845. [11]-275 pp. Contemp calf,
hinges sl cracking, some scuffing.
(Reese) **$500 [≈£312]**

Lawrence-Archer, J.H. (ed.)
- Monumental Inscriptions of the British West
Indies, from the Earliest Date. London:
Chatto & Windus, 1875. 1st edn. 4to. xii,442
pp. W'engvs throughout. Annotations. Orig
cloth, rebacked.   *(Gough)* **£75 [≈$120]**

The Laws of Jamaica ...
- The Laws of Jamaica, passed by the
Assembly, and confirmed by His Majesty in
Council, April 17, 1684 ... London: 1684. [ii],
xxii, 151, [1] pp. Fldg map (torn at folds).
Contemp calf, hinge cracked but cords sound.
The Phillipps - Lord Macartney copy.
(Reese) **$2,000 [≈£1,250]**

Lay, G. Tradescant
- The Chinese as they are: their Moral, Social,
and Literary Character ... Language ... Arts
and Sciences. London: 1841. 1st edn. 8vo. xii,
342, [2 blank] pp. Frontis, text ills. Lacks
half-title. Crnr of 1 leaf torn affecting a few
letters. Rec bds.   *(Fenning)* **£38.50 [≈$62]**

Lay, William & Hussey, C.M.
- A Narrative of the Mutiny, on Board the Ship
Globe, of Nantucket, in the Pacific Ocean ...
Two Years on the Mulgrave Islands ... New
London: Lay & Hussey, 1828. 1st edn. 168
pp. Sl fraying & foxing, 1 sgntr starting, a few
minor marg tears. Old calf.
(Reese) **$1,500 [≈£937]**

Layard, Sir Austen Henry
- Discoveries in the Ruins of Nineveh and
Babylon; with Travels in Armenia, Kurdistan
and the Desert: being the Result of a Second
Expedition ... London: 1853. xxiii,686 pp.
Fldg frontis, maps, plans, plates. Scattered
foxing. Contemp calf gilt, rebacked.
(Reese) **$250 [≈£156]**
- Discoveries among the Ruins of Nineveh and
Babylon; with Travels in Armenia,
Kurdistan, and the Desert: being the Result
of a Second Expedition ... New York:
Putnam, 1853. 1st US edn. 8vo. xxiv,687 pp.
Num maps & plates, text ills. Orig cloth, sl
worn.   *(Worldwide Antiqu'n)* **$45 [≈£28]**
- Nineveh and Babylon. A Narrative of a
Second Expedition to Assyria during the
years 1849, 1850 & 1851. Abridged by the
Author from his larger Work. London:
Murray, 1867. 12mo. iv,413 pp. Num text

ills. Orig pict cloth gilt, spine top crnr sl
chipped.   *(Terramedia)* **$30 [≈£18]**
- Nineveh and Its Remains: with an Account of
a Visit to the Chaldaean Christians of
Kurdistan ... London: 1849. 2 vols. xxx,[2],
399; xii,495 pp. Maps, plans, plates. Occas sl
foxing. Contemp polished calf gilt, lacks 1
label, some wear to extremities.
(Reese) **$200 [≈£125]**
- Nineveh and Its Remains: with an Account of
a Visit to the Chaldaean Christians of
Kurdistan ... New York: Putnam, 1849. 2
vols in one. viii,326; ii,373 pp. Map, 2
frontis, num plates, num text ills. Orig half
mor, a.e.g., worn, spine cracked & chipped at
hd.   *(Worldwide Antiqu'n)* **$125 [≈£78]**

Leake, William Martin
- Travels in the Morea. London: Murray,
1830. 1st edn. 3 vols. 8vo. 17 maps & plans,
13 plates. Occas foxing. Orig green cloth,
paper labels, spines chipped & laid down.
(Terramedia) **$600 [≈£375]**

Lear, Edward
- Journal of a Landscape Painter in Corsica.
London: 1870. xvi,272 pp. Frontis, plates,
text ills. A few sl traces of foxing. Fine-
grained mor gilt extra, gilt inner dentelles,
a.e.g., spine sunned, some edge wear. Part of
a note sgnd by the author laid in.
(Reese) **$475 [≈£296]**

Leared, Arthur
- Marocco and Moors: Being an Account of
Travels ... Second Edition, revised and edited
by Sir Richard F. Burton. London: Sampson
Low; New York: Scribner & Welford, 1891.
8vo. Orig red cloth, paper spine label
(remainder iss).   *(Book Block)* **$195 [≈£121]**

Leask, Thomas
- The Southern African Diaries of Thomas
Leask, 1865-1878. Edited by J.P.R. Wallis.
London: Chatto & Windus, Oppenheimer
Series, 1954. 1st edn. Tall 4to. lxvi,253 pp.
Fldg map, port frontis. Orig dec pink maroon
cloth gilt.   *(Terramedia)* **$80 [≈£50]**

Leatham, A.E.
- Sport in Five Continents. Edinburgh &
London: Blackwood, 1912. 1st edn. 8vo.
x,333, 50 advt pp. Frontis, num plates. Orig
pict green cloth, t.e.g., spine sl scratched.
(Terramedia) **$100 [≈£62]**
- Sport in Five Continents. Edinburgh: 1912.
10,333 pp. Ills. Orig cloth, sl rubbed.
(Reese) **$65 [≈£40]**

Lechevalier, Jean Baptiste
- Description of the Plain of Troy: with a Map of that Region ... Translated from the Original not yet Published ... Notes ... by Andrew Dalzel. Edinburgh: for T. Cadell, London, 1791. 1st edn. 4to. 4 maps. Contemp half calf gilt, rubbed.
(Ximenes) **$500 [≈ £312]**

Le Comte, Louis Daniel
- Memoirs and Observations ... Made in a late Journey Through the Empire of China. London: Tooke, 1697. 1st English edn. 8vo. Advts at end. Frontis & 3 plates (2 fldg, 1 full-page), half-page plate & chart. Calf, rebacked, jnt reprd, sl loose in bndg. Wing L.831.
(Rostenberg & Stern) **$345 [≈ £215]**

Lee, Charles
- The Centenary of "Bradshaw". London: The Railway Gazette, 1940. 48 pp. Ills. Orig cloth backed ptd bds. *(Duck)* **£25 [≈ $40]**

Lee, Henry
- Memoirs of the War in the Southern Department of the United States. Philadelphia: Bradford & Inskeep ..., 1812. 1st edn. 2 vols. 8vo. 423; 486 pp. Frontis ports (offset). 1 section pulled, portion of 1 page missing. Orig three qtr leather, labels rubbed. *(Schoyer)* **$300 [≈ £187]**

Lee, Mrs John Clarence
- Across Siberia Alone. An American Woman's Adventures. New York, London & Toronto: John Lane, Bell, Cockburn, 1914. 1st edn. 12mo. 220 pp. Frontis, plates. Orig brown cloth, sl worn. *(Terramedia)* **$30 [≈ £18]**

Lee, Laurie & Keene, Ralph
- We Made a Film in Cyprus. London: Longmans Green, 1947. Only edn. Med 8vo. xii,92 pp. Ills, map endpapers. Orig brown cloth. Dws reprd. *(Piccadilly)* **£20 [≈ $32]**

Lee, S.M.
- Glimpses of Mexico and California. Boston: Geo. H. Ellis, 1887. Sm 8vo. 124 pp. Orig cloth, spine extremities sl rubbed.
(Karmiole) **$50 [≈ £31]**

Leeder, S.H.
- Modern Sons of the Pharaohs. A Study of the Manners and Customs of the Copts of Egypt. London: Hodder & Stoughton, [ca 1920]. 8vo. 355 pp. Photo plates. Orig pict grey cloth, front cvr sl warped. *(Terramedia)* **$50 [≈ £31]**

Leeper, David R.
- The Argonauts of 'Forty-Nine. Some Recollections of the Plains and the Diggings. South Bend: 1894. 146,xvi pp. Ills. Cloth gilt.
(Reese) **$150 [≈ £93]**

Lees, J.A. & Clutterbuck, W.J.
- B.C. 1887. A Ramble in British Columbia. London: 1888. 8vo. Fldg map, plates. Half calf. *(Farahar)* **£55 [≈ $88]**

Leet, Ambrose
- A Directory of the Market Towns, Villages, Gentlemen's Seats and other Noted Places in Ireland ... added a General Index of Person's Names ... Dublin: Smith, 1814. 2nd edn. Calf, rebacked. *(Emerald Isle)* **£75 [≈ $120]**

Leffingwell, Ernest de K.
- The Canning River Region Northern Alaska. Washington: GPO, USGS Professional Paper 109, 1919. 4to. 251 pp. Maps (inc 6 fldg in pocket), num photo ills. Sm repr to title. Rec cloth. *(High Latitude)* **$95 [≈ £59]**

Leigh, Charles
- The Natural History of Lancashire, Cheshire and the Peak, in Derbyshire. Oxford: 1700. Folio. Port, cold map, 24 plates. Some signs of use, outer marg of title trimmed. Calf, rebacked. *(Wheldon & Wesley)* **£180 [≈ $288]**

Leigh, Samuel
- Leigh's New Pocket Road-Book of England & Wales ... Third Edition, carefully revised. London: for Samuel Leigh, 1831. 12mo. [2], 486, [2 advt] pp. Engvd table of prices, fldg cold map, engvd title, 55 county maps. Orig green roan gilt. *(Fenning)* **£75 [≈ $120]**

Leighton, John
- Paris under the Commune: or, The Seventy-Three Days of the Second Siege ... London: Bradbury, Evans, 1871. 1st edn. xvi, 396, ctlg pp. Fldg frontis, 4 other fldg plates, fldg plan, 83 other ills. Lacks 1 port plate. Orig pict cloth, faded, rear endpaper torn.
(Box of Delights) **£50 [≈ $80]**

Leith-Adams, A.
- Field and Forest Rambles, with Notes and Observations on the Natural History of Eastern Canada. London: 1871. 8vo. xvi,333 pp. Fldg map, frontis. Orig cloth gilt.
(Henly) **£45 [≈ $72]**

Leland, Charles Godfrey
- The Union Pacific Railway, Eastern Division, or, Three Thousand Miles in a

Railway Car. Philadelphia: 1867. 95 pp. Half mor.   *(Reese)* $175 [≈ £109]

Lempriere, William
- A Tour from Gibraltar to Tangier, Sallee, Mogodore, Santa Cruz, and Tarudant; and thence over Mount Atlas to Morocco ... Philadelphia: 1794. xi,330 pp. Foxed. Sgntr clipped from title marg. Contemp calf, few sm worm holes in spine, lacks front free endsheet.   *(Reese)* $250 [≈ £156]

Leslie, L.A.D.
- Wilderness Trails in Three Continents. London: 1931. 8vo. Ills. Orig bndg.
                          (Grayling) £35 [≈ $56]

Lester, C. Edwards
- The Life and Voyages of Americus Vespucius ... New Haven: 1852. 431 pp. Ills. Occas foxing. Orig cloth, spine gilt extra, some edge wear.   *(Reese)* $85 [≈ £53]

Lester, John E.
- The Atlantic to the Pacific. What to See and How to See It. London: 1873. 293 pp. Frontis, 2 maps, ills. Ink inscrptn. Cloth, a.e.g.   *(Reese)* $100 [≈ £62]

Letter(s) ...
- A Letter to the Reverend Mr. Geo. Lewis ... see Ziegenbalg, Bartholomew & Grundler, Johann Ernest.
- Letters concerning the Present State of the French Nation ... see Young, Arthur.
- Letters from Scandinavia ... see Thomson, William.
- Letters from the Caucasus and Georgia ... see Freygang, Madame de.
- Letters from the North of Italy ... see Rose, William Stewart.
- Letters to a Friend in England, on the Actual State of Ireland. London: James Ridgway, 1828. Tall 8vo. 115 pp. Contemp blue qtr calf, red label.   *(Jarndyce)* £75 [≈ $120]
- Letters to a Nobleman, on the Conduct of the War in the Middle Colonies ... see Galloway, Joseph.

Letts, J.M.
- A Pictorial View of California; Including a Description of the Panama and Nicaragua Routes ... By a Returned Californian. New York: Henry Bill, 1853. 8vo. 224,[1 advt] pp. 48 litho plates. Sl foxing. Orig gilt dec black cloth, extremities rubbed, spine faded.
                          (Heritage) $400 [≈ £250]

Leveson, Henry Astbury, 'The Old Shekarry'
- The Forest and the Field. By "The Old Shekarry". London: Saunders Otley, 1867. 2nd edn. xix,551,xxiv pp. Port frontis, 8 engvs. Orig green cloth gilt.
                 (Bates & Hindmarch) £55 [≈ $88]
- Sport in Many Lands. By H.A.L., 'The Old Shekarry'. London & New York: Warne, 1890. Wide 8vo. xlvi,587,advt pp. Frontis, num plates. Orig green cloth gilt, sl worn.
                     (Terramedia) $75 [≈ £46]
- Sport in Many Lands: Europe, Asia, Africa and America, etc. etc. By H.A.L. 'The Old Shekarry'. London: Warne, 1890. Orig blue pict cloth gilt, spine a little dull, sl shaken.
                    (Waterfield's) £35 [≈ $56]

Lewis, A.G.
- Sport, Travel and Adventure. London: 1915. 8vo. Ills. Sl foxing. Orig bndg, sl rubbed, spine faded.   *(Grayling)* £32 [≈ $51]

Lewis, Harold
- The Church Rambler. A Series of Articles on the Churches in the Neighbourhood of Bath. Bath: 1876-78. 2 vols. 12mo. Num engvd plates. Orig dec cloth gilt, sm nick at hd of 1 spine.   *(Ambra)* £42 [≈ $67]

Lewis, John Delaware
- Across the Atlantic. London: 1851. 1st edn. 8vo. xii,274 pp. Orig cloth, inner jnts weak.
                      (Young's) £35 [≈ $56]

Lewis, John W.
- The Life, Labors, and Travels of Elder Charles Bowles, of the Free Will Baptist Denomination, Together with and Essay on ... the African Race ... Also, An Essay on the Fugitive Law ... Watertown: 1852. 8vo. 286 pp. Orig green cloth.
                    (Karmiole) $250 [≈ £156]

Lewis, M.G.
- Journal of a West India Proprietor, Kept during a Residence in the Island of Jamaica. London: Murray, 1834. 1st edn. Tall 8vo. 408 pp. Advt leaf before half-title. Orig cloth, spine relaid.   *(Schoyer)* $100 [≈ £62]

Lewis, Meriwether & Clark, William
- History of the Expedition ... to the Sources of the Missouri, thence across the Rocky Mountains, and down the River Columbia to the Pacific Ocean ... Philadelphia: 1814. 1st edn. 2 vols. Fldg map, 5 text maps. Orig ptd bds, 1 bd detached, spines worn. Cloth box.
                   (Reese) $20,000 [≈ £12,500]

- History of the Expedition under the Command of Captains Lewis and Clarke [sic] ... New York: 1842. 1st abridged edn, edited by Paul Allen. New York: Harper's, 1842. 2 vols. Fldg map (split on 1 fold). Vol 1 title loose. Orig cloth.   *(Reese)* **$250 [≈£156]**
- Travels in the Interior Parts of America ... Discoveries made in Exploring the Missouri, Red River and Washita ... London: 1807. 1st London edn. 116 pp. Fldg table. Occas sl foxing. Mod cloth & mrbld bds, t.e.g., others untrimmed   *(Reese)* **$500 [≈£312]**

Lewis, Samuel
- A Topographical Dictionary of England ... with Historical and Statistical Descriptions ... Fifth Edition. London: S. Lewis & Co, 1842. 4 vols. 8vo. Orig brown cloth, spines faded & chipped at ends. Lord George Lennox's booklabels.   *(Waterfield's)* **£45 [≈$72]**
- A Topographical Dictionary of Ireland. London: Lewis, 1837. 2 vols. 4to. Fldg linen backed map of Ireland added at end of vol 1. Mod cloth.   *(Emerald Isle)* **£110 [≈$176]**
- A Topographical Dictionary of Ireland. London: Lewis, 1837. 2 vols. 4to. Mod cloth bds.   *(Emerald Isle)* **£85 [≈$136]**

Leys, Norman
- Kenya. London: Hogarth Press, 1925. 2nd edn. 8vo. 409 pp. Ills. Orig pink-brown cloth.   *(Terramedia)* **$50 [≈£31]**

Liberty, Arthur Lasenby
- Spring-Time in the Basque Mountains. London: Grant Richards, 1901. Sm 4to. xx,299 pp. Map. Orig blue cloth, t.e.g. Pres copy.   *(Piccadilly)* **£25 [≈$40]**

Life ...
- The Life and Explorations of David Livingstone ... see Livingstone, David.
- The Life of the late Gen. William Eaton ... see Prentiss, Charles.

Lillingston, Luke
- Reflections on Mr. Burchet's Memoirs. or, Remarks on his Account of Captain Wilmot's Expedition to the West-Indies. London: 1704. 171 pp. Calf, rebacked, some wear to crnrs.   *(Reese)* **$1,250 [≈£781]**

Lindley, Augustus F.
- A Cruise in Chinese Waters, being a Log of "The Fortuna", containing Tales of Adventure in Foreign Climes ... London, Paris & New York: Cassell, [ca 1870]. 4th edn. 8vo. vi, 256 pp. Num ills. Orig cloth, a.e.g., edges sl rubbed, some tears in spine.

     (Worldwide Antiqu'n) **$45 [≈£28]**

Lindsay, Lord
- Letters from Egypt, Edom, and the Holy Land. London: Bell & Daldy, 1866. New edn. Sm 8vo. xi,458 pp. 2 maps (1 fldg), 35 (of 38) plates. Half mor gilt, t.e.g., lib number on spine.   *(Worldwide Antiqu'n)* **$45 [≈£28]**

Lindsay, M.
- Sledge. The British Trans-Greenland Expedition 1934. London: (1935). 1st edn. 8vo. [xii],342 pp. 5 maps (1 cold & fldg), 49 photo plates (inc 2 fldg panoramas), 12 text ills. Orig cloth, dull.   *(Bow Windows)* **£36 [≈$57]**

Lindsay, W.S.
- History of Merchant Shipping and Ancient Commerce. London: Sampson Low, 1874-76. 1st edn. 4 vols. Roy 8vo. 4 frontis, num ills. A few minor tears. Orig cloth, uncut, spines dull & sl worn.   *(Duck)* **£350 [≈$560]**

Lindsey, David Moore
- A Voyage to the Arctic in the Whaler Aurora. Boston: Dana Estes, [1911]. 1st edn.   *(Terramedia)* **$100 [≈£62]**

Linklater, Eric
- The Northern Garrisons. London: HMSO, 1941. 1st edn. Maps. Orig ptd wraps.   *(Hannas)* **£10 [≈$16]**

Linnaeus, Carl
- Lachesis Lapponica, or a Tour in Lapland, now first published from the Original Manuscript Journal ... by J.E. Smith. London: 1811. 2 vols. 8vo. 55 text ills. Contemp calf gilt, reprd.   *(Wheldon & Wesley)* **£350 [≈$560]**

Linton, John
- A Handbook of the Whitehaven and Furness Railway, being a Guide to the Lake District of West Cumberland and Furness. London: & Whitehaven, 1852. 1st edn. Sm 8vo. 134, 18 advt pp. Fldg map, 12 plates. Orig cloth gilt, jnts cracked, spine ends chipped.   *(Hollett)* **£90 [≈$144]**

Lisiansky, Urey
- A Voyage round the World, in the Year 1803, 4, 5, & 6 ... London: 1814. 1st English edn. xxi,388 pp. 8 cold charts (3 fldg), 3 plates. Lacks the 2 aquatint views. Occas traces of sl foxing. Later half calf, partly unopened.   *(Reese)* **$2,500 [≈£1,562]**

Lisser, H.G. de
- Twentieth Century Jamaica. Kingston: 1913. 208,advt pp. Port. Scattered foxing. Orig stiff pict cvrs, spine worn.   *(Reese)* **$60 [≈ £37]**

A Little Tour in Ireland ...
- See Hole, S. Reynolds.

Little, W.J. Knox
- Sketches & Studies in South Africa. London: Isbister, 1899. 1st edn. 8vo. 328 pp. Orig maroon cloth.   *(Terramedia)* **$45 [≈ £28]**

Livingstone, David
- The Last Journals ... London: 1874. 2 vols. 360; 346 pp. Advts at end of both vols. Maps. Orig cloth, sl wear at hd of spines.
    (Trophy Room Books) **$350 [≈ £218]**
- The Last Journals ... London: Murray, 1874. 2 vols. Fldg map (darkened) in pocket, port, maps, ills. Orig purple cloth gilt, shelfwear, spines faded, tear hd of vol 2.
    (Parmer) **$125 [≈ £78]**
- The Last Journals ... Edited by Horace Waller. New York: Harper & Bros, 1875. 1st Amer edn. 8vo. 541,advt pp. Lge fldg map in pocket, frontis, many tissued plates. Orig pict gilt blue cloth, front cvr sl spotted.
    (Terramedia) **$100 [≈ £62]**
- The Life and Explorations of David Livingstone ... London: J.G. Murdoch, [ca 1875]. 1st edn. 4to. viii,632 pp. Addtnl chromolitho title, 20 litho plates ptd in sepia on a ochre ground. Orig pict gilt mor, a.e.g., extremities a little worn.
    (Claude Cox) **£30 [≈ $48]**
- Livingstone's Travels and Researches in South Africa ... From the Personal Narrative of David Livingstone ... Philadelphia: 1858. xiv,9-440 pp. Frontis, title vignette, engvs. Sl foxing, dampmarks. Orig cloth, stamped in blind & gilt, some wear to extremities.
    (Reese) **$100 [≈ £62]**
- Missionary Travels & Researches in South Africa ... London: Murray, 1857. 1st edn, 1st iss. Lge 8vo. ix,687 pp. 47 ills & maps. Panelled mor gilt.   *(Hollett)* **£120 [≈ $192]**
- Missionary Travels & Researches in South Africa ... London: Murray, 1857. 1st edn. 8vo. 687 pp. 2 fldg maps, fldg frontis, num plates. Minor foxing. Orig brown cloth, rear hinge cracked internally.
    (Terramedia) **$300 [≈ £187]**
- Missionary Travels & Researches in South Africa. New York: Harper & Bros, 1858. 1st Amer edn (?). 732,advt pp. Frontis, maps (2 fldg), chart, num ills. Sl foxing. Orig embossed cloth gilt, crnrs rubbed.
    (Parmer) **$90 [≈ £56]**

- A Popular Account of Missionary Travels and Researches in South Africa. London: 1861. 8vo. x,436 pp. Fldg frontis, vignette title, fldg map, 13 plates. Sl spotting. Orig cloth, inner hinges strengthened.
    (Bow Windows) **£35 [≈ $56]**
- Travels and Researches in South Africa ... Philadelphia: J.W. Bradley, 1859. 440 pp. Frontis, ills. Some foxing & staining. Lacks rear endpapers. Orig embossed red cloth, soiled & rubbed.   *(Parmer)* **$45 [≈ £28]**

Livingstone, David & Charles
- Narrative of an Expedition to the Zambesi and its Tributaries ... New York: Harper, 1866. 1st Amer edn. 8vo. xxii, 638, [6 advt] pp. Fldg map (sm marg tear), fldg frontis, plates, text ills. Orig brown cloth gilt, some wear to spine ends.   *(Parmer)* **$125 [≈ £78]**
- Narrative of an Expedition to the Zambezi and its Tributaries. New York: Harper, 1866. 1st Amer edn, in a variant publisher's bndg. 8vo. xxii, 638 pp. Fldg map, dble page frontis, plates & ills. Orig green cloth, spine lettering sl faded. *(Terramedia)* **$100 [≈ £62]**

Lloyd, Albert B.
- Uganda to Khartoum. Life and Adventures on the Upper Nile. London: Fisher Unwin, 1906. 1st edn. 8vo. xii,312 pp. Lge cold fldg map, frontis & 7 other photo plates. Orig pict red cloth gilt.   *(Terramedia)* **$150 [≈ £93]**

Lloyd, L.
- The Field Sports of Northern Europe. A Narrative of Angling, Hunting and Shooting in Sweden and Norway. London: Hamilton, Adams, 1885. Enlgd & rvsd edn. 8vo. 416,advt pp. Orig blue cloth.
    (Terramedia) **$40 [≈ £25]**
- The Field Sports of the North of Europe. Angling, Hunting, Shooting in Sweden and Norway. London: 1885. 8vo. Orig cloth, sl rubbed & marked.   *(Grayling)* **£50 [≈ $80]**
- Scandinavian Adventures. Vol 2 [only]. London: 1854. Roy 8vo. xi,546 pp. 6 tinted plates. 35 text figs. Orig dec cloth, sm tear in 1 jnt.   *(Wheldon & Wesley)* **£35 [≈ $56]**

Locher, A.
- With Star and Crescent. A Full and Authentic Narrative of a Recent Journey with a Caravan from Bombay to Constantinople ... Philadelphia: Aetna Pub Co, 1891. 12mo. 634 pp. 15 plates. Orig pict brown cloth, sl worn.   *(Terramedia)* **$25 [≈ £15]**

Lock, H.O.
- Dorset. Painted by Walter Tyndale and A.

Heaton Cooper. London: A. & C. Black, 1925. 1st edn. 22 cold plates. Inscrptn on f.e.p. Orig cloth.   *(Old Cathay)* £18 [≈ $28]

Lock, William George
- Askja. Iceland's Largest Volcano, with a Description of the Great Lava Desert in the Interior. Charlton, Kent: the author, 1881. 1st edn. 8vo. Lge fldg map. Orig cloth.
(Hannas) £45 [≈ $72]

Lockman, John
- Travels of the Jesuits, into Various Parts of the World: particularly China and the East-Indies ... Spanish Settlements in America. London: T. Piety, 1762. 2nd edn, crrctd. 2 vols. 8vo. 2,vi,xxiv,488; 6,4,507, 24,19 pp. 5 fldg maps, fldg plate. Mod calf.
(Adelson) $650 [≈ £406]

Lockwood, Joseph
- Guide to St. Helena, Descriptive and Historical, with a Visit to Longwood, and Napoleon's Tomb. St. Helena: 1851. [5],106,42 pp. Occas spotting & foxing, pencil notes. Limp cloth, paper label, cloth worn & discold, spine perished but cords sound.
(Reese) $200 [≈ £125]

Loder, Robert
- The History of Framlingham in the County of Suffolk ... Woodbridge: by & for R. Loder, 1798. 1st edn. 4to. xii,453,[1 blank],[2] pp. 10 engvd plates. Early MS notes on title. A few sl marks. Contemp bds, uncut, later cloth spine sl worn at ends.
(Bow Windows) £180 [≈ $288]

Lodge, R.B.
- Bird-Hunting through Wild Europe. London: Robert Culley, (1908). 8vo. 333,[2 advt] pp. 124 photo ills. Orig gilt dec cloth, t.e.g.   *(Blackwell's)* £40 [≈ $64]

Loftie, William John
- Kensington: Picturesque and Historical. London: Leadenhall Press, 1888. Large Paper. List of subscribers. Maps. Over 300 ills, some cold, by William Luker, Jun. Orig buckram, spine sl chafed, cvrs sl marked.
(Coombes) £15 [≈ $24]
- Orient Line Guide. Chapters for Travellers by Sea and by Land Illustrated. The Third Edition, re-written ... London: Sampson Low ..., 1889. 4to. xxxvii,[2],439 pp. Addtnl dec title by Kate Greenaway, 81 views, maps, &c. Orig cloth backed bds gilt, edges sl worn.
(Fenning) £48.50 [≈ $78]

Loggan, David
- Cantabrigia Illustrata. Edited ... by J.W. Clark. Cambridge: Macmillan & Bowes, 1905. Lge folio. [75] ff. Orig cloth & bds, sl soiled, crnrs worn.   *(Schoyer)* $50 [≈ £31]

Loiterings ...
- Loiterings among the Lakes of Cumberland and Westmoreland ... see Mogridge, George.

Lomas, John
- Spain. Illustrated by Edgar T. Wigram and Joseph Haddon. London: A. & C. Black, 1925. 8vo. vii,383 pp. Map, 22 cold plates. Orig blue cloth.   *(Piccadilly)* £16.50 [≈ $27]
- Spain. Painted by Edgar V. Wigram and Joseph Haddon. London: A. & C. Black, 1925. 1st edn thus. Map, 22 cold plates. Orig cloth.   *(Old Cathay)* £19 [≈ $30]

Londonderry, Charles William Stewart, Marquis of
- Recollections of Tour in the North of Europe in 1836-1837. London: Bentley, 1828. 1st edn. 2 vols. 8vo. 2 maps, 5 ports. Orig black cloth, uncut, spines sl worn. *(Hannas)* £65 [≈ $104]

Long, Edward
- The History of Jamaica ... London: T. Lowndes, 1774. 1st edn. 3 vols. Lge 4to. 16 maps & engvs (lacks 1 plate, of Jamaica Environs). Title trimmed. Later cloth, mor labels.   *(Jenkins)* $485 [≈ £303]

Longstaff, G.B.
- Butterfly Hunting in Many Lands. Notes of a Field Naturalist. London: 1912. 8vo. xx,729 pp. 16 plates (7 cold). Sl foxing. Orig cloth, trifle used. *(Wheldon & Wesley)* £50 [≈ $80]

Lord, J.
- Duty, Honor, Empire: The Life and Times of Colonel Richard Meinertzhagen. London: 1971. 412 pp. Ills. Orig bndg. Dw.
(Trophy Room Books) $100 [≈ £62]

Lord, W. & Baines, T.
- Shifts and Expedients of Camp Life. London: 1876. 734 pp. Nearly 400 ills. Marg repr to frontis. Half leather, raised bands.
(Trophy Room Books) $750 [≈ £468]

Lorimer, Norma
- By the Waters of East Africa. British East Africa, Uganda, and the Great Lakes. London: Robert Scott ..., 1917. 8vo. x,342 pp. Fldg map, 73 photo plates. Orig blue cloth stamped in black, sl rubbed.
(Karmiole) $45 [≈ £28]

Loring, W.W.
- A Confederate Soldier in Egypt. New York: Dodd, Mead, [1884]. 1st edn. 8vo. xviii,450 pp. Fldg map, frontis, num plates. Orig pict green cloth gilt.   *(Terramedia)* **$100 [≈£62]**

Loskiel, George Henry
- History of the Mission of the United Brethren among the Indians of North America ... Translated ... by Christian Ignatius La Trobe. London: for the Brethren's Society, 1794. 1st English edn. 2 vols in one. 8vo. xii, 159, 234, 233, [22] pp. Lacks map. Half calf. *(Young's)* **£95 [≈ $152]**

Loti, Pierre
- Morocco. Translated from the French by W.P. Baines. London: Werner Laurie, [ca 1910]. 8vo. vi,335,advt pp. Cold frontis, other photo plates. Orig pict brown cloth. *(Terramedia)* **$25 [≈£15]**

Loughborough, John
- The Pacific Telegraph and Railway, an Examination of all the Projects for the Construction of these Works ... St. Louis: 1849. xx,80 pp. 2 fldg maps (sl splitting at 1 fold). Sm lib mark on title. Later half mor. *(Reese)* **$2,500 [≈£1,562]**

Lovett, Richard
- Irish Pictures. Drawn by Pen and Pencil. London: 1888. 4to. 224 pp. Orig gilt dec cloth, a.e.g. *(Moorhead)* **£15 [≈ $24]**
- London Pictures Drawn with Pen and Pencil. London: RTS, 1890. Lge 8vo. 224 pp. 130 ills. Some foxing. Inscrptn on reverse of frontis. Orig pict cloth, a.e.g., crnr tips rubbed. *(Bow Windows)* **£25 [≈ $40]**

Lovett, Richard (ed.)
- Welsh Pictures drawn with Pen and Pencil. With Seventy-Two Illustrations. London: RTS, [ca 1890]. 1st edn. Sm folio. 192, 8 illust ctlg pp. Ills. Orig pict cloth, sl rubbed & soiled. *(Claude Cox)* **£15 [≈ $24]**

Low, A.P.
- Cruise of the Neptune: Report on the Dominion Government Expedition to Hudson Bay and Arctic Islands ... 1903-1904. Ottawa: GPO, 1906. 1st edn. 8vo. xvii,355 pp. Fldg map in pocket, frontis, photo plates, ills. Orig brown cloth, front hinge cracked. *(Parmer)* **$95 [≈£59]**

Low, Sidney
- Egypt in Transition. With an Introduction by the Earl of Cromer. New York: Macmillan,

1914. 1st Amer edn. 8vo. xxiv,316,advt pp. Ports. Orig green cloth gilt. *(Terramedia)* **$40 [≈£25]**

Lowry, Walker
- Tumult at Dusk, being an Account of Ecuador, its Indians, its Conquerors, its Colonists ... San Francisco: Grabhorn Press, 1963. One of 100. Folio. 160 pp. Fldg map. Parchment, gilt device, spine v sl soiled. Plastic slipcase. *(Reese)* **$350 [≈£218]**

Lowth, Alys
- Doreen Coasting, With Some Account of the Places She Saw and the People She Encountered [Red Sea to Kenya, Zanzibar & Zimbabwe]. London: 1912. 8vo. 294 pp. Frontis, num photo plates. Orig pict blue cloth gilt, sl worn. *(Terramedia)* **$30 [≈£18]**

Lowther, H.
- From Pillar to Post. London: 1912. 3rd edn. 304 pp. Ills. Orig bndg. *(Trophy Room Books)* **$100 [≈£62]**

Lozano, Pedro
- A True and Particular Relation of the Dreadful Earthquake which happened at Lima ... Description ... of ... Peru ... London: Osborne, 1748. 1st English edn. xxiii,341,3 advt pp. 9 fldg maps & plates. Occas browning & perf lib marks. 19th c half mor, rehinged. *(Young's)* **£190 [≈ $304]**

Lubbock, Basil
- The China Clippers. Second Edition. Glasgow: 1914. 8vo. xvi, 387, xxxiii, [iii blank] pp. 10 plans (sev fldg), 18 plates, chart, Sail plan. Tiny marg tear & crease in 1 leaf. Orig cloth, illust upper cvr. *(Bow Windows)* **£25 [≈ $40]**

Lubbock, Sir John, Baron Avebury
- Pre-historic Times, as illustrated by Ancient Remains, and the Manners and Customs of Modern Savages. Fourth Edition. London: Norgate, 1878. 8vo. xxx,655 pp. 4 litho plates (2 cold), 228 text ills. Orig cloth, sides unevenly faded. *(Claude Cox)* **£25 [≈ $40]**

Lumholtz, Carl
- Among Cannibals ... Four Year's Travels in Australia ... Camp Life with the Aborigines of Queensland. New York: Scribner's, 1889. 1st edn in English. 8vo. xx,395 pp. 2 fldg maps, frontis, num plates (3 cold). 1 leaf loose. Orig pict grey cloth, sl rubbed & shaken. *(Terramedia)* **$150 [≈£93]**
- Among Cannibals ... Four Year's Travels in Australia ... Aborigines of Queensland. New

York: Scribner's, 1902. 8vo. xx,395 pp. Port, maps, 4 chromolithos, w'cuts. Orig green cloth, sl soiled. Author's pres inscrptn.
(Parmer) **$90 [≈ £56]**

Lunn, Sir Arnold H.M.
- A Century of Mountaineering, 1857-1957. London: 1957. 1st edn. Roy 8vo. 263 pp. Cold & other plates. Orig cloth gilt.
(Fenning) **£24.50 [≈ $40]**

Lyall, Robert
- Travels in Russia, the Krimea, the Caucasus, and Georgia. London: for T. Cadell; & W. Blackwood, 1825. 1st edn. 2 vols. 8vo. Half-titles. W'cut vignettes in text. Contemp calf, spines worn, Signet Library arms on cvrs.
(Hannas) **£120 [≈ $192]**

Lyell, D.
- The Hunting and Spoor of Central African Game. London: 1929. 334 pp. Ills. Orig bndg. *(Trophy Room Books)* **$325 [≈ £203]**
- Memories of an African Hunter. MA: [ca 1933]. 267 pp. Ills. Orig bndg. Dw.
(Trophy Room Books) **$400 [≈ £250]**

Lyman, George D.
- John Marsh, Pioneer. The Life Story of a Trail-Blazer on Six Frontiers. New York: 1930. One of 150, signed. 394 pp. Cloth. Slipcase. *(Reese)* **$125 [≈ £78]**

Lynch, Jeremiah
- Egyptian Sketches. London: 1890. 8vo. 250 pp. Frontis, other full-page plates. Orig pict light blue cloth gilt, hinges sl shaken.
(Terramedia) **$75 [≈ £46]**
- Three Years in the Klondike. London: Edward Arnold, 1904. 8vo. [8],280 pp. Fldg map, 24 photo plates. Orig cloth, uncut.
(High Latitude) **$85 [≈ £53]**
- Three Years in the Klondike. London: Edward Arnold, 1904. 1st edn. 280 pp. Fldg map, 24 plates inc frontis. Orig bndg, crnrs sl worn. *(Parmer)* **$125 [≈ £78]**

Lynch, Thomas Kerr
- A Visit to the Suez Canal. London: Day & Son, 1866. 1st edn. Slim roy 8vo. 72 pp. Errata slip. Fldg map, 10 tinted litho plates (inc vignette title), 2 w'cuts. Sl foxing on some plates. Orig dec cloth, loose (due to gutta-percha bndg). Cloth case.
(Schoyer) **$175 [≈ £109]**

Lynch, W.F.
- Narrative of the U.S. Expedition to the River Jordan. Philadelphia: 1849. 8vo. 508, advt

pp. Frontis, num plates & text ills. Scattered foxing. Contemp qtr mor, front cvr detached, rear hinge tender. *(Terramedia)* **$50 [≈ £31]**
- Narrative of the United States' Expedition to the River Jordan and the Dead Sea. Philadelphia: Lea & Blanchard, 1850. 7th edn, rvsd. 8vo. 509,52 advt pp. 2 fldg maps (1 reprd), 28 plates. Sl foxing. Orig cloth, edges v rubbed, spine ends chipped.
(Worldwide Antiqu'n) **$65 [≈ £40]**

Lyon, George Francis
- A Brief Narrative of an Unsuccessful Attempt to reach Repulse Bay, through Sir Thomas Rowe's "Welcome", in H.M.S. Griper in the Year 1824. London: Murray, 1825. 1st edn. 8vo. Fldg map, 7 litho plates. List of plates. Contemp half calf gilt. Ilchester b'plate.
(Hannas) **£190 [≈ $304]**
- A Brief Narrative of an Unsuccessful Attempt to reach Repulse Bay through Sir Thomas Rowe's "Welcome", in H.M.S. "Griper" in the Year 1824. London: Murray, 1825. 1st edn. xvi,198 pp. Fldg map, 7 plates. Sl foxed. Leather, sl worn. *(Parmer)* **$295 [≈ £184]**
- A Brief Narrative of an Unsuccessful Attempt to reach Repulse Bay, through Sir Thomas Rowe's "Welcome", in H.M.S. Griper in the Year 1824. London: Murray, 1825. 1st edn. 8vo. xvi,198 pp. Fldg map, 7 plates. Stain on top edge of 1/2 the pp. Rec cloth.
(Schoyer) **$150 [≈ £93]**
- A Narrative of Travels in Northern Africa in the Years 1818, 19 and 20 ... London: Murray, 1821. 4to. xii,383 pp. Fldg map, frontis, 16 hand cold litho plates. Mod calf backed bds. *(Sotheran)* **£750 [≈ $1,200]**
- A Narrative of Travels in Northern Africa in the Years 1818, 19 and 20 ... London: Murray, 1821. 1st edn. 4to. xii,383 pp. Fldg map, 17 hand cold plates. Half calf gilt, bds faded. *(Hollett)* **£550 [≈ $880]**
- The Private Journal ... during the Recent Voyage of Discovery under Captain Parry. London: Murray, 1824. 1st edn. 8vo. xiv,468 pp. Lge fldg map, 7 plates. 2 ff (pp 103-6) lacking & supplied in facs. Contemp half calf, sometime rebacked.
(Claude Cox) **£60 [≈ $96]**
- The Private Journal ... during the Recent Voyage of Discovery under Captain Parry. London: Murray, 1825. New edn. xi,468 pp. Fldg map, 7 plates. Old red mor, a.e.g., sl rubbed. *(High Latitude)* **$200 [≈ £125]**

Lyon, John
- The History of the Town and Port of Dover, and of Dover Castle; with a Short Account of the Cinque Ports. Dover: for the author ...,

1813-14. 1st edn. 2 vols. 4to. 18 plates (some fldg). Some spotting & offsetting. Contemp tree calf, rebacked. *(Young's)* £110 [≈ $176]

Lysachy, A.M.
- Joseph Banks in Newfoundland and Labrador, 1766. His Diary, Manuscripts and Collections. London: Faber, 1971. 1st edn. 4to. 512 pp. 12 cold plates, 9 facs, 105 monochrome ills & maps, 6 text figs. Orig cloth gilt. Dw.   *(Hollett)* £60 [≈ $96]

Lysons, Daniel & Samuel
- Magna Britannia ... Volume the Sixth, containing Devonshire. London: for Thomas Cadell, 1822. 2 vols. 4to. 34 plates. Contemp half calf, rather rubbed, rebacked.
(Waterfield's) £150 [≈ $240]

Macalister, R.A.S.
- A Century of Excavation in Palestine. London: RTS, [1926]. 8vo. 335 pp. Frontis map, plates. Orig blue cloth.
(Terramedia) $50 [≈ £31]

Macarius
- The Travels of Macarius, Patriarch of Antioch. Written by his attendant Archdeacon, Paul of Aleppo ... Part the First ... Translated by F.C. Balfour. London: Murray, 1829. Folio. 114 pp. Addtnl engvd half-title for the Earl of Mount-Norris. Qtr mor, rubbed.   *(Terramedia)* $150 [≈ £93]

MacBride, Mackenzie
- Wild Lakeland. Painted by A. Heaton Cooper. London: A. & C. Black, 1928. 2nd edn. Map, 32 cold plates. Orig cloth. Dw chipped, price-clipped, top of spine missing.
(Old Cathay) £17 [≈ $27]

McCagg, Ezra Butler
- Six Weeks of Vacation in 1883. Chicago: McDonnell, 1884. 1st edn. 12mo. 152 pp. Sl offsetting. Ex-lib. Orig limp vellum, sl rubbed.   *(Worldwide Antiqu'n)* $65 [≈ £40]

MacCann, William
- Two Thousand Miles' Ride through the Argentine Provinces ... London: Smith, Elder, 1853. 2 vols. 8vo. xiv,295,12 advt; x,324 pp. Fldg map, 6 plates. Orig green pict cloth, rebacked in mor.
(Adelson) $475 [≈ £296]

McClintock, Walter
- The Old North Trail or Life, Legends and Religion of the Blackfeet Indians. London: Macmillan, 1910. 8vo. xxvi,539 pp. Fldg map, cold frontis, 7 cold ills, num photo ills.

Rec blue half leather, ex-lib.
(Bates & Hindmarch) £60 [≈ $96]
- The Old North Trail. Or Life, Legends & Religion of the Blackfeet Indians. London: Macmillan, 1910. 1st edn. 8vo. xxvi,539 pp. Fldg map, cold frontis, 7 cold & num other plates, ills. Orig pict gilt blue cloth, ex-lib, bookplate.   *(Terramedia)* $80 [≈ £50]

M'Clung, John
- Sketches of Western Adventure ... Maysville, Ky.: L. Collins, 1832. 1st edn. 12mo. [3]-360 pp. Lacks half-title (as usual). A few minor reprs. Unfoxed. Contemp sheep, rubbed, recased.
(M & S Rare Books) $1,150 [≈ £718]

M'Clure, Robert
- The Discovery of the North-West Passage by H.M.S. Investigator ... Edited by Commander Sherard Osborn ... London: 1856. 1st edn. xiv, 405 pp. Fldg map, 4 tinted litho plates. Orig cloth, spine relaid, orig endpapers.   *(High Latitude)* $395 [≈ £246]

M'Clymont, J.A.
- Greece. London: Black, 1906. 1st edn. 8vo. xii,235,4 advt pp. Fldg map, 75 cold plates. Orig cloth, t.e.g., sl rubbed.
(Worldwide Antiqu'n) $65 [≈ £40]

McCormick, A.B.
- The Alps. Painted by Martin Conway. London: A. & C. Black Colour Book, (1904). One of 300, sgnd by the publishers. 70 cold plates. Orig cloth, t.e.g., endpapers sl foxed, fine.   *(Old Cathay)* £275 [≈ $440]

McCormick, William Thomas
- A Ride Across Iceland in the Summer of 1891. London: Digby, Long, 1892. 1st edn. 8vo. Port. Orig dec cloth.
(Hannas) £65 [≈ $104]

McCracken, H.
- Alaska Bear Trails. New York: 1931. 1st edn. 260 pp. Ills. Orig bndg. Dw.
(Trophy Room Books) $125 [≈ £78]

McCulloch, John Ramsay
- A Dictionary, Practical, Theoretical, and Historical, of Commerce and Commercial Navigation ... Edited by Henry Vethake. Philadelphia: 1840. 2 vols. xi,[1],767; 803 pp. Foxed, 2 sgntrs starting. Orig cloth, edgeworn.   *(Reese)* $200 [≈ £125]

McCutcheon, J.
- In Africa: Adventures in Big Game Hunting

Country. IN: 1910. One of 250 deluxe, sgnd. 402 pp. Num ills. Orig bndg, slipcase.
(Trophy Room Books) **$500 [≈ £312]**

McCutcheon, John T.
- In Africa. Hunting Adventures in the Big Game Country. Indianopolis: [1910]. 4to. 420 pp. Frontis, num photo plates, cartoon ills. Orig pict olive green cloth gilt, new endpapers.   *(Terramedia)* **$150 [≈ £93]**

McDanield, H.F. & Taylor, N.A.
- The Coming Empire; or, Two Thousand Miles in Texas on Horseback. New York: 1877. 389 pp. Sm lib stamp on title. Cloth, hd of spine sl nicked, lib mark on spine.
(Reese) **$175 [≈ £109]**

Macdonald, George
- The Gold Coast, Past and Present: A Short Description of the Country & Its People. London: Longmans, 1898. 1st edn. Sm 8vo. ix, 352 pp. Frontis & num plates, inc map. Orig maroon cloth gilt, sl rubbed.
(Terramedia) **$140 [≈ £87]**

Macdonald, James
- Travels through Denmark and Part of Sweden ... London: for Richard Philips, 1809. 1st edn. 2 vols. Sm 8vo. Fldg map, lge fldg table. Contemp half calf, lacks a label.
(Hannas) **£75 [≈ $120]**
- Travels through Denmark and Part of Sweden ... London: for Richard Philips, 1809. 2 vols. Sm 8vo. Fldg map, lge fldg table. Contemp half calf, rebacked.
(Sanders) **£45 [≈ $72]**

MacDonald, William
- The Conquest of the Desert. London: Werner Laurie, [ca 1913]. 197 pp. Map, num plates. Orig green cloth, pict onlay. Dw frayed.
(Parmer) **$75 [≈ £46]**

McElwaine, Eugene
- The Truth about Alaska the Golden Land of the Midnight Sun. N.p.: the author, 1901. 8vo. xxi,23-445 pp. 2 maps, photo ills. Orig dec cloth, 2 sm stains on back cvr.
(High Latitude) **$95 [≈ £59]**

McFall, Crawford
- With the Zhob Field Force, 1890. New York: Macmillan, 1895. 8vo. 232 pp. Tinted frontis & half-title, num plates & ills. Orig green cloth, sl rubbed. *(Terramedia)* **$200 [≈ £125]**
- With the Zhob Field Force. London: 1895. 232 pp. Ills. Orig bndg.
(Trophy Room Books) **$250 [≈ £156]**

MacFarlane, Charles
- Constantinople in 1828. A Residence of Sixteen Months in the Turkish Capital and Provinces etc. Second Edition. London: Saunders & Otley, 1829. 2 vols. 8vo. [i], xxviii,517; [ii],viii,491 pp. 2 cold & 2 fldg plates. Sl foxing. Mod bds, untrimmed.
(Piccadilly) **£225 [≈ $360]**

MacGahan, J.A.
- Under the Northern Lights. London: Sampson Low ..., 1876. viii,339 pp. Fldg map, 8 plates, text ills. 2 ff of prelims carelessly opened. Orig dec cloth, minor edge wear.   *(High Latitude)* **$225 [≈ £140]**

McGarvey, J.W.
- Lands of the Bible. A Geographical and Topographical Description of Palestine, with Letters of Travel in Egypt, Syria, Asia Minor, and Greece. Philadelphia & London: Lippincott, 1881. 8vo. Frontis, 3 maps & plans, 34 plates, text ills. Contemp half mor sl rubbed.   *(Sanders)* **£35 [≈ $56]**

MacGovern, William Montgomery
- To Lhasa in Disguise. A Secret Expedition through Mysterious Tibet. New York & London: Century, 1924. 1st edn. 8vo. xii,462 pp. 37 plates. Orig cloth.
(Worldwide Antiqu'n) **$40 [≈ £25]**

MacGowan, J.
- Pictures of Southern China. London: RTS, 1897. 320 pp.. Frontis, num ills. Sl shaken. Orig gilt illust cloth.   *(Lyon)* **£45 [≈ $72]**
- Side-Lights on Chinese Life. Illustrated by Montague Smyth. London: Kegan Paul, 1907. 1st edn. 12 cold plates, 34 other ills. Orig gilt dec bndg, spine sl sunned.
(Old Cathay) **£33 [≈ $52]**

MacGregor, Charles Metcalfe
- Wanderings in Balochistan. London: 1882. 1st edn. 315 pp. Port, plates, fldg map in pocket. 315 pp. Fldg map in pocket (few reprs to verso), plates. Contemp three qtr calf, mrbld bds, calf worn, spine chipped, reprs to jnts, rear bd gnawed at ft.
(Reese) **$200 [≈ £125]**

MacGregor, James
- The Rob Roy on the Jordan, Nile, Red Sea & Gennesareth, etc. A Canoe Cruise in Palestine and Egypt and the Waters of Damascus. Fourth Edition. London: Murray, 1874. 8vo. Frontis & 3 other chromolitho plates, 8 maps, text ills. Orig red cloth gilt, sl worn.   *(Sanders)* **£25 [≈ $40]**

Macintyre, D.
- Hindu-Koh. Wanderings and Wild Sport on and beyond the Himalayas. London: Blackwood, 1891. New edn. 8vo. xviii,362 pp. Frontis, 31 ills. Orig pict cloth gilt.
(Bates & Hindmarch) £80 [≈ $128]

Mackaness, George
- The Life of Vice-Admiral Bligh, R.N., F.R.S. New York & Toronto: Farrar & Rinehart, [ca 1931]. 2 vols in one. 369; 348 pp. Fldg map, ills. A few marg ink notes. Dw worn.
(Parmer) $65 [≈ £40]

Mackay, A.M.
- A.M. Mackay, Pioneer Missionary of the Church Missionary Society in Uganda. By his Sister. New York: Armstrong & Son, 1890. Author's Edition. 12mo. 480 pp. Frontis, cold fldg map. Orig green cloth gilt.
(Terramedia) $50 [≈ £31]

McKee, Lanier
- The Land of Nome. A Narrative Sketch of the Rush to Our Bering Sea Goldfields. The Country, its Mines and People, and the History of a Great Conspiracy 1900-1901. New York: Grafton Press, [ca 1902]. 12mo. ix,[3], 260 pp. Orig cloth.
(High Latitude) $75 [≈ £46]

McKenney, Thomas L.
- Sketches of a Tour to the Lakes, of the Character and Customs of the Chippeway Indians ... Baltimore: 1827. 494 pp. 29 plates. V foxed. Orig cloth, leather label, worn, bit gnawed at spine ends, some insect damage to jnts. Slipcase.
(Reese) $375 [≈ £234]

Mackenzie, Alexander
- Voyages from Montreal ... in the Years 1789 and 1793 ... Account of the Fur Trade ... London: Cadell ..., 1801. 1st edn. 4to. 412 pp. Frontis port, 3 fldg maps. Some offsetting to title & 1 map. Contemp calf, rebacked, mor label. *(W. Thomas Taylor)* $2,000 [≈ £1,250]
- Voyages from Montreal ... London: 1801. 1st edn. 412,2 errata pp. Frontis port, 3 fldg maps. Contemp elab gilt three qtr calf, some repr.
(Jenkins) $1,750 [≈ £1,093]

Mackenzie, Compton
- Greek Memories. London: Cassell, 1932. 1st (suppressed) edn. 8vo. x,588 pp. Frontis. Orig black cloth, top edge v sl spotted. Dw.
(Piccadilly) £160 [≈ $256]
- Greek Memories. London: Chatto & Windus, 1939. 8vo. xxiv,455 pp. 8 ills. Orig red cloth.
(Piccadilly) £12.50 [≈ $20]

Mackenzie, D.R.
- The Spirit-Ridden Konde. A Record of the Interesting but Steadily Vanishing Customs & Ideas Gathered during Twenty-Four Years' Residence Amongst the Shy Inhabitants of the Lake Nyasa Region. Philadelphia: 1925. 1st edn. 8vo. Map, plates. Orig blue cloth gilt.
(Terramedia) $125 [≈ £78]

Mackenzie, E.
- An Historical, Topographical and Descriptive View of the County of Northumberland ... Newcastle: 1825. 2nd edn, enlgd. 2 vols. 4to. iv,499; x,515 pp. Fldg map, 15 plates. Sl browning, few dampstains. Old half calf gilt, rubbed & scraped, 1 bd cracked.
(Hollett) £85 [≈ $136]
- An Historical, Topographical, and Descriptive View of the United States of America, and of Upper and Lower Canada, with an Appendix ... Newcastle upon Tyne: [1819]. xv, [9]-712 pp. Fldg map (1 tear), fldg plan, plates. Later three qtr cloth, paper label.
(Reese) $600 [≈ £375]

McKenzie, Frederick A.
- From Tokyo to Tiflis: Uncensored Letters from the [Russo-Japanese] War. London: 1905. 8vo. 340 pp. Lge fldg map, frontis, photo plates. Orig pict cloth gilt.
(Terramedia) $100 [≈ £62]

Mackenzie, Sir George Steuart
- Travels in the Island of Iceland during the Summer of the Year 1810. Edinburgh: Constable ..., 1811. 1st edn. 4to. xx,483 pp. Lge fldg map, 1 other map, 15 plates (inc 8 mtd hand cold aquatints), 15 text vignettes. Lacks the 4 tables. Mod half mor, uncut.
(Claude Cox) £300 [≈ $480]

Mackenzie, Georgianna Muir & Irby, Adelina Paulina
- Travels in the Slavonic Provinces of Turkey-in-Europe. London & New York: Strahan, 1866. 1st edn. 8vo. Fldg cold map (mtd), 3 other fldg maps, 19 plates. Some soiling of text. Orig cloth, gilt spine, worn, spine recased.
(Trebizond) $275 [≈ £171]

Macky, John
- A Journey through Scotland ... Being the Third Volume, which compleats Great Britain. By the Author of the Journey thro' England. London: for J. Pemberton ..., 1723. 8vo. Contemp calf.
(Falkner) £30 [≈ $48]

M'Leod, John
- Voyage of His Majesty's Ship Alceste ... London: 1818. 2nd edn. 8vo. 323 pp. 5

aquatint plates. Mod cloth.
(Argosy) **$200 [≈ £125]**
- Voyage of His Majesty's Ship Alceste ...
London: Murray, 1818. 2nd edn. 8vo. vi,323
pp. 6 plates (5 hand cold). "Original cloth",
edges rubbed, slight tears in spine, externally
unmarked ex-lib.
(Worldwide Antiqu'n) **$180 [≈ £112]**
- Voyage of His Majesty's Ship Alceste ...
London: 1819. 3rd edn. vi,339 pp. Fldg map,
port, 4 aquatint plates. Occas traces of foxing
or soiling, offsetting from map. Mod cloth,
leather label.
(Reese) **$175 [≈ £109]**

McLeod, Lyons
- Travels in Eastern Africa; with the Narrative
of a Residence in Mozambique. London:
Hurst & Blackett, 1860. 1st edn. 2 vols. 8vo.
viii,341,[ii]; vi,347,[i],[8 advt] pp. Fldg map,
2 frontis (1 cold). Mod qtr mor.
(Sotheran) **£650 [≈ $1,040]**

MacMichael, William
- Journey from Moscow to Constantinople, in
the Years 1817, 1818. London: Murray,
1819. 1st edn. 4to. vi,[ii],272 pp. 6 aquatint
plates. Sm loss to engvd surface of frontis.
Contemp gilt dec half calf, a few scrapes to
bds. Littlecote b'plate.
(Sotheran) **£500 [≈ $800]**

Macmillan, Alexander (ed.)
- Seaports of the Far East. Historical and
Descriptive. Commercial and Industrial
Facts, Figures and Resources. London:
Collingridge, 1925. 2nd edn, enlgd. 529 pp.
Cold map, num ills. Orig dec green cloth gilt.
(Lyon) **£125 [≈ $200]**

McNamara, John J.
- In Perils of Mine Own Countrymen. Three
Years on the Kansas Border. By A
Clergyman. New York & Auburn: 1856. 240
pp. Sl stain to text, foxing. Ptd wraps bound
into cloth. *(Reese)* **$125 [≈ £78]**

McQuade, James
- The Cruise of the Montauk, to Bermuda, the
West Indies and Florida. New York: Thomas
R. Knox, 1885. 8vo. xvi,442 pp. Frontis,
num ills. Orig dark green dec cloth.
(Karmiole) **$65 [≈ £40]**

McSkimin, Samuel
- The History and Antiquities of the County of
the Town of Carrickfergus, from Earliest
Records to 1839, also a Statistical Survey of
said County. Belfast: Cleeland, 1909. New
edn. 537 pp. Orig bndg.
(Emerald Isle) **£85 [≈ $136]**

Madagascar: Its Mission and Its Martyrs ...
- See Prout, Ebenezer.

Magoun, F.A.
- The Frigate "Constitution" and other
Historic Ships. Salem, MA: Marine Research
Society, 1928. 1st trade edn. Folio. 157 pp. 16
plans, 30 plates, num text ills. Orig cloth.
Dw. *(Schoyer)* **$200 [≈ £125]**

Mahaffy, J.P.
- Rambles and Studies in Greece. Philadelphia:
Coates, 1900. Ills. Orig pict red cloth gilt.
(Terramedia) **$50 [≈ £31]**

Mahony, James
- The Book of the Baltic ... London: Effingham
Wilson ..., 1857. 8vo. [xxii advt], 160 pp.
Advts to pastedowns & endpapers. W'engvs
throughout. V occas spotting or thumbing.
Orig gilt dec green cloth, back cvr sl cockled.
(de Beaumont) **£78 [≈ $124]**

Maillart, Ella K.
- Forbidden Journey, from Peking to Kashmir.
London: 1937. 8vo. Fldg map, plates. Orig
cloth. *(Farahar)* **£25 [≈ $40]**

Maistre De La Tour, --.
- The History of Ayder Ali Khan, Nabob -
Bahader: or, New Memoirs concerning the
East Indies. Dublin: William Porter, '1774'
[=1784]. 2 vols in one, continuously
paginated. Contemp calf, brown label.
(Jarndyce) **£90 [≈ $144]**

Maitland, William
- The History of Edinburgh, from its
Foundation to the Present Time ...
Edinburgh: Hamilton, Balfour & Neill, 1753.
Folio. viii, 518 pp. Fldg city plan, 19 engvd
plates (1 fldg). Occas spotting & browning.
Contemp calf, rebacked, crnrs reprd.
(Frew Mackenzie) **£350 [≈ $560]**

Malcolm, Alexander
- Letters of an Invalid from Italy, Malta, and
South of France [1826-1828]. London:
William Clowes & Son, 1897. 1st edn. One of
50. 8vo. Port. Contemp half calf, t.e.g., by
Morrell, jnts cracked. *(Hannas)* **£45 [≈ $72]**

Malcolm, Sir John
- A Memoir of Central India, including Malwa,
and Adjoining Provinces ... London: 1824.
2nd edn, crrctd. 2 vols. 8vo. 2 fldg maps (1
cold). Contemp calf gilt, upper jnt reprd.
(Farahar) **£150 [≈ $240]**
- A Memoir of Central India, including Malwa,

and Adjoining Provinces. Third Edition. London: 1832. 2 vols. 8vo. 2 fldg maps (1 cold). Contemp half calf.
(Argosy) **$150 [≃ £93]**
- The Political History of India, from 1784 to 1823. London: 1826. 2 vols. 8vo. Calf, rebacked.   *(Farahar)* **£140 [≃ $224]**

Manat, J. Irving
- Aegean Days. London: Murray, 1913. 8vo. xii,405 pp. Num plates. Sl foxing. Orig gilt dec red cloth.   *(Terramedia)* **$40 [≃ £25]**

Mangourit, M.O.B.
- Travels in Hanover, during the Years 1803 and 1804 ... London: Richard Phillips, 1806. 88,index pp. Mod half cloth.
(Reese) **$100 [≃ £62]**

Maning, Frederick Edward
- Old New Zealand; a Tale of the Good Old Times. By "A Pakeha Maori". Auckland: Robert J. Creighton & Alfred Scales, 1863. 2nd edn. 8vo. Cloth backed bds, new calf spine.   *(Stewart)* **£95 [≃ $152]**

Manning, Samuel & Green, S.C.
- English Pictures Drawn with Pen and Pencil. New Edition, revised. London: RTS, [1889]. Imperial 8vo. viii,216,8 advt pp. Chromolitho frontis, num w'engvd ills. Orig pict gilt & dec silk finish turquoise cloth, a.e.g.
(Claude Cox) **£20 [≃ $32]**

Mansfield, Charlotte
- Via Rhodesia. A Journey through Southern Africa. London: Stanley Paul, (1911). 1st edn. Lge 8vo. xiii,430 pp. 2 cold maps (1 fldg, with sm tear), 144 ills. Orig bndg with pict onlay.
(Schoyer) **$60 [≃ £37]**

Manstein, Baron de
- Memoirs of Russia. From the Year 1727 to the Year 1744. Translated from the Original Manuscript ... Second Edition, carefully Corrected ... London: 1773. Sm 4to. xxvi,416, index pp. 10 maps (9 fldg), frontis. Rec qtr mor.   *(Terramedia)* **$450 [≃ £281]**

Mantell, Gideon Algernon
- Geological Excursions round the Isle of Wight and along the adjacent Coast of Dorsetshire. London: 1854. 3rd edn. Cr 8vo. xxii,356,2,32 advt pp. Fldg cold map, 19 plates, text figs. Orig cloth.
(Henly) **£45 [≃ $72]**

Maraini, Fosco
- Secret Tibet. London: Hutchinson, 1952.

8vo. 251 pp. Photo frontis, 60 photo ills. Orig bndg. Dw. *(Bates & Hindmarch)* **£25 [≃ $40]**

Marcoy, Paul
- A Journey Across South America from the Pacific Ocean to the Atlantic Ocean. London: Blackie & Son, 1871-73. 1st edn in English. 2 vols. Folio. 11 maps, 600 w'engvs. Contemp three qtr dark green mor, a.e.g., vol 1 rebacked.   *(Jenkins)* **$450 [≃ £281]**
- Travels in South America ... see also Saint-Cricq, Laurent de.

Marcy, Randolph B.
- Explorations of the Red River of Louisiana, in the Year 1852 ... With Reports on the Natural History of the Country. Washington: Tucker, 1853. 1st edn. 310 pp. 2 lge fldg maps in sep cloth folder. 65 plates. Orig cloth.
(Jenkins) **$525 [≃ £328]**

Margoliouth, D.S.
- Cairo, Jerusalem & Damascus. Three Chief Cities of the Egyptian Sultans. London: Chatto & Windus, 1907. 8vo. xvi,301 pp. Num cold plates, line drawings. Unopened, spine sl discold.   *(Parmer)* **$75 [≃ £46]**
- Cairo, Jerusalem and Damascus. Three Chief Cities of the Egyptian Sultans. With Illustrations in Color by W. Tyrwhitt. New York: Dodd, Mead, 1907. 8vo. xiii,473 pp. Num cold plates. Orig light brown cloth.
(Terramedia) **$50 [≃ £31]**

Mariana, Juan de
- The general history of Spain ... Translated from the Spanish by Capt. John Stevens. London: for R. Sare ..., 1699. 1st edn in English. Folio. [9 ff, with c1 bound after a2], "563" [≃ 564],'95 [≃ 91] pp, 6 ff. Some foxing. 2 tears (no loss). Old half calf. Wing M.599.   *(Ramer)* **$650 [≃ £406]**

Mariette-Bey, Auguste
- The Monuments of Upper Egypt. A Translation of the 'Itineraire de la Haute Egypte' ... Revised with Notes and Additions by Lysander Dickerman. Boston: Mansfield & Dearborn, 1890. 12mo. 335 pp. Frontis map, num plates. Orig pict gilt maroon cloth.
(Terramedia) **$50 [≃ £31]**

Mariner, William
- An Account of the Natives of the Tonga Islands ... see Martin, John.

Marjoribanks, Alexander
- Travels in New Zealand. London: Smith, Elder, 1846. 12mo. viii,9-174,4 pp. Fldg map

cold in outline. Half calf.
(Adelson) **$285 [≈ £178]**

Markham, Clements R.
- A History of the Abyssinian Expedition. With a Chapter Containing an Account of the Mission & Captivity of Mr. Rassam & his Companions ... London: Macmillan, 1869. 1st edn. 8vo. xii,484 pp. 5 maps (4 fldg). Contemp half mor, sl rubbed.
(Terramedia) **$500 [≈ £312]**
- Peruvian Bark. A Popular Account of the Introduction of Cinchona Cultivation into British India, 1860-1880. London: 1880. Cr 8vo. xxiii,550 pp. 3 maps, 3 ills. Sm blind stamp on title. Orig cloth, trifle used.
(Wheldon & Wesley) **£40 [≈ $64]**
- Travels in Peru and India. London: 1862. 8vo. xviii,572 pp. 2 fldg maps, 15 plates. Half mor. *(Wheldon & Wesley)* **£120 [≈ $192]**

Markham, Clements R. (ed.)
- Narratives of the Mission of George Bogle to Tibet and of the Journey of Thomas Manning to Lhasa. Edited with Notes and Introduction and the Lives ... London: 1879. 2nd edn. 362 pp. Fldg maps, ills. Sm perf stamp on title & verso of a few plates. Half leather.
(Trophy Room Books) **$1,750 [≈ £1,093]**

Marmontel, Jean Francois
- The Incas: or, the Destruction of the Empire of Peru. London: for J. Nourse ..., 1777. 1st English edn. 2 vols. 12mo. Half-titles. Contemp calf, worn, rebacked. Bibliotheca Lindesiana b'plate. *(Hannas)* **£320 [≈ $512]**

Marsh, John & Waite, H. Stirling
- The Story of Commander Allen Gardiner, R.N., with Sketches of Missionary Work in South America. London: James Nisbet, 1867. 1st edn. 176 pp. Frontis, 3 cold maps, 1 cold fldg map facing title. Polished prize calf gilt.
(Jenkins) **$200 [≈ £125]**

Marshall, John
- A History of the Colonies planted by the English on the Continent of North America ... Philadelphia: Abraham Small, 1824. 1st edn thus. 8vo. 486 pp. Leather, backstrip cracked, lacks label. *(Schoyer)* **$65 [≈ £40]**
- The Life of George Washington. Philadelphia: C.P. Wayne, 1804-07. 1st 5 vols. 8vo. Port frontis in vol 1 (some offsetting onto title). Orig tree calf, later reback, some light wear on crnrs. Harmar Denny's sgntr on titles.
(Schoyer) **$200 [≈ £125]**

Marshall, Robert
- Arctic Wilderness. Edited, with an Introduction, by George Marshall. Berkeley: Univ of Calif Press, 1956. 1st edn. xxvi,171 pp. Fldg map, photo ills. Orig cloth. Dw.
(High Latitude) **$25 [≈ £15]**
- North Doonerak, Amawk and Apoon. Another Letter to Friends about Arctic Exploration between June 23 and July 16, 1939. N.p.: privately ptd, [1939]. [iv],31,[3] pp. Dble-page map. Orig stiff ptd wraps.
(High Latitude) **$50 [≈ £31]**

Marshall, William
- The Rural Economy of Norfolk ... London: Cadell, 1787. 1st edn. 2 vols. 8vo. xix,400; [xvi],392,[4] pp. Fldg map. Sl worm in vol 1 gutters & some margs of vol 2. Section Cc vol 2 misfolded. Orig bds, untrimmed.
(Blackwell's) **£140 [≈ $224]**
- The Rural Economy of the West of England. London: for G. Nicol ..., 1796. 1st edn. 2 vols. 8vo. 2 advt ff in vol 2. Fldg map. Sl spotting of vol 1 title. Mod mottled calf, uncut. *(Claude Cox)* **£140 [≈ $224]**

Martin, Annie
- Home Life on an Ostrich Farm. London: George Philip & Son, 1890. 1st edn. 288 pp. 10 ills. Orig dec cloth gilt.
(Hollett) **£45 [≈ $72]**

Martin, John
- An Account of the Natives of the Tonga Islands in the South Pacific Ocean. Compiled and arranged from the extensive communications of Mr. William Mariner ... Boston: Ewer, 1820. 1st US edn. 8vo. 461 pp. Fldg map (2 sm tears), frontis. Contemp mor, sl worn *(Worldwide Antiqu'n)* **$125 [≈ £78]**

Martin, Percy Falcke
- Egypt, Old and New. A Popular Account of the Land of the Pharoahs ... New York: Doran, 1923. Sq 8vo. 224 pp. Fldg map, 45 mtd cold plates, 72 other ills. Orig bndg, pict onlay, spine sl rubbed. *(Schoyer)* **$45 [≈ £28]**
- Mexico's Treasure House (Guanajuato). New York: The Cheltenham Press, 1906. Roy 8vo. 259,ix pp. 49 plates. Orig cloth, sl warped.
(Gemmary) **$100 [≈ £62]**

Martin, Robert Montgomery
- History of Nova Scotia, Cape Breton, the Sable Islands, New Brunswick ... London: Whittaker, British Colonial Library Series Vol 6, 1837. 1st edn. Sm 8vo. viii, 364, [24 advt] pp. 2 fldg cold maps, engvd frontis. Sm stamp on series title. Rec paper bds.

(Fenning) **£75 [≈ $120]**
- The Hudson's Bay Territories and Vancouver's Island ... Policy of the Hon'ble Hudson's Bay Corporation. London: Boone, 1849. viii,175 pp. Fldg map frontis. Orig cloth, spine faded.
(High Latitude) **$210 [≈ £131]**
- Statistics of the Colonies of the British Empire in the West Indies, South America, North America, Asia, Austral-Asia, Africa ... London: 1839. Lge thick 8vo. 602,304 pp. Fldg map, fldg table, plates. Some offsetting from plates, sl foxed. Three qtr calf.
(Reese) **$450 [≈ £281]**

Martine, George, 1635-1712
- Reliquae Divi Andreae, or the State of the Venerable and Primital See of St Andrews ... With some Historical Memoirs ... Primates thereof ... St. Andrews: James Morison, 1797. 1st edn. 4to. viii,[2],256 pp. 3 plates (browned). Old qtr calf, rebacked.
(Young's) **£100 [≈ $160]**

Martineau, Harriet
- A Complete Guide to the English Lakes ... Windermere: John Garnett ..., [1855]. 1st edn. 8vo. [iv],iii,[i], ii,iv,[ii], 233,xviii pp. Half-title. 16 plates of views, 6 outline plates (2 fldg). Orig pale olive cloth, gilt spine, sl faded & marked. *(Burmester)* **£100 [≈ $160]**

Martyn, Benjamin
- Reasons for Establishing the Colony of Georgia ... With Some Account of the Country ... London: for W. Meadows, 1733. 2nd edn. Sm folio. 48 pp. Map. Lacks frontis. Crimson mor gilt, gilt inner dentelles.
(Reese) **$2,000 [≈ £1,250]**

Martyn, Thomas
- A Tour through Italy ... London: 1791. xxxix, 480, index pp. Fldg hand cold map. Occas sl foxing. Contemp calf, rebacked.
(Reese) **$200 [≈ £125]**

Marvin, Charles
- Reconnoitring Central Asia. Pioneering Adventures in the Region lying between Russia and India. London: Swan Sonnenschein, 1886. 3rd edn. 421 pp. Ills. Orig pict green cloth gilt.
(Terramedia) **$150 [≈ £93]**
- Reconnoitring Central Asia. Pioneering Adventures in the Region lying between Russia and India. London: Swan Sonnenschein, 1885. 8vo. xix,421,2 advt pp. Fldg map, frontis, 7 ills. Ex-lib. Rec red half leather. *(Bates & Hindmarch)* **£40 [≈ $64]**

Mason, Michael Henry
- Where the River Runs Dry. London: Hodder & Stoughton, (1934). Tall 8vo. xv,220 pp. Map, 18 photos, 31 sketches. Orig pict cloth.
(Schoyer) **$40 [≈ £25]**

Mason, Winfield Scott
- The Frozen Northland. Life with the Eskimo in his Own Country. Cincinnati: [ca 1910]. 12mo. 160 pp. 2 maps, 8 photo plates. Orig gilt titled blue cloth, pict onlay.
(Parmer) **$175 [≈ £109]**

Maspero, G.
- Life in Ancient Egypt and Assyria. Translated from the French. New York: Appleton, 1895. Sm 8vo. cv,376,advt pp. Num ills. Orig cloth, sl worn.
(Terramedia) **$35 [≈ £21]**

Maspero, G., et al.
- History of Egypt, Chaldea, Syria, Babylonia and Assyria. Edited by A.H. Sayce. Translated by M.L. McClure. London: Grolier Society, [1903]. 13 vols. 8vo. Over 1000 plates & ills. Contemp half mor, gilt dec spines, sl rubbed.
(Terramedia) **$600 [≈ £375]**

Masson, Rosaline
- Edinburgh. Painted by John Fulleylove. London: A. & C. Black Colour Book, 1904. 1st edn. 21 cold plates. Extensive foxing. Orig dec cloth. *(Old Cathay)* **£15 [≈ $24]**

Mather, Cotton
- Magnalia Christi Americana: Or, the Ecclesiastical History of New-England ... London: 1702. 1st edn. Folio. Fldg map (reprd). Lacks the blank after Book VI & the 2 errata ff found in a few copies. Sl soiling. 19th c mor gilt, a.e.g., by de Coverly, sl rubbed.
(M & S Rare Books) **$2,500 [≈ £1,562]**

Mather, Samuel
- An Attempt to Shew, that America must be known to the Ancients ... added an Appendix, concerning the American Colonies ... By an American Englishman. Boston: J. Kneeland, 1773. [5],6-35 pp. Neat lib marks. Three qtr mor. *(Reese)* **$400 [≈ £250]**

Mathew, Frank
- Ireland. Painted by Francis S. Walker. London: A. & C. Black Colour Books, Twenty Shilling Series, 1912. 1st reprint. 79 cold plates. Orig dec cloth, t.e.g., fine.
(Old Cathay) **£60 [≈ $96]**

Mathews, G.B.

- A Narrative of the Proceedings of His Majesty's Fleet in the Mediterranean ... Including an accurate Account of the late Fight near Toulon ... By a Sea-Officer. London: for J. Millan, 1744. 1st edn. 8vo. viii,112,[viii] pp. 4 fldg maps, engvd table. Orig cloth, sl worn.   *(Bickersteth)* £148 [≈ $236]

Matthews, Henry

- The Diary of an Invalid being the Journal of a Tour in Pursuit of Health in Portugal, Italy, Switzerland and France in the Years 1817, 1818 and 1819 ... Second Edition. London: Murray, 1820. 8vo. Some spotting. Contemp half calf, spine relaid.
(Waterfield's) £65 [≈ $104]

Matthews, Herbert

- Eyewitness in Abyssinia, with Marshal Badoglio's Forces to Addis Ababa. London: 1937. 8vo. Map, plates. Orig cloth.
(Farahar) £35 [≈ $56]

Maturin, Mrs Fred (Edith)

- Petticoat Pilgrims on the Trek. London: Eveleigh Nash, 1909. 8vo. 335 pp. Port. Orig pict cloth, spine darkened.
(Schoyer) $40 [≈ £25]

Maugham, R.

- Portuguese East Africa. London: 1906. 340 pp. Ills. Orig bndg.
(Trophy Room Books) $150 [≈ £93]

Maugham, Reginald Charles F.

- The Republic of Liberia ... London: (1920). 8vo. 299 pp. Fldg map, 37 ills. Orig dec cloth. Dw.   *(Schoyer)* $35 [≈ £21]

Maughan, William Charles

- The Alps of Arabia. Travels in Egypt, Sinai, Arabia and the Holy Land. London: Henry King, 1875. New edn. 8vo. xvi,374,32 advt pp. Frontis map. Marg dampstain. Orig pict gilt cloth, edges of cvrs touched by dampstain, front hinge cracked.
(Terramedia) $50 [≈ £31]

Maundrell, Henry

- A Journey from Aleppo to Jerusalem. New Haven: 1814. 16mo. Text darkened, some foxing. Orig mrbld bds, rebacked in paper, bds worn, lacks front free endpaper.
(Reese) $100 [≈ £62]
- A Journey from Aleppo to Jerusalem ... Boston: Simpkins, 1836. 12mo. xvi,271 pp. Frontis. Sl foxing. Orig cloth, edges a little rubbed.   *(Worldwide Antiqu'n)* $65 [≈ £40]

Mawe, John

- Travels in the Interior of Brazil ... London: Longman ..., 1812. 1st edn. 4to. vi, 366,[21] pp. Map, plates (1 cold). Leather, mod spine, mrbld endpapers.
(Parmer) $1,750 [≈ £1,093]
- The Voyager's Companion, or Shell Collector's Pilot ... London: the author ..., 1825. 4th edn. Sm 8vo. viii,75,[i advt] pp. 2 hand cold plates. Frontis offset. Drab mor grain paper (?) bds, title label to front cvr, later cloth spine. *(de Beaumont)* £78 [≈ $124]

Mawson, Sir Douglas

- Australasian Antarctic Expedition 1911-1914: Geographical Narrative and Cartography. Sydney: 1942. 4to. 366 pp. 2 fldg maps in pocket, 7 map plates, 124 plates, 30 text figs. Orig wraps, sl rubbed & faded.
(Parmer) $250 [≈ £156]
- The Home of the Blizzard ... London: Heinemann, 1915. 1st edn. 2 vols. Lge 8vo. xxx,349; xiii,338 pp. 3 fldg maps in pocket, maps, plates. Orig silver & gilt cloth, minor mark across vol 2 front cvr.
(High Latitude) $295 [≈ £184]
- Home of the Blizzard. Philadelphia: Lippincott, 1915. 2 vols. 349; 338 pp. 3 fldg maps, num cold & b/w plates. Orig blue cloth, somewhat worn, silver titles sl faded.
(Parmer) $375 [≈ £234]
- Macquarie Island - Its Geography and Geology. Sydney: 1943. 4to. 194 pp. Fldg map, 3 fldg plates in pocket, 37 photo plates. Some creasing, minor dampstain. Orig wraps, new paper spine. *(Parmer)* $125 [≈ £78]

Maxwell, Donald

- A Dweller in Mesopotamia. Being the Adventure of an official Artist in the Garden of Eden. London: John Lane, 1921. 4to. xii, 124 pp. 16 cold & 12 b/w plates, 34 ills. Orig cloth & bds, partly unopened, some edges worn.   *(Schoyer)* $40 [≈ £25]

Maxwell, Marius

- Stalking Big Game with a Camera. With a Monograph on the African Elephant ... London: Heinemann, 1925. 1st trade edn. Folio. xxiv, 206 pp. Lge fldg frontis, num plates, some fldg. Orig blue cloth, sl worn.
(Terramedia) $100 [≈ £62]
- Stalking Big Game with a Camera in Equatorial Africa. With a Monograph on the African Elephant. London: 1925. Reprint of the imperial 4to ltd edn of 1924. Roy 4to. xxiv,206 pp. 113 photo plates. Orig cloth.
(Wheldon & Wesley) £45 [≈ $72]
- Stalking Big Game with a Camera. With a

Monograph on the African Elephant. New
York: 1926. 331 pp. Ills. Orig bndg.
      (Trophy Room Books) **$50 [≈ £31]**
- Stalking Big Game with a Camera in
Equatorial Africa with a Monograph on the
African Elephant. London: 1925. Lge 4to
edn. Num ills. Orig bndg. Dw.
      (Trophy Room Books) **$250 [≈ £156]**

May, George
- A Descriptive History of the Town of
Evesham ... Evesham & London: 1845. 8vo.
Frontis, 5 plates, 1 plan, num text engvs.
Final leaf of subscribers (torn without loss).
Orig cloth, sl worn. *(Sanders)* **£125 [≈ $200]**

Maydon, H.C.
- Big Game of India. London: 1937. 253 pp.
Ills. Orig bndg.
      (Trophy Room Books) **$125 [≈ £78]**

Maydon, H.C. (ed.)
- Big Game Shooting in Africa. London: Seeley
Service, Lonsdale Library, 1932. 8vo. 445 pp.
Frontis, 140 ills, map on front endpapers. Sl
foxing to 1st & last few pp. Orig bndg. Dw.
      (Bates & Hindmarch) **£60 [≈ $96]**
- Big Game Shooting in Africa. London: 1951.
8vo. Ills. Endpapers & foredges foxed. Orig
bndg. Dw.   *(Grayling)* **£40 [≈ $64]**

Mayer, A.M.
- Sport with Gun and Rod in American Woods
and Waters. London: 1883. 2 vols. Sm folio.
Num engvd plates, text ills. Orig cloth, some
rubbing.   *(Grayling)* **£90 [≈ $144]**

Meade, Herbert
- A Ride through the Disturbed Districts of
New Zealand; together with some Account of
the South Sea Islands. London: Murray,
1871. 2nd edn. 8vo. xi,375 pp. Frontis, 2 fldg
maps, text engvs. Mod cloth.
      (Adelson) **$325 [≈ £203]**

Means, Philip Ainsworth
- Ancient Civilizations of the Andes. New York
& London: Scribner's, 1931. 1st edn. Lge
8vo. xviii,586 pp. Map, cold frontis, photo
plates. Orig blue cloth, pict gilt spine.
      (Terramedia) **$75 [≈ £46]**

Meares, John
- Voyages made in the Years 1788 and 1789,
from China to the Northwest Coast of
America. London: Logographic Press, 1791.
2 vols. Plates & maps. Lacks the 2 fldg maps.
Orig calf, moderate wear.
      (Jenkins) **$385 [≈ £240]**

Measom, George
- The Official Illustrated Guide to the North-
Western Railway ... London: W.H. Smith &
Son ..., [preface dated June 1859]. Post 8vo.
[vi],574,[2],[184,8 advt] pp. Frontis, 360 ills,
fldg advt plate. Occas sl marking. Contemp
half calf, gilt spine, sl worn.
      (Duck) **£75 [≈ $120]**

Medford, Macall
- Oil without Vinegar, and Dignity without
Pride: or, British, American, and West-India
Interests Considered ... Second Edition ...
London: 1807. xv,110,[7] pp. Fldg chart. Lib
stamps. Disbound.   *(Reese)* **$100 [≈ £62]**

Meek, A.S.
- A Naturalist in Cannibal Land [New Guinea].
London: 1913. 8vo. xviii,238 pp. 36 ills. Orig
cloth, trifle used.
      (Wheldon & Wesley) **£35 [≈ $56]**

Meikle, R.
- After Big Game. London: 1915. 327 pp. Fldg
map, ills. Orig bndg.
      (Trophy Room Books) **$125 [≈ £78]**

Meinertzhagen, R.
- Army Diary 1899-1926. London: 1960. 301
pp. Ills. Orig bndg. Dw.
      (Trophy Room Books) **$250 [≈ £156]**

Melek-Hanum
- Thirty Years in the Harem: or, the
Autobiography of Melek-Hanum Wife of
H.H. Kibrizli-Mehemet-Pasha. London:
1876. 8vo. Faint stamp on title. Orig cloth,
worn, shaken.   *(Farahar)* **£35 [≈ $56]**

**Melland, Frank Hume & Cholmeley,
Edward H.**
- Through the Heart of Africa, being an
Account of a Journey on Bicycles and on Foot
from Northern Rhodesia past the Great
Lakes, to Egypt ... Boston: 1912. 8vo.
xvii,305 pp. Fldg map, 80 ills. Orig cloth,
t.e.g., nick on spine.   *(Schoyer)* **$50 [≈ £31]**

Mellon, James
- African Hunter. London: 1975. 1st edn.
Folio. Num ills. Orig bndg.
      (Grayling) **£120 [≈ $192]**
- African Hunter. New York: 1975. 1st edn.
Num ills. Orig bndg, mint.
      (Trophy Room Books) **$200 [≈ £125]**

Melville, George
- In the Lena Delta. A Narrative of the Search
for Lieut-Commander DeLong and his

Companions ... Boston: Houghton Mifflin, 1885. 1st edn. xiii,[3],497 pp. Maps, plates. Orig dec cloth. *(High Latitude)* **$85 [≈ £53]**

Melville, Lewis
- The Thackeray Country. London: Adam & Charles Black, 1905. 1st edn. 8vo. Fldg map, 50 plates. Orig green cloth gilt.
(Clark) **£15 [≈ $24]**

Memoirs ...
- Memoirs Relative to Egypt, Written in that Country during the Campaigns of General Bonaparte, in the Years 1798 and 1799, by the Learned and Scientific Men who accompanied the French Expedition. London: R. Phillips, 1800. 8vo. 459,5 advt pp. 2 plates. Contemp half calf.
(Moon) **£250 [≈ $400]**

Memorandums ...
- Memorandums of a Residence in France in the Winter of 1815-16, including Remarks on French Manners and Society etc. London: Longman ..., 1816. 8vo. x,404 pp. Old half calf, mrbld sides, new label, trifle rubbed.
(Piccadilly) **£42 [≈ $67]**

Men and Manners in America ...
- See Hamilton, Thomas.

Menefee, C.A.
- Historical and Descriptive Sketch Book of Napa, Sonoma, Lake and Mendocino ... Napa City: 1873. 356 pp. Port, ills. Cloth, scuffed, edgeworn. Author's pres inscrptn.
(Reese) **$275 [≈ £171]**

Mennie, Donald
- The Pageant of Peking. Comprising 66 Vandyck Photogravures ... from Photographs ... Shanghai: A.S. Watson, 1922. 3rd edn. Folio. viii,40 pp. 66 mtd gravure plates. Orig silk over bds, gilt spine stripped, cvrs worn.
(Charles B. Wood) **$150 [≈ £93]**
- The Pageant of Peking. Comprising 66 Vandyck Photogravures ... from Photographs. Shanghai: A.S. Watson, 1922. 3rd edn. Folio. 40 pp. 66 mtd plates. Orig purple silk gilt, spine faded. *(Lyon)* **£165 [≈ $264]**

Menocal, A.G.
- Report of the U.S. Nicaragua Surveying Party, 1885. Washington: GPO, Senate Document 99, 1886. 4to. 54 pp. 11 fldg plates, 56 full page views. Contemp qtr mor, spine v rubbed & cracked at some edges.
(Terramedia) **$80 [≈ £50]**

Menpes, Dorothy
- Britanny. Painted by Mortimer Menpes. London: A. & C. Black Colour Books, Twenty Shilling Series, 1905. 1st edn. 75 cold plates. Orig dec cloth, t.e.g., fine.
(Old Cathay) **£55 [≈ $88]**
- Britanny. Painted by Mortimer Menpes. London: A. & C. Black Colour Book, 1905. One of 350, sgnd by Mortimer Menpes. 75 cold plates. Orig cloth, t.e.g., spine v sl darkened. *(Old Cathay)* **£135 [≈ $216]**
- Britanny. Painted by Mortimer Menpes. London: A. & C. Black Colour Books, 1912. Reprint. 75 cold plates. Orig dec cloth, spine v sl faded. *(Old Cathay)* **£45 [≈ $72]**
- Japan. Painted by Mortimer Menpes. London: A. & C. Black Colour Books, Twenty Shilling Series, 1901. 100 cold plates. Orig dec dark blue cloth, t.e.g., hd of spine chipped. *(Old Cathay)* **£20 [≈ $32]**
- Japan - A Record In Colour. London: A. & C. Black Colour Books, 1901. One of 600, sgnd by Menpes. 100 cold plates. Orig cloth, t.e.g., minor stains & marks to bds, spine sl darkened. *(Old Cathay)* **£125 [≈ $200]**
- Japan. Painted by Mortimer Menpes. London: A. & C. Black Colour Books, Twenty Shilling Series, 1902. Reprint. 100 cold plates. Orig dec dark blue cloth, t.e.g., top bd bubbled, crnrs bumped.
(Old Cathay) **£30 [≈ $48]**
- Japan. Painted by Mortimer Menpes. London: A. & C. Black Colour Books, Twenty Shilling Series, 1904. Cold plates. Orig dec cloth, top spine split, superfluous colour pictures pasted to f.e.p.
(Old Cathay) **£13 [≈ $20]**
- Japan. Painted by Mortimer Menpes. London: A. & C. Black Colour Books, Twenty Shilling Series, 1905. Reprint. 75 cold plates. Orig dec blue grey cloth, faded & sl stained here & there.
(Old Cathay) **£20 [≈ $32]**
- Paris. Painted by Mortimer Menpes. London: A. & C. Black Colour Books, 1910. One of 500, unsgnd. 76 cold plates, num text ills. Orig cloth, foxing to endpapers, fine. Dw, chipped & torn.
(Old Cathay) **£195 [≈ $312]**
- Paris. Painted by Mortimer Menpes. London: A. & C. Black Colour Books, 1910. One of 500, unsgnd. 76 cold plates, num text ills. Orig cloth, spotting to endpapers, spine v sl faded. *(Old Cathay)* **£175 [≈ $280]**
- Venice. Painted by Mortimer Menpes. London: A. & C. Black Colour Books, 1904. One of 500, sgnd by Mortimer Menpes. 100 cold plates. Orig dec cloth, t.e.g., spine sl darkened. *(Old Cathay)* **£145 [≈ $232]**

- World Pictures. Painted by Mortimer
Menpes. London: A. & C. Black Colour
Books, Twenty Shilling Series, 1902. 1st edn.
100 cold plates. Orig cloth, t.e.g., crease on
front bd.   *(Old Cathay)* **£35 [≈$56]**
- World Pictures. Painted by Mortimer
Menpes. London: A. & C. Black Colour
Books, Twenty Shilling Series, 1902. 1st edn.
100 cold plates. Orig dec cloth, t.e.g., rubbed.
Sgnd by M. Menpes.
                                (Old Cathay) **£30 [≈$48]**

Menpes, Mortimer, et al.
- France. Painted by Gordon Home. London:
A. & C. Black Colour Books, Twenty Shilling
Series, 1918. 2nd edn. Map, 64 cold plates.
Orig dec cloth.   *(Old Cathay)* **£55 [≈$88]**
- France. Painted by Gordon Home. London:
A. & C. Black Colour Books, Twenty Shilling
Series, 1918. 2nd edn. Map, 64 cold plates.
Pencilled marginalia. Orig dec cloth, some
grubbiness to spine & rear bd, rear jnt
splitting.   *(Old Cathay)* **£23 [≈$36]**

Meredith, Louisa Anne, nee Twamley
- Notes and Sketches of New South Wales,
during a residence in that Colony from 1839
to 1844. London: Murray, 1844. 1st edn. 8vo.
Half-title. Lacks advts at end. Contemp half
mor, gilt spine, sl worn. Bound with John H.
Drummond Hay's Western Barbary, 1844.
                                (Sanders) **£40 [≈$64]**
- Some of My Bush Friends in Tasmania,
Native Flowers, Berries and Insects drawn
from Life. London: 1860. Imperial 4to. Cold
title & 14 cold plates inc 2 page-borders.
Occas sl foxing & soiling. Orig cloth gilt,
a.e.g., rebacked.
                    (Wheldon & Wesley) **£280 [≈$448]**

Merrill, Selah
- Ancient Jerusalem. New York: Fleming H.
Revell, [1908]. 1st edn. 4to. 419 pp. Frontis,
num plates, 58 typographic maps & charts.
Orig gilt dec maroon cloth.
                                (Terramedia) **$150 [≈£93]**
- East of the Jordan. A Record of Travel and
Observation in the Countries of Moab Gilead
and Bashan ... New York: Scribner, 1883.
8vo. xvi,550,6 advt pp. Fldg plate, 70 ills.
Foredge marg affected by damp. Orig cloth,
edges rubbed, sl soiled.
                        (Worldwide Antiqu'n) **$50 [≈£31]**

Messiter, C.A.
- Sport and Adventures among the North
American Indians. London: 1890. 8vo. ills.
Orig cloth, sl rubbed.
                                (Grayling) **£80 [≈$128]**

Metcalfe, C.J.
- The Channel Islands: Historical and
Legendary Sketches. London: Simpkin,
Marshall, 1852. 8vo. 6 plates. Green morocco
grain cloth, some sl wear to spine ends, sl
scuffing.   *(Waterfield's)* **£40 [≈$64]**

Metropolitan Improvements ...
- See Shepherd, Thomas H.

Meyers, William H.
- Sketches of California and Hawaii by William
H. Meyers Gunner, U.S.N. aboard the
United States Sloop-of-War 1842 - 1843. [San
Francisco]: 1970. One of 450. Folio. Port,
cold plates. Orig cloth over bds, paper spine
label.   *(Reese)* **$225 [≈£140]**

Michaux, F. Andrew
- Travels to the West of the Alleghany
Mountains in the States of Ohio, Kentucky
and Tennessee. London: 1805. 2nd edn. 8vo.
xii, 294 pp. Orig bds, uncut, jnts weak. The
Phillips copy inscrbd HMC with press mark.
                                (Henly) **£350 [≈$560]**

Michler, Nathaniel
- Routes from the Western Boundary of
Arkansas to Santa Fe and the Valley of the Rio
Grande. [Washington]: 31st Cong., 1st Sess.,
1850. 12 pp. The map mentioned in the text
was not issued with report. Later wraps.
                                (Reese) **$100 [≈£62]**

Middiman, Samuel
- Select Views in Great Britain, Engraved from
Pictures and Drawings by the most Eminent
Artists, with Descriptions. London: Boydell,
[1813]. 1st coll edn. 4to. 52 plates (8 v foxed,
others v minor marg foxing). Elab embossed
black leather.   *(Hartfield)* **$395 [≈£246]**
- Select Views of Great Britain engraved by S.
Middiman from Pictures and Drawings by
the most Eminent Artists with Descriptions.
London: Boydell, 1812. Oblong 4to. 63 plates
(dated 1784-1792), with tissue guards.
Contemp roan, a.e.g., rather rubbed.
                            (Waterfield's) **£265 [≈$424]**

Midgley, Samuel
- Hallifax, and its Gibbet-Law Placed in a True
Light. Together with a Description of the
Town ... London: J. How, for William
Bently, at Hallifax, 1708. 1st edn. 12mo.
Frontis (shaved at foredge). Contemp black
mor gilt, spine relaid, gilt & gauffered edges.
                                (Hannas) **£140 [≈$224]**
- See also Bentley, John.

Miege, Guy
- The New State of England Under Their Majesties K. William and Q. Mary. In Three Parts ... London: 1693. 2nd edn. 12mo. [xxxiv], 280,468 pp. Outer edge cropped with some loss to side-notes. Engvd title cropped. Old sheep, worn. Wing M.2020.
(Young's) **£40 [≈ $64]**
- A Relation of Three Embassies from His Sacred Majestie Charles II to the Great Duke of Moscovie, the King of Sweden, and King of Denmark ... London: for John Starkey, 1669. 1st edn. 8vo. 2 ports (frontis laid down). 3 advt pp. Contemp calf, rebacked. Wing M.2025.
(Hannas) **£240 [≈ $384]**

Mikkelsen, Ejnar
- Lost in the Arctic. Being the Story of the 'Alabama' Expedition, 1909-1912. London: Heinemann, 1913. 1st edn. Lge 8vo. xviii,399, 1 pp. Fldg map, frontis, num plates. Orig orange brown cloth, ex-lib, tear across hd of spine. *(Terramedia)* **$50 [≈ £31]**

Miles, Nelson A.
- Personal Recollections and Observations of General Nelson A. Miles Embracing a Brief View of the Civil War ... Chicago: 1896. 1st edn, 1st iss. Thick 4to. 590 pp. Port, ills. Orig pict gilt cloth, some edge wear.
(Reese) **$200 [≈ £125]**

Milford, John
- Norway, and Her Laplanders, in 1841: with a Few Hints to the Salmon Fisher. London: Murray, 1842. 1st edn. Half-title. No advt ff. Early scarlet mor gilt, a.e.g.
(Hannas) **£210 [≈ $336]**

Mill, Hugh Robert
- The Record of the Royal Geographic Society 1830-1930. London: RGS, 1930. Lge 8vo. 35 plates, 1 chart. Orig cloth gilt. Dw sl chipped at lower edge. *(Hollett)* **£35 [≈ $56]**

Millais, J.G.
- A Breath from the Veldt. London: 1899. Folio. 346 pp. Num ills inc photogravures with tissue guards. Orig bndg.
(Trophy Room Books) **$600 [≈ £375]**
- Far Away Up the Nile. London: Longmans, 1924. 4to. x,254 pp. frontis, 49 ills. Orig red cloth, sl string marks to front cvr.
(Bates & Hindmarch) **£75 [≈ $120]**
- Newfoundland and its Untrodden Ways. London: 1907. Imperial 8vo. Ills. Orig bndg.
(Grayling) **£70 [≈ $112]**
- Newfoundland and its Untrodden Ways. London: 1907. Roy 8vo. xvi,340 pp. 2 maps,

86 plates (6 cold). Sl foxing. Cloth, rather faded. *(Wheldon & Wesley)* **£60 [≈ $96]**
- Newfoundland and its Untrodden Ways. London: Longmans, 1907. 4to. 340 pp. Ills. Orig maroon cloth, stamped in blind with a moose & hunter. *(Moon)* **£95 [≈ $152]**
- Newfoundland and its Untrodden Ways. With Illustrations by the Author & from Photographs. London: Longmans, 1907. 1st edn. Lge 8vo. xvi,340 pp. Num tissued plates (6 cold). Orig pict maroon cloth gilt.
(Terramedia) **$325 [≈ £203]**
- A Sportsman's Wanderings. MA: 1920. 298 pp. Ills. Orig bndg.
(Trophy Room Books) **$50 [≈ £31]**
- Wanderings and Memories. London: 1919. 8vo. Ills. Orig bndg. *(Grayling)* **£30 [≈ $48]**
- Wanderings and Memories. London: 1919. 8vo. Ills. Orig bndg, sl marked..
(Grayling) **£25 [≈ $40]**

Millard, David
- A Journal of Travels in Egypt, Arabia Petraea, and the Holy Land, during 1841-2. Rochester: 1843. 352 pp. Occas dampstain & trace of foxing, sgntr starting. Orig cloth, rubbed. *(Reese)* **$165 [≈ £103]**

Miller, George
- A Description of the Cathedral Church of Ely; with Some Account of the Conventual Buildings. Illustrated with Engravings. London: Luke Hansard ..., 1808. 2nd edn. 8vo. xii,174 pp. 10 plates (sl browned). Orig bds, uncut, rebacked. *(Young's)* **£38 [≈ $60]**

Miller, William, 1769-1844
- The Costume of the Russian Empire. Illustrated ... With Descriptions in English and French. London: for William Miller, 1803. Folio. 73 cold plates (watermarked 1823). Sl foxing & offsetting. Red straight grained mor gilt, a.e.g., hinges & some edges sl rubbed. *(Thornton's)* **£600 [≈ $960]**

Miller, William
- The Balkans, Roumania, Bulgaria, Servia and Montenegro. London: Fisher Unwin, Story of the Nations Series, 1896. 3rd imp. 8vo. xix,476 pp. Fldg map, ills. Old mor & cloth, faded & rubbed. *(Piccadilly)* **£24 [≈ $38]**
- Travels and Politics in the Near East. London: Fisher Unwin, 1898. 8vo. xxiv,515 pp. Fldg map in pocket (1 fold reprd). Num photo ills. Orig black cloth, sl worn.
(Piccadilly) **£50 [≈ $80]**

Miller, W.
- Greek Life in Town and Country. London:

Newnes, 1905. 8vo. x,311 pp. 28 photos. Sl spotting. Orig dec cloth, cvrs rather stained, edges sl frayed.   *(Piccadilly)* £15 [≈ $24]

Millet, Samuel A.
- A Whaling Voyage in the Bark "Willis" 1849-1850. Boston: privately ptd, 1924. One of 50. vi,[3],46 pp. 8 ills. Endpapers v sl foxed. Mrbld paper over bds.
      (Parmer) $250 [≈ £156]

Millin, A.L.
- Travels through the Southern Departments of France. Performed in the Years 1804 and 1805. London: Richard Phillips, 1808. 280 pp. 4 cold plates. 2 sm holes in blank marg, some ff darkened or with sl foxing. Mod half cloth.   *(Reese)* $125 [≈ £78]

Mills, Lady Dorothy
- The Road to Timbuktu. London: Duckworth, 1924. 1st edn. 8vo. 262 pp. Frontis & other photo plates. Orig light blue cloth, spine sl sunned.
      (Terramedia) $60 [≈ £37]

Mills, Robert
- Memorial of Robert Mills, respecting a New Route to the Pacific Ocean ... Feb. 15, 1848. [Washington: 1848]. 7 pp. Fldg map. Selfwraps, stitched.   *(Reese)* $150 [≈ £93]

Milne, Mrs Leslie
- Shans at Home. With Two Chapters on Shan History and Literature by Rev. Wilbur Willis Cochrane. London: Murray, 1910. 1st edn. xxiv, 289 pp. Cold frontis, 103 ills. Orig dec cloth gilt, spine sl rubbed & faded.
      (Hollett) £55 [≈ $88]

Milne, William C.
- Life in China. London: Routledge, 1857. 1st edn. Sm 8vo. x,517 pp. 2 fldg maps (only, of 4). Contemp polished calf gilt, rubbed.
      (Claude Cox) £15 [≈ $24]

Milner, J.
- Inquiry into Certain Vulgar Opinions Concerning the Catholic Inhabitants and Antiquities of Ireland [Milner's Tour 1807 in Ireland]. London: Keating, 1808. Orig owner's comments at hd of title. Half leather.
      (Emerald Isle) £50 [≈ $80]

Milner, Thomas
- Russia: Its Rise and Progress, Tragedies and Revolutions. London: Longman, 1856. 1st edn. 8vo. xv,[i],500 pp. Frontis. Orig red cloth gilt, spine faded.
      (Burmester) £55 [≈ $88]

Milner, Revd Thomas
- The Gallery of Geography. A Pictorial & Descriptive Tour of the World. Glasgow: M'Phun & Son, [ca 1872]. 2 vols. Sm thick 4to. 20 chromolithos, 8 steel engvd plates, 12 cold maps.   *(Hollett)* £75 [≈ $120]

Milton, Viscount & Cheadle, W.B.
- North-West Passage by Land ... London: Cassell, Petter & Galpin, [ca 1868]. 7th edn. 8vo. xxiv,394 pp. 8 w'engvd plates. Contemp half calf.   *(Gough)* £48 [≈ $76]

Mitchell's School Atlas ...
- Mitchell's School Atlas: comprising the Maps and Tables designed to accompany Mitchell's School and Family Geography. Philadelphia: E.H. Butler, 1859. 4to. 32 maps (inc Texas, sm stain in blank marg), 9 tables. Calf backed ptd bds, rubbed, edges worn.
      (Reese) $250 [≈ £156]

Mittelholzer, W., et al.
- By Airplane toward the North Pole. An Account of an Expedition to Spitzbergen in the Summer of 1923. Translated by E. and C. Paul. London: (1925). 1st edn. 8vo. 178 pp. Fldg map frontis, 3 maps, 32 plates. Orig cloth.   *(Berkelouw)* $75 [≈ £46]

Mitton, G.E.
- Buckinghamshire and Berkshire. Painted by Sutton Palmer. London: A. & C. Black, 1929. 2nd edn. Map, 32 cold plates. Orig cloth.
      (Old Cathay) £16 [≈ $25]
- Cornwall. Painted by G.F. Nicholls. London: A. & C. Black Colour Book, 1915. 1st edn. 24 cold plates. Orig dec cloth.
      (Old Cathay) £33 [≈ $52]
- Cornwall. Painted by G.F. Nicholls. London: A. & C. Black, 1915. 1st edn. 8vo. Frontis & 19 other cold plates, all titled on tissue guards. Orig cloth, gilt spine, sl soiled.
      (Sanders) £25 [≈ $40]
- Cornwall. Painted by G.F. Nicholls. London: A. & C. Black Colour Book, 1915. 1st edn. 24 cold plates. Orig dec cloth, bds sl affected by damp.   *(Old Cathay)* £23 [≈ $36]
- Cornwall. Painted by G.F. Nicholls. London: A. & C. Black, 1925. 2nd edn, with an addtnl chapter on the Scilly Isles. 8vo. Frontis & 31 other plates. Orig cloth.
      (Sanders) £18 [≈ $28]
- Cornwall. Painted by G.F. Nicholls. London: A. & C. Black, 1925. 2nd edn, with addtnl chapter. 32 cold plates. Orig cloth.
      (Old Cathay) £19 [≈ $30]
- Normandy. Painted by Nico Jungman. London: A. & C. Black Colour Book, 1905.

1st edn. 40 cold plates. Orig cloth, t.e.g., spine discold as usual, minor wear to extremities.   *(Old Cathay)* **£23 [≈ $36]**

- The Scenery of London. Painted by Herbert Marshall. London: A. & C. Black Colour Books, Twenty Shilling Series, 1905. 1st edn. 75 cold plates. Orig dec cloth, t.e.g., wear to extremities & minor staining to rear bd.
        (Old Cathay) **£135 [≈ $216]**

- The Thames. Painted by Mortimer Menpes. London: A. & C. Black Colour Books, Twenty Shilling Series, 1906. 1st edn. 75 cold plates. Orig grey, green & white dec cloth, minor rubbing to spine & front bd, half inch waterstain on front bd, minor scuffing.
        (Old Cathay) **£95 [≈ $152]**

- The Thames. Painted by Mortimer Menpes. London: A. & C. Black Colour Books, Twenty Shilling Series, 1906. 1st edn. 75 cold plates. Orig grey, green & white dec cloth, spine darkened, rubbed & worn, front bd crinkly, rubbed with sl stains, endpapers browned.   *(Old Cathay)* **£65 [≈ $104]**

- The Thames. Painted by Mortimer Menpes. London: A. & C. Black Colour Books, Twenty Shilling Series, 1906. 1st edn. 75 cold plates. Orig grey, green & white dec cloth, spine worn & shabby.   *(Old Cathay)* **£55 [≈ $88]**

The Modern Traveller Series ...
- Modern Traveller. A Popular Description, Geographical, Historical and Topographical, of the Various Countries of the Globe. Mexico and Guatemala. London: 1825. 1st edn. 2 vols. 12mo. vi,371; iv,320 pp. Fldg map, 3 plates. Occas spotting. Contemp half mor, sl rubbed.   *(Young's)* **£34 [≈ $54]**
- See also Conder, Josiah.

Moens, William John Charles
- English Travellers and Italian Brigands. A Narrative of Capture and Captivity. Second Edition, Revised, with Additions. London: Hurst & Blackett, 1866. Fldg map, frontis (loose), plates. Orig cloth, backstrip chafed.
        (Wreden) **$65 [≈ £40]**

Moffat, Robert
- Missionary Labours and Scenes in Southern Africa ... London: John Snow, 1842. 8vo. xv, 624 pp. Cold frontis, fldg map, 6 plates. New half mor.   *(Adelson)* **$325 [≈ £203]**

Mogg, Edward
- A New Travelling Map of England, Wales and Scotland. London: 1818. Hand cold fldg map. 720 x 600 mm. A few place names underlined in pencil. Orig slipcase.
        (Robertshaw) **£20 [≈ $32]**

Mogridge, George
- Loiterings among the Lakes of Cumberland and Westmoreland. London: RTS, [1849]. Sm sq 8vo. viii,208 pp. Baxter frontis, 6 w'engvd plates. Some thumbing or dusting. Orig gilt dec cloth, a.e.g., rubbed, gilt dulled.
        (de Beaumont) **£38 [≈ $60]**

Molesworth, Robert, Viscount
- An Account of Denmark, as it was in the Year 1692 ... London: ptd in the year, 1694. 1st edn. 8vo. [lii],271 pp. Contemp sprinkled calf, gilt spine, mor label, upper jnt reprd. Wing M.2382A. Contemp inscrptn dated 6 Feb 1693 (i.e. 1694).
        (Pickering) **$650 [≈ £406]**

Molina, J. Ignatius
- The Geographical, Natural, and Civil History of Chili. Translated from the Original Italian ... Added, Notes ... By the English Editor. London: Longman ..., 1809. 1st London edn. 2 vols. 8vo. Fldg frontis map (foxed). Orig bds, rebacked, crnrs sl worn.
        (Schoyer) **$185 [≈ £115]**

Mollien, Gaspard T.
- Travels in Africa, to the Sources of the Senegal and Gambia, in 1818. London: Richard Phillips, 1820. 8vo. ix,128 pp. Fldg map, 4 plates. Mod buckram, uncut.
        (Adelson) **$225 [≈ £140]**

Monckton, C.A.W.
- Last Days in New Guinea being Further Experiences of a New Guinea Resident Magistrate. London: Bodley Head, 1922. 2nd edn. 8vo. x,287,4 advt pp. Fldg map, photo frontis, 54 ills. Orig bndg, rear hinge weak.
        (Bates & Hindmarch) **£30 [≈ $48]**

Moncrieff, A.R. Hope
- Belgium - Past and Present, (The Cockpit of Europe). London: A. & C. Black Colour Book, 1920. 1st edn. Map, 32 cold plates. Orig cloth, 1 or 2 sm watermarks to front bd.
        (Old Cathay) **£25 [≈ $40]**
- Belgium Past and Present. London: A. & C. Black, 1920. Sm 4to. xii,210 pp. Map, 32 cold plates. Orig dec red cloth, spine v sl faded, foredge sl foxed.   *(Piccadilly)* **£22.50 [≈ $36]**
- Belgium Past and Present. The Cockpit of Europe. London: A. & C. Black, 1920. 1st edn. 8vo. xii,210 pp. Map, 32 cold plates. Orig gilt dec red cloth.
        (Terramedia) **£30 [≈ £18]**
- Bonnie Scotland. Painted by Sutton Palmer. London: A. & C. Black Colour Book, (1904). One of 500, sgnd by Moncrieff. 75 cold

plates. Orig cloth, t.e.g., spine ends v sl rubbed.   (*Old Cathay*) £175 [≈ $280]

- Bonnie Scotland. Painted by Sutton Palmer. London: A. & C. Black Colour Book, (1904). One of 500, sgnd by Moncrieff. 75 cold plates. Orig cloth, t.e.g., occas v minor rubbing, some scuff marks to rear bd & sl darkening to the cloth.
(*Old Cathay*) £125 [≈ $200]

- Essex. Painted by L. Burleigh Bruhl. London: A. & C. Black Colour Books, Twenty Shilling Series, 1909. 1st edn. Fldg map, 75 cold plates. Orig dec cloth, t.e.g., endpapers sl foxed, else fine.
(*Old Cathay*) £85 [≈ $136]

- Highlands and Islands of Scotland. Painted by William Smith. London: A. & C. Black, 1929. 3rd edn. Map, 32 cold plates. Orig cloth.   (*Old Cathay*) £17 [≈ $27]

- The Isle of Wight. Painted by A. Heaton Cooper ... London: Adam & Charles Black, 1908. 8vo. viii,176,4 advt pp. Fldg map, 24 cold plates. Orig dec cloth, sm nick on back cvr edge. Worn dw.   (*Schoyer*) $50 [≈ £31]

- London. London: A. & C. Black Colour Book, 1910. 1st edn. 32 cold plates. Orig bright red gilt dec pict cloth, t.e.g.
(*Old Cathay*) £35 [≈ $56]

- London. London: A. & C. Black Colour Book, 1916. 2nd edn. 32 cold plates. Orig cloth, spine faded. (*Old Cathay*) £20 [≈ $32]

- The Peak Country. Painted by W. Biscombe Gardner. London: A. & C. Black Colour Books, Six Shilling Series, 1908. 1st edn. 24 cold plates. Orig deep blue cloth, t.e.g.
(*Old Cathay*) £33 [≈ $52]

- The Peak Country. Painted by W. Biscombe Gardner. London: A. & C. Black Colour Books, Six Shilling Series, 1908. 1st edn. 24 cold plates. Orig brown cloth, t.e.g.
(*Old Cathay*) £25 [≈ $40]

- Surrey. Painted by Sutton Palmer. London: A. & C. Black Colour Books, Twenty Shilling Series, 1909. Reprint. Map, 75 cold plates. Orig dec blue & green cloth, minor scuffs to rear bd, minor rubbing to front bd.
(*Old Cathay*) £43 [≈ $60]

- Surrey. Painted by Sutton Palmer. London: A. & C. Black Colour Books, Twenty Shilling Series, 1909. Reprint. Map, 75 cold plates. Orig dec blue & green cloth, gilt school stamp to rear bd, v minor wear to extremities.
(*Old Cathay*) £43 [≈ $68]

- Surrey. Painted by Sutton Palmer. London: A. & C. Black, (1912). 8vo. xi,252,8 advt pp. Map,.75 cold plates with captioned tissues. Some foxing. Orig dec cloth, t.e.g.
(*Bow Windows*) £45 [≈ $72]

- Surrey. Painted by Sutton Palmer. London:

A. & C. Black, 1912. 8vo. xi,252 pp. Fldg map, 75 cold plates. Orig cloth, lower cvr wrinkled & dampmarked, rest unaffected.
(*Coombes*) £15 [≈ $24]

- Surrey. Painted by Sutton Palmer. London: A. & C. Black, 1922. 2nd edn, rvsd. Map, 32 cold plates. Foredges sl foxed. Orig cloth.
(*Old Cathay*) £19 [≈ $30]

Monson, Ronald A.

- Across Africa on Foot. London: Elkin Mathews & Marrot, 1936. 8vo. xiv,386 pp. 5 maps, 93 photos. Dw torn.
(*Schoyer*) $35 [≈ £21]

Montagu, Lady Mary Wortley

- Letters ... written during her Travels in Europe, Asia and Africa ... New Edition. London: Becket & De Hondt, 1769. 3 vols. Sm 8vo. Contemp half calf.
(*Hannas*) £65 [≈ $104]

Montague, Charles

- Tales of a Nomad, or Sport and Strife. London: 1894. 8vo. Orig cloth.
(*Grayling*) £40 [≈ $64]

Montbard, G.

- Among the Moors. (Morocco). New York & London: Scribner's, Sampson Low, 1894. 4to. 281 pp. Port frontis, title vignette, num ills. Orig gilt dec green cloth, front inner hinges cracked.   (*Terramedia*) $90 [≈ £56]

Monteith, Robert

- Description of the Islands of Orkney and Zetland ... Reprinted from the Edition of 1711 ... Edinburgh: Stevenson, 1845. 8vo. red & black title, 82 pp. 2 lge fldg maps. Three qtr mor gilt, t.e.g.
(*Hollett*) £150 [≈ $240]

- Description of the Islands of Orkney and Zetland ... Reprinted from the Edition of 1711 ... Edinburgh: Stevenson, 1845. One of 145. 8vo. 2 fldg maps. Orig red cloth, paper label (chipped), unopened.
(*Clark*) £65 [≈ $104]

Montgomery, H.B.

- The Empire of the East [Japan]. London: Methuen, 1908. 1st edn. 8vo. xii,307,advt pp. Cold frontis, num plates. Orig violet cloth gilt.   (*Terramedia*) $75 [≈ £46]

Montgomery, Rutherford G.

- High Country [hunting in the Colorado mountains]. New York: Derrydale Press, [1938]. 1st edn. One of 950. 8vo. 248 pp. Frontis, num photo plates. Orig pink &

brown cloth, gilt mor labels, unopened.
(Terramedia) **$125 [≈ £78]**

Moor, Edward
- Oriental Fragments by the Author of the
Hindu Pantheon. London: Smith, Elder,
1834. 8vo. viii,[i],537 pp. 24 pp inserted
advts. Orig cloth, uncut, spine faded.
Author's pres inscrptn. *(Lamb)* **£60 [≈ $96]**

Moore, Clarence B.
- Aboriginal Sites on Tennessee River.
reprinted from Journal of the Academy of
Natural Sciences of Philadelphia.
Philadelphia: 1915. Folio. Over 250 pp. Num
ills & plates (4 cold). Sl lib marks. Orig
maroon cloth, spine ends sl chipped.
(Terramedia) **$300 [≈ £187]**
- Antiquities of the St. Francis, White & Black
Rivers, Arkansas. Reprinted from the Journal
of the Academy of Natural Sciences of
Philadelphia, Volume XIV. Philadelphia:
P.C. Stockhausen, 1910. Folio. Ca 110 pp. 19
cold plates. Orig maroon cloth, sl worn.
(Terramedia) **$300 [≈ £187]**

Moore, Decima & Guggisburg, F.G.
- We Two in West Africa. New York:
Scribner's, 1909. 8vo. xvi,368 pp. Fldg map
of the Gold Coast, frontis, num ills. Orig pict
maroon cloth gilt. *(Terramedia)* **$100 [≈ £62]**

Moore, John, 1730-1802
- A Journal of a Residence in France, from the
Beginning of August, to the Middle of
September, 1792 ... London: for G.G. & J.
Robinson, 1793. 1st edn. 2 vols. 8vo. Fldg
map cold in outline. Orig speckled calf,
contrasting mor labels.
(Bickersteth) **£140 [≈ $224]**
- A Journal during a Residence in France ...
Dublin: P. Byrne, 1793. 1st Irish edn. 2 vols.
Lge 12mo. Fldg cold map & leaf of
explanation. Half-titles, advt leaf. Contemp
calf, 1 label sl chipped.
(Hartfield) **$225 [≈ £140]**
- Journal of a Residence in France from the
beginning of August, to the middle of
September, 1792 ... London: for G.G. & J.
Robinson ..., 1793. New edn. 2 vols. 8vo.
[iv],502; 618,[2] pp. Fldg map cold in outline.
Contemp calf, jnts weak. Sir Robert Peel's
b'plate. *(Young's)* **£75 [≈ $120]**
- A View of Society and Manners in France,
Switzerland, and Germany: With Anecdotes
relating to some Eminent Characters.
London: 1780. 3rd edn, crrctd. 2 vols. 8vo.
xvi,451; xv, 440 pp. Occas sl trace of foxing.
Contemp speckled calf, gilt spines relaid, vol
1 jnts worn. *(Reese)* **$250 [≈ £156]**

- A View of Society, and Manners in France,
Switzerland, and Germany: With Anecdotes
relating to some Eminent Characters.
London: for A. Strahan ..., 1786. 6th edn,
crrctd. 2 vols. 8vo. xvi,420; xii,420 pp. Old
calf, rebacked. *(Young's)* **£55 [≈ $88]**

Moore, S.S. & Jones, T.W.
- The Traveller's Directory, or a Pocket
Companion, shewing the Course of the Main
Road from Philadelphia to New York ...
Philadelphia: Mathew Carey, 1802. 1st edn. 2
ff, 52 pp. 38 engvd maps on 22 ff. Some
foxing. Orig calf, hinges cracking.
(Reese) **$2,750 [≈ £1,718]**

Morden, W.
- Across Asia's Snows and Deserts. New York:
1927. 413 pp. Ills. Orig bndg.
(Trophy Room Books) **$200 [≈ £125]**

More, R. Jasper
- Under the Balkans. Notes on a Visit to the
District of Philoppopolis in 1876 ... London:
Henry S. King, 1877. 8vo. xii,272 pp. Fldg
map, 8 ills. Orig dec green cloth.
(Piccadilly) **£20 [≈ $32]**

Moreland, A. Maud
- Through South Westland. A Journey to the
Haast and Mount Aspiring, New Zealand.
London: Witherby, 1911. 8vo. xviii,219 pp.
Fldg map, 48 plates. Orig bndg.
(Schoyer) **$60 [≈ £37]**

Morell, John Reynell
- Algeria: The Topography and History,
Political, Social and Natural of French Africa.
London: 1854. 1st edn. 8vo. W'engvd plates,
2 text ills. Orig cloth, a.e.g., spine sl faded.
(Robertshaw) **£55 [≈ $88]**

Morgan, Dale L. & Wheat, Carl I.
- Jedediah Smith and his Maps of the American
West. San Francisco: 1954. One of 530. Lge
folio. 86 pp. 7 fldg facs maps. Cloth.
(Reese) **$600 [≈ £375]**

Morgan, John
- Several Voyages to Barbary. Containing an
Historical and Geographical Account of the
Country ... [maps & plans] Designed by
Captain Henry Boyde. London: Olive Payne
..., 1736. 2nd English edn. 12mo. 146,158
pp. 2 fldg maps, 4 fldg panoramas (sm reprs).
Rec cloth. *(Schoyer)* **$250 [≈ £156]**

Morgan, William
- Pocket-Book of the Roads ... see Ogilby, John
& Morgan, William.

Morrell, Z.N.
- Flowers and Fruits in the Wilderness; or, 46 Years in Texas. St. Louis: 1882. 412 pp. Orig cloth. *(Jenkins)* **$485** [≈ £303]

Morris, F.O.
- The Ancestral Homes of Britain. London: Bell & Daldy, 1868. 4to. iv,91 pp. Cold frontis & title opening, 39 cold plates. Some spotting, bruising to a few ff, some edge dusting. Orig elab dec cloth gilt, a.e.g. *(de Beaumont)* **£135** [≈ $216]
- A Series of Picturesque Views of the Seats of the Noblemen and Gentlemen of Great Britain and Ireland. London: Mackenzie, [ca 1860-80]. 6 vols. 4to. 240 colour-ptd plates. Orig dec cloth, a.e.g. *(Charles B. Wood)* **$500** [≈ £312]
- A Series of Picturesque Views of Seats of Noblemen and Gentlemen of Great Britain and Ireland. Edinburgh: Mackenzie, [ca 1870]. 7 vols, inc 'Autograph' vol. 240 chromolitho plates. Occas sl foxing. Orig pict brown cloth gilt. *(Gough)* **£195** [≈ $312]
- A Series of Picturesque Views of Seats of the Noblemen and Gentlemen of Great Britain and Ireland. London: Mackenzie, [1880]. 1st edn. 4to. 240 tissued cold plates. Orig elab gilt dec red mor, spines sl darkened & sl rubbed. *(Terramedia)* **$750** [≈ £468]
- A Series of Picturesque Views of Seats of the Noblemen and Gentlemen of Great Britain and Ireland. London: Mackenzie, n.d.. 6 vols. 4to. Chromolitho plates & extra titles. Orig dec cloth gilt extra, a.e.g. *(Hollett)* **£220** [≈ $352]

Morris, James
- Sultan in Oman. London: 1957. 8vo. 2 maps, cold frontis, plates. Orig cloth. *(Farahar)* **£20** [≈ $32]

Morris, William Gouverneur
- Report upon the Customs District, Public Service, and Resources of Alaska Territory. Washington: GPO, 1879. 8vo. 163 pp. 11 plates inc fldg map. Sm lib stamp on 1 page. New cloth. *(High Latitude)* **$65** [≈ £40]

Morrison, George Ernest
- An Australian in China being the Narrative of a Quiet Journey across China to Burma. London: Horace Cox, 1895. 2nd edn. 299 pp. Frontis, map, plates. Orig maroon cloth gilt. *(Lyon)* **£115** [≈ $184]

Morse, Jedidiah
- The American Geography ... with a particular Description of Kentucky, The Western Territory, and Vermont ... Second Edition. London: Stockdale, 1792. 8vo. xvi, 536 pp. 2 fldg maps, fldg table of distances. 2 closed tears in maps without loss. Rec half calf. *(Clark)* **£220** [≈ $352]
- The American Geography ... with particular Descriptions of Kentucky, The Western Territory, and Vermont ... Second Edition. London: Stockdale, 1792. 8vo. xvi,536 pp. 2 fldg maps, fldg table. Contemp calf, outer hinges a bit weak. *(Karmiole)* **$350** [≈ £218]

Morse, Jedidiah & Richard C.
- The Traveller's Guide: or Pocket Gazetteer of the United States. New-Haven: 1823. 324 pp. Orig calf, mor backed. *(Jenkins)* **$45** [≈ £28]

Mortimer, J.R.
- Forty Years' Researches in British and Saxon Burial Mounds of East Yorkshire ... London: 1905. 4to. Cold frontis, 125 plates. Contemp qtr mor, t.e.g. *(Waterfield's)* **£200** [≈ $320]

Morton, Edward
- Travels in Russia, and a Residence at St. Petersburg and Odessa, in the Years 1827-1829 ... London: Longman, Rees, 1830. 1st edn. 8vo. Half-title. Orig cloth, mor label. Author's pres copy. *(Trebizond)* **$250** [≈ £156]

Morton-Cameron, W.H. (compiler)
- Present Day Impressions of Japan ... London: 1919. Lge thick 8vo. [xii],932 pp. Cold fldg map, 8 cold plates, sev hundred text ills. Orig brown mor, gilt spine, a.e.g., cvr edges a trifle rubbed. *(Bow Windows)* **£375** [≈ $600]

Moryson, Fynes
- An History of Ireland from the Year 1599 to 1603, with a Short Narration of the State of the Kingdom from 1169, to which is added a Description of Ireland. Dublin: Powell, 1735. 2 vols. Calf. *(Emerald Isle)* **£200** [≈ $320]
- An Itinerary: Containing His Ten Yeeres Travell through the Twelve Dominions ... Glasgow: 1907-08. One of 1000. 4 vols. 8vo. 17 plates. Some foxing. Orig cloth, t.e.g., spines a little faded. *(Bow Windows)* **£80** [≈ $128]

Moseley, H.N.
- Notes by a Naturalist. An Account of Observations made during the Voyage of H.M.S. "Challenger" round the World in the Years 1872-1876. London: 1892. New rvsd edn. 8vo. xxiv,540 pp. Fldg cold map, port, text figs. Orig cloth, trifle used. *(Wheldon & Wesley)* **£40** [≈ $64]

Moser, J.F.
- Alaska. Hydrographic Notes, Sailing Directions, and Charts of Surveys relating to the Vicinity of Prince William Sound, Cook Inlet, Kadiak Island ... Washington: GPO, 1899. 4to. Title, 121-142 pp. 6 fldg charts, 3 plates. Orig ptd wraps, sl soiled & frayed.
(High Latitude) **$60 [≈£37]**

Mosquera, Tomas C. de
- Memoir on the Physical and Political Geography of New Granada. New York: Dwight, 1853. 1st edn in English. 105 pp. Lge fldg map. Orig dec buff wraps.
(Jenkins) **$225 [≈£140]**

Mosse, A.
- My Somali Book. London: 1913. 309 pp. Ills. Orig bndg.
(Trophy Room Books) **$95 [≈£59]**
- My Somali Book. London: 1913. 309 pp. Ills. Orig bndg, good only.
(Trophy Room Books) **$60 [≈£37]**

Mouat, Frederic J.
- Adventures and Researches ... Andaman Islanders. London: 1863. 1st edn. 8vo. 4 plates. Lacks map & half-title. Contemp half calf. *(Fenning)* **£45 [≈$72]**

Moule, Thomas
- Winkles's Architectural and Picturesque Illustrations of the Cathedral Churches of England and Wales ... see Winkles, H. & B.

Mounteney-Jephson, A.J.
- Emin Pasha and the Rebellion at the Equator. A Story of ... Experiences in the Last of the Soudan Provinces, with the Revision ... of Henry M. Stanley. London: 1890. 8vo. xxiv,490,2 advt pp. Fldg map, facs letter, 22 plates. Orig pict cloth, spine sl faded.
(Adelson) **$160 [≈£100]**
- Emin Pasha and the Rebellion at the Equator. A Story of ... Experiences in the Last of the Soudan Provinces, with the Revision ... of Henry M. Stanley. London: 1890. 2nd edn. 8vo. xxiv, 490, [2 advt] pp. Num plates. Orig cloth, v rubbed, sl shaken.
(Worldwide Antiqu'n) **$65 [≈£40]**
- Emin Pasha - Rebellion at the Equator. New York: Scribner, 1890. 1st Amer edn. 8vo. 490 pp. Fldg map, facs, ills. Title detached. Orig dec green cloth gilt, some shelfwear, rear hinge tender. *(Parmer)* **$75 [≈£46]**

Mountfort, G.
- Portrait of a Desert. The Story of an Expedition to Jordan. London: Readers Union, 1966. 8vo. Map, 68 plates (some cold). Orig cloth.
(Wheldon & Wesley) **£25 [≈$40]**
- Portrait of a River, the Wildlife of the Danube from the Black Sea to Budapest. London: 1962. Roy 8vo. 207 pp. Cold frontis, 56 photo plates. Orig cloth.
(Wheldon & Wesley) **£25 [≈$40]**
- Portrait of a Wilderness (Coto Donana). London: (1958) 1968. Roy 8vo. Num cold & other plates. Orig cloth. Dw.
(Wheldon & Wesley) **£20 [≈$32]**
- The Vanishing Jungle. The Story of the World Wildlife Fund Expeditions to Pakistan. London: 1969. Roy 8vo. 286 pp. 60 plates (some cold), endpaper maps. Name on title. Orig cloth. Dw sl frayed.
(Wheldon & Wesley) **£40 [≈$64]**

Mudie, Robert
- A Historical Account of His Majesty's Visit to Scotland. Third Edition. London: 1822. 5 lge fldg plates. Contemp half calf, 1 crnr worn.
(Robertshaw) **£26 [≈$41]**

Muir, John
- The Cruise of the Corwin. Boston: Houghton Mifflin, 1917. One of 550 Large Paper. xxxi, 279 pp. 22 ills. Largely unopened. Slipcase sl worn. Inscrbd by the editor, Wm. F. Bodie.
(Parmer) **$350 [≈£218]**
- The Mountains of California. New York: The Century Co, 1894. 1st edn. 8vo. xiii,[3],381 pp. Frontis, maps, text ills. Occas usual sl foxing. Orig pict tan cloth gilt, t.e.g., crnrs sl bumped. *(Heritage)* **$250 [≈£156]**
- The Mountains of California. New York: century, 1911. 8vo. xvi,382 pp. Frontis, 6 maps, 90 ills. Some underlining. Orig illust cloth gilt, spine sl faded.
(Berkelouw) **$150 [≈£93]**
- Our National Parks. Boston: Houghton, Mifflin, 1901. 8vo. xii,370 pp. Frontis, map, 10 plates. Some pencil marking in text. Orig cloth gilt, t.e.g. *(Berkelouw)* **$100 [≈£62]**
- Travels in Alaska. Boston: Houghton Mifflin, 1915. 1st edn. One of 450 Large Paper. 326 pp. Frontis, plates. Ink inscrptn. Cloth backed bds, largely unopened, leather label, sl soiled, label rubbed. *(Reese)* **$150 [≈£93]**
- Yosemite and the Sierra Nevada. Photographs by Ansel Adams. Selections from the Works of John Muir. Edited by Charlotte E. Mauk. Boston: Houghton Mifflin, 1948. 1st edn. 4to. [xxii],132 pp. 64 ff of plates. Orig bndg. Dw sl chipped.
(Karmiole) **$125 [≈£78]**

Muller, Christian
- Journey through Greece and the Ionian Islands in June, July and August 1821. London: Sir Richard Phillips, 1822. Only edn in English. 8vo. Occas sl foxing. Mod paper backed bds.   *(Trebizond)* **$225 [≈£140]**

Muller, Friedrich Max
- Auld Lang Syne. London: 1898-99. 1st & 2nd series. 2 vols. 8vo. Port. Orig cloth, sl worn.
        (Farahar) **£50 [≈$80]**
- The Life and Letters of the Right Honourable Friedrich Max Muller, edited by his Wife. London: 1902. 2 vols. 8vo. 3 ports, 3 plates. Orig cloth.   *(Farahar)* **£50 [≈$80]**
- My Autobiography. A Fragment. London: 1901. 8vo. 6 ports. Orig cloth.
        (Farahar) **£35 [≈$56]**

Mulock, Dinah Maria, later Mrs Craik
- Fair France. Impressions of a Traveller. London: Hurst & Blackett, 1871. 1st edn. 8vo. [4],313,[3],16 advt pp. Orig cloth gilt, sl rubbed.   *(Claude Cox)* **£15 [≈$24]**

Mumey, N.
- Rocky Mountain Dick. Colorado: 1953. One of 500, sgnd. 86 pp. Ills. Orig bndg, mint.
        (Trophy Room Books) **$150 [≈£93]**

Mummery, A.F.
- My Climbs in the Alps and Caucasus. London: Fisher Unwin, 1895. 2nd edn. Sm 4to. xii,360 pp. 11 plates. Some spotting. Orig cloth, rather soiled & marked, jnts cracked.   *(Hollett)* **£120 [≈$192]**

Mundy, Capt.
- Pen and Pencil Sketches, being the Journal of a Tour in India. London: 1832. 2 vols. xiv, [1], 381; 376 pp. Frontis, plates. Offsetting from some plates. Contemp polished calf gilt, wear to outer hinges. *(Reese)* **£275 [≈£171]**
- Pen and Pencil Sketches: being the Journal of a Tour in India. London: 1832. 2 vols. 381; 376 pp. Fldg map, ills. Qtr leather, mrbld bds & endpapers.
        (Trophy Room Books) **$350 [≈£218]**

Mundy, D.L.
- Rotomahana: and the Boiling Springs of New Zealand. A Photographic Series of Sixteen Views ... with Descriptive Notes by Ferdinand Von Hochstetter. London: Sampson, Low ..., 1875. Only edn. Folio. [x],4 pp. Map, 16 autotype plates. Orig dec cloth, a.e.g. *(Charles B. Wood)* **$585 [≈£365]**

Munk, Joseph A.
- Southwest Sketches. New York & London: 1920. x,311 pp. Photo ills. Orig pict cloth.
        (Reese) **$85 [≈£53]**

Munroe, Neil
- Ayrshire Idylls. Illustrated by George Houston. London: A. & C. Black Colour Book, 1912. 1st edn. 20 cold plates, 20 text ills. Orig cloth.   *(Old Cathay)* **£25 [≈$40]**
- The Clyde. Painted by M.Y. and J.Y. Hunter. London: A. & C. Black Colour Books, Twenty Shilling Series, 1907. 1st edn. Fldg map, 67 cold plates. Orig dec cloth, fine.
        (Old Cathay) **£55 [≈$88]**
- The Clyde. Painted by M.Y. and J.Y. Hunter. London: A. & C. Black Colour Books, Twenty Shilling Series, 1907. 1st edn. Fldg map, 67 cold plates. Orig dec cloth, faded.   *(Old Cathay)* **£25 [≈$40]**

Murray, Charles Augustus
- Travels in North-America during the Years 1834, 1835, & 1836 ... New York: 1839. 1st Amer edn. 2 vols. xii,[13]-324; vii,[13]-247 pp. Occas foxing. Vol 1 dampstained on sev ff & rear bd. Orig cloth, paper labels, jnts cracked.   *(Reese)* **$100 [≈£62]**

Murray, The Hon. Henry A.
- Lands of the Slave and the Free: or, Cuba, the United States, and Canada. London: John W. Parker & Son, 1855. 1st edn. 2 vols. 8vo. 2 advt ff at end of both vols. Fldg map, engvd title vignettes, 11 w'engvd plates. Orig cloth gilt, spines sl faded.
        (Bickersteth) **£95 [≈$152]**

Murray, Hugh
- An Encyclopaedia of Geography. London: Longman, Rees ..., 1834. V thick 8vo. xii, 1567,14 advt pp. 82 full-page maps by Sidney Hall, over 1000 text ills. Mod half mor gilt.
        (Hollett) **£40 [≈$64]**
- An Historical and Descriptive Account of British America ... Edinburgh: Cabinet Library, 1839. 1st edn. 3 vols. Sm 8vo. 240, [2], 242-352; 356; 388 pp. 6 maps (2 fldg), 2 plates, a few other ills. Orig cloth, paper labels.   *(Fenning)* **£125 [≈$200]**

Murray, James & Marston, George
- Antarctic Days. Introduced by Sir Ernest Shackleton. London: 1913. 1st edn. 8vo. Ills. Orig cloth.   *(Robertshaw)* **£30 [≈$48]**

Murray, John Fisher
- A Picturesque Tour of the River Thames in its Western Course; including Particular

Descriptions of Richmond, Windsor, and Hampton Court. London: 1862. 8vo. xii,356 pp. 3 maps, num w'engvs. Orig cloth, spine faded with sl wear at tips, stringmark on front cvr. *(Coombes)* **£50 [≃ $80]**

Murray, T. Douglas & White, A.S.
- Sir Samuel Baker, A Memoir. London: Macmillan, 1895. 1st edn. 8vo. xii,437 pp. 4 fldg cold maps, port frontis, other ills. Blind stamp on title. Orig dec brown cloth, lib label removed from spine.
(Terramedia) **$100 [≃ £62]**
- Sir Samuel Baker, A Memoir. London: 1895. 437 pp. Num ills. Orig cloth, recased, new endpapers.
(Trophy Room Books) **$150 [≃ £93]**

Murray, Thomas Boyles
- Pitcairn: the Island, the People and the Pastor; with a Short Account of the Mutiny of the Bounty. London: SPCK, 1853. 2nd edn. 8vo. Half-title (crnr creased). Litho port (lacking another), 9 full-page ills, text ills. Orig pict cloth gilt, quite worn.
(Trebizond) **$125 [≃ £78]**

Murray, W.H.H.
- Daylight Land. The Experiences, Incidents & Adventures, Humorous & Otherwise, which Befell Judge John Doe, Tourist, of San Francisco ... Boston: Cupples & Hurd, 1888. 8vo. 338,advt pp. Orig pict brown cloth gilt, a.e.g. *(Terramedia)* **$35 [≃ £21]**

Musgrave, Sir Richard
- Memoirs of the Different Rebellions in Ireland ... Dublin: ptd by Robert Marchbank, for John Milliken ... & Stockdale, London, 1801. 2nd edn. 4to. x,636, 210,[8] pp. 10 fldg map (1 with old repr). Orig three qtr leather, rubbed, crnrs worn. *(Schoyer)* **$350 [≃ £218]**

Musson, Spencer C.
- La Cote d'Emeraude. [The Emerald Coast of Brittany]. Painted by J. Hardwicke Lewis. London: A. & C. Black Colour Book, 1912. 1st edn. 20 cold plates. Orig dec cloth, bds & spine sl discold, upper bd bumped at edge.
(Old Cathay) **£25 [≃ $40]**
- Sicily. Painted by Alberto Pisa. London: A. & C. Black Colour Books, Twenty Shilling Series, 1911. 1st edn. Map, 48 cold plates. Neat stamp at ft of title. Orig dec cloth, t.e.g., minor wear to spine ends.
(Old Cathay) **£50 [≃ $80]**
- Sicily. Painted by Alberto Pisa. London: A. & C. Black Colour Books, Twenty Shilling Series, 1911. 1st edn. Map, 48 cold plates. Foxing to prelims & foredge. Orig dec cloth,

t.e.g., extremities sl worn.
(Old Cathay) **£37 [≃ $59]**
- The Upper Engadine. Painted by J. Hardwicke Lewis. London: A. & C. Black Colour Books, Six Shilling Series, 1907. 1st edn. 24 cold plates. Orig dec cloth, t.e.g., spine sl discold. *(Old Cathay)* **£29 [≃ $46]**
- The Upper Engadine. Painted by J. Hardwicke Lewis. London: A. & C. Black Colour Books, Six Shilling Series, 1907. 1st edn. 24 cold plates. Orig dec cloth, t.e.g., spine faded. *(Old Cathay)* **£23 [≃ $36]**

Mutsu, Iso
- Kamakura: Fact & Legend. In Memoriam J.F. Tokyo: Maruzen Co, 1918. 8vo. lv,ii,308 pp. Fldg map, num photo views. Orig green cloth gilt. *(Karmiole)* **$65 [≃ £40]**

Myer, H.
- Across East African Glaciers. An Account of the First Ascent of Kilimanjaro. London: 1891. 1st English edn. 404 pp. 3 maps, 8 photogravures, 40 ills. V faint blindstamp on title. Orig cloth.
(Trophy Room Books) **$1,250 [≃ £781]**

Myers, P.V.N.
- Remains of Lost Empires: Sketches of the Ruins of Palmyra, Nineveh, Babylon and Persepolis ... New York: Harper, 1875. 1st edn. 8vo. [xiv], 531, 2 advt pp. Frontis & other tissued plates & ills. Orig cloth gilt.
(Terramedia) **$100 [≃ £62]**

N'Zau, Bula
- Pseudonym used by Henry Bailey, q.v.

Nansen, Fridtjof
- Eskimo Life. Translated by William Archer. London: Longmans ..., 1893. 1st English edn. 8vo. xvi, 350, [24 advt] pp. 16 plates. Orig cloth gilt, trifle worn, crnrs of bds sl bumped. *(Hollett)* **£120 [≃ $192]**
- Farthest North. London: 1897. 1st edn. 2 vols. 8vo. xiv,510; x,671 pp. 4 maps, 2 frontis, 16 cold plates, 111 other plates, 92 text ills. The 4 maps detached & loosely inserted. Orig pict cloth gilt.
(Henly) **£145 [≃ $232]**
- 'Farthest North'. London: Constable, 1897. 1st edn. 2 vols. Lge 8vo. xvi,510; xvi,671 pp. 4 fldg maps, etched frontis, 16 cold plates, about 120 full page ills, num other ills in text. Orig cloth gilt, unopened, sl rubbed.
(Claude Cox) **£65 [≃ $104]**
- Farthest North. London: Constable, 1897. 1st edn in English. 2 vols. Lge 8vo. 510; 671 pp. 4 fldg maps, port frontis, 16 cold plates,

111 other plates, 92 text ills. Orig pict cloth, hinges a little loose. *(Schoyer)* **$165 [≈ £103]**
- Farthest North. New York: 1897. 1st Amer edn. 2 vols. 587; 714 pp. Fldg maps in pockets. Orig cloth.   *(Reese)* **$200 [≈ £125]**
- Farthest North ... New York: Harper, 1897. 1st Amer edn (same ills as London edn, but without an index). 2 vols. xi,587; xi,714 pp. 1 + 3 fldg maps in pockets, frontis port, 16 cold plates, 2 gravure plates, 184 text ills. Orig dec cloth, t.e.g. *(Schoyer)* **$125 [≈ £78]**
- Farthest North ... New York: Harper, 1897. 1st US edn. 2 vols. 8vo. x,[4],587; x,[2],729 pp. 4 fldg maps in pockets, num plates, some cold. Orig dec cloth, t.e.g., vol 1 sl marked.
    (High Latitude) **$90 [≈ £56]**
- Farthest North. London: Newnes, 1898. 2nd edn in English. 2 vols. 8vo. Fldg map, cold plate, port, num ills. Sm tears in map without loss. Prize calf gilt, trifle rubbed.
    (Wheldon & Wesley) **£48 [≈ $76]**
- The First Crossing of Greenland. London: Longmans, Green, 1890. 1st edn in English. 2 vols. 8vo. xxii,510; x,509 pp. 5 fldg maps, 12 plates, num text ills. Occas sl foxing. Orig silver dec cloth, spines relaid.
    (High Latitude) **$225 [≈ £140]**
- Hunting & Adventure in the Arctic. Fully Illustrated from Drawings by the Author. London: Dent, 1925. 1st edn. 8vo. 462 pp. 8 plates of maps, num ills. Orig dark grey cloth, sl rubbed.   *(Terramedia)* **$125 [≈ £78]**
- Hunting and Adventure in the Arctic. New York: Duffield, 1925. [viii],462 pp. Maps, 4 photo plates, text ills. Orig cloth. Dw torn but complete.   *(High Latitude)* **$50 [≈ £31]**
- In Northern Mists. London: Heinemann, 1911. 1st edn. 2 vols. Lge 8vo. xi, 384; vi, 416 pp. Mtd cold frontis, maps, text ills. Orig dec cloth, front hinges sl tender.
    (Parmer) **$250 [≈ £156]**
- In Northern Mists. Arctic Exploration in Early Times. New York: Stokes, 1911. 2 vols. Lge 8vo. xviii,384; xiii,420 pp. Mtd cold frontises, num maps & text ills. Orig gilt dec cloth.   *(High Latitude)* **$175 [≈ £109]**
- Through Siberia, the Land of the Future. London: Heinemann, 1914. 3 fldg maps, frontis, 59 plates. Orig dec cloth gilt, spine ends bumped.   *(John Smith)* **£60 [≈ $96]**

Naphegyi, G.
- Guardaia; or Ninety Days among the B'ni Mozab. Adventures in the Oasis of the Desert Sahara. New York & London: Putnam's & S. Low, 1871. 1st edn. 12mo. 348 pp. Frontis, engvd half-title vignette. Orig pict green cloth, sl rubbed. *(Terramedia)* **$100 [≈ £62]**

Napier, Edward Delaval Hungerford Elers
- The Life and Correspondence of Admiral Sir Charles Napier, K.C.B. London: Hurst & Blackett, 1862. 1st edn. 2 vols. 8vo. x,461; iv,415 pp. Frontis port, fldg cold map, other ills. Contemp mor gilt, spine labels, mrbld edges.   *(Terramedia)* **$200 [≈ £125]**

Napier, W.
- The Life and Opinions of Sir Charles James Napier. London: 1857. 2nd edn. 4 vols. 482; 458; 458; 432 pp. Frontis, fldg map. Orig cloth, vol 4 a little loose.
    (Trophy Room Books) **$300 [≈ £187]**

Napier, W.F.P.
- History of the War in the Peninsula ... New Edition, revised by the Author ... London: Barthes & Lowell, 1876. 6 vols. 8vo. 55 maps & plans. Contemp half calf, gilt ruled spines, contrasting gilt labels.
    (Spelman) **£180 [≈ $288]**

Narborough, John
- An Account of Several Late Voyages and Discoveries to the South and North ... Amsterdam & New York: Nico Israel, 1970. Facs of 1694 edn. 442 pp. 2 fldg maps & table, 19 plates. Orig bndg.
    (Parmer) **$110 [≈ £68]**

Narjoux, Felix
- Notes and Sketches of an Architect taken during a Journey in the Northwest of Europe. Translated from the French by John Peto. Boston: Osgood, 1877. 8vo. 442 pp. Num plates. Name stamp on title. Orig pict gilt cloth, inner hinges v sl cracked.
    (Terramedia) **$75 [≈ £46]**

Narrative ...
- A Narrative of the Cruise of the Yacht Maria ... see Davenport, A.H. & Greig, E.H.
- Narrative of the Expedition to the Baltic: with an Account of the Siege and Capitulation of the Danish Fleet. By an Officer employed in the Expedition. London: Brettell & Co ..., 1808. 1st edn. 8vo. 2 fldg cold maps (offset). Half roan, gilt spine sl worn.
    (Hannas) **£65 [≈ $104]**
- A Narrative of the Proceedings of His Majesty's Fleet in the Mediterranean ... see Mathews, Thomas.
- A Narrative of What Passed at Killalla ... see Stock, Joseph.

Nash, Wallis
- Oregon: There and Back in 1877. London: Macmillan, 1878. 1st edn. 8vo. xviii,[iv], 285,

36 ctlg pp. Dble page map, 13 ills. Orig cloth, sl worn.   *(Young's)* **£70 [≈ $112]**

Nathan, Manfred
- The Voortrekkers of South Africa. From the Earliest Times to the Foundation of the Republics. London: 1937. 427 pp. Ills. Internal ex-lib labels. Orig green cloth gilt.
    (Terramedia) **$30 [≈ £18]**

Nattes, John Claude
- See Fittler, James & Nattes, J.C.

Naval Intelligence Handbook
- Indo-China. Naval Intelligence Division. London: Geographical Handbook Series, 1943. xiii,535 pp. Maps (1 fldg in pocket), plates, diags. Orig cloth. *(Lyon)* **£45 [≈ $72]**

Navarrete, Domingo
- The Travels and Controversies of Friar Domingo Navarrete 1618-86. Cambridge: Hakluyt Society, 1960. 8vo. 475 pp. 18 plates & sketch maps. Orig blue cloth gilt.
    (Parmer) **$60 [≈ £37]**

The Navigator ...
- The Navigator, Containing Directions for Navigating the Monongahela ... see Cramer, Zadok.

Naville, Edouard
- Ahnas El Medineh (Heracleopolis Magna). With 'The Tomb of Paheri at El Kab' ... London: Egypt Exploration Fund 11th Memoir, 1894. 1st edn. 2 parts in one vol. Folio. 39, 1; vi,34,2 pp. 27 plates. Orig cloth & bds, ex-lib, rubbed.
    (Terramedia) **$50 [≈ £31]**
- Bubastis, 1887-1889. London: Egypt Exploration Fund, Memoir 8, 1891. 1st edn. Folio. v,71 pp. 54 plates. Orig cloth & bds, ex-lib, sl soiled, sl chipped.
    (Terramedia) **$75 [≈ £46]**
- The Festival Hall of Osorkon II, in the Great Temple of Bubastis (1887-1889). London: Egypt Exploration Fund, 1892. 1st edn. Folio. vi,40 pp. 38 plates. Orig cloth & bds, ex lib, cvrs rubbed, spine ends chipped.
    (Terramedia) **$75 [≈ £46]**
- Goshen and the Shrine of Saft El Henneh, 1885. London: Fourth [actually 5th] Memoir of the Egypt Exploration Fund, 1887. 1st edn. Folio. 25,1 pp. 11 plates (6 fldg). Orig cloth & bds, ex-lib, rubbed.
    (Terramedia) **$50 [≈ £31]**
- The Mound of the Jew and the City of Onias ... London: Egypt Exploration Fund Memoir VII, 1890. Folio. vi,76 pp. Frontis, 26 plates.

Ex-lib. Orig cloth & ptd bds, rubbed.
    (Terramedia) **$75 [≈ £46]**
- The Store-City of Pythom and the Route of the Exodus. London: Egypt Exploration Fund [1st] Memoir, 1885. 1st edn. Folio. viii,31,1 pp. 2 maps, 12 plates. Orig cloth & bds, bndg much browned & broken at spine.
    (Terramedia) **$50 [≈ £31]**
- The Temple of Deir El Bahari. London: Egypt Exploration Fund Memoirs 13, 14, 16, 19, 27, 29, 1894-1908. 1st edn. 6 vols. Lge folio. 174 plates. Ex-lib (external labels only). Orig cloth & ptd bds.
    (Terramedia) **$1,200 [≈ £750]**
- The Temple of Deir El Bahari: Its Plain, its Founders, and its Explorers. Introductory Memoir. London: Egypt Exploration Fund, 12th Memoir, 1894. Folio. vi,[1],31 pp. 14 plates. Orig cloth & bds, front cvr spotted.
    (Terramedia) **$75 [≈ £46]**
- The XIIth Dynasty Temple at Deir El-Bahri. London: Egypt Exploration Fund Memoirs 28, 30 & 32, 1907-13. 3 vols. Folio. Plates & plans, Orig cloth & bds, ex-lib with external labels only.   *(Terramedia)* **$200 [≈ £125]**

Naville, Edouard & Peet, T.E.
- The Cemeteries of Abydos. London: Egypt Exploration Fund, Memoirs 33-35, 1914-14-13. 3 vols. Folio. xii,54; xvi,133; xi,54 pp. 86 plates. Orig bndgs, ex-lib, sl soiled.   *(Terramedia)* **$200 [≈ £125]**

Neale, J.M.
- Notes, Ecclesiological & Picturesque, on Dalmatia, Croatia, Istria, Styria, with a Visit to Montenegro. London: J.T. Hayes, 1861. Sm 8vo. viii,208 pp. Fldg frontis, line ills. Orig purple cloth, spine sl mottled.
    (Piccadilly) **£24 [≈ $38]**

Neale, James
- The Abbey Church of Saint Alban, Hertfordshire. London: [1878]. Lge folio. Chromolitho title, x,36 pp. 59 plates. Orig mor backed cloth, rubbed, hd of spine worn, contents loose due to decay of gutta-percha bndg.   *(Upcroft)* **£40 [≈ $64]**

Necker De Saussure, L.A.
- Travels in Scotland; Descriptive of the State of Manners, Literature, and Science. London: for Sir Richard Phillips, 1821. 1st English edn. 8vo. viii,112 pp. Rec paper cvrd bds.
    (Young's) **£38 [≈ $60]**

Negro Slavery ...
- Negro Slavery; or, a View of some of the more Prominent Features of that State of Society ...

in the United States of America and in the Colonies of the West Indies, especially in Jamaica. London: 4th edn. 1824. [viii],92 pp. Title soiled. Sl foxing. Wraps.
(Reese) **$100 [≃ £62]**

Nesbitt, Frances E.
- Algeria and Tunis Painted and Described. London: Black, 1904. 1st edn. 8vo. ix,229,[2 advt] pp. Fldg map, 70 cold plates. Orig cloth, t.e.g., sl rubbed.
(Worldwide Antiqu'n) **$45 [≃ £28]**

Neufeld, Charles
- A Prisoner of the Khaleefa. Twelve Years' Captivity at Omdurman. New York & London: Putnam's & Chapman & Hall, 1899. 3rd edn. 8vo. xiv,365 pp. Num plates & map & plans. Orig cloth.
(Terramedia) **$100 [≃ £62]**

Neumann, C.F. (translator)
- The History of Vartan, and of the Battle of the Armenians ... by Elisaeus, Bishop of the Arnadunians. Translated from the Armenian. London: Oriental Translation Fund, 1830. 4to. xxiv,111 pp, inc engvd pres leaf. Mod half calf.
(Farahar) **£165 [≃ $264]**

Neve, A.
- Tourist's Guide to Kashmir, Ladakh, Skardo, Etc. London: 1927. 8vo. Fldg map. Orig cvrs.
(Grayling) **£20 [≃ $32]**

Nevius, Helen S.C.
- Our Life in China. New York: Carter & Bros, 1869. vi,504 pp. Frontis, 2 plates. Orig cloth, spine sl faded, sl rubbed, externally unmarked ex-lib.
(Worldwide Antiqu'n) **$65 [≃ £40]**

Nevius, John L.
- China and the Chinese. A General Description of the Country and its Inhabitants ... New York: Harper, 1869. 1st edn. Sm 8vo. 456 pp. Fldg map, ills. Orig cloth, gilt spine, spine faded & extremities sl chipped.
(Karmiole) **$50 [≃ £31]**

New ...
- The New Act of Assembly of the Island of Jamaica ... commonly called, The New Consolidated Act ... Published for the Use of both Houses of Parliament by Stephen Fuller, Esq., Agent for Jamaica. London: 1789. vii,17 pp. Bds.
(Reese) **£600 [≃ $375]**
- The New Brighton Guide ... see Williams, John.
- A New Pocket Companion for Oxford: or, Guide through the University ... New

Edition. Oxford: J. Cooke, 1807. 12mo. Fldg frontis plan, 8 plates. Some browning. Orig blue grey wraps, spine frayed with some loss at ends, crnrs sl dogeared.
(Clark) **£36 [≃ $57]**
- The New State of England ... see Miege, Guy.
- New Travels in the United States ... see Brissot de Warville, Jacques Pierre.
- A New Voyage round the World ... see Defoe, Daniel.

Newcomb, Raymond L. (ed.)
- Our Lost Explorers: The Narrative of the Jeannette Arctic Expedition, as related by the Survivors, and in the Records and Last Journals of Lieut. De Long. Hartford & San Francisco: 1882. 479 pp. Port, plates, ills. Sl foxing. Orig pict gilt cloth, sl worn.
(Reese) **$150 [≃ £93]**

Newell, R.H.
- Letters on the Scenery of Wales ... Instructions to Pedestrian Tourists. London: Baldwin, Cradock & Joy, 1821. 8vo. Fldg frontis, 10 plates (5 cold aquatints, 5 cold etchings). Mod qtr calf.
(Waterfield's) **£225 [≃ $360]**

Newenham, Thomas
- A View of the Natural, Political and Commercial Circumstances of Ireland. London: Cadell & Davies, 1809. 1st edn. 4to. Fldg map. 30 statistical appendices. Mod half calf, uncut.
(Falkner) **£260 [≃ $416]**

Newman, E.M.
- Seeing Egypt and the Holy Land. New York: Funk & Wagnalls, 1928. 8vo. 394 pp. Cold map, over 300 plates & ills. Orig pict gilt green cloth.
(Terramedia) **$30 [≃ £18]**

Newman, Francis William
- Personal Narrative, in Letters, principally from Turkey, in the years 1830-3. London: Holyoake & Co, 1856. 1st edn. 8vo. iv, 117 pp. Occas faint lib stamp. Contemp half calf, gilt spine, sl rubbed.
(Burmester) **£150 [≃ $240]**

Newman, John B.
- Texas and Mexico in 1846 ... New York: J.K. Wellman, 1846. 1st edn. 32 pp. As usual without the map. Sewn.
(Jenkins) **$1,250 [≃ £781]**

Newman, John P.
- The Thrones and Palaces of Babylon and Nineveh from Sea to Sea. A Thousand Miles

on Horseback. New York: Harper, 1876. 1st edn. 8vo. 455,12 advt pp. Num ills. Orig cloth, sl rubbed, rebacked, good ex-lib.
(Worldwide Antiqu'n) **$48 [≈ £30]**

Newth, J.D.
- Austria. Painted by E. Harrison Compton. London: A. & C. Black, 1931. 1st edn. Map, 24 cold plates. Orig cloth, some fading.
(Old Cathay) **£13 [≈ $20]**

Newton, C.T.
- A History of Discoveries at Halicarnassus, Cnidus and Branchidae, being the results of an Expedition sent to Asia Minor by H.M. Government in 1856. London: 1862. Atlas vol only. Lge folio. Litho title, 97 litho plates. Some foxing. Orig cloth, new mor spine.
(Frew Mackenzie) **£1,300 [≈ $2,080]**
- Travels & Discoveries in the Levant. London: Day & Son, 1865. 1st edn. 2 vols. Imperial 8vo. xvi,360; xvi,275 pp. 9 maps, 31 plates (of 32, lacks plate 15 vol 1), 38 text ills. Orig green cloth, gilt spines.
(Gough) **£120 [≈ $192]**

Nicholson, H. Whalley
- From Sword to Share; or a Fortune in Five Years at Hawaii. London: 1881. 348 pp. Fldg map, 9 mtd woodburytype photos. Three qtr mor, front bd detached.
(Reese) **$425 [≈ £265]**

Nicholson, J. & Burn, R.
- The History and Antiquities of the Counties of Westmorland and Cumberland ... London: Strahan & Cadell, 1777. 1st edn. 2 vols. 4to. cxxxiv,630; 615,[8] pp. 2 lge fldg maps. Tree calf gilt, a little rubbed & worn, recased.
(Hollett) **£350 [≈ $560]**

Nicolay, C.G., et al.
- A Manual of Geographic Science, Mathematical, Physical, Historical, and Descriptive. London: John Parker ..., 1859. 1st edn. 8vo. xvi,445, xii,615 pp. Text diags. Orig cloth, sl rubbed. *(Young's)* **£35 [≈ $56]**

Nicolay, Nicholas
- The Navigations, Peregrinations and Voyages, made into Turkie ... Translated out of French by T. Washington ... London: Thomas Dawson, 1585. 1st edn in English. Sm 8vo. 166 ff. 60 engvd plates. Trimmed. 19th c elab gilt mor, a.e.g., labels sl chipped.
(Terramedia) **$2,500 [≈ £1,562]**

Nicoll, James
- An Historical and Descriptive Account of Iceland, Greenland, and the Faroe Islands ...

Second Edition. Edinburgh: 1841. Sm 8vo. Addtnl engvd title, 2 maps, 2 plates. Orig cloth, uncut. Sometimes attrib to Bishop Michael Russell. *(Hannas)* **£35 [≈ $56]**
- An Historical and Descriptive Account of Iceland, Greenland, and the Faroe Islands ... New York: Harper, Family Library, 1841. 1st Amer edn. 12mo. Addtnl engvd title, 2 maps, 1 plate in collation. Orig cloth, sl worn.
(Hannas) **£40 [≈ $64]**

Nicoll, M.J.
- Three Voyages of a Naturalist ... London & New York: Witherby; Scribner's, 1908. 8vo. xxvi, 246 pp. 4 sketch maps, 56 plates, text ills. Endpapers sl foxed. Orig blue cloth, minor shelfwear. *(Parmer)* **$75 [≈ £46]**
- Three Voyages of a Naturalist. London: 1909. 2nd edn. 8vo. xxx,246 pp. 4 sketch maps, 56 plates, text figs. Orig cloth, trifle used. *(Wheldon & Wesley)* **£30 [≈ $48]**

Nicolson, Joseph & Burn, Richard
- The History and Antiquities of the Counties of Westmorland and Cumberland. London: 1777. 1st edn. 2 vols. 4to. 2 maps. Later half calf, sl rubbed. *(Robertshaw)* **£175 [≈ $280]**

Niedieck, P.
- With Rifle in Five Continents. London: Rowland Ward, 1908. 426 pp. Ills. Orig bndg. *(Trophy Room Books)* **$350 [≈ £218]**

Nightingale, Joseph
- London and Middlesex; or, an Historical, Commercial, & Descriptive Survey ... Vol III. Part II. containing the History and Description of the City and Liberty of Westminster. London: J. Harris ..., 1819. 8vo. 40 plates. Mod half calf.
(Waterfield's) **£90 [≈ $144]**

Nile Notes of a Howadji ...
- See Curtis, George William.

Niles, G.G.
- Bog-Trotting for Orchids. New York: 1904. 8vo. xvi,310 pp. 24 cold & 46 plain plates. Orig cloth. *(Wheldon & Wesley)* **£35 [≈ $56]**

Niles, John Milton
- A View of South-America and Mexico, comprising their History, their Political Condition, Geography ... New York: 1825. 2 vols in one. iv,223; 242 pp. Port. Light to moderate foxing. Contemp mottled calf, gilt spine, scuffed, sm chip at spine.
(Reese) **$100 [≈ £62]**

Nimmo, Joseph
- Report on the Internal Commerce of the U.S. ... The Range and Ranch Cattle Industry of Texas. Washington: 1885. 562 pp. 5 lge fldg maps. Tables. Orig (US Govt Doc) sheep, mor labels.   *(Jenkins)* **$1,500 [≈ £937]**

Noble, J.
- The Cape and South Africa. Cape Town: J.C. Juta, 1878. 12mo. xvi,218,20 pp. Advts. Map. Orig ptd bds, worn.
          (Berkelouw) **$150 [≈ £93]**

Noble, Louis Legrand
- After Icebergs with a Painter: A Summer Voyage to Labrador and around Newfoundland. New York: 1861. 336 pp. 6 tinted litho plates. Orig cloth, spine sunned, hd of spine worn.   *(Reese)* **$850 [≈ £531]**
- After Icebergs with a Painter: A Summer Voyage to Labrador and around Newfoundland. New York: 1861. 1st edn. 336 pp. 6 tinted litho plates by Frederick Church. Orig cloth. *(Jenkins)* **$600 [≈ £375]**

Noel, Baptist W.
- Notes of a Tour in Switzerland in the Summer of 1847. London: James Nisbet, 1848. 1st edn. 8vo. viii,308 pp. 6 plates. Occas sl foxing; label removed from pastedown. Orig cloth gilt extra, spine faded, edges trifle rubbed.   *(Hollett)* **£75 [≈ $120]**

Noel, Gerard T.
- Arvendel; or, Sketches in Italy and Switzerland ... London: James Nisbet ..., 1826. Only edn. 8vo. [viii],123 pp. Orig ptd bds, uncut, spine reprd.   *(Young's)* **£75 [≈ $120]**

Nohara, Komakichi
- The True Face of Japan: A Japanese on Japan. London: 1936. 1st English edn. 8vo. 288 pp. 25 photo ills. Some foxing. Orig cloth, dust marked.
          (Bow Windows) **£28 [≈ $44]**

Nolan, E.H.
- The Illustrated History of the British Empire in India and the East ... London: [1859?]. 2 vols. Thick 4to. viii, viii, 804; [6], 772 pp. Engvd titles, ports, num plates & maps (some tinted). Occas foxing. Three qtr calf, some wear to extremities.   *(Reese)* **$150 [≈ £93]**

Nolhac, Pierre de
- Versailles and the Trianons.. London: Heinemann, 1906. One of 100, sgnd. 55 mtd cold plates. Orig vellum gilt, a little marked & bowed.   *(Gough)* **£125 [≈ $200]**

Nolte, Vincent
- Fifty Years in Both Hemispheres or, Reminiscences of the Life of a Former Merchant. New York: 1854. 1st edn in English. xxii,[11]-484 pp. Three qtr pebbled calf, extremities rubbed. *(Reese)* **$150 [≈ £93]**

Norden, Hermann
- White & Black in East Africa. A Record of Travel & Observations in Two African Crown Colonies. Boston: Small Maynard & Co, 1924. Thick paper. 8vo. 304 pp. Fldg map, num plates. Orig green cloth, spine lettering sl faded. *(Terramedia)* **$75 [≈ £46]**

Nordhoff, Charles
- Northern California, Oregon, and the Sandwich Islands. New York: Harper, 1874. 1st edn. 256 pp. Map, port, num ills. Orig cloth, minor shelfwear.
          (Parmer) **$135 [≈ £84]**
- Peninsular California. Some Account ... chiefly of the Northern Half of Lower California. New York: Harper, 1888. 1st edn. 130,6 pp. 2 maps, frontis, 11 plates. Orig cloth gilt, hinges starting, crnrs bumped.
          (Berkelouw) **$75 [≈ £46]**

Norie, John William
- New and Extensive Sailing Directions for the Navigation of the North Sea ... Seventh Edition ... augmented ... by J.S. Hobbs. London: Charles Wilson, 1846. 8vo. xvi,202, [2] pp. Mod bds, orig wraps with title label bound in.   *(Hannas)* **£90 [≈ $144]**

Norman, Henry
- All the Russias. Travels and Studies in Contemporary European Russia, Finland, Siberia, the Caucasus and Central Asia. London: Heinemann, 1902. 1st edn. 8vo. xvi, 476 pp. Fldg map, frontis, num plates. Orig cloth, t.e.g.   *(Terramedia)* **$100 [≈ £62]**
- The Peoples and Politics of the Far East. Travels and Studies ... London: Fisher Unwin, 1895. 1st edn. 8vo. xvi,608 pp, advt leaf. Cold frontis, 4 maps, 48 plates (occas sl foxing). Orig cloth gilt, t.e.g.
          (Fenning) **£55 [≈ $88]**

Norman, Philip
- London Vanished and Vanishing. London: A. & C. Black Colour Books, 1905. One of 250, sgnd by Norman. 75 cold plates. Orig cloth, t.e.g., bds discold & sl stained & worn, esp spine.   *(Old Cathay)* **£150 [≈ $240]**
- London Vanished and Vanishing. London: A. & C. Black Colour Books, Twenty Shilling Series, 1905. 1st edn. Cold plates. Orig dec

cloth, wear to spine ends, 1 crnr bruised.
(Old Cathay) £69 [≈ $110]

North, Allan, publisher
- Middlesex, Biographical and Pictorial. Published Only for Subscribers: 1907. 4to. Unpaginated. Num ills. Orig qtr vellum & cloth, a.e.g. *(Coombes)* £20 [≈ $32]

North, F.J., et al.
- Snowdonia, the National Park of North Wales. London: New Naturalist, 1949. 1st edn. 8vo. xviii,469 pp. 6 maps, 40 cold & 32 plain plates, 25 diags. Orig cloth, sl faded. Dw. *(Wheldon & Wesley)* £28 [≈ $44]

Northall, John
- Travels through Italy. Containing New and Curious Observations on that Country ... London: Hooper, 1766. 1st edn. 8vo. [viii], 476, [xii] pp. Fldg frontis map (outer marg dusty), 5 fldg plates. A few plate & page edges a little dusty. Rec half calf.
(Clark) £140 [≈ $224]

The Northern Traveller ...
- See Disturnell, John.

Northey, W. & Morris, C.
- The Ghurkas. Their Manners, Customs, Country. With a Foreword by C.G. Bruce. London: 1928. 282 pp. Fldg map, ills. Orig cloth. *(Trophy Room Books)* $175 [≈ £109]

Northrop, Henry Davenport
- The Flowery Kingdom and the Land of the Mikado. Or China, Japan and Corea. Phila: Bell, [1894]. 4to. [xvi],624 pp, in dble column. Num plates & ills. Orig pict cloth.
(Terramedia) $40 [≈ £25]

Notes and Reflections ...
- Notes and Reflections during a Ramble in Germany ... see Sherer, J. Moyle.

Nourse, Charles Francis
- Narrative of the Second Arctic Expedition made by Charles F. Hall ... see Hall, Charles Francis.

O'Bryen, Denis
- A View of the Present State of Ireland, with an Account of the Origin and Progress of the Disturbances in that Country; and a Narrative of Facts, addressed to the People of England. By an Observer. London: J.S. Jordan, 1797. 41 pp. Disbound. *(Jarndyce)* £65 [≈ $104]

O'Connor, Jack
- Game in the Desert. Illustrated by T.I. Harter. New York: 1939. 1st edn. One of 950. 4to. Cold frontis, num other plates. Orig green imitation snakeskin cloth.
(Terramedia) $600 [≈ £375]

O'Donovan, E.
- The Merv Oasis. Travels and Adventures East of the Caspian During the Years 1879-80-81 including Five Months' Residence among the Tekkes of Merv. New York: 1883. 1st Amer edn. 2 vols. 502; 500 pp. Maps (1 fldg), ills. Orig cloth.
(Trophy Room Books) $300 [≈ £187]
- The Merv Oasis. Travels and Adventures East of the Caspian During the Years 1879-80-81, including Five Months' Residence among the Tekkes of Merv. New York: Putnam, 1883. 1st Amer edn. 2 vols. 8vo. Fldg map in pocket, maps, facs. Orig cloth, sl worn ex-lib.
(Worldwide Antiqu'n) $125 [≈ £78]

O'Reilly, Bernard
- Greenland, and Adjacent Seas, and the North-West Passage to the Pacific Ocean, illustrated in a Voyage to Davis's Strait, during the Summer of 1817. London: 1818. 1st edn. 4to. 3 maps, 18 plates (sm lib stamp in crnr). Final advt leaf. Contemp calf, rebacked. *(Hannas)* £160 [≈ $256]
- Greenland, the Adjacent Seas, and the Northwest Passage to the Pacific Ocean, illustrated in a Voyage to Davis's Strait, during the Summer of 1817. New York: 1818. 1st Amer edn. 8vo. 3 fldg maps (some splits at folds). Some foxing. Contemp 3/4 calf, rubbed, jnts worn. *(Parmer)* $225 [≈ £140]

O'Rell, Max
- John Bull & Co. The Great Colonial Branches of the Firm ... London: 1894. 322 pp. Frontis, ills. Orig pict cloth.
(Reese) $100 [≈ £62]

O'Sullivan, Florence
- The History of Kinsale [Co. Cork]. Dublin: J. Duffy, 1916. 1st edn. 8vo. x,240 pp. 3 lge fldg maps, 7 plates. Portion of flyleaf torn away. Orig cloth gilt. *(Fenning)* £65 [≈ $104]

Oakes, William
- Scenery of the White Mountains: with Sixteen Plates, from the Drawings of Isaac Sprague. Boston: Crosby & Nichols, [1848]. 1st (only) edn. Folio. The plates foxed, 1 or 2 heavily. Orig cloth, spine & crnrs worn.
(M & S Rare Books) $425 [≈ £265]

Oates, Frank
- Matabeleland and the Victoria Falls. A Naturalist's Wanderings in the Interior of South Africa. London: Kegan Paul, 1881. 1st edn. xliii,383,32 advt pp. Half-title. Port, 6 chromolithos, 9 cold lithos, 4 fldg maps, 3 plates. Orig pict cloth gilt, recased.
(Hollett) **£275 [≃ $440]**
- Matabeleland and the Victoria Falls. A Naturalist's Wanderings in the Interior of South Africa. London: 1889. 2nd edn. 383 pp. Num cold & b/w ills. Orig cloth. Pres copy from the author's daughter.
(Trophy Room Books) **$450 [≃ £281]**

Ober, Frederick A.
- Camps in the Caribbees: The Adventures of a Naturalist in the Lesser Antilles. Edinburgh: David Douglas, 1880. 1st edn. 8vo. xviii, 366 pp. Frontis, num plates & ills. Contemp half mor, gilt spine, by George Quinton, sl rubbed.
(Terramedia) **$100 [≃ £62]**
- A Guide to the West Indies and Bermudas. New York: 1908. 1st edn. ix,522 pp. 5 fldg maps, frontis, plates. Orig cloth gilt.
(Reese) **$90 [≃ £56]**

An Observer in the Near East ...
- An Observer in the Near East. Illustrated by Photographs by the Author and Princess Xenia of Montenegro. London: Eveleigh Nash, 1907. 8vo. 309 pp. Fldg map, num ills. Orig green cloth, rubbed, sm nick in spine.
(Piccadilly) **£32 [≃ $51]**

Ockley, Simon
- The Conquest of Syria, Persia, and Aegypt, by the Saracens ... London: R. Knaplock ..., 1708. 1st edn. 8vo. xxiv,[iv], 391,[xix] pp. Occas spotting & marg browning. Rebound in contemp style panelled calf. A 2nd vol was publ in 1718.
(Frew Mackenzie) **£225 [≃ $360]**

Odenheimer, W.H.
- Jerusalem and its Vicinity. A Series of Lectures on the Sacred Localities ... Philadelphia: Butler & Co, 1855. 8vo. vii, 218, advt pp. Frontis, 7 plates (foxed). Contemp calf, gilt label, dec spine, a.e.g.
(Terramedia) **$100 [≃ £62]**

Ogden, Peter Skene
- See Finlayson, Duncan.

Ogilby, John & Morgan, William
- Ogilby's and Morgan's Pocket-Book of the Roads ... The Eleventh Edition, Corrected

and Improved ... London: for J. Brotherton ..., 1752. 12mo. [40],17-166,[2 blank] pp. Lge fldg map (tear, no loss). Contemp gilt ruled calf.
(Fenning) **£48.50 [≃ $78]**
- The Traveller's Pocket-Book; or, Ogilby and Morgan's Book of the Roads Improved and Amended ... London: J. Brotherton ..., 1770. 5th edn. Sm sq 8vo. vi,315 pp. 1 or 2 sm tears, occas sl soiling. Old calf, spine ends chipped, hinges tender, sl shaken.
(Hollett) **£35 [≃ $56]**

Ogilvy, James S.
- A Pilgrimage in Surrey. London: 1914. 2 vols. 4to. xii,324; xi,481 pp. 94 cold plates. 1st few ff vol 1 dampstained. Orig cloth, dampmarked.
(Coombes) **£18 [≃ $28]**

Olafsen & Povelsen
- Travels in Iceland: performed by order of His Danish Majesty ... London: Richard Phillips, 1805. 162 pp. Fldg frontis map, 3 plates. Occas trace of foxing. Mod half cloth, t.e.g.
(Reese) **$100 [≃ £62]**

'An Old Bushman'
- See Wheelright, H.W.

Old New Zealand ...
- See Maning, Frederick Edward.

'The Old Shekarry'
- See Leveson, H.A.

Oldfield, Thomas Hinton Burley
- An Entire and Complete History, Political and Personal of the Boroughs of Great Britain [together with the Cinque Ports]. London: for G. Riley ..., 1792. 1st edn. 3 vols. 8vo. Half-title vol 1, errata leaf vol 2. Frontis in vols 2 & 3. Early calf gilt, sl rubbed.
(Hannas) **£250 [≃ $400]**
- An Entire and Complete History, Political and Personal of the Boroughs of Great Britain ... London: for G. Riley ..., 1792. 1st edn. 3 vols. 8vo. Half-titles. Orig bds, uncut, rebacked.
(Young's) **£165 [≃ $264]**

Oliphant, Laurence
- Haifa or Life in Modern Palestine. Edited by Charles A. Dana. New York: Harper, 1887. 1st edn. 8vo. vi,369 pp. Orig cloth, sl rubbed, spine ends frayed, lib number on spine.
(Worldwide Antiqu'n) **$75 [≃ £46]**
- Haifa, or Life in Modern Palestine. Edited by Charles A. Dana. New York: Harper, 1887. 1st edn. Sm 8vo. vi,369,6 advt pp. Perf lib stamp. Orig brown cloth gilt, lib labels clumsily removed. *(Terramedia)* **$35 [≃ £21]**

- Minnesota and the Far West. London: William Blackwood & Sons, 1855. 8vo. xiii, [i],306,advt pp. Half-title. Tinted frontis, fldg map, 14 ills. Orig cloth gilt, recased, new endpapers. *(Hollett)* £85 [≈ $136]
- Narrative of the Earl of Elgin's Mission to China and Japan in the Years 1857, 58, 59. Edinburgh: Blackwood, 1859. 1st edn. 2 vols. 8vo. xiv,492,16 advt; xi,496 pp. 5 maps, 20 cold plates. Some foxing. Orig blue pict cloth, rubbed. *(Adelson)* $425 [≈ £265]
- Narrative of the Earl of Elgin's Mission to China & Japan in the Years 1857, '58, '59. Edinburgh: Blackwood, 1859. 2 vols. 8vo. xiii, 492; xi,496 pp. Maps, cold lithos, w'engvs. Orig calf, gilt spines, reprd. *(Lyon)* £275 [≈ $440]
- Narrative of the Earl of Elgin's Mission to China and Japan in the Years 1857, '58, '59. New York: Harper & Bros, 1860. 1st US edn. 8vo. xvi,645 pp. Num plates (1 cold), num text ills. V sl foxed. Orig cloth, sl rubbed, externally unmarked ex-lib.
(Worldwide Antiqu'n) $175 [≈ £109]
- The Russian Shores of the Black Sea ... London: Wm. Blackwood & Sons, 1853. 2nd edn, rvsd & enlgd. 8vo. xv,380,16 advt pp. 2 maps (1 lge fldg), 33 tinted lithos. A few spots. Orig cloth gilt, new endpapers.
(Hollett) £65 [≈ $104]

Oliphant, Margaret
- Jerusalem. Its History and Hope. London: Macmillan, 1891. 1st edn. 8vo. xxiii,515 pp. Num plates & ills. Orig cloth, edges sl rubbed. *(Worldwide Antiqu'n)* $65 [≈ £40]

Ollier, Edmund
- Cassell's Illustrated History of the Russo-Turkish War. London, Paris & New York: [ca 1879-80]. 2 vols. Lge 4to. 576; 583 pp. Num plates, maps, ills. Contemp red qtr mor, mrbld bds, moderately rubbed.
(Terramedia) $50 [≈ £31]

Oman, Charles
- Castles. London: GWR, 1926. 1st edn. Lge 8vo. xii,232 pp. 2 maps (1 in pocket), 2 cold plates, over 170 other ills. A few sl marks. Orig linen backed bds.
(Bow Windows) £24 [≈ $38]

Oman, J. Campbell
- The Brahmans, Theists and Muslims of India. Studies of Goddess-Worship in Bengal ... Curious Festivals, Ceremonies and Faquirs. London: Fisher Unwin, 1907. 1st edn. 8vo. xv,342 pp. Num plates. Orig pict maroon cloth. *(Terramedia)* $100 [≈ £62]

Orient Line Guide ...
- See Loftie, William J.

Orr, C.W.J.
- The Making of Northern Nigeria. London: Macmillan, 1911. 1st edn. 8vo. 306 pp. 4 maps. Rec half cloth.
(Terramedia) $40 [≈ £25]

Orton, James
- The Andes and the Amazon; or, Across the Continent of South America. With a New Map of Equatorial America ... New York: Harper, 1870. Sm 8vo. 356 pp. Num ills. 3 pp sl discold by newspaper clippings laid in. Orig green cloth gilt, spine extremities sl rubbed. *(Karmiole)* $50 [≈ £31]

Osborn, Chase S.
- The Andean Land. Chicago: McLurg, 1909. 1st edn. 2 vols. 8vo. xv,312; ix,331 pp. Num photo plates. Orig pict blue cloth, photo onlay, sl rubbed. *(Terramedia)* $60 [≈ £37]

Osborn, Henry S.
- Palestine Past and Present, with Biblical, Literary and Scientific Notices. Philadelphia: James Callen & Son, 1859. 1st edn. Lge 8vo. [viii],600 pp. 2 lge fldg maps, num plates & ills, inc 6 cold plates. Orig maroon cloth, spine sunned & cracked at 1 crnr.
(Terramedia) $100 [≈ £62]

Osborn, Sherard
- The Discovery of the North-West Passage ... see M'Clure, Robert.
- My Journal in Malayan Waters; or, the Blockade of Quedah. Second Edition. London: Routledge ..., 1860. Sm 8vo. xvi,360 pp. Fldg cold map, 4 tinted lithos. Sgntrs pulled. Orig purple cloth, spine sunned, backstrip damaged. *(Schoyer)* $115 [≈ £71]
- Stray Leaves from an Arctic Journal; or, Eighteen Months in the Polar Regions in Search of Sir John Franklin's Expedition ... New York: Putnam, 1852. 1st US edn. 12mo. 216 pp. Sev sm text ills. Orig cloth, faded. *(High Latitude)* $60 [≈ £37]

Ossendowski, Ferdinand
- Man and Mystery in Asia. In Collaboration with Lewis Stanton Palen. New York: Dutton, 1924. 1st edn in English. xvi, 343 pp. Frontis, endpaper maps. Orig cloth, spine faded, light stain on cvr.
(Wreden) $45 [≈ £28]

Oswald, Elizabeth Jane
- By fell and Fjord, or, Scenes and Studies in

Iceland. Edinburgh: Blackwood, 1882. 1st edn. 8vo. Errata slip. Fldg map, text ills. Orig dec cloth, uncut.   *(Hannas)* **£75 [≈$120]**

Oswald, Felix
- Alone in the Sleeping Sickness Country. London: Kegan Paul, 1915. 8vo. xii,219 pp. Fldg cold map, plates. Orig red cloth gilt.
    (Karmiole) **$65 [≈£40]**
- Alone in the Sleeping-Sickness Country. London: Kegan Paul, 1923. 2nd imp. 8vo. xii, 219 pp. Frontis with fldg cold map & over 70 plates. Cloth.   *(Terramedia)* **$30 [≈£18]**

Oswell, William Cotton
- William Cotton Oswell: Hunter and Explorer. Introduction by F. Galton. London: 1910. 2 vols. 289; 267 pp. Maps, ills. Orig bndg.
    (Trophy Room Books) **$1,000 [≈£625]**

Otley, Jonathan
- A Concise Description of the English Lakes ... Keswick: 1823. 12mo. 130 pp. Errata pasted inside rear cvr. Fldg cold frontis map (2 reprs to fold on verso). Contemp three qtr calf, gilt spine, edgeworn & rubbed.
    (Reese) **$85 [≈£53]**

Otter, William
- The Life and Remains of the Rev. E.D. Clarke, Professor of Mineralogy in the University of Cambridge. London: 1824. 4to. xii,670 pp. frontis. Frontis & title foxed & browned, other pp lightly spotted. New qtr calf gilt.   *(Baldwin)* **£75 [≈$120]**

Ottley, W.J.
- With Mounted Infantry in Tibet. London: Smith Elder, 1906. 8vo. xiii,275,4 advt pp. Frontis, 47 ills, plans. Orig cloth, faded & stained. *(Bates & Hindmarch)* **£135 [≈$216]**

Ouchterlony, John
- The Chinese War: An Account of all the Operations of the British Forces from the Commencement to the Treaty of Nanking. London: Saunders & Otley, 1844. xx,522 pp. 53 ills. Rebound in half leather.
    (Lyon) **£125 [≈$200]**

Overbury, Sir Thomas, the elder
- His Observations on His Travailes upon the State of the xvii Provinces as they stood Anno Dom. 1609. The Treatie of Peace being then on foote. [London]: 1626. 1st edn. 4to. [2],28 pp. Minute hole in 1 leaf. Mod half calf. STC 18903.   *(Hannas)* **£230 [≈$368]**

Owen, C.H.
- Sketches in the Crimea, taken during the Late War ... London: 1856. Oblong folio. Title, 5 ff, bearing 8 images in chromolitho, inc title. Occas sl foxing. Orig half calf & gilt cloth, edgeworn, spine relaid, new endpapers.
    (Reese) **$2,000 [≈£1,250]**

Owen, D,J,
- The Port of London Yesterday and Today. A History, with a Survey of the Docks ... London: PLA, 1927. 4to. 106 pp. Plans, ills. Orig bndg.   *(Book House)* **£25 [≈$40]**

Owen, David D.
- Report of a Geological Survey of Wisconsin, Iowa, and Minnesota; and incidentally of a Portion of Nebraska Territory. Philadelphia: Lippincott, 1852. 1st edn. Folio. 638,[1] pp. Sev lge fldg cold maps, 27 plates, ills.
    (Jenkins) **$275 [≈£171]**

Owen, J.
- Travels into Different Parts of Europe in the Years 1791 and 1792, with Familiar Remarks on Places Men and Manners. London: 1796. 1st edn. 2 vols. 8vo. Errata leaf. Tree calf.
    (Henly) **£60 [≈$96]**

Owen, John & Bowen, Emanuel
- Britannia Depicta or Ogilby Improv'd ... London: Tho. Bowles, 1730. 4th edn. Sm 4to. [iii], 273 pp. Engvd title, 273 maps engvd on both sides of the leaf. Sl dampstain affecting endpapers & foredge but only 1 or 2 maps. Contemp calf, rebacked, crnrs bumped.
    (Frew Mackenzie) **£685 [≈$1,096]**

Pacific Coast Pilot ...
- See Dall, William H.

Page, F.B.
- Prairiedom: Rambles and Scrambles in Texas or New Estremadura, By a Suthron. New York: Paine & Burgess, 1845. 1st edn. 12mo. 166 pp. Fldg map (1 sm repr). Orig maroon half leather over brown cloth, hinges strengthened with Japanese tissue.
    (W. Thomas Taylor) **$850 [≈£531]**

Page, John Lloyd Warden
- An Exploration of Exmoor & the Hill Country of West Somerset. London: 1893. 3rd edn. 8vo. Map, ills. Prelims & foredge sl spotted. Orig cloth gilt. *(Ambra)* **£18 [≈$28]**
- The North Coast of Cornwall. Its Scenery, Its People, Its Antiquities & Its Legends. With an Appendix on the Geology by W.A.E. Ussher. London: [1897]. 8vo. Map, ills. Orig

cloth gilt. *(Ambra)* £16 [≈ $25]
- The Rivers of Devon from Source to Sea. With Some Account of the Towns and Villages on their Banks. London: 1893. 1st edn. 8vo. Ills. Orig cloth.
(Ambra) £21 [≈ $33]
- The Rivers of Devon from Source to Sea. With Some Account of the Towns and Villages on their Banks. London: Seeley, 1893. 1st edn. Sm 8vo. xv,348,advt pp. Fldg map, frontis, num plates. Sl foxing. Orig pict green cloth gilt. *(Terramedia)* $25 [≈ £15]

Page, Thomas J.
- La Plata, the Argentine Confederation, and Paraguay. Being a Narrative of the Exploration of the Tributaries of the River La Plata ... New York: 1859. xxii,632 pp. Fldg cold map, frontis, plates. Contemp three qtr calf, spine gilt extra, rubbed, some edgewear.
(Reese) $150 [≈ £93]

Pages, Pierre Marie Francois de
- Travels round the World in the Yeares 1767 ... 1771. Translated from the French. Dublin: for P. Byrne ..., 1791. 1st Irish edn. 8vo. Contemp calf. *(Falkner)* £120 [≈ $192]

Pagitt, Ephraim
- Christianographie, or the Description of the Multitude and Sundry Sorte of Christians in the World not Subject to the Pope ... London: T.P. & W.J. for Matthew Costerden, 1635. 1st edn. Sm 4to. [24],156,56,[16] pp. 4 fldg maps. Errata leaf. Old calf, worn, rebacked.
(Karmiole) $350 [≈ £218]

A Pakeha Maori (pseud.)
- See Maning, Frederick Edward.

Palgrave, William Gifford
- Essays on Eastern Questions. London: Macmillan, 1872. 1st edn. 8vo. vii, 349, [2 advt] pp. Orig cloth, rebacked.
(Worldwide Antiqu'n) $85 [≈ £53]
- Narrative of a Year's Journey through Central and Eastern Arabia (1862-63). London & Cambridge: 1865. 1st edn. 2 vols. xii,[1], 466; 398 pp. Half-titles. Frontis port, fldg map, fldg plans. Sl foxing to plans, sm repr to verso of map. Contemp three qtr calf.
(Reese) $350 [≈ £218]
- Narrative of a Year's Journey through Central and Eastern Arabia (1862-63). London: 1866. 3rd edn. 2 vols. Lge 8vo. xii,466,advt; 398,advt pp. Frontis port, lge fldg cold map, 3 town plans. Orig pict gilt green cloth, spine edges sl frayed. *(Terramedia)* $250 [≈ £156]
- Narrative of a Year's Journey through Central

and Eastern Arabia (1862-63). London: Macmillan, 1866-65. 3rd edn. 2 vols. xiv,466; [4],398 pp. Frontis port, fldg map, 4 fldg plans. Orig green cloth gilt, inner hinges starting to crack. *(Karmiole)* $175 [≈ £109]
- Personal Narrative of a Year's Journey through Central and Eastern Arabia (1862-63). London: Macmillan, 1877. Sm 8vo. ix,427,4 advt pp. Engvd title, 5 fldg maps & plans. Orig cloth, sl rubbed, spine ends frayed.
(Worldwide Antiqu'n) $65 [≈ £40]

Pallas, P.S.
- Travels through the Southern Provinces of the Russian Empire in the Years 1793 and 1794. London: 1802-03. 2 vols. 552; 523 pp. Map, 55 engvd plates (some fldg, most cold). Qtr leather.
(Trophy Room Books) $1,100 [≈ £687]
- Travels through the Southern Provinces of the Russian Empire, in the Years 1793 and 1794. London: Stockdale, 1812. 2nd edn. 2 vols. 4to. xxiii,552; xxxii,523 pp. 4 maps, 51 engvd plates (many fldg, all but 7 cold), 29 vignettes (all but 2 cold). Contemp calf.
(Frew Mackenzie) £875 [≈ $1,400]

Palmer, Frederick
- With Kuroki in Manchuria. New York: Scribner's, 1904. Sm 8vo. x,362 pp. 3 maps, frontis, other photo plates by James H. Hare. Orig maroon cloth, sl worn.
(Terramedia) $40 [≈ £25]

Palmer, H.R.
- Sudanese Memoirs; being Mainly Translations of a Number of Arabic Manuscripts relating to the Central and Western Sudan. London: 1928, reprint by Cass, 1967. 3 vols in one. 4to. 81,119,163 pp. 2 fldg maps. Orig bndg. Dw.
(Terramedia) $100 [≈ £62]

Palmer, J.W.
- Up and Down the Irrawaddi; or The Golden Dragon: Being Passages of Adventure in the Burman Empire. New and Revised Edition. New York: Rudd & Carleton, 1859. Sm 8vo. xii,312, 6 advt pp. 2 w'engvs. Orig cloth, b'plate removed. *(Karmiole)* $50 [≈ £31]

Palmer, Sutton & Mitton, G.E.
- Buckinghamshire and Berkshire. London: A. & C. Black Colour Books, Twenty Shilling Series, 1920. 1st edn. 60 cold plates. Orig dec cloth. VG +. *(Old Cathay)* £45 [≈ $72]
- Buckinghamshire and Berkshire. London: A. & C. Black Colour Books, Twenty Shilling Series, 1920. 1st edn. 60 cold plates. Orig dec

cloth. G +.   *(Old Cathay)* **£25 [≈ $40]**

Palmer, W.T.
- The English Lakes. Painted by A. Heaton
Cooper. London: A. & C. Black Colour
Books, Twenty Shilling Series, 1905. 1st edn.
75 cold plates. Orig dec blue-grey cloth, fine.
          (Old Cathay) **£55 [≈ $88]**
- The English Lakes. Painted by A. Heaton
Cooper. London: A. & C. Black Colour
Books, Twenty Shilling Series, 1905. 1st edn.
75 cold plates. Orig dec blue-grey cloth, spine
sl rubbed.   *(Old Cathay)* **£45 [≈ $72]**
- The English Lakes. Painted by A. Heaton
Cooper. London: A. & C. Black Colour
Books, Twenty Shilling Series, 1908. 2nd
edn. 75 cold plates. Orig dec plain grey cloth,
spine sl faded.   *(Old Cathay)* **£35 [≈ $56]**
- The English Lakes. Painted by A. Heaton
Cooper. London: A. & C. Black, 1929.
Reprint. Map, 32 cold plates. Orig cloth.
          (Old Cathay) **£19 [≈ $30]**

Papworth, J.B.
- Select Views of London. London: R.
Ackermann, 1816. 1st edn. Imperial 8vo.
[viii], 159 pp. 76 hand cold plates (5 fldg). 1
fold strengthened on verso. Regency straight
grained blue mor gilt, rebacked.
          (Sotheran) **£3,400 [≈ $5,440]**

Pardoe, Julia
- Beauties of the Bosphorus ... London: Virtue,
1838. 1st edn. 4to. 64 pp. 81 engvd plates by
W.H. Bartlett. Sl foxing. Half mor, worn.
          (Worldwide Antiqu'n) **$195 [≈ £121]**
- The Beauties of the Bosphorus ... London:
[1838]. xii,172 pp. 78 engvd plates. Occas sl
foxing. Contemp elab gilt mor, gilt inner
dentelles, a.e.g., sl rubbed.
          (Reese) **$600 [≈ £375]**
- Traits and Transitions of Portugal. Collected
during a Residence in that Country. London:
Saunders & Otley, 1833. 2 vols. 12mo.
xii,308; iv,338 pp. Later half calf, extremities
sl rubbed.   *(Karmiole)* **$65 [≈ £40]**

Paris ...
- Paris and Its Environs ... see Pugin, Augustus
C. & Heath, Charles.
- Paris As It Was and As It Is ... see Blagdon,
Francis William.

Parish, Woodbine
- Buenos Ayres and the Provinces of the Rio de
la Plata ... London: Murray, 1852. 2nd edn,
enlgd. 8vo. xlii,434,32 advt pp. Advt slip.
Fldg map, 6 plates. Mod cloth.
          (Adelson) **$375 [≈ £234]**

Park, John James
- The Topography and Natural History of
Hampstead, in the County of Middlesex ...
London: 1814.   8vo.   xxi,359,39   pp.
Subscribers. Fldg map (tear), 2 fldg pedigrees,
10 plates. Some foxing & offsetting. Half calf,
spine faded, rubbed. Booklet inserted.
          (Coombes) **£95 [≈ $152]**

Park, Mungo
- The Journal of a Mission to the Interior of
Africa, in the Year 1805 ... London: 1815.
2nd edn, rvsd & enlgd. 4to. [20],373 pp. Lge
fldg map. A few scattered traces of foxing.
Contemp diced calf, gilt spine, jnts worn but
sound.   *(Reese)* **$400 [≈ £250]**
- Travels in the Interior Districts of Africa ...
London: Nicol, 1799. 1st edn. 4to. xxvi, 372,
xcii pp. 3 fldg maps, 6 plates. A few ff sl
browned. Half calf, rubbed.
          (Adelson) **$485 [≈ £303]**
- Travels in the Interior Districts of Africa ...
in the Years 1795, 1796 ... London: 1807. 5th
edn. Map (misfolded, torn), port, 5 plates.
Leather, rubbed, spine ends v rubbed.
          (Parmer) **$190 [≈ £118]**

Parker, A.A.
- Trip to the West and Texas. Concord: 1835.
1st edn. 276 pp. 2 plates. Orig half calf, mrbld
bds.   *(Jenkins)* **$1,500 [≈ £937]**
- Trip to the West and Texas ... With a Brief
Sketch of the Texian War. Concord: 1836.
380 pp. 3 plates. Orig cloth, gilt Lone Star
flag on spine.   *(Jenkins)* **$1,250 [≈ £781]**

Parker, John H.
- The Architectural Antiquities of the City of
Wells. Oxford & London: James Parker,
1866. 1st edn. 8vo. viii,91,8 advt pp. 29
plates, 9 other ills. Orig cloth. Author's
inscrptn.   *(Fenning)* **£36 [≈ $57]**

Parker, Nathan H.
- Iowa As It Is in 1855; A Gazetteer for
Citizens, and a Hand-Book for Emigrants ...
Chicago: 1855. xv,17-264,advt pp. Frontis,
ills, fldg cold map laid in. Orig pict cloth
stamped in blind, spine gilt extra, extremities
worn.   *(Reese)* **$175 [≈ £109]**
- The Minnesota Handbook, for 1856-7. With
a New and Accurate Map. Boston: 1857. 160
pp. Cold fldg map. Orig cloth gilt, spine
chipped, sl staining.   *(Reese)* **$200 [≈ £125]**

Parker, Samuel
- Journal of an Exploring Tour beyond the
Rocky Mountains ... Ithaca, New York: the
author, 1838. 1st edn. 12mo. 371 pp. Lge fldg

map, 1 plate. Sl foxing. Contemp three qtr leather & bds. Cloth case.

(Schoyer) **$450 [≈ £281]**

- Journal of an Exploring Tour beyond the Rocky Mountains ... With a Map of Oregon Territory. Ithaca: 1844. 4th edn. Orig cloth, sl worn. *(Reese)* **$250 [≈ £156]**

Parker, W.B.

- Notes taken during the Expedition commanded by Capt. R.B. Marcy, U.S.A., through Unexplored Texas, in ... 1854. Philadelphia: Hayes & Zell, 1856. 1st edn. 242 pp. *(Jenkins)* **$650 [≈ £406]**

Parkman, Francis

- The Oregon Trail. Sketches of Prairie and Rocky-Mountain Life. Illustrated by Frederic Remington. London: Macmillan, 1892. 8vo. 12 plates, 64 text ills. Orig dec mor gilt, rebacked & reprd. *(Hollett)* **£95 [≈ $152]**

Parkyns, Mansfield

- Life in Abyssinia: being Notes collected during Three Years' Residence and Travels in that Country. London: 1853. 2 vols. xiii,425; iv,432 pp. Fldg map, plates. Orig pict gilt cloth, edge wear, front hinge of vol 2 cracked, sm tear at hd of 1 jnt. *(Reese)* **$300 [≈ £187]**

- Life in Abyssinia. Being Notes collected during Three Years' Residence and Travels in that Country. New York: Appleton, 1854. 1st Amer edn. 2 vols. 350,10 advt; 355,4 advt pp. 13 plates. Occas sl foxing. Orig cloth, pict spine, crnrs sl worn. *(Schoyer)* **$150 [≈ £93]**

Parry, Hubert

- Notes on Old Teignmouth. Exeter: 1914. 4to. Ills. Orig cloth. *(Ambra)* **£34 [≈ $54]**

Parry, J.D.

- An Historical and Descriptive Account of the Coast of Sussex. London: 1833. Large Paper. Roy 8vo. xii,435 pp. Engvd title, fldg map (offset), 6 plates (foxed). Later half mor. *(Henly)* **£85 [≈ $136]**

Parry, William Edward

- Journal of a Voyage for the Discovery of a North-West Passage from the Atlantic to the Pacific ... London: Murray, 1821. 1st edn. 4to. [8],xxix,[3],310, clxxix pp. Errata slip. 20 plates & maps, some fldg. New half calf. *(High Latitude)* **$475 [≈ £296]**

- Journal of a Second Voyage for the Discovery of a North-West Passage ... London: Murray, 1824. 4to. [8],xxx,[2],571 pp. 39 plates & maps. Sm blind stamp on title. New half calf. *(High Latitude)* **$475 [≈ £296]**

- Journal of a Second Voyage ... London: 1824. 1st edn. 4to. 38 (of 39, lacks a general chart) plates. Contemp half calf.

(Fenning) **£125 [≈ $200]**

- Journal of a Third Voyage for the Discovery of a North-West Passage ... London: Murray, 1826. 4to. xxviii,186,[2],151 pp. 11 plates & maps, inc 2 fldg. Contemp half calf, rebacked. *(High Latitude)* **$600 [≈ £375]**

- Three Voyages for the Discovery of a North-West Passage from the Atlantic to the Pacific, and Narrative of an Attempt to Reach the North Pole. New York: Harper's Family Library, 1840. 2 vols. 12mo. Port, frontis in vol 2. Sl foxing. Orig ptd cloth, edge wear. *(Reese)* **$150 [≈ £93]**

Partington, C.F. (ed.)

- National History and Views of London and Its Environs ... London: Alan Bell, [vol 2] Simpkin & Marshall, 1834. 1st edn. 2 vols. [2], 208,[iv]; viii,216 pp. 2 frontis, 2 addtnl engvd titles, 555 engvs in 111 plates. A few sm defects. Mod half mor.

(Claude Cox) **£120 [≈ $192]**

Paterson, Daniel

- A New and Accurate Description of all the Direct and Principal Cross Roads in England and Wales ... Seventh Edition, Corrected, and Greatly Improved ... London: for T. Carnan, 1786. 8vo. Fldg map (sl dusty). Orig sheep, sl worn, lacks blank flyleaves.

(Fenning) **£45 [≈ $72]**

- A New Description of all the Direct and Principal Cross Roads in Great Britain ... Twelfth Edition ... London: 1799. 8vo. xvi, lxii,[ii] pp,702 columns,704-759 pp. 2 maps. Sm wormhole through maps & title. Contemp sheep, rubbed, jnt cracked.

(Bickersteth) **£24 [≈ $38]**

- A New and Accurate Description of all the Direct and Principal Cross Roads in England and Wales, and Part of the Roads of Scotland ... Fifteenth Edition. London: for the proprietor, 1811. 8vo. 8 fldg maps. Contemp tree calf, gilt spine, minor wear.

(Clark) **£65 [≈ $104]**

Paton, Maggie Whitecross

- Letters and Sketches from the New Hebrides. London: Hodder & Stoughton, 1894. 2nd edn. 8vo. xi,382 pp, advt leaf. A few spots. Lib label on pastedown. Orig cloth gilt, sl used, labels removed from spine, front jnt cracking. *(Hollett)* **£50 [≈ $80]**

Patterson, A.H.

- Nature in Eastern Norfolk. London: 1905. 8vo. 352 pp. 12 cold plates. Sl foxing. Orig

cloth.   *(Baldwin)* **£25 [≈ $40]**
- Notes of an East Coast Naturalist. London: 1904. Cr 8vo. xiii,304 pp. 12 cold plates by Frank Southgate. Orig cloth, trifle used.
                (Wheldon & Wesley) **£30 [≈ $48]**
- Wild Life on a Norfolk Estuary. London: 1907. 8vo. xv,352 pp. 40 ills. Half-title rather foxed, minor foxing elsewhere. Orig cloth, trifle worn. *(Wheldon & Wesley)* **£35 [≈ $56]**

Patterson, J.H.
- In the Grip of the Nyika. Further Adventures in British East Africa. London: Macmillan, 1909. 1st British edn. 8vo. xiv, 389 pp. 9 maps, num photo ills. Endpapers browned. Orig cloth.   *(Parmer)* **£135 [≈ £84]**
- In the Grip of the Nyika. Further Adventures in British East Africa. London: Macmillan, 1909. 8vo. xiv,389,2 advt pp. Ills. Orig blue cloth gilt, t.e.g.
           (Bates & Hindmarch) **£40 [≈ $64]**
- In the Grip of the Nyika. London: 1910. 389 pp. Map, ills. Orig bndg.
        (Trophy Room Books) **$75 [≈ £46]**
- The Maneaters of the Tsavo. London: 1908. 4th imp. Orig bndg, as new. Dw.
       (Trophy Room Books) **$150 [≈ £93]**
- The Man-Eaters of Tsavo, and Other East African Adventures. London: Macmillan, 1908. 8vo. 338 pp. Frontis, ills. Orig pict blue cloth gilt, t.e.g.   *(Terramedia)* **$100 [≈ £62]**

Payer, Julius
- New Lands within the Arctic Circle. Translated from the German. New York: 1877. 8vo. xxxiv,399,[6 advt] pp. Chromolitho frontis, map, num text w'cuts. Orig dec cloth gilt, spine ends sl defective, sl bumped, jnts cracked.
                (Hollett) **£120 [≈ $192]**

Payne, Edward J. (ed.)
- Voyages of the Elizabethan Seamen to America. Select Narrative from the 'Principal Navigations' of Hakluyt. Oxford: 1893. 2nd edn. 2 vols. Ports, plates. Orig cloth gilt, a bit rubbed.   *(Reese)* **$125 [≈ £78]**

Payton, E.W.
- Round About New Zealand. Being Notes from a Journal of Three Years Wandering in the Antipodes. London: Chapman & Hall, 1888. 8vo. Fldg map, 20 plates. Orig pict cloth gilt, 1 crnr sl damp marked.
                (Stewart) **£60 [≈ $96]**

Pearce, Richard
- Marooned in the Arctic - Diary of the MacAlpine Aerial Expedition. N.p: Northern

Miner, n.d. 8vo. 71 pp. Map, 5 photo plates. Orig cloth, crnrs sl worn. Author's inscrptn.
                (Parmer) **$400 [≈ £250]**

Pearson, H.J.
- Three Summers Among the Birds of Russian Lapland. London: R.H. Porter, 1904. 1st edn. 8vo. xvi,216 pp. Fldg map, 68 photo plates. Orig green cloth gilt.
                (Gough) **£110 [≈ $176]**

Peary, Robert E.
- Nearest the Pole ... London: Hutchinson, 1907. 1st British edn. xx,411 pp. 2 fldg maps, 65 plates. Orig gilt dec blue cloth.
                (Parmer) **$125 [≈ £78]**
- The North Pole. Its Discovery in 1909 under the Auspices of the Peary Arctic Club ... New York: Stokes, 1910. 2nd edn. Lge 8vo. xxii,373 pp. Lge fldg cold frontis, num other plates (some cold). Orig pict blue cloth gilt.   *(Terramedia)* **$125 [≈ £78]**
- Northward Over The 'Great Ice' ... London: Methuen, 1898. 2 vols. 8vo. 521; 625 pp. Fldg map, num ills. Orig pict blue cloth, sl rubbed & soiled. *(Terramedia)* **$150 [≈ £93]**

Pease, Alfred E.
- Biskra and the Oases and Desert of the Zibans with Information for Travellers. London: Stanford, 1893. 8vo. xvi,112 pp. 3 maps, 8 photo ills. Orig green cloth gilt, recased.
           (Bates & Hindmarch) **£30 [≈ $48]**

Pease, Sir Joseph & Currie, Sir Donald
- The Story of a Three Weeks' Trip to Norway in the Steam Yacht Iolanthe ... [Durham?]: for private circulation, 1890. 1st edn. Sm 4to. Fldg map. 47,[3],iii-lviii pp, blank leaf. Red & black title. Orig cloth.
                (Hannas) **£180 [≈ $288]**

Peck, George W.
- Melbourne, and the Chincha Islands; with Sketches of Lima and a Voyage round the World. New York: 1854. 8vo. Frontis, vignette maps. Half calf.
                (Farahar) **£95 [≈ $152]**
- Melbourne, and the Chincha Islands; with Sketches of Lima, and a Voyage round the World. New York: Scribner, 1854. Sm 8vo. 294 pp. Frontis, w'cut map. Some foxing. Orig cloth gilt, front cvr stained.
                (Karmiole) **$65 [≈ £40]**

Peltier, Jean-Gabriel
- The Late Picture of Paris; or, A Faithful Narrative of the Revolution of the Tenth of August. London: for the author, 1792-93. 2

vols. 8vo. Fldg map. Stained. Qtr calf, hinges weak, 1 cvr detached.
(Rostenberg & Stern) **$150 [≈ £93]**

Pemberton, Edward
- Travels of His Royal Highness the Duke D'Angouleme, through several Departments of France in 1817 ... London: E. Cox & Son, 1819. Sole edn. 8vo. Port frontis. Contemp bds, rebacked, cvrs worn.
(Trebizond) **$300 [≈ £187]**

Pembroke, George Herbert, 13th Earl of
- See Herbert, George Robert Charles, 13th Earl of Pembroke.

Pendergrast, Garrett Elliott
- A Physical and Topographical Sketch of the Mississippi Territory, Lower Louisiana, and a Part of West Florida. Philadelphia: 1803. 34 pp. Scattered spotting & staining. Disbound, in plain blue wraps.
(Reese) **$2,500 [≈ £1,562]**

Pendlebury, J.D.S.
- The Archaeology of Crete. An Introduction. London: Methuen, 1939. 1st edn. xxxii,400 pp. 43 photo plates at end, text ills. Orig green cloth. Dw.
(Frew Mackenzie) **£40 [≈ $64]**

Pennant, Thomas
- The History of the Parishes of Whiteford and Holywell. London: for B. & J. White ..., 1796. 1st edn. 4to. [viii],328 pp. 2 titles with engvd vignettes, 22 plates. A few spots, sl offsetting from plates. Old polished half calf gilt, uncut, sl rubbed. *(Hollett)* **£185 [≈ £296]**
- The Journey from Chester to London. London: for Wilkie & Robinson ..., 1811. 8vo. viii, 622 pp. Frontis, 4 ports. Panelled & diced calf gilt, gilt & blind ornamental borders, spine sl faded & sl rubbed at ends.
(Hollett) **£85 [≈ £136]**
- The Journey from Chester to London. London: B. White, 1782. 1st edn. 4to. iv,452, [vi] pp. Engvd title with vignette, 22 plates (some a little offset). Contemp tree calf, rebacked, crnrs a little worn.
(Clark) **£160 [≈ $256]**
- Some Account of London. Third Edition. Dublin: for John Archer, 1791. 1st irish edn. Roy 8vo. iv, [8 subscribers], [2],479,[8] pp. Engvd title, fldg map, 15 plates. Contemp calf gilt, minor signs of use.
(Fenning) **£75 [≈ $120]**
- Some Account of London. The Fifth Edition, with Considerable Additions. London: 1813. Thick 8vo. viii, 660 pp. Fldg frontis map,

engvd title, plates (some fldg). Orig paper bds, paper label chipped, spine chipped, front bd nearly detached but cords sound.
(Reese) **$100 [≈ £62]**
- Some Account of London ... Fifth Edition, with considerable Additions. London: J. Faulder ..., 1813. 8vo. Addtnl engvd title, 14 plates (1 fldg), all sl spotted. Mod qtr calf.
(Waterfield's) **£100 [≈ $160]**

Pennecuik, Alexander, M.D.
- A Geographical and Historical Description of the Shire of Tweeddale. With a Miscelany [sic] and Curious Collection of Select Scotish Poems. Edinburgh: John Moncur, 1715. 1st coll edn. 4to. Few pp sl stained. Contemp calf, rebacked. Lord Eliock's b'plate.
(Hannas) **£350 [≈ $560]**

Pennefather, Frederick William
- A Handbook for Travellers in New Zealand. London: Murray, 1893. 1st edn. Later iss, with leaf of 'Addenda' on pink paper inserted. Sm 8vo. Half-title, 4 advt ff at end. 15 maps & 2 loose maps in pockets. Orig red cloth, spine faded. *(Hannas)* **£85 [≈ $136]**

Pennell, Elizabeth Robins
- French Cathedrals. Monasteries and Abbeys and Sacred Sites of France. Illustrated by Joseph Pennell. New York: Century, 1909. 1st trade edn. Tall 8vo. 424 pp. 38 tinted plates, 23 full page b/w ills, 134 text ills. Orig dec cloth gilt, t.e.g. *(Schoyer)* **$50 [≈ £31]**

Pennell, Joseph & Elizabeth Robins
- A Canterbury Pilgrimage. London: Seeley, 1885. Fcap 4to. 78 pp. Frontis & ills by the authors. Occas minor spotting. Orig pict dec cloth, a.e.g., front hinge tender.
(Duck) **£30 [≈ $48]**

Penny, F.E.
- Southern India. Painted by Lady Lawley. London: A. & C. Black Colour Books, Twenty Shilling Series, 1914. 1st edn. Map, 50 cold plates. Orig dec orange cloth, t.e.g., v. fine. *(Old Cathay)* **£65 [≈ $104]**
- Southern India. Painted by Lady Lawley. London: A. & C. Black Colour Books, Twenty Shilling Series, 1914. 1st edn. Map, 50 cold plates. Orig dec orange cloth, t.e.g.
(Old Cathay) **£55 [≈ $88]**

Penzer, N.M.
- An Annotated Bibliography of Sir Richard Francis Burton. London: 1923. One of 500 deluxe, sgnd. 351 pp. Orig bndg, fine.
(Trophy Room Books) **$750 [≈ £468]**

- The Harem. Philadelphia: Lippincott, n.d.
Lge 8vo. 277 pp. Fldg plans, ills. Orig red
cloth.   *(Parmer)* **$65 [≈£40]**

Percival, A. Blayney
- A Game Ranger's Notebook. Edited by E.D.
Cuming. New York: George Doran, [1924].
1st Amer edn. 8vo. xviii,373 pp. Lge map,
frontis, num other photo plates. Orig red
cloth, spine sl sunned.
               (Terramedia) **$100 [≈£62]**
- A Game Ranger's Notebook. London: 1927.
369 pp. Fldg map, ills. Orig cloth, v fine.
        (Trophy Room Books) **$125 [≈£78]**

Percival, Robert
- An Account of the Island of Ceylon ...
London: Baldwin, 1803. 1st edn. 4to. xii,420
pp. 4 fldg maps. Rebacked with half calf, gilt
dec spine, orig mrbld bds.
      (Frew Mackenzie) **£320 [≈$512]**

**Percy,   Elizabeth,   Duchess   of
Northumberland**
- A Short Tour made [to the Netherlands] in
the Year One Thousand Seven Hundred and
Seventy One. London: ptd in the year, 1775.
1st edn. 8vo. [2],89 pp. Orig mrbld wraps,
uncut & largely unopened, spine defective.
                 (Hannas) **£120 [≈$192]**

Perkins, James
- A Tour Round the Globe. Letters to the "City
Press." London: W.H. & L. Collingridge,
City Press, privately ptd for the author, 1891.
1st edn. 8vo. 76 pp. Orig blue cloth.
      (W. Thomas Taylor) **$300 [≈£187]**

Perkins, Justin
- A Residence of Eight Years in Persia, among
the Nestorian Christians; with Notices of the
Mahommedans. Andover: Allen, Morrill &
Wardwell, 1843. 1st edn. 8vo. xx,512 pp.
Fldg map, 27 plates (24 hand cold). Sl foxed.
Orig cloth, edges sl rubbed.
      (Worldwide Antiqu'n) **$350 [≈£218]**

Perrin du Lac, M.
- Travels Through the Two Louisianas, and
among the Savage Nations of the Missouri ...
London: 1807. 1st English edn. 106,[2] pp.
Mod half cloth, untrimmed.
                  (Reese) **$400 [≈£250]**

Perry, Amos
- Carthage and Tunis. Providence: 1860. 4to.
560 pp. 1 ill. Orig green cloth, sm ex-lib
markings.   *(Terramedia)* **$100 [≈£62]**

Perry, John
- The State of Russia under the Present Czar ...
London: Benjamin Tooke, 1716. 1st edn.
8vo. [x],280 pp. Lge fldg map by Moll.
Contemp panelled calf, hd of spine sl worn, v
sl stain on upper cvr.
          (Frew Mackenzie) **£280 [≈$448]**
- The State of Russia under the Present Czar ...
London: 1716. viii,280 pp. Fldg map.
Contemp calf, hinges sl worn, hd of spine
reprd.   *(Reese)* **$450 [≈£281]**

Perry, Matthew Calbraith
- Narrative of the Expedition of an American
Squadron to the China Seas and Japan ...
Compiled ... by Francis L. Hawks. New
York: Appleton, 1856. 1st public edn. 624 pp.
Errata tipped in. Maps & plates (some fldg).
Orig cloth gilt.   *(Jenkins)* **$200 [≈£125]**
- Narrative of the Expeditions of an American
Squadron to the China Seas and Japan ...
Compiled ... by Francis L. Hawks. New
York: 1857. 2nd edn. 4to. 537 pp. 6 maps, 83
chromolitho plates of views, 3 other cold
plates, 3 plates of diags. 19th c 3/4 mor,
rubbed.   *(Heritage)* **$750 [≈£468]**

Perry, Richard
- The Jeannette: and a Complete and Authentic
Narrative Encyclopedia of all Voyages and
Expeditions to the North Polar regions ...
Chicago: 1882. 840 pp. Frontis, ills. Orig dec
cloth, some wear to extremities.
                   (Reese) **$150 [≈£93]**

Peters, Carl
- The Eldorado of the Ancients. London:
Pearson, 1902. 1st edn. Thick 8vo. x,447 pp.
2 fldg maps. Orig rust cloth, extremities
rubbed.   *(Karmiole)* **$65 [≈£40]**

Peters, John Punnett
- Nippur or Explorations and Adventures on
the Euphrates. The Narrative of the
University of Pennsylvania Expedition to
Babylonia in the Years 1888-1890. New York
& London: Putnam, 1897. 1st edn. 2 vols.
8vo. 2 fldg maps in pocket. 63 plates & ills.
Orig cloth, edges sl rubbed, lib number on
spine.   *(Worldwide Antiqu'n)* **$140 [≈£87]**
- Nippur, or Explorations and Adventures on
the Euphrates ... New York & London: 1898.
2nd edn. 2 vols. 8vo. 2 fldg maps in pocket.
Num plates & ills. Orig pict cloth.
              (Terramedia) **$200 [≈£125]**

Petrie, Graham
- Tunis, Kairouan and Carthage. Described
and Illustrated ... London: Heinemann, 1908.

Lge 8vo. xiv,252 pp. 48 cold plates, captioned tissue guards. Orig pict cloth, t.e.g.
(Schoyer) **$45 [≈ £28]**

Petrie, W.M. Flinders
- Ehnasia, 1904. London: Egypt Exploration Fund, 26th Memoir, 1905. Folio. viii,41 pp. 44 plates. Orig qtr cloth, ptd bds, sl rubbed & soiled.   *(Terramedia)* **$50 [≈ £31]**
- Naukratis. London: Egypt Exploration Fund, Memoirs 3 & 6, 1886-88. 2 vols. Folio. viii, 100; vi,92 pp. 69 plates. Orig cloth & bds, ex-lib, sl worn.   *(Terramedia)* **$175 [≈ £109]**
- Prehistoric Egypt. London: 1920. 1st edn. 4to. viii,54 pp. 53 plates. Orig half cloth, paper sides dust marked.
(Bow Windows) **£40 [≈ $64]**
- Researches in Sinai. New York: Dutton, 1906. 2nd printing. Sm 4to. xxiii,280,2 advt pp. 4 maps, 186 ills on 98 plates. V sl foxing. Orig cloth, edges sl rubbed & soiled, spine ends frayed.
(Worldwide Antiqu'n) **$125 [≈ £78]**
- Tanis. [Followed by his] Nebesheh and Defeneh. London: Egypt Exploration Fund Memoirs 2 & 4, 1883-84. 1st edn. 3 parts in 2 vols. Folio. viii,3; 44; viii,116 pp. Frontis, 2 fldg plans, 79 plates. Sl browned. Orig cloth & bds, rubbed, ex-lib.
(Terramedia) **$175 [≈ £109]**
- Ten Years Digging in Egypt. 1881-1890. London: RTS, 1892. Sm 8vo. 201 pp. Num ills. Orig maroon cloth.
(Terramedia) **$50 [≈ £31]**

Petrie, W.M. Flinders, et al.
- Abydos, Parts I-III. London: Egypt Exploration Fund, Memoirs 22 & 24, 1902-03. Lge 4to. 60; viii,56; vi,60 pp. 205 plates. Orig cloth & bds, ex-lib, bndg bit soiled, sl rubbed. *(Terramedia)* **$250 [≈ £156]**

Pfeiffer, Ida
- A Journey to Iceland, and Travels in Sweden and Norway. Translated from the German ... by Charlotte Fenimore Cooper. New York: Putnam's Library for the People, 1852. 1st edn of this trans. 12mo. 274 pp. Lge fldg map. Orig brown cloth, spine extremities sl rubbed.   *(Karmiole)* **$50 [≈ £31]**
- Journey to Iceland: and Travels in Sweden and Norway. From the German by Charlotte Fenimore Cooper. London: Bentley, 1852. 1st English edn. 8vo. Half mor, gilt spine.
(Hannas) **£70 [≈ $112]**
- The Last Travels ... Inclusive of a Visit to Madagascar with an Autobiographical Memoir of the Author ... New York: Harper, 1861. 1st Amer edn. 12mo. xxxvii,281,6 advt

pp. Litho port frontis. Orig purple cloth, spine lettering faded.   *(Schoyer)* **$65 [≈ £40]**
- Visit to Iceland and the Scandinavian North. Translated from the German. London: Ingram, Cooke, 1852. 1st edn of this trans. 8vo. 8 tinted plates inc addtnl engvd title. Orig embossed cloth. *(Hannas)* **£70 [≈ $112]**
- A Visit to Iceland and the Scandinavian North. London: Ingram, Cooke, National Illustrated Library, 1852. 1st edn thus. 8vo. xvi, 354 pp. Cold frontis & title, 6 cold ills. Occas spotting. Orig blind stamped cloth, spine extremities & crnrs rubbed with some loss.   *(de Beaumont)* **£68 [≈ $108]**
- Visit to the Holy Land, Egypt, and Italy. Translated from the German ... Second Edition. London: Ingram, Cooke, 1853. 8vo. Frontis, addtnl title with vignette (dated 1852), 6 tinted plates. Orig patterned cloth gilt spine, sl dampmarked.   *(Sanders)* **£35 [≈ $56]**

Philby, H. St. John
- Across Arabia: from the Persian Gulf to the Red Sea. London: reptd from the Geographical Journal, 1920. 8vo. Fldg map. Blue ptd sewn wraps. Pres ALS by Philby inserted.   *(Dalian)* **£175 [≈ $280]**
- Arabian Jubilee. New York: John Day Co, [1953]. 1st Amer edn. 8vo. xiv,280 pp. Num photo plates. Orig black cloth. Dw.
(Terramedia) **$75 [≈ £46]**
- The Empty Quarter being a Description of the Great South Desert of Arabia known as Rub' al Khali. New York: 1933. 1st Amer edn. 433 pp. Lge cold fldg map, num ills. Orig bndg. Dw.
(Trophy Room Books) **$125 [≈ £78]**
- Saudi Arabia. London: Benn, 1955. 1st edn. 8vo. Fldg map, ills. Orig blue buckram. V sl nicked dw.   *(Dalian)* **£45 [≈ $72]**

Phillipps-Wolley, Clive
- Sport in the Crimea and Caucasus. London: Bentley, 1881. 8vo. x,370 pp. Later cloth.
(Schoyer) **$65 [≈ £40]**
- A Sportsman's Eden [Canada]. London: 1888. 8vo. V sl foxing. Orig pict cloth, v sl rubbed.
(Grayling) **£75 [≈ $120]**

Philosophical ...
- A Philosophical Survey of the South of Ireland ... see Campbell, Thomas.

Phipps, Constantine John
- A Voyage towards the North Pole ... London: 1774. viii,253 pp. 3 fldg maps, 12 fldg plates & plans. Orig calf, rebacked, crnrs bumped, calf somewhat singed on edges.
(Reese) **$900 [≈ £562]**

Picart, Bernard
- The Ceremonies and Religious Customs of the Various Nations of the Known World; with Additions and Remarks Omitted by the French Author. London: 1741. Folio. 21 plates. Tear reprd. Sl marg stain on 1st 50 pp. Marg worm hole at end. Contemp calf, sl worn.   *(Farahar)* **£150 [≈ $240]**

A Pictorial View of California ...
- See Letts, J.M.

The Picture of Parsonstown ...
- See Cooke, Thomas L.

Picturesque ...
- Picturesque America. A Pictorial Delineation of the ... Picturesque Features of the North American Continent ... London: Cassell, [ca 1890]. 8 vols. Folio. 8 frontis, 40 steel engvd plates, over 900 w'engvs. Orig gilt dec red cloth, a.e.g., spines faded, sl worn.
                          (Rankin) **£300 [≈ $480]**
- Picturesque America ... see also Bryant, William Cullen (ed.).
- Picturesque Europe ... London: Cassell, [ca 1870]. 4 vols. 4to. Each vol with engvd title, 24 engvd plates, num text ills. Orig gilt dec red cloth, a.e.g.   *(Spelman)* **£65 [≈ $104]**
- Picturesque Europe ... London: Cassell, Petter & Galpin, [1876/7]. 4 vols in 10 divisions. 4to. Each vol 288 pp. 70 steel engvs inc the 10 pict titles, num w'engvs. Occas sl spotting. Orig pict cloth gilt, a.e.g., inner hinges broken, somewhat soiled & worn.
                      (Claude Cox) **£135 [≈ $216]**
- Picturesque Europe ... London: Cassell, Petter, Galpin & Co, n.d. 5 vols. Lge 4to. Num steel engvd plates after Birket Foster & others. Mor gilt extra, a.e.g., spine ends sl damaged & a trifle chipped, 1 bd detached, some hinges a little weak.
                          (Hollett) **£220 [≈ $352]**
- Picturesque Europe ... see also Taylor, Bayard (ed.).
- A Picturesque Handbook to Carlingford Bay and Vicinity ... see Byrne, P.
- The Picturesque Mediterranean. Its Cities, Bays and Islands. With Illustrations on Wood ... New York: Cassell, [ca 1880]. 2 vols. Folio. vii,280; viii,288 pp. Num plates & text engvs. Orig pict gilt green cloth, elab dec front cvr, a.e.g., spine sl dulled.
                      (Terramedia) **$200 [≈ £125]**
- The Picturesque Mediterranean. Its Cities, Shores and Islands. With Illustrations on Wood ... New York: Cassell, [ca 1880]. 1st edn. 2 vols. Folio. vii,280; viii,288 pp. Num w'engvs. Orig cloth, a.e.g., sl rubbed.

(Worldwide Antiqu'n) **$175 [≈ £109]**
- Picturesque Representations of the Dress and Manners of the Austrians ... see Alexander, William.

Pidgeon, Daniel
- An Engineer's Holiday or Notes of a Round Trip from Long. 0 to 0. London: 1882. 2 vols. xiv,342; xii,342 pp. Advts. Half-titles. Orig cloth gilt, extremities worn, hinges cracked.
                          (Reese) **$200 [≈ £125]**

Pierce, W.H.
- Thirteen Years of Travel and Exploration in Alaska ... Edited by Prof. and Mrs. J.H. Carruth. Lawrence, KS: Journal Pub Co, 1890. 12mo. vii,[2],10-224 pp. 3 w'cut ills. Orig cloth, hd of spine pulled, bit of wear.
                   (High Latitude) **$175 [≈ £109]**

Pigott, R.
- Twenty Five Years of Big Game Hunting. London: 1928. 307 pp. 64 ills. Orig bndg.
                   (Trophy Room Books) **$200 [≈ £125]**
- Twenty-Five Years Big Game Hunting. London: 1928. 8vo. Ills. V sl foxing. Orig bndg, v sl rubbed. *(Grayling)* **£85 [≈ $136]**

Pike, Albert
- Prose Sketches and Poems, Written in the Western Country. Boston: Light & Horton, 1834. 1st edn. 200 pp. Extremities foxed. Orig cloth gilt. *(Jenkins)* **$2,250 [≈ £1,406]**

Pike, Nicholas
- Sub-Tropical Rambles in the Land of the Aphanapteryx. Personal Experiences, Adventures, & Wanderings in and around the Island of Mauritius. London: 1873. 8vo. 3 fldg maps, 15 plates, num text ills. Contemp calf, gilt spine laid down, new label.
                          (Farahar) **£225 [≈ $360]**

Pike, Warburton
- The Barren Ground of Northern Canada. London: 1892. 8vo. 2 fldg maps. Orig cloth, worn, lib label on upper cvr.
                          (Farahar) **£75 [≈ $120]**

Pike, Zebulon M.
- Exploratory Travels through the Western Territories of North America ... London: Longman, Hurst ..., 1811. 1st English edn. 4to. xx,436 pp. 2 maps. Fldg map sl foxed & offset. 1 tear reprd. Mod qtr leather.
                          (Parmer) **$2,395 [≈ £1,496]**
- Exploratory Travels through the Western Territories of North America ... London: Longman, Hurst ..., 1811. 1st edn. 4to. xx,

436 pp. 2 fldg maps. Lacks half title. Usual offsetting from maps. Contemp calf, spine relaid.
(W. Thomas Taylor) **$2,000 [≈ £1,250]**
- Exploratory Travels through the Western Territories of North America ... Denver: 1889. 1st reprint. 4to. 394 pp. Port. Cloth, sl worn.   *(Reese)* **$150 [≈ £93]**

Pinckard, George
- Notes on the West Indies; written during the Expedition under the Command of the late General Sir Ralph Abercromby ... London: 1806. 3 vols. [24],448; [20],472; [20],456 pp. Lge 8vo. Half-titles correctly in vols 1 & 2 only. Contemp polished calf, mor labels.
(Reese) **$600 [≈ £375]**

Pindar, Peter (i.e. John Wolcot)
- Royal Recollections on a Tour to Cheltenham. Gloucester, Worcester, and Places Adjacent, in the Year 1788. The Fourteenth Edition. London: '1779' [misprint for 1789]. Binder's cloth.
(Ambra) **£68 [≈ $108]**

Pinkerton, Robert
- Russia: or, Miscellaneous Observations on the Past and Present State of that Country and its Inhabitants ... London: 1833. [8], 486, [2] pp. Half-title. 8 hand cold litho views. Contemp three qtr mor, bit of wear at edges.
(Reese) **$350 [≈ £218]**

Pinks, William J.
- The History of Clerkenwell. With Additions by the Editor, Edward J. Wood. London: Charles Herbert, 1881. 2nd edn. Lge thick 8vo. xx, 800 pp. Hand cold fldg map, nearly 200 w'engvd ills. Orig pict cloth gilt, crnrs sl rubbed, spine sl faded, recased.
(Hollett) **£95 [≈ $152]**

Piotrowski, Rufin
- My Escape from Siberia. Translated with the Express Sanction of the Author, by E.S. ... London: Routledge ..., 1863. 1st English edn. 8vo. xxiv,386,6 advt pp. Litho frontis, fldg map in pocket at end. Orig blue cloth, a little soiled & faded.   *(Claude Cox)* **£45 [≈ $72]**

Piozzi, Hester Lynch
- Observations and Reflections made in the Course of a Journey through France, Italy, and Germany. Dublin: H. Chamberlaine ..., 1789. 1st Dublin edn. 8vo. Half-title evidently not called for. Contemp calf, gilt spine, front hinges a bit tender.
(Trebizond) **$225 [≈ £140]**

Pittman, Philip
- The Present State of the European Settlements on the Mississippi; with a Geographical Description of that River. London: 1770. viii,99 pp. 5 fldg maps, 3 plans (2 fldg). Trace of marg staining. Tall untrimmed copy, never bound, rear wrapper present. Cloth case.
(Reese) **$3,750 [≈ £2,343]**

Plaisted, Bartholomew
- A Journey from Calcutta in Bengal, by Sea, to Busserah; from thence across the Great Desert to Aleppo: and from thence to Marseilles, and through France, to England ... London: for J. Newbery, 1757. 1st edn. 12mo. Mod half calf, gilt spine.
(Ximenes) **$500 [≈ £312]**

Planche, James Robinson
- Descent of the Danube from Ratisbon to Vienna during the Autumn of 1827, with Anecdotes and Recollections ... London: James Duncan, 1828. 1st edn. 8vo. xv,320 pp. Litho frontis view, map, vignette. Orig cloth, backstrip relaid, label chipped.
(Schoyer) **$110 [≈ £68]**

Planta, Edward
- A New Picture of Paris; or, The Stranger's Guide ... Environs of Paris ... Tenth Edition, much enlarged ... London: Samuel Leigh, 1818. Lge 12mo. xx,64, *63-*64, 65-458, 12 advt pp. 8 maps, plans, tables, plates. Some sm tears, no loss. Orig roan gilt.
(Fenning) **£45 [≈ $72]**

Playfair, G.M.H.
- The Cities and Towns of China. A Geographical Dictionary. Hong Kong: Noronha & Co, 1879. Lge 8vo. lviii,428,32 pp. Orig cloth, spine relaid, crnrs bumped.
(Karmiole) **$150 [≈ £93]**

Plumptre, Anne
- Narrative of a Residence in Ireland during the Summer of 1814 and that of 1815. London: Colburn, 1817. 1st edn. 4to. Plates. Mod half maroon mor, uncut.
(Emerald Isle) **£250 [≈ $400]**

A Pocket Companion for Oxford ...
- A Pocket Companion for Oxford ... Public Edifices, and Buildings of the Colleges ... New Edition, with Additions. Oxford: for R. Clements ..., 1756. 12mo. viii,107,[i],4 pp. Frontis & 7 plates (inc 1 in duplicate). Some soiling. 1 tear. Rec half mor.
(Clark) **£65 [≈ $104]**

Podmore, St. Michael
- Rambles and Adventures in Australasia, Canada, India ... London: 1909. 8vo. Ills. Orig cloth, a bit worn. *(Grayling)* **£35 [≈ $56]**

Poinsett, Joel R.
- Notes on Mexico, made in the Autumn of 1822, accompanied by a Historical Sketch of the Revolution ... and Present State of the Country. Philadelphia: Carey & Lea, 1824. 1st edn. vi,357 pp, errata leaf. Lacks the fldg map. Orig bds, ptd label, scuffed.
(Jenkins) **$225 [≈ £140]**

Poiret, Jean Louis Marie
- Travels Through Barbary ... In the Years 1785 and 1786, and Containing an Account of the Customs and Manners of the Moors, and the Bedouin Arabs. Translated from the French. London: C. Forster, [1789]. 1st English edn. 12mo. 336 pp. Rec cloth.
(Schoyer) **$110 [≈ £68]**

Polack, Joel S.
- Manners and Customs of the New Zealanders ... and Remarks to Intending Emigrants. London: James Madden, 1840. 2 vols. 8vo. xxxiv, 288; xviii,304 pp. Fldg map, 3 plates, text ills. Orig cloth, rubbed, spines chipped.
(Adelson) **$485 [≈ £303]**

Poletika, Pierre
- A Sketch of the Internal Condition of the United States of America, and of their Political Relations with Europe. By a Russian ... From the French, by an American, with Notes. Baltimore: 1826. 1st edn in English. 8vo. [7],163 pp. Orig qtr cloth, spine splitting. *(M & S Rare Books)* **$250 [≈ £156]**

Pollington, Viscount
- Half Round the Old World. Being Some Account of a Tour in Russia, the Caucasus, Persia, and Turkey, 1865-66. London: Moxon, 1867. 1st edn. 8vo. iv,403 pp. Lge fldg map. Sl foxing. Orig cloth, edges sl rubbed, b'plates removed.
(Worldwide Antiqu'n) **$95 [≈ £59]**

Polo, Marco
- The Most Noble and Famous Travels ... together with the Travels of Nicolo de' Conti. Edited ... by N.M. Penzer. Argonaut Press: 1929. One of 1050, this copy out of series (review copy?). 4to. lx,381 pp. Cold frontis, plate, 11 maps.t Orig qtr vellum.
(Bickersteth) **£80 [≈ $128]**

Pommerol, Mme. Jean
- Among the Women of the Sahara. From the

French ... by Mrs Arthur Bell. London: Hurst & Blackett, 1900. 1st English edn. 8vo. [viii], 343,[4 advt] pp. 90 ills. Orig cloth gilt, trifle soiled. *(Hollett)* **£45 [≈ $72]**

Pompeii ...
- See Clarke, George.

Ponting, Herbert G.
- In Lotus-Land Japan. London: 1922. New & rvsd edn. Lge 8vo. xii,306 pp. 8 cold & 80 b/w plates. Some dust & finger marks, sgntr erased from endpapers. Orig cloth, spine gilt dull, tiny tear ft of upper jnt.
(Bow Windows) **£50 [≈ $80]**
- In Lotus-Land Japan. London: Macmillan, 1910. 1st edn. 8vo. xvi,395 pp. 8 cold & 96 b/w ills. Orig pict gilt dec cloth, crnrs & edges worn. *(Parmer)* **$125 [≈ £78]**

Poole, G.A. & Hugall, J.W.
- An Historical & Descriptive Guide to York Cathedral and its Antiquities ... York: R. Sunter, [1850]. 4to. xiii,213 pp. 40 litho plates (2 cold, one in 2 colours, 2 dble page). Orig plain glazed bds, rebacked with calf, crnrs worn. *(Spelman)* **£50 [≈ $80]**

Poole, Reginald Stuart
- The Cities of Egypt. London: Smith, Elder, 1882. 1st edn. 8vo. xii,215 pp. Fldg map, 1 ill. Orig cloth, externally unmarked ex-lib.
(Worldwide Antiqu'n) **$75 [≈ £46]**

Pooley, Charles
- An Historical and Descriptive Account of the Old Stone Crosses of Somerset. London: 1877. Roy 8vo. Map, 20 litho plates, text ills. Orig cloth, inner hinges tender.
(Ambra) **£32 [≈ $51]**

Portal, Sir Gerald
- The British Mission to Uganda in 1893. Edited with a Memoir by Rennell Rodd ... London: Edward Arnold, 1894. 1st edn. 8vo. xlvi,351 pp. Engvd frontis port, woodburytype port, fldg cold map, 37 ills from photos. Orig pict cloth, sl rubbed.
(Schoyer) **$100 [≈ £62]**

Porter, J.L.
- Five Years in Damascus, with Travels and Researches in Palmyra, Lebanon, the Giant Cities of Bashan, and the Hauran. London: Murray, 1870. 2nd edn, rvsd. Sm 8vo. xvi,339 pp. Fldg map (torn with loss), num ills. Orig cloth, edges rubbed, lib sticker on spine. *(Worldwide Antiqu'n)* **$45 [≈ £28]**
- The Giant Cities of Bashan and Syria's Holy

Places. New York: Thomas Nelson, 1884.
12mo. [v],377 pp. Orig brown cloth, front
inner hinge cracked.
(Terramedia) **$35 [≈ £21]**

Porter, Sir Robert Ker
- A Narrative of the Campaign in Russia
during the Year 1812. London: Longman,
[1813]. Slim 4to. xii,282 pp. Frontis, 2 part-
cold fldg plans. 1 plan torn without loss.
Frontis & title foxed. Contemp half leather.
(Bates & Hindmarch) **£90 [≈ $144]**
- Travelling Sketches in Russia and Sweden
during the Years 1805, 1806, 1807, 1808.
London: 1813. 2nd edn. 2 vols. 4to. 41 engvd
plates (3 fldg, 28 hand cold, 13 tinted).
Offsetting from most plates. Rec half calf, vol
1 uncut, vol 2 cut down (3/4 inch shorter).
(Young's) **£280 [≈ $448]**

Porter, Robert P.
- The Full Recognition of Japan ... Economic
Progress of the Japanese Empire to 1911.
London: OUP, 1911. 1st edn. 8vo. x,789 pp.
7 cold maps. Orig pict gilt blue cloth.
(Terramedia) **$125 [≈ £78]**

Porteus, Beilby
- A Letter to the Governors, Legislatures, and
Proprietors of Plantations in the British West-
India Islands. London: 1808. 48 pp. Ptd
wraps, stitched, a bit chipped, worn at spine.
(Reese) **$125 [≈ £78]**

Portlock, Nathaniel
- A Voyage round the World; but more
particularly to the North-West Coast of
America ... London: for John Stockdale ...,
1789. 1st edn. Lge 4to. xii,384,xl pp. Frontis
port, fldg maps, plates. Frontis & title backed.
Ex-lib. Old style calf.
(Wreden) **$1,200 [≈ £750]**

The Post Chaise Companion ...
- The Post Chaise Companion: or, Travellers
Directory through Ireland ... Dublin: J. &
J.H. Fleming, [1803]. 3rd edn. 8vo. [ii],
xxvii,660,19 pp. Lge fldg map, 5 plates. Orig
bds, uncut, respined. Variously attributed to
R. Lewis or William Wilson.
(Young's) **£110 [≈ $176]**

Postans, Mrs.
- Cutch or Random Sketches during a
Residence in One of the Northern provinces
of Western India interspersed with Legends
and Traditions. London: 1839. 1st edn. 283
pp. Engvs. Orig cloth.
(Trophy Room Books) **$450 [≈ £281]**

Postl, Karl
- The Cabin-Book; or, National
Characteristics. By Charles Sealsfield
[pseud.]. London: Ingram Cooke, 1852. 1st
English edn, 1st illust edn. 296,[4] pp.
Vignette title, plates. Orig green pict
blindstamped cloth gilt extra, spine sl faded.
(Jenkins) **$450 [≈ £281]**
- Life in the New World; or, Sketches of
American Society. By Charles Sealsfield. New
York: J. Winchester, 1844. 1st edn in
English. 349 pp. Orig cloth.
(Jenkins) **$225 [≈ £140]**

Pote, Joseph
- Les Delices de Windsor; or, a Description of
Windsor Castle, and the Country Adjacent ...
Eton: ptd by Joseph & Thomas Pote, 1755.
1st edn. 12mo. 2 advt ff. Frontis, 2 plates, sev
text ills. Contemp (orig?) dark blue bds, calf
spine, spine worn, jnts weak.
(Ximenes) **$150 [≈ £93]**

Potter, John, 1674?-1747
- Archaeologia Graeca: or, the Antiquities of
Greece. The Sixth Edition. London: for H.
Knaplock ..., 1740. 2 vols. 8vo. Num plates.
Contemp calf. *(Hannas)* **£15 [≈ $24]**

Potter, T.R.
- The History and Antiquities of Charnwood
Forest ... London: 1842. 1st edn. 4to. xii,
192,80 pp, inc Subscribers. Engvd vignette
title, frontis, dedic, 3 plates, 14 tinted litho
plates, 1 cold plate, cold map, cold section. A
few marks. Old half calf, rebacked.
(Bow Windows) **£125 [≈ $200]**

Pottinger, Sir Henry
- Flood, Fell and Forest. London: 1905. 2 vols.
8vo. Num ills. Orig cloth.
(Grayling) **£80 [≈ $128]**

Pouqueville, F.C.H.L.
- Travels through the Morea, Albania, and
Several Other Parts of the Ottoman Empire,
to Constantinople, during the Years 1798,
1799, 1800 and 1801 ... London: Richard
Phillips, 1806. 192 pp. Fldg map, plates
(some fldg). Occas foxing. Mod half cloth,
t.e.g. *(Reese)* **$150 [≈ £93]**

Powell, Alexander
- Marches of the North. From Cape Breton to
the Klondike. London: Appleton, 1931. 1st
edn. 8vo. x,311 pp. Fldg map, num plates.
Orig green cloth. *(Terramedia)* **$50 [≈ £31]**

Powell, E.
- Beyond the Utmost Purple Rim [Somaliland and Abyssinia]. New York: 1925. 431 pp. Ills. Orig bndg. Dw.
(Trophy Room Books) **$55 [≃ £34]**

Power, W. Tyrone
- Sketches in New Zealand, with Pen and Pencil. From a Journal kept in that Country from July 1846, to June 48. London: Longman, Brown ..., 1849. 8vo. xlviii,290 pp. 8 tinted plates. Lib stamp on title. Mod half calf. *(Adelson)* **$300 [≃ £187]**

Poyser, Arthur
- The Tower of London. Painted by John Fulleylove. London: A. & C. Black Colour Book, 1908. 1st edn. Map, 22 cold plates. Neat inscrptn on title. Orig cloth, t.e.g., spine sl faded & discold, split at hd of jnt.
(Old Cathay) **£36 [≃ $57]**

Praeger, Robert Lloyd
- The Way That I went. An Irishman in Ireland. Dublin: Hodges, 1937. 1st edn. Roy 8vo. Orig dark blue cloth.
(Emerald Isle) **£48 [≃ $76]**
- The Way That I went. An Irishman in Ireland. Dublin: 1939. 394 pp. Map. Orig bndg. Dw. *(Emerald Isle)* **£25 [≃ $40]**
- The Way That I Went. London: 1939. 2nd edn. 8vo. xiv,394 pp. Map, 39 plates, 12 figs. Orig cloth. *(Baldwin)* **£25 [≃ $40]**

Prairiedom ...
- Prairiedom ... by a Suthron ... see Page, F.B.

Pratt, A.
- To the Snows of Tibet through China. London: 1892. 1st edn. 268 pp. Frontis, fldg map, 29 plates, text ills. Orig blue cloth.
(Trophy Room Books) **£400 [≃ $250]**

Pratt, Samuel Jackson
- Gleanings in England; descriptive of the Countenance, Mind and Character of the Country. London: Strahan, for Longman & Rees, 1801. 1st edn. 2 vols. 8vo. Half-titles, advt leaf. Contemp tree calf, gilt spines sl rubbed. *(Hannas)* **£85 [≃ $136]**

Prentiss, Charles
- The Life of the late Gen. William Eaton; Several Years an Officer in the United States' Army, Consul at the Regency of Tunis on the Coast of Barbary ... Brookfield: E. Merriam, 1813. 1st edn. 8vo. viii,448 pp. Lacks port frontis (as usual). Rec leather.
(Schoyer) **$125 [≃ £78]**

Prescott, William H.
- History of the Conquest of Mexico ... New York: Harper, 1843. 1st edn. 3 vols. 488; 480; 524 pp. 2 maps, 3 ports, 1 facs. Orig black cloth, gilt spines, fine.
(M & S Rare Books) **$500 [≃ £312]**
- History of the Conquest of Peru with a Preliminary View of the Civilization of the Incas. Boston: 1847. 1st edn, 1st state. 2 vols. Ports. Occas foxing. Orig cloth, some chipping at spine ends. *(Reese)* **$85 [≃ £53]**

The Present State of the West Indies ...
- The Present State of the West Indies, containing an Accurate Description of what Parts are Possessed by the Several Powers in Europe ... London: 1778. Sm folio. iv,95 pp. Fldg cold map. Old mrbld wraps, sl dog-eared. Cloth box. *(Reese)* **$1,500 [≃ £937]**

Price, David (translator)
- Memoirs of the Emperor Jahangueir, written by Himself; and translated from a Persian Manuscript. London: Oriental Translation Fund, 1829. 4to. vi,141 pp, inc engvd pres. Mod half calf. *(Farahar)* **£155 [≃ $248]**

Price, Julius Mendes
- From the Arctic Ocean to the Yellow Sea. The Narrative of a Journey in 1890 and 1891, Across Siberia, Mongolia, the Gobi Desert and North China. New York: Scribner's, 1892. 1st Amer edn. 8vo. xxiv,384 pp. Cold fldg map, frontis, plates, ills. Orig cloth gilt.
(Terramedia) **$150 [≃ £93]**
- From the Arctic Ocean to the Yellow Sea. The Narrative of a Journey in 1890 and 1891, Across Siberia, Mongolia, the Gobi Desert and North China. New York: Scribner's, 1892. 8vo. xxiv,380 pp. Cold fldg map, port, 142 ills. Orig pict cloth, rubbed, hd of spine reprd. *(Schoyer)* **$65 [≃ £40]**
- The Land of Gold. The Narrative of a Journey through the West Australian Goldfields in the Autumn of 1895 ... London: Sampson Low, 1896. 1st edn. 8vo. xix,204 pp. Fldg map, port, num ills. Dec endpapers. Orig pict gold cold cloth, spine darkened.
(Moon) **£200 [≃ $320]**

Prichard, H. Hesketh
- Hunting Camps in Wood and Wilderness. With a Foreword by F.C. Selous. London: Heinemann, 1910. 1st edn. Sm 4to. xiv,274,[2 advt] pp. Port frontis, 77 ills. A few damp spots. Orig cloth gilt, spine sl faded, minor wear to edges. W. & M. Mason's b'plate. *(Hollett)* **£110 [≃ $176]**
- Hunting Camps in Woods & Wilderness.

With a Foreword by F.C. Selous. New York & London: Sturgis & Heinemann, 1910. 1st Amer edn. Lge 8vo. xx, 274 pp. Num photo plates. Orig red cloth gilt, edges of front cvr darkened. *(Terramedia)* **$75 [≈£46]**
- Hunting Camps in Wood and Wilderness. London: 1910. 4to. Some foxing. Orig bndg. *(Grayling)* **£25 [≈$40]**
- Through Trackless Labrador. London: 1911. 4to. Ills. V sl foxing. Orig bndg. *(Grayling)* **£50 [≈$80]**
- Through Trackless Labrador. London: Heinemann, 1911. 1st edn. Sm 4to. xv,254 pp. 97 ills. Orig pict cloth gilt, trifle faded, front jnt cracked, a few damp spots. *(Hollett)* **£100 [≈$160]**

Priest, Josiah
- American Antiquities, and Discoveries in the West ... Third Edition Revised. Albany: Hoffman & White, 1833. 400 pp. Fldg map, 2 engvd plates (1 fldg). Text sl foxed. Contemp calf gilt, extremities sl rubbed. *(Karmiole)* **$150 [≈£93]**

Priest, William
- Travels in the United States of America, 1793-1797, with the Author's Journals of his Two Voyages across the Atlantic. London: J. Johnson, 1802. 1st edn. [10],214 pp. Cold frontis. Waterstained & spotted. Foxed. Half calf. *(Jenkins)* **$200 [≈£125]**

Prime, E.D.G.
- Forty Years in the Turkish Empire; or, Memoirs of Rev. William Goodell, by his Son-in-law. New York: Carter, 1876. 1st edn. Sm 8vo. xii,489,12 advt pp. Orig cloth, sl rubbed. *(Worldwide Antiqu'n)* **$48 [≈£30]**

Prime, William C.
- Boat Life in Egypt and Nubia. New York: Harper, 1857. 8vo. 498,advt pp. Orig red cloth gilt, spine bit sloped & sl chipped at ends. *(Terramedia)* **$60 [≈£37]**

Prior, James
- Voyage along the Eastern Coast of Africa, to Mosambique, Johanna, and Quiloa; to St. Helena; to Rio de Janeiro, Bahia, and Pernambuco in Brazil, in the 'Nisus', Frigate. London: Sir Richard Phillips, 1819. 1st edn. 2 fldg maps, 1 plate. Mod cloth backed bds. *(Trebizond)* **$225 [≈£140]**

Pritchard, W.T.
- Polynesian Reminiscences; or, Life in the South Pacific Islands. London: 1866. xii,428 pp. Frontis, tinted plates. Orig cloth gilt,

backstrip reprd, cloth a bit rumpled, worn at outer hinges. *(Reese)* **$275 [≈£171]**

Prout, Ebenezer
- Madagascar: Its Mission and Its Martyrs. London: London Missionary Society, 1863. 2nd edn, enlgd. 8vo. viii,167 pp. Title vignette, engvd map frontis. Orig dec cloth. *(Schoyer)* **$45 [≈£28]**

Prudden, T. Mitchell
- On the Great American Plateau. New York & London: Putnam's, 1906. 1st edn. 12mo. viii, 243, advt pp. Fldg map, frontis, num photo plates. Orig pict brown cloth gilt. *(Terramedia)* **$30 [≈£18]**

Pruen, Septimus Tristram
- The Arab and the African. Experiences in Eastern Equatorial Africa during a Residence of Three Years. London: Seeley, 1891. xi,338, [2 advt] pp. Port, 8 plates, 2 text maps. Orig cloth, sl rubbed. *(Adelson)* **$160 [≈£100]**
- The Arab and the African: Experiences in Eastern Equatorial Africa during a Residence of Three Years. London: Seeley, 1891. 1st edn. Cr 8vo. xi,338,[2 advt] pp. 22 plates & ills. Orig cloth gilt. *(Fenning)* **£45 [≈$72]**

Prus, Madame
- A Residence in Algeria. Translated from the French. London: William Pickering, 1852. 1st edn. 8vo. vii,332,[4 advt] pp. Orig cloth, paper label. *(Frew Mackenzie)* **£115 [≈$184]**

Pugin, Augustus C. & Heath, Charles
- Paris and Its Environs ... With Topographical and Historical Descriptions ... London: 1831. 4to. ii,[4],202 pp. Engvd titles. 200 engvd plates on 100 ff. Some foxing & offsetting. Orig cloth, leather label, worn at extremities, front hinge broken. *(Reese)* **$400 [≈£250]**

Pumpelly, Raphael
- Across America and Asia. Notes of a Five Years' Journey around the World and of Residence in Arizona, Japan and China. New York: Leypoldt & Holt, 1870. 4th edn, rvsd. 8vo. xvi,454 pp. 4 maps, 25 ills. Orig cloth. *(Worldwide Antiqu'n)* **$45 [≈£28]**
- Geological Researches in China, Mongolia, and Japan, 1862-1865. Washington: 1866. 1st edn. Folio. 143 pp. Cold maps, fldg plates. Orig ptd wraps. Half mor slipcase. *(Jenkins)* **$200 [≈£125]**

Purdy, John
- The New Sailing Directory for the Gulf of Venice and the Eastern or Levantine Division of the Mediterranean Sea ... London: 1834. [28], 282 pp. Orig paper bds, paper labels, spine chipped, front bd detached, rear bd loose.   *(Reese)* **$100 [≈ £62]**

Putnam, George P.
- The Southland of North America. Rambles & Observations in Central America during the Year 1912. New York & London: Putnam's, 1913. Sm 8vo. xiv,425 pp. Fldg map, frontis, num other photo plates. Orig green cloth.
                    (Terramedia) **$40 [≈ £25]**

Pyne, J.B.
- The Lake Scenery of England. Drawn on Stone by T. Picken. London: Day & Son, [1859]. Imperial 8vo. [ii],vii pp. Cold litho title, 24 cold litho views, each with page of ptd text. 1 plate loose, sl spotting. Orig pict cloth gilt, a.e.g., hd of spine sl worn.
                    (Bickersteth) **£160 [≈ $256]**

Quatrefages, A. de
- The Rambles of a Naturalist on the Coasts of France, Spain and Sicily. Translated by E.C. Otte. London: 1857. 2 vols. Post 8vo. Orig cloth, jnts loose, bndg of vol 2 sl stained.
                    (Wheldon & Wesley) **£35 [≈ $56]**
- The Rambles of a Naturalist on the Coast of France, Spain and Sicily. Translated by E.C. Otte. London: Longman ..., 1857. 2 vols. Sm 8vo. xx,355,32 advt; viii,375 pp. Orig green cloth.   *(Karmiole)* **$75 [≈ £46]**

Quiller-Couch, M. & L.
- Ancient & Holy Wells of Cornwall. London: 1894. 1st edn. 8vo. Ills. Orig cloth, top bd sl scratched.   *(Ambra)* **£28 [≈ $44]**

Quillinan, Dorothy, nee Wordsworth
- Journal of a Few Months' Residence in Portugal, and Glimpses of the South of Spain. London: Moxon, 1847. 2 vols. 8vo. [8],xvi, [2], 242,[2]; [4],248 pp. Orig green cloth, gilt spines.   *(Karmiole)* **$100 [≈ £62]**

Quincey, J. Wong
- Chinese Hunter. London: 1939. 8vo. Ills. Orig cloth.   *(Grayling)* **£85 [≈ $136]**

Quisenberry, Anderson C.
- Lopez's Expeditions to Cuba 1850 and 1851. Louisville, 1906. Lge 4to. 172 pp. Port, plates. Cloth. Orig wraps bound in.
                    (Reese) **$125 [≈ £78]**

Rabin, Chaim
- Ancient West-Arabian. London: 1951. 8vo. Maps. Orig cloth.   *(Farahar)* **£20 [≈ $32]**

Radford, George
- Yorkshire by the Sea ... Leeds: Richard Jackson, 1891. One of 300. Sm folio. 192 pp. 12 etchings & 26 text ills by J.A. Symington. A few spots. Orig vellum gilt extra over heavy bevelled bds, a.e.g.   *(Hollett)* **£250 [≈ $400]**

Ragg, Lonsdale & Laura
- Venice. Painted by Mortimer Menpes. London: A. & C. Black Colour Books, Twenty Shilling Series, 1916. New edn, with new text (replacing previous text by Dorothy Menpes). 75 cold plates. Orig white dec turquoise cloth.   *(Old Cathay)* **£45 [≈ $72]**
- Venice. Painted by Mortimer Menpes. London: A. & C. Black Colour Books, Twenty Shilling Series, 1916. New edn. 75 cold plates. Orig white dec turquoise cloth, bds rubbed & worn.
                    (Old Cathay) **£33 [≈ $52]**

The Railway Guide of New South Wales ...
- The Railway Guide of New South Wales, (for the Use of Tourists, Excursionists, and Others) ... Sydney: Thomas Richards, Govt Printer, 1879. Post 4to. [ii],122 pp. Chromolitho title, fldg map, 6 plates, num ills. Sl used. Orig cloth, sl used & marked.
                    (Duck) **£335 [≈ $536]**

Rainsford, W.S.
- The Land of the Lion. London: 1909. 8vo. Ills. Orig pict cloth, rubbed & frayed.
                    (Grayling) **£70 [≈ $112]**

Raleigh, Sir Walter
- A Discourse of Sea-Ports ... see Digges, Sir Dudley.
- Judicious and Select Essayes and Observations ... London: T.W. for Humphrey Mosele [sic], 1650. 1st edn. 8vo. 8 pp advts. 4 sep title-pages. Frontis port. A few smudges. Early 19th c calf gilt, elab gilt spine with nautical motifs. Wing R.170.
                    (Trebizond) **$650 [≈ £406]**

Ramsden, A.R.
- Assam Planter. Tea Planting and Hunting in the Assam Jungle. London: 1945. 8vo. Orig cloth.   *(Farahar)* **£15 [≈ $24]**

Ramsden, Douglas M.
- Tramping through Iceland. Liverpool: Henry Young & Sons, 1931. 1st edn. 8vo. Fldg map, 3 plates. Orig cloth.   *(Hannas)* **£40 [≈ $64]**

Ramseyer, F.A. & Kuhne, J.
- Four Years in Ashantee ... Edited by Mrs Weitbrecht, with Introduction by Rev. Dr. Gundert ... New York: 1875. 1st Amer edn. 8vo. Frontis, 3 plates. 1 tear reprd. Occas spotting. Half calf. *(Farahar)* £150 [≈ $240]

Ranken, George (ed.)
- Windabyne. A Record of By-gone Times in Australia. Related by Reginald Crawford, Strath-clyde Maranoa in 1880. London: Remington, 1895. 1st edn. 8vo. Half-title. Lacks final f.e.p. Orig dec blue cloth, sl stained. *(Hannas)* £35 [≈ $56]

Rankin, Daniel J.
- The Zambesi Basin and Nyasaland. London: Blackwood, 1893. 1st edn. vi,277 pp. 3 fldg maps, 10 plates. Mod half mor gilt. *(Hollett)* £85 [≈ $136]

Rankin, N.
- Antarctic Isle. Wild Life in South Georgia. London: 1951. 8vo. 383 pp. 138 plates. Orig cloth. *(Wheldon & Wesley)* £28 [≈ $44]

Raphael, John R.
- Through Unknown Nigeria. London: Werner Laurie, [1914?]. 8vo. xxiii,361 pp. Cold frontis, 60 ills. Orig cloth. *(Schoyer)* $50 [≈ £31]

Rasmussen, Knud
- Greenland by the Polar Sea ... the Story of the Thule Expedition ... New York: Stokes, [1921]. Lge 8vo. xxiii,327 pp. Fldg map, num plates. Orig dec green cloth, minor wear. *(Parmer)* $125 [≈ £78]
- Greenland by the Polar Sea ... the Story of the Thule Expedition ... London: Heinemann, 1921. Lge 8vo. xxiii,327 pp. Fldg map, num plates. Orig dec green cloth, spine faded. *(Parmer)* $125 [≈ £78]

Rasmussen, S.E.
- London: The Unique City. London: 1937. Rvsd edn. 8vo. 104 pp. Num photo ills. Orig cloth. *(Henly)* £22 [≈ $35]

Ratcliffe, Dorothy Una
- Icelandic Spring. With Decorations by Barbara Arnason. London: The Bodley Head, 1950. 1st edn. 4to. Endpaper maps. Orig cloth. *(Hannas)* £55 [≈ $88]

Ratti, Abate Achille
- Climbs on Alpine Peaks. Translated by J.E.C. Eaton ... London: Fisher Unwin, 1923. 1st English edn. 136 pp. Frontis, map,

20 ills. Half-title sl spotted, 1 plate reprd. Mod blue half levant mor gilt. *(Hollett)* £65 [≈ $104]

Rawlinson, George
- History of Ancient Egypt. London: 1881. 1st edn. 2 vols. 8vo. 554; 567,advt pp. Cold map, num plates, ills. Orig brown cloth gilt, inner hinges sl cracked, sm tear vol 1 spine. *(Terramedia)* $100 [≈ £62]

Ray, John
- Observations Topographical, Moral and Physiological made in a Journey through part of the Low-Countries, Germany, Italy and France ... London: 1673. 8vo. [xv],499, [vii], 115 pp. Port, 3 plates (part of 1st supplied in facs). Mod calf, antique style. *(Wheldon & Wesley)* £220 [≈ $352]
- Travels through the Low Countries, Germany, Italy and France ... added An Account of the Travels of Francis Willughby, Esq., through great Part of Spain ... London: 1738. 2nd edn. 2 vols. 8vo. iv,428; [x],489, [ii], 120 pp. 3 figs. Calf, spine ends & hinges worn. *(Baldwin)* £275 [≈ $440]

Ray, Patrick Henry
- Report on the International Polar Expedition to Point Barrow, Alaska ... Washington: GPO, 1885. 4to. 695 pp. Fldg map, plates (some cold). Orig cloth, dull & scuffed. *(High Latitude)* $100 [≈ £62]

Read, George H.
- The Last Cruise of the Saginaw. Boston & New York: 1912. 127 pp. Port, ills. Orig pict cloth. *(Reese)* $100 [≈ £62]

Read, Samuel
- Leaves from a Sketch Book. Pencillings of Travel at Home and Abroad. London: Sampson Low, 1875. Folio. xii,224 pp. Ills. Occas foxing & spotting, mainly marginal. Orig green cloth gilt, a.e.g., front endpaper loose. *(Lamb)* £120 [≈ $192]

Reade, W. Winwood
- Savage Africa: Being the Narrative of a Tour in Equatorial, Southwestern & Northwestern Africa, with Notes on the Habits of the Gorilla ... New York: Harper, 1864. 1st Amer edn. 8vo. [xi],452,advt pp. Fldg map (tear reprd), plates, ills. Rebound in cloth. *(Terramedia)* $150 [≈ £93]
- Savage Africa. A Tour in Equatorial, Southwestern, Northwestern Africa ... Habits of the Gorilla ... New York: 1864. Engvd plates, text ills. Half mor, hinges strengthened, crnrs rubbed.

(Grayling) **£150 [≈ $240]**

Reading, Joseph
- The Ogowe Band: A Narrative of African Travel. Philadelphia: 1890. 1st edn. Sl worn & shaken.   *(Terramedia)* **$100 [≈ £62]**
- The Ogowe Band: A Narrative of African Travel. Philadelphia: 1890. 2nd edn. Tall 8vo. xv,278 pp. Frontis, num photo plates. Orig pict grey green cloth gilt.
    (Terramedia) **$100 [≈ £62]**

Reasons for Establishing the Colony of Georgia ...
- See Martyn, Benjamin.

Recollections ...
- Recollections of an Excursion to the Monasteries of Alcobaca and Batalha ... see Beckford, William.

Redding, Cyrus
- An Illustrated Itinerary of the County of Lancaster. London: How & Parsons, 1842. 4to. Frontis, map, 6 steel-engvd & 1 w'engvd plates, text engvs. Occas sl foxing. New half calf over old mrbld bds.
    (Sanders) **£100 [≈ $160]**

Redding, M.W.
- Antiquities of the Orient Unveiled. Hartford: 1874. Lge 8vo. 421,advt pp. Cold frontis of Jerusalem, fldg cold map, num other plates. Orig gilt dec green cloth.
    (Terramedia) **$50 [≈ £31]**

Reed, William
- The Phantom of the Poles. New York: Walter S. Rockey, 1906. 8vo. 281 pp. 21 ills. Orig green cloth, light edgewear.
    (Parmer) **$100 [≈ £62]**

Reeve, Henry F.
- The Gambia. Its History, Ancient, Medieval & Modern. Together with Geographical, Geological and Ethnographical ... London: Smith, Elder, 1912. 1st edn. Lge 8vo. xv,288 pp. Lge fldg map, num photo plates. Orig maroon cloth gilt, ex-lib, spine edges cracked.
    (Terramedia) **$75 [≈ £46]**

Reeves, Hon. W.P.
- New Zealand. Painted by F. and W. Wright. London: A. & C. Black Colour Books, Twenty Shilling Series, 1908. 1st edn. Fldg map, 75 cold plates. Orig dec cloth. VG + /F-.
    (Old Cathay) **£55 [≈ $88]**
- New Zealand. Painted by F. & W. Wright. London: A. & C. Black Colour Books, Twenty Shilling Series, 1908. 1st edn. Fldg map, 75 cold plates. Orig dec cloth. VG.
    (Old Cathay) **£45 [≈ $72]**

Reid, W. Max
- The Mohawk Valley: Its Legends & History. New York: Putnam's, 1901. 1st edn. 8vo. xii, 455,advt pp. Frontis & other photo plates. Orig blue cloth gilt, front hinge sl cracked internally.   *(Terramedia)* **$75 [≈ £46]**

Reinbeck, G.
- Travels from St. Petersburgh through Moscow, Grodno, Warsaw, Breslaw, &c. to Germany; in the Year 1805: In a Series of Letters. London: Richard Phillips, 1807. 160 pp. Mod half cloth.   *(Reese)* **$125 [≈ £78]**

Remarks ...
- Remarks on Several Parts of Italy ... see Addison, Joseph.

Remy, Jules & Brenchley, Julius
- A Journey to Great Salt Lake City. London: W. Jeffs, 1861. 1st edn in English. 2 vols. Fldg map, plates. Orig bndg, new spines.
    (Jenkins) **$400 [≈ £250]**

Rennell, James
- The Geographical System of Herodotus Examined and Explained ... London: Rivington, 1830. 2nd edn, rvsd. 2 vols. 8vo. xxiv,535; vi, 472 pp. Port frontis, 11 fldg maps. Contemp polished calf, gilt spines.
    (Frew Mackenzie) **£98 [≈ $156]**

Rennie, S.
- Bhotan and the Story of the Dooar War including Sketches of a Three Months' residence in the Himalayas and Narrative of a Visit to Bhotan in 1865. London: 1866. 408 pp. Lge fldg map. Orig green cloth, recased.
    (Trophy Room Books) **$400 [≈ £250]**

Reresby, Sir John
- The Travels and Memoirs ... States and Courts of Europe, During the Time of Cromwell's Usurpation ... London: 1813. Lge 8vo. xii,412 pp. 40 plates (12 hand cold). Green half mor, elab gilt spine, by Riviere (ca 1900).   *(Karmiole)* **$200 [≈ £125]**

Reuilly, J.
- Travels in the Crimea, and along the Shores of the Black Sea, performed during the Year 1803. London: Richard Phillips, 1807. 84 pp. Plates. Occas trace of foxing, sl offsetting from plates. Mod half cloth, t.e.g.
    (Reese) **$100 [≈ £62]**

Rey, Guido
- The Matterhorn. London: Fisher Unwin, 1908. 2nd edn. Sm 4to. 336 pp. 35 plates, some tinted & tipped-in. Orig cloth, rubbed & damped, v scraped, front jnt cracked, endpapers spotted.   *(Hollett)* **£125 [≈ $200]**

Reynolds, John
- Sketches of the Country on the Northern Route from Belleville, Ill., to the City of New York and Back by the Ohio Valley. Belleville: 1854. 1st edn. 264 pp. Orig cloth.
  (Jenkins) **$775 [≈ £484]**

Reynolds-Ball, Eustace A.
- The City of the Caliphs. A Popular Study of Cairo and its Environs and the Nile and its Antiquities. Boston: Estes & Lauriat, (1897). 8vo. 20 plates. Orig pict cloth gilt, uncut, t.e.g.   *(Stewart)* **£30 [≈ $48]**

Rhodes, F.
- Pageant of the Pacific. Being the Maritime History of Australasia ... Sydney: Thwaites, (1936). 2 vols. Lge 8vo. 411; 478 pp. Port. Endpapers sl foxed. Orig cloth, extremities sl rubbed.   *(Karmiole)* **$150 [≈ £93]**

Ricaut, Sir Paul
- See Rycaut, Sir Paul.

Rice, W.
- Indian Game from Quail to Tiger. London: 1884. 8vo. Orig cloth, rubbed, inner hinge weak.   *(Grayling)* **£35 [≈ $56]**

Rich, Claudius James
- Narrative of a Residence in Koordistan. And of the Site of Ancient Nineveh; with a Journal of a Voyage down the Tigris ... London: James Duncan, 1836. 1st edn. 2 vols. 8vo. xxxiii,398; viii,410 pp. 13 maps & plates. Orig green cloth, sl worn & shaken.
  (Terramedia) **$400 [≈ £250]**

Rich, Virtulon
- Western Life in the Stirrups. A Sketch of a Journey to the West in the Spring & Summer of 1832. Chicago: Caxton Club, 1965. 1st edn. Sm 4to. xix,81 pp. Map, port, plates. Orig half cloth & bds. Prospectus laid in.
  (Wreden) **$45 [≈ £28]**

Richards, Capt. & Clarke, Lieut.-Col.
- Report on the Maritime Canal connecting the Mediterranean at Port Said ... (Suez Canal) ... London: HMSO, 1870. 2 maps, 13 charts. Spine worn & scuffed..   *(Parmer)* **$95 [≈ £59]**

Richards, Fred
- A Persian Journey, being an Etcher's Impressions of the Middle East. London & Toronto: Cape, 1931. 1st edn. Sm 4to. 240 pp. 48 plates. Orig cloth, sl rubbed.
  (Worldwide Antiqu'n) **$65 [≈ £40]**

Richards, Matthew W.
- Rambles in Sweden. Being Notes of a Tour made in the Summer of 1873. London: for private circulation only, 1875. 1st edn. Mtd photo, sgnd by the author (as always). Text w'cuts. Orig cloth, a.e.g. Author's pres copy.
  (Hannas) **£45 [≈ $72]**

Richardson, William
- The Monastic Ruins of Yorkshire ... With Historical Descriptions by Revd. Edward Churton. York: Robert Sunter ..., 1843. 2 vols. Lge folio. 60 tinted litho plates by Day & Hague, title & fldg map. Rather spotted as usual. Contemp half mor gilt, a.e.g.
  (Hollett) **£650 [≈ $1,040]**

Richtofen, Ferdinand P.W.
- Baron Richtofen's Letters, 1870-1872. Shanghai: "North-China Herald", [1872]. 1st edn. 4to. [4],149 pp. 2 ills (1 fldg). Perf lib stamp on title. Old bds, disbound.
  (M & S Rare Books) **$200 [≈ £125]**

Rickards, Constantine George
- The Ruins of Mexico. Vol. I [all published]. London: Shrimpton, 1910. 1st edn. Folio. viii,154,viii pp. Frontis gravure, 261 mtd photos. Orig pict gilt cloth.
  (Jenkins) **$335 [≈ £209]**

Ricketts, Charles
- Pages from a Diary in Greece. Edited by Paul Delany. Edinburgh: The Tragara Press, 1978. One of 150. 8vo. 57 pp. Frontis. Orig blue cloth.   *(Piccadilly)* **£22.50 [≈ $36]**

Ridger, A.L.
- A Wanderer's Trail. A Faithful Record of Travel in Many Lands. New York: Henry Holt, 1914. 1st edn. 8vo. 403 pp. Frontis, num plates. Orig maroon cloth, t.e.g.
  (Terramedia) **$30 [≈ £18]**

Riggs, Stephen R.
- Mary and I. Forty Years with the Sioux ... Chicago: Holmes, (1880). 8vo. xxii,388 pp. 3 litho ports on 2 plates. Old marg waterstain on both plates. Orig green cloth, sl soiled.
  (Karmiole) **$45 [≈ £28]**

Riley, Athelstan
- Athos or the Mountain of the Monks. London: Longmans, Green, 1887. 8vo. xvi,409 pp. Map, full-page plates & w'cuts in text. Orig red cloth, spine sl rubbed & faded. *(Piccadilly)* **£52 [≃ $83]**

Rimmer, Alfred
- Rambles round Eton and Harrow. London: 1882. Large Paper Edition de Luxe. One of 250. xi,290 pp. 52 ills. Orig bds, parchment spine, uncut, v rubbed, stain on lower bd. *(Coombes)* **£12.50 [≃ $20]**

Rink, Henry
- Danish Greenland Its People and Its Products. London: 1877. 1st edn in English. xvii,468 pp. Fldg map, 15 plates. Frontis. A few ff sl foxed. Polished calf, spine gilt extra, prize b'plate. *(Reese)* **$125 [≃ £78]**
- Danish Greenland. Its People and Products. Edited by Dr. Robert Brown. London: Henry S. King, 1877. 1st English edn. 8vo. Fldg map, 16 plates. Orig pict cloth, inner hinge cracked. Traces of removed label from title & 1st p of text. *(Hannas)* **£160 [≃ $256]**
- Tales and Sketches of the Eskimo ... Edinburgh & London: Blackwood, 1875. 1st English edn. 8vo. xii,[2],472 pp. 6 plates (2 fldg), text ills. Orig dec brown cloth, somewhat worn at spine, upper hinge weak. *(Parmer)* **$300 [≃ £187]**

Ritchie, Leitch
- A Journey to St. Petersburg and Moscow ... London: Longman, Rees, Heath's Picturesque Annual, 1836. 8vo. [viii],256 pp. 25 engvd plates (some spotting & browning). Scarlet mor gilt, a.e.g., rather worn at edges. *(Hollett)* **£50 [≃ $80]**
- Scott and Scotland ... London: Longman, Rees ..., Heath's Picturesque Annual, 1835. 8vo. viii,256 pp. 21 engvd plates by George Cattermole. Some browning. Lacks front free endpaper. Scarlet mor gilt, a.e.g., a little rubbed. *(Hollett)* **£40 [≃ $64]**
- Travelling Sketches on the Sea-Coasts of France. London: Longman, Rees ..., Heath's Picturesque Annual, 1834. 8vo. [iv],256 pp. 21 engvd plates by Clarkson Stanfield (a little browned). Scarlet mor gilt, a.e.g., a little worn. *(Hollett)* **£50 [≃ $80]**
- Wanderings by the Seine. With 20 Engravings from Drawings by J.M.W. Turner ... London: for the proprietor ..., (1834). 1st edn. 8vo. 256 pp. Addtnl engvd title, 1 engvd vignette, 19 plates. Tissues. Contemp black calf, a.e.g., sl rubbed. *(Young's)* **£70 [≃ $112]**

Robbins, Alfred F.
- Launceston, Past and Present. A Historical and Descriptive Sketch. Launceston: 1888. 1st edn. 8vo. Sl spotting to foredge & prelims. Orig cloth. *(Ambra)* **£43 [≃ $68]**

Robbins, Archibald
- A Journal, comprising an Account of the loss of the Brig Commerce, of Hartford ... Western Coast of Africa ... Sufferings ... upon the Desert of Zahara ... Rochester, New York: E. Peck ..., 1818. 12mo. 375 pp. Fldg map (foxing, creased). Contemp calf, worn but sound. *(Ramer)* **$250 [≃ £156]**

Roberts, David
- The Holy Land, Syria, Idumea, Arabia, Egypt & Nubia ... With Historical Descriptions by the Revd. George Croly. London: Day & Son, 1855. 6 vols in 3. 4to. 249 (of 250) tinted lithos. Minor marg dampstain affecting about half the set. Orig cloth, spines relaid. *(Frew Mackenzie)* **£1,500 [≃ $2,400]**

Roberts, Emma
- Hindostan: Its Landscapes, Palaces, Temples, Tombs. The Shores of the Red Sea ... Himalaya Mountains Illustrated in a Series of Views ... London: Fisher, Son & Co, 1845. 2 vols. 128; 103 pp. 2 frontis, num engvs. Orig elab gilt maroon cloth, a.e.g., rebacked. *(Lyon)* **£275 [≃ $440]**
- Indostan Its Landscapes, Palaces, Temples, Tombs; The Shores of the Red Sea ... Himalaya Mountains Illustrated in a Series Views ... London: [ca 1845]. 2 vols. 4to. 128; 104 pp. 2 frontis, engvd titles, plates. Contemp polished calf gilt extra, a.e.g. *(Reese)* **$550 [≃ £343]**

Roberts, Emma & Elliott, Robert
- Views in India, China, and on the Shores of the Red Sea ... London: Fisher &c., n.d. 2 vols in one. 4to. 68,64 pp. Baxter-ptd cold frontis, 61 steel engvd plates. A few spots. Half calf gilt, sl rubbed. *(Hollett)* **£150 [≃ $240]**

Roberts, James H.
- A Flight for Life and an Inside View of Mongolia. Boston & Chicago: Pilgrim Press, [1903]. 1st edn. 12mo. 402 pp. Frontis. Orig maroon cloth, t.e.g. Author's signed presentation. *(Terramedia)* **$50 [≃ £31]**

Roberts, Orlando W.
- Narrative of Voyages and Excursions on the East Coast and in the Interior of Central America ... Edinburgh: Constable's

Miscellany 17, 1827. 1st edn. Lge 12mo. 302 pp. Engvd vignette series title, fldg engvd map. Orig roan backed cloth, headband chipped. *(Fenning)* £68.50 [≈ $110]

Roberts, Peter
- The Cambrian Popular Antiquities; or An Account of some Traditions, Customs and Superstitions of Wales ... London: 1815. 1st edn. 8vo. [ii],viii,353,[1] pp. Half-title. 9 cold aquatint plates, 1 other plate. Lacks advts. Some signs of age. Contemp calf, sl rubbed. *(Bow Windows)* £295 [≈ $472]

Robertson, Sir George Scott
- Chitral. The Story of a Minor Siege. London: Methuen, 1898. 8vo. x,363,40 advt pp. 5 maps & plans, frontis, 31 ills. Orig cloth, v worn. *(Bates & Hindmarch)* £50 [≈ $80]
- The Kaffirs of Hindu Kush. London: Lawrence & Bullen, 1896. 1st edn. Lge 8vo. xx, 658 pp. Fldg map, num plates & ills. Orig pict cloth gilt. *(Terramedia)* $500 [≈ £312]

Robertson, John P. & William P.
- Letters on Paraguay: Comprising an Account of a Four Years' Residence in that Republic, under the Government of the Dictator Francia. London: Murray, 1838. 1st edn. 2 vols. 8vo. xxviii,359; x,342 pp. Fldg map, port, plate. Orig brown cloth, rebacked. *(Adelson)* $375 [≈ £234]

Robertson, Wilfrid
- Zambezi Days. London: Blackie, 1936. 8vo. 196 pp. Photo frontis, 15 photo ills. Orig bndg. Worn dw. *(Bates & Hindmarch)* £35 [≈ $56]

Robertson, William
- An Historical Disquisition concerning the Knowledge which the Ancients had of India; and the Progress of Trade with that Country ... London: for A. Strahan ..., 1791. 1st edn. 4to. xii,364,[10] pp. 2 fldg maps. Contemp qtr calf, rebacked. *(Young's)* £85 [≈ $136]
- An Historical Disquisition concerning the Knowledge which the Ancients had of India ... Dublin: John Ershaw for G. Burnet ..., 1791. 1st Dublin edn. 8vo. vi,[ii],349,[xv] pp. 2 fldg maps. Contemp calf, gilt spine, label, upper jnt cracked, new endpapers. *(Clark)* £40 [≈ $64]
- An Historical Disquisition concerning the Knowledge which the Ancients had of India ... Philadelphia: Young, 1792. 1st US edn. 8vo. 420 pp. Sl foxing. Contemp calf, rear cvr detached. *(Worldwide Antiqu'n)* $50 [≈ £31]

Robins, William
- Paddington: Past and Present. London: for the author, [1853]. 8vo. xv,200 pp. 2 views. Orig cloth, spine sl worn & faded. *(Coombes)* £20 [≈ $32]

Robinson, Charles H.
- Hausaland. or, Fifteen Hundred Miles through the Central Soudan. London: Sampson Low ..., 1896. 1st edn. 8vo. xvi,304 pp. Fldg map, 17 plates, 15 ills. Orig cloth gilt, mainly unopened. *(Fenning)* £95 [≈ $152]

Robinson, F.K.
- Whitby: its Abbey, and the Principal Parts of the Neighbourhood. Whitby: S. Reed, 1860. 8vo. Fldg map, 2 engvd & 2 litho plates, w'engvd text ills. Orig blue cloth. *(Sanders)* £35 [≈ $56]

Robinson, George
- Three Years in the East ... London [ptd in Paris]: 1837. viii,416 pp. 5 fldg maps. Scattered foxing. Contemp mor gilt, gilt inner dentelles, front free endsheet excised. *(Reese)* $175 [≈ £109]

Robinson, John
- An Account of Sweden. London: Goodwin, 1694. 8vo. Calf, front cvr detached. Wing R.1690. *(Rostenberg & Stern)* $235 [≈ £146]
- An Account of Sveden: Together with an Extract of the History of the Kingdom. The Second Edition. London: for Tim Goodwin, 1711. [4],85,[3] pp. Some foxing. Contemp calf gilt, worn, spine chipped. *(Reese)* $300 [≈ £187]

Robinson, William
- The History and Antiquities of the Parish of Tottenham ... Middlesex: for the author, 1818. 1st edn. 8vo. Lge fldg map, 18 plates (some spotting). Contemp half calf. *(Robertshaw)* £65 [≈ $104]

Robo, Etienne
- Mediaeval Farnham: Everyday Life in an Episcopal Manor. Farnham: 1935. 4to. xiii,326 pp. 24 ills. Sl foxing. Orig buckram, some fading. *(Coombes)* £25 [≈ $40]

Rochefort, C. de
- The History of Barbados, St. Christophers, Mevis, St. Vincents, Antego, Martinico, Monserrat, and the rest of the Caribby-Islands ... London: 1665. Folio. [viii],352, [16] pp. 9 plates. Sl waterstain, 9 ff browned. Contemp calf, rebacked, crnrs reprd.

(Wheldon & Wesley) £800 [≈ $1,280]

Rochon, Alexis de
- A Voyage to Madagascar, and the East Indies ... to which is added a Memoir on the Chinese Trade. London: Robinson, 1792. 8vo. 4,xlix,2,475 pp. Fldg map. Orig mrbld bds, rebacked in calf.   *(Adelson)* $325 [≈ £203]

Rock, James L. & Smith, W.I. (eds.)
- Southern and Western Texas Guide for 1878. St. Louis: 1878. 282 pp. Frontis, ills. Lacks the map as usual. Cloth, some edge wear.
(Reese) $150 [≈ £93]

Rockhill, W.W.
- The Land of the Lamas. Notes of a Journey through China, Mongolia and Tibet. New York: 1891. 1st edn. 398 pp. 2 maps, num ills. Orig cloth.
(Trophy Room Books) $750 [≈ £468]
- The Land of the Lamas. Notes of a Journey through China, Mongolia and Tibet. New York: 1891. 1st edn. 398 pp. 2 maps, num ills. Later bndg.
(Trophy Room Books) $500 [≈ £312]

Rockwell, Charles
- The Catskill Mountains and the Region Around. Their Scenery, Legends, and History; with Sketches in Prose and Verse ... New York: 1873. Sm 8vo. Text ills. Orig cloth.   *(Farahar)* £35 [≈ $56]

Rodd, Francis Rennell
- People of the Veil being an Account of the ... Tuareg Tribes which inhabit the Mountains of Air or Asben in the Central Sahara. London: Macmillan, 1926. 8vo. xvi,504 pp. 11 maps & diags, 51 photo plates. Orig bndg, ex-lib.   *(Bates & Hindmarch)* £40 [≈ $64]

Rodgers, John
- British Cities - York. London: Batsford, 1951. 1st edn. Num photo ills. Orig bndg. Dw by Brian Cook, price-clipped.
(Old Cathay) £17 [≈ $27]

Rodway, James
- In the Guiana Forest. Studies of Nature in Relation to the Struggle for Life. Chicago: McLurg, 1912. New enlgd edn. Sm 8vo. 326 pp. Photo plates. Orig pict green cloth, sl worn.   *(Terramedia)* $30 [≈ £18]

Rogers, Fairman
- A Manual of Coaching. London: Lippincott, 1900. 8vo. 34 plates. Orig pict gilt maroon cloth, v sl marked, rear inner jnt weak.

(Waterfield's) £150 [≈ $240]

Rogers, Sir John
- Sport in Vancouver and Newfoundland. London: 1912. 8vo. Ills. Some foxing. Orig bndg, rubbed.   *(Grayling)* £20 [≈ $32]

Rogers, Sir John, et al
- Hunting Big Game. London: 1897. 8vo. Ills. Orig bndg, sl worn.   *(Grayling)* £35 [≈ $56]

Rogers, Robert
- Journals of Major Robert Rogers: containing An Account of the several Excursions he made under the Generals who commanded upon the Continent of North America, during the late War ... London: 1765. viii,236,iv pp. Calf, rebacked, crnrs reprd.
(Reese) $1,850 [≈ £1,156]

Rogers, Robert W.
- A History of Babylonia and Assyria. New York: 1900. 2 vols. Lge 8vo. 429; 418 pp. Orig cloth gilt.   *(Terramedia)* $60 [≈ £37]

Rohde, E.S.
- Oxford's College Gardens. London: 1932. Roy 8vo. xiv,193 pp. Cold frontis, 23 cold & 8 plain plates. A little foxing, v sl ink stain on a few outer margs. Orig cloth, sl bubbled.
(Wheldon & Wesley) £28 [≈ $44]

Rokeby, Matthew Robinson-Morris, Baron
- Considerations on the Measures carrying on with respect to the British Colonies in North America. London: R. Baldwin, [1774]. The issue dated at the end: April, 1774, with the catchword 'ties' on p 154. 160 pp. Disbound.
(Jarndyce) £180 [≈ $288]

Rollin, Charles
- The Ancient History of the Egyptians, Carthaginians, Assyrians ... Translated from the French. London: Knapton, 1734-39. 1st edn in English. 13 vols in 14 (vol 11 in 2 vols). 8vo. 55 (of 56, lacks plate 38) fldg plates & maps. Orig calf & orig bds, sl worn.
(Bickersteth) £185 [≈ $296]
- The Ancient History of the Egyptians, Carthaginians, Assyrians ... Translated from the French. London: for J. Rivington ..., 1768. 5th edn. 7 vols. 8vo. 14 fldg maps, 10 plates. Sl foxing. Contemp calf, edges sl rubbed, sl scuffed, a few spine ends chipped.
(Worldwide Antiqu'n) $225 [≈ £140]

Ronaldshay, Lord
- On the Outskirts of Empire in Asia. London: 1904. 408 pp. Ills. Rebound in buckram.

(Trophy Room Books) $225 [≈ £140]
- Sport and Politics under an Eastern Sky. London: 1902. 8vo. Ills. Orig cloth, a bit rubbed.   *(Grayling)* £75 [≈ $120]
- Sport and Politics under an Eastern Sky. London: Blackwood, 1902. 8vo. xxiv,423 pp. 2 fldg maps, frontis, num photo ills. Orig pict cloth, recased.
          (Bates & Hindmarch) £145 [≈ $232]

Roosevelt, Kermit
- The Happy Hunting Grounds. New York: Scribners, 1920. Autographed edn, sgnd. Dw torn.   *(Terramedia)* $25 [≈ £15]

Roosevelt, Theodore
- African Game Trails. New York: 1910. Roy 8vo. xvi,529 pp. Map, num ills. Rather foxed. Inscrptn on title. Cloth.
          (Wheldon & Wesley) £55 [≈ $88]
- African Game Trails. London: Murray, 1910. 1st edn. Lge 8vo. xvii,534,8 advt pp. Ills. Orig pict cloth gilt.   *(Hollett)* £140 [≈ $224]
- African Game Trails, an Account of the African Wanderings of an American Hunter-Naturalist. New York: 1910. Roy 8vo. xvi, 529 pp. Map, num ills. Rather foxed. Inscrptn on title. Orig cloth.
          (Wheldon & Wesley) £55 [≈ $88]
- African Game Trails. New York: Syndicate, 1910. Roy 8vo. xxiv,584 pp. Port frontis, 7 cold & 36 b/w plates, over 150 text ills. Orig dec cloth, worn.   *(Berkelouw)* $100 [≈ £62]
- African Game Trails. New York: Scribners, 1910. 4to. xxiii,529 pp. Frontis port, num other plates. Orig pict green cloth, sl damp staining at edges.   *(Terramedia)* $50 [≈ £31]
- Hunting Trip of a Ranchman. 1886. 8vo. Ills. Orig bndg, spine relaid, crnrs rubbed.
          (Grayling) £30 [≈ $48]
- The Outdoor Pastimes of an American Hunter. New York: 1905. 1st edn. 369 pp. Ills. Orig bndg, with gilt cougar head on cvr.
          (Trophy Room Books) $85 [≈ £53]
- Ranch Life and the Hunting Trail. London: Fisher Unwin, [1888]. 1st edn. 4to. viii,186 pp. Illust by Remington. Orig dec cloth gilt extra, bumped, spine worn & torn, upper hinge cracking, jnts tender.
          (Hollett) £160 [≈ $256]
- Through the Brazilian Wilderness. London: Murray, 1914. 1st edn. Lge 8vo. xiv,374 pp. Map, num ills. Half-title & frontis spotted. Orig cloth gilt, untrimmed, spine faded.
          (Hollett) £35 [≈ $56]
- Through the Brazilian Wilderness. London: 1914. 8vo. Ills. Orig bndg, spine faded & sl rubbed.   *(Grayling)* £50 [≈ $80]

- The Wilderness Hunter. An Account of the Big Game of the United States and its Chase with Horse, Hound & Rifle. New York & London: Putnam's, Knickerbocker Press, [1893]. 1st edn. xvi,472 pp. Orig pict beige cloth, somewhat shabby.
          (Terramedia) $75 [≈ £46]

Roper, Edward
- By Track and Trail. A Journey through Canada. London: 1891. 8vo. Fldg map, num plates (2 spotted). Orig pict cloth, spine sl worn.   *(Farahar)* £45 [≈ $72]
- By Track and Trail. A Journey through Canada. London: 1891. 8vo. Plates, text ills. Sl foxing. Orig cloth, rubbed.
          (Grayling) £75 [≈ $120]

Roscoe, Revd John
- The Baganda; an Account of their Native Customs & Beliefs. London: Macmillan, 1911. 1st edn. 8vo. xix,547 pp. 2 fldg maps, frontis, num other ills. Orig dec pict green cloth gilt, hinges cracked internally.
          (Terramedia) $100 [≈ £62]
- The Baganda. An Account of their Native Customs and Beliefs. London: 1911. 8vo. 2 fldg tables, num plates. Orig cloth.
          (Farahar) £85 [≈ $136]
- The Soul of Central Africa. A General Account of the Mackie Ethnological Expedition. London: Cassell, 1922. 1st edn. Bndg stained & sunned at spine, front hinge cracked.   *(Terramedia)* $50 [≈ £31]

Roscoe, Thomas
- The Tourist in Italy. Illustrated ... by Samuel Prout. London: Robert Jennings & William Chaplin, 1831. 1st edn. 8vo. viii,271 pp. Frontis, addtnl engvd title & 26 plates. Tissue guards. Orig mor, a.e.g. Landscape Annual for 1831.   *(Claude Cox)* £55 [≈ $88]
- The Tourist in Italy. Illustrated from Drawings by J.D. Harding, London: Jennings & Chaplin, 1832. 1st edn. 8vo. [4],iv,288,8 advt pp. Frontis, addtnl engvd title & 24 plates. Sl marg spotting. Orig mor, sm split in hinge. The 3rd Landscape Annual.
          (Claude Cox) £55 [≈ $88]
- The Tourist in Italy. London: Landscape Annual, 1833. 8vo. viii,271,4 advt pp. Frontis, addtnl engvd title & 24 plates by J. Harding. Sm waterstain to top of title & frontis. Mor, a.e.g.   *(Henly)* £25 [≈ $40]
- The Tourist in Italy. Illustrated from Drawings by J.D. Harding, London: Jennings & Chaplin, 1833. 1st edn. 8vo. [8],271 pp. Frontis, addtnl engvd title & 24 plates. Orig green mor, sl rubbed. The 4th Landscape

Annual.   *(Claude Cox)* **£55 [≈ $88]**
- The Tourist in Italy. Illustrated from Drawings by J.D. Harding, London: 1833. 271 pp. Half-title. Frontis, engvd title, 23 engvd plates (of 24, lacks plate 1). Scattered foxing, sgntr starting. Contemp calf, gilt inner dentelles, a.e.g., jnts rubbed.
        (Reese) **$100 [≈ £62]**
- The Tourist in Spain. Andalusia. Illustrated from Drawings by David Roberts. London: Robert Jennings, 1836. 1st edn. 8vo. xii,280,4 advt pp. 21 plates (sl foxed). Orig green mor, extremities rubbed, hd of spine sl worn. Landscape Annual for 1836.
        (Claude Cox) **£80 [≈ $128]**
- The Tourist in Switzerland and Italy. Illustrated from Drawings by S. Prout. London: Jennings, 1830. 1st edn. 8vo. [8],278 pp. Addtnl engvd title & 25 plates. Tissue guards. Orig green mor gilt, a.e.g. Landscape Annual for 1830. *(Claude Cox)* **£65 [≈ $104]**
- The Tourist in Switzerland and Italy. Illustrated from Drawings by S. Prout. London: Jennings, 1830. 1st edn. 8vo. [8],278 pp. Addtnl engvd title & 25 plates. Frontis & engvd title foxed in margs. Orig mor, rather rubbed.   *(Claude Cox)* **£45 [≈ $72]**
- The Tourist in Switzerland and Italy. Illustrated from Drawings by S. Prout. London: Jennings, Landscape Annual, 1830. 8vo. 25 steel engvd plates. Orig green mor gilt, sl worn.   *(Hollett)* **£45 [≈ $72]**
- Wanderings and Excursions in North and South Wales. London: Tilt & Simpkin, 1836 & n.d. 1st edn. 2 vols. 8vo. [xiv],261; xii,268 pp. 99 engvd plates & vignettes. Some foxing to plates. Contemp red half mor, gilt dec spines, sl worn, jnts & crnrs rubbed.
        (Gough) **£125 [≈ $200]**

Rose, T. & Allom, Thomas
- Westmorland Illustrated ... see Allom, Thomas & Rose, T.

Rose, William Stewart
- Letters from the North of Italy. Addressed to Henry Hallam Esq. London: Murray, 1819. 2 vols in one. xii,339; viii,229,errata,8 advt pp. Some dampstaining to vol 2. Mod qtr calf.
        (Piccadilly) **£48 [≈ $76]**

Rosenberg, F.
- Big Game Shooting in British Columbia and Norway. London: 1928. 8vo. Ills. Orig bndg, v sl rubbed.   *(Grayling)* **£55 [≈ $88]**
- Big Game Shooting in British Columbia and Norway. London: 1928. 8vo. Ills. Sl foxing. Orig bndg, v sl rubbed & marked.
        (Grayling) **£40 [≈ $64]**

Rosenmueller, E.F.C.
- Views of Interesting Places in the Holy Land: with a Brief Sketch of the Principal Events Associated with them. Philadelphia: [ca 1832]. Oblong 4to. 36 pp. 8 lithos. Occas sl foxing. Half calf, some wear to spine, front hinge sl cracking.   *(Reese)* **$1,250 [≈ £781]**

Ross, Frederick
- The Ruined Abbeys of Britain. Illustrated ... by H.F. Lydon. London: William Mackenzie, [ca 1880]. Lge folio. viii,288 pp. 13 cold plates, num other plates & text figs. Front sgntr loose. Orig pict gilt orange-brown cloth, a.e.g., front inner hinge cracked.
        (Terramedia) **$325 [≈ £203]**
- The Ruined Abbeys of Britain. London: William Mackenzie, n.d. Folio. viii,288 pp. 12 chromolithos by Fawcett of Driffield after A.F. Lydon, num num text w'cuts. Orig cloth gilt, rather rubbed & marked, upper hinge reprd, front jnt roughly reprd.
        (Hollett) **£60 [≈ $96]**
- The Ruined Abbeys of Britain. London: n.d. 2 vols. Folio. 12 cold plates & num w'engvs in the text by A.F. Lydon. Sl foxing in text. Orig pict gilt cloth, a.e.g.   *(Henly)* **£95 [≈ $152]**
- The Ruined Abbeys of Britain. London: (1882). 1st edn. Folio. 288 pp. 12 cold plates, with tissue guards, 11 other ills, by A.F. Lydon. Orig pict gilt cloth.
        (Argosy) **$350 [≈ £218]**

Ross, Sir James Clark
- Narrative of a Second Voyage in Search of a North-West Passage ... London: Webster, 1835. 740 pp. Frontis, ills, fldg plates (some cold). Orig cloth.   *(Jenkins)* **$725 [≈ £453]**
- A Voyage of Discovery and Research in the Southern and Antarctic Regions, during the Years 1839-1843. London: Murray, 1847. 2 vols. 8vo. 15 plates & maps, some fldg. Orig cloth, faded, sm 19th c lib sticker on front pastedown.   *(High Latitude)* **$995 [≈ £621]**

Ross, Sir John
- Narrative of a Second Voyage in Search of a North-West Passage ... London: Webster, 1835. 2 vols. Lge 4to. 2 frontis, 8 maps & plans (1 cold, 1 fldg), 39 plates (19 hand cold). Some foxing & browning. Recased using orig cloth on sides & spine, sl rubbed & soiled.
        (Sotheran) **£500 [≈ $800]**
- Narrative of a Second Voyage in Search of a North-West Passage ... London: Webster, 1835. 4to. xxxiv,740 pp. Fldg chart, 30 plates (9 cold). Contemp leather.
        (Bates & Hindmarch) **£335 [≈ $536]**
- Narrative of a Second Voyage in Search of a

North-West Passage ... London: Webster, 1835. 1st edn. 4to. xxiv,740 pp. Lge fldg map, 5 other maps, 25 litho plates (9 cold). Mor, rebacked. *(Parmer)* **$800 [≈£500]**
- See also Williams, Edwin (compiler).

Rous, Francis
- Archaeologiae Atticae Libri Septem ... Containing the Description of the Citties ... within the Athenian Territories ... Oxford: 1658. A. Lichfield & H. Hall, 5th edn, enlgd. Sm 4to. Final index leaf defective. A few marg tears. Mod half mor. *(Stewart)* **£50 [≈$80]**

Rovings in the Pacific ...
- Rovings in the Pacific from 1837 to 1849, with a Glance at California. By a Merchant long resident at Tahiti. London: Longman ..., 1851. 2 vols in one. xii,351; xi,371 pp. 4 cold ills. Some fingermarks. Orig navy cloth, recased. *(Box of Delights)* **£30 [≈$48]**

Rowe, Samuel
- A Perambulation of the Ancient and Royal Forest of Dartmoor and the Venville Precincts ... Exeter & London: 1896. 3rd edn, by J.B. Rowe. One of 250 Large Paper. Lge thick 8vo. xvi,516 pp. Frontis, 5 maps, 23 plates, text ills. Orig buckram, cvrs dust marked. *(Bow Windows)* **£95 [≈$152]**

Rowlands, Henry
- Mona Antiqua Restaurata; An Archaeological Discourse on the Antiquities ... of The Isle of Anglesey ... Second Edition Corrected and Improved. London: J. Knox, 1766. 4to. xvi, 357, [ii] pp. Map, 12 plates. Orig calf gilt, elab gilt spine relaid. *(Gough)* **£125 [≈$200]**

Royal Geographical Society
- Supplementary Papers Vol 1. London: 1886. 650 pp. Num fldg maps. Orig cloth. *(Trophy Room Books)* **$300 [≈£187]**

Royal Recollections ...
- Royal Recollections on a Tour to Cheltenham ... see Pindar, Peter.

Rudolph, Franz Karl Joseph, Crown Prince of Austria
- Travels in the East Including a Visit to Egypt and the Holy Land. London: Bentley, 1884. 4to. xi,380 pp. 93 ills. Orig dec cloth gilt, spine a little faded & sl torn at ft. *(Hollett)* **£95 [≈$152]**
- Travels in the East Including a Visit to Egypt and the Holy Land. London: bentley, 1884. 4to. xi,380 pp. 88 plates, 5 text ills. Lib stamps on back of plates. Lib buckram, lib

number on spine. *(Worldwide Antiqu'n)* **$185 [≈£115]**

Rundall, L.P.
- The Ibex of Sha-Ping and Other Himalayan Studies. London: 1915. 4to. Mtd cold plates, text ills. Orig bndg, v sl rubbed. *(Grayling)* **£35 [≈$56]**

Rundall, Thomas
- Narrative of Voyages toward the North-West, in Search of a Passage to cathay and India. 1496 to 1631 ... London: Hakluyt Society, 1849. 4,xix,259 pp. 2 fldg maps, ills. Orig pict cloth gilt, partly unopened. Paper wrapper. *(Reese)* **$125 [≈£78]**

Ruschenberger, William Samuel Waithman
- Narrative of a Voyage Round the World, During the Years 1835,36, and 37; including a Narrative of an Embassy to the Sultan of Muscat and the King of Siam ... London: Bentley, 1838. 1st English edn. 2 vols. 8vo. 4 litho plates. Contemp cloth backed bds, sl worn *(Heritage)* **$1,000 [≈£625]**

Russan, A.
- Mighty Hunters. Some of the Adventures of Richard and Helen Carson in the Forests and on the Plains of Chiapas in Mexico. London: 1909. 8vo. Ills. 5 words on 1 page underlined in red. Orig cloth, sl dulled & snagged on spine. *(Grayling)* **£25 [≈$40]**

Russel, Mrs C. (ed.)
- General Rigby, Zanzibar and the Slave-Trade. With Journals, Despatches, Etc. Edited by his Daughter Mrs. Charles E.B. Russel. London: Allen & Unwin, [1953]. 1st edn. 8vo. 404 pp. Fldg map. Blue cloth. *(Terramedia)* **$100 [≈£62]**

Russell, John
- Shakespeare's Country. London: Batsford, 1942. 1st edn. Num photo ills. Orig bndg. Dw by Brian Cook. *(Old Cathay)* **£25 [≈$40]**
- A Tour in Germany, and in Some of the Southern Provinces of the Austrian Empire, in 1820,'21 & '22. New Edition with Additions. London: Constable's Miscellany, 1828. 2 vols. 12mo. viii,285; vi,288 pp. Addtnl engvd title. Orig linen bds, paper labels. *(Claude Cox)* **£15 [≈$24]**

Russell, W.S.
- Pilgrim Memorials, and Guide for Visitors to Plymouth Village ... Boston: privately ptd, 1851. 8vo. viii,148 pp. Fldg map, 6 plates. Foxed. Orig cloth, spine faded.

(Berkelouw) **$200 [≈ £125]**

Russell, William Howard
- A Diary in the East during the Tour of the Prince and Princess of Wales. London: Routledge, 1869. 1st edn. 8vo. Half-title. 6 cold plates. Text vignettes. Contemp half calf gilt.   *(Trebizond)* **$200 [≈ £125]**
- The Prince of Wales's Tour: A Diary in India. New York: 1878. 8vo. 552 pp. Frontis, plates & ills. Orig pict green cloth gilt, minor defects.   *(Terramedia)* **$40 [≈ £25]**

Russell-Jeaffreson, Joseph
- The Faroe Islands. London: Sampson Low, 1898. 1st edn. 8vo. Fldg map, 16 plates. Orig cloth, sl worn.   *(Hannas)* **£65 [≈ $104]**

Ruston, Arthur G. & Witney, Denis
- Hooton Pagnell. The Agricultural Evolution of a Yorkshire Village. London: 1934. 1st edn. 8vo. 12 plates. Orig cloth, sl rubbed.
                                  (Robertshaw) **£15 [≈ $24]**

Rutland, John Henry Manners, Duke of
- A Tour through Part of Belgium and the Rhenish Provinces. London: for Rodwell & Martin, 1822. 1st edn. 4to. 13 litho plates. Some pencil scribbles on title verso & a few preliminary ff. Later brown half mor.
                                  (Hannas) **£260 [≈ $416]**

Rutter, Eldon
- The Holy Cities of Arabia. London & New York: Putnam's, [1930]. 8vo. 593 pp. Num fldg maps, plans, plates. Orig blue cloth gilt.
                                  (Terramedia) **$100 [≈ £62]**

Rutter, John
- A Description of Fonthill Abbey ... including a List of its Paintings, Cabinets, and other Curiosities. Second Edition, enlarged and corrected. Shaftesbury: 1822. 8vo. Frontis. Orig wraps, lacks spine.
                                  (Robertshaw) **£30 [≈ $48]**

Ruttledge, Hugh
- Everest 1933. London: Hodder & Stoughton, 1934. 1st edn. Thick 4to. xv,390 pp. 4 fldg maps, 59 plates, 3 diags. Orig cloth gilt, spine trifle faded, extremities minimally rubbed.
                                  (Hollett) **£40 [≈ $64]**

Ruxton, George F.
- Adventures in Mexico and the Rocky Mountains. New York: Harper, 1848. 1st Amer edn. 12mo. 312 pp. Foxing. Orig cloth, spine faded, extremities sl chipped.
                                  (Karmiole) **$100 [≈ £62]**

- Adventures in Mexico and the Rocky Mountains. New York: Harper, 1848. 1st Amer edn. 312 pp. Orig cloth, rebacked.
                                  (Jenkins) **$235 [≈ £146]**

Ryan, Frederick W.
- Malta. Painted by Vittorio Boron. London: A. & C. Black Colour Book, 1910. 1st edn. Map, 20 cold plates. Orig cloth, t.e.g. Dw.
                                  (Old Cathay) **£65 [≈ $104]**

Ryan, William Redmond
- Personal Adventures in Upper and Lower California, in 1848-9; with the Author's Experience at the Mines ... London: 1851. 2 vols in one. x,347; vi,413 pp. Plates (occas foxing). Stamp in marg of preface. Rec half calf.   *(Reese)* **$300 [≈ £187]**
- Personal Adventures in Upper and Lower California, in 1848-9; with the Author's Experience at the Mines ... London: William Shoberl, 1851. 2nd edn (?). 2 vols. 8vo. x, 347, [1], [6 advt]; vi, 413, [1] pp. 2 litho frontis, 21 litho plates. Orig cloth, sl worn & shaken.   *(Heritage)* **$550 [≈ £343]**

Rycaut, Sir Paul
- The Present State of the Ottoman Empire ... London: John Starkey & Henry Brome, 1668. 1st edn. 4to. 2 blanks, [xiii], 218 pp. Frontis & 29 other text engvs. Occas browning & sm holes. Contemp calf, gilt dec spine, hinges cracked.   *(Terramedia)* **$600 [≈ £375]**

Sabin, Joseph
- A Dictionary of Books relating to America ... New York: Sabin, 1868-1936. 1st edn. 29 vols. 8vo. Black buckram. [With] Molnar's Author-Title Index to Sabin. New York: Scarecrow, 1974. 3 vols. 8vo. Blue cloth.
                                  (Terramedia) **$2,000 [≈ £1,250]**

Sacheverell, William
- An Account of the Isle of Man ... London: for J. Hartley ..., 1702. 1st edn. 8vo. [xv], 175, 1 advt pp. Contemp panelled calf, rebacked.
                                  (Young's) **£130 [≈ $208]**

Saint-Cricq, Laurent de
- Travels in South America from the Pacific Ocean to the Atlantic Ocean. By Paul Marcoy [pseud.]. London: Blackie, 1875. 2 vols. 525 w'engvs. Contemp three qtr green mor over blue mrbld bds, t.e.g., light cvr wear.
                                  (Jenkins) **$200 [≈ £125]**
- See also Marcoy, Paul.

St. John, Bayle
- Adventures in the Libyan Desert and the

Oasis of Jupiter Ammon. New York: Putnam; London: Murray, 1849. 1st edn. 12mo. 244 pp. Frontis. V foxed. Orig cloth, rubbed, crnrs sl worn, old stain on crnr of back cvr, sm hole in spine.   *(Schoyer)* **$50 [≈ £31]**

St. John, Charles
- Natural History and Sport in Moray. London: 1882. 8vo. Etched plates, text ills. Some light foxing. Orig bndg, spine rather rubbed & frayed.   *(Grayling)* **£60 [≈ $96]**
- Short Sketches of the Wild Sports and Natural History of the Highlands. London: 1893. New edn. Roy 8vo. xxiii,319 pp. Ills. Orig cloth.   *(Wheldon & Wesley)* **£18 [≈ $28]**
- A Tour in Sutherlandshire. With Extracts from the Field-Books of a Sportsman and Naturalist. London: 1884. 2nd edn. 2 vols. Plates, text ills. Orig bndg.   *(Grayling)* **£60 [≈ $96]**
- Wild Sports and Natural History of the Highlands. 1878. 1st illust edn. 8vo. Text engvs. Orig pict gilt cloth, sl rubbing & bubbling.   *(Grayling)* **£23 [≈ $36]**
- Wild Sports and Natural History of the Highlands. 1878. 8vo. Text engvs. Contemp half mor.   *(Grayling)* **£55 [≈ $88]**
- Wild Sports and Natural History of the Highlands. London: 1893. 8vo. Text engvs throughout. Orig cloth, spine sl faded & rubbed.   *(Grayling)* **£20 [≈ $32]**
- Wild Sports and Natural History of the Highlands. Edited by Sir H. Maxwell. Edinburgh: 1919. Cr 4to. xxx,472 pp. 39 plates (29 cold). Orig buckram, uncut.   *(Wheldon & Wesley)* **£30 [≈ $48]**
- Wild Sports and Natural History of the Highlands. Edited by Sir Herbert Maxwell. Edinburgh: 1927. Roy 8vo. xxx,472 pp. 39 plates (29 cold). Orig cloth. Dw.   *(Wheldon & Wesley)* **£35 [≈ $56]**
- Wild Sports and Natural History of the Highlands. 1927. 8vo. 39 cold plates by George D. Armour & E. Alexander. Orig bndg. Dw.   *(Grayling)* **£30 [≈ $48]**

St. John, J.A.
- Egypt and Nubia. London: Chapman & Hall, 1845. 1st edn. 8vo. viii,472 pp. Num engvs. Sl foxed. Half mor, hinges cracked.   *(Worldwide Antiqu'n)* **$145 [≈ £90]**

St. Marie, Count
- Algeria in 1845. A Visit to the French Possessions in Africa. London: Bentley, 1846. 1st edn. Sm 8vo. vii,284 pp. Frontis. Sm tear in title. Orig cloth, worn, tears in spine, rear cvr detached, backstrip defective.   *(Worldwide Antiqu'n)* **$45 [≈ £28]**

St. Sauveur, A.G. de
- Travels through the Balearic and Pithusian Islands, performed between the Years 1801 and 1806 ... London: Richard Phillips, 1808. 156 pp. Frontis. Occas moderate to heavy foxing. Mod cloth & mrbld bds, t.e.g.   *(Reese)* **$150 [≈ £93]**

St. Vincent, J.B.G.M. Bory de
- Voyage to, and Travels through the Four Principal Islands of the African Seas, performed by Order of the French Government ... London: Richard Phillips, 1805. 212 pp. 2 maps, 5 plates. Occas sl foxing & offsetting. Mod half cloth, t.e.g.   *(Reese)* **$200 [≈ £125]**

Sala, George Augustus
- America Revisited: From the Bay of New York to the Gulf of Mexico, and from Lake Michigan to the Pacific. London: 1882. 1st edn. 2 vols. 8vo. [xx],314; xii,326 pp. Nearly 400 engvs (inc 54 plates). Sl foxing. Green half calf, gilt spines, labels.   *(Bow Windows)* **£150 [≈ $240]**
- Dutch Pictures; with some Sketches in the Flemish Manner. London: Tinsley Bros, 1861. 1st edn. xii,339,[5 advt] pp. Orig cloth, gilt spine.   *(Claude Cox)* **£20 [≈ $32]**

Salaman, M.C.
- London Past and Present ... Edited by Charles Holme. London: The Studio, 1916. 1st edn. Lge 8vo. viii,194 pp. Num ills, inc cold. 1 fldg ill rather creased & spotted. Text browned. Orig cloth, t.e.g.   *(Bow Windows)* **£25 [≈ $40]**

Sale, Lady
- A Journal of the Disasters in Affghanistan, 1841-2. London: Murray, 1843. 1st edn. 8vo. xvi,451,12 advt pp. 2 maps. Orig pict pink cloth gilt, uncut, spine faded & reprd at hd.   *(Gough)* **£125 [≈ $200]**

Salmon, Thomas
- The Foreigner's Companion Through the Universities of Cambridge and Oxford, and the Adjacent Counties. London: for William Owen, 1748. 1st edn. 2 parts in one vol. 12mo. Contemp half vellum, mrbld bds, sl rubbed, vellum soiled, cracks starting at ends of jnts.   *(Sanders)* **£135 [≈ $216]**
- The Modern Gazetteer: or, a Short View of the Several Nations of the World ... Fifth Edition, with Additions. London: 1758. 12mo. [xxxvi],[465],3 advt pp. Dark stain upper marg of 1st half of book. Orig sheep, rubbed, spine ends sl worn.   *(Bickersteth)* **£25 [≈ $40]**

Sampson, G.V.
- Statistical Survey of the County of Londonderry. Dublin: Graisberry, 1802. Maps & plates. Calf.
(Emerald Isle) **£200 [≃ $320]**

Sanderson, George P.
- Thirteen Years among the Wild Beasts of India ... Third Edition. London: 1882. Sm 4to. 387 pp. Cold frontis, 23 plates inc sev maps. Orig pict gilt cloth.
(Argosy) **$125 [≃ £78]**
- Thirteen Years among the Wild Beasts of India ... Sixth Edition. London: W.H. Allen, 1896. 8vo. Num ills. Orig green cloth gilt, a little shaken. *(Waterfield's)* **£25 [≃ $40]**

Sandys, John Edwin
- An Easter Vacation in Greece ... London: Macmillan, 1887. 8vo. xvi,175 pp. Map, plan. Orig green cloth, v sl loose.
(Piccadilly) **£28 [≃ $44]**

Sansom, George
- A History of Japan to 1867. London: The Cresset Press, 1958-61-64. 3 vols. 8vo. 58 ills on plates & others in text. Orig cloth, some cvrs dust marked.
(Bow Windows) **£115 [≃ $184]**
- The Western World and Japan. London: The Cresset Press, 1950. 8vo. xvi,543 pp. 6 plates, ills. Light stain at ft of frontis & title & on foredge of some ff. Orig cloth.
(Bow Windows) **£40 [≃ $64]**

Sarbadhicary, S.B.
- Sojourn in the West; with Its Brief Ancient History. Alahabad: 1900. Sm narrow 4to. [xiii],160 pp. Occas spotting & smudging. Orig cloth backed ptd bds, some edge wear.
(Reese) **$150 [≃ £93]**

Sargent, Winthrop (ed.)
- The History of an Expedition against Fort Du Quesne in 1755. Under Major-General Braddock, Generalissimo of H.B.M. Forces in America ... Philadelphia: 1855. 1st edn. Lge 8vo. [xiv],423 pp. 9 fldg maps & plans. Orig cloth, ex-lib, spine ends sl chipped.
(Terramedia) **$140 [≃ £87]**

Sarmiento, Domingo F.
- Life in the Argentine Republic in the Days of the Tyrants ... From the Spanish ... With a Biographical Sketch of the Author, by Mrs. Horace Mann. New York: Hurd & Houghton, 1868. 1st Amer edn. 12mo. xxxv,400 pp. Orig three qtr mor, mrbld bds.
(Schoyer) **$50 [≃ £31]**

Sartorius, C.
- Mexico. Landscapes and Popular Sketches ... London: 1859. 4to. 202 pp. 18 steel engvs. Cloth, somewhat shaken, a few ff loose.
(Reese) **$1,200 [≃ £750]**

Sarytschew, Gawrila
- Account of a Voyage of Discovery to the North-East of Siberia, the Frozen Ocean, and the Northeast Sea. London: 1806-07. Only English edn. 2 vols in one. 70,80 pp. 3 fldg plates, 2 cold plates of natives. Antique half calf & mrbld bds. *(Reese)* **$850 [≃ £531]**

Saulcy, F. de
- Narrative of a Journey round the Dead Sea and in the Bible Lands in 1850 and 1851. Edited with Notes by Count Edward de Warren. London: Bentley, 1853. 2 vols. 8vo. xi,586; ii,658 pp. 2 fldg plates. Sev lib stamps. Orig cloth, lacks backstrips, cvrs loose. *(Worldwide Antiqu'n)* **$250 [≃ £156]**

Saunders, William
- Through the Light Continent; or, The United States in 1877-8. London: Cassell, Petter & Galpin, 1879. 1st edn. 8vo. x,409, [6] pp. Orig cloth gilt. *(Fenning)* **£35 [≃ $56]**

Savage, James
- A Genealogical Dictionary of the First Settlers in New England ... Boston: Little, Brown, 1860. 1st edn. 4 vols. 8vo. xv, 516; 599; 664; 714 pp. Mod buckram.
(Terramedia) **$150 [≃ £93]**

Savage-Landor, A. Henry
- Across Coveted Lands or a Journey from Flushing (Holland) to Calcutta, Overland. New York: Scribner, 1903. 1st edn. 2 vols. viii, 461; viii, 459 pp. 2 fldg maps, 123 plates. Ex-lib. Orig cloth, edges rubbed.
(Worldwide Antiqu'n) **$75 [≃ £46]**
- Across Unknown South America. Boston: Little, Brown, 1913. 2 vols. 8vo. xxiii,377, xvi,439 pp. Port, 2 fldg maps, 8 cold plates, num photo ills. Orig blue pict cloth, sl rubbed. *(Adelson)* **$135 [≃ £84]**
- Across Unknown South America. London: Hodder & Stoughton, 1913. 2 vols. 4to. xxiv, 432; xvi,504 pp. Frontis, 8 cold plates, 2 maps, 259 ills. Orig blue cloth, string mark to vol 2 front bd.
(Bates & Hindmarch) **£85 [≃ $136]**
- Across Widest Africa. London: Hurst & Blackett, 1907. 2 vols. xv,396; xii,512 pp. Lge fldg cold map, 160 ills. Orig gilt lettered cloth. *(Thornton's)* **£75 [≃ $120]**
- Across Widest Africa ... A Twelve Months'

Journey from Djibuti to Cape Verde. New York: 1907. 2 vols. 4to. xv,396; xii,511 pp. Lge fldg cold map, num plates. Orig dec blue grey cloth gilt. *(Terramedia)* **$200 [≈ £125]**
- The Gems of the East. Sixteen Thousand Miles of Research Travel among Wild and Tame Tribes of Enchanting Islands. New York & London: Harper, 1904. 1st edn. 8vo. xi,567 pp. Fldg map, num plates, plans, diags. Ex-lib. Orig cloth, sl rubbed.
(Worldwide Antiqu'n) **$35 [≈ £21]**
- In the Forbidden Land. An Account of a Journey in Tibet ... London: Heinemann, 1898. 2 vols. 8vo. xx,320; xvi,263 pp. Frontis, fldg map, 8 cold plates, 246 ills. Orig pict cloth, a little bumped & worn.
(Bates & Hindmarch) **£100 [≈ $160]**
- In the Forbidden Land. An Account of a Journey in Tibet ... London: 1899. 8vo. [xxviii], 508 pp. Fldg map, 251 ills. 1 or 2 marks, front fly leaf removed. Orig illust cloth. *(Bow Windows)* **£70 [≈ $112]**
- Tibet and Nepal. London: A. & C. Black Colour Books, Twenty Shilling Series, 1905. 1st edn. 75 cold plates. Orig cloth, v minor discolouration to bds.
(Old Cathay) **£75 [≈ $120]**

Savary, Claude Etienne
- Letters on Egypt ... Second Edition. London: Robinson, 1787. 2 vols. 8vo. ix,467; 490,[xiv] pp. 3 fldg maps, 1 fldg plan. Orig calf, later cloth spines. *(Schoyer)* **$135 [≈ £84]**

Saville, Frank
- The High Grass Trail. Being the Difficulties & Diversions of Two: Trekking & Shooting for Sustenance in the Dense Bush Across British Central Africa. London: 1924. 1st edn. 8vo. 255 pp. Frontis & other photo plates. Orig pict red cloth gilt, sl worn.
(Terramedia) **$60 [≈ £37]**

Saville-Kent, W.
- The Great Barrier Reef of Australia; its Products and Potentialities. London: [1893]. Imperial 4to. xviii,387 pp. Fldg map, 64 plates (16 cold). Orig cloth, trifle used, refixed. *(Wheldon & Wesley)* **£150 [≈ $240]**
- The Naturalist in Australia. London: 1897. 4to. xv,302 pp. Port, 9 cold & 50 collotype plates, num ills. 1 plate taped in & with short marg. Orig cloth, trifle used, inner jnts reprd.
(Wheldon & Wesley) **£150 [≈ $240]**

Sayce, A.H. (ed.)
- History of Egypt, Chaldea, Syria, Babylonia and Assyria ... see Maspero, G., et al.

Scale, Bernard
- An Hibernian Atlas ... London: Laurie & Whittle, 1798. Sm sq 4to. Engvd & illust title & dedic pp, engvd contents page, 37 hand cold engvd maps. Sl offsetting. Orig three qtr lea, bds v rubbed, crnrs worn, 3 inches of front jnt split, spine ends worn.
(Schoyer) **$750 [≈ £468]**

Scale, Bernard & Richards, William
- Directions for Navigating into the Bay of Dublin ... Dublin: for the proprietors by S. Powell & Son, 1765. 1st edn. 8vo. [2],32,[3 subscribers],[1 advt] pp. With the preliminary leaf, sgnd "a", dated June 3, 1765. 8 engvd charts. Sl marg browning. Rec wraps.
(Fenning) **£650 [≈ $1,040]**

Scenes ...
- Scenes and Impressions in Egypt and in Italy. London: Longman, 1825. 3rd edn. 8vo. iv,435 pp. Contemp calf, maroon label, hinges cracked, cvr almost detached.
(Terramedia) **$100 [≈ £62]**
- See also Sherer, J. Moyle.

Scheffer, Johannes
- The History of Lapland ... Oxford: at the Theater, 1674. 1st English edn. Probably 1st iss. Folio. Addtnl engvd title, fldg map, 25 lge w'cuts in text. Contemp panelled mottled calf, gilt spine (carelessly reprd), a.e.g. Wing S.851A. *(Hannas)* **£950 [≈ $1,520]**
- The History of Lapland ... Oxford: at the Theater, sold by George West & Amos Curtein, 1674. 1st English edn, later iss. Folio. Addtnl engvd title, fldg map, 25 lge w'cuts in text. Minor marg tears. Contemp calf, gilt spine, hd of spine worn. Wing S.851.
(Hannas) **£850 [≈ $1,360]**

Schevill, Ferdinand
- The Balkan Peninsula and the Near East ... London: Bell & Sons, 1922. 8vo. viii,558 pp. 15 maps. Sm lib stamps. Orig green cloth.
(Piccadilly) **£24 [≈ $38]**

Schillings, C.G.
- Flashlights in the Jungle. A Record of Hunting Adventures and of Studies of Wild Life in Equatorial East Africa. New York: Doubleday, Page, 1906. Lge 8vo. xxx,[2],782 pp. 302 photo ills. Orig bndg.
(Parmer) **$100 [≈ £62]**
- In Wildest Africa. London: Hutchinson, 1907. 1st English edn. 2 vols. 8vo. vi,318; 319-716,2 advt pp. Num ills. Orig dec cloth, moderate wear & spotting to bds.
(Parmer) **$140 [≈ £87]**

- In Wildest Africa. New York & London: Harper, 1907. 1st Amer edn. 8vo. xvi,716 pp. Num photo ills. Orig dec brown cloth, sl soiled, hinge reprd.   *(Parmer)* **$65 [≈£40]**
- In Wildest Africa. London: 1907. 2 vols. Num ills. Orig cloth. *(Grayling)* **£60 [≈$96]**
- With Flashlight and Rifle [Hunting etc in East Africa]. London: 1906. 2 vols. 8vo. Ills. Orig bndg, sl rubbed, hinges a bit weak.
     (Grayling) **£45 [≈$72]**

Schliemann, Henry
- Ilios: the City and the Country of the Trojans ... including an Autobiography of the Author. London: Murray, 1880. 1st English edn. 4to. xvi,800 pp. 6 fldg plans, 32 pp of litho plates, num text ills. Orig pict gilt cloth, t.e.g., spine faded & sl worn at ends
     (Claude Cox) **£75 [≈$120]**
- Mycenae: A Narrative of Researches and Discoveries at Mycenae and Tyrins. New York: Scribner's, 1880. New edn, enlgd. 4to. lxviii, 404 pp. 33 plates & plans (4 cold, many fldg), num ills. Orig maroon cloth, a.e.g., ex-lib, v sunned.   *(Terramedia)* **$75 [≈£46]**
- Tiryns. New York: Scribner's, 1885. 385 pp. Plates, some cold, some fldg, ills. Orig elab gilt dec cloth, crnrs & spine ends v sl worn.
     (Parmer) **$200 [≈£125]**
- Tiryns: The Prehistoric Palace of the Kings of Tiryns, The Results of the Latest Excavations. New York: 1885. !st Amer edn. Tall thick 8vo. Map, 24 chromolithos, 4 plans, 188 w'cuts. Orig dec gilt cloth.
     (Argosy) **$125 [≈£78]**

Scholes, James Christopher
- History of Bolton. Bolton: 1892. 1st edn. 8vo. xii,[iv],555 pp. 42 ills. Mod polished half calf gilt, t.e.g., orig bds with gilt coat of arms retained, new endpapers.
     (Hollett) **£75 [≈$120]**

Schoolcraft, Henry R.
- Information respecting the History Condition and Prospects of the Indian Tribes of the United States ... Philadelphia: 1853-56. 5 vols. Imperial 8vo. 274 (of 275) plates (some cold / fldg). Lacks the map of Creek county in vol 5. Occas marks. Mod half oasis.
     (Frew Mackenzie) **£620 [≈$992]**
- Narrative of an Expedition through the Upper Mississippi to Itasca Lake, the actual Source of this River ... New York: Harper, 1834. 1st edn. 8vo. 2,308 pp. 5 maps (2 fldg). Lib stamps on title & verso of 1 map. Mod buckram.   *(Adelson)* **$275 [≈£171]**

Schrader, Frank Charles
- A Reconnaissance in Northern Alaska across the Rocky Mountains ... in 1901. Washington: GPO, 1904. 4to. 139 pp. 16 plates inc 4 maps (2 fldg). Half leather & cloth.   *(Parmer)* **$125 [≈£78]**

Schroeder, Francis
- Shores of the Mediterranean, with Sketches of Travel. New York: Harper, 1846. Only edn. 2 vols. 12mo. 13 plates. Pervasive light foxing. Orig embossed cloth, gilt spines, minor wear.   *(Trebizond)* **$180 [≈£112]**

Schroeder, Henry Alfred & Peters, Laurence A.
- Shirt-Tail and Pigtail. Nonchalant Adventures in Central Asia. New York: Minton, Balch, 1930. 1st edn. 8vo. xiv,316 pp. 31 photo plates. Orig cloth, sl faded & rubbed.   *(Worldwide Antiqu'n)* **$45 [≈£28]**

Schuchhardt, C.
- Schliemann's Excavations. An Archaeological and Historical Study. Translated from the German ... Appendix ... Introduction by Walter Leaf. London: Macmillan, 1891. 1st English edn. 8vo. xxxii, 363, [4 advt pp]. Num maps, plans, ills. Orig cloth, fine.
     (Frew Mackenzie) **£115 [≈$184]**
- Schliemann's Excavations: An Archaeological and Historical Study. Translated from the German ... Appendix ... London: Macmillan, 1891. 1st edn. 8vo. xxxii, 363, advt pp. Frontis port, num plates & plans. Some crnrs sl dampstained. Orig blue cloth, lib labels removed.   *(Terramedia)* **$100 [≈£62]**

Schultz, Christian
- Travels on an Inland Voyage through the States of New York, Pennsylvania, Virginia ... New York: Isaac Riley, 1810. 1st edn. 2 vols in one. 18,207; 8,204 pp. 5 fldg maps, 3 plates. Orig tree calf.
     (Jenkins) **$1,000 [≈£625]**

Schuster, W. Morgan
- The Strangling of Persia: A Record of European Diplomacy and Oriental Intrigue. London: 1912. 8vo. 378,advt pp. Frontis, num photo plates. Orig green cloth gilt, minor wear.   *(Terramedia)* **$75 [≈£46]**

Schuyler, Eugene
- Turkistan: Notes of a Journey in Russian Turkistan, Khokand, Bukhara, and Kuldja. New York: Scribner, Armstrong, 1876. 1st edn. 2 vols. 8vo. xii,411; vii,463 pp. 3 fldg maps, num plates & ills. Orig pict gilt cloth, sl worn.   *(Terramedia)* **$500 [≈£312]**

- Turkistan. Notes of a Journey in Russian Turkistan, Khokand, Bukhara, and Kuldja. New York: 1877. 2 vols. 8vo. 3 fldg maps, plates. Orig cloth, spine ends sl worn, labels removed from spines.
(Farahar) **£125 [≈ $200]**

Schwatka, Frederick
- Report of a Military Reconnaissance in Alaska, made in 1883. Washington: GPO, 1885. 8vo. 121 pp. 20 lge fldg maps, ills. Old half calf, orig ptd front wrapper bound in, a bit rubbed, wrapper frayed.
(High Latitude) **$85 [≈ £53]**

Schweinfurth, G.
- The Heart of Africa. Three Years' Travel and Adventures in the Unexplored Regions of Central Africa from 1868 to 1871. London: 1878. 3rd edn. 2 vols. Cr 8vo. Sl foxed. Orig cloth. *(Wheldon & Wesley)* **£35 [≈ $56]**
- The Heart of Africa. New York: 1874. 2 vols. 512; 559 pp. Ills. Orig bndg.
(Trophy Room Books) **$375 [≈ £234]**

Scidmore, Eliza R.
- China: the Long-lived Empire. London: Macmillan, 1900. 1st UK edn. 8vo. xv,[2],466 pp. 50 plates, other ills. Orig cloth.
(Fenning) **£35 [≈ $56]**

Scoresby, William
- An Account of the Arctic Regions, with a History and Description of the Northern Whale-Fishery. Edinburgh: 1820. 1st edn. 2 vols. 8vo. 21 (of 24) plates. Contemp half calf. *(Fenning)* **£135 [≈ $216]**
- The Arctic Regions and the Northern Whale-Fishery. London: [1849]. 2 vols in one. 16mo. 192; 192 pp. Frontis. Orig pict cloth gilt, a.e.g., extremities rubbed, front hinge loosened, ink inscrptn. *(Reese)* **$200 [≈ £125]**
- Journal of a Voyage to the Northern Whale-Fishery ... in the Summer of 1822 in the Ship Baffin of Liverpool. Edinburgh: Constable, 1823. 1st edn. 8vo. xliii,472 pp. 2 fldg maps, 6 plates. Some offsetting. Rebound in qtr calf. *(Frew Mackenzie)* **£450 [≈ $720]**

Scott, A.
- Scinde in the Forties. London: 1912. 201 pp. Ills. Orig black cloth.
(Trophy Room Books) **$200 [≈ £125]**

Scott, Hugh
- In the High Yemen. London: 1942. 8vo. 4 maps (1 fldg), num plates inc a fldg panorama. Orig cloth, unevenly faded.
(Farahar) **£45 [≈ $72]**

- In the High Yemen. London: 1942. 8vo. xix, 260 pp. 66 plates (2 fldg), num maps & ills in text. Orig cloth.
(Worldwide Antiqu'n) **$45 [≈ £28]**

Scott, John
- Sketches of Manners, Scenery &c. in the French Provinces, Switzerland and Italy. With an Essay on French Literature. Second Edition. London: for Longman ..., 1821. vi, 519 pp. Lower inner crnr dampstained throughout. Contemp half calf, hd of spine reprd. *(Claude Cox)* **£20 [≈ $32]**

Scott, R.F.
- Scott's Last Expedition. London: Smith, Elder, 1913. 2nd edn. 2 vols. 8vo. xxvi,633; xvi,534 pp. 2 fldg maps, 15 cold plates, 11 gravures, 3 dble page & 247 b/w plates, other ills. Orig blue cloth. *(Gough)* **£65 [≈ $104]**

Scott, Sir Walter
- The Border Antiquities of England and Scotland ... London: Longman ..., 1814. 2 vols. Lge 4to. Engvd title, 90 steel engvd plates. A little spotting. Orig de luxe bndg of straight grained maroon mor gilt extra, a.e.g., a trifle rubbed. *(Hollett)* **£275 [≈ $440]**
- The Border Antiquities of England and Scotland. London: Longman ..., '1814' [≈ ca 1823-26]. 4th edn. 2 vols. 4to. 94 plates. Contemp half mor, a little rubbed.
(Waterfield's) **£125 [≈ $200]**

Scott, William
- The Riviera. London: A. & C. Black Colour Books, Twenty Shilling Series, 1907. 1st edn. Map, 75 cold plates. Orig dec cloth, hd of front bd sl grazed. *(Old Cathay)* **£43 [≈ $68]**

Scott-Stevenson, Mrs
- Our Home In Cyprus. London: Chapman & Hall, 1880. 1st edn. 8vo. xxv,[i],332 pp. Fldg map, frontis, 7 full page ills. Orig pict gilt green cloth, sl rubbed. Inscrbd pres copy from Ronald Storrs.
(Frew Mackenzie) **£110 [≈ $176]**

The Scottish Tourist ...
- The Scottish Tourist, and Itinerary; or, A Guide to the Scenery and Antiquities of Scotland and the Western Islands ... Edinburgh: Stirling & Kenney, 1832. 4th edn, enlgd. xvi,432 pp. 2 lge fldg maps, 6 other maps, 15 engvd plates. Few spots. Contemp half calf gilt. *(Hollett)* **£75 [≈ $120]**

Scrope, W.
- The Art of Deer Stalking. London: 1839. 2nd edn. 8vo. Tinted litho plates, some heavily

foxed. Orig cloth, spine dulled with sl snags.
(Grayling) **£150 [≈ $240]**
- Days of Deer Stalking. London: 1894. 8vo.
Ills. Orig bndg, sl rubbed.
(Grayling) **£30 [≈ $48]**

Scull, Marshall E.
- Hunting in the Arctic & Alaska. Philadelphia:
John C. Winston Co, 1914. 1st edn. 8vo. 304
pp. 11 maps, num plates. Orig blue cloth gilt,
t.e.g., sl worn.   *(Terramedia)* **$100 [≈ £62]**

Scully, William
- Brazil: Its Provinces and Chief Cities.
London: Murray,   1866.   12mo.
xv,398,errata,2 advt pp. Lge fldg map. Orig
cloth, spine ends chipped, ex-lib.
(Adelson) **$60 [≈ £37]**

Seabrook, William
- The White Monk of Timbuctoo. New York:
Harcourt Brace, [1934]. 1st edn. 8vo. xii,279
pp. Ills. Orig red cloth.
(Terramedia) **$45 [≈ £28]**

Sealsfield, Charles (pseud.)
- See Postl, Karl.

Seeman, Berthold
- Viti: An Account of a Government Mission to
the Vitian or Fijian Islands in the Years
1860-61. Cambridge: Macmillan, 1862. 8vo.
xv, 447, 24 advt pp. Map, 4 tinted plates. 1st
3 ff sl foxed. Ex-lib. Orig green cloth, rubbed.
(Adelson) **$225 [≈ £140]**

Seidenfaden, Erik
- Guide to Bangkok. With Notes on Siam.
Siam: Royal State Railway Dept, 1927. 1st
edn. iii,320,xxxii pp. Cold frontis, 2 fldg
maps, cold plates, num ills. Orig elab gilt
green cloth.   *(Lyon)* **£45 [≈ $72]**

Select Views of London ...
- See Papworth, J.B.

Selfridge, Thomas O.
- Reports of Explorations and Surveys to
Ascertain the Practicability of a Ship-Canal
between the Atlantic and Pacific Oceans by
way of the Isthmus of Darien. Washington:
1874. 4to. 268 pp. 17 fldg maps (some fold
splits), 14 litho plates. Later cloth.
(Reese) **$450 [≈ £281]**

Selous, F.C.
- African Nature Notes and Reminiscences.
London: 1908. 356 pp. Ills. Rebound in
buckram, orig spine label laid on.

(Trophy Room Books) **$175 [≈ £109]**
- African Notes and Reminiscences. London:
1908. 8vo. Ills. Orig bndg, spine dulled.
(Grayling) **£80 [≈ $128]**
- A Hunter's Wanderings in Africa. London:
1893. 3rd edn. 8vo. Ills. Rather browned.
Mod half mor.   *(Grayling)* **£90 [≈ $144]**
- A Hunter's Wanderings in Africa. London:
1928. 8vo. Ills. Orig bndg.
(Grayling) **£40 [≈ $64]**
- Hunting Trips in British North America.
London: 1907. 8vo. Ills. Orig cloth, sl
marked, sm tear in upper spine reprd, crnrs
bumped.   *(Grayling)* **£120 [≈ $192]**
- Recent Hunting Trips in British North
America ... London & New York: Witherby &
Scribner's, 1907. 1st edn. 8vo. 400 pp. 65 ills.
Orig pict green cloth gilt, t.e.g.
(Terramedia) **$300 [≈ £187]**
- Recent Hunting Trips in British North
America. London: Witherby, 1907. 1st edn.
8vo. 400 pp. 65 ills. A little spotting. Orig
cloth gilt, sl worn, jnts tender.
(Hollett) **£80 [≈ $128]**
- Recent Hunting Trips in British North
America. London: 1907. 395 pp. Ills. Orig
bndg.   *(Trophy Room Books)* **$200 [≈ £125]**
- Sport and Travel East and West. London:
1901. 8vo. Ills. Orig cloth.
(Grayling) **£100 [≈ $160]**
- Sport and Travel East and West. London:
1901. 8vo. Ills. Orig cloth, bndg variant, cvrs
sl marked.   *(Grayling)* **£100 [≈ $160]**
- Sport and Travel East and West. London:
1900. 311 pp. Orig pict gilt cloth.
(Trophy Room Books) **$200 [≈ £125]**
- Sunshine and Storm in Rhodesia. London:
1896. 2nd edn. 8vo. xxix,290 pp. Map,
frontis, 8 plates, 8 text figs. Orig buckram,
trifle used, spine darkened, cloth sides sl
bubbled.   *(Wheldon & Wesley)* **£55 [≈ $88]**
- Sunshine and Storm in Rhodesia. London:
1896. 2nd edn. 8vo. Orig buckram, sl
browned.   *(Grayling)* **£90 [≈ $144]**
- Sunshine and Storm in Rhodesia. London:
1896. 2nd edn, variant. 8vo. Orig red cloth,
black title.   *(Grayling)* **£90 [≈ $144]**
- Travel and Adventure in Southeast Africa.
London: Rowland Ward, 1893. 503 pp. Map,
num ills. Orig bndg.
(Trophy Room Books) **$350 [≈ £218]**
- Travels and Adventures in South East Africa
... London: 1893. 1st edn. 8vo. Fldg map, ills.
Orig cloth, sl rubbed & soiled. Sir Douglas
Brooke's b'plate.   *(Grayling)* **£120 [≈ $192]**
- Travels and Adventures in South East Africa
... London: 1893. 1st edn. 8vo. Fldg map, ills.
Lower edges v marginally discold by damp.

Orig cloth, sl marked.

(Grayling) **£90 [≈ $144]**

- Travel and Adventures in South East Africa ... Eleven Years spent on the Zambesi and its Tributaries. London: 1893. 3rd edn. 8vo. Fldg cold map, ills. Foredge of a few ff sl marked. Mod half mor gilt.

(Grayling) **£120 [≈ $192]**

- Travels and Adventure in South East Africa ... London: Rowland Ward, 1893. 1st edn. 8vo. xviii,503,4 advt pp. Fldg map, 23 plates. Orig pict cloth, sl rubbed.

(Adelson) **$325 [≈ £203]**

Selous, Percy & Bryden, H.A.
- Travel and Big Game. New York: Longmans, Green, 1897. Tall 8vo. 195 pp. 6 ills by Whymper. Sl foxed. Tissue guards darkened. Orig pict gilt green cloth, sl faded & soiled.

(Parmer) **$125 [≈ £78]**

Semon, R.
- In the Australian Bush and on the Coast of the Coral Sea. London: 1899. 8vo. xv,552 pp. 4 maps, 86 ills. Sl foxing. Sgntr & blind stamp on title. Cloth.

(Wheldon & Wesley) **£110 [≈ $176]**

Semple, Robert
- Observations on a Journey through Spain and Italy to Naples and thence to Smyrna and Constantinople ... London: 1807. 1st edn. 2 vols. Sm 8vo. xiv,222; 4,249 pp. Sl foxing. Contemp calf, edges rubbed, hinges cracked, some chips to spine.

(Worldwide Antiqu'n) **$250 [≈ £156]**

Senior, Nassau William
- A Journal kept in Turkey and Greece in the Autumn of 1857 and the Beginning of 1858. London: Longman, Brown ..., 1859. 1st edn. 8vo. xi,[3],372 pp. 2 cold fldg maps, 2 cold litho plates. Lacks half-title. Contemp half calf.   *(Fenning)* **£145 [≈ $232]**

Senn, Nicholas
- In the Heart of the Arctics. Chicago: W.B. Conkey, [1907]. 1st edn. Sm 8vo. 336 pp. 75 ills. Orig pict cloth gilt, t.e.g.

(Schoyer) **$60 [≈ £37]**

- In the Heart of the Arctics. Chicago: W.B. Conkey, [1907]. 336 pp. 75 photo ills. Front endpaper spotted. Orig pict cloth blue gilt.

(Parmer) **$95 [≈ £59]**

A Sentimental Journey ...
- A Sentimental Journey through France and Italy ...see Sterne, Laurence.

Series ...
- A Series of Indoostan Letters by a Traveller ... see Burges, Barthalomew.

Seton-Karr, Sir Henry
- My Sporting Holidays. London: Edward Arnold, 1904. 8vo. 367,advt pp. Frontis & other plates. Orig blue cloth gilt.

(Terramedia) **$60 [≈ £37]**

- Ten Years Wild Sports in Foreign Lands. London: 1889. 8vo. Orig bndg, sl rubbed.

(Grayling) **£80 [≈ $128]**

Seume, J.G.
- A Tour through Part of Germany, Poland, Russia, Sweden, Denmark, &c. during the Summer of 1805. London: Richard Phillips, 1807. 102,index pp. Mod half cloth, t.e.g.

(Reese) **$100 [≈ £62]**

Several Voyages to Barbary ...
- See Morgan, John.

Seymour, Henry D.
- Russia on the Black Sea and Sea of Azov: being a Narrative of Travel in the Crimea and Bordering Provinces ... London: Murray, 1855. 1st edn. 8vo. xxiv,361,32 advt pp. 3 fldg maps, 3 plates. Orig cloth, spine reprd.

(Fenning) **£55 [≈ $88]**

- Russia, the Black Sea and Sea of Azov. Being a Narrative of Travel in the Crimea and Bordering Provinces ... London: Murray, 1855. 1st edn. 8vo. xviii,361 pp. Frontis, fldg map, 3 plans, 1 plate. Orig tan cloth, much faded & a bit spotted.

(Terramedia) **$200 [≈ £125]**

Shackleton, Ernest H.
- The Heart of the Antarctic ... Philadelphia: Lippincott, 1909. 1st edn. 2 vols. Lge 8vo. liii,365,1; xvi,450,1 pp. 2 lge fldg maps & chart in pocket, num photo plates. Orig pict blue & silver cloth.

(Terramedia) **$500 [≈ £312]**

- The Heart of the Antarctic ... London: Heinemann, 1909. 1st edn. 2 vols. Lge 8vo. xlviii,372; xv,418 pp. Fldg maps & plans, num plates (many cold), text diags. Orig cloth, upper cvrs blocked in silver, t.e.g.

(Frew Mackenzie) **£225 [≈ $360]**

Sharp, Samuel
- Letters from Italy, describing the Customs and Manners of that Country, in the Years 1765, and 1766 ... London: for Henry & Cave ... Rivington ... F. Newbery, [1767]. 3rd edn. 8vo. Contemp calf, gilt spine.

(Ximenes) **$225 [≈ £140]**

- Letters from Italy, describing the Customs and Manners of that Country, in the Years 1765 and 1766. London: [ca 1770]. 3rd edn. 8vo. Contemp calf, upper jnt cracked but firm, lacks label. *(Robertshaw)* **£38 [≈ $60]**

Shaw, Barnabas
- Memorials of South Africa. New York: 1841. 1st Amer edn. 317 pp. Occas foxing. Contemp calf, rebacked. *(Reese)* **$125 [≈ £78]**

Shaw, D.A.
- Eldorado or California as Seen by a Pioneer. Los Angeles: 1900. 313 pp. Port. Cloth, hinge cracking. *(Reese)* **$200 [≈ £125]**

Shaw, George A.
- Madagascar and France. With Some Account of the Island ... London: RTS, 1885. 1st edn. 8vo. 320 pp. Fldg map (short tear, no loss), 16 plates. A few marg pencil notes. Orig cloth gilt. *(Fenning)* **£45 [≈ $72]**
- Madagascar and France. With Some Account of the Island ... London: RTS, 1885. 8vo. 320 pp. Fldg map, 17 ills. Orig pict gilt cloth, unopened. *(Schoyer)* **$60 [≈ £37]**

Shaw, Richard Norman
- Architectural Sketches from the Continent. Views and Details from France, Italy and Germany. London: Day & Son, [1858]. 1st edn. Lge folio. [xiii],100 pp. Engvd title & 100 plates. 1st & last few ff sl foxed. Contemp half mor, a.e.g., rubbed, cloth sl spotted. *(Terramedia)* **$200 [≈ £125]**

Shaw, Robert Barkley
- Visits to High Tartary, Yarkand, and Kashgar (formerly Chinese Tartary) and Return Journey over the Karakoram Pass. London: 1871. 1st edn. 486 pp. Fldg litho map, tinted litho frontis, plates. Orig cloth. *(Trophy Room Books)* **$700 [≈ £437]**
- Visits to High Tartary, Yarkland, and Kashgar (formerly Chinese Tartary), and Return Journey over the Karakoram Pass. London: Murray, 1871. 1st edn. xvi,486 pp. 2 fldg maps, 7 plates (4 tinted in colours), text ills. Contemp half gilt, sl rubbed & worn. *(Hollett)* **£240 [≈ $384]**

Shaw, Stebbing & Brydges, Sir Samuel Egerton
- The Topographer for the Year 1789 [1790, 1791] ... London: for Robson & Clarke, 1789-91. All published. 4 vols. 8vo. viii, 582,[10]; vi,[ii], 392,[20]; [x],3-398, 9-28, [4]; vii,[i], [14],362 pp. 51 plates. Contemp half russia, worn, hinges cracked or broken. *(Claude Cox)* **£30 [≈ $48]**

Shaw, Thomas
- Travels or Observations relating to Several Parts of Barbary and the Levant. The Third Edition, Corrected, with Some Account of the Author. Edinburgh: Johnstone ..., 1808. 2 vols. 8vo. [xxxiv],462; [vi],440 pp. 34 maps & plates. Sl foxing. Half mor, sl rubbed. *(Terramedia)* **$200 [≈ £125]**

Shaw, Thurston
- Igbu Ukwu. Northwestern Univ Press: 1976. 1st edn. 2 vols (text & plates). Thick 4to. Over 514 plates. Orig bndg. Dws. *(Terramedia)* **$200 [≈ £125]**

Shaw, W. Teignmouth W.
- Kent. Painted by W. Biscombe Gardener. London: A. & C. Black Colour Books, Twenty Shilling Series, 1907. 1st edn. 73 cold plates. Orig dec cloth, t.e.g., fine. *(Old Cathay)* **£55 [≈ $88]**

Shaw, William
- Cullybackey. The Story of an Ulster Village. Edinburgh: Macdonald, 1913. 199 pp. Ills. Orig bndg. *(Emerald Isle)* **£55 [≈ $88]**

Shearer, Frederick E. (ed.)
- The Pacific Tourist. J.R. Bowman's Illustrated Trans-Continental Guide of Travel, from the Atlantic to the Pacific Ocean ... New York: 1886. 4to. 372 pp. Ills, tables. Cloth gilt, loose in bndg. *(Reese)* **$100 [≈ £62]**

Shebbeare, John
- Letters on the English Nation by Batista Angeloni, a Jesuit who resided many years in London. London: 1755. 1st edn. 2 vols. 8vo. Old ownership stamps on titles. Contemp calf, rubbed, vol 1 rebacked & upper jnt split, upper cvr of vol 2 detached. *(Robertshaw)* **£45 [≈ $72]**

Sheffield, F.
- How I Killed the Tiger. Being an Account of my Encounter with a Royal Bengal Tiger. Also an Appendix of General Information about India. London: 1902. 8vo. Ills. Orig cloth, sl discold. *(Grayling)* **£50 [≈ $80]**

Sheil, Lady
- Glimpses of Life and Manners in Persia, with Notes on Russia, Koords, Toorkomans, Nestorians, Khiva, and Persia. London: 1856. 8vo. Frontis, 6 plates. Occas spotting, name on title. Mod half calf. *(Farahar)* **£300 [≈ $480]**

Sheldon, Charles

- The Wilderness of the North Pacific Coast Islands. A Hunter's Experiences ... New York: Scribner's, 1912. xvi,246 pp. Maps (1 fldg), photo plates. Orig cloth, t.e.g.
(High Latitude) **$150 [≈ £93]**
- The Wilderness of the Upper Yukon. A Hunter's Explorations for Wild Sheep in the Sub-Arctic Mountains. New York: Scribner's, 1911. 1st edn. xxi,354 pp. 4 maps, cold frontis, photo plates. Orig cloth, t.e.g., new endpapers. *(High Latitude)* **$150 [≈ £93]**
- The Wilderness of the Upper Yukon. A Hunter's Explorations for Wild Sheep in Sub-Arctic Mountains. New York: Scribner's, 1911. 1st edn. 8vo. 354 pp. Maps, cold frontis, other plates. Orig pict green cloth gilt, sl nicked. *(Terramedia)* **$400 [≈ £250]**

Shepard, Elihu H.

- The Autobiography of Elihu H. Shepard, Formerly Professor of Languages in St. Louis College. St. Louis: George Knapp, 1869. 276 pp. 2 mtd orig photos. Orig black cloth, spine extremities sl chipped. Family inscrptn.
(Karmiole) **$100 [≈ £62]**

Shepherd, Charles William

- The North-West Peninsula of Iceland: being the Journal of a Tour in ... 1862. London: Longmans, Green, 1867. 1st edn. 8vo. Fldg map, 2 cold lithos. Orig cloth.
(Hannas) **£85 [≈ $136]**
- The North-West Peninsula of Iceland: being the Journal of a Tour in ... 1862. London: Longmans, Green, 1867. 1st edn. 8vo. Fldg map, 2 cold lithos. Lib stamp on title. Orig cloth, spine a little worn.
(Hannas) **£65 [≈ $104]**

Shepherd, Thomas H.

- Metropolitan Improvements or London in the Nineteenth Century. London: Jones & Co, 1827. 2 vols. 4to. 161 pp. Ca 350 pp of plates. Mor backed bds, bds rubbed, extremities bumped. *(Reese)* **$500 [≈ £312]**
- Metropolitan Improvements; or, London in the Nineteenth Century: being a Series of Views ... by Thomas H. Shepherd ... [descriptive text] by James Elmes. London: Jones & Co, 1829. 4to. vi,172,ii pp. Engvd title & 85 plates, plan. Sl marked. Orig buckram, sl worn.
(Box of Delights) **£120 [≈ $192]**
- Modern Athens Displayed in a Series of Views: or Edinburgh in the Nineteenth Century. London: Jones, 1829. 8vo. 89 pp. Ca 250 pp of plates. Mor backed bds, extremities worn. *(Reese)* **$350 [≈ £218]**

Sheppard, T.

- Geological Rambles in East Yorkshire. London: n.d. 8vo. xi,235 pp. Frontis, cold fldg map, 53 text ills. Orig cloth, soiled.
(Henly) **£17 [≈ $27]**
- Geological Rambles in East Yorkshire. London: [1903]. 8vo. xi,235 pp. Maps & 53 figs. Orig cloth.
(Wheldon & Wesley) **£28 [≈ $44]**

Sherer, J. Moyle

- Notes and Reflections during a Ramble in Germany. London: Longman, Rees ..., 1826. 1st edn. 8vo. iv,400 pp. A few spots. Half calf gilt, surface of leather rather pitted.
(Hollett) **£65 [≈ $104]**
- Scenes and Impressions in Egypt and Italy. Third Edition. London: Longman ..., 1825. 8vo. Orig cloth backed bds, uncut & partly unopened, crnrs sl worn, label a little chipped. *(Clark)* **£45 [≈ $72]**
- Sketches of India: written by an Officer for Fire-side Travellers at-home. London: Longman, Hurst ..., 1824. 2nd edn. 8vo. iv, 358 pp. A few spots. Half calf gilt, surface of leather rather pitted. *(Hollett)* **£65 [≈ $104]**

Sherson, Erroll

- Townshend of Chitral and Kut. London: Heinemann, 1928. 8vo. 411 pp. Frontis, 7 ills. Ex-lib. Rec red half leather, green label.
(Bates & Hindmarch) **£45 [≈ $72]**

Shields, G.O. (ed.)

- The Big Game of North America. Habits, Habitat, Haunts, Characteristics, and How, When, Where to Hunt It. London: 1890. 8vo. Ills. Orig cloth. *(Grayling)* **£100 [≈ $160]**

Shields, George O.

- Cruisings in the Cascades ... Chicago: Rand, McNally, 1889. 8vo. 339, 12 advt pp. Frontis, num text ills. Orig pict cloth, sl rubbed. *(Adelson)* **$95 [≈ £59]**

Shiels, Archie W.

- Seward's Icebox. A Few Notes on the Development of Alaska 1867-1932. Bellingham, WA: privately printed, [ca 1933]. One of 500. 8vo. 419,[3] pp. Orig cloth. Dw. Inscribed by Shiels.
(High Latitude) **$70 [≈ £43]**

Shirley, Evelyn Philip

- Some Account of the Territory or Dominion of Farney in the Province and Earldom of Ulster. London: Pickering, 1845. 4to. 211 pp. Half calf. *(Emerald Isle)* **£125 [≈ $200]**

Shoberl, Frederic (ed.)
- Persia; containing a Description of the Country ... Illustrated with Twelve Coloured Engravings. Philadelphia: 1834. 2nd Amer edn. 12mo. 181 pp. 12 cold plates. Text foxed. Old calf, worn & loose.
  (M & S Rare Books) **$125 [≈ £78]**
- Turkey ... see Castellan, A.L.
- The World in Miniature ... Africa ... London: for R. Ackermann, [1821]. 4 vols in 2. 16mo. Cold engvd title to vol 1, 4 cold frontis, cold plates, maps. Calf gilt, a.e.g., wear to jnts, chip to hd of 1 spine. *(Reese)* **$850 [≈ £531]**
- The World in Miniature: Tibet and India beyond the Ganges ... London: Ackermann, [1822]. 12mo. xi,1,352 pp. 12 hand cold plates (dated 1824). Orig bds, rebacked in green cloth. *(Terramedia)* **$200 [≈ £125]**

Short ...
- A Short History of Barbados ...see Frere, George.
- A Short Survey or History of the Kingdom of Sveden ... London: for Michael Sparke, sold by James Boler, 1632. 1st English edn. 2 parts in one vol. 4to. Intl & final blanks in 2nd part. Lacks intl blank in 1st part. Mod calf. STC 23518 & 13458. *(Hannas)* **£850 [≈ $1,360]**
- A Short Tour made in the Year One Thousand Seven Hundred and Seventy One ... see Percy, Elizabeth, Duchess of Northumberland.

Short, Bertie
- Between the Indian Flags. Allahabad: 1894. 8vo. 2 port frontis. Orig cloth, sl worn.
  (Farahar) **£100 [≈ $160]**

Shufeldt, Robert W.
- Reports of Explorations & Surveys to ascertain the practicality of a Ship-Canal between the Atlantic & Pacific Oceans ... Washington: GPO, 1872. 1st edn. Lge 4to. 151 pp. 20 fldg maps, 10 litho plates. Perf lib stamp in title. Orig green cloth.
  (Terramedia) **$250 [≈ £156]**

Sidney, Samuel
- The Three Colonies of Australia. New South Wales, Victoria, South Australia ... London: Ingram, Cooke, 1852. 1st edn. 8vo. 425, 2 appendix pp. Num plates & ills. Contemp qtr mor, sl rubbed & darkened.
  (Terramedia) **$200 [≈ £125]**
- The Three Colonies of Australia. New South Wales, Victoria, South Australia ... Auburn: 1854. 1st Amer edn. Sm 8vo. 408 pp. 10 plates. 2 lib b'plates. Orig green cloth gilt, sl soiled, extremities sl frayed.

(Karmiole) **$150 [≈ £93]**

Siggins, A.
- Shooting with Rifle and Camera [Tanzania]. London: 1931. 368 pp. Ills. Orig bndg. Author's pres copy.
  (Trophy Room Books) **$100 [≈ £62]**

Silliman, Benjamin
- A Journal of Travels in England, Holland, and Scotland, and of Two Passages over the Atlantic, in the Years 1805 and 1806 ... Boston: 1812. 2 vols in one. 336; 359 pp. 3 fldg plans. Dampstained, scattered foxing, 1 tear without loss. Mod cloth.
  (Reese) **$100 [≈ £62]**

Silver, A.P.
- Farm-Cottage, Camp and Canoe in Maritime Canada, or the Call of Nova Scotia to the Emigrant and Sportsman. London: [ca 1910]. 8vo. Ills. Orig bndg, sl rubbed.
  (Grayling) **£30 [≈ $48]**

Simmonds, P.L.
- The Arctic Regions & Polar Discoveries during the Nineteenth Century. With an Account of the New British Exploring Expedition Fitted Out in 1875 ... London & New York: Routledge, 1878. 9th edn. 16mo. xvi, 387 pp. Fldg map. Contemp mor, rubbed. *(Terramedia)* **$35 [≈ £21]**
- Sir John Franklin and the Arctic Regions. London: Routledge, 1851. xvi,375 pp. 2 fldg maps, frontis. Prize calf, some wear & scuffing. *(Parmer)* **$125 [≈ £78]**
- Sir John Franklin and the Arctic Regions: with Detailed Notices of the Expeditions in Search of the Missing Vessels under Sir John Franklin ... Buffalo: 1852. xvii,[25]-396 pp. Fldg map, plates, ills. Orig pict cloth, gilt spine, extremities frayed.
  (Reese) **$200 [≈ £125]**

Simpson, Henry I.
- The Emigrant's Guide to the Gold Mines ... Adventures with the Gold Diggers of California. New York: Joyce & Co, 1848. The 5-cent iss without map. 30,[2] pp. Later half mor. *(Jenkins)* **$950 [≈ £593]**

Simpson, J.H.
- Report of Explorations across the Great Basin of the Territory of Utah for a Direct Wagon-Route from Camp Floyd to Genoa, in Carson Valley in 1859. Washington: GPO, 1876. 1st edn. Folio. 518 pp. 25 plates & maps. Contemp three qtr mor, raised bands, gilt.
  (Jenkins) **$425 [≈ £265]**

Simpson, Thomas
- Narrative of the Discoveries on the North Coast of America, effected by the Officers of the Hudson's Bay Company during the Years 1836-39. London: Bentley, 1843. xix,419 pp. 2 maps. Rec half calf, t.e.g.
(High Latitude) **$500 [≃ £312]**
- Narrative of the Discoveries on the North Coast of America, effected by the Officers of the Hudson's Bay Company during 1836-39. London: Bentley, 1843. 1st edn. xix,419 pp. 2 fldg maps. Orig dec cloth. Half mor slipcase. John R. Bartlett's copy, sgnd on title.
(Jenkins) **$350 [≃ £218]**

Simpson, William
- Meeting the Sun: A Journey all round the World, through Egypt, China, Japan, and California ... London: 1874. 413,advt pp. Frontis, ills. Elab gilt cloth, a bit worn, crnrs bumped. *(Reese)* **$110 [≃ £68]**

Singer, Caroline
- White Africans and Black. New York: Norton, 1929. 4to. 120 pp. Illust by Cyrus Baldridge. Dec endpapers. Orig dec cloth. Sgnd by author & illustrator.
(Parmer) **$50 [≃ £31]**

Singh, A.
- Tiger Haven. London: 1973. 8vo. Num cold & other ills. Orig bndg. dw.
(Grayling) **£20 [≃ $32]**

Singh, Bhawani
- Travel Pictures The Record of a European Tour. London: Longmans, 1912. 8vo. xiv,287 pp. Photo frontis, 96 photo ills. Orig bndg, sl stained. *(Bates & Hindmarch)* **£25 [≃ $40]**

Sinigaglia, Leone
- Climbing Reminiscences of the Dolomites. Translated by Mary Alice Vialls. London: 1896. 1st edn in English. 8vo. xxiv,224 pp. Cold map, 39 plates. Some marks. Orig pict cloth, spine ends a little worn, short tear & sm hole in lower jnt.
(Bow Windows) **£185 [≃ $296]**

Sinker, Robert
- Memorials of the Hon. Ion Keith-Falconer, M.A. Cambridge: Deighton, Bell ..., 1888. 1st edn. 8vo. viii,280 pp. Port. Orig cloth, faded. *(Burmester)* **£25 [≃ $40]**

A Six Weeks Tour ...
- A Six Weeks Tour through the Southern Counties of England and Wales ... see Young, Arthur.

Skelton, Joseph
- Pietas Oxoniensis or Records of Oxford Founders. Oxford: for J. Skelton by J. Parker, 1828. 1st edn. Large Paper. Lge 4to. iv,96 pp. Engvd title & 25 guarded plates on india paper. Orig half roan, rubbed, 1 inch section lost from spine. Subscriber's copy.
(Claude Cox) **£48 [≃ $76]**

Skelton, R.A., et al.
- The Vinland Map & The Tartar Relation. New Haven & London: Yale UP, 1965. Lge 4to. xii, 291 pp. Num facs plates & maps. Cloth. Dw. *(Terramedia)* **$30 [≃ £18]**

Sketch(es) ...
- A Sketch of the Internal Condition of the United States of America ... By a Russian ... see Poletika, Pierre.
- Sketches of India ... see Sherer, J. Moyle.
- Sketches of the West ... see Grinnell, Joseph B.

Skinner, Captain Thomas
- Excursions in India; including a Walk over the Himalaya Mountains, to the Sources of the Jumna and the Ganges. London: Colburn & Bentley, 1832. 1st edn. 2 vols. 8vo. 2 frontis (somewhat foxed). Contemp half calf gilt, some wear. *(Trebizond)* **$350 [≃ £218]**
- Excursions in India; including a Walk over the Himalaya Mountains to the Sources of the Jumna and the Ganges. London: 1832. 2 vols. 330; 312 pp. Frontises. Half leather, v fine.
(Trophy Room Books) **$500 [≃ £312]**

Skrine, C.P.
- Chinese Central Asia. With an Introduction by Sir Francis Younghusband. Boston & New York: Houghton, Mifflin, 1926. 1st Amer edn. 8vo. xvi,306 pp. Lge fldg map, cold frontis, num photo plates inc 2 panoramic views. Sl foxing. Orig cloth, spine lettering sl rubbed. *(Terramedia)* **$100 [≃ £62]**

Sladen, Douglas
- Carthage and Tunis. Philadelphia: 1906. 2 vols. 8vo. 311; 663 pp. Cold frontis in vol 2, 4 cold & num photo plates, ills. Orig cloth, exlib, rubbed. *(Terramedia)* **$50 [≃ £31]**
- Egypt and the English. London: Hurst & Blackett, 1908. 8vo. xxviii,568,advt pp. Map, 40 photo ills. Orig gilt dec red cloth, edges sl foxed, bds smudged. *(Parmer)* **£40 [≃ $25]**
- Queer Things About Egypt. Philadelphia & London: Lippincott, Hurst & Blackett, 1911. 1st edn. 8vo. xxi,428 pp. Fldg map, frontis, num photo plates. Orig maroon cloth gilt, spine sl sunned. *(Terramedia)* **$75 [≃ £46]**

- Segesta, Selinunte, and the West of Sicily. London: 1903. 1st edn. Sm 4to. Num ills. Orig cloth, sl soiled, spine rather dull. Pres copy.   *(Robertshaw)* **£18 [≃ $28]**

Slatin Pasha, Rudolph C.
- Fire and Sword in the Sudan. A Personal Narrative of Fighting & Serving the Dervishes, 1879-1895. Translated by Major F.R. Wingate. London & New York: 1896. 1st edn. 8vo. xviii,636 pp. 2 fldg maps, frontis, num plates. Orig pict green cloth gilt, sl shaken.   *(Terramedia)* **$200 [≃ £125]**
- Fire and Sword in the Sudan. A Personal Narrative of Fighting and Serving the Dervishes, 1879-1895. Translated by F.R. Wingate. London & New York: Arnold, 1896. 1st edn. 8vo. xix,635 pp. 2 fldg maps, frontis, 21 plates. Sl foxed. Orig cloth, sl rubbed. *(Worldwide Antiqu'n)* **$75 [≃ £46]**
- Fire and Sword in the Sudan. A Personal Narrative of Fighting and Serving the Dervishes, 1879-1895 ... London: Edward Arnold, 1896. 3rd edn. Thick 8vo. xviii,636, 32 advt pp. 2 fldg plans, frontis port, 21 plates. Orig cloth gilt, sl worn & marked.
                 (Hollett) **£85 [≃ $136]**
- Fire and Sword in the Sudan. A Personal Narrative of Fighting and Serving the Dervishes, 1879-1895. London: Edward Arnold, 1897. Popular Edition. 8vo. xviii,416 pp. 2 maps, frontis, 21 ills. Orig maroon cloth gilt.   *(Bates & Hindmarch)* **£35 [≃ $56]**

Sleeman, W.H.
- Rambles and Recollections of an Indian Official. London: Hatchard, 1844. 1st edn. 2 vols. 8vo. xii,478; vii,[i],459 pp. 32 chromolithos. Occas sl spotting. Orig pict gilt crimson cloth, by Westleys.
          (Frew Mackenzie) **£250 [≃ $400]**

Slingsby, William Cecil
- Norway, the Northern Playground. Sketches of Climbing and Mountain Exploration ... Edinburgh: David Douglas, 1904. 1st edn. 8vo. 9 maps, 32 plates & text ills. Lib stamp on verso of maps & plates. Orig cloth, uncut, headband snagged. *(Hannas)* **£240 [≃ $384]**

Sloan, J.M.
- Galloway. Painted by James Faed, Junr. London: A. & C. Black Colour Books, Six Shillings Series, 1908. 1st edn. 24 cold plates. Orig dec blue cloth, hd of spine reprd.
                 (Old Cathay) **£39 [≃ $62]**

Sloane, Hans
- A Voyage to the Islands Madera, Barbados, Nieves, S. Christophers and Jamaica, with the Natural History ... London: 1707-25. 4 vols. Folio. Lge fldg map, 284 dble-page plates. 4 plates restored with xerox. 2 blank crnrs restored. Contemp calf, sl rubbed.
          (Wheldon & Wesley) **£2,400 [≃ $3,840]**

Smiles, Samuel
- Round the World: Including a Residence in Victoria, and a Journey by Rail across North America. New York: 1872. 289,advt pp. Map, ills. Orig cloth, spine faded, wear to extremities, hinges starting.
                 (Reese) **$75 [≃ £46]**

Smith, A.
- Through Unknown African Countries. London: 1897. 471 pp. Ills. Orig bndg, elephant head on front, edge of front cvr damaged.
          (Trophy Room Books) **$500 [≃ £312]**

Smith, A.H.
- The Place-Names of Gloucestershire. London: 1964-65. 4 vols. Fldg map in pocket. Orig cloth.   *(Ambra)* **£45 [≃ $72]**

Smith, Agnes
- Through Cyprus. London: Hurst & Blackett, 1887. 1st edn. 8vo. ix,351 pp. Fldg map, frontis, title vignette, 3 full page ills. Orig gilt dec blue cloth, spine extremities chipped, cvrs sl rubbed.
          (Frew Mackenzie) **£85 [≃ $136]**

Smith, Albert Richard
- To China and Back: being a Diary kept, Out and Home. [London]: for the author, Egyptian Hall, 1859. 1st edn. Sm 8vo. 60 pp, final advt leaf. W'engvd frontis. Mod qtr mor.
                 (Hannas) **£75 [≃ $120]**

Smith, Amanda
- An Autobiography. The Story of the Lord's Dealings with Mrs. Amanda Smith, the Colored Evangelist. Containing an Account of her Life Work of Faith, and her Travels ... Chicago: Meyer & Brother, 1893. 1st edn. Orig cloth gilt.   *(Minkoff)* **$285 [≃ £178]**

Smith, Arthur H.
- China in Convulsion. New York: 1901. 2 vols. Maps, plates. Orig pict gilt cloth, a bit soiled, partly unopened. *(Reese)* **$125 [≃ £78]**

Smith, Charles
- The Ancient and Present State of the County and City of Cork, a Natural, Civil, Ecclesiastical, Historical and Topographical Description Thereof. Dublin: Wilson, 1774. 2nd edn, with addtns. 2 vols. Maps, plates.

Diced calf, rebacked.
(Emerald Isle) **£245 [≈ $392]**
- The Ancient and Present State of the County and City of Cork, a Natural, Civil, Ecclesiastical, Historical and Topographical Description Thereof. Dublin: Wilson, 1774. 2nd edn, with addtns. 2 vols. Maps, plates. Rec cloth. *(Emerald Isle)* **£175 [≈ $280]**

Smith, E. Quincy
- Travels at Home and Abroad. New York: 1911. 3 vols. Ills. Cloth, sl stains to 1 vol.
(Reese) **$125 [≈ £78]**

Smith, Edmond Reuel
- The Aracaunians; or, Notes of a Tour among the Indian Tribes of Southern Chili. New York: Harper, 1855. 1st edn. 12mo. 7 full-page & 10 text engvs. Occas sl foxing, endpapers discold. Orig cloth, gilt spine.
(Trebizond) **$160 [≈ £100]**

Smith, Francis Hopkinson
- Venice of To-day. Illustrated by the Author. New York: Henry T. Thomas, 1896. Lge folio. [22],160 pp. 42 mtd plates (20 cold), num text ills, many cold. Contemp dark green half mor gilt, spine faded, orig wraps bound in. *(Karmiole)* **$150 [≈ £93]**

Smith, George
- The Chaldean Account of Genesis. New York: Scribner, 1876. 1st Amer edn. Lge 8vo. xvi, 319, advt pp. Mtd photo frontis, num other plates, ills, decs. Orig pict maroon cloth gilt, edges of spine sl frayed.
(Terramedia) **$100 [≈ £62]**

Smith, Revd George
- A Narrative of an Exploratory Visit to each of the Consular Cities of China, and to the Islands of Hong Kong and Chusan ... New York: 1847. [16],467 pp. Frontis, fldg map, plates. Occas foxing. Later three qtr mor.
(Reese) **$250 [≈ £156]**

Smith, H. Clifford
- Buckingham Palace: its Furniture, Decoration and History. With Introductory Chapters on the Building and Site by Christopher Hussey. London: Country Life, [1930]. 4to. xxiii,300 pp. 351 plates. Orig cloth, uncut, crnrs bumped, some marking on cvrs. *(Coombes)* **£40 [≈ $64]**

Smith, H. Maynard
- Frank, Bishop of Zanzibar. Life of Frank Weston, 1871-1924. London: SPCK, (1926). 1st edn. 8vo. xi,326 pp. Frontis port, other photo plates. Orig brown cloth gilt.

(Terramedia) **$60 [≈ £37]**

Smith, Herbert H.
- Brazil. The Amazons and the Coast. London: Sampson, Low, Marston, 1879. 8vo. xv,644 pp. Fldg map, text ills. Mod buckram.
(Adelson) **$85 [≈ £53]**

Smith, Horace S. (compiler)
- Visit to the City of Prague by Sir Charles Wakefield, Acting Lord Mayor, and a Deputation of the Corporation of the City of London. Chiswick Press: for private circulation, 1921. 4to. 124 pp. Num ills. Orig black buckram, t.e.g. *(Piccadilly)* **£25 [≈ $40]**

Smith, Sir James Edward
- A Sketch of a Tour on the Continent. London: 1807. 2nd edn, with addtns & crrctns. 3 vols. 8vo. A few pp carelessly opened. Orig bds, uncut, jnts cracked, spines partly defective.
(Wheldon & Wesley) **£120 [≈ $192]**

Smith, Captain John
- Generall Historie of Virginia, New England ... Ohio: Rainbird, 1966. Facs edn. Ltd edn. Folio. xiv,248 pp. Map, engvd title, 2 ports, 4 plates. Orig vellum gilt. Orig box.
(Gough) **£60 [≈ $96]**
- The True Travels, Adventures, & Observations ... in Europe, Asia, Affrica, and America ... New York: Rimington & Hooper, The Georgian Press, 1930. One of 327. Folio. [xxiv], 80 pp. Port, facs title, fldg plate. Orig buckram, slipcase. *(Gough)* **£40 [≈ $64]**

Smith, John Thomas
- Antiquities of London and its Environs ... London: 1791. 1st edn. Lge 4to. 96 engvd plates (2 ptd in bistre). 1 plate marg reprd. Contemp red half calf, raised bands, mor label, sl rubbed. *(Young's)* **£130 [≈ $208]**

Smith, John Thomas & Hawkins, J.S.
- Antiquities of the City of Westminster ... London: J.T. Smith ..., 1807. 1st edn. 4to. xvi,276 pp. 2 variant title-pages. 36 engvd plates (inc 1 litho, 14 hand cold), some highlighted in gold). Contemp half calf, mrbld bds. *(Gough)* **£395 [≈ $632]**

Smith, Michael
- A Geographical View of the Province of Upper Canada ... containing a Complete Description of Niagara Falls ... New York: for the author, August, 1813. 2nd edn. 12mo. 118, [1] pp. Contemp mrbld wraps, some wear. *(M & S Rare Books)* **$150 [≈ £93]**

- A Geographical View of the Province of Upper Canada ... containing a Complete Description of Niagara Falls ... Trenton, [N.J.]: Nov, 1813. 3rd edn, rvsd. 12mo. 117, [1] pp. Frontis of Perry's Victory. Text browned. Contemp leather backed bds.
(M & S Rare Books) **$200 [≈ £125]**

Smith, Sir Ross
- 14,000 Miles through the Air. New York: Macmillan, 1922. 1st Amer edn. 8vo. xiv,136 pp. Frontis, map, plates. Orig cloth. Dw sl chipped.   *(Berkelouw)* **$150 [≈ £93]**

Smith, Thomas (ed.)
- Hand-Book for Visitors to Harrow on the Hill; containing a Topographical and Historical Account of the Parish of Harrow and the Grammar School ... With a Directory ... London: 1850. 120 pp. Ills. Orig cloth, spine faded & chafed. *(Coombes)* **£30 [≈ $48]**

Smith, Tom C.
- History of the Parish of Chipping in the County of Lancaster, with some Account of the Forests of Bleasdale and Bowland. Preston: for the author by C.W. Whitehead, 1894. 1st edn. 276 pp. Lge fldg map frontis, 2 plates, 11 fldg pedigrees. Orig bndg.
(Box of Delights) **£90 [≈ $144]**

Smith, W.C.G.
- Observations on China and the Chinese. New York: Carleton, 1863. 8vo. 216 pp. Orig dec green cloth, spine extremities sl frayed.
(Karmiole) **$75 [≈ £46]**

Smith, William
- An Authentic Journal of the Expedition to Belleisle, and of the Siege of the Citadel of Paris ... London: for G. Woodfall, & M. Cooper, 1761. 8vo. iv,48 pp. Fldg map. Title dusty. Disbound.   *(Bickersteth)* **£35 [≈ $56]**

Smith, William, 1727-1803
- A Brief State of the Province of Pennsylvania ... London: for R. Griffiths, 1755. 1st edn. 12mo. Half-title,45 pp. Contemp wraps, untrimmed. Cloth case.
(Schoyer) **$500 [≈ £312]**

Smith, William, d.1793
- The History of the Province of New-York, from the First Discovery to the Year 1732 ... London: for Thomas Wilcox, 1757. 1st edn. 4to. 12,255 pp. Fldg frontis (sl worn). Sl browning. A few marg tears. Contemp sheep, rubbed, rear inner hinge reinforced.
(M & S Rare Books) **$500 [≈ £312]**

Smollett, Tobias
- A Journal of the late Expedition to Carthagena, with Notes. In Answer to a late Pamphlet; entitled, An Account of the Expedition to Carthagena. London: 1744. 59 pp. Half calf.   *(Reese)* **$450 [≈ £281]**
- Travels through France and Italy ... London: for R. Baldwin, 1766. 1st edn. 2 vols. 8vo. [iv],372; [iv],296 pp. V sl marg worm in 4 ff, not affecting text. Contemp calf, spines rubbed & sl chipped at hd.
(Finch) **£225 [≈ $360]**
- Travels through France and Italy. London: for R. Baldwin ..., 1778. 2 vols. Sm 8vo. 291; 290 pp. Old calf gilt, rather rubbed, edges rather darkened.   *(Hollett)* **£75 [≈ $120]**

Smyth, C. Piazzi
- Madeira Meteorologic. Being a Paper on the Above Subject Read before the Royal Society, Edinburgh, on the 1st of May 1882. Edinburgh: David Douglas, 1882. 1st edn. Cr 4to. viii,83 pp. 2 plates, ills & tables. Occas sl thumbing. Orig cloth, t.e.g., uncut.
(Duck) **£25 [≈ $40]**

Smyth, J.F.D.
- A Tour in the United States of America ... London: 1784. 2 vols. 400;455,errata pp. Half-title. A few pencil scorings & notes. Contemp calf, edgeworn, spine extremities sl chipped, hinges broken but cords intact. Subscriber's copy with b'plate.
(Reese) **$750 [≈ £468]**

Smyth, Warington W.
- A Year with the Turks or Sketches of Travel in the European and Asiatic Dominions of the Sultan. New York: 1854. 1st Amer edn. x, [11]-251, advt pp. Fldg cold frontis map. Some traces of foxing. Orig cloth, sunned, worn at extremities.   *(Reese)* **$100 [≈ £62]**

Smythe, F.
- Climbs in the Canadian Rockies. New York: 1950. 260 pp. Ills. Orig bndg. Dw.
(Trophy Room Books) **$45 [≈ £28]**

Smythe, F.S.
- The Valley of Flowers. London: 1938. 1st edn. 8vo. xiii,322 pp. 2 maps, 16 cold plates. Orig cloth, ex-lib.
(Wheldon & Wesley) **£25 [≈ $40]**

Smythe, Sarah M.
- Ten Months in the Fiji Islands. Oxford: Henry & Parker, 1864. 8vo. xviii,282 pp. 4 maps, 10 plates (4 cold). Mod cloth.
(Adelson) **$285 [≈ £178]**

'Snaffle" (i.e. Robert Dunkin)
- Gun, Rifle and Hound in East and West. By "Snaffle". London: Chapman & Hall, 1894. 8vo. 376 pp. Frontis, num plates. Orig pict green cloth gilt, unopened.
(Terramedia) **$100 [≈ £62]**
- Gun, Rifle and Hound in East and West. By "Snaffle". London: 1894. 8vo. Ills. Orig bndg.   *(Grayling)* **£45 [≈ $72]**
- In the Land of the Bora. Or Camp Life and Sport in Dalmatia and the Herzegovina. London: 1897. 8vo. Ills. Orig bndg, spine faded, crnrs sl bumped.
(Grayling) **£45 [≈ $72]**
- The Land of the Bora. Or Camp Life and Sport in Dalmatia and the Herzegovinia, 1894-5-6. London: Kegan Paul, 1897. 1st edn. 8vo. 406 pp. Frontis, other plates. Orig pict gilt green cloth.
(Terramedia) **$125 [≈ £78]**

Snell, F.J.
- North Devon. Painted by Henry B. Wimbush. London: A. & C. Black Colour Books, Six Shilling Series, 1906. 1st edn. 26 cold plates. Orig cloth, t.e.g., fine.
(Old Cathay) **£33 [≈ $52]**

Soane, E.B.
- To Mesopotamia and Kurdistan in Disguise. With Historical Notices of the Kurdish Tribes and the Chaldeans of Kurdistan. London: Murray, 1912. 1st edn. 8vo. ix,410 pp. Fldg map, 6 plates. Orig cloth, sl worn ex-lib, lib number on spine.
(Worldwide Antiqu'n) **$65 [≈ £40]**

Sola, A.E.
- Klondyke - Truth and Facts of the New Eldorado. London: Mining & Geog Inst, [ca 1897]. 4to. 92 pp. 3 maps, 17 plates. Orig green cloth gilt, rear cvr v sl spotted.
(Parmer) **$300 [≈ £187]**
- Klondyke: Truth and Facts of the New El Dorado. London: Mining & Geog Institute, [ca 1897]. Lge 8vo. [x],102 pp. 4 maps, 28 ills. Sl spotting, a few finger marks, 2 short tears. Lacks flyleaf. Orig gilt illust cloth, lower cvr a little marked.
(Bow Windows) **£155 [≈ $248]**

Somerset, H. Somers
- The Land of the Muskeg. With a Preface by A. Hungerford Pollen. London & Philadelphia: Heinemann & Lippincott, 1895. 1st edn. 8vo. xxxi, 248 pp. 4 maps (2 fldg), num plates & ills. Orig pict red cloth, new endpapers, sl soiled.
(Terramedia) **$175 [≈ £109]**

Somner, William
- A Treatise of the Roman Ports and Forts in Kent. To which is prefixt the Life of Mr. Somner. Oxford: at the Theater ..., 1693. 2nd (?) edn. 8vo. [x],118,[2], 117,[15] pp. Port. Contemp panelled calf, rubbed. Wing S.4669.   *(Young's)* **£95 [≈ $152]**

Somner, William & Batley, N.
- The Antiquities of Canterbury, in Two Parts, The Suburbs and Cathedral and Canturia Sacra. London: 1703. Folio. Frontis, 19 plates (1 torn & reprd). Sheep, a little worn.
(Henly) **£180 [≈ $288]**

South Sea Bubbles ...
- See Herbert, George Robert Charles, 13th Earl of Pembroke, & Kingsley, George Henry.

Southesk, James Carnegie, Earl of
- Saskatchewan and the Rocky Mountains. Edinburgh: Edmonston & Douglas, 1875. 1st edn. xxx,448 pp. 2 fldg maps, lithos, engvs. Orig blue cloth gilt, spine sl faded, partly unopened.   *(Parmer)* **$250 [≈ £156]**
- Saskatchewan and the Rocky Mountains. Edinburgh: Edmonston & Douglas, 1875. 1st edn. xxx,448 pp. 2 fldg maps, 9 plates, text engvs. Orig blue cloth, spine ends starting.
(Adelson) **$285 [≈ £178]**

Southey, Robert
- Journal of a Tour in the Netherlands in the Autumn of 1815. Boston: Houghton Mifflin, 1902. One of 519. Sm 8vo. 274 pp. Orig cloth & mrbld bds, untrimmed.
(Schoyer) **$50 [≈ £31]**

Southworth, Alvan S,
- Four Thousand Miles of African Travel. A Personal Record of a Journey up the Nile & through the Soudan to the Confines of Central Africa ... New York & London: Baker Pratt; Sampson, Low, 1875. 1st edn. 8vo. xi,381 pp. Fldg map, plates. Orig pict gilt cloth, sl worn.   *(Terramedia)* **$150 [≈ £93]**

Sowerby, A. de Carle
- A Naturalist's Holiday by the Sea, being a Collection of Essays on Marine, Littoral, and Shore-Line Life of the Cornish Peninsula ... London: Routledge, 1923. 8vo. xvi,262 pp. 21 plates, 21 text ills. Orig blue cloth gilt.
(Blackwell's) **£25 [≈ $40]**
- A Naturalist's Note-Book in China. Shanghai: 1925. Roy 8vo. 270 pp. 20 plates, num text figs. Sl foxing. Orig cloth.
(Wheldon & Wesley) **£50 [≈ $80]**

- A Naturalist's Note-Book in China. Shanghai: 1925. [xii],270 pp. Errata tipped in. 20 plates, num text ills. Orig dec cream cloth.
(Lyon) **£150 [≈ $240]**

Spallanzani, L.
- Travels in the Two Sicilies and some Parts of the Apennines ... London: 1798. 4 vols. 8vo. 11 plates. Cloth.
(Wheldon & Wesley) **£300 [≈ $480]**

Sparks, Jared
- The Life of John Ledyard, the American Traveller. Cambridge: Hilliard & Brown, 1828. 1st edn. xii,325 pp. Sl foxing at end. Orig bds, label.   *(Jenkins)* **£385 [≈ £240]**
- Memoirs of the Life and Travels of John Ledyard, from his Journals and Correspondence. London: Colburn, 1828. 1st London edn. 8vo. Lacks half-title. Contemp polished calf gilt, jnts weak.
(Hannas) **£380 [≈ $608]**

Sparrman, Anders
- A Voyage to the Cape of Good Hope ... Translated from the Swedish Original ... Second Edition, Corrected. London: for G.G. & J. Robinson, 1786. 2 vols. 4to. Final advt leaf. Frontis (marg repr), map, 9 plates. Sl stains. Contemp calf, rebacked & recrnrd.
(Hannas) **£300 [≈ $480]**

Spears, John R.
- The Gold Diggings of Cape Horn. A Study of Life in Tierra del Fuego & Patagonia. New York & London: Putnam's, 1895. 1st edn. Sm 8vo. 319 pp. Frontis map, other plates & ills. Orig green cloth. Author's pres copy.
(Terramedia) **$90 [≈ £56]**
- Illustrated Sketches of Death Valley, and Other Borax Deserts of the Pacific Coast. Chicago: 1892. 226 pp. Plates. Orig cloth gilt, light wear.   *(Jenkins)* **£225 [≈ $14,118]**

Speedy, Tom
- The Natural History of Sport in Scotland with Rod and Gun. London: 1920. 4to. Ills. Orig bndg, sl rubbed, inner hinge sprung.
(Grayling) **£30 [≈ $48]**
- Sport in the Highlands and Lowlands of Scotland with Rod and Gun. London: 1886. 2nd edn. 8vo. Plates, text ills. Orig bndg. Author's sgnd pres copy.
(Grayling) **£50 [≈ $80]**
- Sport in the Highlands and Lowlands of Scotland. With Rod and Gun. Edinburgh & London: Blackwood, 1886. 2nd edn. 8vo. 444, advt pp. Frontis, ills. Orig green cloth gilt.   *(Terramedia)* **$60 [≈ £37]**

Speight, Harry
- Lower Wharfedale. London: [Bradford ptd] Stock, 1902. 1st edn (?). 532,ctlg pp. Maps, ills, 16 pedigrees. Orig pict cloth, sl marked.
(Box of Delights) **£45 [≈ $72]**
- Nidderdale and the Garden of the Nidd: A Yorkshire Rhineland ... London: Elliot Stock, 1894. 1st edn. 514,[4 advt] pp. Fldg map, num ills. Orig pict cloth gilt, hinges v sl rubbed, upper hinge just cracking.
(Hollett) **£90 [≈ $144]**
- Upper Nidderdale, with the Forest of Knaresborough ... London: Elliot Stock, 1906. 1st edn. 367,lxxii,[xvi] pp. Fldg map (a few spots to verso), fldg pedigree, num ills. Orig pict cloth gilt.   *(Hollett)* **£75 [≈ $120]**

Speke, John Hanning
- Journal of the Discovery of the Source of the Nile. Edinburgh: Blackwood, 1864. 2nd edn. Thick 8vo. Fldg map, 25 plates, text ills. Orig brown pict cloth, a.e.g., rubbed, spine ends sl frayed.   *(Adelson)* **$350 [≈ £218]**
- Journal of the Discovery of the Source of the Nile. New York: Harper, 1864. 1st Amer edn. 8vo. 590,[6 advt] pp. Fldg map, num ills. Some mainly marg dampstaining. Orig cloth, edges rubbed, sl soiled, spine ends chipped, tears in spine.
(Worldwide Antiqu'n) **$125 [≈ £78]**
- Journal of the Discovery of the Sources of the Nile. New York: 1864. 1st Amer edn. 8vo. [xxx],390 pp. 2 maps (1 fldg, 1 cold). Num plates & ills. Orig dark brown cloth gilt, spine reprd.   *(Terramedia)* **$200 [≈ £125]**
- Journal of the Discovery of the Source of the Nile. New York: Harper, 1864. 1st Amer edn. 8vo. xxx,[1],32-590,advt pp. Fldg map (torn). Orig embossed cloth, minimal foxing to edges.   *(Parmer)* **$225 [≈ £140]**

Spence, Sydney A.
- Antarctic Miscellany - Books, Periodicals & Maps. Surrey: Simper, 1980. Ltd edn. Ills. Leather-look paper over bds.
(Parmer) **$65 [≈ £40]**

Spencer, Edmund
- Travels in Circassia, Krim-Tartary, &c. ... London: 1839. 3rd edn. 2 vols. xxii,392; xi, 415 pp. Fldg map (2 sm reprs), 2 cold frontis, text vignettes. Occas foxing. Contemp three qtr calf, chipped spines relaid, crnrs reprd, rubbed, some edge wear.
(Reese) **$250 [≈ £156]**

Spencer, J.A.
- The East: Sketches of Travel in Egypt and the Holy Land. New York: Putnam; London:

Murray, 1850. 1st edn. 8vo. 7 (of 8) tinted plates, 4 other plates, 3 text ills. Sl foxing. Orig cloth, spine torn & chipped at ends.
(Worldwide Antiqu'n) **$75 [≈ £46]**

Spilsbury, F.B.

- Account of a Voyage to the Western Coast of Africa; performed by His Majesty's Sloop Favourite, in the Year 1805 ... London: Richard Phillips, 1807. 43 pp. 8 plates (3 fldg). Occas sl foxing & offsetting. Mod half cloth, t.e.g.   *(Reese)* **$200 [≈ £125]**

Spittel, R.L.

- Wild Ceylon: describing in particular the Lives of the Present Day Veddas. Ceylon: The Colombo Apothecaries Co, 1924. 1st edn. 8vo. [xviii], 260 pp. Fldg map, frontis, num plates. Orig light brown cloth, sl worn.
(Terramedia) **$50 [≈ £31]**

The Sportsman in Ireland ...

- See Allan, Robert.

Spruce, Richard

- Notes of a Botanist on the Amazon & Andes being Records of Travel on the Amazon and Its Tributaries ... Edited by Alfred R. Wallace. London: Macmillan, 1908. 1st edn. 2 vols. Frontis port, 7 maps, 71 ills. Orig green cloth, t.e.g., spines recased. Boxed.
(Jenkins) **$325 [≈ £203]**

Spry, William James J.

- The Cruise of Her Majesty's Ship "Challenger" ... New York: 1877. 1st Amer edn. 8vo. 388,advt pp. Fldg map, frontis, 8 plates, 38 text ills. Orig cloth.
(Argosy) **$75 [≈ £46]**

Squier, E.G.

- Nicaragua: Its People, Scenery, Monuments. And the Proposed Interoceanic Canal ... New York: Appleton, 1852. 2 vols. 8vo. xxi,424; 452 pp. Panoramic fldg frontis, 4 maps (1 fldg), plates (sev tinted), text ills. Sl foxing. Orig cloth, 1 bd stained & spotted.
(Terramedia) **$280 [≈ £175]**
- Notes on Central America; particularly the States of Honduras and San Salvador ... New York: Harper, 1855. 1st edn. [2],397 pp. 5 fldg maps, 1 text map, 8 tinted lithos, 3 w'cut views. Some browning. Half mor.
(Jenkins) **$325 [≈ £203]**
- Peru ... London: Macmillan, 1877. 1st English edn (from Amer sheets). Contemp three qtr calf, mrbld bds, elab gilt spine, contrasting labels. *(Jenkins)* **$225 [≈ £140]**
- Peru. Incidents of Travel and Exploration in

the Land of the Incas. New York: Harper, 1877. 8vo. xx,599 pp. Map, 14 plates, num text ills. Orig pict cloth, rubbed, ex-lib.
(Adelson) **$175 [≈ £109]**

Squire, Ephrain George

- Waikna; or, Adventures on the Mosquito Shore by Samuel A. Bard [pseud.]. New York: Harper, 1855. 8vo. 366 pp. 56 ills, vignettes, & maps. Orig green cloth, faded, spine extremities sl rubbed. *(Karmiole)* **$75 [≈ £46]**

Stanford, Edward, publisher

- A Map of the Environs of London extending Twenty-Five Miles from the Metropolis. London: [ca 1880]. Cold dissected linen backed map. Fldg into orig cloth cvrs. Spine reprd on cvrs.   *(Coombes)* **£30 [≈ $48]**
- Stanford's Library Map of London and its Suburbs. London: [ca 1897]. 24 sheets combined into 4 sheets, each measuring 36 x 31 ins plus margins. Cold dissected linen backed, fldg into mor slipcase. Edges of slipcase rubbed.   *(Coombes)* **£85 [≈ $136]**

Stanford, John Frederick

- Rambles and Researches in Thuringian Saxony. London: John W. Parker, 1842. 1st edn. 8vo. Lge fldg map, geneal table, 4 litho ports, 2 w'cut plates. Orig cloth, uncut, spine worn.   *(Hannas)* **£30 [≈ $48]**

Stanhope, Philip Dormer

- Genuine Memoirs of Asiaticus, in a Series of Letters to a Friend, during Five Years Residence in different Parts of India ... London: for G. Kearsley, 1784. 1st edn. 12mo. Some worming. Contemp half calf, rebacked, orig label preserved, sl worn.
(Ximenes) **$125 [≈ £78]**

Stanley, Arthur P.

- Sinai and Palestine in connection with their History. London: Murray, 1856. 535 pp. Fldg cold maps. Rebound in paper over bds.
(Parmer) **$45 [≈ £28]**
- Sinai and Palestine. London: 1873. New edn. 8vo. lviii,560,32 pp. Cold section, 6 cold maps, 5 w'cut maps. Orig cloth, spine faded.
(Henly) **£35 [≈ $56]**
- Sinai and Palestine. In Connection with their History. New York: 1883. 8vo. 641 pp. Num cold fldg maps. Orig brown cloth.
(Terramedia) **$50 [≈ £31]**

Stanley, Henry M.

- The Autobiography ... Edited by Dorothy Stanley. Boston & New York: Houghton Mifflin, 1909. 1st edn. 551,index pp. Fldg

map, 16 gravures. Orig red cloth, some shelfwear & spotting, hinges sl weak.
(Parmer) **$40 [≃ £25]**

- The Congo and the Founding of its Free State. London: Sampson Low ..., 1885. 2 vols. xxvii,528; x,483 pp. 2 fldg maps, num ills. Half leather, mrbld edges, some scuffing & wear to edges.   *(Parmer)* **$300 [≃ £187]**

- The Congo and the Founding of its Free State. New York: Harper, 1885. 2 vols. xxvii, 528; x, 483 pp. 2 fldg maps in pockets, num ills. Orig elab dec green cloth, moderate wear & fading to spines.   *(Parmer)* **$300 [≃ £187]**

- Coomassie and Magdala. The Story of Two British Campaigns in Africa. London: 1891. 2nd edn. 402 pp. Ills. Orig dec red cloth.
(Trophy Room Books) **$200 [≃ £125]**

- How I Found Livingstone. Travels, Adventures and Discoveries in Central Africa. London: 1872. 2nd edn. 8vo. Fldg map. Orig bndg, sl rubbed.
(Grayling) **£50 [≃ $80]**

- How I Found Livingstone: Travels, Adventures & Discoveries in Central Africa ... New York: Scribner's, 1873. Thick 8vo. xxiii,736,lxxix pp. Num plates. Lacks 1 of the fldg maps, other maps with sl reprs at edges. Orig pict green cloth.
(Terramedia) **$100 [≃ £62]**

- In Darkest Africa ... London: Sampson Low ..., 1890. Subscribers Edition. 22 parts in 6 vols. Sm 4to. 165 w'cut ills & maps. Orig pict cloth gilt, extremities minimally worn.
(Hollett) **£95 [≃ $152]**

- In Darkest Africa ... London: Sampson Low, 1890. 2 vols. 8vo. xv,529; xv,472,2 advt pp. 4 maps, num ills. Orig cloth, crnrs sl bumped & rubbed.
(Bates & Hindmarch) **£85 [≃ $136]**

- In Darkest Africa ... New York: Scribner's, 1890. 1st Amer edn. 2 vols. 8vo. 2 steel engvs, 150 ills & maps. Orig dec dark green cloth, rubbed & bumped.   *(Parmer)* **$150 [≃ £93]**

- In Darkest Africa ... New York: Scribner's, 1890. 1st Amer edn. 2 vols. 8vo. xiv,547; xvi,540 pp. Maps (inc 3 lge fldg in rear pocket), 2 steel engvs, 150 w'engvs & maps. Orig three qtr red leather & mrbld bds, hole in 1 jnt, spine ends & crnrs worn.
(Schoyer) **$100 [≃ £62]**

- In Darkest Africa. New York: 1890. 2 vols. 548; 540 pp. Fldg pocket map. Orig dec cloth.
(Trophy Room Books) **$150 [≃ £93]**

- My Dark Companions and their Strange Stories. New York: 1893. 319 pp. Ills. Plain cloth, gilt stamped spine.
(Trophy Room Books) **$200 [≃ £125]**

- My Early Travels in America and Asia. New York: 1895. 2 vols. 325; 424 pp. Orig bndg.

(Trophy Room Books) **$265 [≃ £165]**

- Story of Emin's Rescue as told in Stanley's Letters. New York: Harper & Bros, 1890. 8vo. 176 pp. Map, 3 ports. Orig red cloth, sl soiled.   *(Parmer)* **$60 [≃ £37]**

- Through the Dark Continent or the Sources of the Nile ... New York: 1878. 1st Amer edn. 2 vols. xiv,522; ix,566 pp. Lge fldg cold map (sm fold tears) in pocket of each vol, 2 ports, maps, plates, text ills. Contemp three qtr calf, spines gilt extra, edgeworn, rubbed.
(Reese) **$225 [≃ £140]**

- Through the Dark Continent ... London: 1899. 2 vols. 8vo. xxxii,400; xii,419 pp. Frontis, 32 plates, 7 maps (1 sl torn), text ills. Vol 2 title reprd. A few sl marks. Orig pict cloth, faded, sl marked.
(Bow Windows) **£125 [≃ $200]**

Stansbury, Howard

- Exploration and Survey of the Valley of the Great Salt Lake of Utah. Washington: R. Armstrong, 1853. 495 pp. 2 fldg maps, plates.
(Jenkins) **$450 [≃ £281]**

Stanyan, Abraham

- An Account of Switzerland. Written in the Year 1714. London: for Jacob Tonson, 1714. 1st edn. Large Paper. 8vo. Sl foxing of title & following ff. 19th c polished calf, rebacked.
(Hannas) **£85 [≃ $136]**

Stapp, William

- The Prisoners of Perote: Containing a Journal Kept by the Author, who was captured by the Mexicans at Mier. Philadelphia: Zieber, 1845. 1st edn. 12mo. 164 pp. Some foxing & staining. Orig brown ptd wraps.
(W. Thomas Taylor) **$1,500 [≃ £937]**

Stark, Freya

- The Coast of Incense. London: Murray, 1953. 1st edn. 8vo. Map, plates, decs after Reynolds Stone. Orig cloth. Dw frayed. Signed by the author. *(Sanders)* **£15 [≃ $24]**

- Riding to the Tigris. London: Murray, 1959. 1st edn. 8vo. Plates. Bookplate scar on free endpaper. Orig cloth. price-clipped dw. Signed by the author. *(Sanders)* **£10 [≃ $16]**

- Beyond Euphrates. London: Murray, 1951. 1st edn. 8vo. Map, plates, decs after Reynolds Stone. Orig cloth. Sl nicked dw. Signed by the author.   *(Sanders)* **£15 [≃ $24]**

- East is West. London: Murray, 1945. 1st edn. 8vo. Frontis, map, plates. Orig cloth. Soiled & clipped dw. Signed by the author.
(Sanders) **£12 [≃ $19]**

- Ionia. A Quest. London: Murray, (1954). 1st

edn. 8vo. xxiv,263 pp. 56 pp of ills. B'plate on free endpaper. Dw. *(Schoyer)* **$20 [≃£12]**

- The Lycian Shore. London: 1956. 1st edn. 204 pp. Ills. Orig cloth. Dw.
(Trophy Room Books) **$80 [≃£50]**

- Riding to the Tigris. London: Murray, (1959). 1st edn. 8vo. xi,114 pp. Fldg map, 39 ills. Dw. *(Schoyer)* **$20 [≃£12]**

- Seen in the Hadhramaut. London: Murray, 1938. 1st edn. 4to. 130 photo plates. Orig cloth. Sl nicked dw. *(Dalian)* **£65 [≃$104]**

- The Southern Gates of Arabia. New York: [1936]. Lge 8vo. 327 pp. Map, num plates. Orig bndg. *(Terramedia)* **$40 [≃£25]**

- Space, Time & Movement in Landscape. Compton Chamberlayne: The Compton Press, [1969]. 1st edn. One of 500, sgnd. Lge oblong 8vo. Port, 121 plates. Orig morocco backed mrbld bds, gilt spine, by Zaehnsdorf. Slipcase. *(Sanders)* **£80 [≃$128]**

- Traveller's Prelude. London: Murray, 1950. 1st edn. 8vo. Map, plates, decs by Reynolds Stone. Orig cloth. Frayed dw. Signed by the author. *(Sanders)* **£15 [≃$24]**

Starke, Mariana
- Information and Directions for Travellers on the Continent. London: Murray, 1828. 6th rvsd edn. Cr 8vo. Fldg plan. Contemp calf, crnrs worn, new spine.
(Stewart) **£65 [≃$104]**

Starr, Frederick
- In Indian Mexico: A Narrative of Travel & Labour. Chicago: Forbes & Co, 1908. 1st edn. 8vo. xi,425 pp. Frontis, num photo plates. Orig maroon cloth, ft of rear cvr sl spotted. Author's pres copy.
(Terramedia) **$100 [≃£62]**

Statement ...
- Statement Respecting the Earl of Selkirk's Settlement upon the Red River ... see Halkett, John.

Statham, Col. J.C.R.
- With My Wife Across Africa: By Canoe and Caravan. London: Simpkin Marshall, (1924). 1st edn. 8vo. 323 pp. 3 maps, frontis, plates. Orig pict light green cloth, lacks front flyleaf.
(Terramedia) **$60 [≃£37]**

Stebbing, Edward Percy
- Jungle Byways in India. Leaves from the Note-Book of a Sportsman and Naturalist. London & New York: John Lane, 1909. 8vo. Num plates & ills. Orig green cloth.
(Terramedia) **$50 [≃£31]**

- Jungle By-Ways in India. London: 1911. 8vo.

Ills. V sl foxing. Lacks front endpaper. Orig bndg, v sl rubbed. *(Grayling)* **£25 [≃$40]**

- Stalks in the Himalaya. Jottings of a Sportsman Naturalist. London: Bodley Head, 1912. 8vo. xxviii,321,18 advt pp. Frontis, num ills. Occas sl foxing. Orig green cloth.
(Bates & Hindmarch) **£80 [≃$128]**

Stebbing, Henry
- The Christian in Palestine; or, Scenes of Sacred History, Historical and Descriptive ... Illustrated from Sketches taken on the Spot by W.H. Bartlett. London: George Virtue, 1847. 4to. 78 plates (1 dble-spread). Contemp purple roan, rubbed.
(Waterfield's) **£160 [≃$256]**

Stedman, J.G.
- Narrative of a Five Years' Expedition against the Revolted Negroes of Surinam... London: J. Johnson, 1806. 2nd edn, crrctd. 2 vols. 4to. xviii,423,[4]; iv,419,[5] pp. 81 plates (13 engvd by William Blake). Contemp diced half russia, spines gilt, jnts sl rubbed.
(Gough) **£575 [≃$920]**

Steel, Flora Annie
- India. Painted by Mortimer Menpes. London: A. & C. Black Colour Books, Twenty Shilling Series, 1905. 1st edn. 75 cold plates. Orig dec cloth, fine.
(Old Cathay) **£55 [≃$88]**

- India. Painted by Mortimer Menpes. London: A. & C. Black Colour Books, Twenty Shilling Series, 1905. 1st edn. 75 cold plates. Orig dec cloth, spine v sl rubbed, rear bd bumped. *(Old Cathay)* **£40 [≃$64]**

- India. Painted by Mortimer Menpes. London: A. & C. Black Colour Books, Twenty Shilling Series, 1912. 75 cold plates. Orig dec cloth, spine sl faded & rubbed, sm split at top, shaken. *(Old Cathay)* **£15 [≃$24]**

- India. Painted by Mortimer Menpes. New Edition, revised by H. Clive Barnard. London: A. & C. Black, 1923. Map, 32 cold plates. Orig cloth. *(Old Cathay)* **£13 [≃$20]**

Steele, John
- Across the Plains in 1850. Chicago: 1930. One of 350. 234 pp. Ills. Cloth. Slipcase.
(Reese) **$125 [≃£78]**

Steevens, G.W.
- From Capetown to Ladysmith. An Unfinished Record of the South African War. Edited by Vernon Blackburn. London: William Blackwood, 1900. 1st edn. 8vo. x,180 pp. Sketch map, lge fldg map at end. Some light spotting. Orig cloth, uncut.
(Claude Cox) **£18 [≃$28]**

Stefansson, Vilhjalmur
- The Adventure of Wrangel Island ... based on the Diary of Errol Lorne Knight ... New York: Macmillan, 1925. 1st edn. Roy 8vo. xxx, 424 pp. Fldg map, frontis, 32 plates. Orig cloth gilt. Sgnd by the author.
  (Berkelouw) **$200 [≈ £125]**
- The Friendly Arctic. New York: Macmillan, 1932. Thick 8vo. xxxii,784 pp. Frontis, 9 maps (4 fldg, 2 in pocket), 68 plates. Orig cloth gilt, uncut. Chipped dw.
  (Berkelouw) **$125 [≈ £78]**
- The Mountain of Jade. New York: Macmillan, 1926. 1st edn. 12mo. 236 pp. Orig cloth. Dw sl worn. *(Parmer)* **$40 [≈ £25]**
- My Life With The Eskimo. New York: Macmillan, 1922. 8vo. ix,527 pp. 2 lge fldg maps, num photo plates. Orig blue cloth.
  (Terramedia) **$75 [≈ £46]**
- Not by Bread Alone. New York: 1946. 1st edn. 8vo. xviii,340 pp. Orig cloth. Dw.
  (Berkelouw) **$50 [≈ £31]**
- Not by Bread Alone. New York: Macmillan, 1946. 1st edn. 8vo. 339 pp. Orig green cloth, light wear to extremities. Later issued as "Fat of the Land". *(Parmer)* **$50 [≈ £31]**
- Ultima Thule. Further Mysteries of the Arctic. New York: 1940. 1st edn. 8vo. viii, 384 pp. Ills, maps, illust endpapers. Orig cloth. Chipped dw. *(Berkelouw)* **$65 [≈ £40]**
- Unsolved Mysteries of the Arctic. New York: 1939. 1st edn. 8vo. xviii,382 pp. 4 maps. Orig cloth. Dw partly missing.
  (Berkelouw) **$75 [≈ £46]**

Stein, Sir Aurel
- Ancient Khotan. Detailed Report of Archaeological Explorations in Chinese Turkestan ... New York: 1975. Reprint of 1907 edn. 3 vols in one. Fldg cold map, 34 + 119 plates, ills. Orig dec red cloth.
  (Lyon) **£185 [≈ $296]**
- An Archaeological Tour in Upper Swat and Adjacent Hill Tracts. Calcutta: 1930. 115 pp. 2 lge fldg maps, 8 plans at end, 66 full-page plates in text. Half leather, orig wraps bound in. *(Trophy Room Books)* **£750 [≈ £468]**
- On Ancient Central Asian Tracks ... London: 1933. 1st edn. 342 pp. Fldg map, num plates, panoramas, cold ills. Orig bndg.
  (Trophy Room Books) **$650 [≈ £406]**
- On Ancient Central Asian Tracks ... New York: 1964. 2nd edn. 342 pp. Fldg map, num plates, panoramas, cold ills. Orig bndg. Dw.
  (Trophy Room Books) **$40 [≈ £25]**
- On Ancient Central Asian Tracks. London: Macmillan, 1933. 1st edn. 8vo. xxiv,342,[2 advt] pp. Lge fldg cold map, 147 ills.

Rebound in half mor, gilt spine, blue label.
  (Frew Mackenzie) **£300 [≈ $480]**
- Personal Narrative of a Journey of Archaeological and Geographical Exploration in Chinese Turkestan. London: 1903. 1st edn. 524 pp. Lge fldg map, gravure frontis, num ills. Orig bndg.
  (Trophy Room Books) **$600 [≈ £375]**

Steinbeck, John & Ricketts, E.E.
- Sea of Cortez, a Journal of Travel and Research with Materials for a Source Book on the Marine Animals of the Panamic Faunal Province. New York: 1941. 1st edn. Roy 8vo. x,598 pp. 40 plates (8 cold). Inscrptns on title & endpapers. Orig cloth.
  (Wheldon & Wesley) **£80 [≈ $128]**

Steinmetz, Andrew
- Japan and her People. London: Routledge ..., 1859. 12mo. xii,4,447 pp. 4 plates, text ills. Orig red pict cloth gilt, rubbed.
  (Adelson) **$120 [≈ £75]**

Stephen, James, d. 1832
- England Enslaved by her Own Slave Colonies. A Address to the Electors and People of the United Kingdom. London: 1826. 2nd edn. 68 pp. Self-wrappers, stitched, unopened. *(Reese)* **$75 [≈ £46]**

Stephens, John L.
- Incidents of Travel in Greece, Turkey, Russia, and Poland ... New York: 1838. 2 vols. 268; 275 pp. Fldg map, text ills. Scattered foxing, sev ink sgntrs. Cloth.
  (Reese) **$275 [≈ £171]**
- Incidents of Travel in Yucatan. London: 1843. 2 vols. 8vo. xii,459; xvi,458,advt pp. Fldg map, 2 fldg frontis. Some browning & foxing. Orig dec cloth gilt, a little worn & faded, spines brown & v sl frayed at ends.
  (Dillons) **£245 [≈ $392]**

Sterndale, R.A.
- Seonee, or Camp Life on the Satpura Range. London: 1887. 8vo. Ills. Orig bndg, sl rubbed. *(Grayling)* **£45 [≈ $72]**

Sterne, Laurence
- A Sentimental Journey Through France and Italy. By Mr. Yorick. London: for T. Becket, 1768. 1st edn. Probable earlier iss, with pp 34 & 35 in vol 2 misnumbered as 33 & 34. 2 vols. 12mo. Contemp calf, mor labels, spines a trifle rubbed.
  (W. Thomas Taylor) **$1,250 [≈ £781]**
- A Sentimental Journey through France and Italy. By Mr. Yorick. London: for Becket &

De Hondt, 1768. 1st edn. 2 vols in one. Sm 8vo. Subscribers' list. Lacks half-titles. Some sl stains. Early 19th c half calf, rubbed.
(Hannas) **£280 [≃ $448]**
- A Sentimental Journey through France and Italy. By Mr Yorick. The Second Edition. London: Becket & De Hondt, 1768. 2 vols. Sm 8vo. Half-titles. 20 pp subscribers in vol 1. Orig calf, gilt spines, contrasting labels, ft of vol 1 spine v sl worn.
(Bickersteth) **£160 [≃ $256]**
- A Sentimental Journey through France and Italy. London: P. Miller & J. White, 1774. A pirated edn. Contains also 'A Political Romance'. 8vo. 328 pp. 19th c half calf, gilt spine.
(Spelman) **£85 [≃ $136]**

Steuart, John R.
- A Description of some Ancient Monuments, with Inscriptions, still existing in Lydia and Phrygia ... London: James Bohn, 1842. 1st & apparently only edn. Folio. [6],14,[1] pp. 17 mtd tinted litho plates. Orig roan backed mrbld bds, ptd paper label on cvr.
(Fenning) **£285 [≃ $456]**

Stevens, Charles E.
- Anthony Burns: A History. Boston: John P. Jewett & Co, 1856. 1st edn. [xiv],295 pp. Frontis & other plates. Orig brown cloth, spine sunned. *(Terramedia)* **$45 [≃ £28]**

Stevens, E.S.
- By Tigris and Euphrates. London: Hurst & Blackett, 1923. 1st edn. 8vo. 349 pp. Frontis & 70 ills on 48 plates. Orig cloth, spine ends sl frayed, rubbed & soiled, lib number on spine. *(Worldwide Antiqu'n)* **$65 [≃ £40]**

Stevens, John
- The History of Persia ... Exact Description of all its Dominions ... London: Brown, 1715. 1st edn. 8vo. xiv,416 pp. Some marg notes, a few MS ff inserted. Half mor, shelfworn, lib number on spine, spine ends frayed.
(Worldwide Antiqu'n) **$350 [≃ £218]**

Stevens, Thomas
- Around the World on a Bicycle ... New York: 1894. 2 vols. xvii,547; xiv,477 pp. Cold frontis in vol 1, port, ills. Orig pict cloth, a bit rubbed, spine ends frayed.
(Reese) **$200 [≃ £125]**

Stevenson, Robert Louis
- Edinburgh. Picturesque Notes. With Etchings by A. Brunet-Debaines ... London: Seeley, Jackson & Halliday, 1879. 1st edn. Folio. [8],40 pp. 6 orig etchings, 12 w'cut text ills. Orig dec brown cloth gilt, a.e.g., spine extremities sl

frayed.   *(Karmiole)* **$175 [≃ £109]**

Stevenson, William B.
- A Historical and Descriptive Narrative of Twenty Years' Residence in South America, containing Travels in Arauco, Chile, Peru, and Colombia ... London: Hurst, Robinson, 1825. 1st edn. 3 vols. 8vo. 7 plates (sl foxed). New cloth.   *(Adelson)* **$650 [≃ £406]**

Stevenson-Hamilton, J.
- The Low-Veld: its Wild Life and its People. London: 1929. 1st edn. 8vo. [xii],288 pp. 16 plates, map endpapers. Orig cloth, trifle used. Author's pres copy.
(Wheldon & Wesley) **£40 [≃ $64]**

Stewart, Charles (translator)
- The Mulfuzat Timury, or Autobiographical Memoirs of the Moghul Emperor Timur ... Translated into English. London: Oriental Translation Fund, 1830. 4to. xvi,154,[12] pp, inc engvd pres leaf. Mod half calf.
(Farahar) **£175 [≃ $280]**

Stewart, Charles S.
- Journal of a Residence in the Sandwich Islands, during the years 1823, 1824, and 1825 ... London: Fisher, Son & Jackson, 1828. 2nd edn. 12mo. xxiv,25-407,1 advt pp. Fldg map, 3 plates. New cloth.
(Adelson) **$325 [≃ £203]**
- A Visit to the South Seas, in the U. S. Ship Vincennes, during the Years 1829 and 1830. Including Notices of Brazil, Peru, Manila, the Cape of Good Hope, and St. Helena ... New York: 1833. 2nd edn. 2 vols. 323; 312 pp. Half cloth & bds, leather labels.
(Reese) **$275 [≃ £171]**

Stewart, James
- Lovedale South Africa. Edinburgh: Andrew Elliot, 1894. 4to. 110 pp. Photo ills. Wear to cvrs, esp spine.   *(Parmer)* **$60 [≃ £37]**

Stewart, Julian H. (ed.)
- Handbook of South American Indians. Washington: Smithsonian Bureau of Amer Ethnology, 1946-59. 1st edn. 7 vols (inc smaller index vol). 8vo. Num fldg maps, charts, photo plates, diags. Lge pocket map in vol 6. Orig olive green cloth.
(Terramedia) **$600 [≃ £375]**

Stewart, Milton
- From Nile to Nile: Rambles of a Kansan in Europe, Palestine and Africa. Wichita: 1888. 8vo. 498 pp. Frontis, ills. Orig orange cloth gilt, moderate cvr wear.
(Terramedia) **$50 [≃ £31]**

Stieler, Karl, et al.
- The Rhine from Its Source to the Sea. Philadelphia: Henry Coates, [1898]. New edn, rvsd. 2 vols. 8vo. vii,303; vii,318 pp. Fldg map, num tissued plates. Orig gilt dec red cloth. Orig cloth gilt, dw, gilt slipcases.
(Terramedia) **$75 [≈ £46]**

Stiff, Edward
- The Texan Emigrant, being a Narration of the Adventures of the Author in Texas. Cincinnati: Conclin, 1840. 1st edn. 367,[1] pp. Lacks the map & plates. Later cloth, mor label.
(Jenkins) **$850 [≈ £531]**

Stigand, C.H.
- To Abyssinia through an Unknown Land ... Journey through Unexplored Regions of British East Africa ... London: Seeley & Co, 1910. 8vo. xvi,17-346,16 advt pp. 2 maps, 36 photo ills. Occas foxing. Orig gilt dec orange cloth, sl worn.
(Parmer) **$145 [≈ £90]**

Stisted, Georgiana M.
- The True Life of Capt. Sir Richard F. Burton, written by his Niece ... with the Authority and Approval of the Burton Family. London: 1896. 8vo. Port. Orig blue buckram, sl worn.
(Farahar) **£30 [≈ $48]**

Stock, Eugene
- The Story of the Fuh-Kien Mission of the Church Missionary Society. London: Seeley, Jackson ..., 1877. 1st edn. 8vo. 272 pp. Fldg cold map, 34 ills. Orig red cloth stamped in black & gilt, rear bd a little stained.
(Young's) **£25 [≈ $40]**

Stock, Joseph
- A Narrative of What Passed at Killalla, in the County of Mayo, and the Parts Adjacent, during the French Invasion in the Summer of 1798. By an Eye-Witness. Dublin, Printed. London: reptd for J. Hatchard & J. Wright, 1800. 8vo. 182 pp. Later cloth.
(Schoyer) **$125 [≈ £78]**

Stockley, C.H.
- Shikar. London: 1928. 162 pp. Ills. Orig bndg. *(Trophy Room Books)* **$250 [≈ £156]**
- Shikar. Tales of a Sportsman in India. London: 1928. 8vo. Ills. Orig bndg, v sl worn.
(Grayling) **£70 [≈ $112]**
- Stalking in the Himalayas and Northern India. London: 1936. 251 pp. Ills, endpaper maps. Orig bndg.
(Trophy Room Books) **$200 [≈ £125]**
- Stalking in the Himalayas and Northern India. London: Jenkins, 1936. 8vo. 254,2

advt pp. Frontis, 36 photo ills, endpaper map. Orig bndg. Worn dw.
(Bates & Hindmarch) **£90 [≈ $144]**
- Stalking in the Himalayas and Northern India. London: 1936. 8vo. Ills. Orig bndg, spine rather rubbed & dulled.
(Grayling) **£60 [≈ $96]**

Stoddard, S.R.
- Lake George; Saratoga, Luzerne and Schroon Lake. Albany: 1874. Cr 8vo. Fldg map, num text ills. Orig cloth. *(Farahar)* **£30 [≈ $48]**

Stokes, Frank
- Belgium. Illustrated by Frank Brangwyn. London: 1916. One of 150, on Japan vellum. 52 ills by Brangwyn. Orig vellum, bds sl bowed, ribbons broken.
(Gekoski) **£90 [≈ $144]**

Stolberg, Frederic Leopold, Count
- Travels through Germany, Switzerland, Italy, and Sicily. Translated by Thomas Holcroft. London: Robinson, 1796-97. 2 vols. 4to. xx,506; xi,656 pp. Fldg map (cloth-backed), 19 fldg plates. Crnr of vol 1 title reprd. Contemp calf, rubbed, spines worn, hinges reprd. *(Bernett)* **$550 [≈ £343]**

Stone, Arthur L.
- Following Old Trails. Missoula: 1913. Cloth, cvr soiled, sl edge wear. Pres copy.
(Reese) **$275 [≈ £171]**

Stone, S.
- In and Beyond the Himalayas. Sport and Travel in the Abode of Snow. London: 1896. 330 pp. Engvd frontis by Whymper, ills. Orig pict gilt red cloth.
(Trophy Room Books) **$675 [≈ £421]**

Stoneham, C.T.
- Big Stuff: The Lure of Big Game. London: 1954. 191 pp. Ills. Orig bndg. Dw.
(Trophy Room Books) **$90 [≈ £56]**
- Wanderings in Wild Africa. London: 1932. 286 pp. Ills. Orig bndg.
(Trophy Room Books) **$100 [≈ £62]**
- Wanderings in Wild Africa. London: 1932. 3rd imp. 8vo. Ills. Sl foxing. Orig bndg.
(Grayling) **£18 [≈ $28]**

Stonehouse, B.
- Wideawake Island. The Story of the B.O.U. Centenary Expedition to Ascension. London: 1960. 8vo. 224 pp. 21 plates (1 cold). Orig cloth. *(Wheldon & Wesley)* **£25 [≈ $40]**

Storer, James Sargant & Greig, John

- Ancient Reliques: or, Delineations of Monastic, Castellated, & Domestic Architecture ... London: Clarke, 1812-13. 1st edn. 2 vols. 8vo. 100 plates inc 2 addtnl engvd titles & 2 tail-pieces. Sl marg water stain to 14 plates. Later mor gilt, t.e.g.
(Claude Cox) **£45 [≈ $72]**

- The Antiquarian and Topographical Cabinet; containing a Series of Elegant Views of the Most Interesting Objects of Curiosity in Great britain. London: 1817-19. 2nd edn. 6 vols. Engvs, text ills, vignettes. Some foxing. Contemp three qtr calf, worn.
(Reese) **$175 [≈ £109]**

Storey, H.

- Hunting and Shooting in Ceylon. London: 1907. 2nd edn. 8vo. Ills. Orig cloth.
(Grayling) **£45 [≈ $72]**

- Hunting and Shooting in Ceylon. London: 1907. 365 pp. Fldg map, ills. Orig bndg, fair condition. Port frontis sgnd by the author.
(Trophy Room Books) **$90 [≈ £56]**

The Story of a Three Weeks' Trip ...

- See Pease, Sir Joseph & Currie, Sir Donald.

Stow, John

- A Survey of the Cities of London and Westminster ... Enlarged ... by John Strype. London: 1720. 1st Strype edn. 2 vols. Folio. 70 views, maps & plans. Old ink stain on a few margs. Sl dusty. Contemp calf, sometime rebacked.
(Sotheran) **£1,100 [≈ $1,760]**

Stowe, Harriet Beecher

- Sunny Memories of Foreign Lands. London: Sampson Low, 1854. 1st English edn. 2 vols. 8vo. xii,326,[11 advt dated July 1854]; viii, 424,[2] pp. 2 tinted frontis, text ills. Orig cloth gilt, spines & little faded & chipped at ends, jnts cracking, lacks 1 endpaper
(Hollett) **£45 [≈ $72]**

Strasburger, E.

- Rambles on the Riviera. Translated by O. and B. Casey. London: 1906. Roy 8vo. xxiii, 444 pp. 87 cold ills. Orig pict cloth.
(Wheldon & Wesley) **£30 [≈ $48]**

Strasser, R.

- The Mongolian Horde. London: 1930. 347 pp. Ills. Orig bndg, mint.
(Trophy Room Books) **$75 [≈ £46]**

Stratilesco, Tereza

- From Carpathian to Pindus. Pictures of Roumanian Country Life. London: Fisher Unwin, 1906. 8vo. x,379 pp. Orig bndg.
(Bates & Hindmarch) **£25 [≈ $40]**

Street, George Edmund

- Brick and Marble in the Middle Ages: Notes of Tours in the North of Italy. London: Murray, 1874. 2nd edn, enlgd. Roy 8vo. xxvi, 415 pp. 5 cold litho & 59 w'engvd plates inc frontis, fldg plan, text ills. Orig cloth, t.e.g., sl worn, spine faded. *(Duck)* **£50 [≈ $80]**

Streeter, Thomas W.

- Bibliography of Texas, 1795-1845. Part III, United States and European Imprints relating to Texas. Cambridge: 1906. 1st edn. 2 vols. 4to. Cloth. Dw. *(Reese)* **$500 [≈ £312]**

Streeter, Thomas Winthrop

- The Celebrated Collection of Americana formed by the late Thomas Winthrop Streeter. New York: Parke Bernet Galleries, 1966-70. 7 vols & Index, together 8 vols. Prices realized laid in, & written in by hand. Orig cloth, sl worn.
(Terramedia) **$675 [≈ £421]**

Strickland, Kate

- The Backwoods of Canada being Letters from the Wife of an Emigrant Officer, illustrative of the Domestic Economy of British America. Third Edition. London: Charles Knight, 1838. 8vo. viii,351 pp. Mod half mor.
(Lamb) **£35 [≈ $56]**

Strickland, W. & Marshall, T.W.M.

- Catholic Missions in Southern India to 1865. London: Longmans, Green, 1865. 1st edn. 8vo. viii,240 pp. Orig cloth.
(Fenning) **£45 [≈ $72]**

Strong, Richard (ed.)

- The African Republic of Liberia & The Belgian Congo. Based on ... the Harvard Scientific Expedition, 1926-7. Cambridge: Harvard UP, 1930. 1st edn. 2 vols. 4to. xxvi, [568]; ix,-1064 pp. Num plates, some cold. Orig cloth gilt. Editor's inscrptn.
(Terramedia) **$150 [≈ £93]**

Strutt, J.G.

- Deliciae Sylvarum; or Grand and Romantic Forest Scenery in England and Scotland. London: 1828. Imperial folio. Addtnl engvd title, 12 engvd plates. Green half mor, orig parts wraps bound at end.
(Henly) **£325 [≈ $520]**

Strutt, Joseph or Benjamin

- The History and Description of Colchester ... Colchester: W. Keymer, 1803. 1st edn. 2

vols. 8vo. 276,22; 232,index pp. 6 plates, 1 text ill. Dampstain to 1 frontis & some lower margs. Orig mrbld bds, uncut, spines mostly defective.   *(Frew Mackenzie)* **£60 [≃ $96]**

- The History and Description of Colchester ... Colchester: W. Keymer, 1803. 1st edn. 2 vols. 8vo. [2],276,22; [4],232,4 pp. 6 plates, 1 text ill. Presumably lacks half- titles. Polished calf gilt, red & green labels, by Riviere.
     (Fenning) **£110 [≃ $176]**

Struve, Johann Christian von
- Travels in the Crimea. A History of the Embassy from Petersburg to Constantinople, in 1793 ... London: 1802. vi,[2],393 pp. Occas sl foxing. Contemp mottled calf, gilt spine.   *(Reese)* **$400 [≃ £250]**

Stuart, Granville
- Forty Years on the Frontier as seen in the Journals and Reminiscences of Granville Stuart, Gold-Miner, Trader, Merchant, Rancher and Politician ... Cleveland: Arthur H. Clark, 1925. 2 vols. 8vo. 276; 266 pp. 15 ills. Orig blue cloth, sl rubbed.
     (Karmiole) **$175 [≃ £109]**

Stuart, James
- Historical Memoirs of the City of Armagh for ... 1373 Years. Newry: Wilkinson, 1819. 1st edn. 651,index pp. 5 plates. Some foxing. Antique style half mor.
     (Emerald Isle) **£150 [≃ $240]**
- Three Years in North America. Edinburgh: 1832. 3rd edn, rvsd. 2 vols. 8vo. xii,525; viii,544 pp. Fldg map (sl browned). Rec half calf.   *(Young's)* **£150 [≃ $240]**

Stuart, James & Revett, Nicholas
- The Antiquities of Athens and other Monuments of Greece. Third Edition with Additions. London: Bohn, 1858. 8vo. viii,149, [2] pp. 71 plates, some fldg. Fly leaf removed. Contemp divinity calf, mor label, sl rubbed.   *(Claude Cox)* **£30 [≃ $48]**

Stuart, Villers
- Nile Gleanings: Concerning the Ethnology, History and Art of Ancient Egypt as revealed by Egyptian Paintings and Bas Reliefs ... London: Murray, 1879. 1st edn. Lge 8vo. xx, 431 pp. Cold frontis, 22 cold litho plates, num other tissued plates. Orig cloth, rebacked.   *(Terramedia)* **$150 [≃ £93]**

Stuck, Hudson
- The Ascent of Mount Denali (Mount McKinley). A Narrative of the First Complete Ascent of the Highest Peak in North America. New York: Scribner's, 1914.

1st edn. 8vo. xix, 188 pp. Fldg map, photo plates inc 2 gravures. Orig dec cloth.
     (High Latitude) **$135 [≃ £84]**
- Ten Thousand Miles with a Dog Sled. A Narrative of Winter Travel in Interior Alaska. New York: Scribner's, 1914. 8vo. xix, 420 pp. Fldg map, num photo plates, some cold. Orig dec cloth, minor wear.
     (High Latitude) **$90 [≃ £56]**
- Voyages on the Yukon and its Tributaries. A Narrative of Summer Travel in the Interior of Alaska. New York: Scribners, 1917. 8vo. xvi, 397 pp. 2 fldg maps, photo plates. Orig dec cloth, minor wear & soil.
     (High Latitude) **$90 [≃ £56]**
- A Winter Circuit of Our Arctic Coast. A Narrative of a Journey with Dog-Sleds around the entire Arctic Coast of Alaska. New York: Scribners, 1920. 8vo. x,[4],360 pp. 2 fldg maps, gravure frontis, num photo plates. Orig dec cloth.   *(High Latitude)* **$90 [≃ £56]**

Studley, J.T.
- The Journal of a Sporting Nomad. London: 1912. 8vo. Ills. Review copy, with blind stamp on title. Sl foxing. Orig cloth, sl rubbed.   *(Grayling)* **£35 [≃ $56]**

Sturt, Charles
- Two Expeditions into the Interior of Southern Australia ... London: Smith, Elder, 1833. 1st edn. 2 vols. 8vo. [2],viii,[2], [ix]-lxxx,219; [vi],271 pp. Lacks vol 1 dedic & pp [vii-viii] in vol 2. Fldg map, 14 plates (4 hand cold). 19th c calf, rebacked, rubbed.
     (Heritage) **$2,250 [≃ £1,406]**

Sullivan, Edward
- Rambles and Scrambles in North and South America. London: 1852. viii,[9]-424 pp. A bit spotted. Blindstamped cloth, gilt spine, worn at extremities, hinges loose but sound.
     (Reese) **$400 [≃ £250]**

Sumner, Charles
- White Slavery in the Barbary States. Boston: Jewett & Co ..., 1853. 1st edn. 8vo. 135 pp. Text engvs. Orig brown blind stamped cloth, lacks front endpaper. *(Young's)* **£35 [≃ $56]**

Sussex. Painted by Wilfrid Ball ...
- See Belloc, Hilaire.

Sutcliffe, Thomas
- The Earthquake of Juan Fernandez, as it occurred in the year 1835. Authenticated by the Retired Governor of that Island ... Manchester: 1839. 32,4 pp. 5 plates & maps. Half mor.   *(Jenkins)* **$225 [≃ £140]**

- Sixteen Years in Chile and Peru from 1822 to 1839, by the Retired Governor of Juan Fernandez. London: Fisher Son & Co, [1841]. 1st edn. 8vo. xii,563,[i] pp. Fldg map, 9 plates. Mod half calf gilt by Bayntun.
(Hollett) £160 [≈ $256]

Sutherland, David
- A Tour up the Straits, from Gibraltar to Constantinople ... Second Edition, corrected. London: for the author, sold by J. Johnson, 1790. 8vo. xlvii,372 pp. Light waterstaining at start. Orig calf, lacks label.
(Bickersteth) £48 [≈ $76]

Sutherland, Peter C.
- Journal of a Voyage in Baffin's Bay and Barrow Straits, in the Years 1850-1851 ... London: Longman ..., 1851. 2 vols. 12mo. iii, 506; vii, 363, ccxxxiii pp. 2 fldg maps, 4 cold litho plates, text ills. Orig cloth, rubbed, partly unopened.
(High Latitude) $650 [≈ £406]

Sutton, R.
- Tiger Trails in Southern Asia. MO: 1926. 207 pp. 115 ills. Orig bndg.
(Trophy Room Books) $45 [≈ £28]

Sutton, R.L.
- An African Holiday. USA: 1924. Ills. Orig bndg.
(Grayling) £60 [≈ $96]
- An Arctic Safari. With Camera and Rifle in the Land of the Midnight Sun. London: 1933. 8vo. Ills. Sm lib stamp on title. Orig bndg.
(Grayling) £70 [≈ $112]

Swanton, E.W. & Woods, P. (eds.)
- Bygone Haslemere: a Short History of the Ancient Borough and its Immediate Neighbourhood from Prehistoric Times. London: 1914. 8vo. xii,317 pp. Fldg map, fldg plan, num ills. Orig cloth, faded, wear at edges.
(Coombes) £20 [≈ $32]

Swarbreck, Samuel D.
- Sketches in Scotland Drawn from Nature and On Stone by S.D. Swarbreck. London: 1839. Tall folio. 2 pp of explanation. 27 litho plates, some sl foxed. Orig cloth gilt, crnrs frayed, lacks backstrip.
(Reese) $1,750 [≈ £1,093]

Swayne, H.
- Seventeen Trips to Somaliland and a Visit to Abyssinia. London: Rowland Ward, 1903. 3rd edn. Orig bndg.
(Trophy Room Books) $175 [≈ £109]
- Through the Highlands of Siberia. London: Rowland Ward, 1904. 259 pp. Fldg map, ills,

zebra endpapers. Lib stamp. Orig bndg, tear in spine.
(Trophy Room Books) $200 [≈ £125]

Sweetman, George
- The History of Wincanton, Somerset, from the Earliest Times to the Year 1903. Wincanton: 1903. 1st edn. 8vo. [2],296 pp. 6 plates. Orig cloth. *(Fenning)* £21.50 [≈ $35]

Swift, William T.
- Some Account of the History of Churchdown. Gloucester: 1905. 8vo. Ills. Orig cloth, sl faded, top bds spotted.
(Ambra) £22 [≈ $35]

Swinton, Andrew
- Travels into Norway ... see Thomson, Revd William.

Sydenham, John
- Baal Durotrigensis. A Dissertation on the Antient Colossal Figure at Cerne, Dorsetshire ... With Observations on the Worship of the Serpent and that of the Sun. London: [1843]. 8vo. 65 pp. Frontis. Occas lib stamp. Orig cloth, partly faded, lib mark on spine.
(Ambra) £34 [≈ $54]

Sykes, C.A.
- Service & Sport on the Tropical Nile ... London: Murray, 1903. 1st edn. 8vo. xi,306 pp. Frontis, other plates. Orig pict red cloth gilt, t.e.g., spine edges sl frayed, front endpaper cut out. *(Terramedia)* $60 [≈ £37]

Sykes, Ella C.
- Persia and Its People. New York: Macmillan, 1910. 1st edn. 8vo. xi,356 pp. Fldg map, 20 plates. Orig cloth gilt, edges rubbed, spine ends sl frayed, lib sticker on spine.
(Worldwide Antiqu'n) $65 [≈ £40]

Sykes, Sir P.
- A History of Exploration. From the Earliest Times to the Present Day. New York: 1936. 2nd edn, rvsd. 374 pp. Cold frontis, maps, ills. Orig cloth.
(Trophy Room Books) $100 [≈ £62]

Sylvan's Handbook ...
- Sylvan's Pictorial Handbook to the English Lakes. Liverpool: 1852. 2nd edn. 248 pp. Lge fldg map at end, maps, plates, tables, text engvs. Orig brown cloth, rebacked, new endpapers. *(Box of Delights)* £50 [≈ $80]

Symington, Andrew James
- Pen and Pencil Sketches of Faroe and Iceland.

London: Longman, Green ..., 1862. 1st edn.
8vo. Frontis, num text ills. Orig cloth.
(Hannas) **£75 [≈ $120]**

Symonds, John Addington
- Our Life in the Swiss Highlands. Second
Edition. London: A. & C. Black Colour Book,
1907. 1st edn thus. 20 cold & 1 b/w plates.
Orig cloth.   *(Old Cathay)* **£35 [≈ $56]**
- Our Life in the Swiss Highlands. Second
Edition. London: A. & C. Black Colour Book,
1907. 1st edn thus. 20 cold & 1 b/w plates.
Orig cloth, not bright.
(Old Cathay) **£20 [≈ $32]**

Szechenyi, Z.
- Land of Elephants. Big-Game Hunting in
Kenya, Tanganyika and Uganda. London:
1935. 8vo. Ills. Orig cloth.
(Grayling) **£75 [≈ $120]**
- The Land of Elephants. London: 1935. 208
pp. Map, ills. Orig bndg.
(Trophy Room Books) **$175 [≈ £109]**

Tabler, Edward C. (ed.)
- Trade & Travel in Early Barotseland: The
Diaries of George Westbeech, 1885-1888, and
Captain Norman McLeod, 1875-1876 ...
Berkeley: Univ of Calif Press, 1963. 1st edn.
125 pp. Frontis & other plates. Orig blue
cloth.   *(Terramedia)* **$40 [≈ £25]**

Tacitus
- The Annales ... The Description of
Germanie. [The End of Nero and Beginning
of Galba ... Life of Agricola. The sixth
Edition]. London: 1640. Folio. 2 parts. [vi],
271,[i], [vi],227,[i] pp. Lacks intl blank.
Contemp calf, endpapers sometime renewed.
STC 23948.   *(Finch)* **£160 [≈ $256]**

Taine, Hippolyte Adolphe
- A Tour through the Pyrenees. Translated by
J. Safford Fiske. With Illustrations by
Gustave Dore. New York: Henry Holt, 1875.
Wide 8vo. xvi,523 pp. Num plates & ills.
Contemp half mor, a.e.g.
(Terramedia) **$60 [≈ £37]**

Talbot, P. Amaury
- In the Shadow of the Bush. New York &
London: Doran & Heinemann, 1922. 1st edn.
Thick 8vo. xiv,500 pp. Lge fldg map, cold
frontis, num plates. Orig pict green cloth.
(Terramedia) **$100 [≈ £62]**

Tangye, Harry Lincoln
- In the Torrid Sudan. Boston: Richard
Badger, 1910. 8vo. xii,300 pp. Fldg map, 61

ills. Orig dec cloth, t.e.g., crnrs sl bumped.
(Schoyer) **$40 [≈ £25]**

Tanner, Henry S.
- Memoir   on   the   Recent   Surveys,
Observations, nd Internal Improvements, in
the United States ... Intended to accompany
his new Map of the United States.
Philadelphia: the author ..., 1829. 1st edn.
12mo. 8 advt pp. Faint waterstains. Contemp
red half mor, gilt spine.
(Ximenes) **$250 [≈ £156]**

Tanner, Thomas
- Notitia Monastica or a Short History of the
Religious Houses in England and Wales ...
Oxford: 1695. 1st edn. 8vo. [lxxxiv],288,[38]
pp. Engvd title vignette, 5 plates of arms.
Contemp sprinkled calf, gilt spine, sl rubbed,
hd of spine chipped. Wing T.144.
(Pickering) **$400 [≈ £250]**
- Notitia Monastica: or, an Account of all the
Abbies, Priories, and Houses of Friers,
heretofore in England and Wales ... London:
Bowyer, 1744. Folio. [4],xliv,[10], 722,[54]
pp. Port, 3 plates. Sl marg worm at end.
Contemp calf gilt, sm splits in hinges.
(Claude Cox) **£90 [≈ $144]**
- Notitia Monastica: or, an Account of all the
Abbies, Priories, and Houses of Friers
heretofore in England and Wales ... London:
Bowyer, 1744. Folio. [4],xliv,[x], 722,[53], [1]
pp. Port, 3 plates. A few marks & tears. Old
calf, worn, jnts broken.
(Bow Windows) **£125 [≈ $200]**

Tarr, Ralph S. & Martin, Lawrence
- Alaskan Glacier Studies of the National
Geographic Society in the Yukutat Bay,
Prince William Sound and Lower Copper
River Regions. Washington: National
Geographic Society, 1914. Lge 8vo. xxvii,498
pp. 9 maps in pockets, ills. Orig cloth, front
hinge cracked. *(High Latitude)* **$85 [≈ £53]**

Tattersall, George
- The Lakes of England (Tablets of an
Itinerant). London: (1836). 1st edn. Lge
12mo. xii,86,83*-86*, 87-165,[1] pp, errata
leaf, 24 advt pp. 3 pp subscribers. Engvd title,
fldg map, 41 plates. Orig cloth, t.e.g.
(Fenning) **£110 [≈ $176]**

Taylor, Bayard
- Colorado: A Summer Trip. New York: 1867.
185 pp. Orig cloth, sunned, top of hinges a bit
frayed.   *(Reese)* **$85 [≈ £53]**
- Eldorado, or, Adventures in the Path of
Empire: comprising a Voyage to California,
via Panama ... New York: Putnam; London:

Bentley, 1850. 1st edn. 2 vols. 8vo. 35 pp advts in vol 2. 8 cold plates. Waterstaining on prelims, some foxing. Cloth.
(Wreden) **$175 [≈£109]**

- Eldorado, or Adventures in the Path of Empire; comprising a Voyage to California, via Panama ... London: Bohn, 1850. 1st English edn. 2 vols in one. 8vo. [ii],360 pp. Mod half calf gilt. *(Hollett)* **£55 [≈$88]**

- A Journey to Central Africa ... New York: [1854]. 522 pp. Fldg map, frontis, plates, text ills. Orig pict gilt cloth, extremities worn, somewhat soiled. *(Reese)* **$175 [≈£109]**

- A Journey to Central Africa. New York: Putnam, 1854. Map, ills. Orig green embossed cloth gilt, spine sl faded, some shelfwear. *(Parmer)* **$125 [≈£78]**

- A Journey to Central Africa. New York: Putnam, 1854. 10th edn. 16mo. 522 pp. Fldg map (torn), port frontis, ills. Orig stamped brown cloth, spine ends chipped, shelfwear. *(Parmer)* **$50 [≈£31]**

- Travels in Greece and Russia, with an Excursion to Crete. New York: Putnam, 1859. 1st edn. Sm 8vo. vii,426,advt pp. Frontis, engvd title. Sl foxing. Orig cloth, sl rubbed, faded.
(Worldwide Antiqu'n) **$35 [≈£21]**

- A Visit to India, China, and Japan, in the Year 1853. New York: 1855. xvii,[13]-539 pp. Occas foxing. Orig cloth, scuffed, edgeworn. *(Reese)* **$100 [≈£62]**

Taylor, Bayard (ed.)
- Picturesque Europe ... Illustrated on Steel and Wood by European and American Artists ... New York: Appleton, [1875-78-79]. 1st edn. 3 vols. Sm thick folio. 63 steel engvs inc frontises & half-titles. Other ills. Orig gilt dec half mor, rubbed at edges.
(Terramedia) **$250 [≈£156]**
- See also Picturesque Europe.

Taylor, Charles
- Five Years in China, with Some Account of the Great Rebellion, and a Description of St. Helena. New York: Derby & Jackson, 1860. 1st edn. Sm 8vo. 413 pp. 1 hand cold plate. Sl foxed. Orig cloth, sl rubbed & soiled.
(Worldwide Antiqu'n) **$95 [≈£59]**

Taylor, Fanny M.
- Eastern Hospitals and English Nurses; the Narrative of Twelve Months' Experience in the Hospitals of Koulari and Scutari. By a Lady Volunteer. Third Edition, Revised. London: Hurst & Blackett, 1857. xii,356 pp. 2 lithotints. Orig pict cloth gilt, v sl soiled.
(Duck) **£135 [≈$216]**

Taylor, Fitch W.
- The Broad Pennant: or, a Cruise in the United States Flag Ship of the Gulf Squadron, during the Mexican Difficulties ... New York: 1848. 415,advt pp. Paper sl tanned. Lacks fldg frontis.Orig cloth, spine gilt extra, extremities worn.
(Reese) **$125 [≈£78]**

Taylor, George & Skinner, Andrew
- Maps of the Roads of Ireland Surveyed 1777. London: Published for the Authors as the Act directs 14th Nov. 1778. Sold by G. Nicol ..., [1778]. 1st edn. xvi, 16 subscribers pp. 288 engvd road maps ptd on both sides. General map defective. Old calf, worn.
(Young's) **£90 [≈$144]**

Taylor, J. (ed.)
- The Illustrated Guide to Sheffield. Sheffield: Pawson & Brailsford, 1879. 398, advt pp. Ills. Orig bndg, rebacked.
(Book House) **£35 [≈$56]**

Taylor, James
- The Pictorial History of Scotland ... A.D. 79-1746. London: James S. Virtue, n.d. 2 vols. Lge thick 8vo. Engvd titles, num plates (a little spotting). Extra illust with num steel engvd plates. Scarlet half calf gilt.
(Hollett) **£150 [≈$240]**

Taylor, John
- African Rifles and Cartridges. London: 1948. 1st edn. 8vo. Ills. Orig bndg. Dw.
(Grayling) **£150 [≈$240]**

Taylor, N.
- Ibex Shooting in the Himalayas. London: 1903. 146 pp. Ills. Orig bndg, cvrs spotted. *(Trophy Room Books)* **$250 [≈£156]**

Taylor, Nathaniel A.
- The Coming Empire; or, Two Thousand Miles in Texas on Horseback. New York: 1877. 1st edn. 389 pp. Orig cloth, worn. Half mor slipcase. *(Jenkins)* **$350 [≈£218]**

Taylor, W. Fitch
- The Broad Pennant: or, A Cruise in the United States Flag Ship of the Gulf Squadron, during the Mexican Difficulties ... New York: 1848. 415, advt pp. Paper sl tanned. Lacks frontis. Orig cloth, spine gilt extra, extremities worn. *(Reese)* **$125 [≈£78]**

Teichman, Sir Eric
- Journey to Turkistan. London: Hodder & Stoughton, 1937. 8vo. 221 pp. Lge fldg map,

photo ills, endpaper map. Orig bndg. Dw
reprd.   *(Bates & Hindmarch)* £25 [≈ $40]

Temple, Edmond
- Travels in Various Parts of Peru, including a
Year's residence in Potosi. London: Colburn
& Bentley, 1830. 1st edn. 2 vols. 8vo. xvi,431;
viii,504 pp. Map, 8 plates (5 aquatints). Sl
foxing. Orig cloth, rubbed, new leather labels.
(Adelson) $350 [≈ £218]

Temple, George Theodore
- Norway Pilot, Part II. From the Naze to the
North Cape, thence to Jacob River. London:
for the Hydrographic Office Admiralty, 1894.
8vo. Orig limp cloth.   *(Hannas)* £35 [≈ $56]

Temple, Sir Richard
- Palestine Illustrated. London: Allen, 1888.
1st edn. 4to. xx,296 pp. 4 maps, 32 cold & 2
other plates. A few margs sl affected by damp.
Orig cloth, t.e.g., edges sl rubbed, sl marked.
(Worldwide Antiqu'n) $75 [≈ £46]

Temple, Sir William
- Observations upon the United Provinces of
the Netherlands. The Fourth Edition,
Corrected and Augmented. London: for
Edward Gellibrand, 1680. 12mo. [xvi],320
pp. Title marg sl chipped, Short tear in 1 leaf
with v sl loss. Old calf, upper jnt cracked.
Wing T.659.   *(Bickersteth)* £110 [≈ $176]

Tempsky, G.F. von
- Mitla: a Narrative of Incidents & Personal
Adventures on a Journey in Mexico,
Guatemala & Salvador in the Years 1853 to
1855 ... London: Longman, 1858. 8vo. 436
pp. Cold frontis, fldg map, 14 other plates
(only, of 17). Contemp qtr mor, front bd
detached.   *(Terramedia)* $100 [≈ £62]

Tende, Gaspard de
- An Account of Poland. London: Goodwin,
1698. 8vo. Calf. Wing T.678.
(Rostenberg & Stern) $185 [≈ £115]

Tennent, Sir James Emerson
- Ceylon: An Account of the Island, Physical,
Historical and Topographical ... London:
Longman, 1859. 3rd edn, rvsd. 2 vols. 8vo.
xxxix,643; xvi,663 pp. 2 fldg maps, num
plates & ills. Lib stamps on titles. Flyleaf
loose. Contemp half mor, rubbed.
(Terramedia) $200 [≈ £125]
- The History of Modern Greece ... London:
Colburn, 1845. 2 vols. 8vo. Orig green cloth,
portion of 1 spine glued down & a trifle worn,
ex-lib.   *(Piccadilly)* £60 [≈ $96]

- Sketches of the Natural History of Ceylon ...
London: Longman, 1861. 1st edn. 8vo. xxiii,
500 pp. 10 plates, num engvs. Orig dec cloth.
(Egglishaw) £52 [≈ $83]

Texier, Charles & Pullan, R. Popplewell
- The Principal Ruins of Asia Minor. London:
Day, 1865. Atlas folio. viii,56 pp. Map, 56
plates. Title sl frayed. Lib stamp on all plates
below image. Half mor, edges rubbed, spine
ends frayed & chipped, hinges sl tender.
(Worldwide Antiqu'n) $425 [≈ £265]

Thackeray, Lance
- The Light Side of Egypt ... Preface by George
Ade. London: Adam & Charles Black, 1908.
Oblong 4to. 36 cold plates. Orig pict cloth,
extremities sl worn. *(Terramedia)* $75 [≈ £46]
- The People of Egypt. London: A. & C. Black,
1910. 32 mtd cold plates, 37 b/w ills. Bds v
faded, bowed.   *(Parmer)* $40 [≈ £25]

Thayer, Emma Homan
- Wild Flowers of Colorado. From Original
Water Colour Sketches Drawn from Nature.
New York: Cassell, [1885]. Folio. 24 cold
plates. Orig pict brown cloth, a.e.g., ft of rear
bd damp stained & discold.
(Terramedia) $150 [≈ £93]

Thayer, James Bradley
- A Western Journey with Mr. Emerson.
Boston: 1884. 1st edn. Sq 16mo. 141 pp. Orig
ptd wraps. *(M & S Rare Books)* $75 [≈ £46]

Thesiger, Wilfred
- Arabian Sands. New York: 1959. 326 pp. Ills.
Orig bndg, lacks front free endpaper. Dw.
(Trophy Room Books) $65 [≈ £40]
- The Marsh Arabs. London: Longmans, 1964.
1st edn. 8vo. Ills. Orig green cloth. Sl frayed
dw.   *(Dalian)* £45 [≈ $72]

Thevenot, Jean de
- The Travels ... into the Levant. In Three
Parts ... Newly Done Out of French. London:
H. Clarke, 1687. 1st edn in French. Folio.
[xl],291,1, [ii],200, [ii],114,4 pp. Frontis port,
3 plates. Rec half mor, raised bands.
(Terramedia) $1,500 [≈ £937]
- The Travels ... into the Levant. In Three
Parts ... Newly Done Out of French. London:
John Taylor, 1687. 1st English edn. Lge 4to.
Frontis port, 3 plates. Sm marg water stain at
start. Contemp calf gilt, spine ends chipped,
crnrs rubbed.   *(Sotheran)* £800 [≈ $1,280]
- The Travels ... into the Levant. In Three
Parts ... Newly Done Out of French. London:
H. Clark ..., 1687. 1st English edn. Folio.

[xxxviii],291,1, [iii],200, [ii],114,[iv] pp. 3 plates. Lacks frontis port. 1 ink stain. Minor foxing. Contemp calf, spine relaid. Wing T.887. *(Clark)* **£400 [≈ $640]**

Thicknesse, Philip
- A Year's Journey through France and Part of Spain. Bath: 1777. 2 vols. xvii,295; 245, subscribers pp. Plates, fldg facs. Frontis in vol 1. Some offsetting from plates. Contemp polished calf, mor labels, raised bands, some wear to jnts. *(Reese)* **$600 [≈ £375]**
- A Year's Journey through France, and Part of Spain. The Second Edition, with Additions. London: W. Brown, 1778. 2 vols in one. 8vo. xix, 252; [iv], 316 pp. 10 plates, 2 engvd ff of music. Orig calf, mor label. *(Bickersteth)* **£225 [≈ $360]**
- A Year's Journey through the Pais Bas; or, Austrian Netherlands. Second Edition, with Considerable Additions ... London: for J. Debrett ..., 1786. 8vo. Fldg plate. Contemp half calf, upper jnt weak. *(Hannas)* **£140 [≈ $224]**

Thielmann, Max von
- Journey in the Caucasus, Persia, and Turkey in Asia. Translated by Charles Heneage. London: Murray, 1875. 1st edn. 2 vols. 8vo. xv,308,advt; ix,302,22 advt pp. Fldg map, 14 plates. Orig cloth, edges rubbed, 1 vol rebacked, lib number on spine. *(Worldwide Antiqu'n)* **$135 [≈ £84]**

Thoburn, J.M.
- Indian and Malaysia. Thirty-Three Years a Missionary in India. Cincinnati: Cranston & Curtis, 1892. 1st edn. 8vo. 562 pp. Frontis, num plates. Orig pict grey-green cloth. *(Terramedia)* **$75 [≈ £46]**

Thomas, Bertram
- Alarms and Excursions in Arabia. Indianapolis: Bobbs-Merrill, [1931]. 1st edn. Ills. Orig cloth, sl soiled. *(Terramedia)* **$30 [≈ £18]**
- Arabia Felix: across the Empty Quarter of Arabia. With a Foreword by T.E. Lawrence ... London: Cape, 1932. 1st edn. Roy 8vo. xxix, 397 pp. Fldg map, 45 plates, text figs. Orig cloth, top edge trimmed, other edges uncut. *(Bickersteth)* **£55 [≈ $88]**
- Arabia Felix: Across the Empty Quarter of Arabia. With a Foreword by T.E. Lawrence ... London: 1932. 1st edn. 8vo. xxix,397 pp. Maps, charts, diags, ills. Faint damp mark on frontis. Orig buckram. Dw. *(Bow Windows)* **£75 [≈ $120]**
- Arabia Felix: Across the Empty Quarter of

Arabia. Foreword by T.E. Lawrence. London: Cape, 1932. 1st edn. Lge 8vo. xxix,397 pp. Maps, ills. Orig buckram gilt, uncut, partly unopened. *(Hollett)* **£45 [≈ $72]**

Thomas, Revd Charles W.
- Adventures & Observations on the West Coast of Africa & Its Islands. Historical and Descriptive Sketches of Madeira, Canary, Biafra & Cape Verde Islands ... New York: Negro Univ Press, 1969. Reprint of 1st edn of 1860. 8vo. xvi,479. Frontis. Cloth. *(Terramedia)* **$50 [≈ £31]**

Thomas, David
- Travels through the Western Country in ... 1816. Auburn, New York: David Rumsey, 1819. 1st edn. 420 pp. Fldg map. Foxed. Orig calf, mor label, worn. *(Jenkins)* **$200 [≈ £125]**

Thomas, Edward
- Beautiful Wales. Painted by Robert Fowler ... London: A. & C. Black Colour Books, Twenty Shilling Series, 1905. 1st edn. Cold ills. Orig dec cloth, fine. *(Old Cathay)* **£65 [≈ $104]**
- Beautiful Wales. Painted by Robert Fowler ... London: A. & C. Black Colour Books, Twenty Shilling Series, 1905. 1st edn. Cold ills. News photo pasted to title verso. Orig dec cloth, v minor rubbings & bumps. *(Old Cathay)* **£45 [≈ $72]**
- Oxford. Painted by John Fulleylove. London: A. & C. Black Colour Books, Twenty Shilling Series, 1903. 1st edn. 60 cold plates. Orig dec cloth, t.e.g. *(Old Cathay)* **£59 [≈ $94]**
- Oxford. Painted by John Fulleylove. London: A. & C. Black, (1903). 1st trade edn, 2nd iss. 8vo. xii,265,[i],[2 advt] pp. 60 cold plates, captioned tissues (one with paper fault hole). Some marks. Orig dec cloth, t.e.g., upper crnrs bumped. *(Bow Windows)* **£55 [≈ $88]**
- Oxford. Painted by J. Fulleylove. London: A. & C. Black, 1922. 2nd edn, rvsd. Map, 32 cold plates. Foredges foxed. Orig cloth, v sm graze to hd of spine. Dw chipped. *(Old Cathay)* **£19 [≈ $30]**
- Wales. Painted by Robert Fowler. London: A. & C. Black, 1924. 2nd edn. Map, 32 cold plates. Orig cloth, pin-prick perforation to front bd. *(Old Cathay)* **£23 [≈ $36]**

Thomas, J.
- Travels in Egypt and Palestine. Philadelphia: Lippincott, Grambo, 1853. 1st edn. Sm 8vo. 174,36 advt pp. Engvd title, 2 plates, 1 text ill. Some foxing. Orig cloth, rubbed & faded. *(Worldwide Antiqu'n)* **$65 [≈ £40]**

Thomas, James A.
- A Pioneer Tobacco Merchant in the Orient. Durham, N. Carolina: Duke Univ Press, 1928. 1st edn. 8vo. [6],340 pp. Cold frontis. Orig dec yellow cloth. Author's sgnd pres copy.   *(Karmiole)* **$65 [≈ £40]**

Thomas, Julian
- Cannibals & Convicts: Notes of Personal Experience in the Western Pacific. London: 1886. 8vo. Map, port. Orig dec cloth, sl soiled, recased, new endpapers.
              (Farahar) **£55 [≈ $88]**

Thomas, Margaret
- From Damascus to Palmyra. Painted by John Kelman. London: A. & C. Black Colour Books, Twenty Shilling Series, 1908. 1st edn. Fldg map, 86 cold plates & b/w photos. Pencilled marginalia. Orig dec cloth, t.e.g., gilt on spine bleached.
              (Old Cathay) **£40 [≈ $64]**

Thomas, W.
- Hunting Big Game with Gun and Kodak. New York: 1906. 240 pp. 70 ills. Orig bndg, with photo onlay.
              (Trophy Room Books) **$65 [≈ £40]**
- Trails and Tramps in Alaska and Newfoundland. New York: 1913. 330 pp. Over 100 ills. Orig bndg.
              (Trophy Room Books) **$70 [≈ £43]**

Thompson, Charles
- The Travels of the late Charles Thompson ... Europe, Asia, and Africa ... Adorn'd with Maps ... Reading: Newbery & Micklewright, 1744. 1st edn. 3 vols. 8vo. Red & black titles. 7 hand cold fldg maps, 11 fldg plates. Contemp calf gilt, 1 jnt tender.
              (Finch) **£600 [≈ $960]**
- Travels through Turkey in Asia, the Holy Land, Arabia, Egypt, and other Parts of the World ... London: J. Newbery, 1767. 3rd edn. 2 vols. 12mo. vi,250; 256,xi pp. 11 fldg maps, plans, &c. Contemp speckled calf, gilt spines, red & black labels. Spixworth Park copy.   *(Frew Mackenzie)* **£275 [≈ $440]**
- Travels through Turkey in Asia, the Holy Land, Arabia, Egypt, and other Parts of the World ... London: 1767. 3rd edn. 2 vols. 12mo. vi,250; 256,xi pp. 10 fldg plates & maps. Contemp tree calf, v rubbed, spines chipped. *(Worldwide Antiqu'n)* **$150 [≈ £93]**

Thompson, G. Caton
- The Zimbabwe Culture. Ruins & Reactions. London: Frank Cass, 1971. 2nd edn, with new intro. 299 pp. 63 plates. Orig red cloth.

              (Terramedia) **$100 [≈ £62]**

Thompson, R. Campbell
- A Pilgrim's Scrip. London: John Lane, 1915. 1st edn. 8vo. ix,345,advt pp. Fldg map, frontis, plates. Orig maroon cloth.
              (Terramedia) **$50 [≈ £31]**

Thompson, Ralph
- An Artist's Safari. London: 1970. Folio. Cold plates, num line drawings. Orig bndg. Frayed dw.   *(Grayling)* **£65 [≈ $104]**

Thompson, W. Harding
- Devon, a Survey of its Coasts, Moors & Rivers, with some Suggestions for their Preservation. London: 1930. 4to. Maps, fldg tables, plates. Orig bndg. Dw sl torn.
              (Ambra) **£22 [≈ $35]**

Thompson, W.M.
- The Land and the Book. New York: Harper, [1885]. 3 vols. Thick 8vo. Orig pict gilt brown cloth.   *(Terramedia)* **$100 [≈ £62]**

Thompson, Waddy
- Recollections of Mexico. New York & London: Wiley & Putnam, 1846. 1st edn, 1st iss. x,304,[4 advt] pp. Orig dark brown cloth, title gilt.   *(Jenkins)* **$225 [≈ £140]**

Thomson, Alexander
- Letters of a Traveller, on the Various Countries of Europe, Asia, and Africa ... London: for James Wallis, 1798. 8vo. viii,524 pp. Seemingly lacks half-title. Orig calf, spine a little rubbed.   *(Bickersteth)* **£90 [≈ $144]**

Thomson, Revd Andrew
- In the Holy Land. London: Nelson, 1882. Sm 8vo. [xii],366,advt pp. Frontis, other plates. Orig pict brown cloth, crnr of back cvr sl worn.   *(Terramedia)* **$30 [≈ £18]**

Thomson, Joseph
- Through Masai Land. A Journey of Exploration ... Eastern Equatorial Africa. Boston: Houghton Mifflin, 1884. 4th edn. 8vo. xii,583 pp. 2 fldg cold maps, frontis, plates & ills. Orig cloth, hinges cracked internally.   *(Terramedia)* **$150 [≈ £93]**

Thomson, T.
- Western Himalaya and Tibet. A Narrative of a Journey through the Mountains of Northern India during the Years 1847-48. London: 1852. 1st edn. 501 pp. 2 maps (1 fldg). Orig cloth, spine ends chipped.
              (Trophy Room Books) **$1,000 [≈ £625]**

Thomson, Revd William, 1746-1817

- Letters from Scandinavia, on the Past and Present State of the Northern Nations of Europe. London: Robinson, 1796. 2 vols. xv, [1],471; 475 pp. Occas foxing. Contemp tree calf, jnts reprd. *(Reese)* **$250 [≈£156]**
- Travels into Norway, Denmark, and Russia ... By A. Swinton, Esq. London: for G.G. & J. Robinson, 1792. 1st edn. 8vo. Errata leaf. Frontis. Contemp mottled calf, rebacked. In fact written by Thomson.
  (Hannas) **£160 [≈$256]**

Thornbury, Walter

- Criss-Cross Journeys. London: Hurst & Blackett, 1873. 1st edn. 2 vols. 8vo. Orig cloth, spines darkened, some wear.
  (Young's) **£15 [≈$24]**

Thornton, E. & A.

- Leaves from an Afghan Scrapbook. London: 1910. 225 pp. Ills. Orig bndg, worn through to bds at crnrs.
  (Trophy Room Books) **$200 [≈£125]**

Thornton, Edward

- India, its State and Prospects. London: Parbury, Allen, 1835. 1st edn. 8vo. xx,354 pp, imprint leaf. Rec paper bds. Inscrbd by the author. *(Fenning)* **£38.50 [≈$62]**

Thornton, J. Quinn

- Oregon and California in 1848 ... Including Recent and Authentic Information on the Subject of the Gold Mines of California. New York: Harper, 1855. 2nd edn. 2 vols. Plates. No map. Orig cloth. Author's pres inscrptns.
  (Jenkins) **$275 [≈£171]**

Thornton, Colonel Thomas

- A Sporting Tour through Various Parts of France in the Year 1802 ... London: 1806. 2 vols in one. 4to. Num aquatint plates, sev fldg. A few plates foxed. Contemp half mor, hinges strengthened.
  (Grayling) **£200 [≈$320]**

Three Letters ...

- Three Letters Concerning the Present State of Italy ... see Burnet, Gilbert.

Thunberg, Charles Peter

- Travels in Europe, Africa, and Asia. Performed between the Years 1770 and 1779. London: 1793-95. 1st edn in English. 3 vols (of 4). Some waterstaining to top edge. Later pigskin. *(Reese)* **$300 [≈£187]**

Thurston, Edgar

- Ethnographic Notes in Southern India. Madras: 1906. 8vo. 40 plates. Orig dec cloth gilt, sl worn. *(Farahar)* **£90 [≈$144]**

Tierney, M.A.

- The History and Antiquities of the Castle and Town of Arundel ... London: 1834. 1st edn. 2 vols in one. Thick 8vo. 8 plates, num vignettes & pedigrees. Some foxing & stains on plates. Contemp half mor, sl rubbed.
  (Bow Windows) **£85 [≈$136]**

Tilsley, George Edwin

- Dan Crawford. Missionary and Pioneer in Central Africa. London: Oliphants, (1929). 8vo. xix,609 pp. 4 maps (3 on endpapers), 4 mtd photos, 36 ills. Orig cloth.
  (Schoyer) **$40 [≈£25]**

Timperley, H.W.

- A Cotswold Book. London: 1931. 1st edn. 8vo. Ills by L.S. Lowry. Orig bndg.
  (Ambra) **£26 [≈$41]**

Tindal, William

- The History and Antiquities of the Abbey and Borough of Evesham. Evesham & London: 1794. 4to. Subscribers. Frontis (creased, marg frayed, inscrptn showing through). 5 engvd plates (of 6, lacks plate of 'Gothic Arch'). Lacks half-title. Later half roan, rubbed. *(Sanders)* **£100 [≈$160]**

Todd, John A.

- The Banks of the Nile. London: Black, 1913. 1st edn. 8vo. xv,282,[10 advt] pp. 2 fldg maps, 60 cold plates. Orig cloth, t.e.g., sl rubbed, sl spotting.
  (Worldwide Antiqu'n) **$45 [≈£28]**

Tonkin, J.C. & R.W.

- Guide to the Isles of Scilly. Penzance: 1887. 2nd edn. 8vo. Fldg map (amateur reprs), ills. Orig cloth, sl spotted, rec endpapers.
  (Ambra) **£30 [≈$48]**

Tooley, R.V.

- The Mapping of Australia and Antarctica. Second Revised Edition ... London: Holland Press, 1985. Lge 8vo. 649 pp. 256 plates of maps. Orig cloth. Dw.
  (Terramedia) **$100 [≈£62]**

The Topographer ...

- See Shaw, Stebbing & Brydges, Sir Samuel Egerton.

Torday, E.
- Camp & Tramp in African Wilds. A Record of Adventure ... Around Lake Tanganyika & in Central Africa ... Philadelphia: Lippincott, 1913. 1st edn. 8vo. 315 pp. Fldg map, frontis, num photo plates. Orig pict orange red cloth gilt.   *(Terramedia)* **$100 [≈ £62]**

Torr, James
- The Antiquities of York City. York: G. White, 1719. 8vo. [8],148,[4] pp. Contemp calf, rebacked.   *(Spelman)* **£120 [≈ $192]**

Torrens, H.D.
- Travels in Ladak Tartary and Kashmir. London: 1862. 1st edn. 367 pp. Fldg map frontis, fldg litho plates, ills. Orig cloth, spine sl faded.
                   (Trophy Room Books) **$1,000 [≈ £625]**

Tott, Francois de, Baron
- Memoirs of the Baron De Tott, on the Turks and the Tartars. Translated from the French, by an English Gentleman at Paris, under the immediate inspection of the Baron. Dublin: for L. White ..., 1785. 3 vols. Contemp calf.
                   (Jarndyce) **£150 [≈ $240]**
- Memoirs ... Second Edition. To which are subjoined, the Strictures of M. de Peysonnel ... London: Robinson, 1786. 2 vols. 8vo. xxxv, [i blank], 238, [2 divisional title], 236; [ii],204,287,[10] pp. Contemp qtr calf, mor labels, rubbed, crnrs sl bumped.
                   (Finch) **£100 [≈ $160]**

Tour ...
- A Tour in Ireland in 1775 ... see Twiss, Richard.
- A Tour in Teesdale; including Rokeby and its Environs. Barnard Castle: T. Clifton, 1834. 5th edn. 73 pp. Fldg map frontis, 8 dble page copper engvs. Green cloth, leather label.
                   (Box of Delights) **£50 [≈ $80]**
- A Tour on the Prairies ... see Irving, Washington.
- A Tour through Part of Belgium ... see Rutland, John Henry Manners, Duke of.
- A Tour through the Principal Provinces of Spain and Portugal, performed in the Year 1803 ... London: Richard Phillips, 1806. 77, index pp. Fldg frontis map. Few traces of foxing. Mod half cloth. *(Reese)* **$100 [≈ £62]**

Tovey, Charles
- Wine and Wine Countries; a Record Manual for Wine Merchants and Wine Consumers. London: Hamilton Adams, 1862. 1st edn. xiv, 359 pp. Fldg & other tables. Orig embossed cloth. *(Box of Delights)* **£200 [≈ $320]**

Townshend, F. Trench
- Ten Thousand Miles of Travel, Sport, and Adventure. London: 1869. xiv,275,advt pp. Frontis, title vignette. Occas sl foxing, ink inscrptn. Orig dec cloth, gilt spine, soiled, extremities worn, somewhat shaken.
                   (Reese) **$225 [≈ £140]**

Toynbee, Arnold
- A Journey to China. London: Constable, 1931. 8vo. 345 pp. Fldg map. Orig green cloth.   *(Terramedia)* **$32 [≈ £20]**

Tozer, Henry Fanshawe
- Researches in the Highlands of Turkey; Including Visits to Mounts Ida, Athos, Olympus, and Pelion ... With Notes on ... the Modern Greeks. London: Murray, 1869. 1st edn. 2 vols. Sm 8vo. Fldg map, 5 maps & plans in text, 8 litho plates. Rec cloth, new endpapers.   *(Schoyer)* **$150 [≈ £93]**

Traill, Catherine
- The Backwoods of Canada: being Letters from the Wife of an Emigrant Officer, illustrative of the Domestic Economy of British America. London: Nattali & Bond, (1846). 12mo. 4,352 pp. 2 maps, 15 plates. Half calf, gilt spine, rubbed.
                   (Adelson) **$160 [≈ £100]**

Traits of American-Indian Life ...
- See Finlayson, Duncan.

Trans-Atlantic Sketches ...
- See Harding, W.M.

Trask, Charles
- Norton-sub-Hamdon. In the County of Somerset. Notes on the Parish and the Manor and on Ham Hill. London: 1898. 1st edn. 8vo. Plates, some fldg. Orig buckram.
                   (Ambra) **£42 [≈ $67]**

Travels ...
- Travels in the Crimea ... see Struve, Johann Christian von.
- Travels through Barbary ... see Poiret, Jean Louis Marie.

Treatt, Stella
- Cape to Cairo. The Record of a Historic Motor Journey. Boston: 1927. 8vo. 251 pp. Fldg cold map, frontis, num plates. Orig blue cloth.   *(Terramedia)* **$50 [≈ £31]**
- Sudan Sand. Filming the Baggara Arabs. London: 1930. 8vo. 252 pp. 63 photo ills. Sl foxing & browning. Orig cloth, sl soiled & dulled.   *(Dillons)* **£24 [≈ $38]**

Tregarthen, Greville
- A Sketch of the Progress and Resources of New South Wales. Sydney: 1893. 2nd edn. 47 pp. Diags (some fldg, some cold). Orig ptd wraps, chipped & tanned.
(Reese) **$100 [≈£62]**

Treves, Sir Frederick
- Uganda for a Holiday. New York: 1910. 1st edn. Lge 8vo. xi,233 pp. Fldg map, frontis, num plates. Orig pict light brown cloth, sl soiled & frayed. (Terramedia) **$50 [≈£31]**

Trevor-Battye, Aubyn
- Ice-Bound on Kolguev ... Westminster: Constable, 1895. 1st edn. Lge 8vo. xxviii,458 pp. 3 fldg maps, 25 plates. Orig bndg, cvrs worn & dampstained, hinges cracked.
(Schoyer) **$45 [≈£28]**
- Ice-Bound on Kolguev. Westminster: Constable, 1895. 3rd edn. 453 pp. Num ills. Orig green cloth, sl soiled.
(Parmer) **$75 [≈£46]**

A Trip to Paris ...
- See Twiss, Richard.

Tristram, Henry B.
- The Great Sahara. London: Murray, 1860. 8vo. xv,435 pp. 2 fldg maps, 11 plates. Half mor, rubbed. (Adelson) **$95 [≈£59]**
- The Land of Moab: Travels and Discoveries on the East Side of the Dead Sea and the Jordan. New York: Harper, 1873. 8vo. 416 pp. Frontis, num plates & ills. Orig maroon cloth gilt, lib b'plate.
(Terramedia) **$50 [≈£31]**
- Scenes in the East, consisting of Twelve Coloured Photographic Views of Places mentioned in the Bible ... London: SPCK, 1887. 1st edn. 4to. 49 pp. 12 chromolitho plates. Sl marks. Orig dec cloth gilt, bevelled bds, faint ring mark on upper cvr.
(Hollett) **£85 [≈$136]**
- The Survey of Western Palestine: The Fauna and Flora of Palestine. London: Palestine Exploration Fund, 1884. 1st edn. Lge 4to. xii, 455 pp. 13 litho plates (only, of 20). Perf lib stamp on title, plates stamped on reverse. Orig cloth, hd of spine worn, inner hinge broken. (Terramedia) **$250 [≈£156]**

Troil, Uno Von
- Letters on Iceland ... London: Richardson ..., 1780. 1st English edn. 8vo. Frontis, fldg map. Sl foxing at ends. Contemp calf, jnts cracked.
(Hannas) **£180 [≈$288]**
- Letters on Iceland ... London: Richardson, 1780. 1st edn. 8vo. xxxvi,400 pp. Frontis,

fldg map. Last leaf browned. Orig qtr calf, mrbld bds, vellum tips. Sir John Swinburne's b'plate. (Blackwell's) **£375 [≈$600]**
- Letters on Iceland ... London: Richardson ..., 1780. 1st edn in English. 8vo. xxvi,400 pp. Engvd frontis by Bewick, fldg map. Outer ff sl browned & spotted. Contemp calf, mor label, endpapers sometime renewed, rubbed.
(Hannas) **£240 [≈$384]**
- Letters on Iceland ... Dublin: G. Perrin ..., 1780. 1st Dublin edn. 8vo. xxvi,400 pp. Fldg map, plate. Occas sl spotting. Old calf, worn.
(Young's) **£150 [≈$240]**

Trollope, Anthony
- How the "Mastiffs" Went to Iceland. With Illustrations by Mrs Hugh Blackburn. London: Virtue & Co, 1878. 1st edn. 4to. Cold map, 2 mtd photos, 14 lithos, all unfoxed. Orig dec blue cloth, n.a.e.
(Hannas) **£480 [≈$768]**
- How the "Mastiffs" Went to Iceland. With Illustrations by Mrs Hugh Blackburn. London: Virtue & Co, 1878. 1st edn. 4to. Cold map, 2 mtd photos, 14 lithos, all foxed. Orig dec blue cloth, a.e.g., extremities worn.
(Hannas) **£280 [≈$448]**
- How the "Mastiffs" Went to Iceland ... London: (privately ptd by) Virtue & Co, 1878. 1st edn. 4to. 2 mtd photos, 14 lithos. Contemp calf gilt. (Minkoff) **$750 [≈£468]**
- New South Wales and Queensland. New Edition. London: Chapman & Hall, 1875. 8vo. 209 pp. Fldg cold map. Orig pict bds, some minor wear & chipping.
(Spelman) **£45 [≈$72]**
- Travelling Sketches. (Reprinted from the "Pall Mall Gazette.') London: Chapman & Hall, 1866. 1st edn. 8vo. Orig scarlet cloth, unopened, spine faded. The secondary bndg of about 1926, but with no blocking on spine & no publisher's ctlg as called for by Sadleir.
(Hannas) **£240 [≈$384]**

Trollope, Frances
- Belgium and Western Germany, in 1833 ... Brussels: Ad. Wahlen, 1834. 2 vols in one. 12mo. 252; 232 pp. No half-titles. 2 frontis. Sl spotting. Contemp half calf, rebacked, sides sl rubbed. (Finch) **£75 [≈$120]**
- A Visit to Italy. London: Bentley ..., 1842. 1st edn. 2 vols. 8vo. xii,402,[2 blank]; xii,396 pp. Half-titles. Occas sl marks. Orig cloth, recased, spines faded.
(Bow Windows) **£125 [≈$200]**

Trotter, Philip Durham
- Our Mission to the Court of Marocco in 1880 under Sir John Drummond Hay. Edinburgh:

David Douglas, 1881. 8vo. xviii,310 pp. Fldg
map (2 sm tears), 31 plates. Orig bndg, sm
split in hd of spine, ft of spine badly chipped,
crnrs worn.   *(Schoyer)* **$60 [≈£37]**

A True and Particular Relation ...
- A True and Particular Relation of the
Dreadful Earthquake which happened at
Lima ... see Lozano, Pedro.

Truman, Ben C.
- From the Crescent City to the Golden Gate
via the Sunset Route of the Southern Pacific
Company. New York: 1886. 4to. 100 pp. Ills.
Chromolitho wraps, sl chipped.
        (Reese) **$125 [≈£78]**
- Tourists' Illustrated Guide to the Celebrated
Summer and Winter Resorts of California ...
San Francisco: 1883. 1st edn. 8vo. 256 pp.
Ills. Underlining in cold pencil on a few ff.
New cloth.
        (M & S Rare Books) **$125 [≈£78]**

Tschudi, J.J. von
- Travels in Peru, during the Years 1838-1842
... Translated from the German by
Thomasina Ross. London: David Bogue,
1847. 1st edn in English. 2 advt,506 pp.
Tinted litho frontis (foxed), title vignette.
Orig green cloth, worn spine relaid.
        (Schoyer) **$175 [≈£109]**

Tucci, C.
- Journey to Mustang. Nepal: 1952. 2nd edn.
86 pp. Map, ills. Orig bndg. dw.
        (Trophy Room Books) **$60 [≈£37]**

Tucker, Alfred R.
- Eighteen Years in Uganda & East Africa.
London: Edward Arnold, 1908. 2 vols. 8vo.
xvi,359,advt; xii,388 pp. Cold fldg map, ills.
Orig gilt dec blue cloth, some wear to
extremities.   *(Parmer)* **$200 [≈£125]**
- Eighteen Years in Uganda & East Africa.
London: Edward Arnold, 1911. New edn.
8vo. xvi,362 pp. Fldg map, ills. Orig red
cloth, edges sl foxed.   *(Parmer)* **$50 [≈£31]**

Tucker, J.C.
- To the Golden Goal and Other Sketches. San
Francisco: Privately Printed, 1895. One of
50. 303 pp. Port. Orig dec cloth.
        (Reese) **$275 [≈£171]**

Tucker, Sarah
- Abbeokuta: or, Sunrise within the Tropics:
an Outline of the Origin and Progress of the
Yoruba Mission. London: James Nisbet ...,
1853. 2nd edn. 8vo. vii,278 pp. Fldg map,

plan, 6 plates (2 cold). Spotting. Orig blue
cloth, recased.   *(Young's)* **£60 [≈$96]**
- Abbeokuta; or Sunrise within the Tropics.
(Nigeria). London: James Nisbet, 1853. 3rd
edn. 12mo. vii,278 pp. Fldg map, plan, 6
plates (2 cold). Orig blue cloth, rubbed, spine
ends worn.   *(Adelson)* **$125 [≈£78]**

Tuckey, J.K.
- Narrative of an Expedition to Explore the
River Zaire, usually called the Congo, in
South Africa in 1816. London: Murray, 1818.
1st edn. 4to. lxii,498,[2 advt] pp. Fldg map,
13 plates (1 cold). 4 ff washed, water staining.
Orig bds, uncut, new cloth spine.
        (Claude Cox) **£100 [≈$160]**
- Narrative of an Expedition to Explore the
River Zaire, usually called the Congo, in
South Africa, in 1816 ... London: Murray,
1818. 1st edn. 4to. lxxxii,498 pp, advt leaf.
Fldg map, 13 plates (1 cold). Plates sl
browned, other sl foxing. Mod qtr mor.
        (Terramedia) **$500 [≈£312]**

Tuker, Mildred A.R. & Malleson, Hope
- Rome. Painted by Alberto Pisa. London: A. &
C. Black Colour Books, 1905. One of 250,
sgnd by the publishers. 70 cold plates. Orig
cloth, t.e.g., fine.
        (Old Cathay) **£195 [≈$312]**
- Rome. Painted by Alberto Pisa. London: A. &
C. Black Colour Books, 1905. One of 250,
sgnd by the publishers. 70 cold plates. Occas
foxing. Orig cloth, t.e.g., bds discold towards
a light shade of sepia, spine ends sl stained &
worn.   *(Old Cathay)* **£150 [≈$240]**
- Rome. Painted by Alberto Pisa. London: A. &
C. Black Colour Books, 1905. One of 250,
sgnd by the publishers. 70 cold plates. Some
browning to edges & foxing of endpapers.
Orig cloth, t.e.g., rear bd marked, spine
darkened, some wear to spine ends.
        (Old Cathay) **£85 [≈$136]**

Tully, Richard
- Letters Written during a Ten Years'
Residence at the Court of Tripoli ... London:
Colburn, 1819. 3rd edn. 2 vols. 8vo. xv,375;
ii,396 pp. Fldg map, 6 hand cold plates. 1st
& last few ff sl foxed. Half mor, hinges
cracked, edges rubbed.
        (Worldwide Antiqu'n) **$325 [≈£203]**

Tunnicliff, W.
- Topographical Survey of the Counties of ...
The Dorset Section. Bath: 1791. 8vo. Lge
fldg hand cold map, 8 pp of coats of arms.
Strip torn from foredge marg of last leaf. rec
qtr calf.   *(Ambra)* **£55 [≈$88]**

Tupper, Ferdinand Brock
- The History of Guernsey and its Bailiwick; with Occasional Notices of Jersey. Guernsey: 1854. 1st edn. 8vo. Contemp half calf, rubbed, front inner hinge split, label chipped. *(Robertshaw)* **£48 [≈ $76]**

Turnbull, John
- A Voyage round the World in the Years 1800 ... 1804: In which the author visited Madeira, the Brazils, Cape of Good Hope, the English Settlements of Botany Bay and Norfolk Island ... London: Maxwell, 1813. 2nd edn. 4to. 2,xv,516 pp. Contemp calf, rebacked. *(Adelson)* **$475 [≈ £296]**

Turner, Dawson
- Architectural Antiquities of Normandy. London: J. & A. Arch, 1822. 2 vols in one. Lge 4to. 125 pp. 96 engvd plates (4 dble page) by John Sell Cotman. Some general foxing. Rebound in blue half mor. Sir Kenneth Clark's b'plate. *(Gough)* **£250 [≈ $400]**

Turner, J.M.W.
- Liber Fluviorum; or, River Scenery of France ... Biographical Sketch by Alaric A. Watts. London: 1853. Thick 4to. lvi,336 pp. Engvd title, engvd plates. Tissue guards. A few fox marks. Orig cloth gilt, a.e.g., worn & frayed at extremities, front hinge broken. *(Reese)* **$250 [≈ £156]**

Turner, R.
- A New and Easy Introduction to Universal Geography: in a Series of Letters to a Youth at School ... Fourth Edition ... London: for S. Crowder, 1789. 12mo. [xii],228 pp. Fldg mappemonde & 25 plates & maps (1 with a volvelle). Rec calf antique. *(Bickersteth)* **£65 [≈ $104]**

Turner, Thomas
- Narrative of a Journey, Associated with a Fly, from Gloucester to Aberystwith, and ... through North Wales ... London: for private distribution by C. Whittingham, 1840. 1st edn. 8vo. xii,[iv],222 pp. Port, 11 tissue guarded plates. Green qtr mor, cloth sides. *(Young's)* **£180 [≈ $288]**

Turner, Thomas A.
- Argentina & the Argentines. Notes & Impressions of a Five Years' Sojourn in the Argentine Republic, 1885-90. New York: Scribner's, 1892. 8vo. xvi,370 pp. Num ills. 1 sgntr loose. Orig cloth, spine ends sl chipped. *(Terramedia)* **$75 [≈ £46]**

Turner-Turner, J.
- Three Years Hunting and Trapping in America and the Great North West. London: 1888. Imperial 8vo. Plates, text ills. Orig cloth backed bds, crnrs bumped, edges rubbed, spine rubbed & sl marked. *(Grayling)* **£200 [≈ $320]**

Turnor, Edmund
- Collections for the History of the Town and Soke of Grantham. Containing Authentic Memoirs of Sir Isaac Newton ... London: 1806. 1st edn. Lge 4to. xvi,200 pp. Map, port, 1 plate, 2 text engvs. Without the 8 extra plates sometimes present. Later half calf, spine chipped at ft. *(Burmester)* **£150 [≈ $240]**

Turton, Zouch H.
- To the Desert and Back; or, Travels in Spain, the Barbary States, Italy, etc. in 1875-6. London: 1876. 1st edn. 8vo. Orig dec cloth, inner hinges weak. *(Robertshaw)* **£38 [≈ $60]**

Twain, Mark
- Following the Equator. A Journey Around the World. Hartford, Conn.: 1897. 1st edn. 1st iss, with Hartford imprint. 8vo. 712 pp. Frontis, num plates & ills. Orig blue cloth, cold pict onlay. *(Terramedia)* **$75 [≈ £46]**

Twamley, Louisa Anne
- See Meredith, Louisa Anne, nee Twamley.

Tweedie, Mrs Alec
- Through Finland in Carts. New York: Macmillan; London: Adam & Charles Black, 1898. 8vo. xi,366,2 advt pp. Fldg map, 18 plates. Orig dec cloth, t.e.g. *(Schoyer)* **$40 [≈ £25]**

Twiss, Richard
- A Tour in Ireland in 1775, with a Map and a View of the Salmon Leap at Ballyshannon. London: for the author, 1776. Later qtr sheep. Sgntr of J.P. Mehaffy. *(Emerald Isle)* **£150 [≈ $240]**
- A Trip to Paris, in July and August, 1792. London: at the Minerva Press, sold by William Lane ..., 1793. Sole edn. 8vo. [iv],131 pp. Frontis, 1 plate. Disbound. *(Bickersteth)* **£140 [≈ $224]**

Tyerman, Daniel & Bennet, George
- Journal of Voyages and Travels ... South Sea Islands, China, India &c. ... Edited by James Montgomery. Boston: Crocker & Brewster, 1832. 1st US edn. 3 vols. Sm 8vo. 3 plates. Sl foxing. Orig cloth, worn, tears in spine, cvrs

starting.   *(Worldwide Antiqu'n)* **$75 [≃ £46]**

Tyler, John
- Message from the President ... Proceedings of the Commissioner Appointed to Run the Boundary Line between the United States and the Republic of Texas. Washington: Senate Doc 199, 1842. 1st edn. 8vo. 74 pp. 6 fldg maps. Rec half mor.
      (W. Thomas Taylor) **$850 [≃ £531]**

Tyler, Josiah
- Forty Years among the Zulus. Boston & Chicago: Congregational Sunday-School, 1891. 8vo. 300 pp. 17 plates (1 map). Orig brown cloth gilt, some bumping & wear to ft.
      (Parmer) **$125 [≃ £78]**

Tyndale, Walter
- An Artist in Italy. [London]: Hodder & Stoughton, [1913]. 4to. 307 pp. 26 mtd cold plates. Orig elab gilt bndg.
      (Schoyer) **$45 [≃ £28]**
- Below the Cataracts. London: Heinemann ..., 1907. 1st edn. 8vo. xi,271,50 (plates) pp. 60 cold plates by the author. Orig cloth, sl rubbed, a little dusty.
      (Worldwide Antiqu'n) **$35 [≃ £21]**
- Japan and the Japanese. New York: Macmillan, 1910. 1st edn. 8vo. xii,317 pp. 32 cold plates. Sl foxed. Orig cloth, sl rubbed.
      (Worldwide Antiqu'n) **$45 [≃ £28]**

Tyndall, John
- Hours of Exercises in the Alps. New York: Appleton, 1873. Sm 8vo. 473 pp. Sev plates. Orig cloth, spine ends chipped, tear at ft of spine.   *(Terramedia)* **$40 [≃ £25]**

Tyrell, H. & Haukell, Henry A.
- The History of Russia from the Foundation of the Empire to the Wars with Turkey in 1877 - '78. London: London Printing & Publishing Co Ltd, [ca 1880]. 3 vols. 4to. 8 maps, 8 ports, 32 steel engvd plates. Half calf gilt.   *(Hollett)* **£120 [≃ $192]**

Tyrrell, Henry
- The History of the War with Russia ... London & New York: [1856]. 4 vols in 2. Thick 4to. Fldg maps, engvd titles, ports, plates. Rubberstamps. Occas sl foxing. Contemp three qtr calf, rubbed, worn at edges & jnts.   *(Reese)* **$275 [≃ £171]**

Tyrrell, James W.
- Across the Sub-Arctics of Canada. A Journey of 3,200 Miles by Canoe and Snowshoe through the Barren Lands. London: T. Fisher

Unwin, [1898]. vi,7-280 pp. Fldg map, plates, text ills. Orig dec cloth, sl soiled.
      (High Latitude) **$100 [≃ £62]**

Tyson, George E.
- Arctic Experiences. Containing Capt. George E. Tyson's Wonderful Drift on the Ice-Floe, a History of the Polaris Expedition ... Edited by E. Vale Blake. New York: Harper Bros, 1874. 1st edn. 8vo. 486,advt pp. Num plates & ills. Orig cloth, hd of spine v sl chipped.
      (Terramedia) **$175 [≃ £109]**

Tytler, Patrick Fraser
- Historical View of the Progress of Discovery of the more Northern Coasts of America ... Edinburgh: 1832. 12mo. 444 pp. Fldg map, engvd title. Polished calf, spine gilt extra.
      (Reese) **$225 [≃ £140]**
- Life of Sir Walter Raleigh founded on Original and Authentic Documents. Edinburgh: Oliver & Boyd, Edinburgh Cabinet Library No. XI, 1838. 12mo. Addtnl engvd title, frontis. Orig cloth, largely unopened.   *(Waterfield's)* **£25 [≃ $40]**

Ubique (pseud.)
- See Gillmore, Parker.

Ulloa, Antonio & George Juan de
- A Voyage to South America ... Undertaken by Command of the King of Spain ... with Notes ... Fourth Edition. London: 1806. 2 vols. xxv,479; 419 pp. Map, plates. Lib perf stamps on titles. Contemp three qtr mor, gilt spines, t.e.g., rubbed, some edge wear.
      (Reese) **$175 [≃ £109]**
- A Voyage to South America ... Undertaken by Command of the King of Spain ... with Notes ... By John Adams ... London: Stockdale ..., 1807. 5th edn. 2 vols. 8vo. xxvii, 479; iv, 419, [14] pp. Fldg map, 6 fldg plates. Contemp half calf, gilt spines, v fine.
      (Frew Mackenzie) **£450 [≃ $720]**

Umbra (pseud.)
- See Clifford, Charles Cavendish.

Umlauft, F.
- The Alps. Translated by Louisa Brough. London: Kegan Paul, 1889. 8vo. 523 pp. Num plates & ills. Orig cloth, moderately soiled.   *(Terramedia)* **$100 [≃ £62]**

Upcott, William
- A Bibliographical Account of the Principal Works relating to English Topography. New York: Burt Franklin, 1968. Reprint of the orig 1818 edn. 3 vols. 2 frontis. Orig red

cloth.   *(Karmiole)* **$85 [≈ £53]**

Upham, Samuel C.
- Notes on a Voyage to California via Cape Horn, Together with Scenes in El Dorado in the Years 1849-'50 ... Pioneer Journalism in California ... Philadelphia: the author, 1878. 1st edn. 8vo. 594 pp. 45 ills. Orig gilt dec cloth, 1 crnr worn, spine ends sl worn.
                      (Schoyer) **$225 [≈ £140]**

Urquhart, D.
- The Spirit of the East. Illustrated in a Journal of Travels through Roumeli ... London: Colburn, 1839. 2nd edn. 2 vols. 8vo. xxviii,435; vii,432 pp. Frontis map in vol 1. Orig cloth.   *(Zeno)* **£99.50 [≈ $160]**

Valentine, L.
- Palestine Past and Present. Pictorial and Descriptive. London: Warne, 1893. Cold frontis, addtnl title & 6 other cold plates, num w'engvs in text. Preface leaf loose & frayed in margs. Orig cloth gilt, a.e.g., v damp stained.
                        (Sanders) **£18 [≈ $28]**
- Palestine Past and Present. Pictorial and Descriptive. London: Warne, [ca 1900]. 4to. Cold litho title, 7 cold plates, num text ills. Orig pict cloth gilt, a.e.g.
                        (Stewart) **£30 [≈ $48]**

Vambery, Arminius
- Arminius Vambery. His Life and Adventures. London: Fisher Unwin, 1884. 3rd edn. 8vo. xiii, 370 pp. Photo frontis, 14 ills. Orig cloth gilt, front cvr rippled & stained.
              (Bates & Hindmarch) **£40 [≈ $64]**
- The Coming Struggle for India. London: Cassell, 1885. 12mo. 214 pp. Fldg map. Orig olive green cloth. *(Terramedia)* **$50 [≈ £31]**
- Travels in Central Asia ... New York: Harper, 1865. 1st Amer edn. 8vo. xvi,[2],493, 2 advt pp. Fldg map in pocket, frontis, 11 plates. Orig brown cloth.
                     (Terramedia) **$300 [≈ £187]**
- Travels in Central Asia ... New York: 1865. Lge 8vo. 493, advt pp. Orig cloth, some wear to extremities.   *(Reese)* **$100 [≈ £62]**
- Travels in Central Asia ... New York: 1865. 492 pp. Frontis, lge fldg map. Orig cloth.
             (Trophy Room Books) **$300 [≈ £187]**

Vancouver, George
- A Voyage of Discovery to the North Pacific Ocean, and Round the World ... London: 1798. 1st edn. 3 vols (without the atlas vol). Folio. Half-titles. 18 plates. Occas sl marks. Lib b'plates. Contemp calf, 2 spines relaid, jnts of 2 vols worn, 1 hinge reprd.

                     (Reese) **$3,000 [≈ £1,875]**

Vandeleur, Seymour
- Campaigning on the Upper Nile & Niger. London: Methuen, 1898. 1st edn. 8vo. xxvii, 319, advt pp. Fldg map, port frontis, num other photo plates. Orig pict green cloth gilt, hd of spine chipped, lib labels removed from spine.   *(Terramedia)* **$100 [≈ £62]**

Van De Velde, C.W.M.
- Narrative of a Journey through Syria and Palestine in 1851 and 1852. London: 1854. 2 vols. Fldg map, plan, 2 tinted litho frontis (1 sl waterstained), fldg table of inscrptns. Orig dec cloth, sl worn.
                     (Farahar) **£180 [≈ $288]**

Van Dyke, Theodore S.
- Southern California: Its Valleys, Hills, and Streams; Its Animals, Birds and Fishes ... New York: 1886. 233 pp. Cloth, spine ends sl rubbed.   *(Reese)* **$85 [≈ £53]**

Van Kampen, N.G.
- The History and Topography of Holland and Belgium ... Translated by William Gray Fearnside. Illustrated ... by W.H. Bartlett. London: [1837]. iv,204 pp. Fldg map, engvd title, plates. Occas foxing. Contemp three qtr polished calf, some edge wear.
                     (Reese) **$250 [≈ £156]**

Van Millingen, Alexander
- Constantinople. Painted by Warwick Goble. London: A. & C. Black Colour Books, Twenty Shilling Series, 1906. 1st edn. Fldg map, 63 cold plates. Orig dec cloth, fine.
                   (Old Cathay) **£95 [≈ $152]**

Varley, Telford
- Hampshire. Painted by Wilfrid Ball. London: A. & C. Black Colour Books, Twenty Shilling Series, 1909. 1st edn. Fldg map, 75 cold plates. Orig dec cloth, t.e.g.
                   (Old Cathay) **£49 [≈ $78]**

Vason, George
- An Authentic Narrative of Four Years' Residence at Tongataboo, one of the Friendly Islands, in the South Sea ... London: Longman, 1810. Sole edn. 8vo. Errata leaf at end. Frontis, map. Contemp mrbld bds, rebacked.   *(Trebizond)* **$450 [≈ £281]**

Vassal, Gabrielle M.
- On and Off Duty in Annam [Vietnam]. New York: Appleton, 1910. 8vo. 283 pp. Frontis, num photo plates. Orig pict brown cloth gilt.
                     (Terramedia) **$40 [≈ £25]**

- On and Off Duty in Annam. New York: 1910. xi, 283 pp. Frontis, map, plates. Orig pict gilt maroon cloth.   *(Lyon)* **£55 [≈ $88]**

Vaux, W.S.W.
- Nineveh and Persepolis: An Historical Sketch of Ancient Assyria and Persia, with an Account of the Recent Researches in those Countries. London: Hall, Virtue, 1850. 1st edn. vii,436,[12 advt] pp. Sm 8vo. Fldg map, 12 plates, num text ills. Orig cloth, sl worn.   *(Worldwide Antiqu'n)* **$50 [≈ £31]**

Veitch, James Herbert
- A Traveller's Notes or Notes of a Tour through India, Malaysia, Japan, Corea, the Australian Colonies and New Zealand during the Years 1891-1893. Chelsea: Royal Exotic Nursery, privately ptd, 1896. 219 pp. Fldg map, plates, ills. Orig dec blue cloth.   *(Lyon)* **£195 [≈ $312]**

Venables, R. Lister
- Domestic Scenes in Russia; in a Series of Letters describing a Year's Residence in that Country ... London: Murray, 1839. 8vo. xii, 349 pp. Old half calf, jnts & hd of spine rubbed.   *(Piccadilly)* **£40 [≈ $64]**

Verelst, Harry
- A View of the Rise, Progress, and Present State of the English Government in Bengal ... London: J. Nourse ..., 1772. 4to. [12],148, [4],253 pp. Contemp calf, green label. John Cator's b'plate.   *(Jarndyce)* **£300 [≈ $480]**

Verner, Willoughby
- Sketches in the Soudan. London: R.H. Porter, 1885. Oblong folio. Tinted engvd title, [88] pp. Cold map, 37 cold litho plates. Orig vellum-like spine over ptd bds, soiled, extremities rubbed.   *(Karmiole)* **£450 [≈ £281]**

Vertot d'Aubeuf, Rene Aubert de
- The History of the Revolution in Portugal in the Year 1640 ... Done into English. London: for Mat. Gilliflower &c., 1700. 1st English edn. 12mo. Contemp calf. Wing V.272.   *(Falkner)* **£60 [≈ $96]**
- The Revolutions of Portugal. London: 1721. 1st English edn. 8vo. Frontis. Contemp calf, jnts cracked but firm.   *(Robertshaw)* **£20 [≈ $32]**

Vescelius-Sheldon, Louise
- An I.D.B. in South Africa. New York: John Levell Co, [1888]. 1st edn. 8vo. 206 pp. Num vignettes. Orig pict light brown cloth gilt.   *(Terramedia)* **$50 [≈ £31]**

- Yankee Girls in Zululand. New York: Worthington Co, 1887. 1st edn. Sm 8vo. 287 pp. Num ills & vignettes. Orig pict yellow cloth gilt.   *(Terramedia)* **$75 [≈ £46]**

Vidal, E.E.
- Picturesque Illustrations of Buenos Ayres and Monte Video ... London: 1820, reprint Buenos Aires: 1943. 4to. 24 cold plates (4 fldg). Orig ptd wraps, sl soiled.   *(Farahar)* **£110 [≈ $176]**

View(s) ...
- A View of South-America and Mexico ... see Niles, John Milton.
- A View of the Present State of Ireland ... see O'Bryen, Denis.
- Views on the Tyrol ... see Allom, Thomas.

Vigne, G.T.
- Travels in Kashmir, Ladak, Iskardoo. The Countries adjoining the Mountain Course of the Indus, and the Himala North of the Punjab. London: 1842. 1st edn. 2 vols. 404; 464 pp. Fldg maps, ills. Orig cloth.   *(Trophy Room Books)* **$1,700 [≈ £1,062]**

Vincent, Frank
- Actual Africa, or the Coming Continent; a Tour of Exploration. New York: Appleton, 1895. 1st edn. 8vo. 541 pp. Fldg map, num plates. Orig pict brown cloth gilt, t.e.g.   *(Terramedia)* **$150 [≈ £93]**
- Through and Through the Tropics Thirty Thousand Miles of Travel in Oceanica, Australasia, and India. New York: 1876. xvi, 304, advt pp. Minor marg dampstain. Orig dec cloth, rubbed.   *(Reese)* **$100 [≈ £62]**

Vischer, Hanns
- Across the Sahara: from Tripoli to Bornu. With a Foreword by Sir Harry H. Johnston. London: 1910. 1st edn. 8vo. xix,308,20 advt pp. Fldg map, frontis, num plates. Orig red cloth gilt, front hinge sl shaken.   *(Terramedia)* **$150 [≈ £93]**

A Visit to Texas ...
- A Visit to Texas, being the Journal of a Traveller. New York: Goodrich & Wiley, 1834. 1st edn. 264,[4] pp. 4 plates. Map in facs. Calf.   *(Jenkins)* **$750 [≈ £468]**
- A Visit to Texas: being the Journal of a Traveller through those Parts most interesting to American Settlers ... New York: 1834. iv,[9],264,[4] pp. 3 plates (of 4). Lacks the map. Foxing, marg dampstain. Lacks front free endsheet. Orig cloth, soiled & worn.   *(Reese)* **$600 [≈ £375]**

Vivian, A. Pendarves
- Wanderings in the Western Land. London: 1879. 426,[2],[32] pp. Frontis, plates (2 fldg, 1 cold). Orig gilt pict cloth. Author's pres copy.   *(Reese)* **$250 [≈£156]**

Vivian, H. Hussey
- Notes on a Tour in America. From August 7th to November 17th 1877. London: Edward Stanford, 1878. 1st edn. 8vo. [v],260 pp. Fldg map (reprd). Orig green cloth gilt, recased.   *(Young's)* **£95 [≈$152]**

Vivian, Herbert
- Abyssinia. Through the Lion-Land to the Court of the Lion of Judah. London: Arthur Pearson, 1901. 8vo. xvi,342,2 advt pp. 2 fldg maps, 80 ills. Orig dec cloth, sl rubbed.
            (Schoyer) **$60 [≈£37]**
- Servia. The Poor Man's Paradise. London: Longmans Green, 1897. 8vo. lvi,300 pp. Port frontis, fldg map at end. Orig grey cloth, v sl loose, jnts rubbed.   *(Piccadilly)* **£40 [≈$64]**

Volney, Constantin F.
- Travels through Syria and Egypt ... London: 1787. 1st English edn. 2 vols. xii, 418; iv,500,index,errata pp. Half-titles. 2 fldg maps, 1 fldg plan, 1 fldg plate. Occas sl marks. Contemp French calf gilt, spines rubbed, jnts worn but sound, spine ends vol 1 chipped.   *(Reese)* **$225 [≈£140]**
- Travels through Syria and Egypt ... Translated from the French. London: Robinson, 1787. 1st edn. 2 vols. 8vo. xii,418; iv,500, 15 pp. 5 fldg maps & views. Sl foxed. Half mor, edges rubbed, hinges tender, lib number on spine.
         (Worldwide Antiqu'n) **$350 [≈£218]**

Volonakis, Michael D.
- The Island of Roses and Her Eleven Sisters, or, the Dodecanese from the Earliest Time down to the Present Day. London: Macmillan, 1922. 8vo. xxvi,438 pp. Num maps & ills. Orig blue cloth, t.e.g., 1 crnr sl bumped, foredge sl spotted.
              (Piccadilly) **£48 [≈$76]**
- The Island of Roses and Her Eleven Sisters or, the Dodecanese. London: Macmillan, 1922. 8vo. xxvi,438 pp. 19 maps, num ills (some fldg). Orig gilt dec blue cloth, crnrs bumped, sl wear to extremities.
              (Parmer) **$50 [≈£31]**

Von Haast, Julius
- New Zealand Scenery ... see Gully, John.

Von Hohnel, L.
- The Discovery of Lakes Rudolph and Stefanie. A Narrative of Count Teleki's Hunting and Exploring Expedition to Eastern and Equatorial Africa in 1887 and 1888. London: 1894. 2 vols. 435; 397 pp. Ills. Orig pict gilt blue cloth.
     (Trophy Room Books) **$1,850 [≈£1,156]**

Voss, John Claus
- Venturesome Voyages of Capt. Voss. Tokyo: Geiser & Gilbert, 1913. 1st edn. 8vo. [xvi], 394 pp. Fldg map, ills. Orig cloth, sl soiled & stained. *(W. Thomas Taylor)* **$400 [≈£250]**

Wack, Henry W.
- The Story of the Congo Free State. New York & London: 1905. 8vo. 634 pp. Maps (lge cold fldg map at end), port frontis, num photo ills & plates. Orig orange brown cloth, sl worn.
              (Terramedia) **$40 [≈£25]**

Waddel, L.A.
- Among the Himalayas. Westminster & Philadelphia: Constable & Lippincott, 1900. 2nd edn. 8vo. xvi,452 pp. Fldg map, frontis, plates & ills. Lacks front flyleaf. Orig maroon cloth, top edge of spine sl chipped.
              (Terramedia) **$150 [≈£93]**

Waddington, C.W.
- Indian India as seen by a Guest in Kajasthan. London: 1933. Folio. 168 pp. Map, 30 ills. Orig 2-tone buckram, spine sl dull.
            (Bow Windows) **£48 [≈$76]**

Waddington, George
- A Visit to Greece, in 1823 and 1824. London: Murray, 1825. 1st edn. 8vo. [iii], lix,248,[i] pp. Fldg engvd map & plan. Contemp straight grained mor, gilt spine, label with later ink lettering, spine sl rubbed & sl chipped at ft.
         (Frew Mackenzie) **£120 [≈$192]**

Waddington, George & Hanbury, B.
- Journal of a Visit to Some Parts of Ethiopia. London: 1822. 333 pp. Lge fldg map, ills, some fldg. Half leather.
     (Trophy Room Books) **$800 [≈£500]**

Wade, Henling Thomas
- With Boat and Gun in the Yangtze Valley. Second Edition. Shanghai: 1910. 4to. Map, ills. Orig green cloth, sl marked.
             (Robertshaw) **£85 [≈$136]**

Wainwright, J.M.
- The Pathways and Abiding Places of Our

Lord. Illustrated in the Journal of a Tour through the Land of Promise. New York: Appleton, 1851. 1st Amer edn. Sm 4to. xix,196 pp. Frontis, engvd title, 18 plates by Bartlett. Orig cloth, lacks backstrip.
(Worldwide Antiqu'n) **$110 [≃£68]**

Wait, Benjamin
- Letters from Van Dieman's Land, written during Four Years Imprisonment for Political Offences committed in Upper Canada ... Buffalo: 1843. 356 pp. Fldg map, frontis. Occas foxing, sl marg staining. Contemp half calf. *(Reese)* **$500 [≃£312]**

Wakefield, Edward
- An Account of Ireland, Statistical and Political. London: Longmans, 1812. 2 vols. 4to. 762; 838,index pp. Map, fldg chart. Half calf. *(Emerald Isle)* **£450 [≃$720]**
- New Zealand after Fifty Years. New York & London: Cassell, [1889]. Tall 8vo. ix,236,26 advt pp. Fldg map, 27 ills. Orig pict cloth.
(Schoyer) **$85 [≃£53]**

Wakefield, Priscilla
- The Juvenile Travellers; containing the Remarks of a Family during a Tour through ... Europe ... Ninth Edition. London: for Darton, Harvey & Darton, 1813. 12mo. xii,419,[25] pp. No map (probably not called for). Contemp sheep, hinges cracked, spine ends defective. *(Claude Cox)* **£15 [≃$24]**
- The Juvenile Travellers; containing the Remarks of a Family during a Tour through the Principal States and Kingdoms of Europe. London: for Darton, Harvey & Darton, 1815. 11th edn. 8vo. xii,[ii],422,[22] pp. Fldg hand cold map. Contemp calf, rebacked.
(Claude Cox) **£30 [≃$48]**

Wakefield, W.
- Our Life and Travels in India. London: Sampson Low, 1878. 8vo. xii,452,24 advt pp. Frontis. Orig bndg.
(Bates & Hindmarch) **£30 [≃$48]**

Waldmeier, Theophilus
- The Autobiography of Theophilus Waldmeier, Missionary. Being an Account of Ten Years' Life in Abyssinia & Sixteen Years in Syria. London & Leominster: Partridge & Co, [ca 1886]. 8vo. xiv,339 pp. Frontis, plates. Orig cloth, sl worn.
(Terramedia) **$100 [≃£62]**

Walker, George
- The Costume of Yorkshire in 1814 ... Edited by Edward Hailstone. Leeds: 1885. One of 100 with the plates on japan paper. Folio. 40

cold plates. Occas spotting to text. Rec vellum, gilt spine, orig vellum front cvr laid down on front bd, t.e.g.
(Spelman) **£450 [≃$720]**

Walker, Jeanie Mort
- Life of Capt. Joseph Fry, the Cuban Martyr. Hartford: 1875. 589 pp. Ills. Orig dec cloth gilt. *(Reese)* **$60 [≃£37]**

Walker, John
- The Universal Gazetteer ... Second Edition ... London: Ogilvy & Son, J. Walker ..., 1798. 8vo. Ca 800 pp. 14 fldg maps. New cloth & bds. *(Schoyer)* **$150 [≃£93]**

Wallace, Alfred Russell
- Island Life. London: 1880. 1st edn. 8vo. xvii,526 pp. Ills. Orig cloth.
(Baldwin) **£120 [≃$192]**
- Island Life. London: 1892. 2nd rvsd edn. 8vo. xx, 563 pp. 26 maps & ills. Orig cloth, trifle used. *(Wheldon & Wesley)* **£75 [≃$120]**
- The Malay Archipelago. The Land of the Orang-Utan, and the Bird of Paradise. London: 1869. 2nd edn. 2 vols. 8vo. 9 maps, 51 ills. Blue levant half mor gilt, t.e.g.
(Wheldon & Wesley) **£120 [≃$192]**
- The Malay Archipelago. London: 1883. Cr 8vo. xvi,653 pp. Maps & ills. Lacks the route map & plate 'Wallace's Standard Wing'. Signs of use, margs of plates waterstained. Orig cloth, somewhat used.
(Wheldon & Wesley) **£20 [≃$32]**
- The Malay Archipelago ... London: Macmillan, 1894. 12mo. xvii,515 pp. 10 maps, 8 plates. Orig green cloth, rubbed.
(Adelson) **$70 [≃£43]**
- The Malay Archipelago. The Land of the Orang-Utan and the Bird of Paradise. A Narrative of Travel ... London: Macmillan, 1894. New edn. Sm 8vo. 525 pp. Fldg cold map, other maps & plates. Orig green cloth gilt. *(Terramedia)* **$48 [≃£30]**
- The Malay Archipelago, the Land of the Orang-Utan and the Bird of Paradise ... London: 1902. 8vo. [xx],515 pp. 10 maps, 8 plates, 43 text ills. Orig cloth.
(Bow Windows) **£75 [≃$120]**
- The Malay Archipelago, the Land of the Orang-Utan and the Bird of Paradise ... London: 1906. 8vo. [xx],515,[1] pp. 10 maps, 8 plates, 43 text ills. Orig cloth.
(Bow Windows) **£48 [≃$76]**
- My Life. A Record of Events and Opinions. New Edition, Corrected and Revised. London: Chapman & Hall, 1908. 8vo. xii,408 pp. Facs letters, ports, ills. Orig green cloth, faded & rubbed. *(Blackwell's)* **£25 [≃$40]**

- A Narrative of Travels on the Amazon and Rio Negro, with an Account of the Native Tribes. Second Edition. London: Ward Lock, 1889. 8vo. xvi,363,4 advt pp. 16 maps & ills. Orig cloth, sl rubbed.
(Claude Cox) £20 [≈ $32]
- Tropical Nature, and Other Essays. London: Macmillan, 1878. 1st edn. 8vo. xiii,356 pp, advt leaf. 1 sgntr sl loose. Orig green cloth blocked in black, gilt lettered spine.
(Bickersteth) £125 [≈ $200]

Wallace, Sir Donald Mackenzie
- Russia. New and Enlarged Edition ... London: Cassell, 1905. 2 vols. 8vo. 456; 487 pp. 2 maps, port. Sl foxing. Orig blue cloth.
(Piccadilly) £24 [≈ $38]

Wallace, H.F.
- Stalks Abroad. London: 1908. 8vo. Ills. Orig bndg.
(Grayling) £60 [≈ $96]

Wallace, R.G.
- Memoirs of India: Comprising a Brief Geographical Account of The East Indies ... Designed for the Use of Young Men going out to India. London: Longman ..., 1824. Only edn. 8vo. xxii,504,16 advt pp. Sl soiled at end. New period style half calf, uncut.
(Young's) £120 [≈ $192]

Waller, Zephaniah
- Seven Letters from an Emigrant, to his Friends in England; containing Remarks on ... the United States ... Diss: ptd by E.E. Abbott ..., 1831. 1st edn. 8vo. 38 pp. Rec wraps.
(Burmester) £300 [≈ $480]

Wallis, Mary Davis
- Life in Feejee, or Five Years among the Cannibals ... Boston: 1851. 422 pp. Cloth, top of rear hinge cracking, spine ends worn.
(Reese) $200 [≈ £125]

Walpole, Robert
- Memoirs relating to European & Asiatic Turkey, and Other Countries of the East: edited from Mss. Journals by Walpole. Second Edition. London: Longman ..., 1818. 4to. xxii, 615 pp. Fldg & other engvs & maps. Rec rebound in tan qtr leather, cloth sides.
(Piccadilly) £180 [≈ $288]

Walter, Richard
- A Voyage round the World ... see Anson, George.

Walters, J.C.
- Romantic Cheshire. Illustrated by Frank Greenwood. London: (1930). 1st edn. Tall 8vo. 192 pp. 23 tinted plates, text ills, endpaper maps. Some foxing. Orig cloth.
(Bow Windows) £36 [≈ $57]

Wansey, Henry
- The Journal of an Excursion to the United States of North America, in the Summer of 1794 ... Salisbury: J. Easton ..., 1796. 1st edn. 8vo. xiii,290,[12] pp. Profile of Washington (laid down & reduced), 1 aquatint view. Top inner crnrs stained. New half calf.
(Young's) £85 [≈ $136]

Warburton, Eliot (ed.)
- Hochelaga; or, England in the New World. London: Colburn ..., 1846. 2nd edn. 2 vols. xiv,318,24 advt; iv,368 pp. Frontis. Rather spotted in places, occas heavily. Orig cloth gilt, a little faded & chipped.
(Hollett) £120 [≈ $192]

Warburton, George Drought
- The Conquest of Canada. London: Bentley, 1849. 1st edn. 2 vols. Half-title & errata slip in each vol. Contemp sprinkled calf gilt, hinges rubbed, ex-Signet Library.
(Claude Cox) £45 [≈ $72]

Warburton, Sir Robert
- Eighteen Years in the Khyber 1879-1898. London: Murray, 1900. 8vo. 344 pp. Port frontis, fldg map, 16 photo ills. Orig bndg, hd of spine split, dull.
(Bates & Hindmarch) £55 [≈ $88]

Ward, Herbert
- Five Years with the Congo Cannibals. New York: Robert Bonner's Sons, 1890. 1st edn. Roy 8vo. 308 pp. Num engvd ills. Orig bndg.
(Parmer) $275 [≈ £171]
- Five Years with the Congo Cannibals. New York: Robert Bonner's Sons, 1890. Lge 8vo. 308 pp. 2 maps, 90 ills. Orig pict cloth, hinges cracked.
(Schoyer) $40 [≈ £25]
- A Voice from the Congo, Comprising Stories, Anecdotes, and Descriptive Notes. New York: Scribner's, 1910. 1st edn. 8vo. xvi, 330 pp. Frontis, num plates. Orig cloth gilt, sl worn.
(Terramedia) $100 [≈ £62]
- A Voice from the Congo. Comprising Stories, Anecdotes, and Descriptive Notes. New York: Scribner's, 1910. 1st Amer edn. 8vo. xvi,330 pp. Frontis, 71 plates. Orig gilt dec cloth, t.e.g.
(Schoyer) $45 [≈ £28]

Ward, J.S.M. & Stirling, W.G.
- The Hung Society or the Society of Heaven and Earth. London: Baskerville Press, 1925.

Ltd edn. 3 vols. xv,180; viii,196; vi,148 pp. Cold frontises, plates (some cold), text ills. Orig cloth gilt.   *(Lyon)* **£185 [≈ $296]**

Ward, John
- Our Sudan. Its Pyramids and Progress. London: Murray, 1905. Sm 4to. xxiv,361,1 advt pp. Fldg map, num ills. Orig dec cloth, t.e.g., spine sl rubbed. *(Schoyer)* **$60 [≈ £37]**
- Our Sudan: Its Pyramids & Progress. London: Murray, 1905. Sm 4to. 361 pp. Num plates & ills. Orig pict orange cloth, ex-lib, crack at top edge of spine.
(Terramedia) **$100 [≈ £62]**

Ward, M.N.
- Female Life among the Mormons. A Narrative of Many Years Personal Experience. London: Routledge ..., 1855. 16th thousand. 8vo. vi, 247 pp. Frontis. Contemp black qtr mor.
(Young's) **£55 [≈ $88]**

Wardrop, A.E.
- Days and Nights with Indian Big Game. London: Macmillan, 1923. 8vo. 212 pp. Num plates. Orig pict blue cloth, t.e.g., bottom edges of binding sl rubbed & spotted.
(Terramedia) **$76 [≈ £47]**
- Days and Nights with Indian Big Game. London: Macmillan, 1923. 8vo. ix,212 pp. Frontis, 23 ills. Orig dark blue cloth gilt.
(Bates & Hindmarch) **£50 [≈ $80]**

Warner, Charles Dudley
- In the Levant. Boston: Houghton Mifflin, 1893. 2 vols. 8vo. xiii,290; 291-568 pp. Photogravure ills. Cloth. *(Zeno)* **£75 [≈ $120]**
- In the Levant. Boston & New York: 1895. 2 vols. 8vo. 290; 568 pp. 2 frontis, other tissued plates. Orig red & green cloth.
(Terramedia) **$40 [≈ £25]**
- Mummies and Moslems. Hartford: American Publ Co, 1876. 1st edn. 8vo. 477 pp. Frontis. Orig cloth.   *(Terramedia)* **$50 [≈ £31]**

Warner, L.
- The Long Old Road in China. New York: 1926. 1st edn. 168 pp. 3 maps, ills. Orig bndg, upper right hand crnr & last few pp dampstained, sl faded. Dw.
(Trophy Room Books) **$125 [≈ £78]**

Warner, Richard
- An History of the Abbey of Glaston, and of the Town of Glastonbury. Bath: 1826. 1st edn. One of 250. 4to. 20 plates. Contemp calf, upper jnt split. B'plate of Stoke Rochford Library.   *(Robertshaw)* **£60 [≈ $96]**

Warren, G.K.
- Explorations in the Dacota Country, in the Year 1855. Washington: 1856. 79,[6] pp. 3 fldg maps. Disbound. *(Reese)* **$300 [≈ £187]**

Warren, T. Robinson
- Dust and Foam; or, Three Oceans and Two Continents; Being Ten Years' Wanderings in Mexico, South America, Sandwich Islands, the East and West Indies, Australia and Polynesia. New York: 1859. 397,[5] pp. 2 sgntrs starting. Orig cloth, spine ends frayed.
(Reese) **$150 [≈ £93]**

Warriner, Francis
- Cruise of the United States Frigate Potomac round the World, during the Years 1831-34 ... New York: 1835. 366,advt pp. Plates. Foxed, a few sgntrs starting, rear free endsheet excised. Orig cloth, rubbed & worn.
(Reese) **$200 [≈ £125]**

Waters, David
- The Art of Navigation in England in Elizabethan and Early Stuart Times. London: Hollis & Carter, (1958). Roy 8vo. 87 plates, 43 diags. Orig cloth.   *(Stewart)* **£45 [≈ $72]**

Waterton, Charles
- Wanderings in South America, the North-West of the United States, and the Antilles in the Years 1812, 1816, 1820 and 1824. London: 1825. 1st edn. 4to. vii,326 pp. Half-title. Frontis. Some stains & annotations. Half calf, trifle used.
(Wheldon & Wesley) **£150 [≈ $240]**
- Wanderings in South America ... London: 1836. 3rd edn. 12mo. vii,341 pp. Frontis. Occas fox or smudge mark. Orig polished calf gilt, jnts worn.   *(Reese)* **$100 [≈ £62]**

Watson, Robert Spence
- A Visit to Wazan, the Sacred City of Morocco. London: Macmillan, 1880. 1st edn. 8vo. xv,328 pp. Fldg map, 12 ills. Lib marks. Orig cloth, edges sl rubbed, spine ends sl frayed.   *(Worldwide Antiqu'n)* **$65 [≈ £40]**

Watt, Mrs Stuart
- In the Heart of Savagedom. Reminiscences of Life & Adventure during a Quarter Century ... in the Wilds of East Equatorial Africa. London: Marshall Bros, [ca 1910]. 2nd edn. 8vo. 472 pp. 70 photo plates. Frontis loose. Orig pict maroon cloth, sl worn.
(Terramedia) **$50 [≈ £31]**

Watts, W.
- The Seats of the Nobility and Gentry in a

Collection of the Most Interesting and Picturesque Views. London: W. Watts, 1779. 1st edn. Oblong 4to. 84 plates. Occas light foxing. Rebound in dark blue mor, gilt spine.
(Gough) £350 [≃ $560]

Watts, William Lord
- Across the Vatna Jokull; or, Scenes in Iceland; being a Description of hitherto Unknown Regions. London: Longman, 1876. 1st edn. 8vo. Errata leaf. 2 maps, 2 plates. Good ex-lib. Orig cloth, discold.
(Hannas) £50 [≃ $80]
- Snioland: or, Iceland, its Jokulls and Fjalls. London: Longman, 1875. 1st edn. 8vo. Fldg map, 12 mtd photos. Orig cloth, uncut.
(Hannas) £110 [≃ $176]

Wauters, Alphonse Jules
- Stanley's Emin Pasha Expedition. Philadelphia: Lippincott, 1890. Sm 8vo. xvii, 378,2 advt pp. Fldg map, 33 ills. Orig pict gilt cloth, hinges sl cracked, centre pulled.
(Schoyer) $40 [≃ £25]

Wavell, A.J.B.
- A Modern Pilgrim in Mecca and a Siege in Sanaa. London: Constable, 1912. 1st edn. 8vo. ix,349 pp. Fldg map, 7 plates. Orig cloth, spine ends frayed, sl soiled, lib number on spine. *(Worldwide Antiqu'n)* $45 [≃ £28]

Webber, Charles W.
- Romance of Natural History; or, Wild Scenes and Wild Hunters. Philadelphia: 1852. 610 pp. Frontis, ills. Some foxing. Orig blind-stamped cloth, gilt spine, sunned, frayed at extremities. *(Reese)* $200 [≃ £125]

Webster, John White
- A Description of the Island of St. Michael, comprising an Account of its Geological Structure; with Remarks on the other Azores or Western Islands. Boston: 1821. Only edn. 8vo. 2 fldg maps, 2 plates (some offsetting), fldg table. Mod half calf antique.
(Trebizond) $265 [≃ £165]

Webster, Kimball
- The Gold Seekers of '49. A Personal Narrative of the Overland Trail and Adventures in California and Oregon from 1849 to 1854. Manchester: 1917. 240 pp. Port, plates. Orig pict cloth.
(Reese) $125 [≃ £78]

Webster, William Henry Bayley
- Narrative of a Voyage to the Southern Atlantic Ocean, in the Years 1828, 29, 30 ... in H.M. Sloop Chanticleer ... London:

Bentley, 1834. 1st edn. 2 vols. 8vo. 399; 398 pp. 2 maps, 5 plates (foxed). Lacks half-titles. Rebound in bds, using orig spines.
(Schoyer) $550 [≃ £343]

Weeks, John H.
- Among Congo Cannibals ... Thirty Years' Sojourn Among the Boloki & Other Congo Tribes ... London: Seeley & Co, 1913. 8vo. 351 pp. Fldg map, num photo plates. Orig cloth, spine sl sunned.
(Terramedia) $100 [≃ £62]
- Among Congo Cannibals ... Thirty Years' Sojourn Among the Boloki and other Congo Tribes ... London: Seeley Service, 1913. 8vo. 352 pp. Fldg map, 54 ills. Orig pict cloth.
(Schoyer) $40 [≃ £25]
- Among the Primitive Bakongo. A Record of Thirty Years' Close Intercourse with the Bakongo and Other Tribes of Equatorial Africa ... Philadelphia: Lippincott, 1914. 1st Amer edn. 8vo. xvi,318 pp. Fldg map, ills. Stained in a few places. Orig red cloth, sl soiled. *(Karmiole)* $75 [≃ £46]
- Among the Primitive Bakongo. A Record of Thirty Years' Close Intercourse with the Bakongo and Other Tribes of Equatorial Africa ... London: Seeley, Service, 1914. 8vo. xvi, 318 pp. Fldg map, num photo plates. Orig pict red orange cloth.
(Terramedia) $100 [≃ £62]

Welch, C.
- History of the Tower Bridge and of other Bridges over the Thames built by the Corporation of London. London: Smith, Elder, 1894. 4to. 284 pp. Half leather, uncut, sl frayed. *(Book House)* £120 [≃ $192]

Welch, Charles
- Modern History of the City of London: a Record of Municipal and Social Progress from 1760 to the Present Day. London: 1896. Large Paper. Imperial 4to. xi,492 pp. Errata slip. Num ills. Orig cloth, t.e.g., sl wear at edges & crnrs, some scratching on cvrs.
(Coombes) £25 [≃ $40]

Weld, Isaac
- Travels through the States of North America, and the Provinces of Upper and Lower Canada. London: John Stockdale, 1799. 1st edn. Folio. [24],464 pp. Lge cold fldg map, 3 other maps, 10 plates. Some pp reprd. Later cloth. *(Jenkins)* $375 [≃ £234]

Wellbeloved, Charles
- Eburacum, or York Under the Romans. York: Sunter & Sotheran, 1842. 1st edn. Tall 8vo. x,[2],168 pp. Frontis map, 17 litho plates.

Stamp on title verso. Orig cloth, spine relaid.
(Spelman) **£16 [≈ $25]**

Wellby, M.
- Twixt Sirdar and Menelik. New York: 1901. 409 pp. 55 ills. Orig pict cloth.
(Trophy Room Books) **$275 [≈ £171]**

Weller, Charles H.
- Athens and its Monuments. New York: Macmillan, 1913. 8vo. 412,advt pp. Frontis, num ills. Orig pict blue cloth, t.e.g.
(Terramedia) **$40 [≈ £25]**

Wellman, W.
- The Aerial Age. A Thousand Miles by Airship over the Atlantic Ocean. Airship Voyages over the Polar Sea ... New York: 1911. 1st edn. 8vo. 448 pp. Frontis, 48 plates. Lacks front endpaper. Orig cloth gilt.
(Berkelouw) **$100 [≈ £62]**

Wells, Edward
- An Historical Geography of the Old and New Testament. Oxford: Clarendon Press, 1801. 2 vols. 8vo. 1 leaf loosening. Contemp qtr calf, vellum tips. 3 pen & wash drawings tipped in.
(Waterfield's) **£65 [≈ $104]**

Wells, H.P.
- City Boys in the Woods, or a Trapping Venture in Maine. 1890. Num engvs. Orig pict cloth gilt.
(Grayling) **£60 [≈ $96]**

Weppner, Margaretha
- The North Star and the Southern Cross: being ... a Two Years' Journey round the World. London [& Albany]: 1876. 2 vols. x, 505; vii,504 pp. Engvd title. Orig cloth gilt, some soiling & wear to extremities.
(Reese) **$125 [≈ £78]**

West, Thomas
- The Antiquities of Furness ... London: T. Spilsbury for the author ..., 1774. 1st edn. 4to. [xx], lvi, 288, 3A-3R4 pp. Fldg plan, 3 plates. Contemp calf gilt, edges rubbed, hinges cracked.
(Hollett) **£220 [≈ $352]**

A Western Journey with Mr. Emerson ...
- See Thayer, James Bradley.

Westgarth, William
- Victoria and the Australian Gold Mines in 1857; with Notes on the Overland Route from Australia, via Suez. London: 1857. xvi,466, advt pp. 3 maps (2 fldg). Orig cloth, worn, a bit frayed at spine ends, front hinge broken.
(Reese) **$425 [≈ £265]**

Weston, Edward
- My Camera on Point Lobos. 30 Photographs and Excerpts from E.W.'s Daybook. Yosemite National Park: Virginia Adams; Boston: Houghton Mifflin, 1950. Folio. 79 pp. 30 Weston photos. Spiral-bound in stiff bds, edges sl rubbed.
(Karmiole) **$300 [≈ £187]**

Weston, Edward & Charis Wilson
- California and the West. A U.S. Camera Book with Ninety-Six Photographs. New York: Duell, Sloan & Pearce, (1940). 2nd printing. 4to. [xii],128 pp. 96 photo plates. Orig black cloth. Lightly worn & soiled dw. Inscrbd by Weston.
(Karmiole) **$500 [≈ £312]**

Wey, Francis
- Rome. Containing Three Hundred and Forty-Five Engravings on Wood ... With an Introduction by W.W. Story. London: Chapman & Hall, 1875. Lge 4to. xxi,339 pp. W'engvs throughout. Orig cloth, blocked in gold & black, t.e.g., extremities sl rubbed.
(Claude Cox) **£35 [≈ $56]**

Whately, Richard
- On the Present State of Egypt. Compiled from the Unpublished Journals of Recent Travellers. A Lecture. London: John W. Parker, 1858. 25,6 advt pp. Rec wraps.
(C.R. Johnson) **£25 [≈ $40]**

Wheater, W.
- Some Historic Mansions of Yorkshire and their Associations ... With ... Etched Illustrations ... Leeds: Richard Jackson, 1888-89. One of 150. 2 vols. 4to. 50 plates. Some spotting. 1 gathering loose. Contemp qtr mor, rubbed, backstrip split at hd.
(Waterfield's) **£65 [≈ $104]**

Wheeler, C.H.
- Ten Years on the Euphrates; or, Primitive Missionary Policy Illustrated. Boston & New York: American Tract Society, 1868. 1st edn. Sm 8vo. xx,15-330 pp. 2 fldg maps, 3 plates. Sl foxed. Orig cloth, edges sl rubbed, spine ends sl frayed.
(Worldwide Antiqu'n) **$75 [≈ £46]**

Wheeler, Daniel
- Extracts from the Letters and Journals of Daniel Wheeler now engaged in a Religious Visit to the Inhabitants of some of the Islands of the Pacific Ocean, Van Diemen's Land, and New South Wales. Part 1. London: Harvey & Darton, 1839. 8vo. Orig cloth.
(Waterfield's) **£65 [≈ $104]**

Wheeler, George M.
- Annual Report upon the Geographical Explorations & Surveys West of the One Hundredth Meridian ... Washington: GPO, 1875. 8vo. 196 pp. Fldg map, fldg chart, sev plates. Lower crnrs damp stained. Mod buckram, orig wraps bound in.
(Terramedia) **$50 [≈£31]**
- Preliminary Report Concerning Explorations and Surveys Principally in Nevada and Arizona. Washington: GPO, 1872. 1st edn. Sm folio. 96 pp. Lge fldg map. Orig green cloth, sl worn.
(M & S Rare Books) **$250 [≈£156]**

Wheeler, J. Talboys
- Early Records of British India: A History of the English Settlements in India. London: 1878. 1st edn. 8vo. Orig green cloth.
(Robertshaw) **£25 [≈$40]**

Wheeler, Lucy
- Chertsey Abbey: an Existence of the Past. London: 1905. Large Paper. 8vo. xvi,232 pp. 23 ills inc maps. Orig pict cloth, cvrs spotted.
(Coombes) **£15 [≈$24]**

Wheeler, R.E.M.
- Maiden Castle, Dorset. London: 1943. 1st edn. 4to. Num plates & fldg plans. Orig cloth, partly faded, 2 sm spots to cvrs.
(Ambra) **£55 [≈$88]**

Wheelright, H.W.
- Ten Years in Sweden ... By "An Old Bushman". Landscape, Climate, Domestic Life, Forests, Mines, Agriculture, Field Sports and Fauna of Scandinavia. London: 1865. 8vo. Contemp half mor, spine reprd, crnrs rubbed.
(Grayling) **£90 [≈$144]**
- Ten Years in Sweden: being a Description of the Landscape, Climate, Domestic Life, Forests, Mines, Agriculture, Field Sports, and Fauna of Scandinavia. By "An Old Bushman". London: 1865. 1st edn. 8vo. xvi, 592,[8 advt] pp. Half-title. Rec paper bds.
(Fenning) **£55 [≈$88]**

Whellan & Co., T.
- History and Topography of the City of York; The Ainsty Wapentake; and the East Riding of Yorkshire. Beverley: 1855. 2 vols. 8vo. xiv,694; x,676 pp. Mod half mor.
(Hollett) **£60 [≈$96]**

Whigham, Henry J.
- Manchuria and Korea. London: Isbister, 1904. 1st edn. 8vo. [8],245 pp, advt leaf. Map, 12 plates. Orig cloth gilt.
(Fenning) **£38.50 [≈$62]**

Whishaw, Bernard & Ellen
- Arabic Spain: Sidelights of Her History and Art. London: Smith, Elder, 1912. 8vo. 421 pp. Ills. Orig green cloth, lib labels neatly removed.
(Terramedia) **$75 [≈£46]**

Whitaker, J.
- The Deer-Parks and Paddocks of England. London: 1892. 8vo. Ills. Orig bndg.
(Grayling) **£50 [≈$80]**
- A Descriptive List of the Deer-Parks and Paddocks of England. London: 1892. 8vo. Ills. Orig cloth.
(Grayling) **£55 [≈$88]**

Whitaker, Thomas Dunham
- The History and Antiquities of the Deanery of Craven, in the County of York ... London: Nichols & Son, sold by T. Payne ..., 1805. 1st edn. xii,437,14 pp. Port frontis, 36 plates (2 hand cold, many tinted), num pedigrees. Mod half calf, old label re-used.
(Hollett) **£195 [≈$312]**
- The History and Antiquities of the Deanery of Craven in the County of York. London: & Halifax, 1812. Lge 4to. Port frontis, litho title, plates, pedigrees. Orig bds, rebacked retaining most of orig spine, crnrs & edges worn.
(Hollett) **£135 [≈$216]**
- The History and Antiquities of the Deanery of Craven in the County of York ... Third Edition with many additions and corrections. Edited by A.W. Morant. Leeds: 1878. 4to. Addtnl chromolitho title, num plates. Mod qtr calf, vellum tips. mor label.
(Waterfield's) **£200 [≈$320]**
- An History of the Original Parish of Whalley and Honor of Clitheroe ... London: 1806. 2nd edn, with addtns. 8vo. 483,9 pp. Fldg map frontis, 27 plates, 11 pedigrees. Sm tear to map, some offsetting from plates, final ff browned. Qtr calf gilt, rubbed & worn.
(Hollett) **£140 [≈$224]**
- Loidis and Elmet ... Ducatus Leodiensis ... Leeds: T. Davison & B. Dewhurst, 1816. 1st edns. 2 vols. 404,ii; xvi,xvii,261, 123, 159,12 pp. 2 hand cold & 63 engvd plates, 20 vignettes, 31 pedigrees. Occas sl spotting. Contemp half calf, gilt spines, reprd.
(Gough) **£250 [≈$400]**

White, Arthur Silva
- The Expansion of Egypt under Anglo-Egyptian Condominium. London: Methuen, 1899. 8vo. 473 pp. Fldg cold maps. Orig red cloth.
(Terramedia) **$75 [≈£46]**
- The Expansion of Egypt under Anglo-Egyptian Condominium. London: Methuen,

1899. 1st edn. 8vo. xv,483 pp. 4 cold fldg maps (2 with tears). Tape repr on 2 pp. Orig cloth, mostly unopened, dec spine faded.
(Schoyer) **$60 [≈£37]**

- From Sphinx to Oracle. Through the Libyan Desert to the Oasis of Jupiter Ammon. London: Hurst & Blackett, 1899. 8vo. xv,277 pp. 2 cold fldg maps, 21 plates, 36 text ills. Tape repr to 1 leaf. Orig gilt pict cloth.
(Schoyer) **$60 [≈£37]**

White, Ernest William
- Cameos from the Silver-Land; or the Experiences of a Young Naturalist in the Argentine Republic. London: Van Voorst, 1881. 1st edn. 2 vols. 436; 527 pp. Lge cold fldg map. Orig cloth. *(Jenkins)* **$225 [≈£140]**

White, George Francis
- Views in India ... London & Paris: Fisher, Son & Co, 1836. 1st edn. Folio. 137,index, subscribers pp. Engvd vignette title, 29 plates. Occas foxing. Contemp three qtr mor, t.e.g., a trifle rubbed & darkened.
(Reese) **$600 [≈£375]**

White, Gilbert
- The Natural History and Antiquities of Selborne. London: 1789. 1st edn. 4to. v, title-page with vignette, 468, [2] pp, errata sheet. 6 plates. Later red mor. Qtr mor case.
(Baldwin) **£900 [≈$1,440]**
- The Natural History and Antiquities of Selborne. London: 1789; reptd Scolar Press, 1970. Facs of the 1st edn. 4to. Plates. Red three qtr Levant mor gilt, t.e.g.
(Bow Windows) **£155 [≈$248]**
- The Natural History and Antiquities of Selborne. New Edition, to which are added The Naturalist's Calendar; Observations ... Poems. London: 1813. Mitford's edn. 4to. x, title vignettes, 585 pp. 9 plates (1 hand cold). 1 plate a little spotted. Later calf gilt.
(Baldwin) **£175 [≈$280]**
- The Natural History of Selborne, to which are added the Naturalists Calendar, Miscellaneous Observations, and Poems. London: 1822. 2 vols. 8vo. 4 plates (1 cold). Buckram, t.e.g. *(Henly)* **£120 [≈$192]**
- The Natural History of Selborne ... London: 1835. Captain T. Brown's 5th edn. 12mo. xii,356 pp. Frontis, 1 plate, 2 ills. Some v light marg staining & foxing. Orig bds, new spine label. *(Baldwin)* **£25 [≈$40]**
- The Natural History of Selborne ... London: 1837. New edn by E.T. Bennett. 8vo. xxiv,640 pp. 46 engvs. Name on title. Orig cloth. *(Baldwin)* **£40 [≈$64]**
- The Natural History of Selborne ... London:

1844. Harting's 3rd edn. 8vo. xxii, 568 pp. Engvs by Bewick & others. Minor spotting. Contemp prize tree calf, hinges reprd.
(Baldwin) **£40 [≈$64]**
- Natural History of Selborne. London: 1853. Brown's 9th edn. 12mo. xii,348 pp. Addtnl title with hand cold vignette, 14 hand cold plates. Orig bndg, a.e.g. *(Henly)* **£25 [≈$40]**
- The Natural History of Selborne. Edited by J.E. Harting. London: 1875. 1st Harting edn. 8vo. xx,532 pp. 60 ills. Orig cloth gilt, a.e.g.
(Henly) **£40 [≈$64]**
- The Natural History of Selborne ... London: 1876. The standard edn of E.T. Bennett rvsd by J.E. Harting. 2nd edn. 8vo. xxii, 532 pp. Bewick engvs. Contemp prize calf, 1 hinge reprd, 1 cracked but sound.
(Baldwin) **£40 [≈$64]**
- The Natural History of Selborne ... London: 1877. Edited by T. Bell. 2 vols. 8vo. Ills. Orig cloth, sl worn & faded.
(Baldwin) **£95 [≈$152]**
- Natural History and Antiquities of Selborne. London: 1883. 6th Buckland edn. Cr 8vo. xxix,480,32 pp. Num ills. Orig cloth, partly unopened. *(Henly)* **£20 [≈$32]**
- The Natural History of Selborne. Edited by J.E. Harting. London: 1887. 5th Harting edn. 8vo. xxii,568 pp. 60 ills. Orig pict cloth gilt, a.e.g. *(Henly)* **£30 [≈$48]**
- The Natural History of Selborne. Edited by J.E. Harting. London: 1890. 8th Harting edn. 8vo. xxii,568 pp. 60 ills. Orig pict cloth gilt, a.e.g. Thomas Ashton's b'plate.
(Henly) **£35 [≈$56]**
- The Natural History of Selborne. London: 1898. Jesse & Jardine's edn. Cr 8vo. xxiv, 416,32 pp. Frontis, 40 hand cold plates. Orig cloth. *(Henly)* **£30 [≈$48]**
- The Natural History and Antiquities of Selborne ... Edited by R. Bowdler Sharpe. London: 1900. One of 160 Large Paper, signed. 2 vols. Thick 4to. Num ills by Keulemans, Railton & Sullivan. Some tissues in vol 1 browned. Vellum gilt, t.e.g., vol 1 spine dulled. *(Hollett)* **£375 [≈$600]**
- The Natural History and Antiquities of Selborne. Edited by R. Bowdler Sharpe. London: 1900. 2 vols. 8vo. 99 plates by Keulemans, Railton & Sullivan, 69 text ills, inc 2 facs letters. Half green mor gilt.
(Wheldon & Wesley) **£180 [≈$288]**
- The Natural History and Antiquities of Selborne. Edited by R. Bowdler Sharpe. London: 1900. 2 vols. 8vo. 99 plates by Keulemans, Railton & Sullivan, 69 text ills, inc 2 facs letters. Orig cloth, t.e.g., 2 faint stains on vol 2 spine.
(Wheldon & Wesley) **£120 [≈$192]**

- The Natural History of Selborne. London: 1902. 1st Kearton edn. Roy 8vo. xvi,294 pp. 124 ills. Orig green cloth gilt.
(Henly) £25 [≈ $40]
- The Works in Natural History ... Natural History of Selborne; The Naturalist's Calendar ... added A Calendar and Observations by W. Markwick. London: 1802. 2 vols. 8vo. 4 plates (2 cold). Contemp calf. The 2nd edn of White's Selborne.
(Wheldon & Wesley) £200 [≈ $320]

White, John
- Sketches from America ... Canada ... The Rocky Mountains ... The Irish in America ... London: Sampson Low, 1870. 373,advt pp. Orig purple cloth, faded. Author's pres copy.
(Emerald Isle) £55 [≈ $88]

White, Stewart Edward
- The Land of Footprints [Hunting adventures, mostly in East Africa]. Garden City & New York: Doubleday, 1912. 1st edn. 12mo. x,440 pp. Num photo plates. Orig pict dark green cloth, spine lettering sl rubbed.
(Terramedia) $40 [≈ £25]
- The Land of Footprints. Garden City: Doubleday Page, 1912. 8vo. x,440 pp. Num photo ills. Orig pict cloth.
(Parmer) $50 [≈ £31]
- The Rediscovered Country. Garden City: Doubleday, Page, 1915. 1st edn. 8vo. xiii, [2],3-358 pp. Map (sl worn), ills. Orig gilt dec green cloth.
(Parmer) $45 [≈ £28]

White, Revd T.H.
- Fragments of Italy and the Rhineland. London: William Pickering, 1841. 1st edn. 8vo. Red & black title. Errata leaf. Orig purple cloth, paper label rubbed & chipped, hd of spine frayed.
(Clark) £36 [≈ $57]

White, Walter
- To Mont Blanc and Back Again. London: 1854. 12mo. xvi,208 pp. Half mor, some edge wear.
(Reese) $50 [≈ £31]

White, William
- History, Gazetteer and Directory of the County of Devon including the City of Exeter ... Sheffield: 1890. 3rd edn. 8vo. Lacks map as usual. Orig cloth, front inner hinge broken with cloth partly split, damp mark to back cvr.
(Ambra) £74 [≈ $118]

Whitehead, C.E.
- The Campfires of the Everglades. Or Wild Sports of the South. 1891. 8vo. Ills. Orig cloth, spine sl faded & rubbed.

(Grayling) £80 [≈ $128]

Whitehead, J.
- Exploration of Mount Kina Balu, North Borneo. London: 1893. Folio. xii,317 pp. 32 plates (14 cold), 21 text figs. Sl foxed at beginning. Orig dec cloth, front cvr trifle warped.
(Wheldon & Wesley) £700 [≈ $1,120]

Whitelocke, Bulstrode
- A Journal of the Swedish Embassy, in the Years 1653 and 1654 from the Commonwealth of England, Scotland, and Ireland. London: Becket & De Hondt, 1772. 1st edn. 2 vols. 4to. Half-titles. Contemp calf, spines v worn.
(Hannas) £85 [≈ $136]

Whitney, Caspar
- On Snow-Shoes to the Barren Grounds - 2800 Miles after Musk-Oxen and Wood-Bison. London: Osgood McIlvaine, 1896. 1st edn. 8vo. x,324 pp. 114 ills. Orig pict cloth gilt, t.e.g., trifle worn & bumped.
(Hollett) £120 [≈ $192]

Whitney, Casper
- Jungle Trails and Jungle People. Travel, Adventure and Observation in the Far East. New York: Scribners, 1905. 1st edn. 8vo. 310 pp. Frontis, num plates. Orig pict blue cloth, a few spine letters rubbed out.
(Terramedia) $45 [≈ £28]

Whitney, Harry
- Hunting with the Eskimos. The Unique Record of a Sportsman's Year Among the Northernmost tribes ... New York: Century Co, 1910. 1st edn. 8vo. xvi,453 pp. Fldg map, frontis, num plates. Lower edge sl damp stained. Orig dec blue cloth gilt.
(Terramedia) $100 [≈ £62]

Whitworth, Charles, Lord
- An Account of Russia as it was in the Year 1710. Strawbery Hill Press: 1758. 8vo in 4s. Errata leaf at end. Title vignette. Faint off-set throughout. Contemp sprinkled calf gilt, lacks label, jnts cracking but firm, extremities v sl worn.
(Sanders) £285 [≈ $456]

Who's Who in China ...
- Who's Who in China: Biographies of Chinese. Containing the Pictures & Biographies of China's Best Known ... Leaders. Shanghai: China Weekly Review, [ca 1931]. 4th edn. 512,25 advt pp. Num photos. Discreet lib stamp. Orig cloth gilt.
(Lyon) £75 [≈ $120]

Whymper, Edward
- Scrambles Amongst the Alps. With Additional Material ... Revised & Edited by H.E.G. Tyndale. London: 1936. xi,393 pp. 5 fldg maps, port frontis, num ills. Endpapers v sl foxed. Top edge sl marked. Orig cloth, sl soiled, spine browned. *(Dillons)* £36 [≈ $57]

Wigram, Edgar T.A.
- Northern Spain. London: A. & C. Black Colour Books, Twenty Shilling Series, 1906. 1st edn. Fldg map, 75 cold plates. Orig dec cloth, t.e.g.　　*(Old Cathay)* £40 [≈ $64]
- Northern Spain. London: A. & C. Black Colour Books, Twenty Shilling Series, 1906. 1st edn. Fldg map, 75 cold plates. Orig dec cloth, t.e.g., spine sl rubbed.
　　　　　　　(Old Cathay) £38 [≈ $60]

Wilber, C.D.
- The Great Valleys and Prairies of Nebraska and the Northwest. Omaha: 1881. 3rd edn. 382, advt pp. Lge fldg map. Lib stamp & b'plate. Orig gilt dec cloth, hinges tender.
　　　　　　　(Reese) $85 [≈ £53]

Wilde, William R.
- The Beauties of the Boyne and its Tributary, the Blackwater. Dublin: McGlashan, 1850. 2nd edn, enlgd. Map, ills. Orig bndg, spine reprd. Author's pres copy.
　　　　　　　(Emerald Isle) £45 [≈ $72]

Wiley, William H. & Wiley, Sara King
- The Yosemite, Alaska, and the Yellowstone. London: Offices of "Engineering", [1893]. 4to. xx, 230 pp. 157 ills, maps. Orig blue cloth gilt, extremities sl rubbed. The dedicatee's copy. *(Karmiole)* $250 [≈ £156]

Wilhelm, Crown Prince of Germany
- From My Hunting Day Book. London: 1912. 8vo. Mtd cold frontis, num other mtd photo plates. Orig cloth, sl rubbed & faded.
　　　　　　　(Grayling) £40 [≈ $64]

Wilkes, Charles
- Narrative of the United States Exploring Expedition, during the Years 1838 ... Philadelphia: Lea & Blanchard, 1845. 1st trade edn. 5 vols text & atlas vol. Lge 4to. Collation as in Howes. Few minor tears & foxing Orig cloth, wear at extremities, some spine reprs.　*(Reese)* $2,500 [≈ £1,562]

Wilkes, J.J.
- Dalmatia. Cambridge: Harvard UP, 1969. 1st edn. 4to. xxvii,572 pp. Fldg map, frontis, 59 plates. Orig cloth. Dw.

　　　　　(Worldwide Antiqu'n) $65 [≈ £40]

Wilkin, Anthony
- Among the Berbers of Algeria. London: Fisher Unwin, 1900. 8vo. xiv,263,8 advt pp. Map, photo ills. Occas sl foxing. Orig gilt dec red cloth.　　*(Parmer)* $45 [≈ £28]
- Among the Berbers of Algeria. New York: [1900]. 8vo. 263 pp. Map, frontis, num photo plates. Orig gilt dec cloth, ft of spine sl stained & discold. *(Terramedia)* $75 [≈ £46]
- On the Nile with a Camera. New York & London: New Amsterdam Book Co, Fisher Unwin, 1897. 1st edn. 8vo. xv,238 pp. Frontis, num other photo plates & ills. Orig gilt dec blue cloth. *(Terramedia)* $75 [≈ £46]

Wilkinson, Henry
- Sketches of Scenery in the Basque Provinces of Spain, with a Selection of National Music ... London: Ackermann, 1838. Folio. vii,48 pp. 12 tinted litho plates. Some foxing. Orig cloth gilt, a.e.g., spine sunned, worn at extremities.　　*(Reese)* $1,250 [≈ £781]

Wilkinson, Hugh
- Sunny Lands and Seas. A Voyage in the S.S. Ceylon ... [India, China & Japan]. London: 1883. 8vo. 324 pp. Fldg map, num plates & ills. Orig cloth.　*(Terramedia)* $35 [≈ £21]

Wilkinson, Sir John Gardner
- The Manners and Customs of the Ancient Egyptians. A New Edition, Revised and Corrected by Samuel Birch. Boston: Cassino, 1883. 3 vols. 8vo. Num plates, some fldg, 7 cold. Contemp half mor, spine labels a bit chipped & edges rubbed.
　　　　　　　(Terramedia) $250 [≈ £156]
- Modern Egypt and Thebes: being a Description of Egypt ... London: Murray, 1843. 1st edn. 2 vols. 8vo. xx,476; iv,591,[2 advt] pp. Fldg map, num ills. Orig cloth, edges rubbed, chips & tears in spines.
　　　　(Worldwide Antiqu'n) $225 [≈ £140]

Wilkinson, William
- An Account of the Principalities of Wallachia and Moldavia: including Political Observations relating to them. London: Longman, Hurst ..., 1820. 8vo. xii,294 pp. Old half calf, new label, jnts rubbed.
　　　　　　　(Piccadilly) £60 [≈ $96]

Willard, T.A.
- The City of the Sacred Well. The Discoveries and Excavations of Edward Herbert Thompson in the Ancient City of Chi-Chenitza with some Discourse on ... the

Mayan Civilization ... London: Heinemann, [ca 1920]. 8vo. xvi,293 pp. Frontis, plates. Orig dec cloth gilt. *(Terramedia)* **$50 [≈ £31]**

William, Prince, of Sweden
- Among Pigmies & Gorillas. With the Swedish Zoological Expedition to Central Africa, 1921. London: 1923. 1st edn. 8vo. 296 pp. Fldg cold map, ills. Orig blue cloth gilt.
(Terramedia) **$80 [≈ £50]**
- Wild African Animals I Have Known. London: [1923]. Folio. 315 pp. Frontis, num plates. Title & frontis loose. Orig blue cloth.
(Terramedia) **$100 [≈ £62]**

Williams, A. Bryan
- Game Trails in British Columbia. Big Game & Other Sport ... New York: Scribner's, 1925. 1st edn. 8vo. 360 pp. Num photo plates. Orig cloth, sl worn.   *(Terramedia)* **$150 [≈ £93]**

Williams, A.F.
- Some Dreams Come True. Cape Town: Howard B. Timmins, 1948. Roy 8vo. 14,590 pp. Frontis port, 3 cold plates, num other ills. Orig cloth. Dw.   *(Gemmary)* **$60 [≈ £37]**

Williams, Edwin, compiler
- Narrative of the Recent Voyage of Captain Ross to the Arctic regions ... and a Notice of Captain Back's Expedition ... New York: Wiley & Long, 1835. 16mo. vi, 7-77, [4], lxxxii-lxxxiv, [3], 68-192 pp. Fldg map frontis. Orig cloth, minor soil, 1 hinge cracked. *(High Latitude)* **$125 [≈ £78]**

Williams, Gardner F.
- The Diamond Mines of South Africa. New York: Macmillan, 1902. 8vo. xix,681 pp. Fldg map, 30 plates (5 cold). Orig cloth, rubbed.   *(Adelson)* **$185 [≈ £115]**

Williams, Helen Maria
- Letters written in France, in the Summer 1790, to a Friend in England; containing Various Anecdotes relative to the French Revolution ... London: for T. Cadell, 1790. 1st edn. 12mo. Half-title. Contemp mrbld bds, rebacked in calf.
(Ximenes) **$350 [≈ £218]**

Williams, Hugh W.
- Select Views in Greece with Classical Illustrations. London: 1829. Special iss on india proof paper. 2 vols in one. Lge 4to. Half-titles. 64 plates. Some tanning & sl foxing. Contemp three qtr calf, rebacked.
(Reese) **$1,000 [≈ £625]**
- Select Views in Greece with Classical

Illustrations. London: 1829. 2 vols in one. Thick 4to. 64 plates. Occas sl tanning & foxing. Elab gilt crimson mor, a.e.g., some wear to extremities, spine sunned.
(Reese) **$650 [≈ £406]**
- Travels in Italy, Greece, and the Ionian Islands in a Series of Letters Descriptive of Manners, Scenery, and the Fine Arts. Edinburgh: 1820. 2 vols. xxii,399; xiv,437 pp. 20 plates (2 fldg). Unobtrusive lib stamps. Contemp three qtr calf, spine reprd.   *(Reese)* **$300 [≈ £187]**

Williams, John, M.D.
- The Rise, Progress, and Present State of the Northern Governments ... or, Observations ... made during a Tour of Five Years ... London: 1777. 1st edn. 2 vols. 4to. Vol 2 has 16 pp index & advts at end (lacking in many copies). Contemp calf, jnts cracked.
(Hannas) **£110 [≈ $176]**

Williams, Joseph
- Narrative of a Tour from the State of Indiana to the Oregon Territory in the Years 1841-2. New York: 1921. One of 250. 95 pp. Cloth.
(Reese) **$85 [≈ £53]**

Williams, Martha N.
- A Year in China; and a Narrative of Capture and Imprisonment, when Homeward Bound on Board the Rebel Pirate Florida ... New York: 1864. Only edn. xvi,362,advt pp. Orig cloth, rubbed, extremities sl frayed.
(Reese) **$150 [≈ £93]**

Williams, Thomas & Calvert, James
- Fiji and the Fijians. Edited by George Stringer Rowe. New York: Appleton, 1859. 1st Amer edn. 2 vols in one. Tall 8vo. x,551 pp. Fldg map, 3 cold plates, 6 engvd plates, num text ills. Orig bndg, spine ends & crnrs sl worn.   *(Schoyer)* **$125 [≈ £78]**
- Fiji and the Fijians. New York: Appleton, 1859. 1st US edn. 8vo. x,551 pp. Fldg map, 3 hand cold plates, 36 ills. 1 leaf frayed. Ex-lib. Orig cloth, crudely rebacked.
(Worldwide Antiqu'n) **$65 [≈ £40]**

Williamson, Alexander
- Journeys in North China, Manchuria, and Eastern Mongolia; with some Account of Corea. London: Smith, Elder, 1870. 1st edn. 2 vols. 8vo. xx,444; viii,442,[1] pp. 2 fldg maps, 8 plates, 8 other ills. Orig cloth gilt, mainly unopened.   *(Fenning)* **£175 [≈ $280]**

Williamson, George C.
- Guildford in the Olden Time. London & Guildford: 1904. One of 100. Fcap 4to. xiii,

270 pp. Num ills. Orig cloth, spine faded & chafed, crnrs bumped. *(Duck)* **£30 [≈ $48]**

Williamson, J.A. (ed.)
- The Cabot Voyages and Bristol Discovery under Henry VII. With the Cartography of the Voyages by R.A. Skelton. Cambridge: 1962. 8vo. Ills & charts (some fldg). Orig cloth. Dw. *(Ambra)* **£15 [≈ $24]**

Williamson, Joseph
- History of the City of Belfast in the State of Maine ... From Its First Settlement in 1770 to 1875. Portland: Loring, 1877. Roy 8vo. 956 pp. Maps, plates. Orig bndg. *(Emerald Isle)* **£85 [≈ $136]**

Williamson, Thomas
- Illustrations of Indian Field Sports selected and reproduced from the Coloured Engravings first published in 1807 ... Westminster: Constable, 1893. Oblong lge 8vo. 10 chromolitho plates. Orig cloth, sl rubbed & faded, spine strengthened, good ex-lib. *(Worldwide Antiqu'n)* **$115 [≈ £71]**

Willis, N.P.
- Out-Doors at Idlewild; or, the Shaping of a Home on the Banks of the Hudson. New York: Scribner ..., 1855. 1st edn. 8vo. xvi,519 pp. Engvd & ptd titles. Frontis. Title spotted as usual. Orig cloth, spine ends worn. W.A. Tonge's b'plate. *(Young's)* **£34 [≈ $54]**

Willis, N.P., et al.
- Picturesque American Scenery. A Series of Twenty-Five Beautiful Steel Engravings from Designs by W.H. Bartlett, George L. Brown ... Troy, N.H.: H.B. Nims & Co, 1884. Folio. [4], 92 pp. 25 steel engvd plates. Orig dec blue cloth gilt, a.e.g. *(Karmiole)* **$150 [≈ £93]**

Willoughby, Howard
- Australian Pictures Drawn with Pen and Pencil ... London: RTS, 1886. Imperial 8vo. 224, 8 advt pp. Fldg cold map, num text ills. Orig pict cloth gilt, a.e.g. *(Bickersteth)* **£50 [≈ $80]**

Willoughby, J.
- East Africa and its Big Game. London: 1899. 312 pp. Fldg map, ills. Orig pict bndg. *(Trophy Room Books)* **$850 [≈ £531]**

Willoughby, William C.
- The Soul of the Bantu. A Sympathetic Study of the Magico-Religious Practices and Beliefs of the Bantu Tribes of Africa. Garden City, New York: Doubleday (with London pasted-over imprint slip), 1928. 1st edn. 8vo.

xxvi,476 pp. Rec calf backed mrbld bds. *(Fenning)* **£45 [≈ $72]**

Wills, Alfred
- 'The Eagle's Nest' in the Valley of Sixt; a Summer Home among the Alps: together with some Excursions among the Great Glaciers. Second Edition. London: Longman ..., 1860. 8vo. Engvd dedic, 2 maps, 12 tinted plates. Orig dec cloth, uncut, sl worn. *(Hannas)* **£40 [≈ $64]**

Wills, C.J.
- In the Land of the Lion and the Sun, or Modern Persia, being Experiences of Life in Persia during a Residence of Fifteen Years ... from 1866 to 1881. London: Macmillan, 1883. 1st edn. 8vo. xvi,446 pp. Cold frontis. Sl foxing. Lib buckram. *(Worldwide Antiqu'n)* **$75 [≈ £46]**

Willyams, Revd C.
- Selection of Views in Egypt, Palestine, Rhodes, Italy, Minorca, and Gibraltar ... London: John Hearne, 1822. Folio. 36 cold aquatints. 3 blank guard ff foxed. Rec half mor, gilt spine. *(Frew Mackenzie)* **£850 [≈ $1,360]**

Willyams, Cooper
- Account of the Campaign in the West Indies in the Year 1794. London: Bensley, 1796. 1st edn. Sm folio. iv,[12],149, [3],62 pp. 2 maps. Lacks 4 plates. Orig bds, rebacked. *(Jenkins)* **$150 [≈ £93]**

Wilmer or Wilmore, John
- The Case of John Wilmore Truly and Impartially Related: or, A looking Glass for All Merchants and Planters that are concerned in the American Plantations. London: 1682. 17 pp. Disbound. Cloth case. Wing W.2883. *(Reese)* **$1,100 [≈ £687]**

Wilson, Alban
- Sport and Service in Assam and Elsewhere. London: 1924. 8vo. Ills. Sl foxed. Orig bndg, sl rubbed. *(Grayling)* **£35 [≈ $56]**
- Sport and Service in Assam and Elsewhere. London: Hutchinson, 1924. 8vo. 320 pp. Frontis, 19 photo ills. Orig bndg. *(Bates & Hindmarch)* **£50 [≈ $80]**

Wilson, Sir Charles
- Picturesque Palestine, Sinai & Egypt ... [with] Lane-Poole, Stanley: Social Life in Egypt ... A Supplement to Picturesque Palestine ... London: Virtue, [1880-84]. 1st edns. 5 vols. Lge 4to. Plates & ills. Orig dec cloth, a.e.g., sm nicks to hd of 2 spines.

(Claude Cox) **£160 [≈ $256]**

- Picturesque Palestine, Sinai and Egypt. London: J.S. Virtue & Co, n.d. 4 vols. 4to. Engvd titles & plates. Stamp on title versos. Orig cloth gilt, sm number at ft of spines. Without the Supplement.
(Spelman) **£140 [≈ $224]**

Wilson, Charles William & Warren, Charles
- The Recovery of Jerusalem. A Narrative of Exploration and Discovery in the City and the Holy Land ... New York: Appleton, 1871. 1st Amer edn. Lge 8vo. xxiv,436,advt pp. Frontis, 7 fldg maps & diags (a few reprd tears), num ills. Orig purple cloth, spine faded.   *(Karmiole)* **$100 [≈ £62]**

Wilson, Daniel
- Letters from an Absent Brother; Containing some Account of Part of a Tour through Parts of the Netherlands, Switzerland, Northern Italy and France in the Summer of 1823. London: George Wilson, 1825. 3rd edn, enlgd. 2 vols. 8vo. Lightly spotted. Mod cloth.   *(Piccadilly)* **£30 [≈ $48]**

Wilson, Ernest H.
- China, Mother of Gardens. Boston: 1929. Roy 8vo. x,408 pp. Map, 61 ills. Orig cloth, trifle used.
(Wheldon & Wesley) **£200 [≈ $320]**
- China: Mother of Gardens. Boston: 1929. Roy 8vo. xi,408 pp. Map, frontis, plates. Orig dec cloth.   *(Lyon)* **£125 [≈ $200]**
- Plant Hunting. Boston: 1927. "Special Autographed Edition", signed. 2 vols. Roy 8vo. 128 plates. Orig rexine.
(Wheldon & Wesley) **£185 [≈ $296]**

Wilson, Revd J. Leighton
- Western Africa; its History, Condition & Prospects. New York: Harper, 1856. 1st edn. Sm 8vo. xii,527 pp. Dble page map, frontis, ills. Orig dark brown cloth, endpapers browned.   *(Terramedia)* **$200 [≈ £125]**

Wilson, John Marius
- The Imperial Gazetteer of England and Wales ... London: A. Fullarton & Co, 1873. 2 vols. Lge thick 8vo. 3 engvd plates, 19 pp of town plans & maps. Half calf gilt.
(Hollett) **£85 [≈ $136]**

Wilson, Revd S.S.
- A Narrative of the Greek Mission; or, Sixteen Years in Malta and Greece ... London: John Snow, 1839. 8vo. xiv,596 pp. 2 w'cuts. Lacks the cold Baxter frontis. Orig green cloth,

spine glued down.   *(Piccadilly)* **£55 [≈ $88]**

Wilson, Samuel
- An Account of the Province of Carolina in America ... London: 1682. 1st edn, 2nd state of text. 27 pp. Lacks the map, not issued in all copies. Foxing. Top marg shaved a bit close in 2 ff, not affecting text. Later three qtr calf.
(Reese) **$5,000 [≈ £3,125]**

Wilson, Lady Sarah
- South African Memories, Social, Warlike & Sporting. From Diaries Written at the Time. London: Edward Arnold, 1909. 2nd imp. 8vo. xii, 331 pp. Ills. Orig cloth.
(Terramedia) **$30 [≈ £18]**

Wilson, Thomas
- A Brief Journal of the Life, Travels, and Labours of Love, in the Work of the Ministry, of that Eminent and Faithful Servant of Jesus Christ, Thomas Wilson ... London: James Phillips ..., 1784. New edn. 12mo. xlviii,98, [2] pp. Old sheep, rebacked.
(Young's) **£35 [≈ $56]**

Wilson, William Rae
- Records of a Route through France and Italy; with Sketches of Catholicism. London: Longman ..., 1835. 1st edn. 8vo. 4 aquatint plates (inc frontis). Some damp staining, mainly of title opening & prelims. Contemp half calf, mrbld bds, extremities rubbed.
(Clark) **£42 [≈ $67]**
- Travels in Norway, Sweden, Denmark, Hanover, Germany, Netherlands, &c. London: Longman, Rees, 1826. Only edn. 8vo. 10 pp of music. Half-title not called for. 7 uncold aquatints. Later 19th c half mor gilt, uncut.   *(Trebizond)* **$275 [≈ £171]**

Winans, W.
- The Sporting Rifle. The Shooting of Big and Little Game, together with a Description of the Principal Classes of Sporting Weapons. London: 1908. Sm folio. Num ills. Orig cloth, sl rubbed.   *(Grayling)* **£100 [≈ $160]**

Winchelsea, Earl of
- An Exact Relation of the Famous Earthquake and Eruption of Mount Aetna, A.D. 1669 ... added a Genuine Letter [by W.B. Earle] ... Journey to the Summit of Mount Aetna, 1766. London: 1775. 1st edn. 8vo. 28,34 pp. Lib stamp on title. 1 plate.
(Robertshaw) **£55 [≈ $88]**

Windham, Francis W.
- Wild Life on the Fjelds of Norway. London: Longman, Green, 1861. 1st edn. 8vo. xvi,273

pp. 2 cold fldg maps, 4 cold litho plates, title vignette, 4 w'cuts. Red half mor gilt, t.e.g.
(Terramedia) **$350 [≃ £218]**

Windus, John
- A Journey to Mequinez; The Residence of the Present Emperor of Fez and Morocco. On the Occasion of Commodore Stewart's Embassy ... London: for Jacob Tonson, 1725. 1st edn. [32],251,[11] pp. 6 fldg plates. Contemp panelled calf, rebacked, outer crnrs worn.
(Karmiole) **$350 [≃ £218]**

Wingate, F.R.
- Ten Years' Captivity in the Mahdi's Camp 1882-1892. London: Sampson Low, 1893. 10th edn. 8vo. xvi,471,32 advt pp. 2 fldg maps, frontis, ills. Orig red cloth gilt, spine & rear bd sl faded.
(Bates & Hindmarch) **£40 [≃ $64]**

Winkles, B.
- Illustrations of the Cathedral Churches of England and Wales. London: Effingham Wilson, 1836-42. 2nd edn. 3 vols. 181 plates. Contemp cloth gilt, sl faded.
(Gough) **£150 [≃ $240]**

Winkles, H. & B.
- Winkles's Architectural and Picturesque Illustrations of the Cathedral Churches of England and Wales ... Descriptions by Thomas Moule. London: 1838-42. 3 vols. Roy 8vo. [4], xx,144; viii,140; xii,160 pp. Addtnl engvd titles, 178 plates. Orig cloth, spines reprd.
(Fenning) **£85 [≃ $136]**

Winthrop, John
- Relation of a Voyage from Boston to Newfoundland, for the Observation of The Transit of Venus, June 6, 1761. Boston, N.E.: Edes & Gill, 1761. 24 pp. 1 diag.
(Jarndyce) **£380 [≃ $608]**

Winthrop, Theodore
- The Canoe and the Saddle. Adventures among the Northwestern Rivers and Forests and Isthmiana. Edinburgh: 1883. 1st edn. 8vo. [iv], 266, 16 advt pp. Orig cloth gilt, extremities trifle rubbed, upper jnt tender.
(Hollett) **£35 [≃ $56]**
- The Canoe and the Saddle or Klalam and Kilckatat. To which are now first added his Western Letters and Journals ... Tacoma: John H. Williams, 1913. Lge 8vo. xxvi,336 pp. Num ills. Vellum-like spine over red cloth gilt, t.e.g.
(Karmiole) **$45 [≃ £28]**

Wise, Henry A.
- Los Gringos: or, an Inside View of Mexico

and California, with Wanderings in Peru, Chili, and Polynesia. New York: 1849. 1st edn. 453 pp. Orig cloth, a bit rubbed.
(Reese) **$250 [≃ £156]**

Wissmann, Hermann von
- My Second Journey through Equatorial Africa from the Congo to the Zambesi in the years 1886 and 1887. London: Chatto & Windus, 1891. 8vo. xiv,326 pp. Fldg map, 32 plates. Orig tan pict cloth, rubbed.
(Adelson) **$275 [≃ £171]**

Withers, Alexander S.
- Chronicles of Border Warfare, or, a History of the Settlement by the Whites, of North-Western Virginia ... Clarksburg, Va.: Joseph Israel, 1831. 1st edn. 12mo. 319, 1 advt pp. Later cloth, leather label. Without the later issued 4-page list of contents.
(Schoyer) **$250 [≃ £156]**

Wittie, Robert
- Scarbrough Spaw, or, a Description of the Nature and Vertues of the Spaw at Scarborough in Yorkshire ... London: Charles Tyus, 1660. 1st edn. Cr 8vo. Errata leaf. 4 ff misbound but present. Contemp sheep, rubbed. Wing W.3231.
(Stewart) **£295 [≃ $472]**

Wittman, William
- Travels in Turkey, Asia-Minor, Syria, and across the Desert into Egypt ... Philadelphia: 1804. 1st Amer edn. 426,advt pp. Half-title. Ex-lib with sm inscrptn, some scattered foxing. Contemp calf, label & extremities worn, front cvr bowed. *(Reese)* **$225 [≃ £140]**

Wolff, Henry Drummond
- Notes taken in Paris, Vienna, Pesth, and Berlin, during the Easter Recess, 1878. [Strictly Private. No. --]. London: William Clowes & Son, 1878. 1st edn. 8vo. 60 pp. Orig blue cloth.
(Hannas) **£30 [≃ $48]**

Wolff, Jens
- Sketches on a Tour to Copenhagen ... London: 1814. 1st edn. Iss with frontis of King of Norway. 4to. Half-title. Inserted 'Note' at end, dated 1820. 9 plates (7 mtd on india paper, 2 hand cold). Num vignettes. Contemp half calf, a.e.g., extremities rubbed.
(Hannas) **£450 [≃ $720]**

Wolff, Joseph
- Narrative of a Mission to Bokhara in the Years 1843-1845 to ascertain the Fate of Colonel Stoddart and Captain Conolly. London: Blackwood, 1852. 6th edn. 8vo.

xxi,346 pp. Orig bndg, recased, lib label on front cvr. *(Bates & Hindmarch)* **£50 [≈ $80]**

Wollstonecraft, Mary
- Letters written during a Short Residence in Sweden, Norway, and Denmark ... London: for J. Johnson, 1796. 1st edn. 8vo. [iv],262, [6] pp, inc final advt leaf. Occas trivial spotting. Orig bds, uncut, sl marked.
(Finch) **£475 [≈ $760]**

Wolverton, Lord
- Five Months Sport in Somaliland. London: 1894. 8vo. Fldg map (foxed). Sl foxing. Orig buckram, spine sl snagged, sm red ink mark on upper cvr. *(Grayling)* **£45 [≈ $72]**

Wood, H.S.
- Shikar Memories. A Record of Sport and Observation in India and Burma. London: 1934. 8vo. Ills. Orig cloth, sl discold & soiled.
(Grayling) **£40 [≈ $64]**

Wood, John
- A Journey to the Source of the River Oxus. With an Essay on the Geography of the Valley of the Oxus. London: Murray, 1872. New edn. 8vo. cvii,280 pp. 2 fldg maps, 1 plate. 1 map reprd with sellotape. Orig cloth, rubbed & soiled, rebacked, lib number on spine.
(Worldwide Antiqu'n) **$65 [≈ £40]**
- A Personal Narrative of a Journey to the Source of the River Oxus by the Route of the Indus, Kabul and Badakhashan ... London: 1841. xv,424 pp. Fldg map. A few ff sl foxed, offsetting from map. Contemp three qtr calf, gilt spine. *(Terramedia)* **$450 [≈ £281]**

Wood, John T.
- Discoveries at Ephesus. Including the Site and Remains of the Great Temple of Diana. London: 1877. 1st edn. 4to. Dble page plan, num litho plates (4 cold). Lib blind stamps on plate margs. Orig pict gilt brown cloth, slit along crnr of edge of spine.
(Terramedia) **$200 [≈ £125]**

Wood, Robert
- An Essay on the Original Genius and Writings of Homer: with a Comparative View of the Ancient and Present State of the Troade ... Dublin: for William Hallhead ..., 1776. 1st Dublin edn. 8vo. xv,[i],294 pp. Lge fldg view. Contemp tree calf. The Downes copy. *(Finch)* **£80 [≈ $128]**

Wood, William Maxwell
- Wandering Sketches of People and Things in South America, Polynesia, California, and Other Places Visited, during a Cruise ...

Philadelphia: 1849. Sole edn. x,[13]-386 pp. Half-title. Lib inscrptn & b'plates. Foxed. Orig cloth, extremities worn, spine ends sl chipped. *(Reese)* **$400 [≈ £250]**

Woods, George
- An Account of the Past and Present State of the Isle of Man ... London: for Robert Baldwin ..., 1811. 1st edn. 8vo. [xii],366 pp. Cold frontis map. Contemp half calf, rebacked. *(Young's)* **£105 [≈ $168]**

Woodward, Ida
- In and Around the Isle of Purbeck. With Thirty-Six Plates in Color by John W.G. Bond. London & New York: John Lane, 1908. 1st edn. Lge 8vo. xiv,237,advt pp. Orig green cloth gilt, front hinge cracked & shaken. *(Terramedia)* **$35 [≈ £21]**

Woodyatt, Nigel
- My Sporting Memories. Forty Years with Note-Book and Gun. Reminiscences of Big-Game Shooting in India. London: Jenkins, 1923. 8vo. 320 pp. Frontis, 22 photo ills. Orig green cloth, foredge foxed.
(Bates & Hindmarch) **£50 [≈ $80]**

Woollen, William Watson
- The Inside Passage to Alaska 1792-1920 with an Account of the North Pacific Coast from the Accounts left by Vancouver ... and from the Author's Journals ... Cleveland: 1924. 2 vols. 8vo. 242; 318 pp. Map, plates. Orig cloth, t.e.g., unopened, almost as new.
(High Latitude) **$125 [≈ £78]**

Wooten, Dudley G.
- A Comprehensive History of Texas, 1685 to 1897. Dallas: W.G. Scarff, 1898. 1st edn. 2 vols. 1741 pp. Maps, ills.
(Jenkins) **$1,650 [≈ £1,031]**

Worcester, Dean C.
- The Philippines, Past and Present. New York: Macmillan, 1914. 1st edn. 2 vols. 8vo. 1023 pp. Num photo plates. Orig dec blue cloth. *(Terramedia)* **$125 [≈ £78]**

Wordsworth, Christopher
- Athens and Attica: Notes of a Tour. Third Edition, Revised. London: Murray, 1855. 8vo. xviii,251 pp, advt leaf. 2 fldg maps (sl torn, without loss), plans, &c. Orig brown cloth, cvrs rather mottled.
(Piccadilly) **£16.50 [≈ $27]**
- Greece, Pictorial, Descriptive, and Historical ... A New Edition Revised, with Notices of Recent Discoveries by H.F. Tozer. London: Murray, 1882. Lge 8vo. xxviii,460,32 advt

pp. Frontis, title vignette, 19 plates, num text engvs. Orig dec cloth, sl rubbed.
(Frew Mackenzie) **£135 [≈ $216]**

- Greece: Pictorial, Descriptive and Historical ... New Edition, Revised ... London: Murray, 1882. Lge 8vo. xxviii,460,32 advt pp. 21 steel engvd plates, num w'engvs. Sl foxing at ends. Orig pict gilt green cloth, t.e.g., spine sl sloped & sl chipped at hd.
(Terramedia) **$100 [≈ £62]**

Wordsworth, Dorothy
- See Quillinan, Dorothy.

Wordsworth, William
- A Complete Guide to the Lakes, comprising minute Directions for the Tourist, with Mr. Wordsworth's Description of the Scenery ... Kendal: J. Hudson, 1843. 2nd edn. ix,vii, '159' [≈ 259] pp. Fldg map at end, frontis (foxed), plans, ills. Orig cloth gilt, jnts sl worn.   *(Box of Delights)* **£90 [≈ $144]**

Workman, F.B. & W.H.
- The Call of the Snowy Hispar. A Narrative of Exploration and Mountaineering on the Northern Frontier of India. London: 1910. 288 pp. 2 lge fldg maps, 113 ills. Orig cloth.
(Trophy Room Books) **$700 [≈ £437]**
- In the Ice World of the Himalaya among the Peaks and Passes of Ladak, Nubra, Suru and Baltistan. New York: Cassell, n.d. [after 1898]. 2nd edn. 204 pp. 2 maps, 65 ills. Orig cloth.   *(Trophy Room Books)* **$200 [≈ £125]**

The World in Miniature ...
- See Shoberl, Frederic (ed.).

Worsaae, J.J.A.
- An Account of the Danes & Norwegians in England, Scotland and Ireland. London: Murray, 1852. 8vo. xxiv,359 pp. Text w'cuts. Mod qtr leather.   *(Piccadilly)* **£52 [≈ $83]**

Worsfold, W. Basil
- Portuguese Nyasaland ... London: Sampson Low ..., 1899. 8vo. ix,295 pp. 2 lge fldg maps in rear pocket, 24 ills. Ex-lib. Orig dec cloth, spine sunned.   *(Schoyer)* **$80 [≈ £50]**

Worth, R.N.
- History of the Town and Borough of Devonport, Sometime Plymouth Dock. Plymouth: 1870. Sm 8vo. Orig bevelled cloth, sm stain to top bd.   *(Ambra)* **£62 [≈ $99]**

Wraxall, Sir Nathaniel William
- Memoirs of the Courts of Berlin, Dresden, Warsaw, and Vienna, In the Years 1777,

1778, and 1779. London: for T. Cadell ..., 1799. 1st edn. 2 vols. 8vo. xii,490; xii,414 pp. Contemp calf, spines worn.
(Young's) **£42 [≈ $67]**

- A Tour round the Baltic, thro' the Northern Countries of Europe ... London: ptd by Luke Hansard & Sons ..., 1807. 4th edn, crrctd & augmented. 8vo. 452 pp. Contemp tree calf, gilt spine, jnts cracked but holding. James Hansard's b'plate.   *(Young's)* **£50 [≈ $80]**
- Tour Through Some Northern Parts of Europe ... London: Cadell, 1775. 2nd edn. 8vo. iv, 411 pp. Fldg map. Contemp calf, gilt spine.   *(Gough)* **£75 [≈ $120]**

Wright, Edward
- Some Observations made in Travelling through France, Italy, &c. in the Years 1720 ... 1722. London: 1730. 1st edn. 2 vols in one. 4to. xiii,[iii],364,[iv]; 365-516,[lxx] pp. 8 pp addenda at end. 41 copper engvd & 1 w'cut plates. Sm reprs. Contemp calf, rebacked.
(Clark) **£250 [≈ $400]**
- Some Observations made in Travelling through France, Italy, &c. in the Years MDCCXXI ... London: 1764. 2nd edn. Thick 4to. xvi,[2],516,[70] pp. Frontis, plates. Sm lib stamp, sl foxing & tanning, marg reprs to a few ff. Antique half calf.
(Reese) **$350 [≈ £218]**

Wright, Frances
- Views of Society and Manners in America; in a Series of Letters from that Country to a Friend in England ... London: Longman ..., 1822. 2nd edn. 8vo. x,483 pp. Fldg map. Piece torn from title not affecting text. Old cloth. The Signet Library copy.
(Young's) **£60 [≈ $96]**

Wright, Revd G.N.
- China, in a Series of Views ... From Original and Authentic Sketches by Thomas Allom ... London: [1843]. 4 vols in 2. 4to. Engvd titles, 124 engvd plates. Contemp polished calf elab gilt, a.e.g., gilt inner dentelles, some wear to outer hinges.   *(Reese)* **$1,500 [≈ £937]**
- An Historical Guide to Ancient & Modern Dublin. London: Baldwin, Craddock & Joy, 1821. 1st edn. 12mo. [viii],442 pp. Lge fldg plan, 17 plates. Contemp half calf, spine ends sl rubbed.   *(Gough)* **£125 [≈ $200]**
- A New and Comprehensive Gazetteer; being a Delineation of the Present State of the World ... London: Thomas Kelly, 1838. 5 vols. Sm 4to. 41 maps, mostly hand cold, 50 engvd plates. Polished half calf gilt, contrasting labels.   *(Hollett)* **£350 [≈ $560]**
- The Rhine, Italy and Greece. In a Series of

Drawings from Nature ... London: Fisher, [1841]. 2 vols in one. 76; 90 pp. 2 engvd titles, 71 tissued plates. Sl offsetting on few plates. Contemp calf, rebacked in mor.
(Terramedia) **$600 [≈ £375]**

- The Shores and Islands of the Mediterranean Drawn from Nature ... London & Paris: Fisher, [ca 1840]. 1st edn. Sm 4to. 156 pp. Fldg map, 63 plates (some foxing & spotting). Elab gilt mor, a.e.g., jnts tender, sl tears.
(Worldwide Antiqu'n) **$260 [≈ £162]**

Wright, Thomas
- The Life of Sir Richard Burton. London: Everett & Co, 1906. 2 vols. 8vo. xxix,31-291; xi,13-291 pp. Half mor gilt.
(Adelson) **$225 [≈ £140]**

Wright, W.H.
- The Grizzly Bear. Narrative of a Hunter-Naturalist; Historical, Scientific, Adventurous. London: 1909. 8vo. Ills. Orig cloth, rather rubbed, inner hinge sprung.
(Grayling) **£25 [≈ $40]**

Wright, William
- An Account of Palmyra and Zenobia. With Travels and Adventures in Bashan and the Desert. New York & London & Edinburgh: Nelson, 1895. 1st edn. Sm 8vo. xviii,394 pp. Num plates & ills. Sm lib stamp on title. Orig cloth.
(Terramedia) **$50 [≈ £31]**
- An Account of Palmyra and Zenobia With Travels and Adventures in Bashan and the Desert. New York & London & Edinburgh: Nelson, 1895. 1st edn. Sm 8vo. xviii,394 pp. Map, num plates & ills. Orig cloth, t.e.g.
(Worldwide Antiqu'n) **$125 [≈ £78]**

Wroth, Lawrence C.
- The Voyages of Giovanni Da Verrazzano, 1524-1528. New Haven: Yale UP, 1970. 4to. xvi, 319 pp. 44 plates of maps & globes. Orig pict cloth. Dw. *(Terramedia)* **$50 [≈ £31]**
- The Voyages of Giovanni Da Verrazzano 1524-1528. New Haven: Yale UP for The Pierpont Morgan Library, 1970. 4to. xvi,322, 44 pp. 44 pp of plates, 24 pp MS facs. Orig blue cloth gilt. Dw. *(Karmiole)* **$65 [≈ £40]**

Wyld, James
- Wyld's New Plan of London and its Vicinity. London: 1867. Cold linen-backed map. Fldg into mrbld endpapers, spine of cvrs worn.
(Coombes) **£25 [≈ $40]**

Wylde, Augustus B.
- Modern Abyssinia. London: Methuen, 1900. 8vo. 506,47 ctlg pp. Frontis, fldg map. Orig

dec cloth, partly unopened, a few sm stains.
(Schoyer) **$60 [≈ £37]**

Wylly, H.C.
- From the Black Mountains to Waziristan. London: 1912. 505 pp. Lge fldg map in pocket, ills. Elab leather bndg.
(Trophy Room Books) **$475 [≈ £296]**

Wyndham, Henry Penryddocke
- A Gentleman's Tour through Monmouthshire and Wales, In the Months of June and July, 1774. London: for T. Evans, 1775. 1st edn. 8vo. [ii],v,[i],218,[ii] pp. Frontis. Early MS marginalia. Near-contemp tree calf, sometime rebacked, sl external fire-damage. *(Finch)* **£75 [≈ $120]**

Wynne, John Huddlestone
- A General History of Ireland. From the Earliest Accounts to the Present Time. London: 1772. 1st edn. 2 vols. 8vo. xxxii, 480,[xii]; 388,[4] pp. Fldg map, 2 fronts, 5 other plates, 2 pp engvd table. Minor damp staining. Contemp vellum, spine gilt faded.
(Clark) **£110 [≈ $176]**

Yates, William Holt
- The Modern History and Condition of Egypt ... Personal Narrative of Travels in that Country ... London: Smith, Elder, 1843. 1st edn. 2 vols. 8vo. 14 plates (1 tinted), 1 text ill. V sl foxing. Orig cloth, sl rubbed, tears in spine, spine ends sl frayed.
(Worldwide Antiqu'n) **$85 [≈ £53]**

Yoakum, Henderson
- History of Texas from its First Settlement in 1685 to its Annexation to the United States in 1846. New York: Redfield, 1855. 1st edn. 1st state, with vol 1 title dated 1855. 2 vols. Maps, plates. Vol 2 title in facs. Calf, mor labels. *(Jenkins)* **$950 [≈ £593]**
- History of Texas from its First Settlement in 1685 to its Annexation to the United States in 1846. New York: Redfield, 1856. 2 vols. Maps, plates. *(Jenkins)* **$950 [≈ £593]**

Yoe, Shway
- The Burman. His Life and Notions. London: Macmillan, 1896. 2nd edn. 8vo. 603 pp. Orig red cloth, sunned, 2 holes in backstrip.
(Schoyer) **$40 [≈ £25]**

Yorick, Mr.
- See Sterne, Laurence.

Young, Arthur
- The Farmer's Tour through the East of

England. London: 1771. 4 vols. 8vo. 29 plates, table. Calf, trifle used.
(Wheldon & Wesley) **£160 [≈ $256]**
- The Farmer's Tour through the East of England ... London: Strahan, 1771. 1st edn. 4 vols. 8vo. Half-title in vol 1. 28 plates (17 fldg), fldg table. Some sl discolouration. Contemp tan calf, some jnts cracked & some spine ends chipped.   *(Blackwell's)* **£210 [≈ $336]**
- General View of the Agriculture of the County of Norfolk; drawn up for the Consideration of the Board of Agriculture ... London: Richard Phillips, 1804. 1st edn. 8vo. xx,532,2 pp. Cold fldg map, 7 plates (sl foxed) & diags. New qtr calf, untrimmed. *(Blackwell's)* **£100 [≈ $160]**
- Letters concerning the Present State of the French Nation ... London: W. Nicoll, 1769. 1st edn. 8vo. iv,[ix],497 pp. Contemp sprinkled calf, sl rubbed, jnts cracking, lacks label.   *(Blackwell's)* **£175 [≈ $280]**
- A Six Weeks Tour through the Southern Counties of England and Wales ... By the Author of The Farmer's Letters. London: for W. Nicholl, 1768. 8vo. Mod qtr calf.
(Waterfield's) **£250 [≈ $400]**
- A Tour in Ireland ... Second Edition. London: H. Goldney, for T. Cadell, 1780. 1st 8vo edn. 2 vols. [2],xxiv,539,[1]; [2],416 pp. 5 engvd plates (3 fldg). Sl later red half calf, gilt spines, crnrs sl rubbed.   *(Fenning)* **£195 [≈ $312]**
- Travels during the Years 1787, 1788, & 1789 ... Kingdom of France ... London: 1794. 2nd edn. 2 vols in one. Lge thick 4to. 629, [3]; 336,[4] pp. 3 fldg maps (1 hand cold). Contemp calf, spine gilt extra, hinges worn, rear broken & loose.   *(Reese)* **£850 [≈ $531]**

Young, Egerton Ryerson
- By Canoe and Dog-Train among the Cree and Salteaux Indians. London: 1892. 1st English edn. 262 pp. Ills. Orig pict cloth, extremities worn, b'plate messily removed.
(Reese) **$50 [≈ £31]**
- By Canoe and Dog-Train among the Salteaux Indians. With an Introduction by Mark Guy Pearse. London: 1898. 8vo. Fldg map, 2 woodburytype ports, text ills. Orig pict cloth gilt.   *(Farahar)* **£30 [≈ $48]**
- Stories from Indian Wigwams and Northern Camp-Fires. London: Charles H. Kelly, 1893. 1st edn. 293,2 advt pp. Frontis, addtnl pict title, plates, ills. Orig pict cloth.
(Wreden) **$48.50 [≈ £30]**

Young, G.O.
- Alaska-Yukon Trophies Won and Lost. Huntington, WV: Standard Publications, 1947. 8vo. [xii],273 pp. Ills. Cloth. Dw.
(High Latitude) **$125 [≈ £78]**

Young, G.W.
- On High Hills, Memories of the Alps. London: (1927). 1st edn. 8vo. xvi,368,[8 advt] pp. 24 plates. Sl foxing. Orig cloth.
(Bow Windows) **£55 [≈ $88]**

Young, R.M.
- Historical Notices of Old Belfast and its Vicinity. Belfast: Marcus Ward, 1896. One of 150. 4to. Orig Irish linen damask. Linen bd slipcase. Author's pres inscrptn.
(Emerald Isle) **£175 [≈ $280]**
- Historical Notices of Old Belfast and its Vicinity. Belfast: Marcus Ward, 1896. Sm 4to. 287, subscribers, advt pp. Ills. Orig bndg.   *(Emerald Isle)* **£50 [≈ $80]**

Young, S. Hall
- Alaska Days with John Muir. New York: Fleming H. Revell, [ca 1915]. 12mo. 226 pp. Map, 12 ills. Orig dec blue cloth.
(Parmer) **$60 [≈ £37]**

Younghusband, Sir Francis
- Kashmir. Painted by Major E. Molyneux. London: A. & C. Black Colour Books, Twenty Shilling Series, 1911. Reprint. Cold plates. Orig dec cloth. Dw.
(Old Cathay) **£75 [≈ $120]**
- Kashmir. Painted by Major E. Molyneux. London: A. & C. Black, 1917. 3rd printing. 8vo. 283 pp. Map, num tissued cold plates. Orig dec Maroon cloth.
(Terramedia) **$85 [≈ £53]**
- South Africa of Today. London: Macmillan, 1898. 1st edn. 8vo. vii,[1],177 pp. 12 photo ills. Orig red cloth, edges sl worn.
(Parmer) **$75 [≈ £46]**

Younghusband, G.J.
- The Story of the Guides. London: Macmillan, 1909. 4th reprint. 8vo. xvi,207 pp. Frontis, 15 ills. Orig bndg, spine sl sunned, some bumping. *(Bates & Hindmarch)* **£45 [≈ $72]**

Younghusband, G.J. & Frank E.
- The Relief of Chitral. London: Macmillan, 1895. 2nd reprint. 8vo. vi,183 pp. Frontis & 23 ills & maps. Orig red cloth gilt.
(Bates & Hindmarch) **£50 [≈ $80]**

Zeisberger, David
- Diary of David Zeisberger, a Moravian Missionary among the Indians of Ohio. Translated from the German Manuscript & edited by Eugene F. Bliss. Cincinnati: 1885. 1st edn. 2 vols. Lge 8vo. 464; 535 pp. Sm lib stamp. Orig cloth. *(Terramedia)* **$150 [≈ £93]**

Catalogue Booksellers Contributing to IRBP

The booksellers who have provided catalogues during 1989 specifically for the purpose of compiling the various titles in the *IRBP* series, and from whose catalogues books have been selected, are listed below in alphabetical order of the abbreviation employed for each. This listing is therefore a complete key to the booksellers contributing to the series as a whole; only a proportion of the listed names is represented in this particular subject volume.

The majority of these booksellers issue periodic catalogues free, on request, to potential customers. Sufficient indication of the type of book handled by each bookseller can be gleaned from the individual book entries set out in the main body of this work and in the companion titles in the series.

Adelson	=	Richard H. Adelson, Antiquarian Bookseller, North Pomfret, Vermont 05053, U.S.A. (802 457 2608)
Ambra	=	Ambra Books, 22 West Shrubbery, Redland, Bristol BS6 6TA, England (0272 741962)
Ampersand	=	Ampersand Books, P.O. Box 674, Cooper Station, New York City 10276, U.S.A. (212 674 6795)
Antic Hay	=	Antic Hay Rare Books, P.O. Box 2185, Asbury Park, NJ 07712, U.S.A. (201 774 4590)
Argosy	=	Argosy Book Store, Inc., 116 East 59th Street, New York, NY 10022, U.S.A. (212 753 4455)
Ars Libri	=	Ars Libri, Ltd., 560 Harrison Avenue, Boston, Massachusetts 02118, U.S.A. (617 357 5212)
Astoria	=	Astoria Books & Prints, 1801 Lawrence Street, Denver, CO 80202, U.S.A. (303 292 4122)
Baldwin	=	Baldwin's Books, Fossil Hall, Boars Tye Road, Silver End, Witham, Essex CM8 3QA, England (0376 83502)
Bates & Hindmarch	=	Bates and Hindmarch, Antiquarian Bookseller, Fishergate, Boroughbridge, North Yorkshire Y05 9AL, England (0423 324258)
Berkelouw	=	Messrs. Berkelouw, Antiquarian Booksellers, 830 N. Highland Ave., Los Angeles, CA 90038, U.S.A. (213 466 3321)
Bernett	=	F.A. Bernett Inc., 2001 Palmer Avenue, Larchmont, N.Y. 10538, U.S.A. (914 834 3026)
Beyer	=	Preston C. Beyer, 752A Pontiac Lane, Stratford, Connecticut 06497, U.S.A. (203 375 9073)
Bickersteth	=	David Bickersteth, 4 South End, Bassingbourn, Royston, Hertfordshire SG8 5NG, England ((0763) 45619)
Blackwell's	=	Blackwell's Rare Books, B.H. Blackwell Ltd., Fyfield Manor, Fyfield, Abingdon, Oxon OX13 5LR, England (0865 390692)
Black Sun Books	=	Black Sun Books, P.O. Box 7916 - F.D.R. Sta., New York, New York 10150-1915, U.S.A. (212 688 6622)
Bookmark	=	Bookmark, Children's Books, Fortnight, Wick Down, Broad Hinton, Swindon, Wiltshire SN4 9NR, England (0793 73693)
Book Block	=	The Book Block, 8 Loughlin Avenue, Cos Cob, Connecticut 06807, U.S.A. (203 629 2990)
Book House	=	The Book House, Grey Garth, Ravenstonedale, Kirkby Stephen, Cumbria CA17 4NQ, England (058 73634)
Bow Windows	=	Bow Windows Book Shop, 128 High Street, Lewes, East Sussex BN7 1XL, England (0273 480780)
Box of Delights	=	The Box of Delights, 25 Otley Street, Skipton, North Yorkshire BD23 1DY, England (0756 60111)

Bromer	=	Bromer Booksellers, 607 Boylston Street, at Copley Square, Boston, MA 02116, U.S.A. (617 247 2818)
Buckley	=	Brian & Margaret Buckley, 11 Convent Close, Kenilworth, Warwickshire CV8 2FQ, England (0926 55223)
Burmester	=	James Burmester, Manor House Farmhouse, North Stoke, Bath BA1 9AT, England (0272 327265)
Castle	=	The Castle Bookshop, 37 North Hill, Colchester, Essex CO1 1QR, England (0206 577520)
Chapel Hill	=	Chapel Hill Rare Books, P.O. Box 456, Carrboro, NC 27510, U.S.A. (919 929 8351)
City Spirit	=	City Spirit Books, 1434 Blake Street, Denver, Colorado 80202, U.S.A. (303 595 0434)
Clark	=	Robert Clark, 24 Sidney Street, Oxford OX4 3AG, England (0865 243406)
Collected Works	=	Collected Works, 3 Melbourne Terrace, Melbourne Grove, London SE22 8RE, England (01 299 4195)
Coombes	=	A.J. Coombes, Bookseller, 24 Horsham Road, Dorking, Surrey RH4 2JA, England (0306 880736)
Claude Cox	=	Claude Cox, The White House, Kelsale, Saxmundham, Suffolk IP17 2PQ, England (0728 602786)
Dalian	=	Dalian Books, David P. Williams, 81 Albion Drive, London Fields, London E8 4LT, England (01 249 1587)
de Beaumont	=	Robin de Beaumont, 25 Park Walk, Chelsea, London SW10 0AJ, England (01 352 3440)
Dillons	=	Dillons, 82 Gower Street, London WC1E 6EQ, England (01 636 1577)
Doyle	=	Mrs. Assia Doyle, Teffont, Salisbury SP3 5QF, England
Duck	=	William Duck, The Glebe House, Brightling, East Sussex TN32 5HE, England (042 482 295)
Edrich	=	I.D. Edrich, 17 Selsdon Road, London E11 2QF, England (01 989 9541)
Egglishaw	=	H.J. Egglishaw, Bruach Mhor, 54 West Moulin Road, Pitlochry, Perthshire PH16 5EQ, Scotland (0796 2084)
Egret	=	Egret Books, 6 Priory Place, Wells, Somerset BA5 1SP, England (0749 79312)
Elgen	=	Elgen Books, 336 DeMott Avenue, Rockville Centre, New York 11570, U.S.A. (516 536 6276)
Emerald Isle	=	Emerald Isle Books, 539 Antrim Road, Belfast BT15 3BU, Northern Ireland (0232 370798)
Falkner	=	Falkner Greirson & Co Ltd, Glenaglogh, Tallow, Co. Waterford, Ireland, Eire (058 56349)
Farahar	=	Clive Farahar, XIV The Green, Calne, Wiltshire SN11 8DG, England (0249 816793)
Fenning	=	James Fenning, 12 Glenview, Rochestown Avenue, Dun Laoghaire, County Dublin, Eire (01 857855)
Finch	=	Simon Finch Rare Books, Clifford Chambers, 10 New Bond Street, London W1Y 9PF, England (01 499 0799)
Firsts & Company	=	Firsts & Company, 1066 Madison Avenue, New York, New York 10028, U.S.A. (212 249 4122)
First Issues	=	First Issues Ltd, 7 York Terrace, Dorchester, Dorset DT1 2DP, England (0305 65583)
Frew Mackenzie	=	Frew Mackenzie plc, 106 Great Russell Street, London WC1B 3NA, England (01 580 2311)
Gach	=	John Gach Books, 5620 Waterloo Road, Columbia, Md. 21045, U.S.A. (301 465 9023)
Gekoski	=	R.A. Gekoski, 33B Chalcot Square, London NW1 8YA, England (01 722 9037)

Gemmary	=	The Gemmary, Inc, PO Box 816, Redondo Beach, CA 90277, U.S.A. (213 372 5969)
Gough	=	Simon Gough Books, 5 Fish Hill, Holt, Norfolk, England (026371 2650)
Grayling	=	David A.H. Grayling, Lyvennet, Crosby Ravensworth, Penrith, Cumbria CA10 3JP, England (09315 282)
Green Meadow Books	=	Green Meadow Books, Kinoulton, Notts NG12 3EN, England (0949 81723)
Greyne	=	Greyne House, Marshfield, Chippenham, Wiltshire SN14 8LU, England (0225 891279)
Handy Book	=	Handy Book, 1762 Avenue Road, Toronto, Ontario M5M 3Y9, Canada (416 781 4139)
Hannas	=	Torgrim Hannas, 29a Canon Street, Winchester, Hampshire SO23 9JJ, England (0962 62730)
Harrison	=	T. Harrison (Books), 25 Clayfields, Wentworth, nr Rotherham, Yorkshire S62 7TD, England (0226 742097)
Hartfield	=	Hartfield, Fine and Rare Books, 117 Dixboro Road, Ann Arbor, MI 48105, U.S.A. (313 662 6035)
Hartley	=	Hartley Moorhouse Books, 142 Petersham Road, Richmond, Surrey TW10 6UX, England (01 948 7742)
Hawthorn	=	Hawthorn Books, 7 College Park Drive, Westbury-on-Trym, Bristol BS10 7AN, England (0272 509175)
Hemlock	=	Hemlock Books, 170 Beach 145th Street, Neponsit, New York 11694, U.S.A. (718 318 0737)
Henly	=	John Henly, Bookseller, Brooklands, Walderton, Chichester, West Sussex PO18 9EE, England (0705 631426)
Heritage	=	Heritage Book Shop, Inc., 8540 Melrose Avenue, Los Angeles, California 90069, U.S.A. (213 659 3674)
High Latitude	=	High Latitude, P.O. Box 11254, Bainbridge Island, WA 98110, U.S.A. (206 598 3454)
Hollett	=	R.F.G. Hollett and Son, 6 Finkle Street, Sedbergh, Cumbria LA10 5BZ, England (05396 20298)
Jarndyce	=	Jarndyce, Antiquarian Booksellers, 46 Great Russell Street, Bloomsbury, London WC1B 3PE, England (01 631 4220)
Jenkins	=	The Jenkins Company, Box 2085, Austin, Texas 78768, U.S.A. (512 444 6616)
C.R. Johnson	=	C.R. Johnson, 21 Charlton Place, London N1 8AQ, England (01 354 1077)
Michael Johnson	=	Michael Johnson Books, Oak Lodge, Kingsway, Portishead, Bristol BS20 8HW, Scotland (2 848764)
Karmiole	=	Kenneth Karmiole, Bookseller, 1225 Santa Monica Mall, Santa Monica, California 90401, U.S.A. (213 451 4342)
Lamb	=	R.W. & C.R. Lamb, Talbot House, 158 Denmark Rd., Lowestoft, Suffolk NR32 2EL, England (0502 564306)
Lewton	=	L.J. Lewton, Old Station House, Freshford, Bath BA3 6EQ, England (022 122 3351)
Limestone Hills	=	Limestone Hills Book Shop, P.O. Box 1125, Glen Rose, Texas 76043, U.S.A. (817 897 4991)
Lyon	=	Richard Lyon, 17 Old High Street, Hurstpierpoint, West Sussex BN6 9TT, England (0273 832255)
Marlborough	=	Marlborough Rare Books Ltd., 144-146 New Bond Street, London W1Y 9FD, England (01 493 6993)
Marlborough B'Shop	=	Marlborough Bookshop, 6 Kingsbury Street, Marlborough, Wiltshire, England (0672 54074)

Mendelsohn	=	H.L. Mendelsohn, Fine European Books, P.O. Box 317, Belmont, Massachusetts 02178, U.S.A. (617 484 7362)
Minkoff	=	George Robert Minkoff Inc., Rare Books, R.F.D., Box 147, Great Barrington, Mass 01230, U.S.A. (413 528 4575)
Minster Gate	=	The Minster Gate Bookshop, 8 Minster Gates, York YO1 2HL, England (0904 621812)
Monmouth	=	Monmouth House Books, Llanfapley, Abergavenny, Gwent NP7 8SN, Wales (060 085 236)
Moon	=	Michael Moon, Antiquarian, Booksellers & Publishers, 41, 42 & 43 Roper Street, Whitehaven, Cumbria CA28 7BS, England (0946 62936)
Moorhead	=	Moorhead Books, Suffield Cottage, Moorhead, Gildersome, Leeds LS27 7BA, England
Mordida	=	Mordida Books, P.O. Box 79322, Houston, Texas 77279, U.S.A. (713 467 4280)
M & S Rare Books	=	M & S Rare Books, Inc., Box 311, Weston, Massachusetts 02193, U.S.A. (617 891 5650)
Nouveau	=	Nouveau Rare Books, Steve Silberman, P.O. Box 12471, 5005 Meadow Oaks Park Drive, Jackson, Mississippi 39211, U.S.A. (601 956 9950)
Oak Knoll	=	Oak Knoll Books, 414 Delaware Street, New Castle, Delaware 19720, U.S.A. (302 328 7232)
Offenbacher	=	Emile Offenbacher, 84-50 Austin Street, P.O. Box 96, Kew Gardens, New York 11415, U.S.A. (718 849 5834)
Old Cathay	=	Old Cathay Fine Books, 106 Park Meadow, Old Hatfield, Hertfordshire AL9 5HE, England (07072 71006)
Parmer	=	J. Parmer, Booksellers, 7644 Forrestal Road, San Diego, CA 92120, U.S.A. (619 287 0693)
Patterson	=	Ian Patterson, 21 Bateman Street, Cambridge CB2 1NB, England (0223 321658)
Piccadilly	=	Piccadilly Rare Books Ltd., Old Knowle, Frant, Kent TN3 9EJ, England (089 275 340)
Pickering	=	Pickering & Chatto Ltd., 17 Pall Mall, London SW1Y 5NB, England (01 930 8627)
Polyanthos	=	Polyanthos Park Avenue Books, 600 Park Avenue, Huntington, NY 11743, U.S.A. (516 673 9232)
Ramer	=	Richard C. Ramer, 225 East 70th Street, New York, N.Y. 10021, U.S.A. (212 737 0222)
Rankin	=	Alan Rankin, 72 Dundas Street, Edinburgh EH3 6QZ, Scotland, Scotland (031 556 3705)
Rayfield	=	Tom Rayfield, The Blacksmiths, Radnage Common, Buckinghamshire HP14 4DH, England (024 026 3986)
Reese	=	William Reese Company, 409 Temple Street, New Haven, Connecticut 06511, U.S.A. (203 789 8081)
David Rees	=	David Rees, 22 Wanley Road, London SE5 8AT, England (01 737 4557)
Reference Works	=	Reference Works, Barry Lamb & David Hollister, 12 Commercial Road, Dorset BH19 1DF, England (0929 424423)
Respess	=	L & T Respess Books, PO Box 236, Bristol, RI 02809, U.S.A.
Rittenhouse	=	Rittenhouse Book Store, 1706 Rittenhouse Square, Philadelphia, Pennsylvania 19103, U.S.A. (215 545 6072)
Roberts	=	Graeme Roberts, 57 Queens Road, Leytonstone, London E11 1BA, England (01 539 7095)
Robertshaw	=	John Robertshaw, 5 Fellowes Drive, Ramsey, Huntingdon, Cambridgeshire PE17 1BE, England (0487 813330)

Rootenberg	=	B & L. Rootenberg, P.O. Box 5049, Sherman Oaks, California 91403-5049, U.S.A. (818 788 7765)
Rostenberg & Stern	=	Leona Rostenberg and Madeleine, Stern, Rare Books, 40 East 88 Street, New York, N.Y. 10128., U.S.A. (212 831 6628)
Sanders	=	Sanders of Oxford Ltd., 104 High Street, Oxford OX1 4BW, England (0865 242590)
Savona	=	Savona Books, 9 Wilton Road, Hornsea, North Humberside HU13 1QU, England (0964 535195)
Schoyer	=	Schoyer's Books, 1404 S. Negley Avenue, Pittsburgh, PA 15217, U.S.A. (412 521 8464)
Sklaroff	=	L.J. Sklaroff, The Bookshop, The Broadway, Totland, Isle of Wight PO39 0BW, England (0983 754960)
John Smith	=	John Smith & Son (Glasgow), 57-61 St. Vincent Street, Glasgow G2 5TB, Scotland (041 221 7472)
Sotheran	=	Henry Sotheran Ltd., 2 Sackville Street, Piccadilly, London W1X 2DP, England (01 439 6151)
Spelman	=	Ken Spelman, 70 Micklegate, York YO1 1LF, England (0904 624414)
Stewart	=	Andrew Stewart, 11 High Street, Helpringham, Sleaford, Lincolnshire NG34 9RA, England (052 921 617)
Sumner & Stillman	=	Summer & Stillman, P.O. Box 225, Yarmouth, ME 04096, U.S.A. (207 846 6070)
W. Thomas Taylor	=	W. Thomas Taylor, 1906 Miriam, Austin, Texas 78722, U.S.A. (512 478 7628)
Temple	=	Robert Temple, 65 Mildmay Road, London N1 4PU, England (01 254 3674)
Terramedia	=	Terramedia Books, 19 Homestead Road, Wellesley, MA 02181, U.S.A. (617 237 6485)
Thornton's	=	Thornton's of Oxford, 11 Broad Street, Oxford OX1 3AR, England (0865 242939)
Tiger Books	=	Tiger Books, Yew Tree Cottage, Westbere, Canterbury Kent CT2 0HH, England (0227 710030)
Transition	=	Transition Books, 209 Post Street, Suite 614, San Francisco, CA 94108, U.S.A. (415 391 5161)
Trebizond	=	Trebizond Rare Books, P.O. Box 2430 - Main Street, New Preston, CT 0677, U.S.A. (203 868 2621)
Trophy Room Books	=	Trophy Room Books, Box 3041, Agoura, CA 91301, U.S.A. (818 889 2469)
Upcroft	=	Upcroft Books Ltd., 66 St. Cross Road, Winchester, Hampshire SO23 9PS, England (0962 52679)
Virgo	=	Virgo Books, Mrs. Q.V. Mason, Little Court, South Wraxall, Bradford-on-Avon, Wiltshire BA15 2SE, England (02216 2040)
Washton	=	Andrew D. Washton, 411 East 83rd Street, New York, New York 10028, U.S.A. (212 751 7027)
Waterfield's	=	Waterfield's, 36 Park End Street, Oxford OX1 1HJ, England (0865 721809)
Waterland	=	Waterland Books, 28 North Street, March, Cambridgeshire PE15 8LS, England (0354 52160)
West Side	=	West Side Books, 113 W. Liberty, Ann Arbor, MI 48103, U.S.A. (313 995 1891)
Wheldon & Wesley ●	= ●	Wheldon & Wesley Ltd., Lytton Lodge, Codicote, Hitchin, Hertfordshire SG4 8TE, England (0438 820370)
Whitehart	=	F.E. Whitehart, Rare Books, 40 Priestfield Road, Forest Hill, London SE23 2RS, England (01 699 3225)
David White	=	David White, 17 High Street, Bassingbourne, Royston, Hertfordshire SG8 5NE, England (0763 243986)

Charles B. Wood	=	Charles B. Wood III, Inc., 116 Commonwealth Avenue, Post Office Box 310, Boston, Massachusetts 02117, U.S.A. (617 247 7844)
Susan Wood	=	Susan Wood, 24 Leasowe Road, Rubery, Rednal, Worcestershire B45 9TD, England (021 453 7169)
Woolmer	=	J. Howard Woolmer, Revere, Pennsylvania 18953, U.S.A. (215 847 5074)
Words Etcetera	=	Words Etcetera, Julian Nangle, Hod House, Child Okeford, Dorset DT11 8EH, England (0258 860539)
Worldwide Antiqu'n	=	Worldwide Antiquarian, Post Office Box 391, Cambridge, MA 02141, U.S.A. (617 876 6220)
Wreden	=	William P. Wreden, 206 Hamilton Avenue, P.O. Box 56, Palo Alto, CA 94302-0056, U.S.A. (415 325 6851)
Xerxes	=	Xerxes, Fine & Rare Books & Documents, Box 428, Glen Head, New York 11545, U.S.A. (516 671 6235)
Ximenes	=	Ximenes: Rare Books, Inc., 19 East 69th Street, New York, NY 10021, U.S.A. (212 744 10021)
Young's	=	Young's Antiquarian Books, Tillingham, Essex CM0 7ST, England (062187 8187)
Zeno	=	Zeno, 6 Denmark Street, London WC2H 8LP, England (01 836 2522)